Lecture Notes in Computer Science　10907

Commenced Publication in 1973
Founding and Former Series Editors:
Gerhard Goos, Juris Hartmanis, and Jan van Leeuwen

More information about this series at http://www.springer.com/series/7409

Margherita Antona · Constantine Stephanidis (Eds.)

Universal Access in Human-Computer Interaction

Methods, Technologies, and Users

12th International Conference, UAHCI 2018
Held as Part of HCI International 2018
Las Vegas, NV, USA, July 15–20, 2018
Proceedings, Part I

 Springer

Editors
Margherita Antona
Foundation for Research
  and Technology – Hellas (FORTH)
Heraklion, Crete
Greece

Constantine Stephanidis
University of Crete
  and Foundation for Research
  and Technology – Hellas (FORTH)
Heraklion, Crete
Greece

ISSN 0302-9743   ISSN 1611-3349   (electronic)
Lecture Notes in Computer Science
ISBN 978-3-319-92048-1   ISBN 978-3-319-92049-8   (eBook)
https://doi.org/10.1007/978-3-319-92049-8

Library of Congress Control Number: 2018944388

LNCS Sublibrary: SL3 – Information Systems and Applications, incl. Internet/Web, and HCI

Printed on acid-free paper

This Springer imprint is published by the registered company Springer International Publishing AG
part of Springer Nature
The registered company address is: Gewerbestrasse 11, 6330 Cham, Switzerland

Foreword

The 20th International Conference on Human-Computer Interaction, HCI International 2018, was held in Las Vegas, NV, USA, during July 15–20, 2018. The event incorporated the 14 conferences/thematic areas listed on the following page.

A total of 4,373 individuals from academia, research institutes, industry, and governmental agencies from 76 countries submitted contributions, and 1,170 papers and 195 posters have been included in the proceedings. These contributions address the latest research and development efforts and highlight the human aspects of design and use of computing systems. The contributions thoroughly cover the entire field of human-computer interaction, addressing major advances in knowledge and effective use of computers in a variety of application areas. The volumes constituting the full set of the conference proceedings are listed in the following pages.

I would like to thank the program board chairs and the members of the program boards of all thematic areas and affiliated conferences for their contribution to the highest scientific quality and the overall success of the HCI International 2018 conference.

This conference would not have been possible without the continuous and unwavering support and advice of the founder, Conference General Chair Emeritus and Conference Scientific Advisor Prof. Gavriel Salvendy. For his outstanding efforts, I would like to express my appreciation to the communications chair and editor of *HCI International News*, Dr. Abbas Moallem.

July 2018

Constantine Stephanidis

HCI International 2018 Thematic Areas and Affiliated Conferences

Thematic areas:

- Human-Computer Interaction (HCI 2018)
- Human Interface and the Management of Information (HIMI 2018)

Affiliated conferences:

- 15th International Conference on Engineering Psychology and Cognitive Ergonomics (EPCE 2018)
- 12th International Conference on Universal Access in Human-Computer Interaction (UAHCI 2018)
- 10th International Conference on Virtual, Augmented, and Mixed Reality (VAMR 2018)
- 10th International Conference on Cross-Cultural Design (CCD 2018)
- 10th International Conference on Social Computing and Social Media (SCSM 2018)
- 12th International Conference on Augmented Cognition (AC 2018)
- 9th International Conference on Digital Human Modeling and Applications in Health, Safety, Ergonomics, and Risk Management (DHM 2018)
- 7th International Conference on Design, User Experience, and Usability (DUXU 2018)
- 6th International Conference on Distributed, Ambient, and Pervasive Interactions (DAPI 2018)
- 5th International Conference on HCI in Business, Government, and Organizations (HCIBGO)
- 5th International Conference on Learning and Collaboration Technologies (LCT 2018)
- 4th International Conference on Human Aspects of IT for the Aged Population (ITAP 2018)

Conference Proceedings Volumes Full List

1. LNCS 10901, Human-Computer Interaction: Theories, Methods, and Human Issues (Part I), edited by Masaaki Kurosu
2. LNCS 10902, Human-Computer Interaction: Interaction in Context (Part II), edited by Masaaki Kurosu
3. LNCS 10903, Human-Computer Interaction: Interaction Technologies (Part III), edited by Masaaki Kurosu
4. LNCS 10904, Human Interface and the Management of Information: Interaction, Visualization, and Analytics (Part I), edited by Sakae Yamamoto and Hirohiko Mori
5. LNCS 10905, Human Interface and the Management of Information: Information in Applications and Services (Part II), edited by Sakae Yamamoto and Hirohiko Mori
6. LNAI 10906, Engineering Psychology and Cognitive Ergonomics, edited by Don Harris
7. LNCS 10907, Universal Access in Human-Computer Interaction: Methods, Technologies, and Users (Part I), edited by Margherita Antona and Constantine Stephanidis
8. LNCS 10908, Universal Access in Human-Computer Interaction: Virtual, Augmented, and Intelligent Environments (Part II), edited by Margherita Antona and Constantine Stephanidis
9. LNCS 10909, Virtual, Augmented and Mixed Reality: Interaction, Navigation, Visualization, Embodiment, and Simulation (Part I), edited by Jessie Y. C. Chen and Gino Fragomeni
10. LNCS 10910, Virtual, Augmented and Mixed Reality: Applications in Health, Cultural Heritage, and Industry (Part II), edited by Jessie Y. C. Chen and Gino Fragomeni
11. LNCS 10911, Cross-Cultural Design: Methods, Tools, and Users (Part I), edited by Pei-Luen Patrick Rau
12. LNCS 10912, Cross-Cultural Design: Applications in Cultural Heritage, Creativity, and Social Development (Part II), edited by Pei-Luen Patrick Rau
13. LNCS 10913, Social Computing and Social Media: User Experience and Behavior (Part I), edited by Gabriele Meiselwitz
14. LNCS 10914, Social Computing and Social Media: Technologies and Analytics (Part II), edited by Gabriele Meiselwitz
15. LNAI 10915, Augmented Cognition: Intelligent Technologies (Part I), edited by Dylan D. Schmorrow and Cali M. Fidopiastis
16. LNAI 10916, Augmented Cognition: Users and Contexts (Part II), edited by Dylan D. Schmorrow and Cali M. Fidopiastis
17. LNCS 10917, Digital Human Modeling and Applications in Health, Safety, Ergonomics, and Risk Management, edited by Vincent G. Duffy
18. LNCS 10918, Design, User Experience, and Usability: Theory and Practice (Part I), edited by Aaron Marcus and Wentao Wang

19. LNCS 10919, Design, User Experience, and Usability: Designing Interactions (Part II), edited by Aaron Marcus and Wentao Wang
20. LNCS 10920, Design, User Experience, and Usability: Users, Contexts, and Case Studies (Part III), edited by Aaron Marcus and Wentao Wang
21. LNCS 10921, Distributed, Ambient, and Pervasive Interactions: Understanding Humans (Part I), edited by Norbert Streitz and Shin'ichi Konomi
22. LNCS 10922, Distributed, Ambient, and Pervasive Interactions: Technologies and Contexts (Part II), edited by Norbert Streitz and Shin'ichi Konomi
23. LNCS 10923, HCI in Business, Government, and Organizations, edited by Fiona Fui-Hoon Nah and Bo Sophia Xiao
24. LNCS 10924, Learning and Collaboration Technologies: Design, Development and Technological Innovation (Part I), edited by Panayiotis Zaphiris and Andri Ioannou
25. LNCS 10925, Learning and Collaboration Technologies: Learning and Teaching (Part II), edited by Panayiotis Zaphiris and Andri Ioannou
26. LNCS 10926, Human Aspects of IT for the Aged Population: Acceptance, Communication, and Participation (Part I), edited by Jia Zhou and Gavriel Salvendy
27. LNCS 10927, Human Aspects of IT for the Aged Population: Applications in Health, Assistance, and Entertainment (Part II), edited by Jia Zhou and Gavriel Salvendy
28. CCIS 850, HCI International 2018 Posters Extended Abstracts (Part I), edited by Constantine Stephanidis
29. CCIS 851, HCI International 2018 Posters Extended Abstracts (Part II), edited by Constantine Stephanidis
30. CCIS 852, HCI International 2018 Posters Extended Abstracts (Part III), edited by Constantine Stephanidis

http://2018.hci.international/proceedings

12th International Conference on Universal Access in Human-Computer Interaction

Program Board Chair(s): **Margherita Antona and Constantine Stephanidis,** *Greece*

- João Barroso, Portugal
- Rodrigo Bonacin, Brazil
- Ingo K. Bosse, Germany
- Anthony Lewis Brooks, Denmark
- Laura Burzagli, Italy
- Pedro J. S. Cardoso, Portugal
- Stefan Carmien, UK
- Vagner Figueredo De Santana, Brazil
- Carlos Duarte, Portugal
- Pier Luigi Emiliani, Italy
- Qin Gao, P.R. China
- Andrina Granić, Croatia
- Simeon Keates, UK
- Georgios Kouroupetroglou, Greece
- Patrick M. Langdon, UK
- Barbara Leporini, Italy
- I. Scott MacKenzie, Canada
- John Magee, USA
- Alessandro Marcengo, Italy
- Troy McDaniel, USA
- Silvia Mirri, Italy
- Ana Isabel Paraguay, Brazil
- Hugo Paredes, Portugal
- Enrico Pontelli, USA
- João M. F. Rodrigues, Portugal
- Frode Eika Sandnes, Norway
- Anthony Savidis, Greece
- Jaime Sánchez, Chile
- Volker Sorge, UK
- Hiroki Takada, Japan
- Kevin Tseng, Taiwan
- Gerhard Weber, Germany

The full list with the Program Board Chairs and the members of the Program Boards of all thematic areas and affiliated conferences is available online at:

http://www.hci.international/board-members-2018.php

HCI International 2019

The 21st International Conference on Human-Computer Interaction, HCI International 2019, will be held jointly with the affiliated conferences in Orlando, FL, USA, at Walt Disney World Swan and Dolphin Resort, July 26–31, 2019. It will cover a broad spectrum of themes related to Human-Computer Interaction, including theoretical issues, methods, tools, processes, and case studies in HCI design, as well as novel interaction techniques, interfaces, and applications. The proceedings will be published by Springer. More information will be available on the conference website: http://2019.hci.international/.

General Chair
Prof. Constantine Stephanidis
University of Crete and ICS-FORTH
Heraklion, Crete, Greece
E-mail: general_chair@hcii2019.org

http://2019.hci.international/

Contents – Part I

Design for All, Accessibility and Usability

A Method for Analyzing Mobility Issues for People with Physical
Disabilities in the Context of Developing Countries.................. 3
    Leticia Maria de Oliveira Camenar, Diego de Faria do Nascimento,
    and Leonelo Dell Anhol Almeida

Mobile-PrivAccess: Method for Analyzing Accessibility in Mobile
Applications from the Privacy Viewpoint Abiding by W3C 18
    Rachel T. Chicanelli, Patricia C. de Souza,
    and Luciana C. Lima de Faria Borges

A Taxonomy for Website Evaluation Tools Grounded
on Semiotic Framework...................................... 38
    Vagner Figueredo de Santana and Maria Cecília Calani Baranauskas

Copy Here, Paste There? On the Challenges of Scaling Inclusive
Social Innovations... 50
    Jennifer Eckhardt, Christoph Kaletka, and Bastian Pelka

Universal Design of ICT for Emergency Management:
A Systematic Literature Review and Research Agenda................ 63
    Terje Gjøsæter, Jaziar Radianti, and Weiqin Chen

When Universal Access Does not Go to Plan: Lessons to Be Learned 75
    Simeon Keates

Categorization Framework for Usability Issues of Smartwatches
and Pedometers for the Older Adults............................ 91
    Jayden Khakurel, Antti Knutas, Helinä Melkas, Birgit Penzenstadler,
    Bo Fu, and Jari Porras

Towards a Framework for the Design of Quantitative Experiments:
Human-Computer Interaction and Accessibility Research 107
    Frode Eika Sandnes, Evelyn Eika, and Fausto Orsi Medola

A Strategy on Introducing Inclusive Design Philosophy to Non-design
Background Undergraduates................................... 121
    Shishun Wang, Ting Zhang, Guoying Lu, and Yinyun Wu

Alternative I/O Techniques, Multimodality and Adaptation

Stabilising Touch Interactions in Cockpits, Aerospace,
and Vibrating Environments   133
    B. I. Ahmad, Patrick M. Langdon, and S. J. Godsill

MyoSL: A Framework for Measuring Usability of Two-Arm Gestural
Electromyography for Sign Language   146
    Jordan Aiko Deja, Patrick Arceo, Darren Goldwin David,
    Patrick Lawrence Gan, and Ryan Christopher Roque

Evaluating Devices for Object Rotation in 3D   160
    Sean DeLong and I. Scott MacKenzie

Interaction Techniques to Promote Accessibility in Games
for Touchscreen Mobile Devices: A Systematic Review   178
    Eunice P. dos Santos Nunes, Vicente Antônio da Conceição Júnior,
    and Luciana C. Lima de Faria Borges

A Collaborative Virtual Game to Support Activity and Social Engagement
for Older Adults   192
    Jing Fan, Linda Beuscher, Paul Newhouse, Lorraine C. Mion,
    and Nilanjan Sarkar

Evaluation of an English Word Look-Up Tool for Web-Browsing
with Sign Language Video for Deaf Readers   205
    Dhananjai Hariharan, Sedeeq Al-khazraji, and Matt Huenerfauth

Gesture-Based Vehicle Control in Partially and Highly Automated Driving
for Impaired and Non-impaired Vehicle Operators: A Pilot Study   216
    Ronald Meyer, Rudolf Graf von Spee, Eugen Altendorf,
    and Frank O. Flemisch

Real-Time Implementation of Orientation Correction Algorithm
for 3D Hand Motion Tracking Interface   228
    Nonnarit O-larnnithipong, Armando Barreto,
    Neeranut Ratchatanantakit, Sudarat Tangnimitchok,
    and Francisco R. Ortega

Haptic Information Access Using Touchscreen Devices: Design Guidelines
for Accurate Perception of Angular Magnitude and Line Orientation   243
    Hari Prasath Palani, G. Bernard Giudice, and Nicholas A. Giudice

Brain Controlled Interface Log Analysis in Real Time Strategy
Game Matches   256
    Mauro C. Pichiliani

M2TA - Mobile Mouse Touchscreen Accessible for Users
with Motor Disabilities   273
Agebson Rocha Façanha, Maria da Conceição Carneiro Araújo,
Windson Viana, and Jaime Sánchez

Multi-switch Scanning Keyboards: A Theoretical Study of Simultaneous
Parallel Scans with QWERTY Layout   287
Frode Eika Sandnes, Evelyn Eika, and Fausto Orsi Medola

Towards Multi-modal Interaction with Interactive Paint   299
Nicholas Torres, Francisco R. Ortega, Jonathan Bernal,
Armando Barreto, and Naphtali D. Rishe

Non Visual Interaction

Nateq Reading Arabic Text for Visually Impaired People.   311
Omaimah Bamasag, Muna Tayeb, Maha Alsaggaf, and Fatimah Shams

Designing a 2×2 Spatial Vibrotactile Interface for Tactile Letter Reading
on a Smartphone.   327
Shaowei Chu and Mei Peng

LêRótulos: A Mobile Application Based on Text Recognition
in Images to Assist Visually Impaired People   337
Juliana Damasio Oliveira, Olimar Teixeira Borges,
Vanessa Stangherlin Machado Paixão-Cortes,
Marcia de Borba Campos, and Rafael Mendes Damasceno

Information Design on the Adaptation of Evaluation Processes' Images
to People with Visual Impairment   355
Fernanda Domingues, Emilia Christie Picelli Sanches,
and Claudia Mara Scudelari de Macedo

Cognitive Impact Evaluation of Multimodal Interfaces for Blind People:
Towards a Systematic Review   365
Lana Mesquita, Jaime Sánchez, and Rossana M. C. Andrade

Keyboard and Screen Reader Accessibility in Complex Interactive Science
Simulations: Design Challenges and Elegant Solutions.   385
Emily B. Moore, Taliesin L. Smith, and Jesse Greenberg

Fair Play: A Guidelines Proposal for the Development of Accessible
Audiogames for Visually Impaired Users   401
Olimar Teixeira Borges, Juliana Damasio Oliveira, Marcia de Borba
Campos, and Sabrina Marczak

Comparison of Feedback Modes for the Visually Impaired:
Vibration vs. Audio.   420
   Sibu Varghese Jacob and I. Scott MacKenzie

Ultrasonic Waves to Support Human Echolocation   433
   Florian von Zabiensky, Michael Kreutzer, and Diethelm Bienhaus

Wayfinding Board Design for the Visually Impaired Based on Service
Design Theory   450
   Wanru Wang and Xinxiong Liu

Designing for Cognitive Disabilities

Design of an Assistive Avatar in Improving Eye Gaze Perception
in Children with ASD During Virtual Interaction   463
   Ashwaq Zaini Amat, Amy Swanson, Amy Weitlauf, Zachary Warren,
   and Nilanjan Sarkar

ICT to Support Dental Care of Children with Autism:
An Exploratory Study   475
   Mariasole Bondioli, Maria Claudia Buzzi, Marina Buzzi,
   Susanna Pelagatti, and Caterina Senette

Design of an Interactive Gesture Measurement System
for Down Syndrome People   493
   Marta del Rio Guerra, Jorge Martin Gutierrez, and Luis Aceves

Assistive Technologies for People with Cognitive Impairments – Which
Factors Influence Technology Acceptance?.   503
   Susanne Dirks and Christian Bühler

Designing Wearable Immersive "Social Stories" for Persons
with Neurodevelopmental Disorder   517
   Franca Garzotto, Mirko Gelsomini, Vito Matarazzo, Nicolo' Messina,
   and Daniele Occhiuto

An AAC System Designed for Improving Behaviors and Attitudes
in Communication Between Children with CCN and Their Peers   530
   Tetsuya Hirotomi

Teaching Concepts with Wearable Technology: Learning Internal
Body Organs   542
   Ersin Kara, Mustafa Güleç, and Kürşat Çağıltay

The Utility of the Virtual Reality in Autistic Disorder Treatment.   551
   Sicong Liu, Yan Xi, and Hui Wang

A Data-Driven Mobile Application for Efficient, Engaging, and Accurate
Screening of ASD in Toddlers   560
Arpan Sarkar, Joshua Wade, Amy Swanson, Amy Weitlauf,
Zachary Warren, and Nilanjan Sarkar

An Interactive Cognitive-Motor Training System for Children with
Intellectual Disability.   571
Caterina Senette, Amaury Trujillo, Erico Perrone, Stefania Bargagna,
Maria Claudia Buzzi, Marina Buzzi, Barbara Leporini,
and Alice Elena Piatti

A Robot-Based Cognitive Assessment Model Based on Visual Working
Memory and Attention Level   583
Ali Sharifara, Ashwin Ramesh Babu, Akilesh Rajavenkatanarayanan,
Christopher Collander, and Fillia Makedon

Effects of E-Games on the Development of Saudi Children with Attention
Deficit Hyperactivity Disorder Cognitively, Behaviourally and Socially:
An Experimental Study   598
Doaa Sinnari, Paul Krause, and Maysoon Abulkhair

Audiovisual Design of Learning Systems for Children with ASD   613
Rafael Toscano and Valdecir Becker

Assisting, Not Training, Autistic Children to Recognize and Share
Each Other's Emotions via Automatic Face-Tracking in a Collaborative
Play Environment   628
Pinata Winoto, Tiffany Y. Tang, Xiaoyang Qiu, and Aonan Guan

Research on the Interactive Design of Wearable Devices
for Autistic Children   637
Minggang Yang and Xuemei Li

Understanding Fine Motor Patterns in Children with Autism
Using a Haptic-Gripper Virtual Reality System.   650
Huan Zhao, Amy Swanson, Amy Weitlauf, Zachary Warren,
and Nilanjan Sarkar

Evaluating the Accessibility of Scratch for Children with Cognitive
Impairments   660
Misbahu S. Zubair, David Brown, Thomas Hughes-Roberts,
and Matthew Bates

Author Index   677

Contents – Part II

Virtual and Augmented Reality for Universal Access

Analysis of the Body Sway While/After Viewing Visual Target Movement
Synchronized with Background Motion 3
   Nao Amano, Hiroki Takada, Yusuke Jono, Toru Tanimura,
   Fumiya Kinoshita, Masaru Miyao, and Masumi Takada

Virtual Reality for Pain Management Among Children and Adolescents:
Applicability in Clinical Settings and Limitations 15
   Barbara Atzori, Laura Vagnoli, Andrea Messeri,
   and Rosapia Lauro Grotto

Virtual Reality Based Assessment of Static Object Visual Search
in Ocular Compared to Cerebral Visual Impairment. 28
   Christopher R. Bennett, Emma S. Bailin, Timothy K. Gottlieb,
   Corinna M. Bauer, Peter J. Bex, and Lotfi B. Merabet

3D Spatial Gaming Interaction to Broad CS Participation. 39
   Santiago Bolivar, Francisco R. Ortega, Maia Zock-Obregon,
   and Naphtali D. Rishe

Using Immersive Virtual Reality Serious Games for Vocational
Rehabilitation of Individuals with Physical Disabilities 48
   Lal "Lila" Bozgeyikli, Evren Bozgeyikli, Andoni Aguirrezabal,
   Redwan Alqasemi, Andrew Raij, Stephen Sundarrao, and Rajiv Dubey

Virtual Reality Interaction Techniques for Individuals
with Autism Spectrum Disorder 58
   Evren Bozgeyikli, Lal "Lila" Bozgeyikli, Redwan Alqasemi,
   Andrew Raij, Srinivas Katkoori, and Rajiv Dubey

Analysis of Human Motion and Cognition Ability with Virtual
Reality System: Basic Mechanism of Human Response 78
   Kouki Nagamune and Keisuke Takata

Effectiveness of Virtual Reality Survival Horror Games for the Emotional
Elicitation: Preliminary Insights Using Resident Evil 7: Biohazard 87
   Federica Pallavicini, Ambra Ferrari, Alessandro Pepe,
   Giacomo Garcea, Andrea Zanacchi, and Fabrizia Mantovani

Mobile Augmented Reality Framework - MIRAR 102
   João M. F. Rodrigues, Ricardo J. M. Veiga, Roman Bajireanu,
   Roberto Lam, João A. R. Pereira, João D. P. Sardo,
   Pedro J. S. Cardoso, and Paulo Bica

Effect of Controlled Consciousness on Sense of Presence and Visually
Induced Motion Sickness While Viewing Stereoscopic Movies   122
   Akihiro Sugiura, Kunihiko Tanaka, Kazuki Ohta, Kazuki Kitamura,
   Saki Morisaki, and Hiroki Takada

Exploring Virtual Reality to Enable Deaf or Hard of Hearing
Accessibility in Live Theaters: A Case Study   132
   Mauro Teófilo, Alvaro Lourenço, Juliana Postal,
   and Vicente F. Lucena Jr.

Use of 3D Human-Computer Interaction for Teaching in the Architectural,
Engineering and Construction Fields   149
   Shahin Vassigh, Francisco R. Ortega, Armando Barreto,
   Katherine Tarre, and Jose Maldonado

The Formulation of Hybrid Reality: Pokémon Go Mania   160
   Chih-yuan Wang and Chen-li Kuo

Accessibility Guidelines for Virtual Environments   171
   Breno Augusto Guerra Zancan, Guilherme Corredato Guerino,
   Tatiany Xavier de Godoi, Daniela de Freitas Guilhermino Trindade,
   José Reinaldo Merlin, Ederson Marcos Sgarbi,
   and Carlos Eduardo Ribeiro

Intelligent Assistive Environments

Ambient Assisted Living and Digital Inclusion: Overview
of Projects, Services and Interfaces   187
   Alessandro Andreadis and Riccardo Zambon

Intelligent Driver Profiling System for Cars – A Basic Concept   201
   Nermin Caber, Patrick M. Langdon, and P. John Clarkson

Development of an Energy Management System for the Charge
Scheduling of Plug-in Electric Vehicles   214
   Dario Cruz, Nelson Pinto, Jânio Monteiro, Pedro J. S. Cardoso,
   Cristiano Cabrita, Jorge Semião, Luís M. R. Oliveira,
   and João M. F. Rodrigues

Designing IoT Solutions for Elderly Home Care: A Systematic Study
of Participatory Design, Personas and Semiotics   226
   Renata de Podestá Gaspar, Rodrigo Bonacin, and Vinícius P. Gonçalves

Participatory Design Approach to Internet of Things: Co-designing a Smart
Shower for and with People with Disabilities   246
   Mexhid Ferati, Ayesha Babar, Kanani Carine, Ali Hamidi,
   and Christina Mörtberg

Security Monitoring in a Low Cost Smart Home for the Elderly 262
*Gabriel Ferreira, Paulo Penicheiro, Ruben Bernardo, Álvaro Neves,
Luís Mendes, João Barroso, and António Pereira*

Understanding the Questions Asked by Care Staff While Eliciting Life
Stories from Older Adults for AAC System Design 274
Haruka Kanetsuku, Tetsuya Hirotomi, and Sachiko Hara

Analysis of Electrogastrograms During Exercise Loads 285
*Fumiya Kinoshita, Kosuke Fujita, Kazuya Miyanaga, Hideaki Touyama,
Masumi Takada, and Hiroki Takada*

Creativity and Ambient Urbanizing at the Intersection of the Internet
of Things and People in Smart Cities. 295
H. Patricia McKenna

Barrier Detection Using Sensor Data from Unimpaired Pedestrians 308
Akihiro Miyata, Iori Araki, and Tongshun Wang

Technologies Applied to Remote Supervision of Exercise in Peripheral
Arterial Disease: A Literature Review 320
Dennis Paulino, Arsénio Reis, João Barroso, and Hugo Paredes

Low-Cost Smart Surveillance System for Smart Cities. 330
*Rúben Pereira, Diogo Correia, Luís Mendes, Carlos Rabadão,
João Barroso, and António Pereira*

Power Assist Control Based on Learning Database of Joint Angle
of Powered Exoskeleton Suitable for Wearer's Posture 340
Katsuya Sahashi, Shota Murai, and Yasutake Takahashi

Performance Sensor for Reliable Operation. 347
*Jorge Semião, Ruben Cabral, Marcelino B. Santos, Isabel C. Teixeira,
and J. Paulo Teixeira*

"I Would Like to Get Close to You": Making Robot Personal Space
Invasion Less Intrusive with a Social Gaze Cue 366
*Stefan-Daniel Suvei, Jered Vroon, Vella V. Somoza Sanchéz,
Leon Bodenhagen, Gwenn Englebienne, Norbert Krüger,
and Vanessa Evers*

A Scoping Study on the Development of an Interactive Upper-Limb
Rehabilitation System Framework for Patients with Stroke 386
*Kevin C. Tseng, Alice M. K. Wong, Chung-Yu Wu, Tian-Sheuan Chang,
Yu-Cheng Pei, and Jean-Lon Chen*

Access to the Web, Social Media, Education, Culture and Social Innovation

Improving Resource Discovery and Access Through User-Controlled
Adaptation: Exploring the Role of Library Metadata   397
  Wondwossen M. Beyene and Marius Wiker Aasheim

SELFMADE – Self-determination and Communication
Through Inclusive MakerSpaces   409
  Ingo K. Bosse, Hanna Linke, and Bastian Pelka

Applying an Implicit Recommender System in the Preparation of Visits
to Cultural Heritage Places.   421
  Pedro J. S. Cardoso, Pedro Guerreiro, Jânio Monteiro,
  and João M. F. Rodrigues

State of Accessibility in U.S. Higher Ed Institutions   437
  Jiatyan Chen

Quo Vadis "Interaction Design and Children, Older and Disabled"
in America and Europe?.   450
  Francisco V. Cipolla Ficarra, Maria V. Ficarra, Eulogia Mendoza,
  and Miguel Cipolla Ficarra

Focus on New Technologies, Editorial and Business Publishing
for International User.   463
  Francisco V. Cipolla Ficarra, Alejandra Quiroga, and Maria V. Ficarra

Picturemarks: Changes in Mining Media and Digital Storytelling   475
  Ole Goethe

Micro-internships on the Margins   486
  Margeret Hall, Michelle Friend, and Markus Krause

Acquisition, Representation and Retrieval of 3D Dynamic Objects   496
  Andreas Kratky

Report A Barrier: Creating and Implementing a Pan-University
Accessibility Reporting System.   511
  Lori Kressin

Open Participatory Democracy in the Basque Country: The Role
of Open Digital Platforms in Public Budgeting and Finance   519
  Álvaro Luna, Xabier Barandiarán, and Alfonso Unceta

A Proposal for a Remote Interactive Class System with Sign
Language Interpretation   530
  Márcio Martins, Jorge Borges, Elsa Justino, Tânia Rocha,
  João Barroso, and Arsénio Reis

Development of Thought Using a Humanoid Robot in an Elementary
School Classroom   541
    Reika Omokawa and Shu Matsuura

A Panorama on Selection and Use of Bioinformatics Tools
in the Brazilian University Context   553
    Vanessa Stangherlin Machado Paixão-Côrtes,
    Walter Ritzel Paixão-Côrtes, Marcia de Borba Campos,
    and Osmar Norberto de Souza

A Personal Emotion-Based Recipe Recommendation Mobile Social
Platform: Mood Canteen   574
    Tsai-Hsuan Tsai, Hsien-Tsung Chang, Chia-Yu Hsu, Shu-Yu Lin,
    Wei-Cheng Yan, and Yi-Cheng Chen

Emerging Social Media and Social Networks Analysis Transforms
the Tourism Industry: Living Green Smart Tourism Ecosystem   583
    Tsai-Hsuan Tsai, Hsien-Tsung Chang, Yu-Wen Lin, Ming-Chun Yu,
    Pei-Jung Lien, Wei-Cheng Yan, and Wei-Ling Ho

Institutional Accessibility Awareness   591
    Brent Whiting

Author Index   603

Design for All, Accessibility and Usability

A Method for Analyzing Mobility Issues for People with Physical Disabilities in the Context of Developing Countries

Leticia Maria de Oliveira Camenar[(✉)], Diego de Faria do Nascimento, and Leonelo Dell Anhol Almeida

Federal University of Technology, Paraná (UTFPR), Curitiba, PR, Brazil
leticia.camenar@gmail.com, df.nascimento93@gmail.com,
leoneloalmeida@utfpr.edu.br

Abstract. In this paper, we propose a method based on studies available in the literature and in the norms that regulate urban accessibility to analyze the problems of urban mobility faced by people with physical disabilities in cities of developing countries. To performing this analysis, we carried out a series of activities through participatory workshops and analysis of route services involving 29 people with physical disabilities or their companions. The results revealed some of the main problems of accessibility found in cities, new ways for tracing routes in map applications, considering accessibility aspects.

Keywords: Urban mobility · Urban accessibility · Physical disabilities

1 Introduction

Urban mobility is one of the main elements for the configuration of the urban structure, since people frequently need to move from a place to another. The concept of mobility has implications on accessibility and due to this reason is necessary that cities provide legislation for ensuring people traffic in an egalitarian way around the urban perimeter [6]. This need and the reality of cities in developing countries represent a gap between urban mobility provided by legislation and urban mobility experienced in the daily lives of people with physical disabilities. This gap is characterized by the fact that cities have historically been built in response to architectural preferences and budget constraints, frequently neglecting the characteristics of people who will move through sidewalks, streets, buildings, bus, and subway entrances, toilets or public agencies [8]. For example, frequently, public spaces have several stairs and few elevators; similarly, the roads have long stretches of sidewalks, however, few of them contain ramps with adequate width and/or inclination.

Considering the urban mobility issue of people with physical disabilities, there are some academic studies developed in the northern hemisphere as Rashid et al. [15], Nuojua et al. [13], Zheng et al. [19], and Tsampoulatidis et al. [17].

© Springer International Publishing AG, part of Springer Nature 2018
M. Antona and C. Stephanidis (Eds.): UAHCI 2018, LNCS 10907, pp. 3–17, 2018.
https://doi.org/10.1007/978-3-319-92049-8_1

These studies present tools to assist the mobility of people with disabilities, however, they consider cultural, social, economic, legislative, and architectural characteristics present in the northern hemisphere, which are quite distinct from the reality found in the context of developing countries.

Therefore, this study aims to analyze the mobility issues faced by people with physical disabilities in large urban centers in the context of developing countries, more specifically in Brazil. We conducted a case study in the city of Curitiba, which has a population of around 1,7 million people. In this case study we decided not to consider small municipalities scenarios, potentially with less favorable contexts, especially to avoid the construction of victimizing scenarios [16]. In this sense, we chose Curitiba because it is a large city, which has a great diversity of urban elements and is one of the best cities in Brazil in terms of urban accessibility [4].

The analysis of mobility problems was conducted by means of a method, which is based on studies available in the literature, Brazilian Association of Technical Standards (ABNT) 9050 standards that regulate urban accessibility in Brazil, and a set of Human-Computer Interaction techniques for involving people. The method is composed of Participatory Workshops and Analysis of Route Services. In order to identify the volunteers' profile who collaborated with the study, both activities also involved the application of a questionnaire that, in cases of severe limitations for reading and/or writing, were applied as structured interviews.

In the Participatory Workshop, which is a workshop model that uses Participatory Design techniques [11] the researchers proposed a series of discussions about mobility experiences in the city. These discussions employed Focus Group, a method that provide conditions for understanding group opinions and experiences more quickly and at lower costs than individual interviews [10]. A mediator led the Focus Group and invited the volunteers to provide opinions within the proposed theme. For this, the mediator used the Scenario technique [2], that, in the Focus Group, described concrete situations faced by physically disabled persons, in order to exemplify to the participants the situations faced in the daily life and also to foment the discussions about the subject.

In the Route Services Analysis, the researchers initially performed a Semistructured Interview about the mobility issues found in the city, similar to the Participatory Workshop, and later carried out two activities involving maps. In the first researchers invited participants to draw a route in a printed map, based on the reading and analysis of text instructions. In the second activity, researchers invited participants to describe a route verbally by analyzing a printed map.

We conducted the activities in October/2016 and involved 29 persons from the Association of the Physically Disabled of Paraná (ADFP). The results of this research provided us some indications to understand mobility issues found in contexts of large cities in developing countries, as well as to identify new ways of describing and visualizing a route that caters to people with physical disabilities as the use of sidewalk-based routes instead of streets [9].

2   Related Work

There are several works that use computing to address problems of urban mobility, these works have different characteristics such as investigate and report problems in the city [15,17] or calculate and provide accessible paths [7,8]. For purposes of analysis, in this study, we selected six papers that apply urban planning methods and route calculations methods. These works will be briefly analyzed taking into account the characteristics of each one of them.

The paper of Rashid et al. [15] aims to provide conditions for wheelchairs users report accessibility problems in the urban environment in real time with a method that uses an application for Nokia N95. This application is intended to provide users with an accessible. Also, users' reports are used to provide new routes that exclude such obstacles.

Zheng et al. [19] analyzed urban traffic and developed a system for managing and constructing traffic maps, where areas that needed adjusts to incorporate accessibility were examined through the maps generated by the application. In this method, the accessibility of a location is determined by a calculus based on a summation of the connectivity of each point of the city represented as a graph. The higher the value of the sum, less accessible is that point in the city and, consequently, that point is marked as not accessible. Once a location is marked as not accessible, the application determines whether that location needs re-planning.

The method of Tsampoulatidis et al. [17] aimed at providing conditions for citizens report problems in the city through an application, available in desktop and mobile versions. The reported problems are automatically transmitted to the public administration. This method considers, in addition to people's opinions about problems found in the urban perimeter, the accessibility and need for urban planning.

Kulakov et al. [7] developed Social Navigator, a routing application that uses a mathematical method based on user evaluations and Dijkstra's method for estimating accessibility. This application provides the flexibility of route variation according to individual constraints reported by users. In addition, the service also provides user feedback functionality to report the conditions of the selected route.

Menkens et al. [8] further investigated user needs through inquiries to potential users of the route planning tool. The results of the study showed that the main problems for wheelchair users are sidewalk constructions, variations in surface pavements, slope, narrow passages, holes or gaps in the streets and sidewalks. In addition, that study also showed there are different profiles of wheelchair users, in this way an accessible path for a wheelchair user is not necessarily usable for another user. For example, while an active wheelchair user (a person who is active and athletic, able to practice sports) can easily overcome low downhills or low curb ramps, however, a wheelchair user dependent on an electric wheelchair may not be able to overcome the same barriers.

Table 1 presents a comparison between the related works by means of the analysis of some characteristics defined by the authors of this study. The first two characteristics refers respectively to the availability of the application code, checking whether the application is open source and the code is publicly available; and the use of open data (i.e. data publicly available and which can be used for various purposes). The analysis of these characteristics showed that no studies use open data and a small number has open source code.

Table 1. Comparative study of Related Work

	Kulakov et al. [7]	Menkens et al. [8]	Rashid et al. [15]	Nuojua et al. [13]	Zheng et al. [19]	Tsampoulatidis et al. [17]
Open code	No	No	No	No	No	Yes
Open data	No	No	No	No	No	No
Required resources	Smart-phone	Smart-phone	Nokia N95	Web browser	Own software	Smartphone and web browser
Collect accessibility information	Yes	Yes	Yes	No	No	Yes
Involves population and public power in application	No	Indirectly	No	No	No	Only in paid version
Quality checking of informed problems	Yes	Yes	Yes	Yes	No	No
Metric for calculation	Streets and collected information	Streets and collected information	Streets and collected information	Streets and collected information	Streets and collected information	Streets and collected information

Next, we analyzed the technological resources needed in each related work and we verified most of them use only widespread technologies as smartphones and web browsers. The fourth characteristic analyzed investigates which works directly collect information about accessibility of the city, this is an important characteristic that provides data which can be used in future studies and was only not found in the studies of Nuojua et al. [13] and Zheng et al. [19].

Other characteristics analyzed were the involvement of the population and public government in the application (in the sense of informing to the public government the problems found in the city), and the quality verification of the problems reported by the population (in the sense of accepting only reports that have at least basic information such as the location and description of the problem). We realize that the involvement of the public power and the population is still limited, however, more than a half of the papers has some form of control of the problems reported.

Finally, we analyzed the metrics employed by each application for calculating routes and verified that all methods are based on streets (rather than sidewalks, where the pedestrians circulate) and in information provided by the population.

3 Our Method

Our method is illustrated in Fig. 1. This method consists in three steps executed sequentially, each step is represented in Fig. 1 by three distinct blocks: Information Sources, Participatory Workshops and Route Services Analysis.

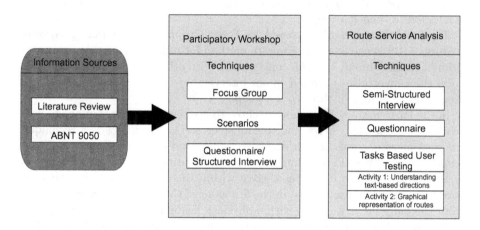

Fig. 1. Our participatory method

In all of the activities of our method (participatory workshop, interviews and task-based activities), all participants received and signed a Informed Consent Form, which was read and explained to the volunteers.

3.1 Information Sources

The initial stage involves analysis of the literature and Brazilian urban accessibility norms. This step aims to identify what was not being addressed by the previous methods and the techniques used by those studies. To reach these objectives, we carried out a literature review. This method of literature review was chosen because it provides the researchers with an in-depth view of the existing works available in the literature. The results of this review allowed us to identify some gaps that were addressed in this research.

Next, we analyzed the particularities of ABNT 9050 [1], which is the norm that regulates urban accessibility of Brazilian cities. This observation is necessary to understand the requirements to be considered to be appropriate for Brazilian context.

Based on these results, the researchers conducted two more steps of analysis: Participatory Workshops and Route Services Analysis.

3.2   Participatory Workshops

The second step of the method employs a workshop model that uses principles and techniques of Participatory Design and is called Participatory Workshop [12]. The choice of the Participatory Workshop was motivated by the fact that this workshop format provides conditions for people democratically exposes their needs and experiences and, also, proposes how computer information systems will be adopted in their daily lives.

The participatory workshop used the Focus Group technique that, according to Morgan [10] is the most appropriate method for individuals develop opinions within a social context, through conversation with other interviewees. In a focus group the conversations are led by an interviewer/mediator who conducts the discussions in groups of three to ten people.

In the Participatory Workshop we chose to use the Scenario technique to permeate the discussions. According to Muller et al. [12] Scenarios is a technique that uses specific stories and/or events to understand concrete situations of participants' daily lives. This technique was chosen because it provides conditions for the participants to insert themselves within the context and to participate more actively in the discussions. In the discussions, the mediator made questions about the daily life of a person with a physical disability, type of transportation used, how they travel on the city sidewalks and how they evaluate sidewalks. In these discussions, the participants had the opportunity to engage in a collective dialogue and contribute with various considerations regarding the proposed themes.

At the end of the activity researchers applied a questionnaire. Ozoki [14] defines a questionnaire as a model, online or printed with questions that the participants must answer in order to provide necessary data in a research, analysis or evaluation. Because of the objectivity of the questionnaires' questions, we decided to use this technique to identify the profile of the interviewees. These questionnaires were also applied as a structured interview in some situations, since the researchers noted that some participants had severe reading and/or writing constraints. The structured interviews according to Vatrapu and Pérez-Quiñones [18] is a type of interview similar to a questionnaire that is composed of predetermined questions that have the characteristic of being short and clearly described, so all the participants can provide a precise answer.

The Participatory Workshop was held in to the Association of the Physically Disabled of Paraná (ADFP), a non-profit organization that provides assistance and rehabilitation to people with physical disabilities, performs physiotherapeutic medical care and promotes the practice of sports to associates. The Participatory Workshop took place at ADFP in October 2016 and was conducted by: an mediator leading the discussion and proposing scenarios, a group of 16 volunteers, and a group of researchers supporting with audio recording, video and group organization. Specifically, on the day of the Workshop, it was also the monthly meeting of families, so the peoples profile who participated in this workshop were wheelchair users, people with reduced mobility and supporters, family members, friends or caregivers.

3.3   Route Services Analysis

The third and last step of our method, articulates semi-structured interviews, questionnaires, and task-based activities.

Semi-structured interviews, according to Blandford [3], combine the characteristics of unstructured interviews with structured interviews using open and closed questions. This interview model was chosen because it enables interviewers to ask questions from the script and also to make explorations from the respondents' responses. In this stage of the work, interviews were conducted with 13 participants who has profile of wheelchair users, crutch user, or supporter. The duration of each interview lasted between 10 and 30 min. In this interviews we asked questions about the daily life of a person with a physical disability, type of transportation used, how they travel on the city sidewalks and how they evaluate sidewalks.

For these activities, two tasks were carried out with the objective of analyzing alternative approaches for presenting routes, considering accessibility aspects. The activities involved 10 of the 13 interviewees. The posture of the researchers who applied these tasks was reactive, they initially explained what was expected to be done and during the accomplishment of the tasks they intervened when questioned or when they noticed that the volunteer expressed difficulties to proceed with the activity.

In the first task the researchers presented a printed version of Fig. 2, which contains a cut-out of a map of the downtown Curitiba and a route drawn from one point to another of the region through sidewalks, curb ramps and crosswalks. Then we invited the volunteers to describe the route presented using imperative phrases, as if they were explaining to another wheelchair user how to make the route indicated on the map.

Fig. 2. Map used in Task 1 Adapted from Google Maps (http://maps.google.com)

For the second task the researchers delivered a printed version of Fig. 3, map of another region of the city accompanied by a textual sequence of 17 directions from one point to another of the map, from these materials the volunteers were asked to draw the route described following the instructions according to an excerpt of a set of instructions:

1. *Go ahead until reach the sidewalk of André de Barros Street;*
2. *Turn left;*
3. *Go ahead until the crosswalk with Desembargador Westphalen Street...*

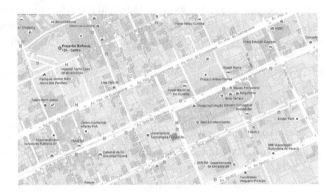

Fig. 3. Map used in the second task. Source: Google Maps (http://maps.google.com)

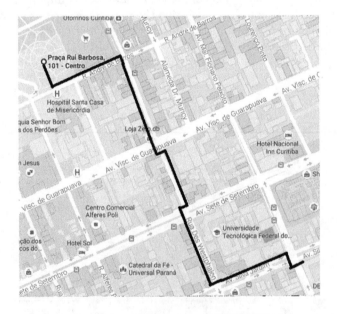

Fig. 4. Trimming from the map used in the second task with the correct dash illustrated. Adapted from Google Maps (http://maps.google.com)

The full dashed path is shown at Fig. 4. At the end of the activities, participants answered the questionnaires (as in the Participative Workshop).

4 Results

This section presents the results of the participatory workshop, interviews, and task-based activities. The volunteers who participated in the participatory workshop are represented in the text with initial G (G1, G2, G3, ...) and the volunteers who answered the interviews are represented with initial E (E1, E2, E3, ...).

Scenario 1: Transportation Used for Locomotion Through the City
Based on the discussion in the participatory workshop and after analyzing the speeches of the semi-structured interviews, we observed that most of the participants use the city's public transportation. However, some of them use a bus line called Acesso[1], created and adapted specifically for people with reduced mobility.

Scenario 2: Accessibility and Issues Experienced in the City
Regarding the accessibility of the city, the 16 participants consider that the city has problems mainly on the sidewalks: "The sidewalks are not adapted for us, wheelchair users, the biggest problem is in the neighborhoods, where accessibility is precarious", said participant E8; "I prefer to walk down the street than on sidewalks, because sidewalks always has something damaged", as reported by E5 participant.

However, we noticed that there was no consensus about the quality of sidewalks: "Bad, lousy, horrible, even more in the region where I live", commented participant E11; "I have already been in a few places where my sister drop my wheelchair and I go alone, so I think it is great", said participant E12. The participant G2 compared the accessibility of urban spaces of Curitiba with the city of Washington, in the United States: "They are a thousand light years ahead of us. It is absurd, my son did not want to leave there because of the ease [for move through the sidewalks], there is not a damaged sidewalk and there is not a hole in the street. He went out with friends to catch subway. It is everything, the whole city". The participant evidenced the disparity of the accessibility in a metropolis of a developed country with the accessibility found in a developing country.

Both wheelchair users with an athletic profile and wheelchair users who always move with help believe that sidewalks have fewer accessibility issues than other participants. Participant E7 believes that this difference of opinion can be explained by the type of disability and difficulty of the wheelchair user: "There may be five wheelchairs here, the only thing that is the same is the wheelchair, because each one has his/her own disability and his/her difficulty. So it is different, it makes a difference".

---

[1] This bus line offers the service of catch disabled persons at home, take them to a health or social care service, and bring them home after care.

Scenario 3: Obstacles Encountered Moving Around the City

Considering the obstacles encountered when moving around the city, the main problem pointed out by all participants is the irregularity of the sidewalks: "It is the sidewalk, ... Is too low or too high", commented E11. In addition to the irregularity of the sidewalks, wheelchair users who are athletes consider holes a major obstacle when moving around. Wheelchair users who cross streets without help commented that other problems are the narrow sidewalks, curb ramps and the type of floor. On the other hand, wheelchair users who need help pointed out that other problems found in public roads are the curb ramps, steps, and holes, "There is no curb ramps. There is a lot of streets in Curitiba that has neither curb ramps and sometimes when curb ramp are present, after the curb ramp there is a step", commented participant E5.

Scenario 4: Slopes

Considering the difficulty of crossing steep slopes streets, 23 participants believe that the two directions have equivalent degrees of difficulty, "The two directions are hard to cross, in both of them I can get hurt if I do not control the wheelchair", commented participant E13, "the companion need to have arm"[2], said participant G4, emphasizing that she needs support in situations like that.

Scenario 5: Longest and Most Accessible Path or Shortest Path but Without Accessibility

The researchers questioned participants about two paths, one shorter but without accessibility and the other much longer with curb ramps and crosswalks to reach from point A to point B, as presented in Fig. 5. Most of the participants reported that they would prefer to use the longer path: "The longer because it gets easier for me because I am going to take a lot more time on the short way, having to dodge the cars because I would have to go down the street and, in the long path, I'll end up getting faster than the other", claimed participant E3. However, three participants, with the athlete profile, mentioned that they would prefer the shortest path: "I would not do the long path, because this tires us too. In the photo here, I would steep my chair, it would fall here on the street, I would cross, and here I would ask help to arrive", reported participant E8.

One variable highlighted in this scenario is whether the wheelchair user is accompanied or not. "If you are accompanied, it becomes easier, but if you are alone ... for me it is impossible to push a wheelchair, because only one hand works [the volunteer has movement restriction in one of the upper limbs], so you always needs to have a person accompanying you, in my case is my son, and he is a strong man", explained the G4 participant.

Results of Route Services Analysis

The first task (describe a route verbally) was performed by 8 participants, identified as E1, E2, ..., E8. Among the 8 participants, the participant E3 showed great difficulty in understanding what should be done. All participants carefully informed the streets that they go through and a minority, represented by the participants E4 and E5, reported in the narration that they use crosswalks, curb

---

[2] Popular expression referring to be strong.

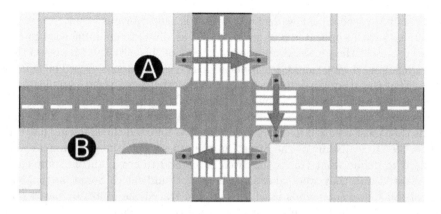

Fig. 5. Scenery used in the workshop

ramps and sidewalks when moving from one point to another of the map. We believe this can be explained by the fact that the participants informed previous experience in using map applications that only indicate the paths by the streets. The ability of participants E4 and E5 to inform more elements than others participants can be explained by the fact that both had access to higher education and are more proficient in using computer technologies when compared to the others. Another interesting point is that not all participants reported the direction (right/left) that they would follow. The result of the first task is shown in Table 2.

Table 2. Elements pointed out by Task 1 participants

	E1	E2	E3	E4	E5	E6	E7	E8
Street	✓	✓	✓	✓	✓	✓	✓	✓
Sidewalk				✓				
Curb ramp				✓	✓			
Crosswalk				✓	✓			
Bicycle path						✓	✓	
Corner	✓							
Road side	✓							
Right/Left	✓	✓		✓	✓			

The analysis of the second task results was based on the routes drawn by participants on the given maps. None of the participants clearly represented that routes passed through sidewalks. The lines of the drawing crossed the center of the streets on the maps and not the edges of the blocks where the sidewalks are. This led to two hypotheses, one is that the text used is not communicating well that it is based on sidewalks and another is that previous experience of the participants with applications of geolocation based on streets influenced in this way to represent the routes. From the volunteers of this activity, 4 reported that they already used Maps and GPS applications on smartphones. Based on this we believe that the other participants have little experience with Maps applications, consequently both hypotheses could be true.

Everyone reached the destination, but there were several errors. The commands that most resulted in errors are those that followed the following pattern: "Cross the street [Name of the Street] in the crosswalk", the participants were confused to define what tracks they were supposed to cross, and in some cases they crossed and they went ahead in the streets indicated. Some participants did not follow the commands until the end and traced the routes by paths they already knew of the city, this may prove that the commands are still complex resulting in the withdrawal of some participants to follow them.

Analysis of the Questionnaires

Based on the questionnaire responses, it was possible to verify that of the 29 respondents 14 (48%) identified themselves as wheelchair users, 5 (17%) identified as friends, spouses, supporters or relatives of a wheelchair user and 10 (34%) were identified as belonging to another profile, among those belonging to another profile there are those who use walking sticks or crutches to move around the city, and also people with other disabilities related to mobility who can walk without objects of support.

Among the group of wheelchair users, segmentation by profiles occurred as follows: 4 (29%) identified themselves as independent wheelchairs users and who easily make long journeys through the city; 7 (50%) have identified themselves as wheelchair users who can easily make some paths, but eventually need support to overcome through some barriers and/or to make long journeys through the city; and 3 (21%) identified themselves as wheelchair users with great difficulty to move through the city, who always need support to overcome barriers in the city.

Regarding the gender issue, it is possible to verify that among the sample analyzed the majority of the users of wheelchairs are men (71%). All wheelchair users who identified themselves as independent profile are men, such percentage can be justified by the fact that men are culturally more physically strong and therefore are able to overcome obstacles more easily. In contrast, all people who identified themselves as supporters of a wheelchair user reported that are women, this percentage occurs due to the social role assigned to women by the patriarchal society, some of them are mothers, and others are professional caregivers.

Among those interviewed, 5 (17%) did not finished elementary school, 11 (38%) did not finished high school, 10 (34%) completed high school and 6 (21%) higher education (complete or incomplete). Of those with complete or incomplete Higher Education, all reported using smartphones, while among those who finished only high school, the number of smartphone users dropped to 70%; Finally, only 54% among volunteers who did not finish high school use smartphones.

5   Final Considerations

This work investigated the problems of urban mobility faced by people with physical disabilities in the Brazilian context through a method composed by three steps: Information Sources, Participatory Workshops and Route Services Analysis.

In Information Sources, the researchers were able to understand research gaps found in the literature. The Participatory Workshop phase employed Scenarios and Focus Group as techniques to promote the discussions. We realized that accessibility is important for mobility in urban spaces, also the main problems found in the city are related to the sidewalks. In the Route Services Analysis phase, Task-Based Activities involving two maps evidenced the participants' experience with map applications that take into consideration only the streets, as Google Maps and OpenStreetMap[3], also the need to adjust the textual instructions proposed by the researchers aiming at providing richer accessibility-related directions.

The questionnaires applied in the Participatory Workshop and in the Route Services Analysis phases pointed out that most of the volunteers declare themselves as wheelchair users. However other profiles emerged, for example, independent wheelchair user and dependent wheelchair user. Another aspect observed is that most of the respondents declared themselves as disabled and men, reflecting data from the National Health Survey of 2013 [5], while most of caregivers are women.

We hoped that this research can be extended to other large urban centers with a similar size of Curitiba. We did not investigate whether this study would apply to small towns, villages and peripheries, but we acknowledge that these scenarios differ in comparison to large centers in quantity of urban elements and in the habits adopted by people. For example, small towns have reduced traffic and it is common for many people to walking on the street and not to use the crosswalk.

Future works involve prototyping and development of applications for smartphones with textual description and graphical representation of the routes; a study about the difficulties of different profiles of people with physical disabilities associated to the different problems of accessibility in urban crossings; proposing tools to assist municipalities in urban planning, based on accessibility data reported by users.

Acknowledgments. We would like to thank EU-BR EUBra-BigSEA project (MCTI/RNP 3rd Coordinated Call), PPGCA, and DAINF.

---

[3] https://www.openstreetmap.org.

References

1. ABNT: NBR 9050. Acessibilidade a edificações, mobiliário, espaços e equipamentos urbanos (2015)
2. Bødker, S., Christiansen, E., Thüring, M.: A conceptual toolbox for designing CSCW applications. DAIMI Rep. Ser. **23**(489) (1994). https://tidsskrift.dk/daimipb/article/view/6983
3. Blandford, A.: Semi-structured qualitative studies. In: The Encyclopedia of Human-Computer Interaction, Interaction Design Foundation, 2nd edn. (2017). https://www.interaction-design.org/literature/book/the-encyclopedia-of-human-computer-interaction-2nd-ed/semi-structured-qualitative-studies
4. IBGE: Censo demográfico 2010: Características urbanísticas do entorno dos domicílios (2010). http://www.ibge.gov.br/home/estatistica/populacao/censo2010
5. IBGE: Pesquisa nacional de saúde 2013: Pessoas com deficiência (2013)
6. Koenig, J.G.: Indicators of urban accessibility: theory and application. Transportation **9**(2), 145–172 (1980). https://doi.org/10.1007/BF00167128
7. Kulakov, K., Shabaev, A., Shabalina, I.: The route planning services approach for people with disability. In: 2015 17th Conference of Open Innovations Association (FRUCT), pp. 89–95, April 2015
8. Menkens, C., Sussmann, J., Al-Ali, M., Breitsameter, E., Frtunik, J., Nendel, T., Schneiderbauer, T.: EasyWheel - a mobile social navigation and support system for wheelchair users. In: Proceedings of the 2011 Eighth International Conference on Information Technology: New Generations, ITNG 2011, pp. 859–866. IEEE Computer Society, Washington (2011). http://dx.doi.org/10.1109/ITNG.2011.149
9. Minetto, R., Kozievitch, N.P., da Silva, R.D., Almeida, L.D.A., de Santi, J.: Shortcut suggestion based on collaborative user feedback for suitable wheelchair route planning. In: ITSC, pp. 2372–2377. IEEE (2016)
10. Morgan, C.: The Focus Group Guidebook. SAGE Publications, Thousand Oaks (1997)
11. Muller, M.J.: Participatory design: the third space in HCI. In: The Human-Computer Interaction Handbook, pp. 1051–1068. L. Erlbaum Associates Inc., Hillsdale (2003). http://dl.acm.org/citation.cfm?id=772072.772138
12. Muller, M.J., Haslwanter, J.H., Dayton, T.: Participatory practices in the software lifecycle. In: Helander, M.G., Landauer, T.K., Prabhu, P.V. (eds.) Handbook of Human-Computer Interaction, pp. 256–300. North-Holland (1997)
13. Nuojua, J., Juustila, A., Räisänen, T., Kuutti, K., Soudunsaari, L.: Exploring web-based participation methods for urban planning. In: Proceedings of the Tenth Anniversary Conference on Participatory Design 2008, PDC 2008, pp. 274–277. Indiana University, Indianapolis (2008). http://dl.acm.org/citation.cfm?id=1795234.1795298
14. Ozok, A.: Survey Design and Implementation in HCI, pp. 151–1169, March 2009
15. Rashid, O., Dunabr, A., Fisher, S., Rutherford, J.: Users helping users: user generated content to assist wheelchair users in an urban environment. In: 2010 Ninth International Conference on Mobile Business and 2010 Ninth Global Mobility Roundtable (ICMB-GMR), pp. 213–219, June 2010
16. Spinuzzi, C.: Tracing Genres Through Organizations: A Sociocultural Approach to Information Design. MIT Press, Cambridge (2003)
17. Tsampoulatidis, I., Ververidis, D., Tsarchopoulos, P., Nikolopoulos, S., Kompatsiaris, I., Komninos, N.: Improvemycity: an open source platform for direct citizen-government communication, pp. 839–842 (2013). http://doi.acm.org/10.1145/2502081.2502225

18. Vatrapu, R., Pérez-Quiñones, M.A.: Culture and usability evaluation: the effects of culture in structured interviews. J. Usability Stud. **1**(4), 156–170 (2006). http://dl.acm.org/citation.cfm?id=2835531.2835533

19. Zheng, X., Zhao, L., Fu, M., Wang, S.: Extension and application of space syntax a case study of urban traffic network optimizing in Beijing. In: Workshop on Power Electronics and Intelligent Transportation System, PEITS 2008, pp. 291–295, August 2008

Mobile-PrivAccess: Method for Analyzing Accessibility in Mobile Applications from the Privacy Viewpoint Abiding by W3C

Rachel T. Chicanelli[(⊠)], Patricia C. de Souza,
and Luciana C. Lima de Faria Borges

Laboratório de Ambientes Virtuais Interativos (LAVI),
Instituto de Computação (IC), Universidade Federal de Mato Grosso (UFMT),
Cuiabá, Brazil
rachelchicanelli@gmail.com, pathycsouza@gmail.com,
lucianafariaborges@gmail.com

Abstract. Despite accessibility is a right ensured by the legislation, it is still a challenge to People with Disability and Limitations (PwDaL), considering Limitations, for instance, those deriving from aging and low literacy. In Digital Systems (DS) restrictions on use by PwDaL are easily found which even more excludes them from society which preponderantly interacts with the technology. Recognizing the importance of ensuring accessibility and privacy to PwDaL we investigated the problems of accessibility and digital privacy in the context of mobile applications and proposed the Mobile-PrivAccess method. This method allows applying the W3C directives to assess the accessibility to mobile applications privacy resources, without the participation of PwDaL. The absence of these users spares unnecessary efforts at the preliminary stages of the application assessment. The method based on an inspection technique is a four-stage structured process with established goals containing support artifacts for specific phases. For applying the method, two professionals with knowledge on and or experience in digital inclusion for PwDaL and/or in the W3C standards are required. For verifying the viability of the method proposed an experiment was performed adopting the proposed method to assess the accessibility of the Waze App [13] in three operating systems, as follows: Android, iOS and Windows Phone. The results demonstrated the viability of the method indicating that Waze meets few success criteria and presents a number of accessibility barriers to different PwDaL profiles.

Keywords: Accessibility guidelines · Accessibility evaluation
Privacy · Waze · Mobile applications

1 Introduction

Accessibility, even though it is a right guaranteed by law, is still a challenge for people with disabilities and limitations (PwDaL) such as those caused by ageing and low literacy. When it comes to digital systems, it is easy to find usability restrictions for this audience, which makes them feel increasingly excluded from a society that nowadays

© Springer International Publishing AG, part of Springer Nature 2018
M. Antona and C. Stephanidis (Eds.): UAHCI 2018, LNCS 10907, pp. 18–37, 2018.
https://doi.org/10.1007/978-3-319-92049-8_2

interacts more than ever by means of technology. Efforts have been made to encourage research in the area, identify accessibility barriers, and propose policies to assist in building solutions, as the Web Accessibility Initiative (WAI) from the World Wide Web Consortium (W3C) has done.

Given the relevance of the accessibility theme, the Brazilian Symposium on Human Factors in Computational Systems (HCI) produced the "Major Research Challenges in HCI in Brazil-GranDIHC-BR'" [1] report in 2012, the same as the Brazilian Society of Computing did in 2006 when launching the Major Challenges for Research in Computer Science in Brazil [2]. The GranDIHC-BR' report [1] listed five major categories. One of these categories was named 'G2-Digital Accessibility and Inclusion'.

Granatto, Pallaro and Bim published in [3] the results of a Systematic Review (SR) that sought to map the evolution of accessibility-related research in HCI since its first edition, covering the period from 1998 through 2015. The objective of this work was to analyze the effects of the launching of the Major Challenges by the BCS – Brazilian Computing Symposium - which had as challenge 4: participatory and universal access of Brazilian citizens to knowledge), as well as the GranDIHC-BR' (which addressed the theme in challenge 2). The SR processed the accepted works on all HCI trails. One of the considerations presented in [3] is that the works that approached accessibility in the investigated period represented approximately 12% of the total; however, given the diversity of topics covered in the HCI Symposium this number did not seem so relevant. The article also sought to answer other questions, such as: what special needs were addressed, and which technologies had already been addressed.

In [4], an analysis was carried out to verify if the HCI publications in Brazil, from 2013 to 2015, had addressed the challenges listed in the GranDIHC-BR'. Among the findings, it is noticeable that most of the articles published in the event (during the analyzed period) had were not related to any of the five challenges and the number of these non-related papers was increasing. The challenge that produced fewer publications was 'G4-Human Values' which deals with 'Privacy in the Connected World' as one of the challenges to be approached.

In order to have control over their privacy when using digital systems, users must have an understanding of the terms of use and the privacy policy as well as control the settings of their privacy preferences. However, researches [5–9] have shown problems related to terms of use and privacy policies regarding readability, clarity, flexibility and compliance with current legislation, such as the Brazilian Civil Rights Framework for the Internet [10]. Additionally, users with no disabilities or other limitations face difficulties controlling their privacy settings.

Aiming to contribute in this context, the discussion presented in this article articulates two GranDIHC-BR' themes-accessibility and privacy proposing a method that allows applying the W3C guidelines to assess the accessibility of mobile application privacy features without the participation of PwDaL. The absence of this user saves an unnecessary effort in the preliminary stages of the app evaluation. This method, based on the inspection technique, is a four-step structured process with specific objectives containing supporting artefacts for specific phases. In order to execute the method, it is necessary to have two knowledgeable and/or experienced professionals in digital inclusion for PwDaL and/or W3C standards.

The article is structured as follows: Sect. 2 presents the bibliography used to support the work of this research; Sect. 3 describes the methodology of the work and the proposed method for this research problem; Sect. 4 presents the results of the application of the proposed method in App Waze evaluation; and finally, the last section presents the research conclusions and suggestions for future work.

2 Related Works

In recent years, technological advances have been noticeable in mobile devices and social networks among other technologies. Faced with this scenario, along with the popularity and ease of technological access, an unpleasant problem arises-abusive data sharing, because of which technological users are at risk of having their privacy violated.

Research works can be found addressing the theme of privacy, also relating it to accessibility; these works may contribute to minimize problems.

Regarding privacy, we highlight works such as [9] which investigates obstacles in privacy and security decision making and seeks for ways to assist in these decision-making tasks. Realizing that it is difficult for users to understand how the collection works, what for, by whom and even when the collected information is stored, and it is difficult to know how to set this environment according to their needs.

As far as the lack of orientation on design aspects for privacy documents is concerned, [7] develops a space for the design of warnings and privacy reports, to better structure those documents, based on a literature review on several systems and the opinion of experts and professionals in the privacy area.

Alternatively, [8] presents works that address guidelines for the design of ubiquitous systems which are aimed to helping trust in and respect for users' privacy. Hence, ten guidelines are drawn up to help and guide the analysis and development of ubiquitous applications, and to ensure users' confidence and the privacy of their data. These guidelines were based on the inspection of the case study of this research.

[6] approaches a research study on privacy policies, which are difficult to understand, very extensive, and offer little or no flexibility to allow users to make adjustments according to their preferences. Based on these issues, an exploratory and qualitative research was carried out on five applications and then a report was drawn which provides the analysis of the privacy problems found, as well as suggestions to improve the users' experience.

Regarding works that investigate privacy issues linked to accessibility issues in mobile devices and the Internet, we highlight [11, 12]. In [11, 12] an accessibility assessment was made by inspecting Facebook's privacy functions with blind users. In [11] the evaluation went through three stages; in the first one, a user profile data collection questionnaire was applied, aiming to analyze the user's experience and knowledge on privacy in the social network. In the second stage, three tasks were performed with different levels of difficulty relating to Facebook's privacy; these tasks were observed and recorded. In the last step, the interviewee was asked to express his/her perception about the interaction with Facebook and on the survey in order to contribute to the improvement of accessibility in Facebook.

No problems were found in the first stage of the evaluation and so, it was concluded that all the interviewees were qualified as active users of Facebook. In the second stage, problems were observed such as the lack of knowledge on privacy settings, a fact that demanded the interviewer's direction. Besides this setback, it was not possible to open the necessary buttons through the keyboard when using the screen reader, causing the interruption of the activity. Thus, it was possible to notice at this stage that it was necessary to take several steps to reach the goal, making the evaluation tiresome. Regarding the last stage, the interviewees reported that, due to their experience and dexterity in the use of the computer, the accessibility to Facebook's privacy functions is an item that needs to be improved.

In [12], Facebook's privacy aspects were assessed considering usability, accessibility, and users' emotional responses to task execution. Three methods were adopted to evaluate accessibility: (i) Simplified Accessibility Assessment (ASA) to assess accessibility to privacy features and (ii) Automatic Assessment based on accessibility guidelines, both of which were carried out by experts, and (iii) Accessibility Test of privacy functionalities by observing visually-impaired users' interaction.

The evaluation made exclusively by the experts clearly showed Facebook's limitations, mainly in issues related to keyboard navigation and texting, in which some privacy options are inaccessible. On the other hand, the evaluation with semiautomatic tools verified the source code adequacy to a set of accessibility guidelines, such as WCAG and e-MAG.

The Accessibility Test based on the observation of users, once more verified that some privacy options are inaccessible, such as the lack of alternative text for reading images. In some situations, there was a need for the intervention of the evaluator, but although the steps to be followed to carry out the task were described, the user was not able to complete the task. Some fields are confusing and disorganized which led the user to follow the wrong path.

This evaluation verified that the accessibility test performed with a visually-impaired user complemented and confirmed the evaluation performed by experts, suggesting that the difficulties in accessing the privacy functions are more critical than those identified in the analytical accessibility assessment. The results made it possible to conclude that a solution to accessibility problems is essential to enable the use of the functions related to privacy in Facebook.

The accessibility and usability assessment were addressed in [5], in which sixty-four site privacy policies were analyzed from the perspective of the Flesch Reading Ease Index, which aims to determine the level of education needed to understand the documents. It was also analyzed whether they meet users' needs and how they can be improved.

It was concluded that the Internet is no longer the exclusive domain of researchers and universities, it is used by people of all kinds and the more people have access to internet, the more diversity increases. For this reason, it is necessary to know if they are not creating a "digital literacy divide", which proves to be disadvantageous for vulnerable people, jeopardizing their security in relation to confusing or intimidating language in privacy policies.

In addition, several researches have been developed aiming to develop a methodology containing recommendations that may help professionals identify characteristics and problems that can be solved or minimized during the interface evaluation. As an example, we can cite [13] that applied an accessibility assessment, based on user inspection and guided by expert-adapted guidelines.

In [14], a guide to the best practices of web accessibility assessment was developed with the participation of visually impaired people. This guide recommends that, before performing the evaluation with the users, other evaluations such as the heuristic evaluation be performed.

One other study [15] brings recommendations for accessibility assessments with the methods used by people involved in web projects, assessing the pros and cons of some accessibility assessment methods and developed recommendations for assessing web accessibility for the visually disabled persons.

In [16] PD4CAT - Participatory Design for Customized Assistive Technology was proposed, a method that helps multidisciplinary teams conceive customized computational solutions by means of PD to actively engage the team (including the disabled person, his/her therapists and caregivers) in the design and development cycle.

3 Methodology

Based on the problems described in the previous sections, the methodology of this work involved the development of a method based on the W3C accessibility documents [17, 18] to assess the accessibility of mobile applications in terms of the autonomy and privacy control of users with disabilities or limitations.

3.1 Web and Mobile Accessibility

W3C is an international community that develops open standards and has as its main objective to develop protocols and guidelines to ensure the growth of the Web [19]. W3C has a working group that deals specifically with web accessibility: the Web Accessibility Initiative (WAI). The WAI working group developed the first version of the Web Content Accessibility Guidelines (WCAG) in mid-1999, a document with several guidelines aimed at making the web accessible to all. In 2008 it released the 2nd version of the Recommendation: WCAG 2.0 [18].

Based on WCAG 2.0 [18], in 2015 the Mobile Accessibility: How WCAG 2.0 and Other W3C/WAI Guidelines Apply to Mobile [17] emerges; a document still in its draft version, which provides guidelines to be applied to mobile web contents and applications, including native and hybrid applications.

Just like WCAG 2.0 [18] the document [17] is organized into four principles named: perceivable, operable, understandable and robust. Summarizing, the four principles have as objectives:

1. Perceivable - ensure that the content and interface components are presented in a way that are perceivable to the user. For example, offering more than one type of media for the same information.

2. Operable - ensure means for the interface and navigation components to be operable, such as ensuring satisfactory reading time and providing all functionalities via keyboard.
3. Understandable - ensure that the information and operation of the interface is evident and easy for users to understand. One example is the need for applications to support both portrait and landscape screen orientations and to provide instructions for custom device and touchscreen manipulation gestures.
4. Robust - seek means to make content robust and sufficient to be reliably interpreted by various types of users, enabling the use of assistive technologies, and using correct and effective markup languages with unique ID attributes. For example, allow keyboard customization in device settings, such as using virtual keyboard.

While in the WCAG 2.0 recommendation [18] each of the four principles has guidelines that are composed by Success Criteria, in document [17] each of the principles brings best practice suggestions in the implementation of the mobile application functionalities in order to meet the diversity of users with disabilities. It is important to point out that [17] can be considered as a complement to the WCAG 2.0 [18] recommendation, since it addresses issues specific to the mobile platform, such as the small size of the screen and the difficulty this causes for the visualization of all content by a person with low vision. For this reason, the design of the Mobile-PrivAccess method considered the success criteria of [18] relevant to mobile applications and the good practices described in [17].

3.2   Mobile-PrivAccess Method

Based on the collected bibliography and the need for a method that evaluates privacy accessibility the method known as Mobile-PrivAccess was developed, assisting in the application of WCAG 2.0 [18] and the good practices established in the document [17]. both from WAI-W3C, to assess whether the disabled user can gain access to and control privacy settings in mobile applications. These documents [17, 18] are written in the form of guidelines to be followed in the design and implementation of web and mobile solutions. The proposed method seeks to facilitate the application of these guidelines in prototypes and off-the-shelf products.

It is still common to find systems that do not meet accessibility recommendations, such as certain limitations found in Facebook [12] and WhatsApp [20].

The method, based on an inspection technique, is a four-stage structured process, with established goals containing support artifacts for specific phases. In order to apply the method, two knowledgeable and/or experienced professionals in digital inclusion for PwDaL and/or in the W3C accessibility standards are required. The stages are:

1. Identifying resources that guarantee the application's privacy.
2. To carry out the inspection, experts separately investigate the accessibility of the privacy resources by adopting assessment tables abiding by the standards [17, 18], considering the users' profiles provided in WAI [21], as illustrated in Fig. 1.
3. Experts gather to discuss and to consolidate the results of the inspection recorded in the tables.

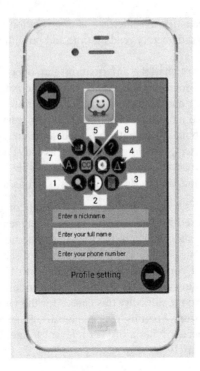

Fig. 1. Interface of profile configuration in Waze meeting principle 1 = perceivable [17, 18]

4. For each of the problems detected by the experts during the assessment for participative design, they present a joint solution in the form of a designed interface prototype.

The first stage of the method involves locating the access to these means: (i) analysis of the privacy configuration options that the App offers and (ii) analysis of the App's Terms of Use and Privacy Policy.

In general, every App has at least two ways to control user privacy: the Term of Use and the Privacy Policy; plus the means of setting privacy within the application itself and via the operating system, when it also provides privacy control features. The Term of Use documents and the Privacy Policy are usually presented in a linked form. The Term of Use is the central document of the legal regiment established between the company holding the App and the user, and describes the application and its rules, as well as the rights and duties of the user [8]. The Privacy Policy, in turn, must inform that user data is collected, stored and distributed, that is, it must provide issues related to the privacy of user data [8].

Based on the description of the wide range of diversity of people and skills, as well as the different types of accessibility barriers imposed to users with certain disabilities and/or limitations, Fig. 1 was produced from [18], summarizing five user profiles. The four principles of the Recommendation [18] and the document [17] aim to address these categories (Table 1).

Table 1. Classification of PwDaL to be served according to WAI [22]

Profile class	User profile
A	People with neurological and cognitive disability
B	People with speech disability
C	People with visual disability
D	People with hearing disability
E	People with physical disability

From [17, 18] four Conformity Assessment Tables were created, each table being related to one of the principles: perceivable, operable, understandable and robust. Each table includes the following items: guideline; quality criteria and/or good practice; and, not-met profiles (according to Fig. 1).

At this stage, each evaluator receives the PwDaL classification table and the conformity assessment tables as well as access to documents [17, 18] for any necessary consultation. Having this material at hand, each evaluator individually inspects the App and fills in the conformity tables. The evaluation should be performed in two sections according to the options identified in step 1 of the method.

Once the inspections are completed in the App, the 3rd stage of the method is started where the evaluators meet to discuss and seek to consolidate the results found. This step ends with the unified production of an accessibility assessment report of the privacy setting means of the inspected application.

The fourth step is developed in a participatory design session [23, 24], aiming to search for solutions that generate prototypes for each accessibility problem found.

The method can be applied in both prototypes (medium and high fidelity) and in off-the-shelf mobile applications.

In order to verify the viability of the proposed method, an experiment was performed adopting the method to assess the accessibility of the Waze App in three operating systems (O. S.): Android, iOS and Windows Phone. This also allowed us to identify the differences in the functioning of the application in each O. S. Waze [25] is a collaborative application in which users may contribute with real-time information on traffic and the area they are driving through, helping users with up-to-date information on what is happening around the route.

The App is available for iOS, Android, Windows Phone and Blackberry operating systems (OS); considering that there are two ways in which to use the App for each operating system (OS): with and without logging in. By choosing not to log in, the user uses the basic features of the App, which focus on calculating routes, but cannot link the App with other social networks and neither can he obtain information from specific users. Even if the user is not being identified, the application remembers all his interaction as well as the routes chosen. If the user logs in, he can edit the map, interact with other users, find where the user's group of friends is at any moment and synchronize with social networks. Consequently, the privacy settings are only possible in this situation.

4   Experiment and Results

This section lists the results of the evaluation of Waze using Mobile-PrivAccess, demonstrating that it does not meet several success criteria and user profiles that are not answered by the App.

Taking into account that it is not always possible to count on the users' performance (PwDaL) in the evaluation of the technology, whether due to their limitations or to the limitation of the technology being used, we emphasize that for this reason the Mobile-PrivAccess method uses specialists in the first instance, not including the PwDaL, and then from these results a new evaluation including PwDaL can be applied, where some of the problems found have already been solved and/or forwarded.

In addition, in this experiment we chose to apply the method on an off-the-shelf product to demonstrate the applicability of such method in an App that is widely used.

4.1   Applying the Method on an Evaluation of Waze

By following the steps of the Mobile-PrivAccess method to evaluate Waze App, the experts involved in the experiment point to the following resources resulting from the application of Step 1 (Identifying resources that guarantee the application's privacy): 1. Privacy Configuration and 2. Terms of Use and Privacy Policy.

Once these resources have been identified, this section is organized into three sub-sections: the first one presents the results of Steps 2 and 3 of the method for the Privacy Setup options; the second one, the results of Steps 2 and 3 of the method for the analysis of the Terms of Use and Privacy Policy and the third one presents results from Step 4 for a variety of user profiles not served by the evaluated App.

It should be noted that the vast majority of accessibility criteria have not been met and the most critical problems are reported here. In addition, as the results found in the analysis of the Android and iOS were very similar, they will be treated in a similar way when comparing them with Windows Phone.

Table 2 shows information on equipment, operating system, and Waze version used in the evaluations.

Table 2. Characteristics of the items used in the evaluations.

O. S.	Version	Smartphone
Windows Phone 8.1 update	Waze 3.7.4.5	Nokia Lumia 928
Android 6.0.1	Waze 4.22.1.0	Asus Zenfone Selfie
iOS 8.1.2	Waze 4.22	iPhone 4 s

About Privacy Settings

After applying Steps 2 and 3 of the Mobile-PrivAccess method to evaluate the Waze Privacy Configuration options in relation to document fulfilment [17, 18], the main problems encountered for each principle are listed below.

Principle 1 - Perceivable

The three OS evaluated by the experts in Waze do not offer the zoom and lens options and do not allow to customize the configuration of the contrast in the Privacy Setup options, frustrating the following criteria of success: Possibility to use zoom by touch and Impossibility to adjust contrast. In this way, the definition of text size is only possible by the configuration of the smartphone itself, which makes it impossible or difficult to interact and read more efficiently to meet the needs of people with neurological, cognitive and visual impairments.

Since [17] is still a draft version, and despite offering some specific criteria for Apps, some features discussed in [18], such as Providing alternatives to time-based media have not been discussed in this paper; thus, the inspection in the App was considered a relevant issue. Windows O.S. provides an explanatory video-a guided tour-on the operation of the App. In iOS and Android O.S., besides the explanatory video, there is a map-editing tutorial (video). However, none of the O.S.s provide any media offering instructions on Privacy Setting options, thus being disadvantageous for people with neurological, cognitive, auditory, and physical disabilities.

Another extremely important factor that has not been predicted in [17] is the possibility of changing the color of the screen source and background. People with visual impairment depend on changing presentation and content to meet their access needs, the same as people with neurological and cognitive impairment do.

Principle 2 - Operable

The interactive elements (fields to be filled in and buttons) are shown together on a small screen, and it is easy to click on them. However, when it is necessary to register, the spaces are small and difficult to handle, making it impossible for people with visual impairment, neurological deficiency, cognitive impairment or physical handicaps to be able to manipulate and consequently configure (success criterion not met: interactive elements - places with sufficient distances from each other). For people who have difficulty typing, people with neurological, cognitive, visual and/or physical disabilities, the application is not operable by touch or physical manipulation through shaking or tilting (device manipulation gestures). In addition, the layout of the keyboard is the same as on the smartphone: very small, making typing difficult. In this way, people with physical disabilities find it difficult to manipulate the keyboard, requiring a physical keyboard.

In spite of the several not-met criteria already described, it was noticed that the interactive elements are shown in an organized way, grouped on a small screen, in accordance with the directive: Set buttons where they are easy to access. In the menu, the elements are large and placed at enough distance from each other, benefiting the interaction of people with visual and physical disabilities.

Principle 3 - Understandable

The App has icons as a question mark to access "Help" (success criteria met: consistent identification) and a house icon to configure the location of the user's home. These icons help people with neurological and cognitive deficits, because they make it possible to remember which path (step by step) the user should follow. On the other hand, the instructions are not easily detectable, accessible and available whenever the user requires, compared to all the other O.S.s.

The privacy configuration does not allow you to automatically set the screen for a particular display orientation (landscape or portrait). Some users use fixed orientation, for example, wheelchair users who use the smartphone on the wheelchair arm (it goes against the Understanding guideline: change the screen orientation - portrait/landscape). Windows O.S. does not offer the possibility of setting the screen in portrait mode, unlike Android and iOS. The absence of this resource makes it impossible for people with neurological, cognitive, visual and/or physical disabilities to access the App.

In Windows O.S., screens are organized according to the same subject (success criterion: end of link and link purpose), but the grouping of interaction elements that perform the same function are mixed. In iOS and Android O.S.s, when they have different interactive elements, these are grouped on the same screen, making it difficult to understand and requiring scrolling to the end to know what features are present on that screen. One example presented was the "Help" screen in the Windows O.S. which is separate from other subjects, but on iOS and Android, this screen is grouped in the settings screen, a completely different subject. This way, the Android and iOS O.S.s are less consistent, considering that this factor is very relevant for people with neurological and cognitive deficiency, since it makes the use of the App easier, without the need to scroll the screen or even go through several interactions to find the subject the user is really interested in.

The deviation in the choice of colors occurs succinctly (guideline: Provide clear indication of what the elements are about, success criteria: consistent identification), with color options in blue, white and sometimes grey using colored letters in blue, black and grey. The links are highlighted in blue. This color supports people who have attention deficit; however, it can turn the use of the App tiring, causing other types of users not to perceive relevant factors in the privacy settings.

On the other hand, the screen layouts work from top to bottom, making the screen organized, which benefits its use by people with neurological, cognitive and/or visual impairment.

Principle 4 - Robust

Regardless of not being mentioned in [18], according to the Robust Principle, the App must provide easy methods for data entry (Principle 4 - Robust - The content must be robust to be reliably interpreted by a wide variety of user agents, including assistive technologies), making it possible to use Assistive Technologies (A.T.). In this way, functions were searched in the device itself and applications that enabled the configuration of mobile devices accessibility.

Windows offers the option to activate the ease of access function, an accessibility function contained in the device itself. However, before activating it, the device language must be set to the English version and this must be done by someone is not visually impaired.

Windows Phone users can choose from various text sizes for the phone. The high contrast theme can be enabled by choosing a theme color for the phone, as well as enabling the narrator, which reads texts aloud. The screen magnifier allows users to use gestures to magnify any screen they are viewing, as well as customizing the browser captions regarding the appearance of captions for videos on Internet Explorer and applications that use the browser to display content [26]. But when trying to access the Waze application, the screen becomes static and the descriptions of the narrator are difficult to understand. Although English is very well pronounced, speech is fast and there is no possibility to change the speed, making it difficult to understand.

The Android Operating System users can activate TalkBack, a function contained in the device with accessibility that helps the visually disabled or those with low vision to interact with their devices [27]. This feature implements spoken feedback, both audible and through vibration, offering the advantage that it is pre-installed on most Android devices. However, it is necessary for someone who is not visually impaired to activate it.

After activating TalkBack and accessing the App it was possible to use it, but the user needs to click on the phrase to listen to what is written. Another relevant factor is that audio in English presents a non-native pronunciation with a strong accent, of those who do not have native English, making understanding difficult.

In the iOS users can activate the VoiceOver function [28] which is a screen reader based on gestures, which allows them to use the iPhone even without being able to see. However, this functionality needs to be enabled by someone who is not visually impaired. After the application is enabled, by clicking three times on the start button, you can hear the description of everything that is displayed on the screen; however, texts are often overlapping.

Finally, it is worth mentioning that all O.S.s made it difficult to return to the standard settings of the device.

About Terms of Use and Privacy Policy
After applying Steps 2 and 3 of the Mobile-PrivAccess method to evaluate the Terms of Use options and the Waze Privacy Policy, it was found that the Terms of Use and the Privacy Policy are static documents, which present very lengthy texts, tiresome and difficult to understand. There is no possibility of interaction in such documents.

In addition, all the O.S.s only allow access to the Privacy Policy through a link within the Terms of Use. However, this provides a clear indication that the element is operable. In this way, the user needs to click on the link to be directed to the Web (Principle 3 - Understanding, grouping of operational elements that perform the same action, success criterion served: end of the link and link purpose), which benefits people with neurological and cognitive disabilities and those with low vision deficiency.

Only in the Windows Phone OS can the user manually increase or decrease the zoom of both the Terms of Use and the Privacy Policy, making it easier for users with low vision (Principle 1 - Perceivable - Zoom, success criterion met: zoom available).

Through the Ease of Access function [26] in Windows Phone OS, TalkBack [27] in the Android OS and VoiceOver [28] in the iOS OS, some problems were identified, such as in Windows Phone, where the narrator's speech is fast, and there is no possibility to change the speed. On Android you cannot click on the phrase to listen to snippets and still on iOS the texts often become confusing and overlapping.

The same as when inspecting privacy settings, some success criteria of the Web Content Accessibility Guidelines [18] were also analyzed, such as resizing text, changing font color, and using the video and audio features. The lack of these last two features consequently leads to not offering the options of sign language and subtitles. In Windows Phone, the web version viewed by the smartphone itself is not responsive. The letters appear scrambled, words are cut, unlike the App version.

Summarizing the results consolidated at the end of Step 3 of the Mobile-PrivAccess method, highlighted the difficulties that users of different profiles [22] face when trying to set the Privacy Configuration and when reading the Terms of Use and Privacy Policy. Table 3 is intended to illustrate the diversity of unmet profiles related only to Principle 1 of the Mobile and Web Guidelines [17, 18] for Waze's review of Terms of Use and Privacy Policy.

Table 3. Results from the analysis of the terms of use and privacy policy according to [17, 18].

Principle 1 – perceivable [17]			
Directive	Non-met success criterion/good practices	Non-served profile	O. S.
Zoom/magnified view	Zoom available	A, C, E	Android and iOS
Zoom/magnified view	Text resizing	A, C, E	All
Contrast	Possibility of adjusting contrast	A, B, C, D, E	All
Principle 1- Perceivable [18]			
Directive	Non-met success criterion/good practices	Non-served profile	O. S.
Text alternatives	Non-textual contente	A, B, C, D	All
Time-based media	Video available	A, C, D	All
	Voice feature available	A, C, D	All
	Captions	A, C, D	All
	Audio-description	A, C, D	All
	Sign language	C, D	All
Distinguishable	Use of colors	A, C, D, E	All
	Contrast	A, C, E	All
	Text resizing	A, C, D, E	All

4.2 Proposal of Accessible Interfaces for Waze

Given the evaluation results obtained, there is a range of problems that should be solved by Waze, problems these that make certain interactions between the App and PwDaL impossible.

Considering this context, and in order to illustrate the support for these limitations, the application of Step 4 of the Mobile-PrivAccess Method proposes interface proto-types for Profile Configuration and Configuration of Terms of Use and Privacy Policy (Figs. 1, 2, 3 and 4), named ideals because they meet the guidelines and success criteria, which were not met in the App regarding Principle 1 - Perceivable, the Accessibility Guidelines for Mobile Environments [17] and Web Content [18].

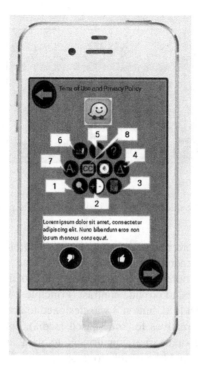

Fig. 2. Interface of terms of use and privacy policy in Waze meeting principle perceivable [17, 18]

Fig. 3. Interface of explanatory video in Waze principle perceivable [17, 18]

In order to make it easier to configure the privacy profile for people with neurological, cognitive, speech, vision, hearing or physical disabilities, a simple standard menu has been implemented for all the screens of the App, as illustrated by buttons 1 to 8, presented in Figs. 1, 2, and 3. This standardized menu provides the best learning and memorization, since it always presents the icons in the same place of the screen, keeping the same design and forms of interaction.

Fig. 4. Interface of explanatory video in Waze principle perceivable [17, 18]

According to [17], in order to satisfy people with neurological and cognitive disabilities and vision impairment, button 1 of Figs. 1, 2 and 3 aims to increase zoom (Principle 1 - Perceivable, Zoom/Enlarge), allowing control of the content size, and button 2, shown in the same figures, to provide contrast (Principle 1-Perceivable-Contrast).

In order to comply with [18], button 3 was designed to activate the audio (Principle 1-Perceivable-Provide alternatives for time-based media), enabling users with neurological, cognitive, vision or hearing impairment to gain access to the App, since without this feature they would be unable to access.

To ensure access to people with neurological, cognitive and vision impairment, the prototype provides the text color options (button 4), text background (button 6), and text size (button 7) shown in Figs. 1, 2 and 3.

For people with neurological and hearing impairment, the prototype offers the possibility of watching an explanatory video (Principle 1-Perceivable-Provide alternatives for time-based medias), also presenting Waze texts in another media as shown in Fig. 3, including playful designs, sound control, captions and the possibility of activating the "sign language" mode, which can be accessed through button 5 as shown in this figure.

When users click on "watch the explanatory video" by pressing button 5, they are directed to the presentation screen, according to Fig. 3, where the standard menu (1 to 8) is shown. Clicking on button 8, to configure the video caption, another menu is displayed, as shown in Fig. 4, which illustrates the explanatory video of the Terms of Use and the Privacy Policy on the screen responsible for setting the video caption.

All the icons in the interfaces were designed following a convention of the users, so that they can accurately interpret and analyze the content, thus becoming evident the role that each element plays and what it refers to.

Interfaces of responsive design are also proposed, as shown in Figs. 1, 2, 3 and 4, which present flexible layout and images based on grids. Thus, according to Principle 1-Perceivable, small size of the screen and meeting the proposal of [29], this design of the App benefits users with visual and auditive impairment.

For the elderly and those who find it difficult to read small texts and click on small elements, there is the possibility of increasing the text size, as well as alternative options of Captcha [30].

The prototype also proposes, although this is not shown in the figures, the search functionality for alternative spellings and correction of misspelt words, which helps mentally and physically impaired people.

As proposed by the specialists, but not shown in the prototype, the pages should be well structured and present a good relationship between them, enabling a good reading sequence and good understanding of the screens, which helps people with cognitive disabilities.

The screens that contain images should provide the transmission of information, such as a caption or else, enable the use of assistive technologies or any other technology that supports PwDaL, avoiding the interruption of activities because of not being able to read what is contained in that area; however, this should be done by developers when implementing the code.

Table 4. Synthesis of accessibility promoted in Waze according to principle perceivable

Served users	Mobile directive and its corresponding number in [17]	Success criterion served/good practices	Button number
A, C, E	Small screen size	Minimum amount of information on the screens	1
		Responsive design	1
A, C, E	Zoom/magnified View	Reasonable standard size for content and touch controls	N/A[a]
		Set the default font size	1,7
		Possibility of enlarging the whole screen	7
		Magnifying lens under the user's finger tip	7
		Enlarge browser viewport when needed -using "Pinch zoom"	N/A
A, C, E	Text resizing	Users must be able to resize text up to 200% without using assistive technology	7
		System fonts should be chosen according to user's preferences	4,7
		Provide control elements on the page to change the text size	7
A, B, C, D, E	Contrast	Minimum contrast: 4.5: 1 or 3: 1 for large-scale text	2
		Improved contrast: 7: 1 or 4.5: 1 for large-scale text	2

[a]The N/A designation for the listing of button numbers in Table 4 stands for "Not Available" and will be developed in the implementation phase of the application code.

Following the same line, the App should have a responsive design, which should be implemented in the programming stage of the App by its developers.

A responsive design allows the screens to have the size proportional to the device and its components should enable control by touch.

In view of these new interface proposals, users with neurological, cognitive, speech, visual, auditive and physical disabilities are included in their access to Waze according to Principle 1 of the guidelines [17, 18]. These inclusions are summarized in Tables 4 and 5.

Thus, according to the results of the method's application, we emphasize the options that promote flexibility in order to meet the different types of users, the guidelines and criteria of success, as well as the good practices and the buttons related to the prototypes presented in this section.

Table 5. Synthesis of accessibility promoted in Waze according to principle perceivable

Served users	Web directive and its corresponding number in [18]	Success criterion served/good practices	Button number
A, B, C, D	Text options	Non-textual content	3,5,8
A, B, C, D	Time-based media	Use explanatory videos in the privacy settings and the terms of use and privacy policy	5
A, C, D		Captions	8
A, C, D		Audio description	3
C, D		Sign language	5
A, C, D, E	Adjustable	Structured pages and good relationship between them. Good reading sequence	N/A
A, C, D, E	Distinguishable	Use of colors	2,4,6,7
A, B, C, D, E		Audio control	3
A, C, E		Contrast (see mobile accessibility considerations related to principle 1-number 2.4)	2
A, C, D, E		Text resizing (see mobile accessibility considerations related to principle 1-number 2.4)	7
A, C, D, E		Possibility of transmitting information instead of text image	N/A

5 Conclusions

Recognizing the importance of ensuring accessibility and privacy to PwDaL, we investigated the problems of accessibility and of digital privacy in the context of mobile applications and proposed the Mobile-PrivAccess Method, which analyses accessibility for mobile applications from the privacy viewpoint abiding by the W3C standards, presenting its viability after assessing it in a case study.

After applying some steps of the method, the results demonstrated that the Waze App only meets a few success criteria and presents many barriers to the accessibility of different profiles of PwDaLs, such as people with neurological, cognitive, speech, visual, auditory and/or physical disabilities.

In addition, advancing in the phases, after assessing the accessibility of this App with Mobile-PrivAccess, it was possible to propose accessible interface solutions for situations where barriers were detected, which created new access resources for this App for PwDaLs, resources that were previously non-existent and provided further exclusion to these users.

It was also found that it is not so costly for application developers to adapt them in a way that makes them accessible to every user profile.

As future work, the proposition is to replicate the method with other mobile applications, besides validating the results, testing them with PwDaL.

In addition, another future work would be to design a new step for the Mobile-PrivAccess method, which would include PwDaL, in order to use this new step of the method to guide the refinement and validation of the results presented in the previous step, which are exemplified in this research work, considering that the current method, in this first stage, only includes the experts.

References

1. Baranauskas, C.C., de Souza, C.S., Pereira, R.: I GranDIHC-BR— Grandes Desafios de Pesquisa em IHC no Brasil. Relatório Técnico. Comissão Especial de Interação Humano-Computador (CEIHC) da Sociedade Brasileira de Computação (SBC), pp. 27–30 (2012)
2. SBC 2006. Grandes Desafios da Pesquisa em Computação no Brasil (2016). http://www.gta.ufrj.br/rebu/arquivos/SBC-Grandes.pdf
3. de Fátima Granatto, C., Pallaro, M., Bim, S.A.: Digital accessibility: systematic review of papers from the Brazilian symposium on human factors in computer systems. In: Proceedings of the 15th Brazilian Symposium on Human Factors in Computer Systems (IHC 2016) (2016). https://doi.org/10.1145/3033701.3033722
4. Bueno, A.O., Ferreira, L.C., Ferreira, V., Anacleto, J.C.: Research trends in HCI in Brazil: an analysis in relation to the GranDIHC-Br. In: Proceedings of the 15th Brazilian Symposium on Human Factors in Computing Systems (IHC 2016) (2016). https://doi.org/10.1145/3033701.3033723
5. Jensen, C., Potts, C.: Privacy policies as decision-making tools: an evaluation of online privacy notices. In: Proceedings of the SIGCHI Conference on Human Factors in Computing Systems (CHI 2004), pp. 471–478 (2004). https://doi.org/10.1145/985692.985752

6. de Souza, P.C., Maciel, C.: Legal issues and user experience in ubiquitous systems from a privacy perspective. In: Tryfonas, T., Askoxylakis, I. (eds.) HAS 2015. LNCS, vol. 9190, pp. 449–460. Springer, Cham (2015). https://doi.org/10.1007/978-3-319-20376-8_40

7. Schaub, F., Balebako, R., Durity, A.L., Cranor, L.F.: A design space for effective privacy notices. In: Eleventh Symposium on Usable Privacy and Security (SOUPS 2015), pp. 1–17 (2015)

8. Yamauchi, E.A., de Souza, P.C., Silva Jr., D.P.: Prominent issues for privacy establishment in privacy policies of mobile apps. In: Proceedings of the 15th Brazilian Symposium on Human Factors in Computing Systems (IHC 2016) (2016). https://doi.org/10.1145/3033701. 3033727

9. Acquisti, A., Adjerid, I., Balebako, R.H., Brandimarte, L., Cranor, L.F., Komanduri, S., Leon, P.G., Sadeh, N., Schaub, F., Sleeper, M., Wang, Y., Wilson, S.: Nudges for privacy and security: understanding and assisting users' choices online. ACM Comput. Surv. **50**(3), 44 (2016). https://doi.org/10.1145/3054926

10. Law No 12.965, Brazilian Civil Rights Framework for the Internet (2014). http://www. planalto.gov.br/CCIVIL_03/_Ato2011–2014/2014/Lei/L12965.htm

11. Pessini, A., Citadin, J., Kemczinski, A., Gasparini, I.: Avaliação da Acessibilidade das Funções de Privacidade do Facebook com Pessoas com Deficiência Visual. Revista Latino-Americana de Inovação e Engenharia de Produção, vol. 1 (2013). https://doi.org/10. 5380/relainep.v1i1.31887

12. Rodrigues, K.R.H., Canal, M.C., Xavier, R.A.C., Alencar, T.S., Neris, V.P.A.: Avaliando aspectos de privacidade no Facebook pelas lentes de usabilidade, acessibilidade e fatores emocionais. In: Companion Proceedings of the 11th Brazilian Symposium on Human Factors in Computing Systems (2012)

13. Billi, M., Burzagli, L., Catarci, T., Santucci, G., Bertini, E., Gabbanini, F., Palchetti, E.: A unified methodology for the evaluation of accessibility and usability of mobile applications. Univ. Access Inf. Soc. **9**(4), 337–356 (2010). https://doi.org/10.1007/s10209-009-0180-1

14. Center, I.A.: White paper: conducting user evaluations with people with disabilities. http:// www.sigaccess.org/wp-content/uploads/formidable/september11_all.pdf, https://doi.org/10. 1016/j.procs.2012.10.006

15. Bach, C.: Avaliação de acessibilidade na web: estudo comparativo entre métodos de avaliação com a participação de deficientes visuais. Master thesis, UNIRIO, Centro de Ciências Exatas e Tecnológicas, Rio de Janeiro (2009)

16. Borges, L.C.L.F., Filgueiras, L.V.L., Maciel, C., Pereira, V.C.: PD4CAT: Um Método de Design Participativo para Tecnologia Assistiva Personalizada. Anais da Escola Regional de Informática da Sociedade Brasileira de Computação - regional de Mato Grosso (ERI 2015) (2015). https://doi.org/10.11606/t.3.2014.tde-18032015-121646

17. Mobile Accessibility: How WCAG 2.0 and Other W3C/WAI Guidelines Apply to Mobile. https://www.w3.org/TR/mobile-accessibility-mapping

18. Web Content Accessibility Guidelines (WCAG 2.0). https://www.w3.org/TR/WCAG20/

19. World Wide Web Consortium (W3C). https://www.w3.org/

20. Silva, C.F., Ferreira, S.B.L., Ramos, J.F.M.: WhatsApp accessibility from the perspective of visually impaired people. In: Proceedings of the 15th Brazilian Symposium on Human Factors in Computer (IHC 2016) (2016). https://doi.org/10.1145/3033701.3033712

21. Web Accessibility Initiative (WAI). https://www.w3.org/WAI/

22. Diversity of Web Users. https://www.w3.org/WAI/intro/people-use-web/diversity#diversity

23. Moffatt, K.: Designing technology for and with special populations and exploration of participatory design with people with aphasia. Dissertation, University of British Columbia, Department of Computer Science, The University of British Columbia (2004)

24. McGrenere, J., Davies, R., Findlater, L., Graf, P., Klawe, M., Moffatt, K., Purves, B., Yang, S.: Insights from the aphasia project: designing technology for and with people who have aphasia. In: ACM SIGCAPH Computers and the Physically Handicapped, no. 73–74, pp. 112–118. ACM (2003). https://doi.org/10.1145/960201.957225
25. Waze. https://www.waze.com/en/
26. Accessibility on my phone. https://support.microsoft.com/enus/help/10664/windows-phone-accessibility-on-my-phone
27. What's talk back? (2015). http://www.samsung.com/br/support/skp/faq/1038671
28. Iphone Accessibility. https://www.apple.com/accessibility/iphone/
29. Marcotte, E.: Responsive web design. http://www.webmastermagazine.es/responsive-webdesign-articulo/2
30. Captcha: Telling Humans and Computers Apart Automatically. http://www.captcha.net

A Taxonomy for Website Evaluation Tools Grounded on Semiotic Framework

Vagner Figueredo de Santana[(✉)]
and Maria Cecília Calani Baranauskas

University of Campinas, Campinas, SP, Brazil
{vsantana, cecilia}@ic.unicamp.br

Abstract. Taxonomies are valuable for providing a standardized way of cataloging elements into categories. In the context of website evaluation tools, providing a structured way for researchers and practitioners to compare and analyze existing solutions is valuable for identifying gaps/trends or to support well-informed decisions during development cycles (from planning to deployment). This paper proposes a taxonomy for classifying website evaluation tools grounded on Semiotic Framework, an artifact from Organizational Semiotics. The taxonomy is structured into 4 main dimensions (i.e., Participant-evaluator interaction; Effort; Automation type; Data source) and considers interaction and efforts involving UI evaluation stakeholders. From the proposed taxonomy, we expect to support consistent characterization of website evaluation tools.

Keywords: User interface evaluation · Usability · Accessibility
Organizational Semiotics

1 Introduction

Accessibility and Usability (A&U) are playing an increasingly important role in the creation of a successful website [5]. User Interface (UI) evaluation is a way of identifying and removing accessibility barriers and usability problems to reach minimum A&U requirements. Due to the volume of data that commonly results from such evaluations, the use of automatic tools is necessary during development cycles. Moreover, the usability of these tools is also essential, because they should not require great effort on the part of the evaluators (when setting up evaluations) or on the part of end users (when participating in an evaluation). Automatic data collection guarantees gathering a vast amount of detailed data, which generally requires substantial effort and time in order to be properly interpreted by humans, in the absence of appropriate automatic data analysis techniques [24].

Evaluation results have direct impact on design rationales and some design decisions can be reconsidered based on them. This is directly related to the fact that the variety of needs and the wide diversity of physical, sensory and cognitive characteristics of users make the design of UI very complex. In addition, due to this diversity, it is almost impossible to consider all users in the design phase [1]. Although it is possible to identify different tasks and ways of using the projected UIs, questions related to different users' needs may appear in a number of contexts of use that were not

M. Antona and C. Stephanidis (Eds.): UAHCI 2018, LNCS 10907, pp. 38–49, 2018.
https://doi.org/10.1007/978-3-319-92049-8_3

foreseen before real usage. Citing ISO's definition, context of use involves the following variables: users, tasks, equipment (hardware, software, and materials), and the social and physical environments in which the product is used [18]. Thus, identifying the most suitable tool for an evaluation or creating a new one involves comparing tools and identifying trends/gaps as well. These steps are usually supported by predefined categories or taxonomies.

This paper contributes with a taxonomy for website evaluation tools –which can be extended for other domains than Web– considering multiple aspects and stakeholders involved in UI evaluation process. The taxonomy was built on top of requirements for evaluation tools elicited in an instance of Semiotic Framework. The taxonomy then summarizes key aspects of website evaluation tools. Finally, we show how the proposed taxonomy can be used for a survey of evaluation tools in order to identify trends and gaps in the state-of-the-art.

This paper is structured as follows: Sect. 2 presents the background for the taxonomy; Sect. 3 present related works; Sect. 4 details the proposed taxonomy; Sect. 5 discusses the taxonomy and paper outcomes.

2 Semiotic Framework

The main theoretical reference considered in this work is Organizational Semiotics (OS) [33]. OS is a discipline that treats information and information systems considering both technical and human aspects [35]. OS counts on a set of methods called MEASUR (Methods for Eliciting, Analyzing and Specifying Users' Requirements), which can be used for understanding, development, management, and use of information systems. MEASUR counts on 5 methods [20]:

- Problem Articulation Method;
- Semantic Analysis Method;
- Norm Analysis Method;
- Communication and Control Analysis;
- Meta-Systems Analysis.

In this work, the OS artifact used is the Semiotic Framework (also called as Semiotic Ladder). The Semiotic Framework (Fig. 1) supports the analysis of information systems in six different layers, contributing to the clarification of what is necessary to produce so that a system can solve not only problems related to the Information Technology (IT) platform (i.e., physical world, empirics, and syntactics), but also considering human information functions of the systems usage [34] (i.e., semantics, pragmatics, and social world). It was used to structure characteristics of website evaluation tools and to support the analysis of multiple stakeholders involved in UI evaluations. In the context of UI evaluation, OS has an important role since as it considers issues and characteristics around stakeholders (user and evaluators) and aspects from physical to social world.

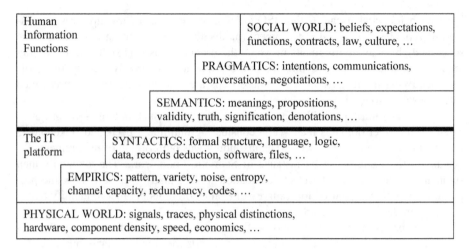

Fig. 1. Semiotic Framework structure.

3   Related Work

Ivory and Hearst [19] proposed a taxonomy of techniques for usability evaluation automation and Hartson et al. [16] presented a comparative study involving remote and non-remote usability tests. These works show that website usability and accessibility automatic evaluation has several characteristics which involve: the participant's location, use of specific tasks, type of interaction between users and evaluators, data source, among others. The choice of each of these characteristics brings pros and cons to the evaluation process and results. In [29], the authors present requirements for website evaluation tools following the Semiotic Framework, exploring each of the framework's layers, summarized next:

- **Social world** – integration of A&U for the target audience of the evaluated website; enable remote testing during real use of the evaluated website; interfere with the Web page operation as minimum as possible; the evaluation report should call administrator's attention to points where users may have faced problems using the website; the tool's widget should allow the customization of its own appearance in order to be gracefully incorporated into the evaluated website's design.
- **Pragmatics** – the tool should require two actions: one to start the capture, which stays valid for future sessions, another to interrupt the capture, which may occur at any time; tool's controls must be gracefully combined with the design of the website being evaluated; the intention passed to the user by the website and controls should result in an integrated experience.
- **Semantics** – provide high levels of abstraction without depending on specific task models, grammars, or events; provide controls representing the status of the tool and user context during the test session; the evaluation report should allow administrators to view, in one spot, data concerning visits of one or more users; if the user can not define settings in a certain environment, the answers and other

data entered by the user should be recorded and kept by the website being evaluated.

- **Syntactics** – use all available data to obtain correlations between them; the combination of the available data in different components may reveal information impossible to obtain independently; use high granularity data to allow the discovery of low and high-level patterns.
- **Empirics** – prevent that processing or transmitting logs interfere with the use of the evaluated interface; the tool should implement safe and effective techniques to transfer logs without impacting on the website usage; the time required to generate the report must consider practical limits if the intention is to retrieve it synchronously to the administrator
- **Physical world** – do not depend on resources or specific configuration of the participants devices (e.g., disk space, bandwidth, etc.); the evaluation tool should include mechanisms to achieve their goals in different configurations of hardware and software.

3.1   Characterizing Evaluation Tools

In this section we present characteristics retrieved from works detailing research involving website evaluation tools. We discuss pros and cons involving each of the characteristics and how they are connected.

Regarding the location of the participant, UI evaluation can be conducted remotely or non-remotely. Remote evaluation means that the user and the evaluator are separated in space and/or time; thus, the user is not required to go to a test environment or lab to participate in the evaluation. Conversely, non-remote evaluations require the user to be present in a controlled environment. Regarding the tasks involved in UI evaluation, the participant can make informal use of the system, when the evaluation requires the completion of freely chosen tasks, or formal use, when it requires the completion of tasks specifically selected for that goal [16, 19].

Considering location and use that participants make of the UI, we have gathered the following arguments. Tests in controlled environments are artificial and may influence the results [26]. It is important that users interact with the application being evaluated in their daily environments, but it is impractical to have evaluators directly observing users' interactions [23]. The remote work setting has become an intrinsic part of usage studies and it is difficult to have it reproduced in a laboratory setting. Moreover, developers often have limited access to representative users for usability testing in the laboratory [16]. Also, the real scenario of use plays an important role when dealing with accessibility due to difficulties in replicating the diversity seen in the configuration of specific hardware and software (e.g., assistive technologies such as screen readers, magnifiers, etc.) used by the participants [4].

Regarding the relationship between users and evaluators, Paternò and Santoro [24] point out aspects in favor of the remote interaction. Remote observation allows the evaluator to observe the actual behavior in real time. Remote questionnaires allow users to provide feedback through a series of questions made available electronically. Critical incidents reported by the user allow users to directly report critical incidents to the evaluator when an incident occurs. Automatic data collection allows the compilation of different types of data regarding user behavior.

Considering the characteristics of those types of interaction, we can make the following considerations. Remote observation depends on the bandwidth of the connection between the user and the evaluator. Remote questionnaires depend on the users' willingness to answer the questionnaire. Critical incidents depend on the user's knowledge in identifying critical incidents. Although automatic data collection has limitations when considering subjective data and the user's behavior in real time, it allows the number of test sessions to scale.

Tools for the automatic evaluation of UI may involve support for data capture (i.e., logging of usage data), analysis (i.e., identification of problems), and critique (i.e., suggestions for improvements) [19]. They may also involve UI adjustments [27]. Considering data capture, there are three main methods used to gather website usage data: capture at the client-side, capture at the server-side, or proxy-based capture. Each of these methods is discussed next.

Capture at the server-side may occur through the use of the Web server access log. This kind of data is the main data source for Web Usage Mining (WUM) tools [25]. WUM is "the process of discovering and interpreting patterns of user access to the Web information systems by mining the data collected from user interactions with the system" [31]. WUM was proposed as an area where Data Mining methods are unified and applied to Web data [25]. Data Mining can be understood as the analysis of large data sets to detect non-trivial relationships and to summarize these relationships in a useful and easy to understand way [15, 36]. Examples of WUM tools were proposed by Spiliopoulou and Faulstich [32], Cooley et al. [9], Chi et al. [8], and Domenech and Lorenzo [11].

Server-side logs have several shortcomings. Their effectiveness is strongly limited by the impossibility of capturing local user interactions and by the validity of the server logs that cannot capture page accesses stored in the browser's cache. If a user clicks on the browser's back button and the content retrieved is a cached Web page, then this will not reach the server and, thus, will not be logged. In addition, interpreting the actions of an individual user is extremely difficult because the methods for capturing and generating server-side logs are not designed for gathering useful usability data [13, 24]. The strength of this approach is the low cost of obtaining the data because they are a natural product of the Web server functioning. However, the identification of the users' tracks and sessions is more complex than when using client-side or proxy-based approaches. In addition, server-side logs do not contain detailed information about users' actions during interaction. Instead, this kind of log contains only Web pages visited by the users (page-views).

Proxy-based capture is an approach in which the tool or data-logger mediates between the user and the websites that she/he accesses. Thus, when the user accesses a Web page, the request is sent first to the proxy's tool that, in turn, accesses the Web page requested by the client, inserts the data-logger into the Web page, and then returns the enhanced page to the client. The strongest aspect of this approach is the possibility of analyzing websites even if the evaluators are not administrators of the website to be studied because this strategy does not require changes in the source code of Web pages or access to Web server logs [28]. However, the proxy-based approach may result in a delayed response time in order to process the Web page and insert the data-logger code and rewrite links so they point to the tool's proxy. In addition, the code inserted into the requested page must deal with any error or incompatibility of the evaluated website. Finally, this type of approach also raises security concerns because this kind of logger can be used for malicious purposes to attack and gather private information such as passwords [10].

Capture at the client-side may be achieved through data-loggers inserted into Web pages or via specifically tailored Web browsers. An interesting characteristic is the highly detailed data available at the client-side. However, it is necessary to include the data- logger in all Web pages to be evaluated or to tailor the Web browser.

Regarding data analysis, critique, and adjustments, different approaches are proposed in the literature. Tools consider task models, heuristics, statistical metrics, Web Usage Mining, among others. The following section presents the proposed taxonomy and how it can be used to structure a comparison among website evaluation tools.

4   A Taxonomy for User Interface Evaluation Tools

Considering the scope of website evaluation tools, the related works, and the main characteristics of website evaluation tools, we propose a taxonomy that considers the interaction between participant and evaluator, as discussed in [24], and the automation type, as presented in [19]. The proposed taxonomy gathers previous contributions and extends them by adding the data source and effort dimensions, as discussed in [27, 28]. The resulting taxonomy consists in the following main dimensions:

1. **Participant-evaluator interaction** – refers to the interaction between evaluators and participants during an evaluation;
2. **Effort** – refers to the effort required from the evaluator and from the participant to setup an evaluation scenario;
3. **Automation type** – refers to the automation characteristics of the tool;
4. **Data source** – refers to the data source considered in the evaluation.

Hence, the proposed taxonomy is structured as follows:

1. Participant-Evaluator Interaction

a. Localization
   (1) Remote
   (2) Non-remote
b. Time
   (1) Synchronous
   (2) Asynchronous
c. Use
   (1) Formal
   (2) Informal

2. Effort

a. Evaluator
    (1) Model development/maintenance (e.g., task model/descriptions, user model)
    (2) Environment configuration (e.g., subscribe, logger insertion)
    (3) No action (e.g., use Web server logs)
b. Participant
    (1) Actions during the test (e.g., select task or indicate task start/finish, indicate that a critical incident occurred)
    (2) Action at the beginning of the test (e.g., access tool's proxy or acceptance)
    (3) No action (i.e., user is unaware of his/her participation in an evaluation)

3. Automation Type

a. Capture
    (1) User expressions (e.g., via camera or eye trackers)
    (2) Physiological signals (e.g., galvanic skin response, heart rate, etc.)
    (3) Ambience (e.g., geo location, luminosity)
    (4) Browser events (e.g., triggered by the user or by the system)
    (5) Customized events (i.e., single, sequenced, or composed)
    (6) Page-views
b. Analysis
    (1) Visual reports
    (2) Statistical reports
c. Critique
    (1) Content
    (2) Structure
    (3) Layout
d. Adjustment
    (1) Content
    (2) Structure
    (3) Layout

4. Data Source

a. Web page data
    (1) Structure (e.g., HTML page)
    (2) Content (e.g., text inside markup tags)
b. User data
    (1) Usage data (e.g., UI events, physiological signals)
    (2) Questionnaire

Having presented the taxonomy, Table 1 provides a panorama of website evaluation tools accounting for the following website evaluation tools:

- DCW (*Descubridor de Conhecimento en la Web*) [11];
- Google Analytics [14];
- LumberJack [8];
- MouseTrack [2];
- MultimodalWebRemUSINE [24];

- UsaProxy [4];
- WAUTER [3];
- Web Usability Probe (WUP) [7];
- Web Utilization Miner [32];
- WebCANVAS [6];
- WebQuilt [17];
- WebRemUSINE [22];
- WebSIFT (Web Site Information Filter) [9];
- WebVIP [21];
- WELFIT [30]
- WET [12].

Table 1. The taxonomy instantiated for website evaluation tools surveyed.

Main dimension	Second level	Third level	Total
Participant-evaluator interaction	Location	Remote	14
		Local	2
	Time	Synchronous	3
		Asynchronous	14
	Use	Formal	6
		Informal	10
Data source	Web page data	Structure	1
		Content	1
	User data	Usage data	15
		Questionnaire	1
Effort	Evaluator	Model/grammar development/maintenance	4
		Environment configuration	8
		No action	5
	Participant	Actions during the test	4
		Action at the beginning of the test	6
		No action	6
Automation type	Capture	User expressions	1
		Physiological signals	0
		Ambience	1
		UI events	10
		Customized events	4
		Page-views	7
	Analysis	Visual reports	11
		Statistical reports	4
	Critique	Content	0
		Structure	0
		Layout	0
	Adjustment	Content	0
		Structure	1
		Layout	1

5 Discussion

In this work we proposed a taxonomy for website evaluation tools grounded on Semiotic Framework. The taxonomy builds on top of requirements elicited in an instance of the Semiotic Framework. Then, characteristics of website evaluation tools were identified and structured in order to compose the proposed taxonomy. Finally, we presented how the proposed taxonomy can be used to provide a panorama of existing tools (Table 1), supporting the analysis of trends/gaps in the state-of-the-art.

In Table 1, in the **Participant-evaluator interaction** dimension, it is possible to observe that the remote and asynchronous evaluations are the most frequently considered by the tools. Regarding use, informal use is somewhat more frequent than formal use. This may be due to the fact that formal use is considered in many tools that capture detailed interactions while informal use is more present in WUM tools. On the **Effort** dimension, considering evaluator efforts to setup and maintain the tool, the attribute that is most commonly shared among the studied tools refers to the environment configuration required by evaluation tools that capture detailed data. When evaluators obtain data from Web server logs, the tool is classified as "no action". Effort on the side of the participants are more equally distributed among the three categories (i.e., actions during the test, action at the beginning of the test, and no action). Selecting tasks is related to evaluation tools that require task models or task descriptions, these being characteristics of tools that consider formal tests. Accessing proxy is related to tools following proxy-based architectures. No user action is frequent in WUM tools. Thus, a promising direction regarding this dimension is to obtain detailed data, thus requiring some environment configuration. In addition, on the part of the participant, the less effort needed the better, except by the necessary condition of accepting to participate in the study, or accessing the proxy, making users aware of the evaluation. Regarding the **Automation type** dimension, capture considering browser events is the most frequent, probably influenced by the JavaScript popularity and easy environment configuration in comparison to evaluations that require logging of user expressions, eye movements, or physiological signals. The ambience data is promising especially when considering mobile applications. Concerning the analysis, graphical reports are commonly used, sometimes in conjunction with statistical reports. Moreover, since the survey produced by Ivory and Hearst [19], few tools provide critique features and, in the context considered in this work (i.e., website evaluation tools), none of the studied evaluation tools provide suggestions on how to treat the problems encountered. Likewise, only one of the evaluation tools considers the adjustment feature. Thus, critique and adjustment represent a potential for exploration in this dimension. Other promising solutions are the capture involving customized events and the analysis via graphical reports, potentially in conjunction with statistical results. Regarding the **Data source** dimension, Table 1 shows that usage data is most commonly considered by these tools.

Moreover, structure, content, and questionnaires may complement usage data and could be combined in new evaluation tools. This combination is a promising direction revealed in this dimension.

Finally, the classification of surveyed tools presented in Table 1 reveals a gap with respect to the combination of WUM techniques with detailed data. Future works involves applying the proposed taxonomy for other domains than the Web in order to evaluate what would be the necessary changes and in which dimensions/levels.

References

1. Abascal, J., Nicolle, C.: Moving towards inclusive design guidelines for socially and ethically aware HCI. Interact. Comput. **17**(5), 484–505 (2005)
2. Arroyo, E., Selker, T., Wei, W.: Usability tool for analysis of web designs using mouse tracks. In: Proceedings of ACM CHI 2006 Conference on Human Factors in Computing Systems. Work-in-Progress, vol. 2, pp. 484–489 (2006)
3. Balbo, S., Goschnick, S., Tong, D., Paris, C.: Leading web usability evaluations to WAUTER. In: AusWeb05 - Australian World Wide Web Conference 2005 (2005)
4. Bigham, J.P., Cavender, A.C., Brudvik, J.T., Wobbrock, J.O., Ladner, R.E.: WebinSitu: a comparative analysis of blind and sighted browsing behavior. In: Pontelli, E., Trewin, S. (eds.) ASSETS, pp. 51–58. ACM (2007)
5. Brajnik, G.: Using automatic tools in accessibility and usability assurance processes. In: Stary, C., Stephanidis, C. (eds.) UI4ALL 2004. LNCS, vol. 3196, pp. 219–234. Springer, Heidelberg (2004). https://doi.org/10.1007/978-3-540-30111-0_18
6. Cadez, I.V., Heckerman, D., Smyth, P., Meek, C., White, S.: Model-based clustering and visualization of navigation patterns on a web site. Data Mining Knowl. Discov. **7**(4), 399–424 (2003)
7. Carta, T., Paternò, F., de Santana, V.F.: Web usability probe: a tool for supporting remote usability evaluation of web sites. In: Campos, P., Graham, N., Jorge, J., Nunes, N., Palanque, P., Winckler, M. (eds.) INTERACT 2011. LNCS, vol. 6949, pp. 349–357. Springer, Heidelberg (2011). https://doi.org/10.1007/978-3-642-23768-3_29
8. Chi, E.H., Rosien, A., Heer, J.: LumberJack: intelligent discovery and analysis of web user traffic composition. In: Zaïane, O.R., Srivastava, J., Spiliopoulou, M., Masand, B. (eds.) WebKDD 2002. LNCS (LNAI), vol. 2703, pp. 1–16. Springer, Heidelberg (2003). https://doi.org/10.1007/978-3-540-39663-5_1
9. Cooley, R., Tan, P.-N., Srivastava, J.: Discovery of interesting usage patterns from web data. In: Masand, B., Spiliopoulou, M. (eds.) WebKDD 1999. LNCS (LNAI), vol. 1836, pp. 163–182. Springer, Heidelberg (2000). https://doi.org/10.1007/3-540-44934-5_10
10. de Santana, V.F., Baranauskas, M.C.C., Henriques, M.A.A.: A framework for web 2.0 secure widgets. In: IADIS, pp. 69– 76 (2011)
11. Domenech, J.M., Lorenzo, J.: A tool for web usage mining. In: Yin, H., Tino, P., Corchado, E., Byrne, W., Yao, X. (eds.) IDEAL 2007. LNCS, vol. 4881, pp. 695–704. Springer, Heidelberg (2007). https://doi.org/10.1007/978-3-540-77226-2_70
12. Etgen, M., Cantor, J.: What does getting WET (web event-logging tool) mean for web usability? In: Proceedings of 5th Conference on Human Factors & the Web (1999)
13. Fenstermacher, K.D., Ginsburg, M.: Mining client-side activity for personalization. In: WECWIS, pp. 205–212 (2002)
14. Google. Google analytics (2018). http://www.google.com/analytics
15. Hand, D., Mannila, H., Smyth, P.: Principles of Data Mining. MIT Press, Cambridge (2001)

16. Hartson, H.R., Castillo, J.C., Kelso, J., Neale, W.C.: Remote evaluation: the network as an extension of the usability laboratory. In: Proceedings of ACM CHI 96 Conference on Human Factors in Computing Systems. PAPERS: Evaluation, vol. 1, pp. 228–235 (1996)
17. Hong, J.I., Heer, J., Waterson, S., Landay, J.A.: WebQuilt: a proxy-based approach to remote web usability testing. ACM Trans. Inf. Syst. **19**(3), 263–285 (2001)
18. International Organization for Standardization ISO. Ergonomic requirements for office work with display terminals (VDTs). part 11: Guidance on usability (1998)
19. Ivory, M.Y., Hearst, M.A.: The state of the art in automating usability evaluation of user interfaces. ACM Comput. Surv. **33**(4), 470–516 (2001)
20. Liu, K.: Semiotics in Information Systems Engineering. Cambridge University Press, Cambridge (2000)
21. National Institute of Standards and Technology NIST. WebVIP (2002). http://zing.ncsl.nist. gov/WebTools/WebVIP/overview.html
22. Paganelli, L., Paternò, F.: Intelligent analysis of user interactions with web applications. In: Proceedings of the 7th International Conference on Intelligent User Interfaces, IUI 2002, pp. 111–118, New York, NY, USA (2002)
23. Paternò, F., Piruzza, A., Santoro, C.: Remote web usability evaluation exploiting multimodal information on user behavior. In: Calvary, G., Pribeanu, C., Santucci, G., Vanderdonckt, J. (eds.) Computer-Aided Design of User Interfaces V, pp. 287–298. Springer, Dordrecht (2007). https://doi.org/10.1007/978-1-4020-5820-2_24
24. Paternò, F., Santoro, C.: Remote usability evaluation: discussion of a general framework and experiences from research with a specific tool. In: Law, E.L.-C., Hvannberg, E.T., Cockton, G. (eds.) Maturing Usability. HIS, pp. 197–221. Springer, London (2008). https://doi.org/10. 1007/978-1-84628-941-5_9
25. Pierrakos, D., Paliouras, G., Papatheodorou, C., Spyropoulos, C.D.: Web usage mining as a tool for personalization: a survey. User Model. User-Adapt. Interact. **13**(4), 311–372 (2003)
26. Rubin, J.: Handbook of Usability Testing: How to Plan, Design, and Conduct Effective Tests, 1st edn. Wiley, Hoboken (1994)
27. de Santana, V.F.: Identificação de padrões de utilização da web mediada por tecnologias assistivas. Master's thesis, Instituto de Computação - Universidade Estadual de Campinas (UNICAMP), Supervisor: Profa. Maria Cecilia Calani Baranauskas (2009)
28. de Santana, V.F., Baranauskas, M.C.C.: A prospect of websites evaluation tools based on event logs. In: Forbrig, P., Paternò, F., Pejtersen, A.M. (eds.) HCIS 2008. IIFIP, vol. 272, pp. 99–104. Springer, Boston, MA (2008). https://doi.org/10.1007/978-0-387-09678-0_9
29. de Santana, V.F., Baranauskas, M.C.C.: Bringing users of a digital divide context to website evaluation using welfit. In: Fatores Humanos em Sistemas Computacionais (IHC 2010). SBC (2010)
30. de Santana, V.F., Baranauskas, M.C.C.: WELFIT: a remote evaluation tool for identifying Web usage patterns through client-side logging. Int. J. Hum.-Comput. Stud. **76**, 40–49 (2015)
31. Shahabi, C., Banaei-Kashani, F.: A framework for efficient and anonymous web usage mining based on client-side tracking. In: Kohavi, R., Masand, B.M., Spiliopoulou, M., Srivastava, J. (eds.) WebKDD 2001. LNCS (LNAI), vol. 2356, pp. 113–144. Springer, Heidelberg (2002). https://doi.org/10.1007/3-540-45640-6_6
32. Spiliopoulou, M., Faulstich, L.C.: WUM: a tool for web utilization analysis. In: Atzeni, P., Mendelzon, A., Mecca, G. (eds.) WebDB 1998. LNCS, vol. 1590, pp. 184–203. Springer, Heidelberg (1999). https://doi.org/10.1007/10704656_12

33. Stamper, R.K.: A semiotic theory of information and information systems/applied semiotics. In: Invited papers for the ICL/University of Newcastle Seminar on 'Information', 6–10 September 1993
34. Stamper, R.K.: Signs of Work: Semiosis and Information Processing in Organisations. Walter de Gruyter, Berlin (1996)
35. Stamper, R.K.: Extending semiotics for the study of organisations. In: Proceedings of Conference on Semiotics and the Information Sciences (1998)
36. Tan, P.-N., Steinbach, M., Kumar, V.: Introduction to Data Mining. Person Education, London (2006)

Copy Here, Paste There? On the Challenges of Scaling Inclusive Social Innovations

Jennifer Eckhardt, Christoph Kaletka[✉], and Bastian Pelka

TU Dortmund University, Dortmund, Germany
{eckhardt,kaletka,pelka}@sfs-dortmund.de

Abstract. This article addresses the question of under which conditions established social innovations aiming at improving social inclusion may be transferred from one specific environmental context to another. Through the example of an in-depth case-study on the PIKSL laboratories in Germany, the authors develop insights into the importance of innovation-friendly ecosystems as preconditions of successful breaching and scaling of social innovations. Previous work (cf. [1]) provides a generic understanding of such an ecosystem and proposes a 'context understand guide', which is applied to the specific use-case of a social innovation initiative and its goal to scale their new solution. On the basis of a working definition of inclusive social innovations and a critical reflexion of scaling concepts the authors draft a framework which is then applied to the PIKSL initiative. In the following, a set of questions is presented to which those inclusive social innovation initiatives can answer who want to systematically plan a dissemination process of their ideas, theories and methodologies. Main outcome of this paper is an instruction of how to apply the context-understanding guide to the scaling process of inclusive social innovations.

Keywords: Scaling · Digital inclusion · Social innovation

1 Introductory Remarks

As digital and physical life-worlds increasingly melt together, a growing number of people and large sections of society are influenced by inherent widespread intersections between these spheres. Not least the success story of mobile devices has led to a normalization of digitization in people's everyday lives, in private, as well as in professional environments. Devices and gadgets at hand seem like catalysts for transformatory tendencies in multiple societal sectors, from shopping over media consumption to the recruitment of service providers and individual transportation.

While relations between customers and companies evolve towards cooperative development of personalized solutions quite rapidly, the social and public service sector and relationships within the formal rehabilitation system are catching up slower. But here also, social practices are adapting and changing. Various legislative renovations facilitate custom-sized solutions aiming at improved participation opportunities in society. Especially people with activity limitations might be able to profit from these developments. Subsumed here under the term "inclusive social innovation", we find

© Springer International Publishing AG, part of Springer Nature 2018
M. Antona and C. Stephanidis (Eds.): UAHCI 2018, LNCS 10907, pp. 50–62, 2018.
https://doi.org/10.1007/978-3-319-92049-8_4

phenomena ranging from new technologies (i.e. 3D-printed body-bound prosthetics) to communication channels (i.e. inclusive language), and new employment possibilities on the first labor market.

People can be unable to use ICT in their living environment due to unavailability and inaccessibility or lack of knowledge and experience. For most people with activity limitations, a 'melting' of digital and physical lifeworlds does not take place to the same degree as for others. Initiatives try to address this digital gap through innovative solutions under the maxima of co-creation and participation [2]. However, these initiatives suffer from various barriers in the process of unfolding their ideas' real potential. Especially when trying to replicate their theory of innovative practice to new contexts, these barriers come into effect.

Accordingly, the common theme and red thread of this article is the question of how already functioning socially innovative solutions can be best transferred to other contexts. Previous research [3] showed the high complexity of factors influencing the development of a social innovation. In order to find out if they help the initiative to breach, if they hold potential to be adapted or if they have be accepted and if possible minimized in their negative effects, these factors need to be understood, identified and categorized. Section 2 is dedicated to present an understanding of the term "inclusive social innovation" as well as to reflect existing theories of scaling processes. Deducted from these presumptions, Subsect. 2.3 focuses on explaining the importance of considering specific contexts and environmental structures of the surrounding in which a functioning solution should be transferred. In paragraph three the authors present an in-depths case study out of the spectrum of inclusive social innovation. The PIKSL-laboratories in Germany are currently working on scaling up their organization. Here, people with so called mental disabilities are working as experts for the own cause, as they are seen as "experts in reducing complexities". The presented generic context-understanding guide is then applied to the PIKSL-laboratories to derive a set of questions to be posed when starting a scaling process (Sect. 3.2).

2 'Scaling' Inclusive Social Innovation

In order to make the ideas of scaling "inclusive social innovations" tangible, the terms and concepts used need further elaboration. As discourses on inclusion and social innovation are heterogeneous and vary in their terminologies, this section functions as a clarification of different notions. Over a working definition of inclusive social innovation, an outline of theories and assumptions on scaling is compiled to critically reflect on the term at itself. To conclude these first theoretical presumptions, a generic understanding of scaling inclusive social innovation is drafted at the end of the chapter.

2.1 Inclusive Social Innovation

Connotations related to the term inclusion still vary greatly in science, as well as in politics and everyday-language. Depending on political, economic and scientific interests in specific fields, the term is conferred with varying semantic concepts and regional specifications. For example, German discourses are often centered on an understanding of inclusion as an educational principle according to which every educational institution should design their structures, practices and organizational alignments in a way that allows everybody to participate in the educational system without obstacles. The underlying maxim can be described as a recognition and appreciation of diversity (cf. [4]). In the last decade, the United Nations Convention on the Rights of Persons with Disabilities (CRPD) changed this perception significantly and brought in a wider scope in the sense of a normative socio-political perspective. Here, the human right to fully participate in all societal subsystems is stressed. This perspective bears a clear destination route: Full participation is the way to the societal objective inclusion, a theoretical angle which holds great potential to describe and analyze social conditions and societal development potentials. The main question to be posed is how a community can eradicate societal exclusion and thereby equalize participation opportunities.

As elaborated in previous work (cf. [3]) social innovations hold great potential to help communities to follow that direction. Social innovation initiatives prompt a new combination or figuration of practices in areas of social action. Provided by certain actors or constellations of actors who cooperate in order to create novel pathways to social and individual needs, these new solutions differentiate from entrenched forms of practice [4]. Dealing with social exclusion, this means inclusive social innovation is *a new combination or figuration of those social practices which tackle societal exclusion in order to equalize participation opportunities for all members of society in all their diversity in all societal subsystems*. All aspects in this working definition need to be further explained and set into the specific context to really determine whether a new solution holds the potential to be an inclusive social innovation. Analyzing prevailing circumstance in specific reference systems might therefore enable statements regarding push-and-pull parameters initiatives are confronted with.

2.2   Assumptions on Scaling

In an extensive scientific literature review on publications about scalability of social enterprises Weber et al. [6] emphasize the heterogeneous use of terms in the discourse on scaling processes. Concepts behind "scalability, transferability, replicability, and adaptability" (ibid.) vary in definitions and, in consequence, are used inconsistently. The majority of definitions of scaling are closely linked to the idea of broadening the social impact of a social business and can be characterized as economy-centric and focused onto organisational aspects. Political and systemic factors are neglected within these models of understanding. In order to create a generic understanding on how to plan a process where a functioning solution is transferred from one environment to another, a broader meaning of scaling which takes environmental factors into account needs to be implemented. Alongside Bradach [7], who emphasizes the possibilities of replication as ability of social innovation initiatives to "move an organisation's theory of change to a new location", the focus shifts towards an ex-ante perspective of scaling, considering environmental predispositions of transferring a specific mode of action.

Weber et al. [6] assemble a ladder of decisions which has to be made when planning a scaling process. As this "Critical Decision-Making Path" points out a set of environmental factors, it might be fruitful to take a closer look at it. While the first three steps within this path refer directly to the initiative to scale up, the four further decisions to make are rather related to the respective contextual parameters. All decisions to be made can be headed with a dimension addressed.

The first decision to be made is to (dis-)agree on the "commitment of leading and executing individuals who drive the scaling process" [6]. The scaling process might already fail if there is not enough will and motivation from the staff involved. Secondly, initiatives and organisations must ensure that the managerial side is sufficiently equipped in terms of personnel competence-wise. A third step is related to the overall structure and modes of operation. It has to be examined, to which degree complexity might be reduced, to get to the heart and core of the innovative character. The degree replicability depends on a high level of complexity reduction. The elements which are the main components of the initiative might then be replicated to other contexts. In a fourth step, these contexts need to be analysed according to verify the given social demand in the respective environment. This stage is a critical point, because a non-existing social demand means the end to the scaling effort. Provided that a social demand is given, the scaling process moves to the question for necessary resources (step 5). It is important to know if the social innovation is capable to obtain relevant resources and whether the context provides them and if they are accessible. A further step towards scaling is the reconciliation consideration if partner organisations might be a fruitful addition to the overall process, and if yes, which ones. The seventh decision to address is related to adaptability. It is a key component and divided into two sub-questions; "Is adaption necessary?" and "Is adaption possible?". Herein lies a high dependency to the sixth step, the context must be clearly examined in order to understand whether conditions of the targeted environment require adaptation or not. If adaption is necessary but impossible, the scaling process is again in danger to terminate.

The following table sums up these steps and shows inherent dimensions addressed as well as the main aspects in question. Also, the left column elucidates the level on which the different steps operate (Table 1).

Table 1. Levels, dimensions and aspects in decisions on scaling, following Weber et al. [6], own representation

	Step	Dimension	Aspects
Micro-level	I	Staff members	Ascertain the degree of commitment of individuals driving the scaling process
	II	Management	Guarantee quality and quantity of management competence within the organization
	III	Structure	Explore the extent to which the SI is able to reduce its complexity determines replicability
Macro-level	IV	Social Demand	Replicability aiming on meeting social demands
	V	Resources	Obtaining resources necessary for increasing social impact
	VI	Partners	Collaboration or not?
	VII	Context	Adaptability – necessary? If yes: possible?

Taking this decision-making path as a basis, it is now essential to further elaborate possibilities to understand ecosystems of social innovation, which addresses in particular the last four steps of the pathway. Under the assumption of the human rights approach to inclusion and taking multi-layered dimensions into account, a wider scope has to be drawn, which is able to consider multiple stakeholders, as well as various contexts coming into play. As it has been shown, inclusion is a process and objective at the same time, making it a complete task and overall challenge for society as a whole. Consequently, planning a scaling process requires to consider this assumption by a multidimensional foundation of variables to be observed, and, at the same time, keeping main obstacles of a scaling process in mind.

2.3   A Generic Understanding of Context-Dependency of a Scaling Process

As it has already been shown, social innovation for inclusion is heavily reliant on a suitable ecosystem and its capacity to accept new practices. This "absorptive capacity", a term deriving from international management studies [8], illustrates the complexity of innovation processes by broadening the perspective: It is not only the innovators, those developing and promoting new solutions for society, but also the individual and collective users and beneficiaries which come into play and decide whether an alternative practice is taken up or not.

To leverage an ecosystem for inclusive social innovation means at the same time to boost society's inclusiveness alongside human rights requirements of full and equal participation opportunities for all citizens. Social innovation initiatives, that have already proven their effectiveness and social impact, hold potential to be equally effective in other contexts, if the transferring process is carefully and thoroughly planned. Scaling must be understood in a wholesome angle, taking various dimensions into account. As theories of innovation show, adoption of social practice is a main factor in the process of successful breaching of social innovation initiatives into society; therefore, all relevant stakeholders need to be kept in mind. Recent research efforts show the strong multi-stakeholder approach social innovation initiatives are based upon: multiple actors from several sectors cooperate while counting on synergies and knowledge transfer to tackle old and new social problems. A theoretical framework therefore needs to build bridges between research, practitioners and policy makers, while focus on the reconfiguration of the interfaces of cross-sector co-operation and the establishment of governance structures to support [9] these modes of action. But aside from relevant stakeholders, it is also mandatory to identify context variables coming into play when thinking about the question how something new might be able to come into a context where pre-existing conditions are implemented and have grown traditionally.

In communication sciences, an equivalent issue occupies scientists and news producers. It is the question, why some news make it into mass media and others remain in the drawer of press agencies and alike. Weischenberg [10] introduced a model which differentiates four contexts of relevance to this issue of diffusion. The four layers (Roles, Functions, Structures and Norms) are arranged in a way that resembles the appearance of an onion, whereby the role-context forms the innermost layer, "functions" are represented on the second layer, structures are reflected on the third and norms is settled on the outer layer. Kaletka et al. [11] transferred this model from media science to the context of social innovation: Based on their model as it becomes visible in the following figure, the "onion" is permeable, which means it may be analysed from the outer to the inner layer or vice versa. But, as the contexts are depended on one another, they all need to be analysed in the course of examination. It has to be noted, that internal factors of a social innovation are not yet involved in this analytical matrix, therefore interrelations are not considered at this point (Fig. 1).

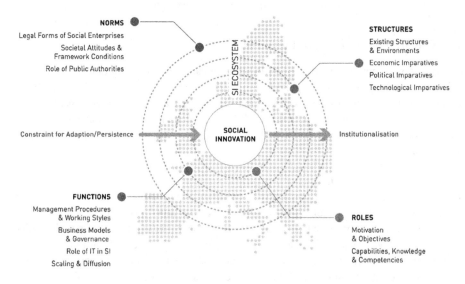

Fig. 1. Contexts of social innovation, cf. [1]

To test the model in synopsis with assumptions on scaling, which were laid out in Sect. 2.2, the PIKSL-laboratories are presented in the next explanations as a use case. The focus lies on a brief description of PIKSL's main operating principles and efforts that have already been implemented to stimulate the targeted scaling process.

3   Case Study: Scaling the PIKSL-Laboratory

Not least stimulated by the CRPD, several developments in recent years have led to a number of renovations within national legislations and standards regarding participation opportunities of people with disabilities and activity limitations. But these new guidelines in favor of a fully inclusive society do not automatically lead to its realization. Especially conservative-corporatist welfare-systems like the German are characterized through a controlling role of the state, whereby market issues play a minor role in comparison to liberal modes of governance.[1] Traditional non-government organizations

---

[1] In "Three worlds of welfare capitalism" (1998) Esping-Andersen differentiates between liberal, conservative-corporatist and social-democratic welfare states, whereby the German is considered to belong to the second type.

are main stakeholders in the field of social services provision, which makes it more difficult for new players and unusual collaborations to position themselves on the market. But nevertheless, these new initiatives which can be described as social innovations gain more and more impact. PIKSL, an initiative from Düsseldorf, Germany, is one of those and dedicated to promote regular employment opportunities for people with activity limitations resulting from the unfavorable interplay between their cognitive and mental abilities and environmental factors. In the following, the initiative is described in detail, whereby the scaling opportunities are in focus of the explanations.

3.1 PIKSL – A Social Innovation on the Rise

PIKSL (Person-centered Interaction and Communication for more Participation) aims at reducing digital barriers and the general complexity of every-day life in order to facilitate an inclusive society and to improve labor market participation possibilities of people with learning difficulties. Founded in 2011, PIKSL now wants to take its ideas and working philosophies to the next level via expanding their organization and moving into new locations.

Working Basis of PIKSL
To centre all efforts on every employee's resources and own potential is one operating principle of PIKSL. The team collaboratively develops innovative ideas to tackle challenges of everyday day life while strictly focusing on the actual needs of people. In its personnel policy, PIKSL relies on a mix of competences of people with and without disabilities. The inclusive team works on simplifying products and services, while people with learning difficulties function as experts in the process of finding suitable solutions for reducing complexity.

Project-bound branches dedicated to different topics and targets are the core of PIKSL's mode of work. While the subproject **PIKSL-TEACHING** employs people with learning difficulties as IT trainers offering inclusive computer classes, **PIKSL-CONSULTING** is specified towards simplifying digital content via identification of digital barriers through people with learning difficulties. These barriers are often not visible for people without activity limitations, but recognisable by people with learning disabilities as experts for their own cause. The service of **PIKSL-CONSULTING** has already been used by large German companies willing to reduce complexity in their web-appearances and to simplify customer service. Within the third branch, **PIKSL-AUDIOGUIDE LINGUISTO,** an innovative approach has been developed to promote interactivity in museums. Scarfs in different colors hold barrier-free audio guide-information, making it easy for people with different perceptions to follow the information. All these branches were already able to produce social impact, and, furthermore one transfer has already taken place as a laboratory opened up in another city, basing their work on the original idea while following the same principles of work.

Feasibility of Scaling PIKSL

Since 2016 PIKSL is supported financially by *SKala*, a funding program by a private foundation investing into social start-ups and non-profit organizations. The SKala-initiative aims at supporting organizations with considerable social impact to grow and transfer their ideas and theories. A feasibility study concerning PIKSL's scalability was an integral component of the support-scheme in its first phase [12]. As PIKSL started in 2011 and is established as a department within the non-government organization "In der Gemeinde leben gGmbH" ("Living in the community" in the legal form of a not-for profit limited enterprise) as well as one successful transfer has already taken place, the main question of the study was not whether or not the underlying concept is working. It rather focused on the exploitation of pathways to secure future financial sustainability to open up new laboratories in new contexts to maximize social impact. In order to exploit these pathways, a strategic reconfiguration of service and product philosophies was necessary. Until then, PIKSL did not operate upon a clear definition of the own services and products. The initiatives reacted to external requests rather than actively promoting the own product and service portfolio. Tailor-made offers for every single customer inquiry required a great deal of energy and ressources, every price setting had to be calculated, every workshop had to be planned individually and the personnel had to be trained anew for every assignment. The demands increase in view of the multiple services offered. This inconsistency regarding product and service placement and distri-bution was identified as a main obstacle of PIKSL's dissemination within the feasibility study. Therefore, top priority was to minimize inconsistencies and to sharpen PIKSL's outward and inward appearance. As a result, the SKala-Team set up a catalogue of products and services offered, whereby the unique selling proposition (people with learning disabilities as experts for reducing complexity in the digital world) was stressed. Pricing for **PIKSL-LEARNING**, the service with the highest social impact, was completely cancelled within this process to even lower the thresholds to participate and to maximize social impact.

Strategy to Scale PIKSL

In the course of reflection of the term scaling (cf. Sect. 2.2), it has been pointed out that scaling does not start with a simple replication of a solution, but with several decisions that have to be made in advance. Alongside the decision-making path Weber et al. introduced, it can be stated that the willingness and readiness as well as a suitable degree of commitment from all members involved have to be ascertained. The feasibility study with its inherent effort can be seen as a major sign for this overall commitment of the relevant stakeholders. Furthermore, quality and quantity of management competences within the organization have to be secured. This has been done by hiring new external experts and via continuing training of the core staff. It is also necessary to reduce the overall complexity of the social innovation initiative. Breaking down PIKSL to its core unique selling proposition meets this precondition. If a solution should be transferred to other contexts, it is essential to actually meet social demands within the targeted new ecosystem. Regarding PIKSL, the social demand is not yet clear-cut. International and national statutory provisions require an inclusive job market, and the overstrained welfare and rehabilitation system calls for alternative solutions, but on a micro-level a social demand cannot be easily defined. Likewise, there is no general rule indicating the amount of ressources that has to be invested and whether or not collaboration should be envisaged. Furthermore it is an open question, if collaboration with external stakeholders is appropriate and practicable. Closely intertwined to these micro-level questions is the issue, if adaptability is necessary, and, if yes, possible. The last four steps within Weber et al.'s [6] scaling decision making-path need further exploration to plan the scaling process. Inherent questions are:

1. Is there a social <u>demand</u> for the solution in the envisaged context? Which internal and external factors might affect the social demand?
2. Which <u>resources</u> are necessary to transfer the solution into the envisaged context? Are there organizational and environmental parameters restricting or promoting the accessibility of resources?
3. Should <u>collaboration</u> with external partners be sought for or not? What does the ecosystem offer, e.g. in terms of possible collaborations?
4. Should PIKSL be <u>adapted</u> to the new environment? Inhowfar? How open is PIKSL itself to adaption processes? How absorptive is the environment?

In the following, these questions are addressed by applying the context understanding guide elaborated in Subsect. 2.3 in order to exemplify a way to coherently examine a possible scaling pathway of PIKSL.

3.2 Generic Understanding of PIKSL's Context

The matrix given below builds on Eckhardt et al.'s [1] work on understanding drivers and barriers for social innovation. It depicts the interplay between the contexts identified and is fortified by the aspects of the decision-making path of scaling, introduced by Weber et al. [6]. In this way the context understanding guide gains a new interrelational perspective and new dimensions (Table 2).

PIKSL's aspiration to scale is taken as a basis for the matrix, whereby the four contexts identified form the analytical layers. To combine assumptions on scaling, especially those considering the ex-ante perspective of predispositions of the process, the questions laid out above are applied and intertwined. As welfare and social policy endeavor to react to social demands and inherent legislative foundations mirror these efforts, the context of *norms* can be read as a direct response to perceived social problems and pressing demands. Interacting external and internal *structures* determine the resources PIKSL might need to bring their solution to light. When the context of *functions* in terms of internal working basis and external modes of governance meet, it gets possible to derive statements regarding the necessity of adapting the organization's practices. The context of *roles* shows inhowfar additional partners are needed or not. Furthermore, it gives hints with regard to the character of these possible partners and the new competences they might bring into the initiative. For an exhaustive analysis, the matrix would need to be applied, until every context crosses with the others. In this first exemplifying step, it was not possible to undergo a full analysis. These issues identified via the decision-making path of a scaling process work as cross-cutting themes

Table 2. Applied context-understanding guide to scaling aspirations of PIKSL

Scaling aspects		Internal factors			
		Norms	**Structures**	**Functions**	**Roles**
External factors	**Norms**	**Social de- mand**	Employees are experts for the own cause = unique selling proposition - compliant to the working principle of full participation and legislative norms.	PIKSL's economic and political work- ing basis meets the social demand (inclusive labour market). ICT is used appropriately.	Staff highly convinced of the social impact of their solution and of the gen- eral aim of equalizing op- portunities.
	Structures	Legislative renovations led improvement of funding oppor- tunities, which have to be ex- ploited.	**Resources**	Technical and spatial infrastruc- tures need to be up-to-date and accessible, adapt- able, available and acceptable.	Staff's compe- tence should be continuously trained, sustain- ability of finance to employ enough people in an inclusive team
	Functions	Do perceptions of ICT in the respective eco- system fit? Modes of action in the welfare system; where are adjusting screws?	Existent adminis- trative traditions need to be reflected to uncover the need and possibility of adaption. Examina- tion of absorptive capacity of the environment.	**Adaption**	Continuous reflection of modes of prac- tices – leaving unnecessary behind, openness to new practices
	Roles	Potential Part- ners as well as local policy makers need to be aware of PIKSL	Partners need to be aware of the social impact PIKSL is able to create via it's unique selling proposition.	Possible partners need to accept main working principles.	**Partners**

to identify relevant internal and external push and pull factors, which extend influence on scaling efforts.

As illustrated, the cross-cutting themes concerning the scaling process are displayed in the cross-column of the table. In the upper row and left column the identified context layers are listed, with external factors to be found on the left and internal, organizational factors displayed in the upper row. In the light grey fields, internal influencing factors within the respective context-interplays are laid out. The red blocks contain aspects on external factors, which need to be considered by planning to transfer a solution.

By taking a closer look at given social demands on the internal spectrum, the high importance of an inclusive working principle as a general rule and its compliance with applicable law are traceable. The unique selling proposition of people with activity limitations as experts for their own cause is a structural component, which is essential to PIKSL and cannot be given up in the endeavors of scaling. Moreover, on the layer of functions it is evident how PIKSL's anchoring in the rehabilitation system meets the social demand of creating an inclusive labour market. Also, on the context of roles it becomes clear that from the staff to the management level the general aim of equalizing participation opportunities is deeply rooted. External existing structures, like political, economic or technical imperatives as well as general environmental factors (includes also i.e. public transportation) also take effect. Focusing on the question if PIKSL is able to acquire needed ressources, the matrix shows in the context of norms that renovations of legislative framework conditions led to new funding schemes promoting an inclusive society. PIKSL's internal structures and economical principles let these new funding possibilities appear achievable if needed (context of functions) and properly accessed (roles). Centered on the issue of necessary and possible adaption, only vague predictions can be made at the moment, as there is no envisaged target context, yet. From external aspects, it is clear that wherever PIKSL is trying to open up new laboratories, these will be placed within an existent system where ICT infrastructures (*functions*), regional or local statutory requirements (*norms*) and administrative realities with specific stake-holders (*roles*) open up and limit opportunities. Regarding possible partners, it has already been decided that cooperation is desired. PIKSL wants to work with external experts, other organizations and, if possible, also with respective public authorities. The four different layers provide first hints towards the possible character of the partners. At first, the relevant stakeholders in the ecosystems need to know about PIKSL, which requires internal resources to spread PIKSL's idea via marketing and other public rela-tion activities. The unique selling proposition needs to be understood and accepted widely by potential partners. As it is the heart of PIKSL which cannot be removed in the scaling process, it is highly necessary to inform and convince possible partners.

4   Conclusion: 'Planning' Scaling by Applying the Decision-Making-Pathway to a Series of Workshops

The application of the "onion-model" to the specific use case of scaling the PIKSL-laboratories supported the identification process of relevant internal and external aspects and promoted an idea of what is important to consider when first planning a scaling process. With a focus on macro-aspects in Weber et al.'s [6], decision-making path, the matrix provides a simple tool when first starting the scaling endeavor. It clarifies PIKSL's multi-faceted character, as a new social enterprise, which is on the one hand driven through new legislations (CRPD; New German Participation Act; enforcing of PWAL participation on the first job market); but also designed to spread new behaviors in society, i.e. acceptance of alternative providers of employment opportunities for PWAL aside from traditional sheltered workplaces. Within the now following scaling process, the described pattern will function as a grid for facilitating a self-reflection process within the PISKL team: By asking questions in accordance to the decision-making-path, researchers will support the social innovation to identify their own core and the conditions of the environment that should be targeted by the scaling process. By this, the described method excels the status of a pure analytical instrument by suggesting moderation questions and their order. It will guide a series of workshops – moderated by researchers and including stakeholders of the innovation giving entity as well as those of the innovation receiving environment - that aim at structuring the process of a) self-reflection of the social innovation (Weber et al.'s [6] steps I–III) and b) the macro-level perspective on the ecosystem of transferring this innovation (Weber et al.'s [6] steps IV–VII).

Through scaling, a new service is to be introduced in the targeted context, which requires a rich knowledge base of that context beforehand. It is not just about doubling a PIKSL laboratory, it is a process, where internal and external factors need to be thought through in the ways, they interact. This article proposes a tested instrument to guide through this scaling process and so contributes to the debate on social innovation, as well as digital inclusion.

Taking a look into the future, it is possible that Germany's inclusiveness of the labor market might improve, as the new German participation Act, ratified at the end of 2016 and implemented also in reaction to the CRPD, holds further potential for alternative solutions and makes it easier for public-private partnerships to position themselves in the rehabilitation system.

References

1. Eckhardt, J., Kaletka, C., Pelka, B.: Inclusion through digital social innovations: modelling an ecosystem of drivers and barriers. In: Antona, M., Stephanidis, C. (eds.) UAHCI 2017. LNCS, vol. 10277, pp. 67–84. Springer, Cham (2017). https://doi.org/10.1007/978-3-319-58706-6_6
2. Howaldt, J., Kaletka, C., Schröder, A., Zirngiebl, M.: Atlas of Social Innovation: New Practices for a Better Future. Sozialforschungsstelle, TU Dortmund University, Dortmund (2018)
3. Eckhardt, J., Kaletka, C., Pelka, B.: New initiatives for the empowerment of people with activity limitations – an analysis of 1,005 cases of (digital) social innovation worldwide. In: Antona, M., Stephanidis, C. (eds.) UAHCI 2016. LNCS, vol. 9737, pp. 183–193. Springer, Cham (2016). https://doi.org/10.1007/978-3-319-40250-5_18
4. Wansing, G.: Was bedeutet Inklusion? Annäherungen an einen vielschichtigen Begriff. In: Degener, T., Diehl, E. (eds.) Handbuch Behindertenrechtskonvention (2015)
5. Howaldt, J., Schwarz, M.: Social innovation: concepts, research fields and inter-national trends. In: Henning, K., Hees, F. (eds.) Studies for Innovation in a Modern Working Environment - International Monitoring, vol. 5 (2010). http://www.sfs-dormund.de/odb/Repository/Publication/Doc%5C1289%5CIMO_Trendstudie_Howaldt_Schwarz_englis che_Version.pdf
6. Weber, C., Kroeger, A., Lambrich, K.: A theoretical model for understanding the scalability of social impact. In: Phan, P.H., Kickul, J., Bacq, S., Nordqvist, M. (eds.) Theory and Empirical Research in Social Entrepreneurship, pp. 112–153. Edward Elgar, Cheltenham, Northampton (2014)
7. Bradach, J.: Going to scale: the challenge of replicating social programs. Stanford Soc. Innov. Rev. **1**(1), 19–25 (2003)
8. Cohen, W.M., Levinthal, D.A.: Absorptive capacity: a new perspective on learning and innovation. Adm. Sci. Q. **35**(1), 128–152 (1990)

9. Domanski, D., Kaletka, C.: Social innovation ecosystems. In: Howaldt, J., et al. (eds.) Atlas of Social Innovation – New Practices for a Better Future, pp. 208–212. Sozialforschungsstelle, TU Dortmund (2018)
10. Weischenberg, S.: Das "Paradigma Journalistik". Publizistik **35**(1), 45–61 (1990)
11. Kaletka, C., Markmann, M., Pelka, B.: Peeling the onion. An exploration of the layers of social innovation ecosystems. Modelling a context sensitive perspective on driving and hindering factors for social innovation. Eur. Public Soc. Innov. Rev. **1**(2), 83–93 (2017)
12. Mews, M.: PIKSL Machbarkeitsstudie (PIKSL Feasability Study) (2017)

Universal Design of ICT for Emergency Management

A Systematic Literature Review and Research Agenda

Terje Gjøsæter[1]([⊠]), Jaziar Radianti[2], and Weiqin Chen[1]

[1] Oslo Metropolitan University, Oslo, Norway
{terje.gjosater,weiqin.chen}@oslomet.no
[2] CIEM, University of Agder, Grimstad, Norway
jaziar.radianti@uia.no

Abstract. The primary objectives of this article are to give a systematic overview of the current state of the emerging research field of Universal Design of Information and Communication Technology (ICT) for Emergency Management, and to highlight high-impact research opportunities to ensure that the increasing introduction of ICT in Emergency Management can contribute to removing barriers instead of adding more barriers, in particular for the elderly and people with disabilities. A systematic review on various literature with respect to Universal Design, ICT and Emergency Management between 2008 to 2018 was employed in this study, and reviewed systematically using a predefined framework. The ultimate goal of this effort is to answer the following questions: (1) How strong is the coverage of research on Universal Design of ICT in Emergency Management in the different categories of Emergency Management ICT tools? (2) What potential next steps in research on Universal Design of ICT in Emergency Management have the highest potential impact in terms of improved Emergency Management and reduced Disaster Risk? We identify a set of gaps in the literature, indicating that there are some challenges where Universal Design is not so much taken into account in the technology development to support the different phases of the crisis management cycle. We also derive a research agenda based on areas that are missing in the literature, to serve a future research in the area of universal design and Emergency Management.

Keywords: Universal Design of ICT · Accessibility · Emergency Management

1 Introduction

Universal Design concerns the design of products and environments to be usable by all people, to the greatest extent possible, without the need for adaptation or specialized design. A prerequisite for Universal Design is *accessibility*. According to WAI/W3C, for the web, accessibility means that people with disabilities can perceive, understand, navigate, and interact with websites and tools, and that they can contribute equally without barriers [1]. In other words, accessibility and usability for the broadest possible diversity of users.

© Springer International Publishing AG, part of Springer Nature 2018
M. Antona and C. Stephanidis (Eds.): UAHCI 2018, LNCS 10907, pp. 63–74, 2018.
https://doi.org/10.1007/978-3-319-92049-8_5

Universal Design in Emergency Management has until now primarily been a research field where the focus has been on the physical environment, buildings and escape routes. However, Universal Design of ICT in Emergency Management and crisis communication can also greatly impact the ability to save people's life in a disaster situation. Practitioners as well as scientists agree that appropriate ICT technology can improve all parts of the disaster management and crisis communication cycle regarding the needs of people with disabilities [1].

However, research indicates that the focus on Universal Design in design of tools and platforms for use in Emergency Management has not been strong enough. To mention two examples: A selection of web-based tools and platforms for crowd-sourcing of information for enhanced public resilience were examined. The results show that none of the tested tools were universally designed and accessible to all users [2]. A study of a set of emergency alert sign-up pages in the northeast of US showed that of 26 webpages that were evaluated, 21 had accessibility issues [3].

To get a more complete overview of the situation concerning Universal Design of ICT for Emergency Management and to highlight future directions for research in this area, the following research questions are proposed: (1) How strong is the coverage of research on Universal Design of ICT in Emergency Management in the different categories of Emergency Management ICT tools? (2) What potential next steps in research on Universal Design of ICT in Emergency Management has the highest potential impact in terms of improved Emergency Management and reduced Disaster Risk?

The rest of the article is organized as follows: Sect. 2 presents the framework that forms the basis of the systematic literature review. Section 3 presents the methodology used, and Sect. 4 provides the results and findings. Section 5 discusses the potential impact of research on different aspects of Emergency Management and proposes a research agenda for future research directions in this area, and Sect. 6 concludes this study.

2 Framework

To understand better the knowledge status and current research on Universal Design and Emergency Management, we need solid framework to analyse the literature.

The four-phase of Emergency Management i.e. preparedness, response, recovery and mitigation is the most acceptable Emergency Management life cycle [4]:

- *Mitigation* seeks to eliminate or reduce the impact of hazards. It also includes the long-term activities to reduce the consequence of the disaster.
- *Preparedness* measures seeks to improve disaster response operations and reduce disaster damage.
- *Response* include activities during a disaster such as evacuation and supplying disaster victims with emergency aids.
- *Recovery* assists the reconstruction of infrastructure and help community return to normal.

Aman et al. [5] examined the use of ICT in Emergency Management, and have defined the following categories where ICT technologies are used:

- *Communication* - Technologies for communication among first-responders, victims and the public, and information creation, dissemination and validation.
- *Event Detection and Assessment* - Technologies used for disaster prevention, early response and damage mitigation.
- *Warning* - Technologies used to alert the public of potential dangers.
- *GIS Supported* Collaboration - Map-based technologies to help in collaboration.
- *Decision Support* - Technologies to aid in decision making.
- *Training* - Tools used in training of first responders for emergency response activities.
- *Navigation* - Technologies that assist in navigating to/from affected areas.
- *Evacuation* - Technologies used to assist in evacuating affected areas or areas under risk.

Universal Design of ICT seeks to ensure that ICT tools are usable and accessible to the widest range of people. It is most achievable through integrating closely with solid development methodologies. In general, a user-centred design approach is required to prioritise the requirements of diverse user groups. This approach, in the context of Universal Design of ICT, involves iterations of requirements, prototyping, and testing with different methods such as review/case study, automatic testing, heuristic testing, and user testing.

In the following, we will use these as the main frameworks to classify tools and technologies in the impact analysis as well as for the prioritization of the items in the research agenda.

3   Method

To better understand the status of art research in Universal Design of ICT for Emergency Management, we have conducted a systematic literature review in this emerging research field.

Based on the research questions, we have identified three topic groups to cover in the literature search:

- Universal Design, covering Universal Design, design for all, and accessibility
- Emergency Management covering crisis management, Emergency Management, disaster management, disaster resilience
- ICT covering Web, technology, digital, mobile, smartphone, computer, internet.

Before conducting the literature search, we defined the following inclusion and exclusion criteria:

- Papers must cover the three topic groups
- Papers must be peer-reviewed scientific journal and conference articles
- Paper must be in English
- Literature review papers are excluded
- Papers published during 2008–2018 are included.

We chose semanticscholar.com as our search database. The search was conducted during 4–5 February 2018. Using search phrase ("Universal Design" OR "Design for all" OR Accessibility) AND ("Crisis Management" OR "Emergency Management" OR "Disaster Management" OR "Disaster Resilience") AND (ICT OR Web* OR Technology OR Digital OR Mobile OR Smartphone OR Computer OR Internet), the search resulted in 1623 papers for 2008–2018.

The 1623 papers were manually checked against the inclusion and exclusion criteria. In the first iteration, the title and abstract were checked first, and if the title and abstract do not give enough information for making a decision, full text was checked. After this iteration, we concluded with a preliminary selection of 33 papers. Three researchers conducted the in-depth review and information extraction of the 33 papers.

We use two frameworks to analyse the relevant papers. First, we use the most acceptable Emergency Management cycle to divide the literature, i.e. preparedness, response, recovery and mitigation [4]. Second, we look at their approach if it is about evaluating existing system, prototyping, model or design or proposal of a system, case study, or about testing such as automated, heuristic and user tests. We also categorize the work based on ICT tools category for Emergency Management as suggested by Aman et al. [5].

4   Literature Review: Overview and Results

4.1   Overview and Further Refinement of the Selection of Papers

As mentioned earlier, we reviewed in-depth 33 papers after manual filtering through Title and Abstract checking. For illustration purpose, few papers were published in the last 10 years discussing Universal Design with respect to the technology for supporting Emergency Management, as seen in Fig. 1. In 2014, 8 papers were published. In 2011 and 2018, there was only 1. However, there may still be more published in 2018.

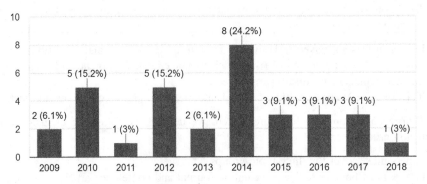

Fig. 1. Publications per year between 2009–2018 on Universal Design and Emergency Management (preliminary selection).

Moreover, the main topics covered by the selected publications based on the in-depth review can be classified as the list seen in the Table 1.

Table 1. Topic coverage in the preliminarily selected literature.

Topics	Reference
Online social network; Web 2.0; social media	[6–10]
Open source intelligence; simulations, e-service	[11–13]
Systematic training, teaching	[14, 15]
Technology mediated citizen participation; disaster resilience; community resilience; user engagement, community-centred crisis system, inclusion, digital divide, social vulnerability	[16–24]
Linguistic, multilingualism	[24]
Accessible technology, assistive technology, alert technology, communication technology	[25–31]
Smartphone technology	[20, 32–34]
Usability, user interface, user testing, universal design	[35, 36]

Nevertheless, our in-depth review showed that some papers still were not really relevant or not at all fulfilled our criteria, and therefore, would not be suitable for further analysis. Some papers used the accessibility term, but in fact, it was about access to information, access to resources or access to the Internet. In other words, in some cases accessibility was to be interpreted as "availability" or "being able to reach or obtain" rather than about design of a system or a technology that could be used by all regardless their impairments. Some papers discussed accessibility and Universal Design in terms of evacuation routes and built environment. Therefore, we discarded 10 papers from being included in the results and analysis. Thus, in the following result we present the analysis of 23 papers.

4.2 Results

Table 2 shows the articles tagged as A1–A33 evaluated across the different criteria described in the framework in Sect. 2 (the gaps in the numbering of the article labels are caused by the discarded articles).

The degree of Universal Design awareness is indicated as:

- *Implicit UD* - there are indications that the awareness of accessibility and diversity of users is there, but it is not discussed),
- *Brief mention of UD* - Universal Design, accessibility or requirements of persons disabilities is mentioned in passing, but without clear signs that it has been taken into account.
- *Explicit UD discussion* - Universal Design is discussed at some length, and is taken into account.
- *UD main topic* - The article is primarily about Universal Design.

Table 2. Articles evaluated across criteria.

Article	Year	Category	Phase	Method	Degree of UD
A1 [7]	2010	GIS, communication	Response	Case study/review	Implicit UD
A5 [17]	2012	Other[a]	Preparedness	Proposal	Explicit UD discussion
A7 [14]	2013	Training	Preparedness	Case study/review	Explicit UD discussion
A8 [16]	2016	Communication	Preparedness	Proposal	Brief mention of UD
A10 [37]	2012	Communication	All	Prototype, user testing	Implicit UD
A11 [18]	2012	Communication	Preparedness, response	Prototype, user testing	Implicit UD
A12 [25]	2009	Communication, Warning	Preparedness	Prototype, Heuristic testing	UD main topic
A13 [19]	2014	Communication, Warning	Preparedness	Prototype, user testing	Implicit UD
A14 [26]	2017	Communication, Evacuation	Preparedness, response	Case study/review	Brief mention of UD
A16 [28]	2017	Communication	Preparedness	Case study/review	Brief mention of UD
A18 [15]	2014	Communication	Preparedness, Response	Proposal, prototype	Explicit UD discussion
A19 [20]	2010	GIS	Preparedness, response	User testing	Brief mention of UD
A20 [38]	2014	Mostly non-EM	Mostly non-EM	Proposal	Explicit UD discussion
A21 [13]	2017	Mostly non-EM	Mostly non-EM	Proposal	Brief mention of UD
A22 [33]	2014	Communication	Preparedness	Prototype	UD main topic
A23 [31]	2014	Communication, Warning	Preparedness, response	Proposal	UD main topic
A24 [21]	2014	Communication, Warning	All	Case study/review	UD main topic
A27 [9]	2016	Communication	Response	Case study/review, Proposal	Explicit UD discussion
A28 [36]	2015	Training	Response	Heuristic testing, user testing	Brief mention of UD
A30 [29]	2013	Communication, warning	Response	Other[b]	Implicit UD

(continued)

Table 2. (*continued*)

Article	Year	Category	Phase	Method	Degree of UD
A31 [34]	2010	Communication	Response	Prototype, user testing	Implicit UD
A32 [10]	2014	Communication, warning	Preparedness, response	Case study/review	Implicit UD
A33 [30]	2010	Warning	Preparedness	Proposal, case study/review, heuristic testing	Explicit UD discussion

[a]Health information system
[b]Optimization of technology solution based on performance evaluation.

4.3   Identified Key Gaps

From our systematic review, and also from comparing with the papers that were *not* included as relevant in the study, we found several key gaps. For example:

- Most of the work on ICT tools and platforms for Emergency Management does not take into account Universal Design nor accessibility.
- Accessibility is used for example in a context of "accessible emergency communication systems" or web that accessible from different devices. It is also used the accessibility in terms of people that have no access to internet in the disaster, and reveal the fact the less educated people has less access to internet.
- Frequently, concerns about access to information and data in general, without a concern for the diversity of users and users with disabilities triggered false positives in the literature search.
- Research issues arise in the areas of data access, data quality, information synthesis, emerging patterns of human behaviour in emergencies, analysis and visualization of nested social networks, implementation of information systems for Emergency Management, privacy, and equity.
- There is a lack of communication support between emergency medical responders and people that are deaf.
- In use of social network in emergency situations, age gap was identified as significantly more severe than the disability gap.
- Good efforts towards accessible tools and platforms exist, but most of them are on the conceptual or at best on the prototype level.
- Awareness about people with disabilities is increasing in Emergency Management, but the concerns are still more commonly focused towards non-ICT issues.
- Awareness about how Universal Design can benefit all users, not only the disabled, was rarely found.
- Research on the use of assistive technology by older adults during disasters is a neglected issue.
- None of the mobile system being reviewed in the study actually considered Universal Design. This highlights the importance of a Universal Design research agenda with respect to Emergency Management systems on mobile devices.

5   Impact Analysis and Research Agenda

As a basis for the research agenda, we will first examine the different categories of Emergency Management ICT tools and platforms in terms of the potential impact of Universal Design. This, together with the identified gaps above, give rise to a prioritized research agenda.

5.1   Impact of Universal Design in Emergency Management

We prioritize the importance of Universal Design in different classes of ICT tools in Emergency Management according to the following issues:

- How many people would be affected by a lack of access?
- How severely are they affected?

From the perspective of information flow, we divide the tools into these distinct classes, with the strongest impact of Universal Design listed first:

1. Information between the public and emergency practitioners. (PEP)
2. Information crowdsourcing concerning emergency situation. (CR)
3. Information among first-responders. (FR)
4. Information among public concerning less-urgent issues such as finding friends and family. (PFF)
5. Information flow among practitioners. E.g. in control rooms and decision makers' offices. (PRR)
6. Non-essential information flow, training, etc. (NIF)

In the first two classes of tools (PEP and CR), we can expect that members of the public are actively avoiding hazards in the affected area, and in addition to any disabilities they will be affected by *situational disabilities* such as reduced ability to interact, type and read on a mobile terminal because of the situation that may involve severe weather, noise, crowds, etc. This, combined with the importance of the communication makes these cases top priority. Concerning the third class of tools (FR), the responders are affected by the same issues, but are trained to come with them and have specialized communication equipment. Additionally, we should also not neglect the importance of Universal Design and usability for communication among practitioners (PRR). Although they are in a controlled environment and trained with the communication and information equipment, the amount of information that needs to be processed makes it important that the interaction with the equipment is as smooth as possible.

Referring back to Aman et al. [39], we prioritize their categories of ICT tools as shown in Table 3.

Table 3. Categories prioritized.

	1. PEP	2. CR	3. FR	4. PFF	5. PRR	6. NIF
Warning	X					
Communication[a]	X	X	X	X		
Navigation			X			
Evacuation			X			
Event detection and assessment					X	
GIS supported collaboration					X	
Decision support					X	
Training						X

[a]Priority 1 to 4, depending on actors and topic of the communication.

We see from the previous section that the selected literature is primarily focused on the preparedness (16 of the 23 selected papers) and response (12 of 23) phases of Emergency Management. Most of the literature is also concerned with the categories of ICT support that we assign the highest priority to; the ones involving the public, and in particular Communication (16 of the 23). However, it is also encouraging to see that Warning category is covered within the existing research in 6 of the 23 papers.

Although these categories are important for future research, we should also not neglect to focus research efforts on the other categories and on the recovery and mitigation phases of the Emergency Management cycle.

5.2 Research Agenda

Based on the impact analysis, Warning systems should have the highest priority in terms of potential impact. We have seen several research efforts in this area, but there is still a way to go towards fully implemented universally designed warning systems that functions well for all users including people with hearing-related disabilities.

Information sharing and crowdsourcing tools are becoming important in disaster resilience, and it is essential that these tools are accessible and usable for as many potential users as possible [2]. This should have a high priority as these tools are affecting many users and their ability to report the situation in their area. Situational disabilities such as being unable to type messages on a mobile phone using virtual keyboard due to cold, wet and shaky hands, noisy background, only using one hand, bumpy roads, eyes are busy observing surrounding areas, can frequently occur in a disaster situation, adding to the importance of the universally designed information sharing tools.

Although Universal Design of ICT for interactions with the public should be highly prioritized, there are also many other important issues such as Universal Design of communication tools, ICT equipment for control rooms, situation visualization tools, situation maps, decision support systems, logistics systems, etc. Emerging technologies such as augmented reality bring a new range of potential barriers and solutions to the table. Technologies like augmented reality can become essential, e.g. in evacuation situations; and assistive technologies facilitating communication between responders and victims can be of great value.

We expect to see the increasing use of wireless technologies to empower people with disabilities regarding individual preparedness (technology outreach), response (warning and reaction), recovery (enable location of accessible shelters) and mitigation (wireless technologies integrated into post-disaster reconstruction).

A standardized framework for accessibility testing and evaluation of tools and technologies for Emergency Management would be very beneficial, as it would simplify the identification of barriers. A selection of relevant and popular tools and platforms for each of these prioritized categories should be evaluated, in order to identify common barriers to create barrier removal strategies and facilitate Universal Design of the next generation of tools.

Awareness must be raised through targeted information to relevant stakeholders with an emphasis on relevant laws and regulations, and consequences of failing to comply with Universal Design. Clear Universal Design-related recommendations and requirements for new acquisitions should be provided. User involvement with a broad diversity of users in all stages of development of new systems, including design and testing, is essential, and must be strongly encouraged. This is where the impact of this emerging research field might be most clearly seen in the future.

6   Conclusions

Given the continuing number of man-made and natural disasters around the world, the development of accessible technologies is clearly very important and has a high potential impact in terms of helping those affected by these disasters. We have conducted a systematic literature review on the last 10 years of research on Universal Design and accessibility of ICT tools and technologies for Emergency Management, and identified gaps as well as trends in this emerging research area. We have highlighted and prioritized the most important research activities needed to bridge these gaps. It is our hope that in the future, Universal Design will be an obvious and obligatory feature of any Emergency Management system. Until then, this research agenda may provide some steps along the way towards that goal.

Some limitations of this study should be mentioned. Only one database (SemanticScholar.org) was searched, and we might have achieved a more complete set of research by adding additional databases such as Scopus, IEEE Xplore and Google Scholar. In addition, a more careful selection of search terms avoiding the frequently ambiguously used term "accessibility", might have contributed to far less false positives to handle in the manual filtering. On the other hand, we might then have run the risk of missing important research where this is the main term used for the efforts to make ICT tools for Emergency Management accessible and usable for all users.

References

1. Bennett, D., Phillips, B.D., Davis, E.: The future of accessibility in disaster conditions: how wireless technologies will transform the life cycle of emergency management. Futures **87**, 122–132 (2017)
2. Radianti, J., Gjøsæter, T., Chen, W.: Universal design of information sharing tools for disaster risk reduction. In: Second IFIP Conference on Information Technology in Disaster Risk Reduction, Sofia-Bulgaria (2017)
3. Wentz, B., et al.: Danger, danger! Evaluating the accessibility of web-based emergency alert sign-ups in the Northeastern United States. Gov. Inf. Q. **31**(3), 488–497 (2014)
4. Lindell, M.K.: Emergency management. In: Bobrowsky, P.T. (ed.) Encyclopedia of Natural Hazards, pp. 263–271. Springer, Dordrecht (2013)
5. Aman, H., Irani, P., Liang, H.-N.: A review of information communication technology applied on common tasks during times of emergency. In: Proceedings of 9th International ISCRAM Conference (2012)
6. Gill, A., Alam, S., Eustace, J.: Using social architecture to analyzing online social network use in emergency management (2014)
7. Li, L., Goodchild, M.F.: The role of social networks in emergency management: a research agenda. In: Managing Crisis and Disasters with Emerging Technologies: Advancements: Advancements. E-pub ahead of print, p. 245 (2012)
8. Huang, C.-M., Chan, E., Hyder, A.A.: Web 2.0 and internet social networking: a new tool for disaster management?-Lessons from Taiwan. BMC Med. Inform. Decis. Mak. **10**(1), 57 (2010)
9. Gray, B., Weal, M., Martin, D.: Social media and disasters: a new conceptual framework (2016)
10. Morris, J.T., Mueller, J.L., Jones, M.L.: Use of social media during public emergencies by people with disabilities. West. J. Emerg. Med. **15**(5), 567 (2014)
11. Backfried, G., et al.: Open source intelligence in disaster management. In: 2012 European Intelligence and Security Informatics Conference (EISIC). IEEE (2012)
12. Lichter, M., Grinberger, A.Y., Felsenstein, D.: Simulating and communicating outcomes in disaster management situations. ISPRS Int. J. Geo-Inf. **4**(4), 1827–1847 (2015)
13. Bell, D., Nusir, M.: Co-design for government service stakeholders. In: Proceedings of 50th Hawaii International Conference on System Sciences (2017)
14. Engelman, A., et al.: Responding to the deaf in disasters: establishing the need for systematic training for state-level emergency management agencies and community organizations. BMC Health Serv. Res. **13**(1), 84 (2013)
15. Kane, S.K., Bigham, J.P.: Tracking@stemxcomet: teaching programming to blind students via 3D printing, crisis management, and Twitter. In: Proceedings of 45th ACM Technical Symposium on Computer Science Education. ACM (2014)
16. Díaz Pérez, P., Carroll, J.M., Cuevas, I.A.: Coproduction as an approach to technology-mediated citizen participation in emergency management (2016)
17. Jan, S., Lurie, N.: Disaster resilience and people with functional needs. N. Engl. J. Med. **367**(24), 2272–2273 (2012)
18. Kuziemsky, C.E., O'Sullivan, T.L., Corneil, W.: An upstream-downstream approach for disaster management information systems design. In: Proceedings of ISCRAM Conference (2012)
19. Meissen, U., Hardt, M., Voisard, A.: Towards a general system design for community-centered crisis and emergency warning systems. In: ISCRAM (2014)

20. Doyle, J., Bertolotto, M., Wilson, D.: Evaluating the benefits of multimodal interface design for CoMPASS—a mobile GIS. GeoInformatica **14**(2), 135–162 (2010)
21. Easton, C.: The digital divide, inclusion and access for disabled people in IT supported emergency response systems: a UK and EU-based analysis. In: ISCRAM (2014)
22. Cinnamon, J., Schuurman, N.: Confronting the data-divide in a time of spatial turns and volunteered geographic information. GeoJournal **78**(4), 657–674 (2013)
23. Aryankhesal, A., Pakjouei, S., Kamali, M.: Safety needs of people with disabilities during earthquakes. Disaster Med. Publ. Health Preparedness 1–7 (2017). https://doi.org/10.1017/dmp.2017.121
24. Flanagan, B.E., et al.: A social vulnerability index for disaster management. J. Homel. Secur. Emerg. Manag. **8**(1) (2011). Article 3
25. Malizia, A., et al.: CAP-ONES: an emergency notification system for all. Int. J. Emerg. Manag. **6**(3–4), 302–316 (2009)
26. McSweeney-Feld, M.H.: Assistive technology and older adults in disasters: implications for emergency management. Disaster Med. Publ. Health Preparedness **11**(1), 135–139 (2017)
27. Moseley, V., Dritsos, S.: Achieving earthquake resilience through design for all. In: International Conference on Interactive Collaborative Learning (ICL). IEEE (2015)
28. Bromley, E., et al.: How do communities use a participatory public health approach to build resilience? The Los Angeles County Community Disaster Resilience Project. Int. J. Environ. Res. Publ. Health **14**(10), 1267 (2017)
29. Ito, A., et al.: A study of optimization of IDDD (Information Delivery System for Deaf People in a Major Disaster). In: First International Symposium on Computing and Networking (CANDAR). IEEE (2013)
30. Malizia, A., et al.: SEMA4A: an ontology for emergency notification systems accessibility. Expert Syst. Appl. **37**(4), 3380–3391 (2010)
31. Onorati, T., et al.: Modeling an ontology on accessible evacuation routes for emergencies. Expert Syst. Appl. **41**(16), 7124–7134 (2014)
32. Maryam, H., et al.: A survey on smartphones systems for emergency management (SPSEM). Int. J. Adv. Comput. Sci. Appl. **7**(6), 301–311 (2016)
33. Hosono, N., et al.: Urgent mobile tool for hearing impaired, language dysfunction and foreigners at emergency situation. In: Proceedings of 16th International Conference on Human-Computer Interaction with Mobile Devices & Services. ACM (2014)
34. Buttussi, F., et al.: Using mobile devices to support communication between emergency medical responders and deaf people. In: Proceedings of 12th International Conference on Human Computer Interaction with Mobile Devices and Services. ACM (2010)
35. Paulheim, H., et al.: Improving usability of integrated emergency response systems: the SoKNOS approach. GI Jahrestagung **154**, 1435–1449 (2009)
36. Stary, C., Cronholm, S.: Method transfer across domains and disciplines: enriching universal access development. Univers. Access Inf. Soc. **14**, 145 (2015). Springer
37. Temnikova, I.P., Orasan, C., Mitkov, R.: CLCM - a linguistic resource for effective simplification of instructions in the crisis management domain and its evaluations (2012)
38. Biswas, P., Langdon, P.: User interface design for developing countries. IEEE (2014)
39. Aman, H., Irani, P., Liang, H.-N.: A review of information communication technology applied on common tasks during times of emergency. In: ISCRAM (2012)

When Universal Access Does not Go to Plan: Lessons to Be Learned

Simeon Keates[✉]

University of Greenwich,
Medway Campus, Chatham Maritime, Kent ME4 4TB, UK
s.keates@gre.ac.uk

Abstract. While the theory of designing for Universal Access is increasingly understood, there remain persistent issues over realising products and systems that meet the goal of being accessible and usable by the broadest possible set of users. Clearly products or service that are designed without even considering the needs of the wider user base are implicitly going to struggle to be universally accessible. However, even products that have been designed knowing that they are to be used by broad user bases frequently still struggle to achieve the ambition of being universally accessible. This paper examines a number of such products that did not achieve, at least initially, the desired level of universal accessibility. Principal recommendations from each case study are presented to provide a guide to common issues to be avoided.

Keywords: Universal access · Robots · Kiosks · Digital television
HCI · Input systems

1 Introduction

The need for universal access (UA) is well established across the globe [1] and is reinforced through legislation in many countries [2].

The theoretical basis for achieving universally accessible products is becoming well established and mature [3]. Most approaches to UA are derived from earlier work in the field of usability by such notable authors as Nielsen [4], Shneiderman [5] and Norman [6]. Their work, in turn, followed that from research centres such as Xerox PARC [7].

Early usability texts focused almost exclusively on able-bodied users and attention to users with functional impairments was comparatively rare. However, as usability methods matured, they began to extend to include accessibility issues that had, up to this point, been considered to be a separate design domain [8]. Different approaches were developed at this time, with different names, such as Universal Design (typically in the US and Japan) (e.g. [9]), Inclusive Design (typically in Europe) (e.g. [10]) and Design for All (also Europe) (e.g. [11]) and these came from different geographical regions, cultures and application areas, such as buildings access, IT equipment or government services. However, all these approaches had a number of common features, including:

© Springer International Publishing AG, part of Springer Nature 2018
M. Antona and C. Stephanidis (Eds.): UAHCI 2018, LNCS 10907, pp. 75–90, 2018.
https://doi.org/10.1007/978-3-319-92049-8_6

- understanding the user wants, needs and aspirations [8], i.e. what they basically want to accomplish (note – these need not be task-driven, but can be focused on experiences or sensations, for example);
- understanding the context of use, i.e. when and where it is to be accomplished; and,
- involving users in the design process, e.g. through participatory design or critical user forums [12].

Second generation methods, such as Countering Design Exclusion (CDE) and user-sensitive design [13] add to or augment these methods, for example:

- understanding where problems lie with existing designs, so that designers can focus on areas with known issues or deficiencies in terms of accessibility and usability (CDE) [8];
- using actors or other representatives/representations of the users to help designers where users may not be available for participatory design (pioneered by the team that developed user-sensitive design) [13]; or,
- using simulations to provide greater understanding (what can be thought of as simulation-assisted design) [14].

However, while there is a substantial and still-growing body of work of how such design ought to be undertaken to achieve an effective Universal Access solution, the reality is that many products are still far from universally accessible [15]. This paper explores examples that were intended to be usable and accessible by the widest possible user base, but failed to do achieve their goal. The examples will cover many areas of functional impairments, whether motor function, vision, hearing or cognitive, and areas of life endeavour [16] rather than focusing solely on computer access. However, the first examples will come from that field.

2   Novel Computer Access Systems

It has long been known that the typical keyboard and mouse arrangement for computer access is innately problematic for those with moderate to severe functional impairments, whether motor impairments or poor vision [17]. Substantial research resources have been applied to the issues, with solutions ranging from very low-tech solutions, such as keyguards and large keyboards, to very high-tech ones such as speech recognition and advanced word prediction. Improved computer processor power and many years of development of the underlying models and algorithms have improved the reliability of such sources of inputs immeasurably. However, the keyboard and mouse still dominate human-computer interaction [18]. It is interesting to explore why, even with the advent of near ubiquitous devices that lack keyboards, such as smart phones and tablets.

An example of why these other technologies rarely manage to displace the keyboard and mouse can be found in the development of Jester, a prototype gesture recognition system developed some time ago [19]. The results from that system are as valid today as they were then.

Users typically consider how well a system performs on three criteria when assessing whether it meets their needs or not:

- Efficiency, i.e. the time taken and effort expended to complete a task;
- Effectiveness, i.e. the ability to complete the task;
- Satisfaction, i.e. user contentedness with the interaction.

Methods for calculating these measures have been formally proposed by the International Standards Organization [20]. Many system designers, though, rarely consider all three of these attributes when evaluating their designs. For example, those developing new computer input systems often focus only on the recognition rate of the software, i.e. what proportion of the input is recognized correctly by the system. However, while the recognition rate is clearly very important, it represents only one contributing element to the three metrics described above, meaning that other elements are being disregarded.

Jester was developed as a means of enabling users with moderate to severe motor impairment to interact with a computer via head and/or hand gestures [21]. Initial results showed that gesture recognition rates of over 90% could be obtained with practice and a small vocabulary of input gestures (left, right, up, down, yes/nod and no/shake) [19]. Much research at the time would have stopped at that point to report the results in the hope that a means of commercialization would be found at that point. The research team did not stop there, though. Figure 1 shows Jester being used with both head and hand input.

Fig. 1. Jester in use. Note the plastic cube mounted on the baseball cap for head gestures and the analogue joystick for hand gesture. Both could be used independently or combined.

When Jester was tested by a hospital-based occupational therapy service [22], they appreciated the novelty of the input, but reported that the users were not sufficiently impressed to consider replacing their existing input systems, such as binary switches, with the new system even though it appeared to offer more freedom and flexibility. Further investigation revealed that while the recognition rate was considered satisfactory, the effort required to produce controlled gestures that Jester could recognize was considerable. Additionally, the time taken to produce and recognize the gestures meant that the throughput, i.e. the rate of useful information transfer between the user and the computer, was lower than for a simple binary switch that took minimal effort to control, was very configurable to a user's personal needs and required very little training to master [23]. The cost of the Jester system was also considered prohibitive.

Attempts to improve the throughput by increasing the usable input gesture vocabulary by combining head and hands gestures proved counter-productive. The cognitive and physical demands placed upon the users were increased significantly to the point where the interaction rate and throughput actually decreased [18]. Gesture recognition is now largely the province of stylus input rather than head and hand movements. The most notable exceptions are to be found in gaming systems, such as the Nintendo Wii and Microsoft Kinect.

There are three key conclusions that can be drawn from the Jester prototype for outcomes that are to be avoided:

1. Do not develop solutions that are too expensive, especially where cheaper options are available.
2. Do not develop solutions that fail to consider all elements of the interaction or focus only on one element of it.
3. Do not develop solutions that place too many demands (whether physical, sensory or cognitive) on the user.

3   Improving the Effectiveness of Existing Input Systems

Sometimes novel solutions for enabling universal access to computer systems can be found from products designed for other uses. One such example was the Logitech Wingman Force Feedback Mouse [24] – henceforth referred to as the Wingman mouse (see Fig. 2). This mouse was developed to enrich gaming experiences by supporting haptic force feedback through the use of a toolkit developed by Immersion. The toolkit enabled the mouse to emulate the feeling of moving over a tactile landscape where the edges of windows could be felt by a small judder of the mouse, for example. Gravity effects could also be added to on-screen elements, actively pulling the cursor into the elements [25].

While such effects can be achieved using solely visual feedback whereby the cursor moves on its own, users typically find such assistance somewhat disorienting as it breaks the relationship between what their eyes see (the cursor location on screen) and their hands/arms feel (the position of the mouse under their hand). The Wingman mouse solved this issue by actually moving the mouse autonomously. The mouse had a metal pin under it that was connected to three motors via three cables arranged 120° apart. The mouse was capable of exerting directional forces of up to 10 Newtons.

User trials were conducted with a range of users with severe motor impairments arising from conditions such as cerebral palsy and muscular dystrophy. Using the Wingman mouse in conjunction with on-screen haptic gravity wells improved the

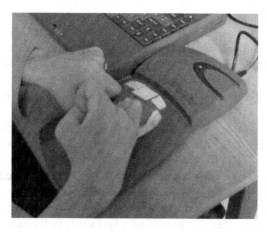

Fig. 2. The Wingman Force Feedback mouse being used by a user with cerebral palsy. Note the user's curled fingers and the hockey tape added to the buttons to stop the user's fingers slipping off them.

average throughput across all the motor-impaired users to something broadly comparable with able-bodied users using an unmodified mouse [23]. Given the level of impairment of the users, this was an astonishing result and offered great potential for improving computer access for many users.

However, Logitech then withdrew the mouse and replaced it with one that had a small oscillator inside it, which could only simulate vibratory output and not move the mouse autonomously. This was extremely unfortunate for those users who stood to benefit from the technology. Informal enquiries found that the reason the mouse was withdrawn was probably connected to a legal case in the US where the parents of a child who had allegedly developed repetitive strain injury from playing on a Sega Rumblepad for several hours a day. Since the forces generated by the Wingman mouse were substantially greater than the Rumblepad, Logitech apparently withdrew the product and replaced it with a re-engineered one as a precautionary measure against possible litigation. The conclusion to be drawn from this example is:

4. Do not develop solutions without considering the risks that may be presented to the users.

4 Introducing New Interaction Paradigms

Looking further afield than computer access, other systems rely upon software-mediated interaction, such as kiosks, information points and smart televisions. One research study into the design of digital set-top boxes undertaken just prior to the switchover of from analogue to digital television provision in the UK highlights some of the issues that can arise where development focuses on the hardware and not on the software.

Prior to the digital switchover, televisions were capable of receiving the analogue signals from an external aerial and could be controlled by a straightforward infrared remote control. After digital switchover, viewers would either have to purchase a new integrated television that could receive and process the digital signals or else purchase a separate set-top box that would change the digital signals into analogue ones that the older televisions could display. Using a set-top box would necessitate the use of a second remote control.

The UK Department of Trade and Industry was concerned that switching off analogue TV signals would lead to some viewers being unable to watch the new digital-only services [26]. They commissioned a company, Scientific Generics, to investigate how many people may potentially have been excluded by the digital switchover. The initial approach to the challenge was to recruit users with significant functional impairments, such as deafness and blindness, to use a range of the new set-top boxes. However, after discussions with specialists in inclusive design, the aim was adjusted to identify users at the boundary of being able to use the new boxes. The idea was that if you could identify those who could just use the system, anyone with more severe functional impairments would most likely be unable to use it [27].

A number of older adults were recruited with a range of minor to moderate functional impairments (see Fig. 3), along with a number of younger users with more severe impairments. The results showed that while there were a number of physical access issues, the biggest causes of exclusion were cognitive in origin. Examples of the confusion were around the use of both remote controls, i.e. the one for the television and the one for the set-top box. To keep costs down, the set-top box designers used cheap generic remote controls that were not designed specifically for the boxes, but could be used to also control VCRs, DVD players and televisions. As a consequence, both remote controls often looked to offer the same functions, but one operated some of them and the other operated the rest of them. The users often got confused over which

Fig. 3. The digital set-top box user trials. Note the pale grey box on top of the television set and the multiple remote controls on the user's lap.

did which. Newer designs for such boxes are now tailored specifically to set-top box operations.

Another area of exclusion was the software interface itself. As part of the user evaluation protocols, users were asked to complete a range of tasks including finding the local weather using the in-built teletext service used in the UK. The analogue teletext pages were structured around a page numbering system that allowed users to navigate either by typing in a three digit page number directly or using four colour-coded "fastext" buttons to jump to common page choices. On Ceefax, the BBC's teletext service, page 100 (the first page) is an index page and each of the "00" pages was the index page for that subsection. For example, pages 100–199 were usually for news, pages 200–299 were for finance, 300–399 were sport, etc. Viewers typically learned the page numbers for their preferred pages, such as page 400 for the weather subsection, or else used the fastext buttons to follow the recommended links to get there.

On the digital television service, the inherent search space was no longer so obviously analogous to navigating a book with sections and subsections. There were no page numbers displayed on the screen and viewers could only navigate using prompts or the cursor keys on the remote control. The mental model used for the navigation was based on web pages, which do not typically use a page numbering system and support much more flexible navigation. This new approach made sense to the designers, who were clearly web-savvy computer users.

However, the older adults in the user session became very confused where they were in the digital teletext service, because this was a completely new way of navigating information and had no signposting to indicate where they were or how they had got there, unlike the old page number system. Following the results of this investigation, page numbers were reintroduced and the older adults found the new design far more usable. It is as important to consider cognitive aspects of interaction as it is to look at the physical ones [28].

The conclusion from this experience is:

5. Do not use inappropriate interaction paradigms.
6. Take time to understand the users – their background, knowledge and experience.

5   Robotic Universal Access Assistants

As discussed earlier, in the early stages of the development of any new and innovative product, the focus is principally on developing the new technology, especially overcoming the inherent engineering challenges to make something that accomplishes the basic task set required [29]. Users typically get overlooked in this early stage of development, not least because if the engineering challenges are significant, there is no guarantee that a feasible product may ever be developed [30]. Instead, designers typically end up designing something that they themselves, regarding themselves as suitable substitutes for the actual end-users [31]. Consequently, the almost inevitable outcome is a product that works best for users who are most like the designer, including attributes such as their knowledge (both background knowledge and detailed knowledge of the product), experiences, capabilities, anthropometrics, and so on [32]. Those who are notably different, which those who would benefit most from a universal access-based approach usually are, do not fare so well. All of these challenges are difficult enough where the hardware platform is widely understood, such as in human-computer interaction. However, when developing systems that involve new hardware, the challenges faced increase.

For example, in the 1990s, the European Union funded a number of research programmes through its TIDE (Telematics for the Integration of Disabled and Elderly people) initiative to develop robotic assistants for users with severe functional impairments. Over $150 m was invested, supporting the development of solutions from office workstations to wheelchair-mounted robots [33]. However, the success of those robots and others developed under similar initiatives was far from satisfactory [34]. Only the Handy 1 robot arm [35] and MANUS wheelchair-mounted robot [36] achieved any degree of successful take-up. Fewer than ten of each of the other robots investigated were produced [34].

Looking at the two more successful robots, the Handy 1 was created by a small British start-up company with a view to being launched as a commercial product. It consisted of a generic robot arm mounted on a mobile base, allowing the design team to focus on the task and the user interaction rather than the development of a brand new robot arm. Attached to the arm was a simple spoon. The users' food was placed in 5 segregated sections of a tray and, through a straightforward interface, the users could feed themselves. This robot allowed many users to feed themselves independently for the first time in their lives. Thus a real need had been identified and a reasonably cheap solution (c. $6000) developed. A second variant was introduced allowing users to apply make-up. Approximately 150 units had been sold by 1997 [34].

The MANUS robot was developed in the Netherlands and it was fundamentally a robot arm mounted on the side of a wheelchair. As such, the robot was inherently mobile, albeit with the disadvantage of making the wheelchair notably wider in certain configurations. The cost was significantly more than the Handy 1 ($35,000), but sales were helped by a pre-existing agreement between the development team and the Netherlands government, which was the largest buyer.

The typical causes of failure in the other robots were illustrated by the EPI-RAID workstation [30] (see Fig. 4). This robot was developed to help a user with severe motor impairments to move documents and books around an adapted office space. Like the Handy 1, it used a generic robot arm, but the arm was mounted on a gantry so it could move around the office space to pick papers and files from shelving and place them on a page-turning device for the user to read. Unlike the Handy 1, where the user sat close to the robot arm so the range of movement required was limited, the EPI-RAID system needed to controllable at a greater distance, with a larger range of possible movement and needed greater accuracy. It also needed to support a wider variety of interactions as a direct consequence of the broader range of functional tasks that it was designed to support.

The focus on meeting the technical challenges of the robot, the gantry and the grippers meant that the user interface was not addressed until quite late in the design process. Furthermore, the complexity of the engineering challenges pushed the cost of the overall system up to at least an order of magnitude more than the Handy 1. User

Fig. 4. The EPI-RAID office workstation consisting of an RTX robot arm mounted on a gantry in a purpose-built office.

trials showed that the technical challenges of the robot had been met, but the user interface was too rudimentary to be useful. To improve it would have required substantial redevelopment, with the commensurate costs that would have pushed the price of the system up even further. The final nail in the coffin was that EPI-RAID was overtaken by other developments in technology. The emerging ready availability of CD-ROMs and the Internet shortly after the commencement of the project made information available on the computer directly without needing to manipulate hard copies, making the concept behind EPI-RAID somewhat redundant.

The other TIDE funded projects suffered from very similar issues, i.e. cost of the system, the time to develop them being too long, being superseded by new technologies and generally too little focus on the user interface, especially its usability and accessibility. The general conclusions to draw from these projects are:

7. Do not focus on the development of the technology to the exclusion of consideration of the user.
8. Develop solutions that meet genuine needs, wants and aspirations of the users.
9. Allow enough development time to ensure the user interface is satisfactory.

6 Access to Information Services

Another set of projects that experienced similar issues to rehabilitation robotics come from almost a decade later and show that while the technology had changed, the underlying issues encountered largely had not.

The UK postal service, Royal Mail, was looking to make its post offices more high-tech and approached a number of suppliers to propose possible solutions to do so. Two solutions were put forward, the Personal Information Point [37] and the Your Guide kiosk [38]. Before these products were rolled out, Royal Mail commissioned user trials to establish whether they were sufficiently usable and accessible. Neither product was introduced following the identification of issues through those user trials.

The first solution, the Personal Information Point (PIP – see Fig. 5), had originally been developed for use in museums to help visitors navigate around the exhibits and also provide more detailed information on those exhibits. It comprised one to three "heads" mounted on a fixed column. Each head held a small LCD panel, approximately 12 cm across, three buttons arranged on both the left and right hand edges of the screen and a telephone handset. The content on the screen could either be static text or video and any auditory output was provided via the telephone handset. It was straightforward to see how the PIP could be used in a museum context with this design.

Fig. 5. The Personal Information Point. Note the telephone handset for audio output, the LCD screen for visual output and the 6 buttons arranged either side of the screen for input. To use the PIP, the user would have to be able to see the screen, hear the audio and simultaneously hold the handset and press the buttons.

However, the proposal was to use this same design in busy and noisier post office environments to provide detailed information about National Savings investments products, such as savings accounts, investment bonds, etc. These products are governed by regulatory rules that require lots of small print to be shown and are intrinsically complex. This was anticipated to result in several screens-worth of information needing to be displayed for each product as well as the ability to compare across products.

The design team was all comparatively young, male, able-bodied and were not used to designing products of this type. The PIP represented something of a departure from their usual product ranges. The target users identified, though, were typical post office customers, with a particular focus on older ladies collecting their pensions. A pre-user trial analysis of the design was undertaken to evaluate where the issues might be expected when users attempted to interact with the PIP.

This pre-trial evaluation highlighted a broad range of issues. For example, the screen was positioned at such a height that while the young, male design team could see it, half the older, female users probably would not have done according to data from anthropometric standards. Similarly, the use of the telephone handset would have presented significant motor and hearing challenges from the requirement to hold the handset and listen to audio output in a fairly noisy environment. The small screen and requirement to display lots of text presented significant vision challenges as the text displayed would either have to be very small or else needed to be presented over multiple screens, which would then have posed memory and motor challenges instead. The use of the six buttons and their rather high location posed motor and dexterity problems with the users potentially needing to raise either arm to push them. The capability demands the would have been placed on the users were evaluated against the prevalence of capability data collected from the 1996/7 Disability Follow-Up Survey [39] – a national survey of c. 8000 people to find out what capability limitations they experienced on a regular basis. An online tool had been developed at the University of Cambridge [40] and an updated version is also available [41].

The results of the pre-study analysis were very surprising. Approximately half of the target population was anticipated to experience significant difficulties using the PIP just from the screen being too high and a quarter of all adult women (not just those over the age of 65) were anticipated to not be able to see the screen. Combining the anthropometric exclusion with the anticipated capability demands resulted in up to 45% of the UK adult population being potentially excluded without even beginning to look at the cognitive demands from the information being displayed on the screen [38].

Royal Mail did not proceed with the PIP and an alternative supplier proposed the Your Guide kiosk (see Fig. 6). This kiosk was much more traditional in design, comprising a large touchscreen positioned at a much lower height. Users could operate the kiosk while standing or seated. A separate "free-phone" telephone was provided adjacent to the kiosk. The kiosk was designed to provide access about the local town, including governmental and council services, utilities contacts, leisure facilities and the like. While the kiosk overall was physically much more accessible than the PIP, the users still could not access the information easily. As with the digital television example earlier, the principal challenges were around some of the design choices, such as the layout of the onscreen keyboard, and the use of icons that the users did not understand. The designers had chosen to use fairly common computer icons, but the users in the trial sessions were not regular computer users, so did not recognize or understand the more abstract icons.

There were still a number of physical access issues, especially for the telephone (see Fig. 7). The telephone cable hung across the keypad, the keys were soft, rubberized ones that needed to be pushed inwards and bent under the user's fingers, and a privacy surround had been added, but was too low so anyone slightly above average height would bang their forehead on it.

The conclusions from both kiosks were:

10. Be mindful of anthropometric issues, especially where the users are very different to the designers.
11. Remember that designers and users are different.
12. Be careful about trying to adopt solutions that are applied outside of the primary use for which they were developed.

Fig. 6. The Your Guide kiosk, its surround and the free-phone telephone. Note the plastic shroud around the telephone and the black foam rubber that had to be added to stop taller people from hitting and hurting their heads.

Fig. 7. The Your Guide telephone. Note the cable obscuring the sunken, rubberized buttons

7   Universal Access Throughout the Interaction

The final example is a fairly straightforward one. Even the best-designed products can be let down by a small, seemingly trivial detail possibly buried somewhere in the chain of interactions between a user and a product or service [42]. It is necessary to check all stages of the interaction to ensure all aspects are accessible.

For example, it is now possible to buy mobile phones (cell phones) with large keys for users with reduced vision and/or limited dexterity. One such example is shown in Fig. 8. The buttons are fairly straightforward to see for everyone with reasonable eyesight. However, Fig. 8 also shows a page from the instruction manual, where the font is notably smaller. While this is probably not going to stop a user from being able to use the phone, it shows that the thinking process across all aspects of the design of the product, which includes packaging and instructions, was not as complete as it might be.

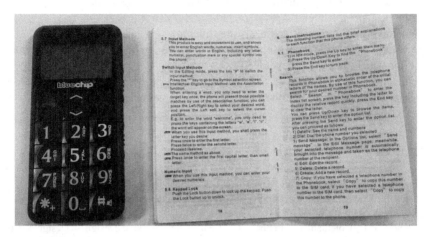

Fig. 8. The Big Button mobile phone and instruction manual. Note the disparity in size between the labels on the keypad and the size of font in the instructions.

The conclusion from this example is:

13. Remember to check all stages of the interaction process from set-up to decommissioning and ensure that they are all equally accessible.

8 Summary

This paper has examined a number of case studies where designers had striven to develop products to meet the needs of the widest possible sets of users, but had not quite achieved the outcomes desired. Each case study highlighted different issues that, taken together, make for a useful set of reminders for all designers:

1. Do not develop solutions that are too expensive, especially where cheaper options are available.
2. Do not develop solutions that fail to consider all elements of the interaction or focus only on one element of it.
3. Do not develop solutions that place too many demands (whether physical, sensory or cognitive) on the user.
4. Do not develop solutions without considering the risks that may be presented to the users.
5. Do not use inappropriate interaction paradigms.
6. Take time to understand the users – their background, knowledge and experience.

7. Do not focus on the development of the technology to the exclusion of consideration of the user.
8. Develop solutions that meet genuine needs, wants and aspirations of the users.
9. Allow enough development time to ensure the user interface is satisfactory.
10. Be mindful of anthropometric issues, especially where the users are very different to the designers.
11. Remember that designers and users are different.
12. Be careful about trying to adopt solutions that are applied outside of the primary use for which they were developed.
13. Remember to check all stages of the interaction process from set-up to decommissioning and ensure that they are all equally accessible.

References

1. Stephanidis, C.: The Universal Access handbook. CRC Press, Boca Raton (2009)
2. Keates, S.: Designing for Accessibility - A Business Guide to Countering Design Exclusion. CRC Press, Mahwah (2007)
3. Clarkson, P.J., Coleman, R., Lebbon, C., Keates, S.: Inclusive Design – Design for the Whole Population. Springer, London (2003). https://doi.org/10.1007/978-1-4471-0001-0
4. Nielsen, J.: Usability Engineering. Morgan Kaufmann, San Francisco (1994)
5. Shneiderman, B.: Designing the User Interface: Strategies for Effective Human-Computer Interaction. Addison-Wesley Longman, Boston (1997)
6. Norman, D.: Affordance, conventions and design. Interactions 6(3), 38–43 (1999)
7. Card, S., Moran, T.P., Newell, A.: The Psychology of Human-Computer Interaction. Lawrence Erlbaum Associates, Mahwah (1983)
8. Keates, S., Clarkson, P.J.: Countering design exclusion – An Introduction to Inclusive Design. Springer, London (2003). https://doi.org/10.1007/978-1-4471-0013-3
9. Goldsmith, S.: Universal Design. Architectural Press, Routledge, Abingdon (2000)
10. Keates, S., Clarkson, P.J., Harrison, L.A., Robinson, P.: Towards a practical inclusive design approach. In: Proceedings of ACM Conference on Universal Usability (CUU 2000), pp. 45–52. ACM Press (2000). https://doi.org/10.1145/355460.355471
11. Stephanidis, C.: Design for all. In: Soegaard, M., Dam, R.F. (eds.) The Encyclopedia of Human-Computer Interaction, 2nd edn. The Interaction Design Foundation (2013)
12. Dong, H., Clarkson, P.J., Cassim, J., Keates, S.: Critical user forums-an effective user research method for inclusive design. Des. J. 8(2), 49–59 (2005). https://doi.org/10.2752/146069205789331628
13. Newell, A.F., Gregor, P., Morgan, M., Pullin, G., Macaulay, C.: User-sensitive inclusive design. Int. J. Univers. Access Inf. Soc. (UAIS) 10(3), 235–243 (2011). https://doi.org/10.1007/s10209-010-0203-y
14. Cardoso, C., Clarkson, P.J.: Simulation in user-centred design: helping designers to empathise with atypical users. J. Eng. Design 23(1), 1–22 (2012)
15. Dong, H., Keates, S., Clarkson, P.J., Cassim, J.: Implementing Inclusive Design: The Discrepancy between Theory and Practice. In: Carbonell, N., Stephanidis, C. (eds.) UI4ALL 2002. LNCS, vol. 2615, pp. 106–117. Springer, Heidelberg (2003). https://doi.org/10.1007/3-540-36572-9_8

16. Keates, S., Kozloski, J., Varker, P.: Cognitive impairments, HCI and daily living. In: Stephanidis, C. (ed.) UAHCI 2009. LNCS, vol. 5614, pp. 366–374. Springer, Heidelberg (2009). https://doi.org/10.1007/978-3-642-02707-9_42

17. Trewin, S., Keates, S.: Computer access for motor impaired users. In: Encyclopedia of Human-Computer Interaction, pp. 92–99. IGI, London (2006)

18. Trewin, S., Pain, H.: Keyboard and mouse errors due to motor disabilities. Int. J. Hum.-Comput. Stud. **50**(2), 109–144 (1999)

19. Keates, S., Robinson, P.: Gestures and multimodal input. Behav. Inf. Technol. **18**(1), 36–44 (1999). https://doi.org/10.1080/014492999119237

20. International Standard Organization (ISO): ISO 9241-11: ergonomic requirements for office work with visual display terminals (VDTs), Part 11: Guidance on Usability Specification and Measures. Technical report. ISO, Geneva (1998)

21. Keates, S., Perricos, C.: Gesture as a means of computer access. Commun. Matters **10**(1), 17–19 (1996)

22. Keates S., Potter R., Perricos C., Robinson P.: Gesture recognition - research and clinical perspectives. In: Proceedings of RESNA 1997, pp. 333–335. RESNA Press, Pittsburgh, Pennsylvania (1997)

23. Keates, S.: Measuring acceptable input - What is "good enough"? Int. J. Univers. Access Inf. Soc. **16**(3), 713–723 (2017). https://doi.org/10.1007/s10209-016-0498-4

24. Hwang, F., Keates, S., Langdon, P.M., Clarkson, P.J.: Movement time for motion-impaired users assisted by force-feedback: effects of movement amplitude, target width, and gravity well width. Int. J. Univers. Access Inf. Soc. **4**(2), 85–95 (2005). https://doi.org/10.1007/s10209-005-0114-5

25. Hwang, F., Keates, S., Langdon, P., Clarkson, P.J.: A haptic toolbar for motion-impaired users. In: Proceedings of the 3rd International Conference on Universal Access in Human-Computer Interaction/11th International Conference on Human Computer Interaction. Springer (2005). ISBN 0-8058-5807-5

26. Carmichael, A., Rice, M., Sloan, D., Gregor, P.: Digital switchover or digital divide: a prognosis for usable and accessible interactive digital television in the UK. Int. J. Univers. Access Inf. Soc. **4**(4), 400–416 (2006). https://doi.org/10.1007/s10209-005-0004-x

27. Keates, S., Clarkson, P.J.: Assessing the accessibility of digital television set-top boxes. In: Keates, S., Clarkson, P.J., Langdon, P.M., Robinson, P. (eds.) Design for a More Inclusive World, pp. 183–192. Springer, London (2004). https://doi.org/10.1007/978-0-85729-372-5_19

28. Keates, S., Adams, R., Bodine, C., Czaja, S., Gordon, W., Gregor, P., Hacker, E., Hanson, V., Kemp, J., Laff, M., Lewis, C., Pieper, M., Richards, J., Rose, D., Savidis, A., Schultz, G., Snayd, P., Trewin, S., Varker, P.: Cognitive and learning difficulties and how they affect access to IT systems. Int. J. Univers. Access Inf. Soc. **5**(4), 329–339 (2007). https://doi.org/10.1007/s10209-006-0058-4

29. Keates, S.: A pedagogical example of teaching universal access. Int. J. Univers. Access Inf. Soc. (UAIS) **14**(1), 97–110 (2015). https://doi.org/10.1007/s10209-014-0398-4

30. Keates, S., Kyberd, P.: Robotic Assistants for Universal Access. In: Antona, M., Stephanidis, C. (eds.) UAHCI 2017. LNCS, vol. 10279, pp. 527–538. Springer, Cham (2017). https://doi.org/10.1007/978-3-319-58700-4_43

31. Cooper, A.: The Inmates are Running the Asylum. SAMS Publishing, Indianapolis (1999)

32. Keates, S., Lebbon, C., Clarkson, P.J.: Investigating industry attitudes to universal design. In: Proceedings of RESNA 2000, pp. 276–278. RESNAPress, Orlando (2000)

33. Buhler, C.: Robotics for rehabilitation – A European (?) perspective. In: Proceedings of the 5th International Conference on Rehabilitation Robotics (ICORR 1997), Bath, UK, pp. 5–11 (1997)

34. Mahoney, R.: Robotic products for rehabilitation: status and strategy. In: Proceedings of the 5th International Conference on Rehabilitation Robotics (ICORR 1997), Bath, UK, pp. 12–17 (1997)
35. Topping, M.J., Smith, J.K.: The development of handy 1. A robotic system to assist the severely disabled. Technol. Disabil. **10**(2), 95–105 (1999)
36. Tijsma, H.A., Liefhebber, F., Herder, J.L.: Evaluation of new user interface features for the Manus robot arm. In: 9th International Conference on Rehabilitation Robotics (ICORR 2005), pp. 258–263. IEEE (2005). https://doi.org/10.1109/icorr.2005.1501097
37. Keates, S., Clarkson, P.J., Robinson, P.: Developing a practical inclusive interface design approach. Interact. Comput. **14**(4), 271–299 (2002). https://doi.org/10.1016/S0953-5438(01)00054-6
38. Keates, S., Clarkson, P.J., Robinson, P.: Design for participation: providing access to e-information for older adults. Int. J. Univers. Access Inf. Soc. (UAIS) **3**(2), 149–163 (2004). https://doi.org/10.1007/s10209-004-0093-y
39. Grundy, E., Ahlburg, D., Ali, M., Breeze, E., Sloggett, A.: Disability in Great Britain. Department of Social Security, Research Report No. 94, Corporate Document Services, London, UK (1999)
40. Clarkson, P.J., Keates, S., Dong, H.: Quantifying design exclusion. In: Clarkson, P.J., Coleman, R., Keates, S., Lebbon, C. (eds.) Inclusive Design: Design for the Whole Population, pp. 422–437. Springer, London (2003). https://doi.org/10.1007/978-1-4471-0001-0_26
41. The Inclusive Design Toolkit. http://www.inclusivedesigntoolkit.com/. Accessed 29 Jan 2018
42. Keates, S.: Pragmatic research issues confronting HCI practitioners when designing for universal access. Int. J. Univers. Access Inf. Soc. (UAIS) **5**(3), 269–278 (2006). https://doi.org/10.1007/s10209-006-0050-z

Categorization Framework for Usability Issues of Smartwatches and Pedometers for the Older Adults

Jayden Khakurel[1(✉)], Antti Knutas[2], Helinä Melkas[1],
Birgit Penzenstadler[3], Bo Fu[3], and Jari Porras[1]

[1] Lapppeenranta University of Technology,
Skinnarilankatu 34, 53850 Lappeenranta, Finland
{jayden.khakurel,helina.melkas,jari.porras}@lut.fi
[2] Lero, the Irish Software Research Centre, Glasnevin, Dublin, Ireland
antti.knutas@lut.fi
[3] California State University, Long Beach, CA, USA
{Birgit.penzenstadler,bo.fu}@csulb.edu

Abstract. In recent years various usability issues related to device character-istics of quantified-self wearables such as smartwatches and pedometers have been identified which appear likely to impact device adoption among the older adults. However, an overall framework has not yet been developed to provide a comprehensive set of usability issues related to smartwatches and pedometers. This study used a two-stage research approach with 33 older participants, applying contextual action theory and usability evaluation methods both to determine perceived usability issues and to formulate a usability categorization framework based on identified issues. Additionally, we prioritized the pre-dominant usability issues of smartwatches and pedometers that warrant imme-diate attention from technology designers, the research community, and application developers. Results revealed predominant usability issues related to the following device characteristics of smartwatches: user interface (font size, interaction techniques such as notification, button location) and hardware (screen size); and of pedometers: user interface (font size, interaction techniques such as notification, button location, and tap detection) and hardware (screen size).

Keywords: Wearables · Usability · Older adults · Framework
User interface · Elderly · Quantified self-technologies · Smartwatches
Pedometers

1 Introduction

Commercially off-the-shelf (COTS) quantified-self wearable devices such as smart-watches, pedometers, and associated applications are seen as a potential medium to: (i) support health self-management among older populations [16]; and (ii) improve physical activities through "Quantified Self" [50]. Despite the potential, compared with their younger counterparts, many older adults have challenges in adopting such

© Springer International Publishing AG, part of Springer Nature 2018
M. Antona and C. Stephanidis (Eds.): UAHCI 2018, LNCS 10907, pp. 91–106, 2018.
https://doi.org/10.1007/978-3-319-92049-8_7

wearable device categories [7]. Previous researchers and practitioners have identified that such challenges are due to: (i) usability issues related to complex interfaces and extensive functionalities [18] that have not been designed to suit them [31]; and (ii) age-related changes in cognitive and physical capabilities [39]. Tedesco et al. [51] state, "wearable technologies are mainly designed to attract a young, sporty and technical affine group of adults." This is a setback facing the older adults when seeking to take advantage of wearables.

To offset such challenges, research has been emerging on identification, evaluation, and analysis of usability issues faced by the older population while using smartwatches and pedometers [9, 22, 43]. Researchers have identified usability issues including button size, screen size, interaction with the screen, iconography, battery, reliability, and accuracy [39, 40, 43]. However, these previous lack an overall framework to provide a comprehensive set of identified usability issues related to specific wearable device categories. This can keep researchers, industry manufacturers, and wearable application developers from understanding most important usability issues that need to be rectified in order to improve adoption of smartwatches and pedometers by the older adults.

While previous studies (see Table 1) have provided insight into various aspects of the usability issues related to wearable devices that the older adults face, they do not directly answer our research questions.

RQ1: What usability issues, related to device characteristics of smartwatches and pedometers, can obstruct the motivation of the older adults to adopt these devices, and how have the issues been categorized? **Rationale**: Identify the range of usability issues of each device category that affect adoption. This enables creation of an overall framework to provide a comprehensive set of usability issues for each device category.

RQ2: What usability issues, related to device characteristics, have a sizable impact on usability needs for smartwatches and pedometers and thus warrant immediate prioritization by technology designers, the research community, and application developers? **Rationale**: Prioritize the predominant usability issues that need immediate potential solutions to improve adoption of smartwatches and pedometers among older adults.

The aim of this study is therefore to: (i) explore the usability issues of specific wearable device categories, i.e. smartwatches and pedometers, by reviewing the literature and applying Contextual Action Theory (CAT) [49], and the Usability Evaluation Method [23] to this study's set of usability experiments among older adults users; and (ii) empirically validate quantitative data gathered from older participants in order to prioritize the predominant usability issues of each device category requiring immediate potential solution. The presented framework and empirically validated result may be valuable for researchers, industry manufacturers, and wearable application developers to improve smartwatches and pedometers for the older adults.

2 Related Work

In order to answer the above research questions, this section details previously identified usability issues faced by older populations while using COTS wearable devices. Table 1 summarizes recent literature on usability issues associated with wearable devices and their associated applications.

Table 1. Usability issues identified by previous researchers.

Citations	Usability issues	Technologies
[40]	Screen size, icons, tapping detection	Web-camera, an accelerometer, and a small Pico projector
[3]	Screen size, font size, and small buttons.	Smart bracelet
[16]	Data accuracy, wearability	Activity trackers
[57]	Interaction with application, resolution of screen	Head mounted devices
[39]	Typography, Data accuracy	Activity trackers
[47]	Font size, icon & button, screen size	dWatch
[48]	Color contrast	smartwatch
[36]	Alert sound from device	Prototype wearable device with sound and haptic feedback
[43]	Location of the button, battery life, design, shape, colour, wearing position, an application using external devices.	Activity trackers
[22]	Typography, button	Wrist device
[41]	Display, battery, comfort, aesthetics	Activity trackers

3 Research Design Process

To answer the research questions, we propose a two-stage research process (see Fig. 1) to measure the issue variables and compare their influence on motivation to adopt smartwatches and pedometers. This study was conducted in two stages, namely Identifying and Prioritizing (see Fig. 1). During the identifying stage, we performed a usability evaluation of devices with older participants to determine perceived usability issues and to formulate a usability categorization framework based on identified issues, whereas in the prioritizing stage, we collected and organized the predominant usability issues into a categorization framework.

3.1 Identifying Stage

The main purpose of this stage was to identify the number of times that usability issues during usability evaluation of devices with older participant throughout the study. First, a general presentation and requirements for participation were provided to participants,

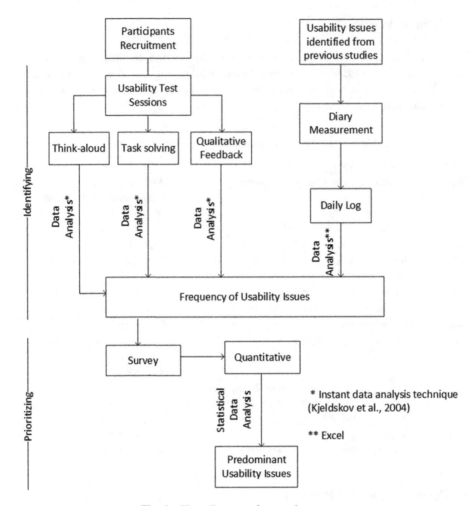

Fig. 1. Flow diagram of research process

followed by a recruitment form, which collected preliminary participants' information such as age, technological knowledge, current use of external devices like smartphones, and consent. Alshamari and Mayhew [2] suggest performing usability tests so that participants can be classified based on their level of systems experience, other individual characteristics. Black [5] point out, "Ideally participants should fall in the middle of the qualification spectrum to ensure that the tests do not result in excessive false positives or false negatives" (p. 7). Based on this suggestion, data obtained from the recruitment form was analyzed and used to select participants for the evaluation study. All participants in the study were presented with an ethical review statement and aspects of informed consent (i.e. participants' right to confidentiality, risks, data storage, the use of anonymized data, the voluntary nature of participation, that no health-related data would be collected), and in turn signed consent forms were obtained. The ethical committees of the Lappeenranta University of Technology and California State University, Long Beach, approved the study.

Thirty-three older participants from Finland and the U.S., with a mean age of 62.46 years (SD = 2.295), were voluntarily recruited to participate in the usability test sessions. This sample size is sufficient based on the recommendation [33] that a group size of 3–20 participants is typically valid, with 5–10 participants demonstrating a sensible baseline range. Participants from both countries were living independently and were interested in using new technology to improve their well-being [27]. The contextual action theory (CAT) explained by Stanton [49] and Usability Evaluation Method (UEM) presented by Ivory and Hearst [23] were applied as foundational methodologies in evaluating COTS wearable devices in this study's set of usability experiments among older users. Stanton et al. [49] states that CAT explains human actions in terms of coping with technology within a particular context and that five phases are associated with contextual actions.

First phase: *Presentation of actual demands and actual resources to participants, consisting of the device, the tasks to be performed on the device, environmental constraints (e.g. time), and so on.* Firstly, participants were presented with functioning wearable COTS devices, i.e. smartwatches and pedometers, to help explore the significance of various types of data for future design, as pointed out by Kanis [26]. No requirements were provided for device selection. Secondly, participants were presented with several experimental tasks (See Appendix A[1] for presented experimental tasks) along with a timeframe, namely two one-hour, controlled environment sessions (i.e. the first and final meetings). As stated by [11], "the idea of momentary memory implies that we don't store our experiences in perfect experimental and temporal fidelity, rather memories are formed from snapshots of the representative moments in an experience" (p. 90). Therefore, participants were asked to use each category of device under real conditions every day for the two weeks between the meet-up sessions (i.e. in a semi-controlled-environment) and to capture the usage in a daily log using the diary method. No specific pre-defined activities such as put on/take off, charge, walk, eat, rest, sleep, or exercise [24] were specified. Participants were requested to return to another one-hour, controlled environment session to return the device and test usability. Finally, participants were told that upon completing the semi-controlled usability evaluation, they would be asked to respond to a survey.

Second phase: *Appraisal of those demands and resources by participants.* As stated by [25], the primary appraisal of an interaction event can result in a negative emotional response such as anxiety or frustration. To reduce such negative emotional response from participants, participants were asked to appraise the demands and resources presented during the first phase, so that their stated perception might help to redirect negative emotional response away from the experiment itself [21].

Third Phase: *Comparison of perceived resources with perceived demands.* In this phase, participants were asked to compare their own perceived resources with

---

[1] https://doi.org/10.5281/zenodo.832159.

perceived demands to determine any imbalance related to the specific properties of smartwatches and pedometers, which could affect participation in the study [49].

Fourth Phase: *Possible degradation of pathways.* Participant appraisal and comparison may reflect the potential for degradation of pathways, i.e. emotional responses and behavioral responses. Such emotional responses may include decreases in user satisfaction and motivation, while potential behavioral responses include an increase in errors and inefficiency.

Fifth Phase: *Appraisal of the effects of these responses on device usage.* The effects of these responses on participant interaction with the devices were gathered through the daily log, which included several kinds of measurements.

Measurements of identifying usability issues
The search strings *"usability issue*", "smartwatch*", "pedometer*", and "wearable*"* were conducted utilizing the digital databases IEEE Xplore, the ACM Digital Library, Science Direct, and Web of Science. After refining the results from the digital databases, the final lists of usability issues were derived from [3, 16, 37, 39, 40, 43, 48].

Participants were asked to keep a diary of their experiences. The diary included several kinds of data, such as: (i) whether devices were worn (*if not, why*); (ii) which activities were undertaken (*e.g. walking, hiking, running, cycling, etc.*); (iii) whether device use motivated physical activity (*and why/why not*); (iv) which applications were used (*if not used, why*); (v) usability issues (*e.g. screen size, icons, interaction techniques, tap detection, font size, button location, data accuracy, screen resolution, device weight, device shape, device size, lack of screen, battery life, and the option to add any missing usability issues*); and (vi) additional comments.

For the purpose of analysis, the usability issues for both device categories (smartwatches and pedometers) have been categorized into two components: hardware and user interface. Specifically, the hardware concerns involve issues related to external look and feel and to internal components such as sensors, processor, memory, power supply, and transceiver [1, 32]. User interface involves issues with various parts through which users interact with the device [1]. Furthermore, the user interface component has been sub-categorized into input and navigation mechanism, based on the work of [1].

The first set of data gathered from the first and final meet up sessions was analyzed using the instant data analysis technique proposed by [29]. The qualitative data obtained from diaries were analysed based on the data analysis framework presented by [10], "which offers an eclectic approach for qualitative diary data analysis" (p. 1514).

The final data set of identifying stage derived from (i) the first and final meet-up sessions and (ii) four weeks of daily logs by the older participants data. The analysis was done using a Microsoft Excel spreadsheet, wherein reported usability issues were assigned (1) to understand the number of times they were reported by participants during the entire evaluation period. This analysis enabled understanding of the breadth and occurrence of reported usability issues in order to find out the most frequent usability issues that could be used as the basis for quantitative analysis.

3.2 Prioritizing Stage

The main purpose of this stage was to collect quantitative data from the participants using an immediate prioritization scale. This study's immediate prioritization scale utilized most usability issues reported by older participants during (i) the usability test sessions (first and final meet-ups) and (ii) four weeks of participants' daily logs. In a survey, participants were asked to rate on a 7 Likert scale (0 = strongly agree to 7 = strongly disagree) how much the identified usability issues correspond with the motivation to adopt. Qualitative data from the survey was analyzed separately in an Excel spreadsheet, using the statistical data analysis language R and the descriptive statistical analysis functions available in R core [42] and the psych library [45].

Data analysis was performed with multiple linear regression [12] in order to test hypotheses to see which variables most influenced the motivation to use the devices. Multiple linear regression modeling was performed using the R core statistics library [42], following the methodological guidelines set out by Weisberg [55, 56] and Laerd Research [30]. Additional multiple linear regression diagnostics were performed using the following R libraries: mctest (multicollinearity diagnostics) [52], MASS (standardized residuals) [53], car (Durbin-Watson Test, outlier testing, Spread-Level and QQ plots) [17], and lmtest (Breusch-Pagan test) [59].

3.3 Results

After analyzing sets of data from the identifying stage (i.e. the first and final meet-up sessions and four weeks of daily logs by the older participants data), we identified 13 usability issues common to pedometers and smartwatches and categorized them into a framework of hardware or user interface related issues (see Fig. 2), with the lack of screen being the only additional issue unique to pedometers. Interaction techniques were a multi-faceted category under user interface. Participants reported that interaction techniques can cause usability issues despite their intended functions of providing feedback to the user that can be perceived without continuous visual attention [19] and engaging users through quantitative or qualitative understanding of underlying data [6] through notification. For example, in this study participants reported usability issues caused by interaction technique sub-categories of both feedback (tactile and kinesthetic) and notification. In addition, on both smartwatches and pedometers, older participants reported issues with data accuracy and connectivity as sub-categories under hardware sensor issues, which was in line with previous research [38, 43].

To understand the important usability issues, we further analyzed the data based on number of times usability issues were reported by the participants during the entire evaluation period. Figures 3, 4, 5 and 6 show the mean and standard deviations of the scores (frequency) of the usability issues related to hardware and user interface and its sub components for both smartwatches and pedometers. This outcome indicates that, screen size, interaction techniques (i.e. feedback and notifications), font size, tap detection, and button location were the most influencing.

Therefore, we focus on screen size, typography (i.e. font size), tap detection, and interaction techniques (i.e. feedback and notifications) and button location to validate and enhance our understanding of the most frequent issues with device characteristics.

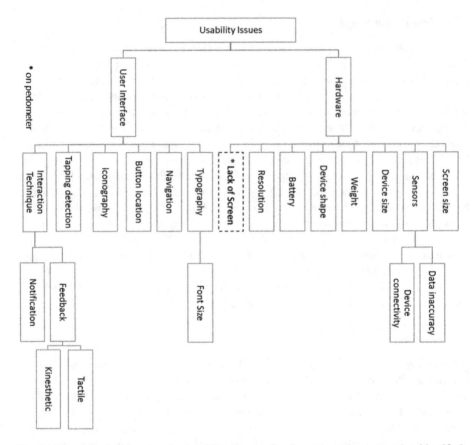

Fig. 2. Categorization framework of usability issues of pedometers and smartwatches identified from the identifying stage of this study.

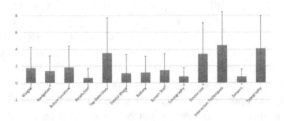

Fig. 3. Descriptive analyses of usability issues related to hardware and user interface for smartwatches

It is in this way that we pursue our proposed process (see Fig. 1) to measure the issue variables and compare their influence on motivation to adopt smartwatches and pedometers. The following section presents the variables used in the statistical research model and hypotheses formulated based on the variables.

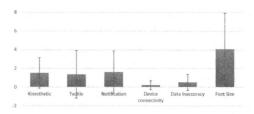

Fig. 4. Descriptive analyses of usability issues related to sub components of hardware and user interface for smartwatches

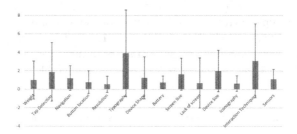

Fig. 5. Descriptive analyses of usability issues related to hardware and user interface for pedometers

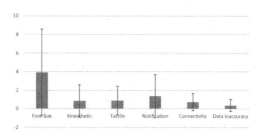

Fig. 6. Descriptive analyses of usability issues related to hardware and user interface and its sub components for smartwatches

3.4   Validity of the Measurement

The hypotheses were tested by creating multiple linear regression models from the issue variables that were most frequently cited as affecting usability. Separate models were created for smartwatches and pedometers. First, a multiple regression was run to predict motivation to adopt smartwatches from screen size, font size, wrist feedback, finger feedback, touch controls, interrupting distractions, and button location perspectives. A second multiple regression was run with those same variables in order to predict motivation to adopt pedometers. In both models there was linearity, as assessed by a plot of studentized residuals against the predicted values. There was independence of residuals, as assessed by a Durbin-Watson statistic of 1.86 in the first model and 2.48 in the second model. There was homoscedasticity, as assessed by visual inspection of a plot of studentized residuals versus unstandardized predicted values and the studentized Breusch-Pagan test. There was no evidence of multicollinearity, as assessed by tolerance values greater than 0.1 and VIF testing. There were no studentized deleted residuals greater than ±3 standard deviations, outlying leverage values, or values for Cook's distance above 1. In the second model two outliers were removed as guided by the regression model diagnostics. The assumption of normality was met in both models, as assessed by a Q-Q Plot.

The first multiple regression model statistically significantly predicted motivation to adopt smartwatches, $F_{(7, 23)} = 3.733$, $p < .01$, adj. $R2 = .39$. Some variables added statistically significantly to the prediction, confirming part of the hypotheses. Regression coefficients and standard errors can be found in Table 2.

The second multiple regression model statistically significantly predicted motivation to adopt pedometers, $F_{(7, 23)} = 3.74$, $p < .01$, adj. $R2 = .39$. Some variables added statistically significantly to the prediction, confirming part of the hypotheses. Regression coefficients and standard errors can be found in Table 3.

Table 2. Multiple Linear regression result for smartwatches

Coefficients:	Estimate	Std. Error	Significance
(Intercept)	8.9416	2.1399	***
Screen size	−0.6115	0.2145	**
Typography (Font Size)	−0.4249	0.1582	*
Button location	−0.5160	0.2229	*
Tap detection	0.1213	0.1518	
Interaction techniques			
Notifications	0.4052	0.1564	*
Kinesthetic	0.1791	0.2432	
Tactile	−0.2958	0.1640	

Table 3. Multiple Linear regression result for pedometers

Coefficients:	Estimate	Std. Error	Significance
(Intercept)	8.7454	2.3928	**
Screen size	−0.5961	0.2145	**
Typography (Font Size)	−0.5139	0.1808	**
Button location	−0.4464	0.2433	
Tap Detection	−0.4272	0.1518	*
Interaction techniques			
Notifications	0.7475	0.2122	**
Kinesthetic	0.2464	0.2620	
Tactile	−0.0801	0.1640	

4   Discussion

The focus of this section is to discuss the results obtained during the identifying and prioritizing stages of this study, based on interpretation and exploration of the retrieved data. The categorization framework explains there are not major differences between the identified usability issues related to smartwatches and pedometers. As both wearable device categories consist of similar features, the only identified difference was due to the pedometer's lack of screen. The main advantage of the categorization framework is that it summarizes and structures usability issues of smartwatches and pedometers identified in previous research and during the identifying stage of this study. If one finds additional usability issues of smartwatches and pedometers in the future, the tree within the framework could be expanded.

During the identifying stage, older participants reflected *three kinds of device usage problems* on both smartwatches and pedometers: short-term, occasional, and long-term issues. Short-term issues, for example those caused by hardware, such as weight, device shape, resolution, device connectivity, sensors (data inaccuracy), and battery, as well as those associated with user interface, such as button location, and iconography, lasted relatively briefly (i.e. the first few days of the study, when participants had their first interactions with the devices) and had minimal effect on device usability. For example, battery could be classified as a short-term issue, because within a few days, participants adjusted to charging the device regularly. Findings regarding short-term usage issues reinforce the statement from [43] that with "increasing time participants were more and more confident in the battery life and thereby decreased the number of charging cycles as well as charged the tracker later and thereby with a lower battery status" (p. 1414). Other identified usability issues, for example those caused by hardware, such as screen size and device size, and by user interface, such as tap detection, font size, interaction techniques, and navigation, appeared either occasionally or throughout the study.

Although participants experienced certain usability issues throughout the study, there was *zero drop-out*. As stated by [25], "Facing an obstacles during the use of technology doesn't necessarily lead to frustration because in the face of goal-incongruent events, the user may still cope with the arising emotions" (p. 73). In practice, the smartwatches and pedometers may have: (i) provided immediate accessibility [46]; and/or (ii) acted as facilitators of behavior change for the older adults due to motivational aspects and objective control [43]. For example, participant feedback indicated that devices facilitated motivation by providing "daily steps," that it was "fun to meet challenges," and that devices "made me aware of sleep patterns" and "aware to move and not to be sedentary for a long period of time." In addition, this study also found though qualitative feedback that users had a positive intention to use devices that are expected to work well, have good design, wearability, and do not raise privacy concerns.

Hypothesis testing revealed that *small screen size* is the main device characteristic related to both smartwatches and pedometers that *needs immediate prioritization* to improve adoption among the older adults. Supporting previous research, this study further reveals that screen size plays a significant role in adoption of wearable devices, in that small screen size restricts user behavior [20] in their ability to move beyond the fixed functionality of a tradition watch and to support a variety of apps [58] through input and output capabilities [20, 44, 58]. As perception of utility has been found to be of great importance for the older adults [46], options to address screen size include creating smartwatches and pedometers with: (i) non-graphical technology designs with led arrays [44] (ii) a larger screen by curving the screen around the wrist [58]; and (iii) the novel gaze interaction technique that enables hands-free input on smartwatches [15], all of which provide better user experience and can lead to a positive opinion from referents, so that older users actively build a positive attitude towards adoption of devices.

In addition, hypothesis results demonstrated that *font size was statistically significantly important* for the older adults in both categories of wearable devices. However, font size had higher significance for pedometers than for smartwatches. Pedometers currently have very limited amounts of screen space, and their visual displays can easily become cluttered with information and widgets [6]. Furthermore, the human eye reads an individual line of text in discrete chunks by making a series of fixations (i.e. brief moments, around 250 ms, when the eye is stopped on a word or word group, and the brain processes the visual information) and saccades (i.e. fast eye movement, usually forward in the text around 8-12 characters, to position the eye on the next section of text) [8]. One study [14] asserts that "individual characteristics such as age, impairments may affect movement of the eyes." Thus significantly longer fixations for smaller fonts [4] on the pedometers may have adversely differentiated the result between two device categories.

Both smartwatches and pedometers provide individuals with various types of *tailored and quantified self-data* supporting daily physical activities, wherever they are and at any time, [28] through notification in the form of audio, visual, and haptic signals [34]. However, results from hypothesis indicate that the older adults are more sensitive towards the disruptions caused by all push notifications. Current smartwatch and pedometer user interfaces may demand users' attention at inopportune moments, [34] e.g. without knowing which context the user is in and featuring repetitiveness in the notification content [35]. Other prioritized, predominant usability issues were button location on smartwatches and tap detection on pedometers. The result related to button location was in line with a previous study [20] indicating that pointing error rate is significantly affected by button size and location on the UI as the index finger taps on a device. However, the tap detection were significantly higher for pedometers, it may be because of (i) variance in touch screen technologies used between two device categories. For example, smartwatch devices evaluated in this study used display with the force touch technology and the pedometers with the monochrome Liquid Crystal Display (LCD) touch screen which has different ways of detecting if user is touching the screen. As tap detection has been found to be of great importance for the older adults with regards to pedometers, options to address improving the touch screen with new sensing technology [54] which could detect how much pressure is been exerted by the older users and display the output based on measurements; (ii) characteristics of older participants. For example, Culen [13] state, "age-related changes constitute challenges of touch and grip" (p. 464).

The above discussion highlights prioritized needs for immediate attention and further investigation by technology designers, the research community, and application developers regarding the predominant issues older adults face when using smart-watches and pedometers. We see two lines of immediate future work: First, the *effect of timing and frequency* using intelligent, sensor driven and/or pre-determined, static notification [35] could be analyzed to gain insight into how the older adults prefer to receive push notifications of "quantified self" data from their smartwatches and pedometers. The findings may help in the design of effective user interfaces to reduce usability issues caused by push notifications and thereby increase device adoption. Second, through a longitudinal study using eye-gazing techniques, future research should look into *which typographical variables* such as font size and font type [4] are most effective for older users of smartwatches and pedometers.

5 Conclusion

This study presented a categorization framework for usability issues of smartwatches and pedometers. Additionally, this paper used multiple linear regression modeling to prioritize the issues predominantly reported during the first 'identifying' stage of the study. "Prioritizing" stage of the study found for (i) pedometers issues of *screen size, Typography (i.e. font size), interaction technique (i.e. notification), and tap detection;* and (ii) smartwatches issues of *screen size, Typography (i.e. font size), interaction technique (i.e. notification); button location* warrant immediate attention by technology designers, the research community, and application developers to increase device adoption among the older adults. The main limitation of this study is the relatively small and non-random sample, meaning the results cannot be generalized. This study can, however, be used as a basis for further studies to: (i) investigate how prioritized predominant usability issues differ when secondary users, such as caregivers or rela-tives, use smartwatches and pedometers on behalf of frail older users; (ii) discover how a categorization framework of usability issues related to smartwatches and pedometers varies across different cultures; (iii) provide information that can serve as a basis for improving adoption by enhancing device characteristics; and (iv) identify the priori-tized predominant usability issues among higher age and frail older users.

Acknowledgments. First author would like to thank Miina Sillanpää Foundation and Second author would like to thank Ulla Tuominen Foundation for their generous support of research.

References

1. Ally, M., Gardiner, M.: Application and device characteristics as drivers for smart mobile device adoption and productivity. Int. J. Organ. Behav. **17**(4), 35–47 (2012)
2. Alshamari, M., Mayhew, P.: Task design: its impact on usability testing. In: 2008 Third International Conference on Internet Web Applications Services, pp. 583–589 (2008)

3. Angelini, L., et al.: Designing a desirable smart bracelet for older adults. In: Proceedings of 2013 ACM Conference Pervasive ubiquitous Computing Adjunct Publication, UbiComp 2013, pp. 425–434 (2013)
4. Beymer, D., et al.: An eye tracking study of how font size and type influence online reading. Br. Comput. Soc. **2**, 15–18 (2008)
5. Black, S.W.: Current Practices for Product Usability Testing in Web and Mobile Applications. University of New Hampshire (2015)
6. Brewster, S., et al.: Multimodal "eyes-free" interaction techniques for wearable devices. In: Proceedings of the Conference Human Factors Computing Systems, CHI 2003. vol. 5, p. 473 (2003)
7. Charness, N., et al.: Aging and information technology use: potential and barriers. Curr. Dir. Psychol. Sci. **18**(5), 253–258 (2009)
8. Chester, R.D.: The psychology of reading. J. Educ. Res. **67**(9), 403–411 (1974)
9. Chiu, C.-J., Liu, C.-W.: Understanding older adult's technology adoption and withdrawal for elderly care and education: mixed method analysis from national survey. J. Med. Internet Res. **19**(11), e374 (2017)
10. Clayton, A.M., Thorne, T.: Diary data enhancing rigour: analysis framework and verification tool. J. Adv. Nurs. **32**(6), 1514–1521 (2000)
11. Cockburn, A., et al.: The effects of interaction sequencing on user experience and preference. Int. J. Hum Comput Stud. **108**, 89–104 (2017)
12. Cohen, J., et al.: Applied Multiple Regression/Correlation Analysis for the Behavioral Sciences, pp. 19–63. Routledge, Abingdon (2013)
13. Culén, A., Bratteteig, T.: Touch-screens and elderly users: a perfect match? In: ACHI 2013 Sixth International Conference on Advances in Computing Interaction, pp. 460–465 (2013)
14. Dowiasch, S., et al.: Effects of aging on eye movements in the real world. Front. Hum. Neurosci. **9**, 46 (2015)
15. Esteves, A., et al.: orbits: gaze interaction for smart watches using smooth pursuit eye movements. In: Proceedings of the 28th Annual ACM Symposium on User Interface Software & Technology, UIST 2015, pp. 457–466 (2015)
16. Fausset, C.B., et al.: Older Adults' Use of and Attitudes toward Activity Monitoring Technologies. In: Proceedings of the Human Factors and Ergonomics Society Annual Meeting. vol. 57, no. 1, pp. 1683–1687 (2013)
17. Fox, J., Weisberg, S.: An R Companion to Applied Regression. Sage, Thousand Oaks (2011)
18. Gudur, R.R., Blackler, A., Popovic, V., Mahar, D.: Ageing, technology anxiety and intuitive use of complex interfaces. In: Kotzé, P., Marsden, G., Lindgaard, G., Wesson, J., Winckler, M. (eds.) INTERACT 2013. LNCS, vol. 8119, pp. 564–581. Springer, Heidelberg (2013). https://doi.org/10.1007/978-3-642-40477-1_36
19. Han, T., et al.: Frictio: Passive Kinesthetic Force Feedback for Smart Ring Output. In: Proceedings of UIST 2017. Figure 2 (2017)
20. Hara, K., Umezawa, T., Osawa, N.: Effect of button size and location when pointing with index finger on smartwatch. In: Kurosu, M. (ed.) HCI 2015. LNCS, vol. 9170, pp. 165–174. Springer, Cham (2015). https://doi.org/10.1007/978-3-319-20916-6_16
21. Harris, D., et al.: Engineering psychology and cognitive ergonomics. Eng. Psychol. Cogn. Ergon. **5639**, 414–423 (2009)
22. Holzinger, A., et al.: Perceived usefulness among elderly people: experiences and lessons learned during the evaluation of a wrist device. In: Proceedings of 4th International ICST Conference on Pervasive Computing Technologies for Healthcare, pp. 1–5 (2010)
23. Ivory, M.Y., Hearst, M.A.: The state of the art in automating usability evaluation of user interfaces. ACM Comput. Surv. **33**(4), 470–516 (2001)

24. Jeong, H., et al.: Smartwatch wearing behavior analysis. Proc. ACM Interact. Mobile, Wearable Ubiquitous Technol. **1**(3), 1–31 (2017)
25. Jokinen, J.P.P.: Emotional user experience: traits, events, and states. Int. J. Hum Comput Stud. **76**, 67–77 (2015)
26. Kanis, H.: Usage centred research for everyday product design (1998)
27. Khakurel, J., Tella, S., Penzenstadler, B., Melkas, H., Porras, J.: Living with smartwatches and pedometers: the intergenerational gap in internal and external contexts. In: Guidi, B., Ricci, L., Calafate, C., Gaggi, O., Marquez-Barja, J. (eds.) GOODTECHS 2017. LNICSSITE, vol. 233, pp. 31–41. Springer, Cham (2018). https://doi.org/10.1007/978-3-319-76111-4_4
28. Kim, S.K., et al.: An analysis of the effects of smartphone push notifications on task performance with regard to smartphone overuse using ERP. Comput. Intell. Neurosci. **2016** (2016)
29. Kjeldskov, J., et al.: Instant data analysis: conducting usability evaluations in a day. In: Proceedings of the Third Nordic Conference on Human-Computer Interaction, pp. 233–240 (2004)
30. Laerd: Multiple regression analysis using SPSS statistics. Laerd Res. Ltd. (2013)
31. Leonardi, C., et al.: Designing a familiar technology for elderly people. Gerontechnology **7**(2), 151 (2008)
32. Liu, C.-C., et al.: Development of a sensor network system for industrial technology education (2010)
33. Macefield, R.: How to specify the participant group size for usability studies: a practitioner's guide. J. Usability Stud. **5**(1), 34–45 (2009)
34. Mehrotra, A., Musolesi, M.: Intelligent notification systems: a survey of the state of the art and research challenges, **1**(1), 1–26 (2017)
35. Morrison, L.G., et al.: The effect of timing and frequency of push notifications on usage of a smartphone-based stress management intervention: An exploratory trial. PLoS One **12**, 1 (2017)
36. Natpratan, C., Cooharojananone, N.: Study of sound and haptic feedback in smart wearable devices to improve driving performance of elders. In: Kim, K.J. (ed.) Information Science and Applications. LNEE, vol. 339, pp. 51–58. Springer, Heidelberg (2015). https://doi.org/10.1007/978-3-662-46578-3_7
37. Paul, G., Irvine, J.: Privacy implications of wearable health devices. In: SIN 2014 Proceedings of 7th International Conference on Security of Information and Networks, p. 117 (2014)
38. Piwek, L., et al.: The rise of consumer health wearables: promises and barriers. PLoS Med. **13**, 2 (2016)
39. Preusse, K.C., et al.: Activity monitoring technologies and older adult users. In: Proceedings of the International Symposium on Human Factors and Ergonomics in Health Care, vol. 3, no. 1, pp. 23–27 (2014)
40. Pulli, P., et al.: User interaction in smart ambient environment targeted for senior citizen. Med. Biol. Eng. Comput. **50**(11), 1119–1126 (2012)
41. Puri, A., et al.: User acceptance of wrist-worn activity trackers among community-dwelling older adults: mixed method study. JMIR mHealth uHealth. **5**(11), e173 (2017)
42. R Development Core Team: R: A Language and Environment for Statistical Computing. Vienna, Austria : the R Foundation for Statistical Computing
43. Rasche, P., et al.: Activity tracker and elderly. In: 2015 IEEE International Conference on Computer and Information Technology; Ubiquitous Computing and Communications; Dependable, Autonomic and Secure Computing; Pervasive Intelligence and Computing (CIT/IUCC/DASC/PICOM), pp. 1411–1416 (2015)

44. Rawassizadeh, R., et al.: Wearables. Commun. ACM. **58**(1), 45–47 (2014)
45. Revelle, W.: psych: procedures for personality and psychological research. R Packag. 1–358 (2016)
46. Rodríguez, I., et al.: Helping elderly users report pain levels: a study of user experience with mobile and wearable interfaces. Mob. Inf. Syst. **2017**, 1–12 (2017)
47. Sin, A.K., et al.: A wearable device for the elderly: a case study in Malaysia. In: Proceedings of the 6th International Conference on Information Technology and Multimedia, pp. 318–323. IEEE (2014)
48. Sin, K.A., et al.: Advances in Visual Informatics. Springer International Publishing, Cham (2015). https://doi.org/10.1007/978-3-319-70010-6
49. Stanton, N.: Ecological ergonomics: understanding human action in context. Taylor & Francis (1994)
50. Swan, M.: Connected car: quantified self becomes quantified car. J. Sens. Actuator Netw. **4**(1), 2–29 (2015)
51. Tedesco, S., et al.: A review of activity trackers for senior citizens: research perspectives, commercial landscape and the role of the insurance industry (2017)
52. Ullah, M.I., Aslam, D.M.: mctest: Multicollinearity Diagnostic Measures (2017). https://cran.r-project.org/package=mctest
53. Venables, W.N., Ripley, B.D.: Modern Applied Statistics with S. Springer, New York (2002). https://doi.org/10.1007/978-0-387-21706-2
54. Vishniakou, S., et al.: Improved performance of zinc oxide thin film transistor pressure sensors and a demonstration of a commercial chip compatibility with the new force sensing technology. Adv. Mater. Technol. **3**, 1700279 (2018)
55. Weisberg, S.: Applied Linear Regression. Wiley, Hoboken (2005)
56. Weisberg, S.: Computing Primer for Applied Linear Regression, Using R (2005)
57. Wulf, L., et al.: Hands free-care free: elderly people taking advantage of speech-only interaction. In: Proceedings of the 8th Nordic Conference on Human-Computer Interaction: Fun, Fast, Foundational, pp. 203–206 (2014)
58. Xu, C., Lyons, K.: Shimmering smartwatches: exploring the smartwatch design space. In: Proceedings of the Ninth International Conference on Tangible, Embedded, and Embodied Interaction, TEI 2014, pp. 69–76 (2015)
59. Zeileis, A., Hothorn, T.: Diagnostic checking in regression relationships. R News **2**(3), 7–10 (2002)

Towards a Framework for the Design of Quantitative Experiments: Human-Computer Interaction and Accessibility Research

Frode Eika Sandnes[1,2(✉)], Evelyn Eika[1], and Fausto Orsi Medola[3]

[1] Department of Computer Science, Faculty of Technology, Art and Design,
OsloMet – Oslo Metropolitan University, Oslo, Norway
{frodes,Evelyn.Eika}@hioa.no
[2] Faculty of Technology, Westerdals Oslo School of Art, Communication and
Technology, Oslo, Norway
[3] FAAC, UNESP, Bauru, Sao Paulo, Brazil
fausto.medola@faac.unesp.br

Abstract. Many students and researchers struggle with the design and analysis of empirical experiments. Such issue may be caused by lack of knowledge about inferential statistics and suitable software tools. Often, students and researchers conduct experiments without having a complete plan for the entire lifecycle of the process. Difficulties associated with the statistical analysis are often ignored. Consequently, one may end up with data that cannot be easily analyzed. This paper discusses the concept sketch of a framework that intends to help students and researchers to design correct empirical experiments by making sound design decisions early in the research process. The framework consists of an IDE, i.e., Integrated (statistical experiment) Development Environment. This IDE helps the user structures an experiment by giving continuous feedback drawing the experimenter's attention towards potential problems. The output of the IDE is an experimental structure and data format that can be imported to common statistical packages such as JASP in addition to providing guidance about what tests to use.

Keywords: Inferential statistics · Design of experiments
Integrated Development Environment · Human computer interaction
Universal accessibility

1 Introduction

There are several challenges faced by students and infrequent users of statistics when designing experiments. These difficulties are evident from the literature [1–3]. Several approaches for remedying the situation have been reported such as teaching in small groups [4], using problem based learning [5], using practical examples [5], and online modes of teaching [6, 7]. Students sometimes establish misconceptions about inferential statistics [8]. Some of the terminology and concepts may be hard to grasp, for example, significance [9], hypothesis testing [10], and p-values [11, 12]. Next, students

© Springer International Publishing AG, part of Springer Nature 2018
M. Antona and C. Stephanidis (Eds.): UAHCI 2018, LNCS 10907, pp. 107–120, 2018.
https://doi.org/10.1007/978-3-319-92049-8_8

and researchers incorrectly use pairs of t-tests instead of an ANOVA test [13, 14]. The notion of parametric versus non-parametric tests is also confusing even for experienced researchers [15]. Several of the tests' titles have individuals' names rather than signaling what the test does. Employing correct tests in specific situations then becomes difficult unless one uses the tests frequently. This problem has given rise to reference sheets such as the ones provided by McCrum-Gardner [16]. Further, statistics is often taught from a theoretical perspective, which might not be easily accessible. We thus take the view of Wood [17], Khait [18], and others who argue for making mathematics and statistics less theoretical and more explorative and practical.

Many students and researchers delay the problem of statistical analysis until after the experiment has been carried out. A researcher may end up with an experiment for which there is no readily available test procedure. This work explores the concept of a workflow where the experimenter makes all the experimental design decisions before the experiment is carried out. The researcher is given feedback on the experimental design at an early stage allowing him or her to explore experiment design ideas before committing to labor-intensive data-collection. Errors are thus prevented during data-input.

Most statistical software tools assume data to be input in a certain way as a prerequisite, while the attention is on data exploration and analysis. Our approach instead focuses on exploring the experimental design at an early stage. Once a suitable design is configured, the subsequent analyses should be straightforward and be conducted more-or-less automatically. The concept revolves around the notion of an IDE (Integrated Development Environment). IDEs are commonly used in software development and facilitate rapid development of quality code. IDEs use mechanisms such as syntax highlighting giving the developer visual feedback during coding. Moreover, systematic feedback and error messages are provided with specific references to the code and to suggested solutions.

2 Statistics in Research and Education–Personal Experiences

The motivation for this work is our extensive use of statistics in our previous work including analyzing students' coursework practices [19], cross cultural differences [20], expectations [21], university preferences [22], motivation [23], language learning [24], cross language effects [25], emotions [26], and prosody [27]. The authors have also applied statistics explicitly in computer science to achieve engineering solutions. Examples include proof of concept real-time license plate recognizer [28], television commercial identification [29], communicating data digitally via paper [30], data mining methods [31], or stochastic optimization [32]. Some of the computer science processes are deterministic, and simple measures of accuracy are sufficiently employed in geo-location based on image content [33], image light intensity [34], image contents [35], and underwater light intensity [36].

Inferential statistics is especially relevant in Human Computer Interaction, universal accessibility [37, 38], and assistive technologies, although it is not the only approach. Inferential statistics is one of the available analysis tools that are relevant in certain situations. For instance, we have used theoretical models [39, 40], graph theory

[41–44], heuristic evaluation [45, 46], qualitative methods via interviews [47], text analysis [48–50], personal accounts [51], visualization [52, 53], design and sketching in two-dimensions [54], pseudo three-dimensions [55, 56], and real three-dimensions [57–59]. We have built concept prototypes such as self-service kiosks [60], multi-view surfaces [61], volunteering services [62], tactile interfaces [63], improved text input interfaces [64], and augmented reality displays [65]. Other approaches included the design and exploration of new methods [66] and artefacts such as new interaction techniques [67], analysis methods [68, 69], interfaces [70–72], navigation tools for the physical world [73] and virtual worlds [74]. Comparative analyses are also common in assistive technology research technologies for motor disabilities [75]. For example, wheelchair research addresses aspects of manual wheelchair design [76, 77], motor assisted wheelchair design [78, 79], chair setup [80], hand-rim design [81, 82], hand pressure effects [83], and wheelchair maneuverability [84].

Within human computer interaction we have used t-tests to compare dyslexic users and non-dyslexic users [85–87], comparing two presentation strategies [88], comparing visual feedback versus no visual feedback [89], comparing two keyboard layouts [90], and comparing left and right scrolling behavior [91]. ANOVAs have been used to analyze how users learn an interface over time (longitudinal) through several sessions of observing practice [92, 93], memory [94, 95], and timing [96].

Computers are claimed to be useful for teaching statistics [97]. The authors have also used Microsoft Excel in teaching and research for many years. Excel has certain challenges as there are no built-in repeated measures analysis functions which are common in human computer interaction. However, one may overcome this short-coming using add-ins such as the one developed my Charles Zainotz [98]. Still, it is claimed that Excel contains several computational inaccuracies [99–101].

We have also used R-Project [102] for more complex functions such as post-hoc testing. Students are also free to use one of the user interface additions to R-Project [103]. More recently, we have started to use JASP in various contexts (Jefferey's Awesome Statistics Package) [104]. We have found this to be a huge improvement upon other statistics software in making statistical analysis available to non-experts.

3 A Statistics IDE

IDEs have been a successful tool for teaching programming [105]. The purpose of the proposed statistics IDE is to help students and researchers develop the following: a clear notion about what is being observed, what the datatypes of the observations are, what factors are altered and what their types are, whether the controlled factors are within-subjects or between-subjects, how many participants will be recruited, among other aspects. The following paragraphs describe the elements of the statistics IDE concept.

3.1 Experiment Definition Editor

The experiment definition editor is used for developing and representing the structure of the experiment. The structure of the notation encourages the experimenter to make clear decisions about what he or she is exploring, what the dependent variables and independent variables are, what datatype these variables have, and whether the factors are within-subjects of between-subjects.

```
1: myExperiment: experiment
2:      (
3:      dependent
4:          (
5:              time: real;
6:          )
7:      independent
8:          (
9:              inputDevice: category (mouse, keyboard, touch);
10:         )
11:  )
12:
13:
14:
15:
ERROR: Keyword within or between missing for independent
factor inputDevice at line 9.
ERROR: participants not defined for experiment myExperiment
at line 12.
```

Fig. 1. Incorrect ANOVA definition.

```
1: myExperiment: experiment
2:      (
3:      dependent
4:          (
5:              satisfaction: integer from 1 to 5;
6:              score: integer from 1 to 5;
7:          )
8:      independent
9:          (
10:             exam: category (oral, essay, paper) within;
11:         )
12:     participants: 10;
13:     )
14:
15:
Within-subjects analysis of variance.
Separate analysis for satisfaction and score.
Non-parametric test: recommending Friedmann test.
Definition analysis successful.
```

Fig. 2. Non-parametric ANOVA definition.

```
1: myExperiment: experiment
2:      (
3:      dependent
4:          (
5:              wpm: real from 0.0 to 200.0;
6:          )
7:      independent
8:          (
9:              inputDevice: category (mouse, touch) within;
10:             context: category (standing, sitting) within;
11:             gender: category (male, female) between;
12:         )
13:     participants: 10;
14:     )
15:
Mixed ANOVA with two within-subjects and one between subject
factors.
WARNING: No non-parametric analysis available.
Definition analysis successful.
```

Fig. 3. Mixed ANOVA definition.

```
1: myExperiment: experiment
2:      (
3:      dependent
4:          (
5:              wpm: real from 0.0 to 200.0;
6:          )
7:      independent
8:          (
9:              experience: real from 0.0 to 10.0;
10:         )
11:     participants: 15;
12:     )
13:
14:
15:
Correlation of factors wpm against experience.
Parametric analysis: Recommending Pearons.
Definition analysis successful.
```

Fig. 4. Correlation definition.

The structure and representation are intended to be simple and to provide guidance by constraints. Syntax highlighting is used for separating keywords from user defined names and data types. If the experimenter misspells a keyword, the mistake is easily identified as the syntax highlighting is not as expected [106].

The IDE also provides feedback if the definition is incorrect. Indentation and free form formatting allow the experimenter to make the definition more readable. Indentation has been shown to improve the understandability of source code [107].

The experiment definitions allow the experimental designs to be easily represented and shared between experimenters for comments and input, for performing formal checks on its feasibility and for generating suitable input forms for the observation data.

Figure 1 shows a simple one-way ANOVA. The dependent variable time is defined as being of interval type while the independent variable being input device is categorical. The input device factor has three levels, namely, mouse, keyboard, and touch display. Here, the experimenter has forgotten to specify whether the independent variable is within-groups or between-groups. Hence, it is unclear whether the treatments should be repeated for each participant or if each participant just receives one treatment. Moreover, the definition does not indicate how many participants the experiment will entail. This feedback helps the experimenter explicitly decide on these details of the experiment and thus correct the definition.

Figure 2 shows an example of a non-parametric repeated measures one-way ANOVA with two dependent variables, namely, satisfaction and score. Both dependent variables are ordinal (integers in a small range). The independent variable exam is categorical with levels oral exam, essay, and exam paper. It is defined as a within-subjects factor meaning that all participants need to be exposed to all three conditions.

The definition declares that 10 participants will be recruited. The IDE recommends that a non-parametric test is used since the data type is ordinal. The feedback indicates that the definition is ok and suggests an appropriate test (Friedman).

Figure 3 shows an example of a mixed multifactor design. Words-per-minute (wpm) is defined as the dependent variable of interval type (real number ranging from 0 to 200). There are three dependent variables, namely, input device, context, and gender. Gender is a between-subjects factor with levels male and female. There are two within-subject factors, input device and context. Input device has the levels mouse and touch, while context has the levels standing and sitting. The experimenter is warned that no non-parametric alternatives exist in the case where the assumptions of the parametric tests are not satisfied. The experimenter therefore has a chance to either proceed with the risk of the data not adhering to the parametric assumptions or to simplify the experiment by reducing the number of factors.

Figure 4 shows the definition of a correlation. Words per minute (wpm) is the dependent variable; experience in years (of interval type ranging from 0 to 10 years) is the independent variable. The IDE recognizes this as a correlation since the independent variable is interval. The IDE also recommends a suitable test (Pearson correlation).

Given an experimental definition, the IDE can also provide help suggesting an experimental setup, such as randomized or Latin square presentation order for within-subject designs. Figure 5 shows an example of this concept based on the experiment definition in Fig. 2. The exam factor has three levels: oral exam, essay exam, and paper exam. The table shows a suggested presentation order for each of the 10 participants. Color-coding is used to reduce the chance of mistakes. With more complex multifactor designs, the benefit of automatically generated presentation sequences become even more useful and the table is directly relating to the level names used in the definition.

3.2   Observations Editor

Once the researcher has specified the experiment, the IDE generates the observation entry form. It is similar to the concepts of a regular spreadsheet such as Excel or the grid editor used in SPSS. The spreadsheet is a versatile and widely understood data entry tool [108]. However, the proposed observation editor distinguishes itself from the traditional spreadsheet in several ways. First, it is a special purpose tool, while the spreadsheet is a general tool.

Next, the names of the columns and the rows cannot be altered as these are set by the experiment definition. It is only possible to enter observations in the empty cells. In

Participant	First	Second	Third
1	oral	essay	paper
2	oral	paper	essay
3	paper	oral	essay
4	paper	essay	oral
5	essay	oral	paper
6	essay	paper	oral
7	oral	paper	essay
8	paper	oral	essay
9	paper	essay	oral
10	essay	paper	oral

Fig. 5. Presentation order.

		Stand Mouse	Stand Touch	Sit Mouse	Sit Touch
Participant 1	Female	yes			
Participant 2	Female	no	8		
Participant 3	Female		1.0		
Participant 4	Female				
Participant 5	Female				
Participant 6	Male				
Participant 7	Male				
Participant 8	Male				
Participant 9	Male				
Participant 10	Male				

Fig. 6. Observation editor. (Color figure online)

other statistical tools, both dependent and independent variable data are coded in the same spreadsheet sometimes causing confusion. Background color-coding is used to indicate the data for the various groups, making it easier to enter the data in the right cells. Finally, justification and text color are used to signal the data type of a value entered into a cell. This is to prevent the user from entering data incorrectly. Excel also performs simple cell datatype visualization, but it is limited to the left justification of text and right alignment of values.

We have chosen the following convention. Categorical data are left aligned with a green text color, ordinal data are right aligned with a blue text color, and interval data are centered on the decimal point with a black color. It is easy to spot cells which have been incorrectly entered.

Figure 6 illustrates an example observation editor rendered from the mixed model example in Fig. 3. The row and column titles give the names of the between- and within-group factor levels; these are not editable. Each group in the editable cells has unique colors making these distinguishable. The example in Fig. 3 shows some incorrectly entered observations, i.e., "yes" and "no", in addition to the ordinal value 8. The color and the alignment help emphasize these differences and give the experimenter a clue that the data are incorrectly entered into the observation editor.

Before the experimenter starts the experiment, the IDE can create a test spreadsheet with dummy values allowing the analysis of the experimental design to be tested before committing to potentially labor-intensive experimentation.

3.3 Statistical Analysis

Once the data are entered into the spreadsheet, the experimenter can start the statistical analysis. Unlike traditional statistics programs that encourage iterative exploration, the tool "compiles" the design and the observations and output the analysis. For instance, if the datatypes are interval, the procedure starts by performing assumption checks for parametric tests. If these are ok, the IDE continues by performing the tests, followed by post-hoc testing if applicable. At all stages, key information is output to the experimenter, including statistics tables with p-values as well as descriptive statistics. These can then readily be used for reports. Similarly, if the assumption checks fail, the appropriate parametric tests are performed if they exist.

If there are problems with the data, these are reported to the experimenter in a similar way in which error messages are reported to developers in traditional IDEs. Alternatively, the output entered in the observation editor can be exported into formats readably by other statistical tools such as R, SPSS, or JASP.

3.4   Interactive Data Explorer

In addition to the verbose textual output provided by running the statistical analysis processor, we also propose the concept of an interactive data explorer. The data explorer is based on the idea of comparing pairs of groups or multiple groups. A p-value needle instrument is used as a metaphor to signal significant differences or no-significance in addition to visualizing the data for the given set by the means of summary statistics and data distributions. The purpose is to help the experimenter get a subjective understanding of the observations.

The observation explorer allows the user to select two or more groups from the set of available groups to produce the visualized output. It is thus clear what the relationship is between the selected groups. These relationships may be slightly harder to read from traditional statistical output. By changing the selected groups, the displayed output responds immediately as it would with a physical probing instrument such as a voltmeter.

Figure 7 illustrates the operation of the interactive data explorer. The group of females using a mouse while standing is compared to males using a mouse while sitting. The selected groups are highlighted. The needle instrument reveals a p-value less than the critical value, indicating that these groups are significantly different.

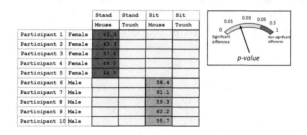

Fig. 7. Interactive data explorer.

4   Preliminary Experiences

Parts of the elements in the framework have been tested on a class of 2nd year undergraduate students of computer science at HiOA, that is, pedagogical learning resources and JSAP. We did not have a working Statistics-IDE ready as yet. The experiences obtained so far are briefly outlined in the following section.

Some of the statistics tools described herein were introduced as the third and last part of a course in human computer interaction. The course was attended by 102 undergraduate students organized into 29 groups with 2 to 5 students each. One group had just one student. The groups were asked to define their own mini-projects based on the materials covered in class. Half-way through the project, the students had to give flash presentations (2–3 min) of their preliminary plans and ideas in class allowing students to learn from other groups and to get feedback from the instructor.

Most students managed to apply statistical analyses using some tool, apart from two groups. The students were free to choose statistics software but JASP was recommended in class. Most groups employed JASP while one group used R and another Excel. The groups employed both within-subject, between-subjects, and mixed designs. About half of the students performed assumptions checks correctly and most groups successfully chose non-parametric tests when the assumptions for the parametric tests were not satisfied. Only one group incorrectly used t-tests when they should have used ANOVAs.

Twenty-four projects involved the comparison of two conditions using t-tests, while four groups used a simple one-way ANOVAs with three levels, and one group had four levels. A handful of groups attempted multifactorial ANOVAs or mixed-design ANOVAs. Most of these also involved post-hoc testing.

Most of the projects (eight) conducted some type of text input experiment. Six of the projects compared voice versus conventional input, five projects compared pointing devices. Three projects compared different widgets for setting date or time. Two projects compared the effectiveness of visualizations. The remaining projects addressed scrolling, navigation, error messages, autocomplete and user authentication.

Based on the feedback, the most challenging areas were how to design good experiments, choosing the right level of detail for the measurements, and isolating sensible independent variables. Some students were also uncertain about the datatype of their dependent variables. Another difficulty was how to interpret the meaning of significance when observing interactions between two or more factors. Some students also wanted the material to be even more clearly organized with a clear separation of the various tutorials. A couple of groups had too ambitious goals with many factors. These were advised to simplify their experimental designs during the presentation session.

5   Conclusions

A concept sketch of a framework that encourages the early design of an experiment in an empirical research project is described and discussed. The framework revolves around an experiment definition. This definition can be checked for correctness and used to provide advice and generate template files for observational data. Strategies such as this may help provide a user-friendly framework that supports and facilitates the statistical analysis for both researchers and students of various levels in the process of designing experiments. Future work includes implementing a prototype of the framework and assessing if it may lower the bar for conducting experiments for students and infrequent users of inferential statistics.

References

1. Phua, K.: How to make the learning of statistics interesting, fun and personally relevant: using progressive material as examples for in-class analysis and to raise social awareness. Radical Stat. **95**, 4 (2007)
2. Gordon, S.: Understanding students' experiences of statistics in a service course. Stat. Educ. Res. J. **3**, 40–59 (2004)
3. Yilmaz, M.R.: The challenge of teaching statistics to non-specialists. J. Stat. Educ. **4**, 1–9 (1996)
4. Garfield, J.: Teaching statistics using small-group cooperative learning. J. Stat. Educ. **1**, 1–9 (1993)
5. Bland, J.M.: Teaching statistics to medical students using problem-based learning: the Australian experience. BMC Med. Educ. **4**, 31 (2004)
6. Chermak, S., Weiss, A.: Activity-based learning of statistics: using practical applications to improve students' learning. J. Crim. Justice Educ. **10**, 361–372 (1999)
7. Gemmell, I., Sandars, J., Taylor, S., Reed, K.: Teaching science and technology via online distance learning: the experience of teaching biostatistics in an online Master of Public Health programme. Open Learn. **26**, 165–171 (2011)
8. Sotos, A.E.C., Vanhoof, S., Van den Noortgate, W., Onghena, P.: Students' misconceptions of statistical inference: a review of the empirical evidence from research on statistics education. Educ. Res. Rev. **2**, 98–113 (2007)
9. Haller, H., Krauss, S.: Misinterpretations of significance: a problem students share with their teachers. Methods Psychol. Res. **7**, 1–20 (2002)
10. Gliner, J.A., Leech, N.L., Morgan, G.A.: Problems with null hypothesis significance testing (NHST): what do the textbooks say? J. Exp. Educ. **71**, 83–92 (2002)
11. Reaburn, R.: Introductory statistics course tertiary students' understanding of p-values. Stat. Educ. Res. J. **13** (2014)
12. Wagenmakers, E.J.: A practical solution to the pervasive problems of p values. Psychon. Bull. Rev. **14**, 779–804 (2007)
13. Skaik, Y.: The bread and butter of statistical analysis "t-test": uses and misuses. Pak. J. Med. Sci. **31**, 1558–1559 (2015)
14. Wu, S., Jin, Z., Wei, X., Gao, Q., Lu, J., Ma, X., Wu, C., He, Q., Wu, M., Wang, R., Xu, J.: Misuse of statistical methods in 10 leading Chinese medical journals in 1998 and 2008. Sci. World J. **11**, 2106–2114 (2011)
15. Yim, K.H., Nahm, F.S., Han, K.A., Park, S.Y.: Analysis of statistical methods and errors in the articles published in the Korean journal of pain. Korean J. Pain **23**, 35–41 (2010)
16. McCrum-Gardner, E.: Which is the correct statistical test to use? Br. J. Oral Maxillofac. Surg. **46**, 38–41 (2008)
17. Wood, M.: Maths should not be hard: the case for making academic knowledge more palatable. High. Educ. Rev. **34**, 3–19 (2002)
18. Khait, A.: Intelligent guesses and numerical experiments as legitimate tools for secondary school algebra. Teach. Math. Appl. **23**, 33–40 (2004)
19. Jian, H.-L., Sandnes, F.E., Huang, Y.-P., Cai, L., Law, K.: On students' strategy-preferences for managing difficult course work. IEEE Trans. Educ. **51**, 157–165 (2008)
20. Jian, H.L., Sandnes, F.E., Huang, Y.P., Huang, Y.M., Hagen, S.: Studies or leisure?: a cross-cultural comparison of Taiwanese and Norwegian engineering students' preferences for university life. Int. J. Eng. Educ. **26**, 227–235 (2010)

21. Jian, H.-L., Sandnes, F.E., Huang, Y.-P., Huang, Y.-M., Hagen, S.: Towards harmonious East-West educational partnerships: a study of cultural differences between Taiwanese and Norwegian engineering students. Asia Pac. Educ. Rev. **11**, 585–595 (2010)

22. Jian, H.L., Sandnes, F.E., Huang, Y.P., Huang, Y.M.: Cultural factors influencing Eastern and Western engineering students' choice of university. Eur. J. Eng. Educ. **35**, 147–160 (2010)

23. Law, K.M., Sandnes, F.E., Jian, H.L., Huang, Y.P.: A comparative study of learning motivation among engineering students in South East Asia and beyond. Int. J. Eng. Educ. **25**(1), 144–151 (2009)

24. Jian, H.-L., Sandnes, F.E., Huang, Y.-P., Law, K., Huang, Y.-M.: The role of electronic pocket dictionaries as an English learning tool among Chinese students. J. Comput. Assist. Learn. **25**, 503–514 (2009)

25. Eika, E., Hsieh, Y.: On Taiwanese pupils' ability to differentiate between English/l/and/r: a study of L1/L2 cross-language effects. First Language 0142723717709106 (2017)

26. Jian, H.-L.: On English speakers' ability to communicate emotion in Mandarin. Can. Mod. Lang. Rev. **71**, 78–106 (2015)

27. Jian, H.-L.: Prosodic challenges faced by L1 English speakers reading Mandarin. ACTA Linguistica Hung. **62**, 35–62 (2015)

28. Huang, Y.-P., Chang, T.-W., Chen, J.-R., Sandnes, F.E.: A back propagation based real-time license plate recognition system. Int. J. Pattern Recogn. Artif. Intell. **22**, 233–251 (2008)

29. Huang, Y.P., Hsu, L.W., Sandnes, F.E.: An intelligent subtitle detection model for locating television commercials. IEEE Trans. Man Cybern. B **37**, 485–492 (2007)

30. Huang, Y.P., Chang, Y.T., Sandnes, F.E.: Ubiquitous information transfer across different platforms by QR codes. J. Mob. Multimedia **6**, 3–13 (2010)

31. Huang, Y.P., Kao, L.J., Sandnes, F.E.: Predicting ocean salinity and temperature variations using data mining and fuzzy inference. Int. J. Fuzzy Syst. **9**, 143–151 (2007)

32. Huang, Y.P., Chang, Y.T., Sandnes, F.E.: Using fuzzy adaptive genetic algorithm for function optimization. In: NAFIPS 2006, Annual Meeting of the North American Fuzzy Information Processing Society, pp. 484–489. IEEE (2006)

33. Sandnes, F.E.: Sorting holiday photos without a GPS: what can we expect from contents-based geo-spatial image tagging? In: Muneesawang, P., Wu, F., Kumazawa, I., Roeksabutr, A., Liao, M., Tang, X. (eds.) PCM 2009. LNCS, vol. 5879, pp. 256–267. Springer, Heidelberg (2009). https://doi.org/10.1007/978-3-642-10467-1_22

34. Sandnes, F.E.: Where was that photo taken? Deriving geographical information from image collections based on temporal exposure attributes. Multimedia Syst. **16**, 309–318 (2010)

35. Sandnes, F.E.: Determining the geographical location of image scenes based on object shadow lengths. J. Sig. Process. Syst. **65**, 35–47 (2011)

36. Gómez, J.V., Sandnes, F.E., Fernández, B.: Sunlight intensity based global positioning system for near-surface underwater sensors. Sensors **12**, 1930–1949 (2012)

37. Whitney, G., Keith, S., Bühler, C., Hewer, S., Lhotska, L., Miesenberger, K., Sandnes, F. E., Stephanidis, C., Velasco, C.A.: Twenty five years of training and education in ICT design for all and assistive technology. Technol. Disabil. **3**, 163–170 (2011)

38. Sandnes, F.E., Herstad, J., Stangeland, A.M., Orsi Medola, F.: UbiWheel: a simple context-aware universal control concept for smart home appliances that encourages active living. In: Proceedings of Smartworld 2017, pp. 446–451. IEEE (2017)

39. Sandnes, F.E., Medola, F.O.: Exploring Russian Tap-Code text entry adaptions for users with reduced target hitting accuracy. In: Proceedings of the 7th International Conference on Software Development and Technologies for Enhancing Accessibility and Fighting Info-exclusion, pp. 33–38. ACM (2016)

40. Sandnes, F.E., Medola, F.O.: Effects of optimizing the scan-path on scanning key-boards with QWERTY-layout for English text. Stud. Health Technol. Inf. **242**, 930–938 (2017)
41. Sandnes, F.E.: Evaluating mobile text entry strategies with finite state automata. In: Proceedings of the 7th International Conference on Human Computer Interaction with Mobile Devices and Services, pp. 115–121. ACM (2005)
42. Sandnes, F.E., Sinnen, O.: A new strategy for multiprocessor scheduling of cyclic task graphs. Int. J. High Perform. Comput. Netw. **3**, 62–71 (2005)
43. Sandnes, F.E.: Scheduling partially ordered events in a randomised framework: empirical results and implications for automatic configuration management. In: Proceedings of LISA, pp. 47–62. USENIX (2001)
44. Rebreyend, P., Sandnes, F.E., Megson, G.M.: Static multiprocessor task graph scheduling in the genetic paradigm: a comparison of genotype representations. Laboratoire de l'Informatique du Parallelisme, Research report no. 98–25. Ecole Normale Superieure de Lyon (1998)
45. Sandnes, F.E., Jian, H.L., Huang, Y.P., Huang, Y.M.: User interface design for public kiosks: an evaluation of the Taiwan high speed rail ticket vending machine. J. Inf. Sci. Eng. **26**, 307–321 (2010)
46. Berget, G., Herstad, J., Sandnes, F.E.: Search, read and write: an inquiry into web accessibility for dyslexics. Stud. Health Technol. Inform. **229**, 450–460 (2016)
47. Sandnes, F.E.: What do low-vision users really want from smart glasses? Faces, text and perhaps no glasses at all. In: Miesenberger, K., Bühler, C., Penaz, P. (eds.) ICCHP 2016. LNCS, vol. 9758, pp. 187–194. Springer, Cham (2016). https://doi.org/10.1007/978-3-319-41264-1_25
48. Eika, E.: Universally designed text on the web: towards readability criteria based on anti-patterns. Stud. Health Technol. Inform. **229**, 461–470 (2016)
49. Eika, E., Sandnes, F.E.: Assessing the reading level of web texts for WCAG2.0 compliance—can it be done automatically? In: Di Bucchianico, G., Kercher, P. (eds.) Advances in Design for Inclusion. Advances in Intelligent Systems and Computing, vol. 500, pp. 361–371. Springer, Cham (2016). https://doi.org/10.1007/978-3-319-41962-6_32
50. Eika, E., Sandnes, F.E.: Authoring WCAG2.0-compliant texts for the web through text readability visualization. In: Antona, M., Stephanidis, C. (eds.) UAHCI 2016. LNCS, vol. 9737, pp. 49–58. Springer, Cham (2016). https://doi.org/10.1007/978-3-319-40250-5_5
51. Sandnes, F.E., Huang, Y., Jian, H.-L.: Experiences of teaching engineering students in Taiwan from a Western perspective. Int. J. Eng. Educ. **22**, 1013–1022 (2006)
52. Sandnes, F.E.: Understanding WCAG2.0 color contrast requirements through 3D color space visualization. Stud. Health Technol. Inform. **229**, 366–375 (2016)
53. Sandnes, F.E.: On-screen colour contrast for visually impaired readers: selecting and exploring the limits of WCAG2.0 colours. In: Black, A., Lund, O., Walker, S. (eds.) Information Design: Research and Practice, pp. 405–416. Routledge (2016)
54. Sandnes, F.E., Jian, H.L.: Sketching with Chinese calligraphy. Interactions **19**, 62–66 (2012)
55. Sandnes, F.E.: Communicating panoramic 360 degree immersed experiences: a simple technique for sketching in 3D. In: Antona, M., Stephanidis, C. (eds.) UAHCI 2016. LNCS, vol. 9738, pp. 338–346. Springer, Cham (2016). https://doi.org/10.1007/978-3-319-40244-4_33
56. Sandnes, F.E.: PanoramaGrid: a graph paper tracing framework for sketching 360-degree immersed experiences. In: Proceedings of the International Working Conference on Advanced Visual Interfaces, pp. 342–343. ACM (2016)

57. Sandnes, F.E.: Sketching 3D immersed experiences rapidly by hand through 2D cross sections. In: Auer, M.E. (ed.) REV2017. LNNS, vol. 22, pp. 1001–1013. Springer, Cham (2017). https://doi.org/10.1007/978-3-319-64352-6_93

58. Sandnes, F.E., Lianguzov, Y., Rodrigues, O.V., Lieng, H., Medola, F.O., Pavel, N.: Supporting collaborative ideation through freehand sketching of 3D-shapes in 2D using colour. In: Luo, Y. (ed.) CDVE 2017. LNCS, vol. 10451, pp. 123–134. Springer, Cham (2017). https://doi.org/10.1007/978-3-319-66805-5_16

59. Sandnes, F.E., Lianguzov, Y.: Quick and easy 3D modelling for all: a browser-based 3D-sketching framework. iJOE **13**, 120–127 (2017)

60. Hagen, S., Sandnes, F.E.: Toward accessible self-service kiosks through intelligent user interfaces. Pers. Ubiquit. Comput. **14**, 715–721 (2010)

61. Hagen, S., Sandnes, F.E.: Visual scoping and personal space on shared tabletop surfaces. J. Ambient Intell. Humaniz. Comput. **3**, 95–102 (2012)

62. Chen, W.-C., Cheng, Y.-M., Sandnes, F.E., Lee, C.-L.: Finding suitable candidates: the design of a mobile volunteering matching system. In: Jacko, J.A. (ed.) HCI 2011. LNCS, vol. 6763, pp. 21–29. Springer, Heidelberg (2011). https://doi.org/10.1007/978-3-642-21616-9_3

63. Lin, M.W., Cheng, Y.M., Yu, W., Sandnes, F.E.: Investigation into the feasibility of using tactons to provide navigation cues in pedestrian situations. In: Proceedings of the 20th Australasian Conference on Computer-Human Interaction: Designing for Habitus and Habitat, pp. 299–302. ACM (2008)

64. Sandnes, F.E.: Reflective text entry: a simple low effort predictive input method based on flexible abbreviations. Procedia Comput. Sci. **67**, 105–112 (2015)

65. Sandnes, F.E., Eika, E.: Head-mounted augmented reality displays on the cheap: a DIY approach to sketching and prototyping low-vision assistive technologies. In: Antona, M., Stephanidis, C. (eds.) UAHCI 2017. LNCS, vol. 10278, pp. 167–186. Springer, Cham (2017). https://doi.org/10.1007/978-3-319-58703-5_13

66. Sandnes, F.E.: Designing GUIs for low vision by simulating reduced visual acuity: reduced resolution versus shrinking. Stud. Health Technol. Inform. **217**, 274–281 (2015)

67. Sandnes, F.E., Huang, Y.P.: From smart light dimmers to the IPOD: text-input with circular gestures on wheel-controlled devices. Int. J. Smart Home **1**, 97–108 (2007)

68. Sandnes, F.E., Zhang, X.: User identification based on touch dynamics. In: 9th International Conference on Ubiquitous Intelligence and Computing and 9th International Conference on Autonomic and Trusted Computing (UIC/ATC), pp. 256–263. IEEE (2012)

69. Sandnes, F.E., Jian, H.-L.: Pair-wise variability index: evaluating the cognitive difficulty of using mobile text entry systems. In: Brewster, S., Dunlop, M. (eds.) Mobile HCI 2004. LNCS, vol. 3160, pp. 347–350. Springer, Heidelberg (2004). https://doi.org/10.1007/978-3-540-28637-0_35

70. Sandnes, F.E., Zhao, A.: A contrast colour selection scheme for WCAG2.0-compliant web designs based on HSV-half-planes. In: Proceedings of SMC2015, pp. 1233–1237. IEEE (2015)

71. Sandnes, F.E., Zhao, A.: An interactive color picker that ensures WCAG2.0 compliant color contrast levels. Procedia Comput. Sci. **67**, 87–94 (2015)

72. Sandnes, F.E., Thorkildssen, H.W., Arvei, A., Buverad, J.O.: Techniques for fast and easy mobile text-entry with three-keys. In: Proceedings of the 37th Annual Hawaii International Conference on System Sciences. IEEE (2004)

73. Gomez, J.V., Sandnes, F.E.: RoboGuideDog: guiding blind users through physical environments with laser range scanners. Procedia Comput. Sci. **14**, 218–225 (2012)

74. Sandnes, F.E., Huang, Y.P.: Translating the viewing position in single equirectangular panoramic images. In: Proceedings of the 2016 IEEE International Conference on Systems, Man, and Cybernetics (SMC), pp. 389–394. IEEE (2016)

75. Medola, F.O., Busto, R.M., Marçal, Â.F., Achour Junior, A., Dourado, A.C.: The sport on quality of life of individuals with spinal cord injury: a case series. Revista Brasileira de Medicina do Esporte **17**, 254–256 (2011)

76. Medola, F.O., Elui, V.M.C., da Silva Santana, C., Fortulan, C.A.: Aspects of manual wheelchair configuration affecting mobility: a review. J. Phys. Ther. Sci. **26**, 313–318 (2014)

77. Lanutti, J.N., Medola, F.O., Gonçalves, D.D., da Silva, L.M., Nicholl, A.R., Paschoarelli, L.C.: The significance of manual wheelchairs: a comparative study on male and female users. Procedia Manuf. **3**, 6079–6085 (2015)

78. Medola, F.O., Purquerio, B.M., Elui, V.M., Fortulan, C.A.: Conceptual project of a servo-controlled power-assisted wheelchair. In: IEEE RAS & EMBS International Conference on Biomedical Robotics and Biomechatronics, pp. 450–454. IEEE (2014)

79. Lahr, G.J.G., Medola, F.O., Sandnes, F.E., Elui, V.M.C., Fortulan, C.A.: Servomotor assistance in the improvement of manual wheelchair mobility. Stud. Health Technol. Inf. **242**, 786–792 (2017)

80. da Silva Bertolaccini, G., Nakajima, R.K., de Carvalho Filho, I.F.P., Paschoarelli, L.C., Medola, F.O.: The influence of seat height, trunk inclination and hip posture on the activity of the superior trapezius and longissimus. J. Phys. Ther. Sci. **28**, 1602–1606 (2016)

81. Medola, F.O., Silva, D.C., Fortulan, C.A., Elui, V.M.C., Paschoarelli, L.C.: The influence of handrim design on the contact forces on hands' surface: a preliminary study. Int. J. Ind. Ergon. **44**, 851–856 (2014)

82. Medola, F.O., Fortulan, C.A., Purquerio, B.D.M., Elui, V.M.C.: A new design for an old concept of wheelchair pushrim. Disabil. Rehabil. Assistive Technol. **7**, 234–241 (2012)

83. Medola, F.O., Paschoarelli, L. C., Silv, D. C., Elui, V. M. C., Fortulan, A.: Pressure on hands during manual wheelchair propulsion: a comparative study with two types of handrim. In: European Seating Symposium, pp. 63–65 (2011)

84. Medola, F.O., Dao, P.V., Caspall, J.J., Sprigle, S.: Partitioning kinetic energy during freewheeling wheelchair maneuvers. IEEE Trans. Neural Syst. Rehabil. Eng. **22**, 326–333 (2014)

85. Berget, G., Mulvey, F., Sandnes, F.E.: Is visual content in textual search interfaces beneficial to dyslexic users? Int. J. Hum.-Comput. Stud. **92–93**, 17–29 (2016)

86. Berget, G., Sandnes, F.E.: Do autocomplete functions reduce the impact of dyslexia on information searching behaviour? A case of Google. J. Am. Soc. Inf. Sci. Technol. **67**, 2320–2328 (2016)

87. Berget, G., Sandnes, F.E.: Searching databases without query-building aids: implications for dyslexic users. Inf. Res. **20** (2015)

88. Sandnes, F.E., Lundh, M.V.: Calendars for individuals with cognitive disabilities: a comparison of table view and list view. In: Proceedings of the 17th International ACM SIGACCESS Conference on Computers and Accessibility, pp. 329–330. ACM (2015)

89. Sandnes, F.E., Tan, T.B., Johansen, A., Sulic, E., Vesterhus, E., Iversen, E.R.: Making touch-based kiosks accessible to blind users through simple gestures. Univ. Access Inf. Soc. **11**, 421–431 (2012)

90. Sandnes, F.E.: Effects of common keyboard layouts on physical effort: implications for kiosks and Internet banking. In: Sandnes, F.E., Lunde, M.T., M., Hauge, A.M., Øverby, E., Brynn, R. (eds.) The Proceedings of Unitech2010: International Conference on Universal Technologies, pp. 91–100. Tapir Academic Publishers (2010)

91. Sandnes, F.E.: Directional bias in scrolling tasks: a study of users' scrolling behaviour using a mobile text-entry strategy. Behav. Inf. Technol. **27**, 387–393 (2008)
92. Sandnes, F.E., Aubert, A.: Bimanual text entry using game controllers: relying on users' spatial familiarity with QWERTY. Interact. Comput. **19**, 140–150 (2007)
93. Sandnes, F.E., Huang, Y.P.: Chord level error correction for portable Braille devices. Electron. Lett. **42**, 82–83 (2006)
94. Sandnes, F.E., Huang, Y.P.: Chording with spatial mnemonics: automatic error correction for eyes-free text entry. J. Inf. Sci. Eng. **22**, 1015–1031 (2006)
95. Sandnes, F.E.: Can spatial mnemonics accelerate the learning of text input chords? In: Proceedings of the Working Conference on Advanced Visual Interfaces, pp. 245–249. ACM (2006)
96. Sandnes, F.E.: Human performance characteristics of three-finger chord sequences. Procedia Manuf. **3**, 4228–4235 (2015)
97. Basturk, R.: The effectiveness of computer-assisted instruction in teaching introductory statistics. J. Educ. Technol. Soc. **8** (2005)
98. Zaiontz, C.: Real statistics using Excel. http://www.real-statistics.com/. Accessed 21 Jan 2017
99. McCullough, B.D., Heiser, D.A.: On the accuracy of statistical procedures in Microsoft Excel 2007. Comput. Stat. Data Anal. **52**, 4570–4578 (2008)
100. Yalta, A.T.: The accuracy of statistical distributions in Microsoft® Excel 2007. Comput. Stat. Data Anal. **52**, 4579–4586 (2008)
101. Mélard, G.: On the accuracy of statistical procedures in Microsoft Excel 2010. Comput. Stat. **29**, 1095–1128 (2014)
102. Crawley, M.J.: The R Book. Wiley, Chichester (2012)
103. Snellenburg, J., Laptenok, S., Seger, R., Mullen, K., Van Stokkum, I.: Glotaran: a Java-based graphical user interface for the R package TIMP. J. Stat. Softw. **49** (2012)
104. Marsman, M., Wagenmakers, E.J.: Bayesian benefits with JASP. Eur. J. Dev. Psychol. **14**, 545–555 (2017)
105. Reis, C., Cartwright, R.: Taming a professional IDE for the classroom. ACM SIGCSE Bull. **36**, 156–160 (2004)
106. Sarkar, A.: The impact of syntax colouring on program comprehension. In: Proceedings of the 26th Annual Conference of the Psychology of Programming Interest Group, pp. 49–58 (2015)
107. Kesler, T.E., Uram, R.B., Magareh-Abed, F., Fritzsche, A., Amport, C., Dunsmore, H.E.: The effect of indentation on program comprehension. Int. J. Man Mach. Stud. **21**, 415–428 (1984)
108. Sandnes, F.E., Eika, E.: A simple MVC-framework for local management of online course material. In: Uskov, V.L., Howlett, R.J., Jain, L.C. (eds.) SEEL 2017. SIST, vol. 75, pp. 143–153. Springer, Cham (2018). https://doi.org/10.1007/978-3-319-59451-4_15

A Strategy on Introducing Inclusive Design Philosophy to Non-design Background Undergraduates

Shishun Wang[1(✉)], Ting Zhang[2], Guoying Lu[1,2], and Yinyun Wu[1,2]

[1] College of Design and Innovation, Tongji University, Shanghai, China
1610947@tongji.edu.cn
[2] College of Design and Art, Shanghai Dianji University, Shanghai, China

Abstract. Focusing on how to integrating design into crossover-education, which is a controversial topic in china's education. And in china, all china's colleges and universities are trying their best to set up crossover education. Cause firstly they all think that it is vital important for the college students to broaden their horizon, secondly, more and more projects need diverse and professional genius to cooperate to be finished. They need to know the design thinking. But the problem is coming, differing from design-major background students, how to make design curriculum transforming a better and easier way to accept and assimilate by the other background students. How to cultivate the design thinking in crossover education, I think, which is the most things we as educator need to concentrate. This paper focuses on how to introduce inclusive design philosophy to non-design background undergraduates. This is one of the parts of a research project "Applied universities' design education reform and practice based on the principle of inclusive design" supported by the Shanghai Education Science Research Program (Grant No. C17067) [1].

Keywords: Inclusive design · Design philosophy · Strategy
Non-background undergraduates

1 Introduction

Since 1998, China has begun to promote general education. Design education, as a means to improve the national aesthetic quality, has become one of the contents of general education. At Fudan University and Shanghai University of Finance and Economics (SUFE), for example, design education is listed as one of the categories of general education courses. With China gradually entering the aging society [2], it is more and more urgent to incorporate the inclusive design concept into design education, not only for design students, but also for non-design background students. Based on this position, the authors' educational practice at SUFE provides a good case.

Inclusive design, which is defined by BS 7000-6:2005 as "a comprehensive, integrated design which encompasses all aspects of a product used by consumers of diverse age and capability in a wide range of contexts, throughout the product's lifecycle from conception to final disposal" [3], the first author has assisted a general course "Design

M. Antona and C. Stephanidis (Eds.): UAHCI 2018, LNCS 10907, pp. 121–130, 2018.
https://doi.org/10.1007/978-3-319-92049-8_9

Art Innovation" at SUFE for 5 semesters. He tries to introduce inclusive design philosophy to those non-design background undergraduates in this course. Some difficulties were met during the teaching process and he clarified the barriers, found several targeted solutions, and summed up a set of conceptual teaching model.

In China, "With the occurrence of a rapidly aging population, the issue of universal access and inclusivity is a challenging and complex one" [4]. Though there are exactly so many practices in crossover education recent years, just like the general curriculum is been built, but it really exists a gap between theories and practice in china. It is hard to find an effective way to find resources and tools of inclusive design in china. So trying to identify the barriers and limitations of integrating inclusive design into china's crossover education is a very important purpose.

Of cause, design discipline has a lot of different branches, so as to understanding how to make design work for crossover education and building up the knowledge base in this area is probably one of the most pressing tasks and challenges for Chinese design educators. As we all known, Inclusive design is one of design disciplines, as a user-centered design approaches. Can we propose a hypothesis that from so many design curriculums, we pick up the most essential and basic ones for them (the crossover education ones) to control by professional systematical learn? Can we use the way in an inclusive perspective to transform the knowledge, integrating design into crossover education? To explore a new world in crossover education through studying the inclusive design thinking. And the next is how to do for the Chinese educators, especially in theoretical and practices. This paper will organize the viewpoint by the actual teaching practice, the design general curriculum in shanghai University of Finance and Economics and a preliminary conceptual framework is proposed to organize the barriers and corresponding actions.

Although part of the work has been done, but there is still a gap between theory and practice. Undergraduate design education, especially for non-design background students, while related courses such as user research and user experience, user-centre factors often embedded a implement course, but seldom see inclusive design as a kind of unique curriculum. Key users involved in the embodiment of the various functions and user research is still limited by time or funds. In addition, it seems that inclusive design method such as characters, scenes and so on need to be translated into Chinese context. In addition, the Chinese version of the website design tools, it is difficult to find resources and inclusive design in the Chinese version of the tool. For example, type in "inclusive design" the jingdong search engine, China's largest online bookstore, the result is zero. This may indicate that it hasn't been able to use inclusive of design of teaching materials in China. The phenomenon of all listed above show that inclusive design is not widely spread as we want in China. This article attempts through the obstacles and limitations will be inclusive design into design education in China.

2 Methodology

Firstly, a literature review related to the inclusive design and design education, especially on the inclusive design education books and some essays about design philosophy (including some design methodology), were carried out. Several books and essays on inclusive design and design philosophy are picked out and six of them refer to the design methodology and inclusive design education, they are:

- Strategy of Design Research [5]
- Inclusive Designing: Joining Usability, Accessibility, and Inclusion [6]
- Designing a More Inclusive World [7]
- Thinking About Design: An Historical Perspective [8]
- Inclusive Design: Design for the Whole Population [9]

According to the reviews and lots of practices and perspectives from the very different books and literatures from home and abroad are synthesized. Of course problems and issues from different counties can be organized and compare with the issues and barriers of inclusive design education from the literature reviews, and adding the first authors' working experience (the first author has been a assistant teacher at Teaching General Curriculum Office of Shanghai University of Finance and Economics for three years), issues focusing on integrating the inclusive design education into the non-background undergraduates were initiated empirically, then demonstrated to expert interview. Hopefully, combined with the barriers of the literature review and issue or ideas from the different expert interview (including the different background experts), some new thoughts relevant the crossover-design education will be come up.

Literature review mainly focused on two areas literature: design education and general education, especially on inclusive design education. But the purpose of literature review and experts interview is to get some perspectives and insights from interdisciplinary experts, especially from teaching administrators from different background university under the Chinese context. Limited by time and funds, only six experts were available to interview at the moment, they are from these two areas:

- Design education who having a general curriculum experience (3 persons on product design, Tongji University)
- Teaching administration (3 persons from teaching affairs office of Tongji University, covering educational theories, teaching organization, and students' innovation projects administration and the others from Shanghai University of Finance and Economics)

Synthesizing different researchers' perspectives through literature review and based on the authors' teaching experience. Main barriers for introducing inclusive design principle to non-design background students were clarified. Then the appropriate education strategies were discussed with several experts. They are from design education and non-design education background. Many good ideas and insights were inspired. After the preliminary education strategies were generated, they were put into practice and quickly get the students' feedback through questionnaire. Through in-depth discussion of some typical teaching cases, a set of conceptual teaching model was initiated.

The experts interview were open-minded and face-to-face, a free talk as the beginning with issues on china's design education situation nowadays and some problems meet in the context of Chinese specific culture, including the challenges and opportunities. Then a more depth discussion about how to integrate inclusive design into exiting China's education system, especially the universal design education among all Chinese populations.

Of course a brief introduction of inclusive design was given from the experts to teaching administration in advance. The preliminary barriers were brought forth and assessed. Perspectives from two-side experts were absorbed and four aspects of barriers were finally clarified. One of the experts from teaching administration suggested a further case study of Tongji University's strategy of integrating sustainability as a whole. It could be a trigger from different angle, that means discuss design issues out of design. Case study gave the authors some clues, and then a conceptual framework was outlined.

3   Literature Review

Literature review mainly focused on two areas literature: design education and general education, and the how to integrate inclusive design into non-background undergraduates through the some design strategies and design philosophy, especially by inclusive design education. By synthesizing different researchers' perspectives through literature

Table 1.   Inclusive design education

Countries	Universities (Time)	Practices	Types of education
China	Tongji University (2010)	User research, inclusive design as courses	2 courses
Japan	Ritsumeikan University in Kyoto (2003)	Inclusive design course towards master students from a wide range of disciplines	Master's course
	Tama Art University (1996)	Collaboration between university and NEC, the university had a revised undergraduate curriculum infused universal design	Undergraduate education
USA	University of California (1973)	Involve users	Traditional design studio
	The Adaptive Environments Center in Boston (1989)	The "Universal Design Education" project	Education project
	Eastern Michigan University (1993)	Infuse universal design throughout undergraduate programs	Interior design education program
	University at Buffalo (1984)	Long history in research, education, practice of accessible design	Research, education, and practice
	San Francisco State University (1990)	Involve with universal design	Product design program
Norway	Several universities across the country (1997)	Adapt the model used by the US "Universal Design Education" project	4 year pilot program
UK	Polytechnic of Central London (1972)	Design for non-average	Diploma course
	The Architectural Association in London	The first qualifying certificate from any institution in the world	Certificate program for people who are already working
	University of the West of England (2002)	BA (Hons) in architecture and planning on the universal design	Undergraduate program
	Royal Society of Arts (1986)	The "New Design for Old" project	Student design awards program
	Glasgow School of Art & University of Glasgow (2004)	Embed inclusive design in a design-centered engineering curriculum	A course
	Helen Hamlyn Centre of RCA (1999)	A series of inclusive design projects undertaken by new graduates of RCA with external partners in a wide variety of contexts	Research associates program

review and based on the authors' teaching experience, critical review focused on inclusive design education was carried out among key publications on inclusive design. From literature review, many practices and cases from different countries were synthesized. Table 1 lists the results:

And from a lot of literature reviews, some inclusive design strategies or design philosophy can be proposed and used by some non-design background education. Telling a perspective how to integrating the inclusive design ideas to non-design undergraduates. It is summarized in Table 2 (Chart 1):

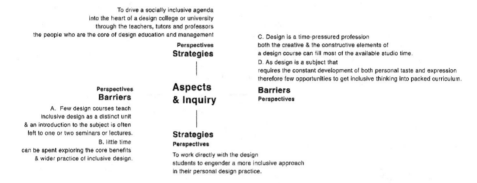

Chart 1. Strategies and barriers of introducing inclusivity into design

During literature review, some perspectives from western researchers like Geheerawo and Donahue [7] about strategies and barriers of introducing inclusivity into design were found, which can bring some insights for Chinese design educators. And an inclusive design thinking of art, the design or non-design background undergraduates can use an inclusive design strategy view from researcher Richard Buchanan. Inclusive design has four orders, respectively symbols, things, action and thoughts. Figuring out the problems of design, and knowing how to solve the problems in inclusive design thinking. Some problems and suggestion about how to deal with will be proposed in the expert interview part.

4   Expert Interview

Speaking of figuring out the problems on how to transfer inclusive design knowledge or design philosophy into non-design background undergraduates. Firstly, knowing the problems of strategies of inquiry or art of design thinking or fields of design problems. Problems of communication symbols, problems of construction things, problems of actions and problems of integrating thoughts are all the steps of upgrading the inclusive design problems. And those also the important part for us to do the expert interview, but cause the complicate of these questions, all school educator are the objects of our interviews, interviews provided information on the barriers from two aspects, one side is from the angle of design education, and on the other side is from the angle of teaching administration. So the perspectives are diverse and can be sorted out in Table 3:

Based on interview results, the barriers of integrating inclusive design into China's non-design education can be preliminarily cataloged into four aspects and corresponding response are initiated: lack of awareness, lack of resources, practical difficulties and cultural factors. So the corresponding response also are illustrated by the Chart 2.

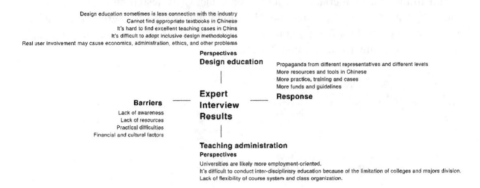

Chart 2. Expert interview results

5   Case Study

A case study of educators of Tongji university and undergraduates of SUFE on mainly talk about inquiry of inclusive design strategies was conducted, based on the discussion and suggestion from the educator and experts home and abroad. A theme called " the inner ability of design discipline" was proposed by Tongji university and cooperated with the undergraduates from SUFE. And it is as a impressive topics in design discipline and a experiment conducted by the undergraduates in SUFE. A vision of how to integrating inquiry of design strategies into non-design background undergraduates, a interdisciplinary courses and general curriculum were conducted in the crossover education issue. It was through five stages'work to realize the mission:

- Stage 1: Education aim redefined
  The education aim need to be redefined since the different purpose between the design background undergraduates and non-design background ones. The education aim was modified from how to build a teaching methods to finally form a design thinking of inclusive sights in the undergraduates' mind. Some stages in the midst of the case study.
- Stage 2: Teaching methods training-encourage to present
  The aim of teaching methods training was to encourage all the non-design background undergraduates to present their ideas first before the educators inform their some strategies. Teaching methods training was integrated into standards model which consists of three levels (standards/ways to realize the standards/methods to evaluate the outcomes) and three aspects (knowledge/abilities/personalities).
- Stage 3: Educational activities modified-activities of design education
  Activities will be modified in this stage, mainly illustrate some design education thinking to the crossover education. According to the new educational standards

organized by the different thoughts or ideas by their presentation. The particular educational activities for the non-design background undergraduates would be conducted. The purpose of this stage is to give them a deep understanding and a specific experience so as to form the course system.

- Stage 4: Course systems reorganized-focus on interaction
  The course systems were reorganized according to the new educational activities standards. The inner ability of design should be saying that is very impressive topic for us design background educators no more than crossover education. The only thing we as educators can do is that according to lots of activities to find out a interactive way for them to understand the inclusive thinking of design strategies. Finally the course systems were revised to reflect inclusive concept and the core courses will be built.

- Stage 5: Core courses building-form the ability of sights
  Based on SUFE-Tongji cooperation about transfer the theoretical discussion into actual emerging practise. The university provided a lot of training opportunities by means of competition, workshops, lunch discussion, etc. 8 course packs towards all the students have been developed.

Although the inquiry of inclusive design strategies originated from the design background education research and it is some means difficult to used in the general curriculum to the non-design background undergraduates. But it is also a inclusive way to integrate some design strategies to non-design background undergraduates, cultivating them can have a better understanding of design thinking so as to cooperated with more different background education people, finally improve the whole project well, or the quality of some projects. And that's also a very important inner ability of design discipline. Five key elements were filtered out within China's talents cultivation system, namely education aim, teaching methods, educational activities, course systems reorganized, and core courses. These elements are hierarchical and successional. The case study gives some inspirations for design education. It may suggest looking inclusive design's integration into China's non-design background education as a whole. Based on this, a conceptual framework was triggered.

6   A Conceptual Framework

Actually, the authors proposed some functional elements; formulated a model of introducing inclusive design principle to non-design background undergraduates; intention to embody the model in the means or materials; synthesis and the form of the solution, definition of the specific need or problem. And also proposed some phases of action of methods of systematic inclusive design: the analytic, the creative and the executive and etc. some cross-shaped charts will be drawn to illustrate the thoughts about how to make inclusive design thinking into crossover education (Chart 3).

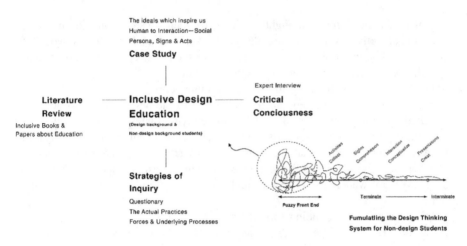

Chart 3. "Cross + 4C Model" framework.

Firstly, cause there's no exact or specific model focusing on integrating design into non-design background students, so according to a lots of literature reviews and experts interview, it needs a procedure to seeking for a system, and we need to find out a quite clear mind through a very fuzzy front end, forming a cross of inclusive design education to guide the non-design background students. So the first step, figuring out the theoretical system of inclusive design education for non-design background students from lots of research and literature review, while seeking out a cross model from the fuzzy front end. And several literature review and experts interview will be proposed and analyzed in this paper.

Secondly, the cross organized by the literature reviews and experts interview from the theoretical fuzzy front end about design review will be as a base to build a practical model. A procedure will be organized as a system of how to do design for non-design background students, proposing 4C model, respectively the collect, comprehension, conceptualize and create, each one corresponding to a specific actions, beginning with very different kinds of activities, it is a vital important way to collect materials. And combined with their own special background sights to comprehend the materials or activities. Then interaction with each other, including the students and teachers, will be carried out, forming a specific concept. In addition, conceptualizing an ambiguous product, another saying, transforming a concept into specific things is not easy, so create a way to encourage non-design background students is more suitable for them.

Finally, an emerging practice, as a model, concrete measures should be proposed, we totally have ten classes in one semester, in each class, we will carry out the different practices, including how to interact, discuss and present. Such as the discussion with each other is face-to-face and open-mind, with a free talk. Educational standards and practices usually determine the graduates' qualities requirements. They are directed by educational aim and meanwhile guide the course system organization. One side has three levels: the standards, ways to realize and how to assess, the other side is at each stage what knowledge should be taught, what abilities students should master, and what personalities should be cultivated. So in the end, the most important for us educators is to impart the way to learn, and for the non-design background students is to grasp the inclusive design thinking to think about objects.

The model suggested that the possible route to introduce inclusive design principle to non-design background undergraduates in China. Inclusive design educators or general education educators may be enlightened by the conceptual model.

7   Conclusion and Future Work

Research is focused on design of inclusive education for non-design in the design of crossover, has carried on the literature review mainly inclusive design on one of the major publications. Gather concentrated reading related papers or chapters. Practice and view synthesis and obstacles of inclusive design in Chinese design education initiated through expert interviews and judgment. A case study is to design the core ability in the simulation on the cross-border education and explore. On this basis, the preliminary framework to generate inclusive design in the fuzzy front. Framework suggests the feasibility of the route will be inclusive design integrated into the crossover design education in China. It shows the potential of the possibility of the application design, teachers and teaching management. However, the framework is mainly based on the empirical research. More literature review and practice may happen in the future to improve the framework.

Acknowledgments. The authors would like to thank Tongji University and SUFE together hold the Symposium on Inclusive Design whereby this study was oral presented and got some feedback from the participants. Special thanks to Associate Professor Guoxin Wu, Mr. Guoqiao Qiu for their suggestions and thanks to the support by Shanghai Education Scientific Research Project, No. C17067.

References

1. Ting, Z., Shishun. W.: Design Applied College Student Cultivation System: Innovation Research Based on the Theory of Inclusive Design. Shanghai Education Scientific Research Project, No. C17067. January 2017–December 2018
2. National Bureau of Statistics of the People's Republic of China. http://www.stats.gov.cn/tjsj/zxfb/201602/t20160229_1323991.html
3. BS 7000-6:2005 Design management systems. Managing inclusive design. Guide, British Standards Institution, London (2005)
4. Macdonald, A.S.: The inclusive challenge: a multidisciplinary educational approach. In: Clarkson, J., Langdon, P., Robinson, P. (eds.) Designing Accessible Technology, pp. 3–12. Springer, London (2006). https://doi.org/10.1007/1-84628-365-5_1
5. Buchanan, R.: School of Design Carnegie Mellon University. Strategies of Design Research: Productive Science and Rhetorical Inquiry
6. Langdon, P.M., Lazar, J., Heylighen, A., Dong, H.: Inclusive Designing: Joining Usability, Accessibility, and Inclusion. Springer, Switzerland (2014). https://doi.org/10.1007/978-3-319-05095-9

7. Gheerawo, R.R., Donahue, S.J.: Introducing user-centred design methods into design education. In: Keates, S., Clarkson, J., Langdon, P., Robinson, P. (eds.) Designing a More Inclusive World, pp. 21–30. Springer, London (2004). https://doi.org/10.1007/978-0-85729-372-5_3
8. Buchanan, R.: School of Design Carnegie Mellon University. Thinking About Design: An Historical Perspective
9. Ostroff, E.: International design education strategies. In: Clarkson, J., Coleman, R., Keates, S., Lebbon, C. (eds.) Inclusive Design: Design for the Whole Population, pp. 336–355. Springer, London (2003). https://doi.org/10.1007/978-1-4471-0001-0_21

Alternative I/O Techniques, Multimodality and Adaptation

Stabilising Touch Interactions in Cockpits, Aerospace, and Vibrating Environments

B. I. Ahmad[1(✉)], Patrick M. Langdon[2], and S. J. Godsill[1]

[1] Signal Processing and Communications Laboratory (SigProC),
Department of Engineering, University of Cambridge, Cambridge, UK
{bia23,sjg30}@cam.ac.uk
[2] Engineering Design Centre (EDC), Department of Engineering,
University of Cambridge, Cambridge, UK
pml24@cam.ac.uk

Abstract. Incorporating touch screen interaction into cockpit flight systems is increasingly gaining traction given its several potential advantages to design as well as usability to pilots. However, perturbations to the user input are prevalent in such environments due to vibrations, turbulence and high accelerations. This poses particular challenges for interacting with displays in the cockpit, for example, accidental activation during turbulence or high levels of distraction from the primary task of airplane control to accomplish selection tasks. On the other hand, predictive displays have emerged as a solution to minimize the effort as well as cognitive, visual and physical workload associated with using in-vehicle displays under perturbations, induced by road and driving conditions. This technology employs gesture tracking in 3D and potentially eye-gaze as well as other sensory data to substantially facilitate the acquisition (pointing and selection) of an interface component by predicting the item the user intents to select on the display, early in the movements towards the screen. A key aspect is utilising principled Bayesian modelling to incorporate and treat the present perturbation, thus, it is a software-based solution that showed promising results when applied to automotive applications. This paper explores the potential of applying this technology to applications in aerospace and vibrating environments in general and presents design recommendations for such an approach to enhance interactions accuracy as well as safety.

Keywords: Interactive displays · Bayesian inference · Target assistance
Turbulence

1 Introduction

In the development of aviation cockpit interfaces, a key step has been the movement from conventional mechanical controls (such as joysticks, trackballs, dials, switches, levers, and buttons [1]), and analogue displays to electronic "glass cockpits". This facilitated the introduction of touch screens into cockpits. They bring several advantages to the manufactures as well as operators (e.g. pilots) due to their ability to:

© Springer International Publishing AG, part of Springer Nature 2018
M. Antona and C. Stephanidis (Eds.): UAHCI 2018, LNCS 10907, pp. 133–145, 2018.
https://doi.org/10.1007/978-3-319-92049-8_10

(1) offer additional design flexibilities by combining the display-input-feedback functionalities in one module, simplifying complex dial arrays and providing better visibility, salience and flexibility of display of critical flight information,

(2) promote intuitive interactions via free hand *pointing gestures*,

(3) incorporate large quantities of information associated with modern aviation developments (e.g. weather radar, collision avoidance, route control, ALS, autopilot and numerous information related to engine parameters and other on-board systems); amongst others this led to the reductions of space required for the cockpit bulkhead as well as control area, and

(4) being easily updatable via reconfiguring the Graphical User Interfaces (GUIs) in lieu of incurring the prohibitive overheads of repurposing-rewiring hardware panels of mechanical controls.

Thereby, touch screens use in aerospace applications is gaining traction [2–8] and can be viewed as the predominant design choice for modern cockpit HMI, e.g. F-35 Joint Strike Fighter has a full-panel-width 20×8 in. touch screen.

However, air turbulence, accelerations (e.g. constant high G-force) and possibly vibrations due to taxiway roughness can significantly affect the ability of an operator to accomplish on-display target acquisition (pointing and selection) tasks via pointing gestures [3, 4, 8, 9]. This is contrary to classical physical controls of non-touchscreen displays (e.g. joystick, rotary, etc.), which offer mechanical stabilisation of the pointing action, especially that touch screen devices as input technology cannot present discreet button regions and can only be activated by contact with the screen. Accordingly, perturbations could result in erroneous user input and/or unintentional (false) selections. Attempts to rectify such incorrect selections, e.g. by repeating the acquisition task(s), can tie up further of the operator's attention, which can be otherwise available for more essential tasks such as controlling the jet and monitoring its on-board systems. Therefore, interacting with displays under perturbations (e.g. turbulence and vibrations) via *pointing* gestures can be highly effortful-distracting and a key challenge is to develop solutions to notably improve the usability and performance (e.g. accuracy) of touch interactions in aerospace and general vibrating environments [3–9].

On the other hand, touch screens are an integrated part of the modern vehicle environment with several established benefits, similar to those of listed above [10, 11]. However, undertaking a free hand pointing gesture to acquire a target on the display, e.g. a GUI icon, requires devoting a considerable amount of attention (visual, cognitive and physical) that would be instead dedicated to the primary task of driving [12], with potential safety implications [13]. Due to road and driving conditions, the user pointing gesture can be subject to perturbations (e.g. vibrations and lateral accelerations) leading to substantial degradation in the touch accuracy and interaction performance [12, 14]. Therefore, the predictive touch technology [15, 16], which can infer, notably early in the free hand pointing gesture, the intended on-screen item has emerged as an effective solution that can simplify and expedite the selection task, even under perturbations. It can significantly improve the usability of in-car touch screens by reducing distractions and workload associated with interacting with them, under various road and driving conditions.

In this paper, we first consider existing approaches to stabilising the user input in cockpits and then propose applying the predictive touch technology, originally developed for automotive applications, as well as statistical filtering techniques as in [16, 17]. The aim is to substantially improve interactions accuracy as well as perfor- mance and usability of touch screens where perturbations (e.g. due to turbulence, vibrations and high accelerations) can be prevalent and carrying out the "secondary" tasks of interacting with various in-cockpit controls can be highly demanding. Design considerations and recommendations to best utilise the predictive display or touch technology are also presented.

The remainder of this paper is organised as follows. In the next section, we consider existing work in Human-Computer Interaction (HCI); in particular that related to counteracting the impact of perturbations on the user input (finger pointing) in cockpits. We then give a brief overview of the proposed predictive display technology and the adopted Bayesian framework, outlining the flexibilities of this formulation and its requirements in Sect. 3. In Sect. 4, a few design recommendations are highlighted and finally conclusions are drawn in Sect. 5.

2   Related Work and Desired Features

2.1   Related Work

With the proliferation of the increasingly ubiquitous touch screen technology in everyday use, target acquisition (pointing and selection) on a graphical user interface has become part of modern life and a frequent HCI task. The majority of modern software products now employ touch pads, touch screens and stylus entry systems to permit the user to input information in the wide varieties of formats necessitated by complex internet functionalities. For example, on screen keypads and keyboards, 2D mapping information, 2D drawing and art tools, 3D representations, as well as conventional screen buttons with standard selection paradigms such as select on mouse-up if within the button boundaries. Furthermore, a whole generation of new interaction techniques have been developed based on touch screen contact. This includes simple gestures with one finger and more recent multi-touch gesture displays that allow multiple finger contact for pinch or sweep gestures [5, 18]. Touch-based interfaces allow a finger or pointing device to be used as a mouse when in contact with the screen. These can be capacitive or resistive (or both) to allow for the use of gloves or use in wet environments.

In the general HCI area, pointing (e.g. with a mouse cursor) reliability and accuracy is of a key importance for the design of effective GUI. This has triggered an immense interest in approaches that model pointing movements and assist the pointing task by reducing the cursor pointing time and improving its accuracy [19–26]. This can be achieved via pointing facilitation techniques, such as increasing the size of the target icon, altering its activation area, dragging the cursor closer to the target, etc. However, such strategies can be effectively applied only if the intended GUI item is known *a priori* [21–26]. Such studies focus on pointing via a mouse or mechanical-device in a 2D set-up to select a GUI icon(s) and often consider able-bodied computer users in a stationary input situation and do not treat the impact of perturbations on the interactions.

However, the user population is diverse and includes motion impaired, elderly and non-expert users. Similar to users experiencing perturbations induced by environmental factors (e.g. due to road and driving conditions or using a touch screen whilst walking), the pointing-selection task can be challenging for users with a motion-visual impairment [17, 26–30]. One area offering mitigation to these challenges is the design of integrated multimodal display and control technologies for ease of input and task completion [17, 27, 30]. Initially, in the domain of better design for elderly and impaired computer and TV users and in the form of extraordinary user interfaces [31, 32]. This approach assumes that any human user can be impaired (disabled) in their effectiveness by characteristics of their environment, the task, and the design of the user interface they are presented with [32].

On the other hand, the problem of improving touch interactions in cockpits under perturbations is not well explored and innovations in this area are rather limited, unlike touch interactions with a portable devices (e.g. smartphones) under situational-induced impairments, for instance whilst walking [33, 34], or under health-induced impairment [26–32]. Existing approaches to combat the effects of present perturbations in cockpits can be divided into the following two general categories:

1. *Selection Strategy:* utilise a suitable criteria to establish a trigger for the selection action of a GUI item from finger(s) touch, e.g. location of on-screen mouse up/down event, dwell time on a particular interface item, double tap, pressure applied during a touch action and others [35]. This is a well-known issue in the area of HCI and plethora of establish approaches; a selection strategy is an integrated part of most touch screen UI design (including those for displays with multi-touch capabilities). Nonetheless, under perturbations such strategies cannot often effectively differentiate between intentional and noise-induced accidental contacts with the display [36, 37].

2. *Braced Touch Interaction*: allows users to mechanically stabilise selections by bracing their fingers/hand/palm on or around the touch screen. For instance, a bezel edge can be used as in [8] or placing one or more of the hand fingers on the display and utilising eye-gaze fixations on the touched GUI item for ensuring an intentional touch as in [38]. They aim to enable accurate target selection (e.g. using an adequate selection strategy) during high levels of vibration, without impeding interaction performance when vibrations are absent. Such approach face the following key challenges include: (a) discriminating intentional selection from braced contacts and (b) limited interaction area which is often confined to the vicinity of the brace, especially for wide interactive displays, rendering various regions of the touch screen inaccessible. Mitigating the latter often requires moving the hand into awkward postures and/or uncomfortable selection maneuvers since one or more of the hand fingers are used for stabilisation.

2.2   Desired Features

In addition to improving the performance of the cockpit display in terms of accuracy (e.g. minimising erroneous selections) and given the constraints of a typical aerospace environment, a suitable solution should possess the following features:

- *Context dependent:* it is expected to be applicable to a wide range of possible scenarios and cockpit control functionalities. It thus should effectively captures the different accuracy requirements under various conditions, e.g. safety critical control commands versus an interaction to obtain an update on a particular status.
- *Adaptable:* the characteristics of the target acquisition task can be affected by many factors, including the operator's physical ability, prior experience and level of experienced perturbations. The adopted solution should be also independent or easily adaptable to various GUI layout design and able to make use of any available priors on the user's behaviour to refine its performance.
- *Reduces the interactions effort:* the adopted solution should reduce the workload (manual, visual, cognitive) and inattention associated with accomplishing a selection task, unlike with the braced touch interaction. Thereby, it minimises distractions from other critical tasks such as jet control, on-board systems monitoring, etc.

As illustrated below, the proposed predictive technology meets these requirements.

3   Predictive Touch: Intent Inference with Hidden Markov Models

The predictive touch system block diagram is depicted in Fig. 1. Its main aim is to predict the icon the user intends to select, i.e. $\mathcal{D}_I$, as early as possible in the free hand pointing gesture; it then facilitates-expedites the target selection albeit the present perturbations. This system utilises a gesture tracker and other sensory data in conjunction with probabilistic inference algorithms to determine the intended destination on the interactive surface (e.g. touch screen). The prediction results for each of the GUI selectable icons are subsequently used to decide on the intended endpoint and accordingly alter the GUI to assist the selection process. Next, we describe the main building blocks of a predictive touch system.

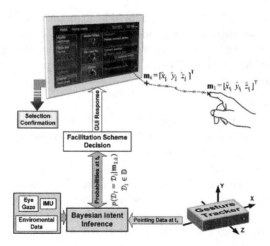

Fig. 1. System block diagram with a complete pointing finger-tip trajectory; $\mathbf{m}_k$ is the finger-tip Cartesian 3D coordinates at time t_k where $t_k > t_1$ [16].

3.1   Pointing Gesture Tracker

It provides, in real-time, the pointing hand/finger(s) locations in 3D, for example at the discrete time instants $t_1, t_2, ..., t_k$. Several such pointing gesture trackers, which can accurately track, in real-time, a pointing gesture in 3D, have emerged lately. They are motivated by a desire to extend HCI beyond traditional keyboard input and mouse pointing. Whilst some trackers are vision-based [39], such as Microsoft Kinect, Leap Motion controller and Nimble UX, others are more amenable to being incorporated into wearables, e.g. [40–43], and thus can be more suitable for a cockpit setting.

3.2   Bayesian Predictor and Statistical Filtering of Noise

Let $\mathbb{D} = \{\mathcal{D}_i : i = 1, 2, ... N\}$ be the set of N selectable items on the display, for example, GUI selectable icons. This key system module calculates the likelihood of each of the selectable interface items, i.e. $\mathcal{D}_i \in \mathbb{D}$, being the intended destination $\mathcal{D}_I$ at a given time instant, e.g. t_k. These probabilities can be expressed by:

$$\mathcal{P}(t_k) = \{p(\mathcal{D}_i = \mathcal{D}_I | \mathbf{m}_{1:k}), i = 1, 2, ..., N\}, \tag{1}$$

such that $\mathbf{m}_{1:k} \triangleq \{\mathbf{m}_1, \mathbf{m}_2, ..., \mathbf{m}_k\}$ are the filtered gesture-tracker observations (can include other sensory data) at the successive time instants $\{t_1, t_2, ..., t_k\}$. For example, $\mathbf{m}_n = [\hat{x}_{t_n} \hat{y}_{t_n} \hat{z}_{t_n}]'$ is the Cartesian coordinates of the pointing finger at t_n. It is noted that data sorting, analysis and association steps are needed prior to utilising the pointing gesture data.

The predictor can use a number of low complexity probabilistic models that are amenable to real-time implementations. A review of these models is given in this [15, 16], showing that they can lead to a Kalman-filter-type implementation of the intent inference routine. Within the Bayesian framework,

$$p(\mathcal{D}_I = \mathcal{D}_i | \mathbf{m}_{1:k}) \propto p(\mathbf{m}_{1:k} | \mathcal{D}_I = \mathcal{D}_i) p(\mathcal{D}_I = \mathcal{D}_i) \tag{2}$$

where the prior $p(\mathcal{D}_i = \mathcal{D}_I)$ on the ith selectable item (independent of the current pointing task) can be attained from semantic data, frequency of use, other sensory data, etc. This makes the adopted formulation particularly appealing as any additional information (if/when becomes available) can be easily incorporated into the inference process via the priors.

Modelling of Intent with HMMs

The Bayesian destination predictor applied here relies on defining a Hidden Markov Model (HMM) of the pointing motion in 3D, effectively capturing the intrinsic influence of the intended on-display endpoint (i.e. interface selectable icon) on the finger/hand movements during the pointing gesture [16, 17]. This is fundamentally distinct from previous HCI research on endpoint prediction in 2D scenarios, which often follow from Fitt's law type analysis and uses deterministic models. The statistical modelling approach employed by a predictive touch system captures the variability among users and their motor capabilities via Stochastic Differential Equations (SDEs), which represent the destination-motivated pointing motion in 3D or even 2D.

Most importantly, a suitable Bayesian formulation with HMMs also allows the flexible and effective modelling of the pointing motion with perturbations via the SDEs. The variability in the pointing movement, e.g. due to the user behavior and/or perturbations, can be introduced through the noise element of the state (position, velocity, acceleration, etc.) evolution equation. Additionally, the noise generated from the employed sensor, e.g. a particular gesture tracker, can be incorporated via the measurement noise in the observation equation. For further details on the modelling aspect of predictive touch, including destination-driven ones and bridged distributions, the reader is referred to [15, 16, 44, 45].

Removing Perturbations: Smoothing Noisy Trajectories

Employing Gaussian and linear motion as well as observation models permits using the efficient Kalman filters to determine (1); typically N or more such filters are needed [15, 16]. When the user input is perturbed, the predictive display system can handle noisy 3D pointing gestures by setting the noise covariance in the motion model relative to the measured (experienced) perturbations. This conforms with the Gaussian and linear modelling assumptions and a higher covariance corresponds to having less certainty in the estimated destination-driven pointing finger position, velocity, etc. This technique is suitable for low to medium perturbation levels that can be represented by Gaussian noise, e.g. driving on smooth to moderately bumpy-paved roads.

The assumption of Gaussian noise in a motion model can be overly restrictive in a highly perturbed environments since the pointing hand/finger can move in a highly erratic manner. It can exhibit sudden unintentional noise-related jump movements or jolts. In such scenarios, the perturbations present can be treated as an additional nonlinear random jump process causing sudden large changes in the pointing finger position and velocity. For example, this can be modelled by the mean-reverting jump-diffusion velocity process [16, 44]. Likelihood estimation for such motion models relies on sequential Monte Carlo (SMC), particle, filtering [44, 46], which is computationally costly compared to Kalman filtering. A practical alternative to applying this computationally-expensive inference procedure N or more times, is to apply the SMC filtering once as a pre-processing stage prior to the destination prediction routine. The objective of this pre-processing stage is to remove the most severe effects of large jolts from the gesture-tracker observations $\mathbf{m}_{1:k}$ at t_k and allow the utilisation of the original linear motion models for intent inference [16]. This approach represents a compromise between effective removal of severe perturbations (jumps) and the computational efficiency of the original models. Figure 2 depicts an example of filtering a highly perturbed pointing trajectory using SMC.

Applying a pre-processing SMC filter or dynamically adjusting the motion model covariance can be guided by additional sensory data, such as changes in the level of experienced perturbations from auxiliary sensors. Additionally, the filtered free-hand pointing gesture can be used not only for pointing, but also for general gesture-based interactions.

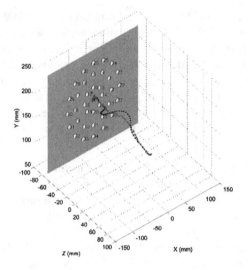

Fig. 2. 3D pointing track before (black) and after (red) applying a variable rate particle filter [44]. (Color figure online)

3.3 Feedback-Decision Scheme

Given the inference results $\mathcal{P}(t_k)$ at time t_k, the GUI is modified (if applicable) to facilitate accomplishing the selection task. For example, the system expands/colours the GUI items based on $\mathcal{P}(t_k)$ or select the predicted intended on-screen item on behalf of the user, i.e. without the user physically touching the display surface. The latter is dubbed *mid-air selection*. Possible criterions for deciding the endpoint of the pointing gesture at t_k (if needed depending on the feedback scheme) include choosing the most probable destination (i.e. Maximum *a Posteriori* estimate), the selectable GUI icon whose probability exceeds a certain threshold and many others. The decision making process within the Bayesian formulation can be addressed, namely in relation to minimising: $\mathbb{E}_{\mathcal{D}_l}[\mathcal{C}(\mathcal{D}^*, \mathcal{D}_l)|\mathbf{m}_{1:k}]$ where $\mathcal{C}(\mathcal{D}^*, \mathcal{D}_l)$ is the cost of deciding $\mathcal{D}^*$ at t_k as the on-screen endpoint given that $\mathcal{D}_l$ is the true intended destination.

3.4 Additional Sensory Data

The availability of additional sensory data such as inertia measurement unit (accelerometer/gyroscope) can enable the system to determine the operating conditions (e.g. whether the user input is noisy) and accordingly modify the applied model and/or adapt its parameters and/or perform smoothing prior to intent prediction. On the other hand, eye-gaze can provide valuable information on the areas of interest on the display. If such information become available, they can be easily incorporated into the Bayesian framework via the priors $Pr(\mathcal{D}_i = \mathcal{D}_l)$, $i = 1, 2, \ldots, N$. Alternatively, additional data can be part of the observations/measurements vectors $\mathbf{m}_{1:k}$.

3.5   Final Remarks

In summary, the developed Bayesian framework for predictive touch enables:

- Handling varying levels of perturbations in the pointing gesture, including those induced by the variability in the pointing behaviour, environment-induced noise (e.g. turbulence, vibrations and accelerations).
- Catering for varying levels of noise due to the sensory technology and inaccuracies in the collected measurements (e.g. inaccurate pointing finger and eye-gaze locations).
- Treatment of irregularly spaced and asynchronous data (e.g. due to the sensory technology) since continuous-time dynamics and observation models are utilised.
- Incorporating contextual information (GUI design, frequency of use, user profile, context as well as history of use, etc.).
- Principled fusion of various sensory data (when available) that can assist facilitating interactions with the touch screen.

Thereby, it meets the desired featured outlined in Sect. 2.

4   Design Recommendations

The main design recommendations stem from the capabilities of the predictive touch approach, enabled by intent prediction. For instance, its robustness with respect to perturbation and applying intrinsic filtering and a principled Bayesian statistical approach. In fact, it is capable of delivering accurate predictions within 30–50% of a movement towards the screen as shown from on-road experimental studies for automotive applications [16, 47]. It is effective when the following criteria are present:

1. for perturbed environments, including in the presence of extreme jumps-jolts in the pointing movement,
2. where tracking data is incomplete, unevenly timed, erratic, and often incorrect (i.e. noisy),
3. for displays or any region of space within the tracking volume that the user may move towards, including non-screen elements (dials, switches, etc.),
4. where reduction of workload or physical stretching is required.

From a design perspective, any device that can offer 3D tracking of user pointing movement and a display may use this approach. For example, a mobile device such as a tablet whilst walking. Unlike bracing approaches or force dependent interactions which are ergonomically inconvenient in a cockpit environment, this technology facilitates usability of interactive displays in general including those that do not have a physical surface to touch (e.g. non-touch displays, 3D projections and HUDs) via mid-air selection and where screens are inaccessible.

5   Conclusions

Consideration of touch screen displays in aviation environments shows that significant issues exist in preventing interaction errors as a result of accidental selection, failure to select, or incorrect selection resulting from external perturbations on both the user and the screen. Three possible solutions to this problem were discussed, namely: (1) utilizing suitable selection strategies (e.g. pressure-based selection), (2) braced interaction, and (3) predictive touch with Bayesian intent prediction. Unlike the former two, the predictive interactive display within a Bayesian framework is well suited to the human centred design of new information-rich and multimodal interfaces in aerospace applications. It can effectively incorporate variabilities in the environment as well as interaction styles, contextual information and additional sensory data (when available), within the stochastic pointing movement and measurement models as well as the modelling priors. Thus, the developed predictive displays framework is a promising approach to achieving substantial significant usability improvements to interactions in cockpits and vibrating environments. Nevertheless, future experimental work is required to substantiate its benefits in aerospace applications.

Intentionality prediction from the tracked pointing movement has the key advantages that Bayesian prediction can be made without and before contact with the screen, reducing workload, and filtering out (suppressing) unintentional perturbations-induced pointing movements (e.g. resulting from vibrations and accelerations). However, a disadvantage of this technology is that the operator's pointing movements (e.g. in 3-D) must be tracked. Nonetheless, plethora of third party solutions (gesture tracking technologies) are now available for use in confined spaces including automotive and aerospace, see [39–43]. This gives rise to a technology that is potentially not restricted to screens of any sort and may also assist or allow free-air gestures in a perturbed vibrating environment.

Acknowledgements. This work was carried out under the University of Cambridge CAPE agreement with Jaguar Land Rover.

References

1. Stanton, N.A., Harvey, C., Plant, K.L., Bolton, L.: To twist, roll, stroke or poke? A study of input devices for menu navigation in the cockpit. Ergonomics **56**(4), 590–611 (2013)
2. ARINC661: Cockpit display system interfaces to user systems. ARINC Specification 661, Supplement 6. Airlines Electronic Engineering Committee (AEEC), p. 216
3. Avsar, H., Fischer, J.E., Rodden, T.: Designing touch-enabled electronic flight bags in SAR helicopter operations. In: Proceedings of the International Conference on Human-Computer Interaction in Aerospace, p. 14. ACM, September 2016
4. Dodd, S., Lancaster, J., Miranda, A., Grothe, S., DeMers, B., Rogers, B.: Touch screens on the flight deck: the impact of touch target size, spacing, touch technology and turbulence on pilot performance. In: Proceedings of the Human Factors and Ergonomics Society Annual Meeting, vol. 58, no. 1, pp. 6–10. SAGE Publications, Los Angeles, September (2014)

5. Hamon, A., Palanque, P., Andre, R., Barboni, E., Cronel, M., Navarre, D.: Multi-touch interactions for control and display in interactive cockpits: issues and a proposal. In: Proceedings of the International Conference on Human-Computer Interaction in Aerospace, p. 7. ACM, July 2014

6. Kaminani, S.: Human computer interaction issues with touch screen interfaces in the flight deck. In: 2011 IEEE/AIAA 30th Digital Avionics Systems Conference (DASC), pp. 6B4–1. IEEE, October 2011

7. Mangion, D.Z., Bécouarn, L., Fabbri, M., Bader, J.: A single interactive display concept for commercial and business jet cockpits. In: ATIO 2011, Conference of the AIAA on Aviation Technology, Integration, and Operations, September 2011

8. Cockburn, A., Gutwin, C., Palanque, P., Deleris, Y., Trask, C., Coveney, A., MacLean, K.: Turbulent touch: touchscreen input for cockpit flight displays. In: Proceedings of the 2017 CHI Conference on Human Factors in Computing Systems, pp. 6742–6753. ACM, May 2017

9. Lin, C.J., Liu, C.N., Chao, C.J., Chen, H.J.: The performance of computer input devices in a vibration environment. Ergonomics 53(4), 478–490 (2010)

10. Burnett, G.E., Porter, J.M.: Ubiquitous computing within cars: designing controls for non-visual use. Int. J. Hum Comput Stud. 55(4), 521–531 (2001)

11. Burnett, G., Lawson, G., Millen, L., Pickering, C.: Designing touchpad user-interfaces for vehicles: which tasks are most suitable? Behav. Inf. Technol. 30(3), 403–414 (2011)

12. Jæger, M.G., Skov, M.B., Thomassen, N.G.: You can touch, but you can't look: interacting with in-vehicle systems. In: Proceedings of the SIGCHI Conference on Human Factors in Computing Systems, pp. 1139–1148. ACM, April 2008

13. Klauer, S.G., Dingus, T.A., Neale, V.L., Sudweeks, J.D., Ramsey, D.J.: The impact of driver inattention on near-crash/crash risk: an analysis using the 100-car naturalistic driving study data. Nat. Highway Traffic Saf. Adm. DOT HS 810, 5942006 (2006)

14. Ahmad, B.I., Langdon, P.M., Godsill, S.J., Hardy, R., Skrypchuk, L., Donkor, R.: Touchscreen usability and input performance in vehicles under different road conditions: an evaluative study. In: Proceedings of the 7th International Conference on Automotive User Interfaces and Interactive Vehicular Applications, pp. 47–54. ACM, September 2015

15. Ahmad, B.I., Murphy, J.K., Langdon, P.M., Godsill, S.J., Hardy, R., Skrypchuk, L.: Intent inference for hand pointing gesture-based interactions in vehicles. IEEE Trans. Cybern. 46(4), 878–889 (2016)

16. Ahmad, B.I., Murphy, J.K., Godsill, S., Langdon, P.M., Hardy, R.: Intelligent interactive displays in vehicles with intent prediction: a Bayesian framework. IEEE Signal Process. Mag. 34(2), 82–94 (2017)

17. Langdon, P., Godsill, S., Clarkson, P.J.: Statistical estimation of user's intentions from motion impaired cursor use data. In: Proceedings of the 6th International Conference on Disability, Virtual Reality and Associated Technologies, ICDVRAT 2006, Esbjerg, Denmark (2006)

18. Benko, H., Wilson, A.D., Baudisch, P.: Precise selection techniques for multi-touch screens. In: Proceedings of the SIGCHI Conference on Human Factors in Computing Systems, pp. 1263–1272. ACM, April 2006

19. MacKenzie, I.S.: Fitts' law as a research and design tool in human-computer interaction. Hum. Comput. Interact. 7(1), 91–139 (1992)

20. Kopper, R., Bowman, D.A., Silva, M.G., McMahan, R.P.: A human motor behavior model for distal pointing tasks. Int. J. Hum Comput Stud. 68(10), 603–615 (2010)

21. McGuffin, M.J., Balakrishnan, R.: Fitts' law and expanding targets: Experimental studies and designs for user interfaces. ACM Trans. Comput. Hum. Interact. (TOCHI) 12(4), 388–422 (2005)

22. Murata, A.: Improvement of pointing time by predicting targets in pointing with a PC mouse. Int. J. Hum. Comput. Interact. **10**(1), 23–32 (1998)
23. Wobbrock, J.O., Fogarty, J., Liu, S.Y.S., Kimuro, S., Harada, S.: The angle mouse: target-agnostic dynamic gain adjustment based on angular deviation. In: Proceedings of the SIGCHI Conference on Human Factors in Computing Systems, pp. 1401–1410. ACM, April 2009
24. Asano, T., Sharlin, E., Kitamura, Y., Takashima, K., Kishino, F.: Predictive interaction using the delphian desktop. In: Proceedings of the 18th Annual ACM Symposium on User Interface Software and Technology, pp. 133–141. ACM, October 2005
25. Lank, E., Cheng, Y.C.N., Ruiz, J.: Endpoint prediction using motion kinematics. In: Proceedings of the SIGCHI Conference on Human Factors in Computing Systems, pp. 637–646. ACM, April 2007
26. Ahmad, B.I., Langdon, P.M., Bunch, P., Godsill, S.J.: Probabilistic intentionality prediction for target selection based on partial cursor tracks. In: Stephanidis, C., Antona, M. (eds.) UAHCI 2014. LNCS, vol. 8515, pp. 427–438. Springer, Cham (2014). https://doi.org/10.1007/978-3-319-07446-7_42
27. Keates, S., Hwang, F., Langdon, P., Clarkson, P. J., Robinson, P.: Cursor measures for motion-impaired computer users. In: Proceedings of the Fifth International ACM Conference on Assistive Technologies, pp. 135–142. ACM, July 2002
28. Gajos, K.Z., Wobbrock, J.O., Weld, D.S.: Automatically generating user interfaces adapted to users' motor and vision capabilities. In: Proceedings of the 20th Annual ACM symposium on User Interface Software and Technology, pp. 231–240, October 2007
29. Domingo, M.C.: An overview of the Internet of Things for people with disabilities. J. Netw. Comput. Appl. **35**(2), 584–596 (2012)
30. Biswas, P., Langdon, P.: Developing multimodal adaptation algorithm for mobility impaired users by evaluating their hand strength. Int. J. Hum. Comput. Interact. **28**(9), 576–596 (2012)
31. Newell, A.F., Gregor, P.: Human computer interfaces for people with disabilities. In: Handbook of Human-Computer Interaction, 2nd edn., pp. 813–824 (1997)
32. Sears, A., Lin, M., Jacko, J., Xiao, Y.: When computers fade: pervasive computing and situationally-induced impairments and disabilities. In: HCI International, vol. 2, no. 03, pp. 1298–1302, June 2003
33. Ng, A., Williamson, J., Brewster, S.: The effects of encumbrance and mobility on touch-based gesture interactions for mobile phones. In: Proceedings of the 17th International Conference on Human-Computer Interaction with Mobile Devices and Services, pp. 536–546. ACM, August 2015
34. Goel, M., Findlater, L., Wobbrock, J.: WalkType: using accelerometer data to accomodate situational impairments in mobile touch screen text entry. In: Proceedings of the SIGCHI Conference on Human Factors in Computing Systems, pp. 2687–2696. ACM, May 2012
35. Zhai, S., Kristensson, P.O., Appert, C., Anderson, T.H., Cao, X.: Foundational issues in touch-surface stroke gesture design—an integrative review. Found. Trends Hum. Comput. Interact. **5**(2), 97–205 (2012)
36. Wang, F., Cao, X., Ren, X., Irani, P.: Detecting and leveraging finger orientation for interaction with direct-touch surfaces. In: Proceedings of the 22nd Annual ACM Symposium on User Interface Software and Technology, pp. 23–32. ACM, October 2009
37. Mayer, S., Gad, P., Wolf, K., Woźniak, P.W., Henze, N.: Understanding the ergonomic constraints in designing for touch surfaces. In: Proceedings of the 19th International Conference on Human-Computer Interaction with Mobile Devices and Services, p. 33. ACM, September 2017

38. Kawalkar, A.N., Roth, H.: Touch screen display user interface and method for improving touch interface utility on the same employing a rules-based masking system. U.S. Patent No. 9,733,707. U.S. Patent and Trademark Office, Washington, DC (2017)
39. Rautaray, S.S., Agrawal, A.: Vision based hand gesture recognition for human computer interaction: a survey. Artif. Intell. Rev. **43**(1), 1–54 (2015)
40. Lu, Z., Chen, X., Li, Q., Zhang, X., Zhou, P.: A hand gesture recognition framework and wearable gesture-based interaction prototype for mobile devices. IEEE Trans. Hum. Mach. Syst. **44**(2), 293–299 (2014)
41. Gupta, H.P., Chudgar, H.S., Mukherjee, S., Dutta, T., Sharma, K.: A continuous hand gestures recognition technique for human-machine interaction using accelerometer and gyroscope sensors. IEEE Sens. J. **16**(16), 6425–6432 (2016)
42. Labrecque, M.: Wearable gesture control: improving the computer interface convenience and accessibility. In: 2014 IEEE Games Media Entertainment (GEM), p. 1. IEEE, October 2014
43. Kim, D., Hilliges, O., Izadi, S., Butler, A.D., Chen, J., Oikonomidis, I., Olivier, P.: Digits: freehand 3D interactions anywhere using a wrist-worn gloveless sensor. In: Proceedings of the 25th Annual ACM Symposium on User Interface Software and Technology, pp. 167–176. ACM, October 2012
44. Ahmad, B.I., Murphy, J., Langdon, P.M., Godsill, S.J.: Filtering perturbed in-vehicle pointing gesture trajectories: improving the reliability of intent inference. In: IEEE International Workshop on Machine Learning for Signal Processing (MLSP), pp. 1–6. IEEE, September 2014
45. Ahmad, B.I., Murphy, J.K., Langdon, P.M., Godsill, S.J.: Bayesian intent prediction in object tracking using bridging distributions. IEEE Trans. Cybern. **41**(1), 215–227 (2018)
46. Cappé, O., Godsill, S.J., Moulines, E.: An overview of existing methods and recent advances in sequential Monte Carlo. Proc. IEEE **95**(5), 899–924 (2007)
47. Ahmad, B.I., Langdon, P.M., Godsill, S.J., Donkor, R., Wilde, R., Skrypchuk, L.: You do not have to touch to select: a study on predictive in-car touchscreen with mid-air selection. In Proceedings of the 8th International Conference on Automotive User Interfaces and Interactive Vehicular Applications, pp. 113–120. ACM, October 2016

MyoSL: A Framework for Measuring Usability of Two-Arm Gestural Electromyography for Sign Language

Jordan Aiko Deja[✉], Patrick Arceo[✉], Darren Goldwin David[✉],
Patrick Lawrence Gan[✉], and Ryan Christopher Roque[✉]

Center for Complexity and Emerging Technologies,
Advanced Research Institute for Informatics, Computing and Networking,
College of Computer Studies,
De La Salle University, Manila, Philippines
{jordan.deja,patrick_arceo,darren_david,patrick_gan,
ryan_roque}@dlsu.edu.ph

Abstract. Several Sign Language (SL) systems have been developed using various technologies: Kinect, armbands, and gloves. Majority of these studies never considered user experience as part of their approach. With that, we propose a new framework that eases usability by employing two-arm gestural electromyography instead of typical vision-based systems see Fig. 5. Interactions can be considered seamless and natural with this way. In this preliminary study, we conducted focus group discussions and usability tests with signers. Based on the results of the usability tests, 90% of respondents found the armband comfortable. The respondents also stated that the armband was not intrusive when they tried to perform their sign gestures. At the same time, they found it aesthetically pleasing. Additionally, we produced an initial prototype from this experiment setup and tested them on several conversational scenarios. By using this approach, we enable an agile framework that caters the needs of the signer-user.

Keywords: Human-centric computing
Human-computer interaction · User studies · Interaction paradigms
Natural language interfaces · Gestural input · Electromyography · Myo

1 Introduction

Sign language (SL) is the primary mode of communication used by the Deaf community (signers). It involves gestural components such as arm, and hand movements. Non-manual signals are also used to convey messages. Combining these different components, sign language on its own is different to comprehend. We applied this framework in the Philippine scenario where statistics show that there is one (1) interpreter for every 53,000 Filipino signers. Human Interpreters

© Springer International Publishing AG, part of Springer Nature 2018
M. Antona and C. Stephanidis (Eds.): UAHCI 2018, LNCS 10907, pp. 146–159, 2018.
https://doi.org/10.1007/978-3-319-92049-8_11

mediate communication between signers and non-signers. Moreover, having sufficient knowledge on sign language is necessary to communicate with signers. This means there is a gap that needs to be addressed for the Deaf community. Several attempts have been made to develop interpreter systems for American Sign Language (ASL) such as [12,13]. However these studies are limited to their visual boundaries and confining environments. We believe that interpreter systems will be more usable if we enable a free, seamless approach to understanding sign language gestures that are not entirely vision-based. In this paper, we intend to discover if we can utilize the Myo Armband as an alternative device that can be used for recognizing sign language. This way, recognizing gestures are not restricted by vision-based constraints such as lighting, angles as the inputs are mostly gestured based. We believe that such interaction design would be considered more usable and would support our proposed framework. This is supported by a discussion of the user insights that we are able to acquire from the user study in the latter parts of this paper. In the long run we envision signers to be able to communicate directly with non-signers by being able to gesture freely while wearing their armbands, sending the message through a mobile device that can be received by non signers. Through this, they would be able to seamlessly send their intended message without the need for an interpreter and in an approach that is empowered by technology (Fig. 1).

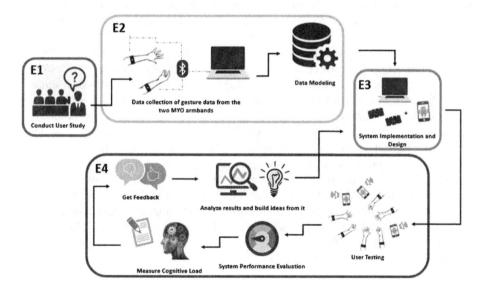

Fig. 1. MyoSL Methodology Framework showing the different components

In this work-in-progress, we discuss our attempts to gather user insights regarding the use of two EMG-based gestural armbands by signers. Also, we attempt to model and identify certain scenarios and expressions that are most convenient and natural. While we understand that there is a large domain at hand, we limited our library of words into a specific scenario. We will also discuss the data collection process and how the EMG data for two gestural devices would look alike which will be then used to generate a model that can identify words. In this study, we have used both American Sign Language (ASL) and Filipino Sign Language (FSL) in order to see if there may be also differences in the terms, gestures and translation. In the succeeding sections we shall also discuss our findings and the next steps needed to complete the study.

2   Related Work

Several systems have been made for sign language interpretation. Each one focuses on different aspects of user needs. [11] created an extendable system which uses a camera placed on top of the brim of a cap to keep track of the hands of the user. The system can track the hands with or without a glove. The usage of gloves does affect the accuracy of the system though. However, for natural scenarios, they stated that the system would be unpleasant for signers since head movements are included in conversational sign language. Signers will also not be able to wear a baseball cap wherever they go. Like the work of [11], SignSpeak, an EU funded project, focuses on recognition and translation of sign language through vision-based input. However, according to [3], difficulties for a vision-based input appear because of different environment assumptions. SignSpeak was only developed for close-world environments with simple backgrounds coupled with special gloves for tracking.

Another vision-based system makes use of the Kinect. The Kinect features a camera with a depth sensor that is capable of tracking body movements [6]. Complex backgrounds and illumination conditions affects hand tracking which makes sign language translation through visual-input difficult. Due to the Kinect's depth sensor, the hand and body action can be tracked easier while maintaining accuracy without the need of special backgrounds [9]. However, practical use of the Kinect is only a partial solution. In terms of portability, its dimensions and the need to be plugged does not allow it to be conveniently carried by the user [5]. To be able to make a portable system, [2] made Sensory Glove. It was designed to translate ASL alphabet into text on a mobile phone. The glove transmits data into an Android phone through bluetooth connection which displays the translated text. Since the system only uses one glove, only a few words can be translated aside from the ASL alphabet. Unfortunately, the glove has an obtrusive design with exposed wires.

3   Methods

3.1   Participants

We have two (2) sets of study groups that participated in this study. The first group involved the thorough understanding of User-Signer needs through a series of User Research studies. The second group took part in the data collection that will be used for the initial model. Eleven (11) signers aged 18–24 were recruited through snowball sampling method in order to take part in the user study part of our framework. The impairments of the participants varied from complete deafness, partial deafness, complete muteness, and partial muteness. They participated in focus group discussions which were used to better help pinpoint the pains and gains of each user type. Additionally, these participants gave insights on the different activities they usually do and its corresponding struggles they experience every day. From these needfinding activities, we were able to derive personas which will be later discussed in the succeeding sections.

Ten (10) signers aged 21–31 were gathered through snowball sampling method took part in the initial usability testing of the two Myo armbands. Their average years of experience in using Sign Language is 9.22 years. The level of expertise varies from beginner (0–10 years), intermediate (10–20), all the way to expert (20 and above). It is important to note that all of the participants are the target end-users of the product. See Table 1 for the demographic information of the usability testing participants.

Table 1. Signer demographics (Usability testing)

Attribute	Min	Max	stdev
Age	21	26	3.24
Years Exp	4	24	7.03

3.2   Study Design

Our methodology in this study has been divided into four (4) major components that define the framework towards a more accessible and usable product. See Table 2 for the specific elements. In short, we can refer to these elements as (E1) User Study, (E2) Data Modeling, (E3) Model Implementation and (E4) Usability Testing. In addition to that, a user-centric design was employed in every stage of this framework. This enables us to have a constant communication and collaboration with our participants from the Deaf community. As seen in Fig. 5, the third and fourth part of the framework is done repetitively. This is designed to continuously develop and improve the system based on the results gathered from the usability tests of the participants. It is also important to note that only the first three parts are included in this paper.

Table 2. Framework elements

E1. Understanding Signer Needs by Conducting Specific User Research
E2. Collecting Data for Sign Language Modeling
E3. Training and Development of a SL Model
E4. Evaluating User Experiences by Testing the Model

User study is an important aspect of the design thinking process which can greatly improve the user experience of a product [8]. In achieving a user-centered design, it is essential to first empathize with the target users. This is done to gain an understanding on the user's needs and preferences as well as their tasks within the context of our system. These are the three (3) main goals of our user study:

1. To know more about the users and determine what is important for them
2. To know the way they do things and why
3. To understand the difficulties and pain points in interpreting Sign Language

In this stage, we conducted Focus Group Discussions (FGD) between eleven (11) signers and two (2) interpreters. FGD is a research strategy where people from similar backgrounds gathered together in order to discuss a specific topic. The participants are chosen purposely based on their common characteristics. It has a facilitator that guides the participants to express their feelings freely in order to have a natural discussion among themselves [1]. It also allows each participant to agree or disagree with each other that can show the range of opinions on how the group thinks about a certain issue in terms of their experiences and beliefs. Based from that, a general view can be established based from the stimulation of ideas of each participant [10]. The main focus of this FGD is to gather opinion on how they feel and think on the context of our study.

3.3 Data Modeling

In order to create the machine learning model using EMG, the ten (10) participants took part in the model building stage. Their average years of experience in sign language is 9.22 years. Most of them started as early as they were born. Each participant wore two Myo armbands in both of his/her forearm and were asked to perform different FSL signs to produce the gesture data. Each sign is done repetitively up to five (5) times to provide a stronger data. The EMG, acceleration, and orientation data of each sign were captured by the armband's 8 EMG Channels Fig. 3 and 3D IMU Sensors. All of the captured data is transmitted to a laptop via Bluetooth. We will sync the data from both of the Myo armbands. This is done so that the data in both armbands are synchronized. Timestamps will be used to ensure the data that are captured at the same time. A sampling rate of 50 hz will be taken from the armbands. An SDK is provided to do this procedure. Once data is gathered, the first and last second of each sign will be trimmed. This process removes noise data. We will have a rest position that will help us determine the start and end of a gesture and make it easier to apply Dynamic Time Warping (DTW) to the sample. After trimming the data, DTW will be applied to be able to standardize the length of the gesture. The reason behind this step is that same gestures can be performed in varying speeds. DTW allows the system to identify which gestures are the same while allowing said gestures to be spread over a variable length of time. With a standardized length, the data will then be normalized to be able to spread the data across a smaller feature space. The normalization will be done by scaling all the data from 0–1. This can be done with the help of tools such as RapidMiner which will automate this step. The data collected will then undergo feature extraction. The study will adapt well-established features from previous studies. Both EMG features, and accelerometer and gyroscope features will be used. Extracted features will be placed under InfoGain attribute evaluator along with the Ranker search technique to determine the features that would be most useful for the dataset (Fig. 2).

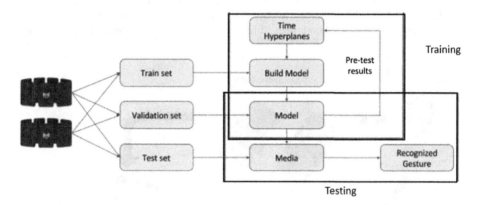

Fig. 2. Data modeling process

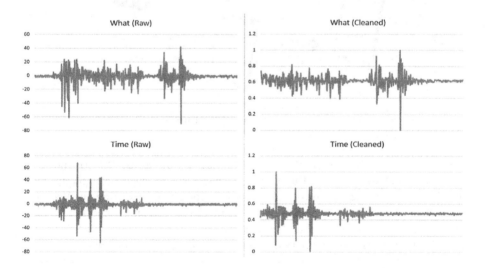

Fig. 3. EMG Visualization of the sign 'Ano' (What) and 'Oras' (Time)

3.4   Model Implementation

The model was initially proposed to be implemented in Android operating system with the help of the Myo SDK (Fig. 4).

The system involves four processes particularly, processing input, recording input, recognition techniques, and projecting output. It utilizes two Myo armbands which are connected to a smartphone. First, the Myo's sensors will capture the data. It will then transmit the data to the computer via Bluetooth. Then, the computer will record the input. Subsequently, recognition techniques will be employed to identify the gestures from the built-in model. Once the application identifies a match in the model, the translation will be voiced out by the speakers of the computer for the non-signers. The translation is also shown on the screen.

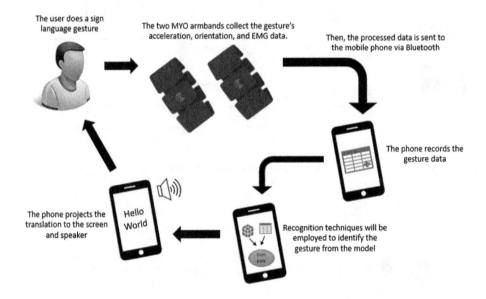

Fig. 4. System architecture

So far we have just started building the dataset of words. We still need to train the model to recognize these words. Concerns were also brought up with regards to the processing power and speed of processing regarding the use of a smartphone. We decided to first build the model to be run on a computer so that the processing time could be handled better. A faster translation and processing time will improve the user experience and make the interaction smoother. With regards to translation the words will first be collected as text and then some NLP techniques will be performed to smooth out the sentences and make them easier on the ears. One example being when the user performs the gestures "what time" "store" "open", the system will then output the phrase "what time will the store open?".

3.5   Usability Testing

Usability testing can be done in several ways, but each of them has these common five characteristics [4]:

1. The objective of each test is to improve the usability of a product
2. The participants are the end-users
3. The participants do real tasks that are associated with the system
4. All actions of the of the participants are observed and recorded
5. The results are analyzed to determine the real problems and to recommend solutions to fix them

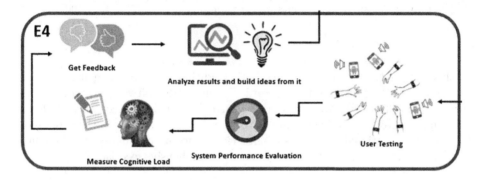

Fig. 5. Usability testing framework

This is done to learn more about the system, specifically its strengths and weaknesses. Additionally, feedbacks from the end-users are solicited. Along the process, both high and low fidelity feedback will be considered and immediately integrated in the system. Here, a usability testing was conducted by allowing the deaf signers to wear the two armbands and run through a low fidelity prototype of the interpreter system. Questions were raised to better understand if the armband was intrusive when it came to the signers gestures. Questions about its level of comfort, weight, and position, gave us insights on how to make the experience more enjoyable for the users. The questions are answered on a 1–4 scale, 1 being the lowest (strongly disagree) and 4 being the highest (strongly agree). See Table 3 for the list of questions about the Myo armband.

3.6   Experiment Design

To validate our framework, we proposed three different experiment setups as seen in Fig. 6 namely (1) Signer-Non-signer conversation with a human interpreter, (2) Signer-Non-signer conversation using only one Myo armband and (3) Signer-Non-signer using two Myo armbands. These experiments will be done in a closed environment with camera recordings to preserve artifacts of this study.

Table 3. Myo Armband Related Questions

Question	Disagree(%)	Agree(%)
MQ1. The armband is comfortable	10%	90%
MQ2. The vibrations are intuitive	0%	100%
MQ3. The placement of the armband is comfortable	0%	100%
MQ4. The aesthetic of the armband is not appealing	20%	80%
MQ5. I can wear the armband for a long period of time	10%	90%
MQ6. I am comfortable with the weight of the armband	20%	80%
MQ7. The armband is not intrusive when I perform my gestures	0%	100%
MQ8. I feel the need to remove the armband after a few minutes	10%	90%
MQ9. It will take time to get used to wearing the armband	10%	90%
MQ10. I am comfortable doing gestures with the armband	0%	100%
Average	8%	92%

In this approach we can benchmark both traditional and existing frameworks as compared to our proposed framework. Furthermore, Software Usability Measurement Inventory (SUMI) [7], and Cognitive Tools will be incorporated. This is to quantitatively measure the impact of the changes we made in the proposed framework. Additionally, a series of interviews and questionnaires will be conducted with the participants. Thus, a more comprehensive feedback is captured.

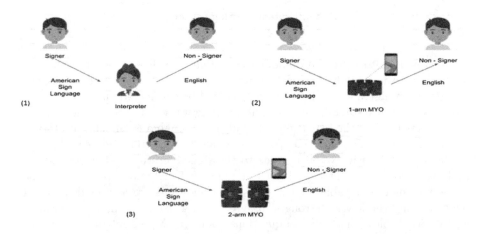

Fig. 6. Experiment design

In the experiments, the participants were given a set of expressions in purchasing scenarios. We ensure that each participants start on equal footing and try to achieve a smooth flow of conversations. While the participants will be communicating with each other, we observed the time it takes for them to respond to the expression, the frustrations they had while conversing, and the total time it took for them to finish the set of expressions. After the experiment, we verified on how the experience was from their conversation with each other.

4   Results

In this preliminary study, there were three results that were produced: the results of the user study, the initial machine learning model, and the user feedback/insights collected during the usability testing.

Based from the results, we discovered that majority of the signers are reliant on interpreters. They stated that interpreters can make their sentences short which is faster than the time it takes if they write or type what they want to say. Furthermore, sign language has a different syntax which makes the grammar of their translations uncommon. The signers also stated that interpreters are highly needed especially in hospital, employment, and purchasing situations. In regards to interpreter systems, they are aware that there are already existing systems. Some of them have already tried some of these systems. One system is a video relay service. A signer connects with the service, and the interpreter relays the interpreted message to the intended person with a telephone. However, majority of the signers stated that these systems are either expensive or available to more developed countries. They end up relying on interpreters, writing, or online messaging. Results of the focus group discussion highlights the existing gap for the Deaf community. We stated awhile ago that there is only one (1) interpreter for 53,000 Filipino signers. Signers expressing that they highly need interpreter will show how a sign language interpretation system will be able to help them. Despite the fact that there are current interpretation systems, its pricing or availability is the problem. Our proposed system uses the Myo armband which is affordable and available in every market.

We also conducted usability tests on a group of nine deaf students. The meeting was facilitated by an interpreter. The goal of the survey was to find out if the signers were comfortable with the armband and if it limits their movement to perform signs. We also wanted to know if they found the aesthetic pleasing and if the vibrations of the armband were intuitive. The results of the initial usability tests showed that 90% of respondents found the armband comfortable. All participants said that the vibrations were intuitive, and they found the placement of the armband comfortable. All participants also responded that the armband was not intrusive when it came to performing gestures. 80% of the participants stated that the aesthetic of the armband was pleasing and would usually go well with what they wear despite the fact that the armband cannot be worn over clothes. They also said that the weight of the armband was comfortable. Regarding the armband's comfortability, 10% did not find it comfortable because of their body size. Since the armband has rubbers to keep it snug to the wearer, different body types react differently to its comfortability. Small frames may have the armband moving up and down their arms, and big frames may have the armband too tight on their arms (Fig. 7).

The armband is comfortable.

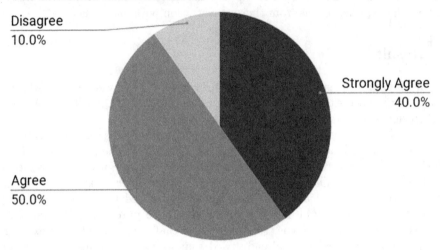

Fig. 7. User feedback

The aesthetic of the armband is appealing.

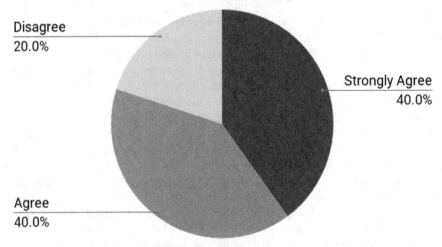

Fig. 8. The aesthetic of the armband is appealing.

The two armbands are worn on both upper forearms of the user. The position allows the armband not to be intrusive when signers will be gesturing signs. The weight and slimness of the armband permits signers to have full range of motion. At the same time, the armband does not tire their arms out. However, 20% did not find the armband aesthetically pleasing due to the fact that it has a futuristic look. Moreover, it may disrupt their fashion style. If the signer is wearing long

The armband is not intrusive when I try to perform my gestures.

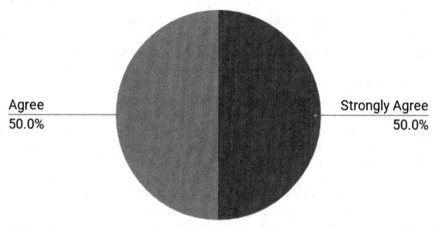

Fig. 9. The armband is not intrusive when I try to perform my gestures.

sleeves, they would have to have a bulge in the middle in their arms which may have made them find the armband not aesthetically pleasing (Figs. 8 and 9).

5   Conclusion

Before any development or data collection was be done, we first decided to conduct specific user research so as to better understand the pain points of our users. This part of the framework is especially effective in determining how to properly address the problems the users encounter and the situation or problem that we want to solve. Through this portion of the research, we were able to find out which specific situations the signers wanted to be able to interact with the hearing.

Ten (10) participants took part in the model building stage to create our machine learning model. Participants wore two Myo armbands their forearms, and each was asked to perform sixty (60) different FSL signs to produce the gesture data five (5) times each. EMG, acceleration, and orientation data of each sign were captured and transmitted to a laptop via Bluetooth.

We then evaluated user experience by testing the model. The participants wore the armband and calibrated it to be able to read their gestures. They were then asked to perform some gestures to see if the software would be able to detect which gesture they were performing. After the activity, they were asked to answer a survey regarding the ease of use of the system. The participants answered questions about how comfortable or intrusive the armband was, and if they found the system intuitive. Based on the results of the survey majority of the users found the system easy to use and the armband comfortable enough to wear for extended periods of time.

6 Future Work

The Myo armband is a promising interface for collecting hand gestures. However, in terms of interpreting sign language, hand gestures are not enough to interpret the entire conversation. Facial expressions and body movement are indeed important in terms of applying context in a given language. A way to capture Facial expressions and integrate them into the system would greatly help in improving this study.

The application was also limited to techniques such as Dynamic Time Warping and Support Vector Machines in our data processing. Although these techniques both yielded quality results. Other variations might provide higher accuracy or faster processing times. In addition to Filipino Sign Language Recognition, this system can be modified for other forms of sign language such as American Sign Language, Chinese Sign Language, etc.

The study could also be extended to include a deeper natural language processing portion in which grammar for different languages could be selected as an output. An example being FSL being the input but the system outputting to spoken english would be a nice quality of life improvement. The implications this has on the system would mean that the part where the data is processed and then compared to templates grammar templates would have to be redone for different languages.

References

1. Research tools: Focus group discussion, January 2009. https://www.odi.org/publications/5695-focus-group-discussion
2. Bukhari, J., Rehman, M., Malik, S.I., Kamboh, A.M., Salman, A.: American sign language translation through sensory glove; signspeak. Int. J. u-and e-Service Sci. Technol. **8**(1), 131–142 (2015)
3. Dreuw, P., Forster, J., Gweth, Y., Stein, D., Ney, H., Martinez, G., Llahi, J.V., Crasborn, O., Ormel, E., Du, W., et al.: Signspeak-understanding, recognition, and translation of sign languages. In: 4th Workshop on the Representation and Processing of Sign Languages: Corpora and Sign Language Technologies (CSLT 2010), Valletta, Malta, pp. 65–73 (2010)
4. Dumas, J.S., Redish, J.: A Practical Guide to Usability Testing. Intellect Books (1999)
5. Filipe, V., Fernandes, F., Fernandes, H., Sousa, A., Paredes, H., Barroso, J.: Blind navigation support system based on microsoft kinect. Procedia Comput. Sci. **14**, 94–101 (2012)
6. Huang, F., Huang, S.: Interpreting american sign language with kinect. J. Deaf Stud. Deaf Educ. Oxford University Press (2011)
7. Kirakowski, J., Corbett, M.: Sumi: the software usability measurement inventory. British J. Educ. Technol. **24**(3), 210–212 (1993)
8. Kittur, A., Chi, E.H., Suh, B.: Crowdsourcing user studies with mechanical turk. In: Proceedings of the SIGCHI Conference on Human Factors in Computing Systems, pp. 453–456. ACM (2008)
9. Lang, S., Block-Berlitz, M., Rojas, R.: Sign Language Recognition with Kinect. Institut für Informatik, Freie Universität Berlin, Bachelor (2011)

10. Langford, J., McDonagh, D.: Focus Groups: Supporting Effective Product Development. CRC Press, Boca Raton (2003)
11. Starner, T., Weaver, J., Pentland, A.: A wearable computer based american sign language recognizer. In: First International Symposium on Wearable Computers, Digest of Papers, pp. 130–137. IEEE (1997)
12. Starner, T., Weaver, J., Pentland, A.: Real-time american sign language recognition using desk and wearable computer based video. IEEE Trans. Pattern Anal. Mach. Intell. **20**(8) (1998)
13. Yang, W., Tao, J., Xi, C., Ye, Z.: Sign language recognition system based on weighted hidden markov model. In: 8th International Symposium on Computational Intelligence and Design (2015)

Evaluating Devices for Object Rotation in 3D

Sean DeLong[(⊠)] and I. Scott MacKenzie

Department of Electrical Engineering and Computer Science,
York University, Toronto, ON M3J 1P3, Canada
{Seand,mack}@cse.yorku.ca

Abstract. An experiment with 12 participants was conducted to compare the performance of a mouse, a mobile phone accelerometer, and a joystick in a 3D rotation task. The 3D rotation task was designed to measure throughput, the user performance metric specified in ISO 9241-9. The mouse had a throughput and error rate of 4.09 bps and 0.88%, respectively, the mobile phone 2.05 bps and 3.46%, and the joystick 2.42 bps and 1.76%. The differences were significant between the mouse and both the mobile phone and joystick, but not between the mobile phone and joystick. There was a significant difference in error rate only between the mouse and mobile phone conditions. The mobile phone condition did not appear to conform to Fitts' law as task index of difficulty had no apparent relationship with movement time. This was most likely caused by reaction time and homing time for that condition.

Keywords: Input devices · User interfaces · Performance measurement
Fitts' law · 3D interfaces · Object orientation

1 Introduction

Advancements in virtual reality (VR) and augmented reality (AR), along with the ever-increasing graphical capabilities of modern computers, emphasizes the need for improved three-dimensional, or 3D, interaction. Given that objects in real 3D space can be described and controlled in six degrees of freedom (DOF), it is reasonable to assert that similar DOFs are needed for an input control to achieve natural interaction in virtual 3D space.

There has been substantial research on methods of input with DOFs higher than the typical two DOF common in traditional inputs like the mouse and capacitive touch. Ortega et al. [15] provide an extensive overview of the technologies and devices supporting higher DOF inputs.

Despite emerging methods of input, the traditional computer mouse remains the primary device for 3D tasks in areas such as 3D modeling, computer-aided design (CAD), and game development. Inputs with only two DOF are also ubiquitous in the video game industry, as joysticks are designed into nearly every controller for Nintendo, Xbox, and PlayStation consoles.

Whether lower DOF devices are better, or even adequate, for 3D tasks seems inconclusive. While there is some evidence that two-DOF inputs are fast and accurate

© Springer International Publishing AG, part of Springer Nature 2018
M. Antona and C. Stephanidis (Eds.): UAHCI 2018, LNCS 10907, pp. 160–177, 2018.
https://doi.org/10.1007/978-3-319-92049-8_12

for 3D selection [18] and 3D object translation [1], other evaluations found that input devices with three DOF are faster for 3D object rotation [e.g., 6].

The research described herein is the first empirical study of 3D object rotation using Fitts' law and the performance measure throughput, as described in ISO 9241-9 [7].[1] In the following section, we review related work and the calculation of throughput, as per the ISO standard with extensions to our technique for 3D rotation. Then, we discuss the methodology and results of our user study. This is followed with our conclusions on user performance with the devices tested and task employed.

2 Related Work

Table 1 gives an overview of research where user studies evaluated devices for 2D and 3D tasks. The table is organized is by task type, with target selection tasks on top and object translation and rotation tasks on the bottom. The table also identifies the performance measurements and the types of inputs.

Table 1. Overview of user studies evaluating methods of 2D and 3D input.

First Author [ref]	Primary Quantitative Performance Measurements	Task Type	Input Method	Input DOF
MacKenzie [11]	Movement Direction Change, Movement Variability, Movement Error, Movement time, Error rate, Throughput	2D target selection	Mouse	2
		2D target selection	Trackball	2
		2D target selection	Joystick (rate control)	2
		2D target selection	Touchpad	2
Natapov [14]	Movement Direction Change, Movement Error, Error rate, Throughput	2D target selection	Joystick (rate control)	2
		2D target selection	Trackball (rate control)	2
Teather [18]	Movement time, Error rate, Throughput	2D target selection	Mouse Cursor	2
		3D target selection	Pen Ray	6
		3D target selection	Pen Touch	2
		3D target selection	Floating Cursor	2
		3D target selection	Sliding Cursor	2

(*continued*)

---

[1] The standard was updated in 2012 as ISO 9241-411 [8]. With respect to performance evaluation, the two versions are the same.

Table 1. (*continued*)

First Author [ref]	Primary Quantitative Performance Measurements	Task Type	Input Method	Input DOF
Young [21]	Movement time, Error rate, Throughput	3D target selection	Gyro-based wearable	6
Bérard [1]	Galvanic skin response, Blood volume pulse amplitude, Heart rate, Session time, Error rate	3D object translation	Mouse	2
		3D object translation	DepthSlider	3
		3D object translation	SpaceNavigator	6
		3D object translation	Free-space	6
Hinckley [6]	Task time, Accuracy	3D object rotation	Mouse- virtual sphere	2
		3D object rotation	Mouse- Arcball	2
		3D object rotation	Magnetic sensor- 3D Ball	3
		3D object rotation	Magnetic sensor - Tracker	3

Additional discussion on the studies in Table 1 is provided in the following sections.

2.1   Degrees of Freedom in Input Devices for 3D Tasks

The number of DOF in an input control determines the mappings to an output display. Interaction where an input device has the same DOFs as an object on an output display can achieve *spatial congruence*, resulting in natural interactions that are easy to learn [9, p. 78]. When there are less DOF in the device than the display, modes or mappings are required. These must be learned, however, and this may impact usability.

Table 1 highlights evaluations of devices with varying DOF. Both mice and joysticks have been evaluated using Fitts' law tasks for target selection in 2D [11, 14]. Since these devices have two DOF, they have a near-congruent relationship with a desktop display, where only the input z-axis requires mapping to the output y-axis. As an example, the 2D control display mappings for the mouse are shown in Fig. 1.

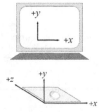

Axis	Control (mouse)	Display (cursor)
x	+	+
y		+
z	+	

Fig. 1. Mapping of mouse control space to cursor display space [9, p. 76]. The plus (+) symbol indicates that positive motion of the control yields positive motion in the display.

The mapping from the z-axis to the y-axis is simple and is easily learned. However, these two–DOF devices require complex mappings to control 3D displays. Consider the translation and rotation of an object in 3D, a task that requires six DOF. A mouse or joystick can only control two DOF at once without mappings or modes. Common practices for 3D rotation with two-DOF devices are to introduce additional graphical controls [2] or to implement a virtual sphere mapping [2, 4–6]. The virtual sphere maps each axis in the two-DOF device to an axis of rotation in the three-DOF display. This is shown in Fig. 2. Note that rotation around the z-axis cannot be controlled.

The translation of an object in 3D can be accomplished with two DOF using multiple viewpoint cameras [1] or ray-casting techniques [18].

In contrast, devices with six DOF can achieve spatial congruence in 3D translation and rotation with one-to-one control-display mappings. Typically, the six DOF are implemented via an accelerometer and magnetic sensor [1, 20, 22]. Such mapping is shown in Fig. 3.

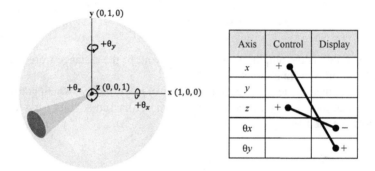

Fig. 2. Virtual sphere mapping of two-DOF controls.

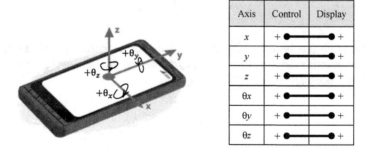

Fig. 3. 3D spatially congruent mapping with a six-DOF input control.

Prior work found that spatially congruent mappings with higher DOF devices do not necessarily make 3D target selection faster or more accurate than with two-DOF devices like the mouse [1, 18]. The robust user performance measure known as throughput has been used for some of these evaluations [18, 21].

Other empirical evidence, such as the work of Hinckley et al. [6], suggests that for the three-DOF task of object rotation, spatial congruency reduces task time compared to the mouse. However, to our knowledge, no such study exists using throughput as a performance measure for 3D rotation.

2.2 Fitts' Law and Throughput for 2D Target Selection

Fitts' law quantifies the relationship between distance, movement time, and accuracy for rapid aimed movements [3]. The usual formulation of this relationship is

$$MT = a + b\,ID \tag{1}$$

where MT is the movement time to complete a target-selection task, a and b are linear regression coefficients, and ID is the index of difficulty, with units "bits". ID was originally defined as

$$ID = \log_2\left(\frac{2A}{W}\right). \tag{2}$$

The A variable is the amplitude of the movement, or the distance from the start of an initial location to a final target of width W.

Fitts also defined the term IP, called the *index of performance*, which quantifies the human information capacity of the motor system. IP has units "bits per second", or "bps", and is defined as

$$IP = ID/MT. \tag{3}$$

MacKenzie proposed a variation of ID according to Shannon's information theory [16], modifying ID to

$$ID = \log_2\left(\frac{A}{W} + 1\right). \tag{4}$$

This variation has been incorporated into an ISO standard for performance measurements of pointing devices. ISO 9241-9 proposes the throughput (TP) measurement [7], which has been refined to

$$TP = \frac{\log_2\left(\frac{A_e}{4.133 \times SD_x} + 1\right)}{MT}. \tag{5}$$

Throughput is the current equivalent of Fitts' index of performance. The A_e term in Eq. 5 is the effective amplitude, which is the amount a participant or cursor moved, rather than what the task specified. The SD_x term is the standard deviation of the selection endpoints, as projected on the task axis.

Throughput's usefulness comes from its robustness and inclusion of both speed and accuracy [10]. Furthermore, if calculated consistently, it provides a basis for between-study comparisons, where device evaluations and findings are directly compared in different studies [16].

2.3   3D Target Selection

Since the emergence of ISO 9241-9, throughput is the standard user performance measure for evaluating of 2D pointing devices, and thus extensive comparisons can be made with existing literature. However, despite throughput being robust enough to describe movements in 3D as well as 2D, the calculation of throughput in 3D tasks is much less common.

Some exceptions are the work of Young et al. [21], where throughput is a performance measure for a 3D arm-mounted inertial controller, and the work of Teather and Stuerzlinger [18], where the throughputs of various 3D pen and cursor inputs are compared with throughputs typical of two-DOF mice and pen devices. Teather et al. [19] designed a system to extend the ISO 9241-9 Fitts' law pointing task into 3D environments, adding a depth component to targets.

2.4   Throughput Calculation for Rotation Tasks

Fitts' law has also been examined in rotation tasks. Meyer et al. [13] conducted 1D rotation experiments using Fitts' original definition of *ID*, shown in Eq. 2. Using an apparatus for measuring wrist rotation, they studied rotation about the wrist joint from an initial angle to a target angle. *A* was defined as the specified rotation, in degrees, from the starting position to the target, and *W* was defined as the specified target range, in degrees. From their experiments, Meyer et al. presented Fitts' law-derived descriptive models for total, primary-submovement, and secondary-submovement endpoint distributions and movement times [13]. Since this work predates the introduction of throughput, index of performance is used instead of throughput in their quantitative analysis.

In more recent work, Stoelen and Akin conducted a 1D rotation Fitts' law experiment using the modified definition of *ID*, shown in Eq. 4 [17]. Throughput was used in their quantitative analysis. They defined the rotational index of difficulty *ID* as

$$ID = \log_2\left(\frac{\alpha}{\omega} + 1\right) \tag{6}$$

where α is the rotation amplitude between a cursor's start and target angle, and ω is the target angle width. These parameters are shown in Fig. 4.

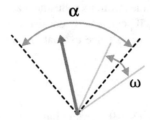

Fig. 4. Definition of α and ω in a rotational index of difficulty (*ID*) [17].

2.5   Defining a Fitts' Law Task for 3D Rotation

The experimental task presented herein was designed to be a spatially congruent interpretation of the 2D Fitts' law task described in the ISO 9241-9 standard. A standard 2D implementation is provided in the FittsTaskTwo software, as shown in Fig. 5.[2]

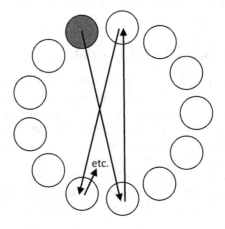

Fig. 5. ISO 9241-9 2D task showing a sequence of 13 targets.

Some challenges were faced in designing a suitable task to test throughput for object rotation in 3D. Firstly, because of the 3D nature of the task, both the cursor and the target become warped when oriented at certain angles in 3D space. For example, when oriented along the *x*-axis, all depth in the *z*-direction of the target range of angles is lost. This removes the user's ability to place the cursor in the center of the target angle range. The image on the left in Fig. 6 illustrates this. It was therefore decided that the target should not be fixed at any orientation other than along *z*-axis perpendicular to the screen. This prevents the true target angle range from becoming distorted.

---

[2] The FittsTaskTwo software download and API are found at http://www.yorku.ca/mack/FittsLawSoftware/.

Fig. 6. A single discrete rotation task.

Furthermore, the target can be represented by a cone because it encompasses a range of angles; however, the cursor can only be represented by a single line. Thus, the cursor becomes foreshortened when oriented in the z-direction, becoming a single point when parallel to it. For this reason, it was decided that the cursor should be fixed in the positive z-direction, facing towards the user. Although this restricts the cursor to a single point, it can be represented by a crosshair and becomes consistent throughout the trials. These issues can be mitigated somewhat if the apparatus includes 3D glasses and head tracking; however, our apparatus was limited to 2D rendering of 3D space.

Combining the above restrictions, the task was designed so that the target, represented by a cone, must be rotated to the cursor, represented by a crosshair and fixed along the z-axis in the positive direction. The target becomes undistorted and circular in shape after being rotated to the cursor. The circular surface of the target cone informs the user if the target is facing in the positive or negative z-direction; the cone is red when on the same side of the z-axis as the cursor, and grey when on the opposing side of the z-axis. Once the target is on the cursor, the user presses ENTER to end the task. Figure 6 shows a single example trial. Like the ISO 9241-9 2D task, subsequent targets alternate in a rotating fashion around the center point. Unlike the standard 2D task, the designed 3D rotation task is a series of discrete tasks, and thus a reaction time component exists. Reaction time was accounted for by starting the task timer only when the cursor leaves a negligible dead zone.

Extending Eq. 6 to 3D, and considering adjustments for the effective index of difficulty, the parameters α and ω are defined as

$$\alpha = \cos^{-1}(\mathbf{A} \cdot \mathbf{z}) \tag{7}$$

and

$$\alpha_e = \alpha + dx. \tag{8}$$

The coefficients in Eqs. 7 and 8 are illustrated in Fig. 7.

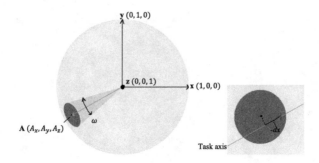

Fig. 7. Amplitude (α), width (ω), and axes definitions.

Recommendations outlined by Soukoreff and MacKenzie [16] were used for Fitts' law model construction. For calculating the effective index of difficulty ID_e, amplitude α was adjusted to the effective amplitude α_e using the angle difference between the cursor and the center of the target at the end of the task, as projected onto the task axis. The target width ω was adjusted to ω_e using the standard deviation SD_x of the task endpoint differences dx. Equation 7 through Eq. 11 were used for throughput calculation:

$$\omega_e = 4.133 \times SD_x \tag{9}$$

$$ID_e = \log_2\left(\frac{\alpha_e}{\omega_e} + 1\right) \tag{10}$$

$$TP = \frac{ID_e}{MT} \tag{11}$$

This is a three DOF task, but only requires two DOF to complete. This has the benefit of removing the need for modes in the two-DOF input conditions, so that the results are more comparable to those obtained in the standard 2D ISO 9241-9 task.

3 Methodology

3.1 Participants

Twelve unpaid participants were recruited from local universities. The participants were a mixture of graduate and undergraduate students. Two of the participants were female, eight were male. Ages ranged from 21 to 28 years. All participants were right-handed, though not by experimental design. Furthermore, all participants use computers daily.

The participants' median response to the number of hours of video games played per week was two to four hours. Two of the participants do not play video games on a regular basis. Only two participants use CAD software, between two to four hours a week. Seven participants had more than two hours of experience using AR or VR technology.

3.2   Apparatus

Hardware. A Microsoft *Surface Pro 4* tablet running Windows 10 ran the experiment for all conditions (Fig. 8a). The tablet configuration included the optional keyboard. Only the ENTER key was used on the keyboard.

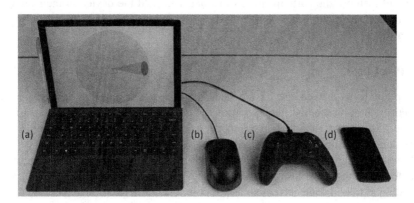

Fig. 8. The host system and input devices. (a) Microsoft *Surface Pro 4* tablet with optional keyboard, (b) Logitech *M-U0026* mouse, (c) Microsoft *Xbox One* game controller, and (d) LG *Nexus 5* mobile phone.

A Logitech *M-U0026* optical USB mouse was used for the mouse condition (Fig. 8b). The default Windows 10 mouse pointer speed was used, with enhanced pointer precision enabled.

A Microsoft *Xbox One* controller was used for the joystick condition (Fig. 8c). Either the left or right thumb stick could be used for object rotation, depending on a participant's preference. Joystick control-display gain was measured as the velocity of sphere rotation, in degrees per second. The gain was linear from 0°/s to 150°/s, corresponding to the joystick's rest position and maximum displacement, respectively.

An LG *Nexus 5* was used for its on-board magnetic gyroscope for the mobile phone condition (Fig. 8d). The gyroscope data were recorded at 50 Hz and streamed over an ad-hoc Wi-Fi network to the remote application on the tablet. The data streaming introduces a 46-ms lag in the system, but was not expected to increase error rates by more than about 5% [12]. Cursor movement was position-control with 1:1 gain (1° of device rotation caused 1° of cursor rotation on the sphere).

Software. The experimental software was developed primarily in JavaScript and compiled using Electron.[3] A Node.js server was hosted on the tablet for all conditions and was responsible for data logging, as well as streaming gyroscope data in the mobile phone tasks. The 3D orientation task was implemented with the three.js library.[4]

---

[3] https://electronjs.org/.

[4] https://github.com/mrdoob/three.js/.

For both the mouse and joystick input methods, the Arcball method of rotation for two-DOF inputs was implemented because of its intuitiveness and ease of implementation [6].

Task. The software implemented the experiment task described in the preceding section. For each input method, the participant performed eight sequences of 19 trials. For each input method, the participant was instructed to hold the device in their preferred hand, then place their other hand on the ENTER key. This was meant to reduce homing time.

3.3   Procedure

When participants arrived, they were seated at the system and familiarized with the task. For each input method, they performed a practice sequence of at least 19 trials to get used to the input method. These practice trials were meant to nullify any learning effects during the timed trials.

After the practice trials, participants were asked to perform all eight sequences continuously. They were instructed to select the targets at a comfortable pace, while proceeding as quickly and accurately as possible. The participants were permitted a rest break after each method of input. An example of a participant performing the experiment task with each input method is shown in Fig. 9.

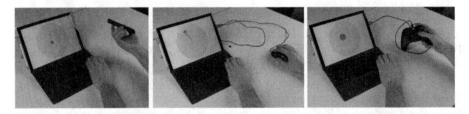

Fig. 9. Input methods: mobile phone (left), mouse (middle), and joystick (right).

A questionnaire was given after the experiment to gather information on how much time they played video games, worked with CAD software, and worked with VR or AR technology. The questionnaire also inquired about participants' impressions of the input methods on a 7-point Likert scale.

3.4   Design

The experiment was a fully within-subjects $3 \times 4 \times 2$ design, with the following independent variables and levels:

Input Method: mobile phone, mouse, joystick

Amplitude (α): $\frac{\pi}{4}, \frac{\pi}{3}, \frac{3\pi}{4}, \frac{5\pi}{6}$

Width (ω): $\frac{\pi}{8}, \frac{\pi}{16}$

The independent variable of primary interest was input method. The amplitude and width independent variables were necessary to ensure the computation of throughput covered a range of task difficulties. The primary dependent variables were movement time, error rate, and throughput.

To offset learning effects the order of presenting the three input methods was counterbalanced. Two participants were assigned to each of the six possible orders.

The amplitude and width variations give way to eight *IDs* ranging from 1.58 bits to 3.84 bits. See Table 2. These were presented in each condition in a random sequence. For each of the eight sequences, 19 trials were performed. Throughput and error rate were calculated for each of the eight sequences.

Table 2. Task amplitudes, widths, and index of difficulties.

α (rads)	$\dfrac{\pi}{4}$	$\dfrac{\pi}{3}$	$\dfrac{\pi}{4}$	$\dfrac{\pi}{3}$	$\dfrac{3\pi}{4}$	$\dfrac{5\pi}{6}$	$\dfrac{3\pi}{4}$	$\dfrac{5\pi}{6}$
ω (rads)	$\dfrac{\pi}{8}$	$\dfrac{\pi}{8}$	$\dfrac{\pi}{16}$	$\dfrac{\pi}{16}$	$\dfrac{\pi}{8}$	$\dfrac{\pi}{8}$	$\dfrac{\pi}{16}$	$\dfrac{\pi}{16}$
ID (bits)	1.58	1.87	2.32	2.66	2.81	2.94	3.70	3.84

In all, there were 12 Participants × 3 Input Methods × 4 Amplitudes × 2 Widths × 19 Trials = 5472 trials.

4   Results and Discussion

After the experiment was finished, the data were imported into a Microsoft *Excel* spreadsheet where summaries of various measures were calculated and charts were created. The statistical tests were performed using the GoStats application.[5]

4.1   Data Adjustment

During many of the trials for the mobile phone condition, participants had to adjust their grip on the device or had trouble mapping the device's orientation to the virtual object's orientation. This usually happened when the target amplitude changed from one sequence to the next, resulting in a task that required a new, drastic rotation. These trials, which typically had movement times greater than two standard deviations from the 19-trial mean, were considered outliers and removed. Using this criterion, 369 of 5472 trials (6.7%) were excluded from analysis.[6] After outlier removal, input method throughput and error rate were calculated by first calculating throughput and error rate on each 19-trial sequence, then averaging these measures to produce values across participants and conditions.

---

[5] Available as a free download at http://www.yorku.ca/mack/HCIbook/.

[6] Prior studies have used three standard deviations away from the mean as recommended by Soukoreff and MacKenzie [16], but like in the work of Wobbrock et al. [20], not all of the outliers were excluded under this criteria.

4.2   Throughput

The grand mean for throughput was 2.86 bps. Figure 10 shows the throughputs for each input method. The mouse throughput of 4.09 bps was about 100% greater than the mobile phone throughput at 2.05 bps and 70% greater than the joystick throughput at 2.42 bps. An ANOVA revealed that input method had a significant effect on throughput ($F_{2,10} = 45.04$, $p < .0001$). A Scheffé post hoc analysis revealed that the difference was significant between the mouse and the mobile phone and the mouse and the joystick, but not between the mobile phone and the joystick.

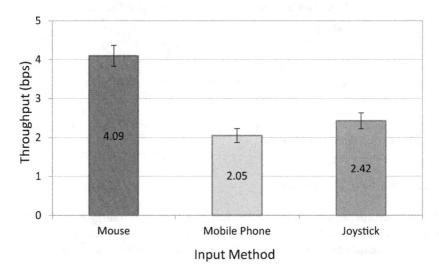

Fig. 10. Throughput by input method. Error bars show $\pm$ 1 *SE*.

The throughputs for the mouse and joystick were similar to values reported in other work [11, 14, 18]. Interestingly, the joystick in this rotation task yielded a higher throughput (2.42 bps) than it did for 2D selection experiments performed by MacKenzie et al. [11] (1.8 bps) and Natapov and MacKenzie [14] (2.01 bps). This suggests that the thumb-controlled joystick is better suited to the 3D rotation task than it is to the 2D target-selection task. However, a true assessment of this would require a within-study comparison of these conditions, to eliminate confounding influences.

Despite the spatially congruent mapping, the mobile phone condition still performed worse than the input methods with less DOF. The possible reasons are discussed below.

4.3   Error Rate

The grand mean for error rate was 2.03%. Figure 11 shows the error rate for each input method. The mouse condition had the lowest error rate of only 0.88%, and the mobile phone condition had the highest error rate of 3.46%. The joystick error rate was about half the mobile phone error rate (1.76%). There was a significant effect of input method on error rate ($F_{2,10} = 10.63$, $p < .001$). A Scheffé post hoc analysis revealed that the error rate only differed significantly between the mouse and mobile phone.

The error rates for each input method were relatively low compared to other research. The mouse in the work of MacKenzie et al. [11] had a throughput and error rate of 4.9 bps and 9.4%, whereas we observed 4.09 bps and 0.88% in the 3D rotation task. This discrepancy might be caused by our participants emphasizing accuracy over speed in the rotation task, along with the relatively large target widths.

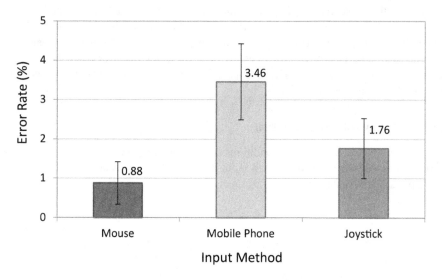

Fig. 11. Error rate by input method. Error bars show ± 1 *SE*.

4.4 Effective Index of Difficulty

Since participants rarely performed the task exactly as specified, the effective index of difficulty ID_e varies. Table 3 shows the specified and effective index of difficulties averaged across participants, along with the standard deviation of endpoints for each condition.

Table 3. Expected index of difficulty (*ID*) and endpoint variation (SD_x) and for each condition the observed effective index of difficulty (ID_e) and standard deviation (SD_x).

Expected		Observed					
		Mouse		Mobile Phone		Joystick	
ID (bits)	SD_x (rads)	ID_e (bits)	SD_x (rads)	ID_e (bits)	SD_x (rads)	ID_e (bits)	SD_x (rads)
1.58	0.095	2.58	0.041	2.08	0.062	2.01	0.065
1.87	0.095	2.86	0.045	2.18	0.073	2.33	0.073
2.32	0.047	3.34	0.024	2.81	0.032	2.53	0.048
2.66	0.047	3.63	0.026	3.04	0.037	3.05	0.036
2.81	0.095	3.79	0.050	3.18	0.107	3.33	0.064
2.94	0.095	3.63	0.058	3.54	0.060	3.32	0.105
3.70	0.047	4.65	0.025	4.24	0.034	4.19	0.034
3.84	0.047	4.86	0.024	4.32	0.035	4.35	0.033

The specified, or "expected", endpoint variation is normalized to a 4% error rate [16], and is calculated as

$$SD_x = \frac{\omega}{4.133}. \tag{12}$$

As for the observed participant behavior, there was a consistent discrepancy between the difficulty of the task specified and the difficulty of the task performed. For all conditions, $ID_e > ID$. This is a natural consequence of participants focusing on accuracy and achieving low error rates. With a low error rate, participants' endpoint variation was lower than the variation expected for a nominal 4% error rate. This tends to push ID_e up, as seen in Table 3.

4.5   Fitts' Law Linear Regression

By averaging the eight sequence conditions separately over all the participants, a linear regression model was created for each input method. The models are shown in Fig. 12 in the plots of movement time vs. ID_e.

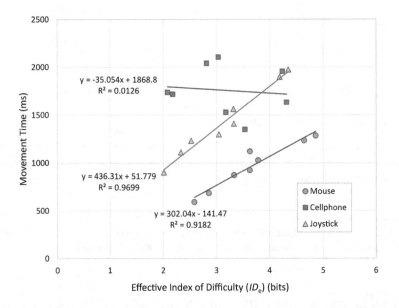

Fig. 12. Movement time (ms) vs. effective index of difficulty (bits) with regression models.

For both the mouse and joystick conditions, the linear regression model fits the data well ($R^2 > .9$), indicating that both conform to Fitts' law. Furthermore, the intercepts are relatively small, within the range outlined by Soukoreff and MacKenzie [16].

These results, along with the resemblance of the 3D rotation throughput to 2D target selection throughput in other work, validate the methodology and task design. The 3D rotation task can be representative of how a device with two DOF might perform in the 2D ISO 9241-9 task.

However, there is no overlooking the exceptionally poor fit of the mobile phone data to the regression model ($R^2 = .0126$). The effective index of difficulty for the mobile phone condition had no apparent impact on the movement time. There are a couple of explanations.

First, the mobile phone condition was not performed single-handed for this task, as originally expected. In many cases, participants had to use both hands to manipulate the mobile phone, taking their second hand from the ENTER key. This doubly impacted homing time, since time was spent moving from the ENTER key both before and after movement to the target.

Reaction time was also not properly eliminated in the mobile phone condition. A negligible dead zone was created at the start of each trial, inside which the movement timer would not start. For the mouse and joystick conditions, this effectively removed reaction time because the dead zone was never left before the participant purposely moved the cursor. However, because the mobile phone operated in position-control and is inherently affected by noise in the magnetic sensor, it frequently triggered a false start, causing the system to record reaction time as well.

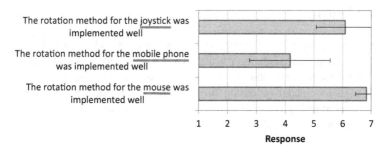

Fig. 13. Seven-point Likert-scale responses on participants' impressions on the implementation of each input method. Higher scores are better. Error bars show $\pm$ 1 *SD*.

4.6 Qualitative Results

Participants provided their impressions on the input methods at the end of the experiment. On a 7-point Likert scale, they were asked to rate how well they thought each input method was implemented (1 = not well, 7 = very well). The results are seen in Fig. 13. From best to worst, the results favored the mouse (6.8), then the joystick (6.1), then the mobile phone (4.2). A Friedman non-parametric test deemed the differences statistically significant ($\chi^2 = 20.4$, $df = 2$, $p < .0001$). All pairwise differences were also significant, as indicated by Conover's F ($p < .05$). The mobile phone rating is quite poor compared to the mouse and joystick ratings. Clearly, there is room for improvement in the mobile phone interaction.

Many participants also described the mobile phone condition as fatiguing, possibly negatively impacting their performance. One participant commented on arm pain when using the mobile phone condition. Another noted, "I had to mind [the] spatial mapping between several things: what I see, hand movements (and its limit), [the] phone, [and the] phone's shape".

5 Conclusion

A novel task for testing two- and three-DOF devices was designed and evaluated. The task used throughput as a performance measure and was intended to support the comparison of two-DOF devices used for 2D selection tasks with higher-DOF devices used for 3D rotation tasks.

The throughput for the mouse and joystick and the corresponding linear Fitts' law equations demonstrate that, with proper control-display mapping, a two-DOF device performs just as well in a 3D rotation task as it does in a 2D target-selection task.

The mobile phone accelerometer, however, did not work well, producing a low value of throughput, a poor Fitts' law model, and an overall negative impression on participants.

6 Future Work

Though the 3D rotation task performed favorably for the standard two DOF inputs, it requires more testing and validation for three DOF inputs. Homing time can be further reduced by introducing a method of rotation confirmation that does not require a free hand, such as a foot pedal or button on each input method. Reaction time can be reduced by implementing a larger dead zone, and then adjusting for its impact on effective amplitude.

References

1. Bérard, F., Ip, J., Benovoy, M., El-Shimy, D., Blum, Jeffrey R., Cooperstock, Jeremy R.: Did "minority report" get it wrong? superiority of the mouse over 3d input devices in a 3d placement task. In: Gross, T., Gulliksen, J., Kotzé, P., Oestreicher, L., Palanque, P., Prates, R.O., Winckler, M. (eds.) INTERACT 2009. LNCS, vol. 5727, pp. 400–414. Springer, Heidelberg (2009). https://doi.org/10.1007/978-3-642-03658-3_45
2. Chen, M., Mountford, S.J., Sellen, A.: A study in interactive 3-D rotation using 2-D control devices. Comput. Graph. **22**, 121–129 (1988)
3. Fitts, P.M.: The information capacity of the human motor system in controlling the amplitude of movement. J. Exp. Psychol. **47**, 381–391 (1954)
4. Henrysson, A., Billinghurst, M., Ollila, M.: Virtual object manipulation using a mobile phone, In: Proceedings of the International Conference on Augmented Tele-Existence, ICAT 2005. ACM, New York (2005)
5. Hinckley, K., Pausch, R., Goble, J.C., Kassell, N.F.: A survey of design issues in spatial input. In: Proceedings of the ACM Symposium on User Interface Software and Technology - UIST 1994, pp. 213–222. ACM, New York (1994)

6. Hinckley, K., Tullio, J., Pausch, R., Proffitt, D., Kassell, N.: Usability analysis of 3D rotation techniques. In: Proceedings of the ACM Symposium on User Interface Software and Technology - UIST 1997, pp. 1–10. ACM, New York (1997)
7. ISO: Ergonomic requirements for office work with visual display terminals (VDTs) - part 9: Requirements for non-keyboard input devices (ISO 9241-9), International Organisation for Standardisation Report Number ISO/TC 159/SC4/WG3 N147 (2000)
8. ISO: Evaluation methods for the design of physical input devices - ISO/TC 9241-411: 2012 (e), International Organisation for Standardisation Report Number ISO/TS 9241-411:2102 (E) (2012)
9. MacKenzie, I.S.: Human-Computer Interaction: An Empirical Research Perspective. Morgan Kaufmann, Waltham (2013)
10. MacKenzie, I.S., Isokoski, P.: Fitts' throughput and the speed-accuracy tradeoff, In: Proceedings of the ACM SIGCHI Conference on Human Factors in Computing Systems - CHI 2008, pp. 1633–1636. ACM, New York (2008)
11. MacKenzie, I.S., Kauppinen, T., Silfverberg, M.: Accuracy measures for evaluating computer pointing devices. In: Proceedings of the ACM SIGCHI Conference on Human Factors in Computing Systems - CHI 2001, pp. 119–126. ACM, New York (2001)
12. MacKenzie, I.S., Ware, C.: Lag as a determinant of human performance in interactive systems. In: Proceedings of the INTERACT 1993 and CHI 1993 Conference on Human Factors in Computing Systems - INTERCHI 1993, pp. 488–493. ACM, New York (1993)
13. Meyer, D.E., Abrams, R.A., Kornblum, S., Wright, C.E., Smith, J.E.K.: Optimality in human motor performance: ideal control of rapid aimed movements. Psychol. Rev. **95**, 340–370 (1988)
14. Natapov, D., MacKenzie, I.S.: The trackball controller, In: Proceedings of the International Academic Conference on the Future of Game Design and Technology - Futureplay 2010, pp. 167–174. ACM, New York (2010)
15. Ortega, F.R., Abyarjoo, F., Barreto, A., Rishe, N., Adjouadi, M.: Interaction Design for 3D User Interfaces: The World of Modern Input Devices. CRC Press, New York (2016)
16. Soukoreff, R.W., MacKenzie, I.S.: Towards a standard for pointing device evaluation: perspectives on 27 years of Fitts' law research in HCI. Int. J. Hum Comput Stud. **61**, 751–789 (2004)
17. Stoelen, M.F., Akin, D.L.: Assessment of Fitts' law for quantifying combined rotational and translational movements. Hum. Factors **52**, 63–77 (2010)
18. Teather, R.J., Stuerzlinger, W.: Pointing at 3D targets in a stereo head-tracked virtual environment. In: Proceedings of the IEEE Symposium on 3D User Interfaces - 3DUI 2011, pp. 87–94. ACM, New York (2011)
19. Teather, R.J., Stuerzlinger, W., Pavlovych, A.: FishTank fitts: a desktop VR testbed for evaluating 3D pointing techniques, In: Proceedings of the Extended Abstracts of the ACM SIGCHI Conference on Human Factors in Computing Systems - CHI 2014, pp. 519–522. ACM, New York (2014)
20. Wobbrock, J.O., Myers, B.A.: The performance of hand postures in front- and back-of-device interaction for mobile computing. Int. J. Hum Comput Stud. **66**, 857–875 (2008)
21. Young, T.S., Teather, R.J., MacKenzie, I.S.: An arm-mounted inertial controller for 6DOF input: design and evaluation. In: Proceedings of the IEEE Symposium on 3D User Interfaces - 3DUI 2017, pp. 26–35. IEEE, New York (2017)
22. Zhai, S., Milgram, P.: Quantifying coordination in multiple DOF movement and its application to evaluating 6 DOF input devices. In: Proceedings of the ACM SIGCHI Conference on Human Factors in Computing Systems - CHI 1998, pp. 320–327. ACM, New York (1998)

Interaction Techniques to Promote Accessibility in Games for Touchscreen Mobile Devices: A Systematic Review

Eunice P. dos Santos Nunes,
Vicente Antônio da Conceição Júnior$^{(\boxtimes)}$,
and Luciana C. Lima de Faria Borges

Institute of Computing, Federal University of Mato Grosso (UFMT),
Cuiabá, MT, Brazil
eunice.ufmt@gmail.com, vicente.junior@live.com,
lucianafariaborges@gmail.com

Abstract. Games for touchscreen mobile devices have become a part of popular culture, reaching beyond the limits of entertainment. However, while touchscreen devices have become one of the most far-reaching gaming platforms, there are very few studies that consider accessibility issues for People with Disabilities (PwD). In this scenario, this work presents the results of a Systematic Review (SR), which allowed to identify interaction techniques/strategies that are being applied in touchscreen devices, in order to promote accessibility of motor-coordination PwD. From the results of the SR, not only interaction techniques that promote accessibility were identified, but also low-cost and short development time adjustment parameters that can improve the interaction of motor-coordination PwD in 3D VEs. We noticed that promoting accessibility adjustments to meet different player profiles considering their limitations in motor coordination can be a differential in the player's experience.

Keywords: Accessibility · Touchscreen mobile device · Games

1 Introduction

Videogames have become a part of popular culture, reaching beyond the limits of entertainment. Government agencies, the military, hospitals, corporations and schools at all levels are using games for training and teaching within different fields of knowledge [1]. With the proliferation of mobile devices, games have broken the barriers of videogame controllers and computer desktops to become commonplace on tablets and smartphones [2].

The number of games employing touchscreen interaction has been steadily increasing for at least a decade [3]. However, while touchscreen devices have become one of the most far-reaching gaming platforms, there are very few studies that consider accessibility issues for People with Disabilities (PwD) [3]. These users still face challenges to interact with the applications and games by using touchscreen [4], due to their individual impairments/disabilities, such as limited motor coordination or loss of

M. Antona and C. Stephanidis (Eds.): UAHCI 2018, LNCS 10907, pp. 178–191, 2018.
https://doi.org/10.1007/978-3-319-92049-8_13

upper limbs (arms and hands) [5], forcing them to seek other alternatives to interact with such devices, such as the use of the feet or the mouth.

It is important to highlight that interacting with mobile devices is more than merely tapping the screen, since it may also involve swiping, sliding, repeated taps, multi-finger tapping, and multi-touch gesture, all of which require good motor control. This creates barriers for the accessibility of many users, especially for people with motor disabilities [6].

A solution presented by Kim et al. [3], proposes to increase the accessibility of PwD based on the personalization of the input controls (physical or virtual), according to each user category.

Therefore, this work, which is part of a larger context that investigates accessibility aspects and interaction techniques for developing games on touchscreen platforms that are accessible to PwD, aims to present the results of a Systematic Review (SR), which seeks to identify interaction techniques/strategies that are being applied in touchscreen devices, especially in the gaming field, to promote accessibility of PwD, more specifically those with motor coordination impairments.

2 Methodology

The methodology applied in this study was the SR process following the PRISMA model (Preferred Reporting Items for Systematic Reviews and Meta-Analyses) [7], based on the searching strings combination applied in the IEEE and ACM database, aiming to find answers for the following research questions:

(1) What interaction techniques/strategies are applied in games for mobile devices to promote accessibility of people with motor coordination disabilities?
(2) What accessibility evaluation parameters are being applied in games for mobile devices?

The SR followed three steps: planning, conducting and extracting results. In the planning stage, an SR protocol was established with guidelines that were followed throughout the review. In the SR conduction stage, primary studies from the last five years (2012–2016) were sought for in order to find new approaches. In the phase of extraction of results, the answers to the research questions were looked into in the studies included in the final selection of the SR.

Figure 1 presents the number of articles included and excluded in the SR process.

As can be observed in Fig. 1, 188 studies were identified by applying search strings. In the preliminary screening phase, 25 articles were selected, out of which 13 articles were included in the final SR selection. These articles sought to answer the research questions posed in the SR protocol.

In relation to the first research question, the main aspects of each work were extracted, such as: interaction type, interaction techniques, which devices were applied in the study and if they allow the customization of control commands.

Concerning the second research question, we identified some parameters to evaluate the PwD user experience in touchscreen devices such as the execution time of a certain task in the game, the rate of errors and hits made by the players and the status of

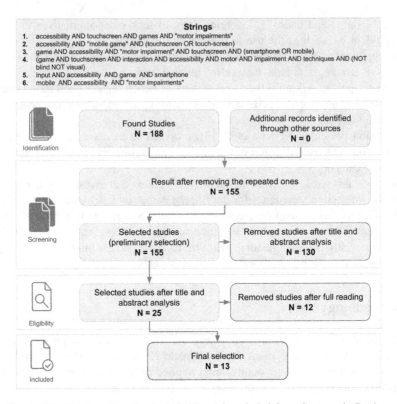

Fig. 1. Distribution of studies included in and excluded from Systematic Review.

the game at the end of the experience, i.e. whether the player was able to complete the task or gave up in the face of the difficulties. These parameters can help in assessing accessibility and proposing improvements in applications, providing a greater technology inclusion.

Section 3 presents the results of the Systematic Review for each research question investigated in this study.

3 Results of Systematic Review

Regarding the first research question, from the results of the SR, two types of interaction were identified: (a) **direct interaction** - when the adopted technique requires touching directly on the device screen [4, 6, 8–10]; (b) **indirect interaction** - when it requires the use of external resources (i.e. controllers, sensors, assistive technology) to aid interaction [11–13]. It should be noted that some of the studies included in the SR present both types of interaction [3, 5, 14–16].

Table 1 shows types of interaction (direct and indirect), interaction techniques and the mobile devices used in the experiments of the reviewed studies.

Table 1. Main interaction techniques identified

Interaction types	Interaction techniques	Mobile devices
Direct	- Extended Thumb [8]	Samsung Galaxy Note
	- Touch Guard [4]	Nexus 5
	- Assistive Touch [6]	IPhone 4S
	- Tap Gesture [9]	IPod Touch 4G
	- Button Touch [10]	Not described
Direct/Indirect	- Touch Gesture, device movement, multi-touch [3]	IPhones, IPads
	- Touch with body [14]	IPads, IPhones and others smartphones.
	- Hierarchical Scanning [5]	Not described
	- Screen resources application and SIRI [15]	IPhones, Android devices
	- Head Mounted, clicker and Tap gesture [16]	IPads, Tablets
Indirect	- Matrix Scan [11]	Samsung Galaxy Mega 6.3
	- Flip Mouse [12]	Android devices
	- Head Tracker [13]	IPad

Direct interaction techniques included adjustments in the size of the buttons as well as applications that reproduce the touch virtually. On the other hand, indirect interaction techniques do not require direct contact with the mobile device's screen, opting for external devices.

An important feature that can be used in external devices that require communication with the device itself is to develop such devices so that they support the use of On-The-Go (OTG) USB cable as suggested by Aigner et al. [12]. OTG cables allow you to connect external devices such as mouse, keyboard and joysticks to Android devices, in addition to being inexpensive. However, some external resources require more electric power and the power supplied by the OTG cable is not enough for its operation. In these cases, some other source of power will have to be used, reducing the mobility that mobile devices provide, or choose to use another approach, such as devices that communicate over Bluetooth.

The following sections describe the contributions of each work presented in Table 1 seeking to highlight the main objective, results obtained, which techniques and interaction strategies were used, and which parameters were used to verify accessibility issues.

3.1 Direct Interaction

More and more users are using mobile devices with larger screens, often making it difficult to reach the farthest regions on the screen. Considering this problem, Lai and Zhang [8] developed and evaluated the ExtendedThumb virtual finger, to make the use of these devices easier using only one hand. ExtendedThumb allows users to configure virtual finger distance in reference to the location of the actual finger touch.

Thirty-six participants were selected for the evaluation process, in which they had an initial time for get acquainted and familiar with the three interaction techniques (including direct touch, MagStick and ExtendedThumb). In the test, a 15 min time was established for the task execution in a game where small white rectangles were randomly highlighted on the screen for the user to select. The features that were analyzed to evaluate the interaction techniques were: difficulty in reaching specific regions, time to complete the task, selection errors and the users' own perceptions. ExtendedThumb obtained the fewest errors when compared with other techniques; however, an average time result was reached, between touch on the screen (faster) and MagStick (slower), considering task completion. Figure 2 shows the ExtendedThumb interaction technique with different distance adjustments of the virtual finger compared with the real finger. Figure 3 shows the test environment that was used in the user experiment [8].

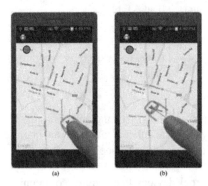

Fig. 2. ExtendedThumb.

Fig. 3. ExtendedThumb test environment.

The study of Zhong et al. [4] sought to reduce the difficulty caused by hand tremor in people with some kind of motor impairment, and they developed an experimental screen assistive system known as Touch Guard, which is an application service that runs in the background of devices providing enhanced touch screen techniques and, once installed, users can enable it and grant the permissions required for the feature to work. Touch Guard was designed for Android OS and is compatible with any application installed on it. In this study, the tests were performed with motor disabled users in a laboratory, in which eight participants with hand problems that affect accuracy were recruited; it is worth mentioning that none of the participants used Assistive Technologies (AT) in their own devices. In the tests, everyone used their own fingers to interact with the screen and the sessions lasted 90 min for each participant.

The experiment started with a brief introduction and an interview to understand the needs of each participant, followed by pre-defined tasks and, ultimately, user feedback for improvements. The data analyzed in the experiment were: time to perform the tasks and error rate. The authors observed that Touch Guard has the potential to solve accessibility issues for people with motor impairment in their hands on their own mobile devices, avoiding the need to purchase and use expensive hardware [4].

Trewin, Swart and Pettick [6] examined physical contact on smartphones with touchscreen. Using interviews and observations, they found that participants with motor coordination deficiency found such smartphones useful and usable; however, tablets offer several important advantages. The study sought to examine the use of touch-screen mobile devices by a group of people with motor disabilities and who are regular users of their devices; the observations focused on screen gestures to identify usability success and failure rates. Finally, the work provides a basis for guiding the development of new techniques to improve physical access to touchscreen mobile devices.

Considering that touchscreen devices are designed to respond to predefined inter-action parameters such as the response time of the recognizers of users' gestures, Montague, Nicolau and Hanson [9] analyzed which variations occur in the interaction of users with motor-coordination disabilities, since due to hand tremors or little control in their movements, this interaction technique can be a challenge. Sudoku was used in the test, in which the following parameters were collected during the four-week period: Touch Location, Touch Offset, Touch Duration, Absolute Touch Movement, Straight-line Touch Movement, Relative Touch Movement, Movement Direction Changes and Target Offset. As a result, the authors identified that not only interaction performance varies significantly between users, but also that an individual user's interaction skills were significantly different between the test sessions. Finally, the authors proposed and evaluated a new gesture recognizer to accommodate individual variables in touchscreen interactions.

A proposal to analyse accessibility issues is presented by Pelegrino et al. [10], suggesting a framework as an interaction technique for games on touch-sensitive screens, verifying how this framework could improve game accessibility and even increase the gameplay experience of users with disabilities or some limitations in motor skills. The proposal presents the use of virtual button controls, as shown in Fig. 4, which adapt to the different contexts of the game, allowing customization of the position and size of the buttons. The work presents how game developers can create specific controls for their games and how to reuse those controls by modifying the layout according to the context of the game. This feature can be used in different ways, thus helping users and changing the layout of buttons.

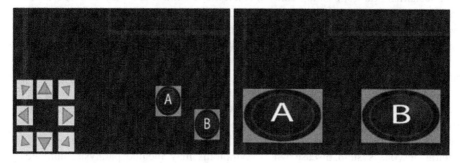

Fig. 4. Basic interface on the left and the adapted interface (right) when just buttons A and B are required [10].

3.2   Indirect Interaction

On the other hand, when physical contact with the screen of mobile devices is impossible for the user, external devices have been used to ensure user interaction. The following studies present the use of some external device as an interaction resource accessible to people with motor-coordination disabilities.

Yadav et al. [11] highlight the growth in the use of touchscreen-based devices, as well as the advances that are emerging day by day. However, the biggest difficulty still is to make these devices fit for the variables of the user's physical abilities. This study focuses on users with motor deficiency and/or difficulties in the movement of the arms.

To understand the interaction challenges, a transversal grid technique was adopted. The technique does not require direct contact with the interfaces but can be controlled using an external switch and minimal arm movements. The accessibility data analyzed in this study were: ease of software use; if the technique has made a touchscreen device more accessible; if the devise was used without much discomfort; if it was possible to navigate the device easily and if the software is an engagement model [11].

For a better evaluation of the method, meetings and interviews were conducted with real users with motor disabilities and their physicians. These interactions aimed to find real problems faced by this group of users and how this technique would be useful in their activities. The method was implemented for the users and their evaluations were recorded for analysis. One of the participants, an attending physician from a well-known neurological department approved the technique and was suggested that it would be helpful for people suffering from Parkinson's Disease and for some cases of paralysis and spinal injuries. Another participant, a physician with experience handling individuals with neurological disorders, considered that the method was significantly valuable and that the design of the switch could increase ease of use [11].

Considering that PwD are often unable to purchase an AT device or the resources available do not fully meet their accessibility needs, Aigner et al. [12] developed an alternative input device known as FLipMouse. The input device enables people with limited motor skills to use computers, smartphones or other electronic devices using their lip or finger gestures. The FLipMouse is based on a joystick and a blow sensor. In addition, two external switches can be connected as additional input resources. The device has a graphical user interface for configuration, offering flexibility in individual settings according to user needs and it is compatible with Android devices via On-The-Go (OTG) USB. The study verified the feasibility of FLipMouse in different user scenarios (games, desktop control, smartphone control and playback of a musical instrument) with people with different motor abilities; a high level of user satisfaction was confirmed, several of the test subjects continued to use the device on a daily basis. According to the authors' qualitative analysis, FlipMouse offers a high degree of adaptability not provided by similar AT products available on the market or described in their related searches.

Manresa-Yee, Roig-Maimó and Varona [13], present a head tracker for mobile devices, based on computer vision techniques, which detects the user's nose, captures its movements and turns them into a position on the screen of the mobile device. The authors performed an initial assessment with four users with multiple sclerosis (MS), central nervous system disease whose symptoms may include paralysis, numbness, spasticity, abnormal sensitivity or visual disturbances. It is worth noting that all users with MS received help in their basic daily activities due to their motor and sensory limitations. Users had control over the movement of their heads, although they had limitations in the extent of their movements and they used wheelchairs. The task completion time is displayed in the results.

3.3 Direct/Indirect Interactions

In the work published by Kim et al. [3], the authors point out that although the gaming platforms currently occupy a position among the most widespread in the world, there are few studies that examine accessibility issues in games. In the study, initial findings were identified from a survey and through a qualitative analysis of popular touchscreen games for IPad/IPhone devices, seeking to find relevant accessibility factors for people with motor coordination disabilities.

The study analyzed approximately 100 games for touch screen mobile devices, collecting information such as target size, gesture type, gender, game speed and penalties (how the game reacts to input errors). The analysis was carried out through a codebook, which was developed using an interactive process described by Kim et al. [3] apud Hruschka et al. Finally, it was possible to identify possible problems or barriers related to accessibility for users with motor coordination disabilities. Few of those games allowed users to customize accessibility resources: 24% require the use of both hands (especially action games), 50% require complex gestures such as swiping or two-finger pinch, and 10% make use of gesture capture. In this study, the authors were able to identify game features that were more accessible, such as the Free Flow game that requires only one hand for interaction and does not require interaction speed [3].

The study of Anthony, Kim and Findlater [14] emphasizes that many of the studies on usability for touchscreen interactions with people with motor impairment have been concentrated at study laboratories with few participants. Although this study did not involve game interactions, it aimed to contribute to use cases, interaction challenges and some home solutions that physically-disabled users are adopting or discovering when using touchscreen mobile devices. The data were collected by analyzing You-Tube public videos and forms filled out by people with motor disabilities.

The above-mentioned author identified two types of interaction in which 91% of the participants used direct interaction (using fingers, hands, or feet), and about 8% interacted indirectly by means of an intermediary device (header pointer). One of the videos demonstrated interaction that uses both touch and intermediary devices [14].

One of the objectives presented in this study Grammenos and Chatziantoniou [5] is related to the inclusion of users with motor and visual impairments as potential players. Next, the authors present an electronic puzzle game that provides support for one player and they describe the main design features of the user interface.

The process of creating the game was carried out during various design and development phases, including evaluation sessions with players with various profiles to assist in creating the user interface, improving gameplay in terms of accessibility, usability and fun. It is worth mentioning that the game consists of main attributes that can be adjusted to better fit the user's abilities [5].

For motor-coordination disabled users, two approaches that employ hierarchical scanning techniques were developed. In both approaches, the first step is to select a jigsaw piece and then make sequential manual changes between the puzzle pieces (using switches) or automatically (at fixed time intervals) and then press another switch when the desired item is in focus [5].

Naftali and Findlater [15] conducted two studies to investigate how smartphones are being used on a daily basis and to discover the true experience of motor-disabled users in the handling of mobile devices.

In the first study a survey was carried out with 16 interviewees. The second study was a little more thorough, including a case study involving four users with disabilities in motor coordination, in which the following techniques were applied: initial interviews lasting 30 min in which information on the following issues was collected: demographic information, medical conditions, model of smartphones that they use, frequency of use of the smartphones and AT that they use; daily sessions on smartphones (10 min), semi-structured interview with small demonstrations (1.5-2 h) and outdoor activities (at malls and other public places). Regarding AT, two users use features of the smartphones themselves to improve accessibility such as: screen magnification and text reader (Android) and a Siri personal assistant as AT [15].

The work of Read et al. [16], describes how children with multiple disabilities use tablet games in their homes. A study was carried out in which 20 children participated in their families; data were collected using daily questionnaires, interviews and observations. A group of six people described some of the difficulties faced by some of the children.

In addition, the authors present six challenges involving children with disabilities for game designers to work on:

"(1) Games that employ 'side-by-side' tablets so parents and children can play together – or games that 'switch' control from parent to child (2) App games as well as web games - web games were underplayed. (3) Games that can be customized in two directions – in terms of 'suitably aged' characters and 'suitably aged' game play (4) Forums are needed for parents of children to be able to use to suggest suitable games for other/similar children (5) Increase the amount of parental choice for simple games to support repetitive gameplay mechanics but with varying content (6) Games should be playable offline" [16].

Interaction techniques for the motor-coordination disabled people were identified such as the head mounted device (used by a child with cerebral palsy), subtle screen touches and others. The study brought gameplay experiences to children with disabilities in the broader context of family and home life. In addition to demonstrating several difficulties faced by these families and identifying a number of challenges for game developers. The study highlights the importance of the industry and academia working together to make a difference [16].

Summarizing, there are several interaction techniques and personalization parameters to promote motor accessibility, which will be considered along the investigation's continuation.

Regarding the second research question, some studies established a set of tasks the users should perform within a specific time frame and then they evaluated parameters such as error rate and task execution time [3, 4, 8].

Interface evaluation methodologies, such as cognitive course, usability test and observation, were adopted in order to verify user-friendliness [6, 11, 14, 15]. It was observed that, although PwD have difficulties in interacting directly with a touchscreen, studies found in academic literature offer interaction techniques/strategies that can render this interaction accessible and extend the gaming scope.

In summary, it should be noted that most studies allow for adjustments and that promoting inclusion is highly relevant as it allows users to customize interaction features.

4 Discussion

From the results of the SR, not only interaction techniques that promote accessibility were identified, but also low-cost and short development time adjustment parameters that can improve the interaction of motor-coordination PwD in 3D VEs, especially in mobile devices. The identified adjustment parameters are shown below.

- Interactive objects adjustment (speed, touch, size, position, time)

Users must be allowed to adjust the movement **speed** of the virtual object in the navigation scenario, so that their experience is not affected. This is because some users may not have enough precision in their movements in order to control, select, or manipulate objects.

It is worth remembering that speed adjustments can be made for both vertical movements (forward and backward) and horizontal movements (character rotation).

In order to evaluate whether the adjustment is appropriate to the needs of the user, we recommend preparing a task such as the user walking in a virtual scenario up to a certain point/location within a pre-set time.

Regarding **touch** sensitivity, users should be able to easily touch objects in the VE, with the inclusion of features such as an object touch area and response time that is appropriate to the user's needs.

We suggest that, after the first touch of the virtual object, the system allow for some time for the object to become interactive again thus avoiding errors caused by multi-touch or inaccuracies.

Regarding the **size** of the virtual objects, Manresa-Yee, Roig-Maimó and Va-rona [13] recommend adopting a minimum size of 76 pixels for any interactive object present in the VE interface.

To evaluate this parameter, we suggest using virtual testing environments similar to those presented by Lai and Zhang [8].

Regarding the **position** of the objects, it may be necessary to adjust the positioning of virtual controls. For example, in virtual joysticks, it is interesting for the user to choose the side at which the control should be available (right/left) in the interface, since users may present different degrees of accuracy in their left and right hands, or they may even lack one of their limbs. Observation may be one way of assessing the adjustment needs of this parameter.

In relation to **time**, it can be related to completing a task or a phase of the game, or as interactive objects showing in the scenario not long enough time for the user to interact. In this case, observation may also be the best way to evaluate this parameter.

- Adjusting control of external devices

Considering that virtual environments may include interaction resources by means of external devices such as hand control and wearables technology, it is important to predict possible interaction adjustments according to the needs of the user, in order to promote accessibility in the VE.

Considering that the parameters for accessibility adjustments presented must service the expected target audience for the VE, we recommend starting a 3D VE project, based on the 3D VE Design Model for PwD proposed by Conceição Junior et al. [18], and adapted as shown in Fig. 5. The model is represented by an Inverted Pyramid, which indicates the levels to be covered during the design phases of a 3D VE. The Inverted Pyramid organizes the levels according to their degree of importance, and the target audience is at the most important level due to the user-centered design methodology.

We adopted the 3D VE Design Model [18] presented in Fig. 5, including a customization step for the specific needs of each user. Mockups are tested in Participative Design sessions to verify through experiments with final users with disabilities which parameters could be adjusted to best serve those users. Mockups are adjusted and presented in new PD sessions until the ideal 3D VE solution is reached. It is important that the user participate in experiments in each development cycle, to verify if the VE is meeting the needs of the user. It is also worth remembering that involving the final user in the design of 3D VE and identifying customizable parameters can provide positive results, such as avoiding having to make adaptations after the 3D VE delivery.

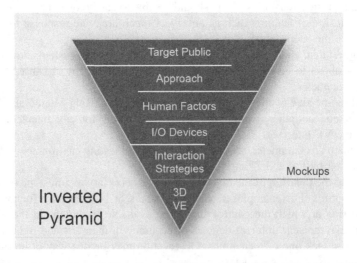

Fig. 5. Proposal for 3D User-Centered VE Design Model (adapted from [18]).

In order to illustrate the application of **Inverted Pyramid** levels, we present a case study of an 11-year-old child with cerebral palsy, called L. In this case, the **Target Audience** corresponds to L: child with cerebral palsy, with motor and speech impairment.

Regarding **Human Factors**, we have as **positive human factors** the fact that L uses the left hand well, and he writes his own name as well as some other words, writes in block letters beginning with the last letter (backward writing), shows motivation to overcome challenges and loves going to school and learning new things; he also enjoys drawing. He shows a good level of understanding, speaks isolated words. His mother reported that the child likes to play on the cell-phone and tablet and is skilled at using touchscreen interaction resources. In these devices, the child usually plays Candy Crush, but also enjoys strategy and simulation games, most especially the Pool game.

On the other hand, we can consider as **negative factors** that L is wheelchair-bound, has limited reading skills, limited vocabulary, and he is not able to form sentences. He pointed out that he does not like to play video games because he finds it difficult to handle the remote control.

When details are included in the levels of the pyramid, the **Approach** to be adopted is based on an educational game to raise awareness of the choice of the best food for a healthy diet. Additionally, the game seeks an approach that stimulates cognitive, motor and social inclusion development.

Regarding **Input/Output Devices**, the use of virtual joysticks was indicated because of the familiarity and ability that L showed in tests performed with some types of controls.

As for **Interaction strategies**, it was necessary to adjust the virtual joystick speed parameter, the size of the virtual control and its position in the interface (left or right), so that L navigated in the VE with greater accessibility considering his limitations.

5 Conclusion

The SR allowed to identify several interaction techniques that are used as accessible alternatives for games of touchscreen devices. In addition, some studies have brought about evaluation parameters, such as how to verify the effectiveness of adjustments and accessibility techniques in 3D VEs.

We noticed that promoting accessibility adjustments to meet different player profiles considering their limitations in motor coordination can be a differential in the player's experience.

From the results achieved, it is possible to recommend accessibility adjustment parameters and relating with the 3D User-Centered VE Design Model for games adapted from [18]. It is worth mentioning that it is important to involve the end user in all stages of game development, avoiding adaptations after the product is delivered.

As for future research, we intend to carry out PD sessions to develop a serious game accessible to PwD in motor coordination in partnership with CRIDAC (Dom Aquino Correa Rehabilitation Center) in the city of Cuiabá, Brazil, in order to validate the interaction techniques and accessibility adjustment parameters that were identified in the SR.

We also intend to investigate whether the error rate in the presented studies can be adopted to verify if the interaction technique reaches an acceptable accuracy rate. Additionally, we can use this data and compare it with the performance of users who do not have motor coordination deficiency in order to achieve a quality rating.

References

1. Michael, D.R., Chen, S.L.: Serious games: games that educate, train, and inform. Education, 31 October, pp. 1–95 (2005)
2. Ara, M.C.C., Jaime, S., Darin, T.G.R., Jogos, A.: Um Estudo das Recomendac¸ oes de Acessibilidade para Audiogames Moveis a a a, November 2004
3. Kim, Y., Sutreja, N., Froehlich, J., Findlater, L.: Surveying the accessibility of touchscreen games for persons with motor disabilitiess: a preliminary analysis. In: Proceedings of the 15th International ACM SIGACCESS Conference Computers and Accessibility, pp. 68:1–68:2 (2013)
4. Zhong, Y., Weber, A., Burkhardt, C., Weaver, P., Bigham, J.P.: Enhancing android accessibility for users with hand tremor by reducing fine pointing and steady tapping. In: Proceedings of the 12th Web for All Conference, pp. 29:1–29:10 (2015)
5. Grammenos, D., Chatziantoniou, A.: Jigsaw together: a distributed collaborative game for players with diverse skills and preferences. In: Proceedings of the 2014 Conference on Interaction Design and Children, pp. 205–208 (2014)
6. Trewin, S., Swart, C., Pettick, D.: Physical accessibility of touchscreen smartphones. In: Proceedings of the 15th International ACM SIGACCESS Conference on Computers and Accessibility, pp. 19:1–19:8 (2013)
7. Moher, D., Liberati, A., Tetzlaff, J., Altman, D.G.: Preferred reporting items for systematic reviews and meta-analyses: the PRISMA statement (reprinted from annals of internal medicine). Phys. Ther. **89**(9), 873–880 (2009)
8. Lai, J., Zhang, D.: ExtendedThumb: a target acquisition approach for one-handed interaction with touch-screen mobile phones. IEEE Trans. Hum.-Mach. Syst. **45**(3), 362–370 (2015)
9. Montague, K., Nicolau, H., Hanson, V.L.: Motor-impaired touchscreen interactions in the wild. In: Proceedings of the 16th International ACM SIGACCESS Conference on Computers & Accessibility, pp. 123–130 (2014)
10. Pelegrino, M., Torok, L., Trevisan, D., Clua, E.: Creating and designing customized and dynamic game interfaces using smartphones and touchscreen. In: 2014 Brazilian Symposium on Computer Games and Digital Entertainment, pp. 133–139 (2014)
11. Yadav, R., Namdeo, S., Dwivedi, K.: Matrix scan: a switch aided screen traversal mechanism for motor disabled. In: 6th International Conference on Mobile Computing, Applications and Services, pp. 168–170 (2014)
12. Aigner, B., David, V., Deinhofer, M., Veigl, C.: FLipMouse: a flexible alternative input solution for people with severe motor restrictions. In: Proceedings of the 7th International Conference on Software Development and Technologies for Enhancing Accessibility and Fighting Info-exclusion, pp. 25–32 (2016)
13. Manresa-Yee, C., Roig-Maimó, M.F., Varona, J.: Mobile accessibility: a head-tracker for users with motor disabilities. In: Proceedings of the XVII International Conference on Human Computer Interaction, pp. 15:1–15:2 (2016)
14. Anthony, L., Kim, Y., Findlater, L.: Analyzing user-generated youtube videos to understand touchscreen use by people with motor impairments. In: Proceedings of the SIGCHI Conference on Human Factors in Computing Systems, pp. 1223–1232 (2013)

15. Naftali, M., Findlater, L.: Accessibility in context: understanding the truly mobile experience of smartphone users with motor impairments. In: Proceedings of the 16th International ACM SIGACCESS Conference on Computers & Accessibility, pp. 209–216 (2014)
16. Read, J.C., Clarke, S., Fitton, D., Joes, R., Horton, M., Sim, G.: Touching base on children's interactions with tablet games. In: Extended Abstracts Publication of the Annual Symposium on Computer-Human Interaction in Play, pp. 61–72 (2017)
17. Hruschka, D.J., Picone-decaro, E., Jenkins, R.A., Carey, J.W.: Reliability in coding open-ended data : lessons learned from **16**(3), 307–331 (2004)
18. Vicente, A., Júnior, C., Borges, L.C.L.D.F., Ramos, K.C., Nunes, E.P.S.: Uma Revisão de Literatura sobre Recomendações de Design de Jogos Digitais 3D para Pessoas com Deficiência. In: 19th Symposium Virtual and Augmented Reality (2017)

A Collaborative Virtual Game to Support Activity and Social Engagement for Older Adults

Jing Fan[1,7(✉)], Linda Beuscher[3,7], Paul Newhouse[4,7],
Lorraine C. Mion[5,6], and Nilanjan Sarkar[1,2,7]

[1] Electrical Engineering and Computer Science Department,
Vanderbilt University, Nashville, TN, USA
jing.fan@vanderbilt.edu
[2] Mechanical Engineering Department, Vanderbilt University,
Nashville, TN, USA
[3] School of Nursing, Vanderbilt University, Nashville, TN, USA
[4] Center for Cognitive Medicine, Department of Psychiatry and Behavioral
Sciences, Geriatric Research Education and Clinical Center, Tennessee Valley
Veterans Affairs Medical Center, Vanderbilt University, Nashville, TN, USA
[5] Center of Excellence in Critical and Complex Care, College of Nursing,
The Ohio State University, Columbus, OH, USA
[6] The Ohio State University, Columbus, OH, USA
[7] Vanderbilt University, Nashville, TN, USA

Abstract. Many older adults suffer from Alzheimer's disease or other dementias and have affected cognitive abilities. In general, physical exercise, cognitive stimulation, and social engagement have been found to be beneficial for the physical and mental health of older adults with and without cognitive impairment. In an effort to address these needs, researchers have been developing human-machine interaction (HMI) systems to administer activity-oriented therapies. However, most of these system, while promising, focus on one-on-one interaction with the computer and thus do not support social engagement by involving multiple older adults. In this paper, we present the design and development of a motion-based collaborative virtual environment (CVE) application to support both activity and social engagement. The CVE task is based on a book-sorting activity and has embedded collaborative components to encourage human-human interaction (HHI). The system records quantitative data regarding users' performance, interaction frequency, and social interaction. A preliminary user study was conducted to validate system usability and test on older adults' tolerance and acceptance of the motion-based user interface (UI) as well as the CVE task. The results showed the usability of the motion-based UI and system capability to assess HMI and HHI from recorded quantitative data. The results from post-test and analysis of audio files indicated that the system might be potentially useful. More user study and data analysis need to be conducted to further investigate the CVE system.

Keywords: Collaborative virtual environment (CVE)
Human-Machine interaction (HMI) · Human-Human interaction (HHI)
Elder care · Dementia

© Springer International Publishing AG, part of Springer Nature 2018
M. Antona and C. Stephanidis (Eds.): UAHCI 2018, LNCS 10907, pp. 192–204, 2018.
https://doi.org/10.1007/978-3-319-92049-8_14

1 Introduction

The number of older adults in the US is increasing dramatically, growing from 35 million in 2000 to an estimated 74 million in 2030 [1]. Many older adults suffer from Alzheimer's disease or other dementias, which affect their memory and/or other cognitive skills such as communication, ability to focus, and reasoning. An additional 15–20% older adults have mild cognitive impairment (MCI) and are at high risk of developing dementia [2]. In addition to the prevalence, Alzheimer's and many other dementias are progressive and costly. In 2017, dementia cost the nation $259 billion [2]. To date, there is no cure to slow or stop Alzheimer's and most dementias. Activity-oriented therapies, including regular physical exercise, cognitive stimulation, and social engagement, have been found to be beneficial for the physical and mental health of older adults with and without cognitive impairment (CI) and may reduce the risk of developing Alzheimer's disease and other dementias [1–4].

In order to mitigate the substantial emotional, financial, and physical burdens of caregivers, researchers have been investigating applications of sensor-based technologies, virtual avatars/environments, and robotics to support the care of older adults [5]. Many systems were designed to assist older adults in aging in place by monitoring their behaviors and providing alarms and reminders through networks of sensors [6, 7]. Animal robots, such as PARO, and telepresence robots, such as Giraff, were developed to provide older adults with social support and reduce their stress [6, 8]. More recently, intelligent systems have been developed to administer activity-oriented therapies. McColl et al. developed a socially assistive robotic (SAR) system Brian to encourage older adults with and without CI during a meal eating activity and a cognitively stimulating activity [9]. Fasola et al. designed a SAR system Bandit to administer physical exercise sessions with older adults [10]. Young et al. developed a platform consisting of a Wii balance board and a virtual environment for the purpose of training older adults' balance function through interacting with virtual tasks [11]. Anderson-Hanley et al. compared the effect of stationary cycling with and without virtual reality tours on older adults' cognition and found that cycling with virtual reality tours had greater potential for preventing cognitive decline [12]. Although these systems were promising in their ability to engage older adults in activity-oriented therapies and potentially benefit their cognitive function, the systems focus solely on one-on-one interaction with the system and thus do not support social engagement by involving multiple older adults simultaneously. Without social interaction with other humans, many older adults feel socially isolated and can suffer from apathy [13].

Research on computer/SAR systems interacting with multiple older adults is still in its early stage. Matsusaka et al. developed a SAR system TAIZO to lead physical exercise session in front of a group of older adults [14]. TAIZO is an open-loop system and does not have the ability to analyze older adults' performance during interaction. Louie et al. developed a SAR system Tangy which can play a bingo game with a group of older adults in a closed-loop fashion [15]. The system can interact with the group as a whole or with each individual. However, it could not capture social interaction among the older adults. In our previous work, we developed a SAR system RAMU that could engage two older adults simultaneously in a physically and cognitively stimulating activity [16]. Although social communications were observed during the interaction, the task was not designed to promote social engagement.

In this work, we designed and developed a novel collaborative virtual environment (CVE) that through human-machine interaction (HMI) actively supports activity and social engagement for older adults with and without CI. In this CVE, two older adults interact with a virtual environment through physical movements. Collaborative components are embedded within the CVE design to encourage human-human interaction (HHI) in addition to HMI. The CVE continuously evaluates older adults' activity compliance and collaboration status in order to provide feedback to keep older adults engaged in both HMI and HHI. We believe that the CVE system with the ability to support social engagement will be more beneficial in enhancing the overall health of older adults than systems focusing solely on older adults' functional ability. In this paper, we present the development of the CVE and the preliminary user study results on system validation and older adults' tolerance and acceptance of the system. The rest of the paper is organized as follows. Section 2 describes the overall system framework and details the design and development of the motion-based CVE application. Section 3 presents the experimental setup and procedure as well as the participants' information. Section 4 provides the results on system usability and participants' interaction including performance, interaction frequency, and conversation duration. Finally, we conclude the paper in Sect. 5 with a discussion of the current results, the limitations, and future directions.

2   System Design

2.1   Overview

The system has two main components: a motion-based CVE application and a robotic facilitator. Figure 1 illustrates the overall system framework. Two users interact with the CVE through a motion-based user interface (UI) using the Kinect sensor [17]. The *Data Management* module is responsible for recording users' real time interaction data. Users' interaction together with the change of the game state trigger audio-visual feedback from the CVE application to support HMI and HHI. In addition, the CVE application sends events to a physically embodied robot through socket communication in order to provide additional feedback and facilitate HMI and HHI. A humanoid robot NAO [18] was used to serve as an artificial intelligent (AI) player, to help users on their motion-based cursor control and to encourage collaboration. In this paper, we focus on the design and development of the motion-based CVE application. The CVE application is based on a sorting activity where older adults sort books with different colors into color-matched collection bins. The Unity game engine [19] was used to develop the 3D book-sorting task shown in Fig. 2. Each user controls one hand cursor in the CVE by upper body movement and hand manipulation. The subsections that follow elaborate on the design of the motion-based UI, the models of computation used to develop the CVE task, and the *data management* module.

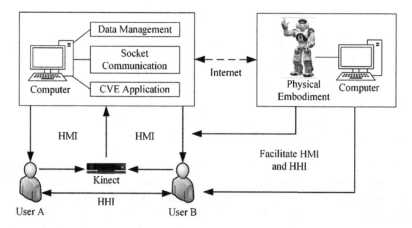

Fig. 1. System framework overview.

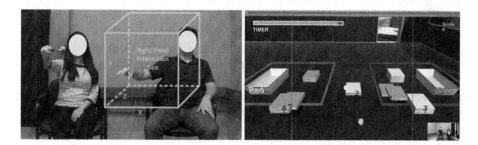

Fig. 2. Two users were interacting with the CVE. (Color figure online)

2.2 Motion-Based UI

We implemented a motion-based UI to introduce physical activity in the CVE task as well as to remove the need for keyboard and mouse, which are not user friendly for older adults. The motion-based UI is designed based on Kinect's skeletal tracking function and hand tracking function. The first step is to map each user's hand joint position to the cursor position in the CVE. This is realized by defining an interaction box for each hand (Fig. 2) and mapping the relative positions of the hand joint with respect to the interaction box to the cursor positions in the CVE. The positions and the sizes of the interaction boxes are defined by each user's left shoulder (SL), right shoulder (SR), left hip (HL), right hip (HR), and spine base (SB) joints and are listed in Table 1. When users move their hands to the left, the hand cursors move to the left of the CVE, otherwise the hand cursors move to the right. Similarly, when users move their hands down, the hand cursors move down, otherwise the hand cursors move up. The hand cursor does not move in the third dimension unless the user is holding onto a book. Users move books closer to them by moving their hands towards their chest and move books away from them by moving their hands away from their chest.

Table 1. Definition of interaction box.

Axis	Left hand		Right hand	
X	$x_{min} = SR_x - 1.15 \cdot 2 \cdot (SR_x - HL_x)$		$x_{min} = SL_x + 0.15 \cdot 2 \cdot (HR_x - SL_x)$	
	$x_{max} = SR_x - 0.15 \cdot 2 \cdot (SR_x - HL_x)$		$x_{max} = SL_x + 1.15 \cdot 2 \cdot (HR_x - SL_x)$	
Y	$y_{min} = HR_y + 0.7 \cdot (SR_y - HR_y)$		$y_{min} = HL_y + 0.7 \cdot (SL_y - HL_y)$	
	$y_{max} = SR_y + 0.7 \cdot (SR_y - HR_y)$		$y_{max} = SL_y + 0.7 \cdot (SL_y - HL_y)$	
Z	$z_{min} = SB_z - 0.5, z_{max} = SB_z$		$z_{min} = SB_z - 0.5, z_{max} = SB_z$	

The second step is to determine which hand is currently controlling the cursor and to allow book manipulation by simple hand gestures. We designed a hierarchical state machine (HSM) to handle hand switching and hand manipulation (Fig. 3). The current control hand is determined by the relative positions of user's left and right hands and interaction boxes. The left hand is interacting (LHI) if its position is within or around the left hand interaction box, similarly for the right hand. When there is no hand cursor and LHI event occurs, left hand is the current control hand that moves the cursor. If only the right hand is interacting (RHI), right hand is set as the current control hand. In the case that both LHI and RHI events occur, the hand that was interacting with the system is set as the current control hand. Kinect's hand state detection algorithm returns five possible hand states, which are closed, lasso, not tracked, open, and unknown. Initially, the *left or right hand cursor* is in *release state*. If *closed* or *lasso hand state* event is detected, the cursor state takes the transition to *grip state*. If *open hand state* is detected, the cursor state becomes *release state*. Cursor movements together with hand manipulations enable users to grip, move, and release virtual objects in the CVE through physical movements.

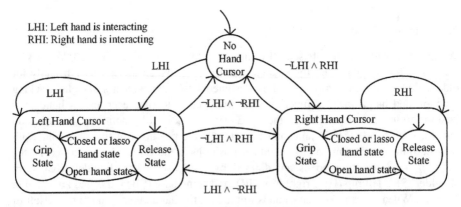

Fig. 3. User interface model.

2.3   CVE Task Design

Main Task. For the purpose of supporting social engagement, we embedded collaborative components in the task so that users have to communicate with each other by verbally exchanging information or physically moving books. The virtual space is divided into two interaction areas, marked by the red and green vertical lines (Fig. 2). Different users' left and right interaction boxes are mapped to different interaction areas. The red cursor can move freely to the left of the green vertical line whereas the green cursor can move freely to the right of the red vertical line. As a result, the virtual space in between the red and green vertical lines is accessible by both users. The red cursor cannot move books inside the green collection bin, and the green cursor cannot move books inside the red collection bin. We refer to the virtual space that is accessible by only the red cursor as red only area (ROA). The green only area (GOA) is defined in the similar way. Notice that some red books are in GOA and some green books are in ROA. These books are designated as 'team bonus' books. Implicit rules for collaboration are attached to these books by varying the scores of the books. If the users collaborate, the score of the book increases. Otherwise, the score of the book decreases or remains low. When the green cursor moves a red team bonus book from GOA inside the red square, it is easy for the red cursor to collect the book. Such a move is called a collaborative move. When red cursor moves a green book away from green cursor's interaction area, i.e., inside ROA, the green cursor is not able to collect the book and the move is called a competitive move. The restricted interaction areas together with the team bonus books form the collaborative components in the CVE task.

The CVE was modeled by timed automata and HSMs to support both continuous and discrete events, state hierarchy, and concurrency. There are models for displaying audio-visual feedback, for online analysis of users' interactions, for movement and score of books, for determining when a book is selected by which user, and for socket communication. It is not possible to present all the models, instead we focus on the HSM model for the books. Figure 4 illustrates the top level model that describes how users change book positions and scores. The *Book Manager* state keeps track of the number of red and green books in the CVE, spawns new books, and removes collected books from the bins. The *Book Position Adjustment* state gradually shifts the books inside the camera view of the CVE in the event users drop the books at the boundaries to guarantee enough visibility of books. Each book has its own concurrent state machines, one for controlling the position and movement of the book, and one for controlling the score of the book. Initially, books are spawned at four locations in the CVE. Users grab a book by moving their hand cursors onto a book and closing their hands (grip cursor state). A selected book is highlighted and moves in the environment following the user's hand cursor. Another user cannot grab and move the book that is currently highlighted. When the book is in *move* state and *release* event is detected, the selected book drops onto the virtual floor by gravity. If the book drops in a color-matched bin, it is collected and removed from the scene (*collect* state). Otherwise, it stays on the floor (*stay* state). The *release* event in Fig. 4 occurs if the user open his/her hand (release cursor state) or the distance between cursor and the book center is above the threshold (200 in pixels). Although a moving book always follows the position of cursor, when the user tries to move the book below the virtual floor, *release* event is triggered and the book goes back to *stay* state. The initial score for each book is 5 points. For team bonus books, *collaborative move* event increases the score to 10 points and *competitive move* event decreases the score back to 5 points. The *countdown timer* state records the remaining interaction time and would end the task after 6 min. There are 6 normal books and 10 team bonus books. Users can achieve a maximum score of 80 points without collaboration and a maximum score of 130 points with collaboration. To win the game, they need to receive at least 100 points.

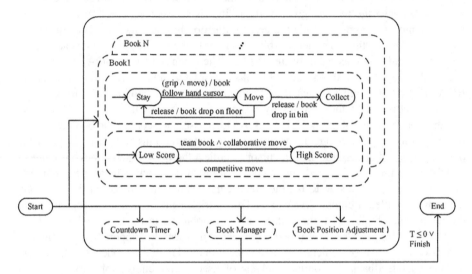

Fig. 4. Hierarchical state machine (HSM) describing movement and score of books.

Post-test Task. The post-test (Fig. 5) is designed to explore users' behaviors when they perform a similar task (book sorting) with unknown information. Users see yellow books and a yellow bin but are not aware of the new collaborative rule that they have to move the same book simultaneously (or together) in the same direction. We were interested to see whether users would communicate with each other to figure out the unknown piece of the task. If they cannot move any yellow books half way through the interaction (3 min in total), the robotic facilitator gives them a hint by asking them to try moving the book together. No score is associated with the yellow books, instead we record how far users move yellow books together and how many books are collected.

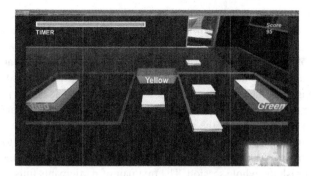

Fig. 5. Post-test task. (Color figure online)

2.4   Data Management

The *data management* module records users' interactions with the CVE application and with each other. These data are stored in csv format in real time and are indexed by timestamps. The performance data file logs the number of books collected for each book type and by each user, the number of collaborative and competitive moves by each user, the time to finish the task, and the total score. The user interaction file logs the motion-based cursor control of each user. These include the interaction hand (left or right), the hand state, the position and type of selected book, and the screen position of the hand cursors. In addition, we record users' conversations as audio files. Audio files are later transcribed to analyze the content of the conversation. All the data are stored in data buffers and written locally when buffers are full or the task ends.

3   Experimental Design

A small user study was conducted with two pairs of older adults. The study was approved by the Vanderbilt Institutional Review Board. Before the experiment, participants completed the Montreal cognitive assessment (MoCA© Version 7.1) [20] to evaluate their cognition. Participants' information is shown in Table 2. In the experiment room,

Table 2. Participant data.

Pair ID	Participant ID	Age	Gender	Cognition	MoCA score
Pair 1	P01	83	Female	MCI	23
	P02	72	Female	Normal	27
Pair 2	P03	71	Female	MCI	25
	P04	77	Female	Dementia	21

there were two chairs, two web cameras, two microphones, a Kinect, a 32-in HD monitor and a NAO robot on the table. An experimenter operated the CVE system and observed older adults' interaction through a one-way mirror in the observation room (Fig. 6). Participants sat approximately two meters away from the monitor and at a 30% angle toward each other. When a single participant played the game with the robot, one chair was positioned directly in front of the table. The experimental procedure had five components or games (Fig. 6). Each participant first interacted independently with the system and then pairs of participants played with each other. In the *Practice* game, the robot taught participants how to interact with the system by arm movement and hand manipulation. The length of the *Practice* depended on how long it took for participants to become familiar with the motion-based UI and collect their first book. Participants then played the main task alone with the robot as the second player. After two older adults completed the single user games, they were paired to play the main task together. They first took turns to play the game and then played simultaneously. Lastly, they completed the *post-test* to finish the whole session. The first pair of participants finished the session in one visit, and the second pair finished single user games in the first visit and paired games in the second visit.

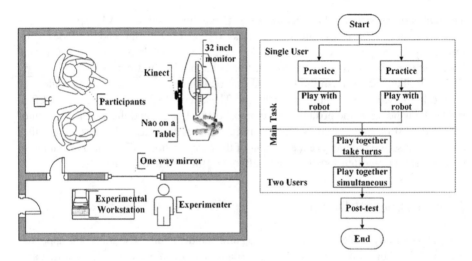

Fig. 6. Experimental setup and procedure.

4   Results

4.1   System Usability

The system worked as designed. For the main task, every collaborative move triggered a rewarding sound and every competitive move triggered an unpleasant sound. Books were spawned correctly, and the movement and score of books followed the HSM model described in Fig. 4. For the post-test task, the yellow books moved in the CVE according to design. When only one participant grabbed a book or two participants tried to move books in different directions, the yellow books did not move. All data files were recorded correctly. Unity was not responsive at the end of one game; for that game the data files were recorded up to the point when the system froze. In the *practice* game, robot NAO taught participants how to interact with the system step by step following the action order in Table 3. When participants successfully performed one action, NAO proceeded to teach the next action. We computed the time duration for participants to learn each motion-based actions. Participants were able to learn most actions quickly, within one minute, and took about a minute to collect one book successfully. P01 took longer to move a book up and down and collect a book. The rest of the participants took longer to move book forward. From the audio files, participants asked questions like "What am I moving up and down?", "Is backward this way and is forward this way?", "This way or that way? When you say forward." This indicates that participants got confused about the instructions related to depth in the virtual environment. There was no need for operator assistance once participants were familiar with the motion-based UI. There were times participants struggled to master *move book forward* action. The depth in the CVE is relatively hard for older adults to perceive correctly. Due to the fact that normal aging or Alzheimer's disease may affect older adults' sensitivity to depth [21, 22], the motion-based actions related to depth in virtual environment can be challenging for older adults.

Table 3. Time takes for older adults to learn motion-based actions.

Order	Actions	P01 (s)	P02 (s)	P03 (s)	P04 (s)
1	Activate motion-based UI	15.687	6.807	6.815	6.800
2	Switch hand	14.155	15.122	24.788	15.264
3	Grab book	20.761	20.593	20.097	20.100
4	Move book left to right	29.180	30.590	30.220	43.695
5	Move book up and down	*99.514*[a]	16.134	15.772	31.388
6	Move book forward	18.295	*90.755*[b]	*96.861*[a]	*103.697*[a,b]
7	Move book backward	32.717	18.859	37.101	57.502
8	Collect book	*68.502*[a]	62.304	57.252	NA

[a]received help from experimenter; [b]confused about system instructions.

4.2 Interaction Data

Table 4 gives the results of participants' main task performance and their interaction frequency as quantified by hand and book movements in the CVE. Collect and collaboration are the number of books collected and the number of books increased score due to collaboration, respectively. Potential collaboration is the number of times participants tried to collaborate but failed to move books into red or green squares. The main reason is that they failed to perform the *move book forward* action correctly. This action is relatively hard as shown in Table 3. Hand movement is the normalized accumulated cursor movement per minute. Averaged book distance is the mean value of the travel distance of books moved by participants. Book movement is the accumulated book movement per minute. These three metrics were calculated as indicators of participants' interaction frequency. If participants were not engaged with the CVE task, they were less likely to interact with the system and all the indicators would have low values. Due to the small sample size, we are unable to draw any conclusions by comparing the results in Table 4. On average, participants' collaboration decreased when playing together, however, potential collaboration complemented the difference. In fact, it is easier to play with the robot than play with another human. When playing with another human, participants need to worry about their own part of the task as well as their peers' performance. The interaction frequency are similar for all the main task games, single or dyad. Note that in *take turns* game, each participant interacted about half the total interaction time. Therefore, hand movement and book movement indicators of *take turns* are relatively low compared to that of the other games. P03 and P04 performed poorly during *take turns* game. *Take turns* game is the first task on their second visit to the lab. P03 did not perform well initially. Since the turn switches after one user successfully collects a book or makes a collaborative move, P04 had very few interaction with the CVE and therefore also collected fewer books.

Table 4. Participants' performance, interaction frequency, and conversation duration.

	Play with robot				Play together - take turns				Play together - simultaneous			
	P01	P02	P03	P04	P01	P02	P03	P04	P01	P02	P03	P04
Collect	8	7	8	7	8	7	3	3	8	6	8	8
Collaboration	4	1	4	2	0	2	0	0	0	1	1	2
Potential collaboration	0	2	1	0	4	2	0	1	4	2	2	1
Hand movement	13.2	22.0	9.4	10.7	5.5	15.3	1.1	3.7	18.1	16.0	12.6	7.5
Averaged book distance	13.8	16.0	4.7	9.1	12.6	13.0	13.9	5.2	7.8	10.8	9.7	9.1
Book movement	64.6	100.2	33.0	48.6	29.3	73.5	6.9	14.7	64.8	75.5	39.8	37.0
Conversation duration (s)	NA	NA	NA	NA	59	62	16	47	48	75	55	75

In terms of the post-test task, P01 and P02 collected one yellow book without help from the robotic facilitator. They moved two yellow books, one had a travel distance of 4.0 and the other had a travel distance of 5.3. P03 and P04 received a hint from the robot to move book together and were able to collect one yellow book. They moved three books in total. The moving distances were 6.2, 1.4, and 6.9 respectively.

Participants talked with each other a lot. Their conversation mostly focused on helping each other with how to move and collect books, how to increase the score of the book, and remind their peers what hand cursor they were controlling. We computed the amount of HHI by counting the time duration they talked directly to each other. The results are listed in Table 4.

5 Discussion and Conclusion

We developed a CVE system for the purpose of supporting activity and social engagement for older adults with and without CI. For activity engagement, we designed a motion-based UI using Kinect to involve older adults' in physical movement, and developed a book-sorting task to involve older adults' in cognitive activity.

For social engagement, we designed collaborative rules to encourage social communication between older adults. Older adults have to collaborate with each other in order to win the game. The system records quantitative data regarding participants' individual and collaborative performance, their interaction frequency with the CVE system, and logs audio data for offline analysis of their social interaction in the form of conversation.

A preliminary user study was conducted with two pairs of older adults. The sample used for the current study is obviously too small to draw any conclusion on the ability of the system to benefit older adults. However, the current results provide insights on the usability and older adults' acceptance of the motion-based UI and the CVE task. The results indicate the difficulty of depth perception and control in virtual environment for older adults. Older adults enjoyed the collaborative virtual game and some indicated their preference to play with another human than with the robot. The results also demonstrate the ability of the CVE system to collect quantitative data needed to assess older adults' performance, interaction frequency, and social communication. Audio data analysis and participants' post-test performance further show promising results that participants were capable of collaboration without knowing the rules and they were talking with each other during game playing.

In the future, we intend to conduct more experiments and collect other modalities of data such as gaze in order to systematically evaluate HMI and HHI. We are also interested in the content of the conversation. The content could help guide the design of better collaborative components as well as system feedback. In addition, we plan to design 2D task instead of 3D task to remove the depth in the collaborative game. The new task will have different difficulty levels to accommodate older adults with different cognition level.

Acknowledgement. This work was supported by the National Institute of Health Grant 1R21AG 050483-01A1.

References

1. Federal Interagency Forum on Aging-Related Statistics: Older Americans 2016: Key Indicators of Well-Being. Federal Interagency Forum on Aging-Related Statistics (2016)
2. Alzheimer's Association: 2017 Alzheimer's disease facts and figures. Alzheimer's Dementia **13**(4), 325–373 (2017)
3. Karp, A., Paillard-Borg, S., Wang, H.-X., Silverstein, M., Winblad, B., Fratiglioni, L.: Mental, physical and social components in leisure activities equally contribute to decrease dementia risk. Dement. Geriatr. Cogn. Disord. **21**(2), 65–73 (2006)
4. Farina, N., Rusted, J., Tabet, N.: The effect of exercise interventions on cognitive outcome in Alzheimer's disease: a systematic review. Int. Psychogeriatr. **26**(1), 9–18 (2014)
5. Ienca, M., Fabrice, J., Elger, B., Caon, M., Pappagallo, A.S., Kressig, R.W., Wangmo, T.: Intelligent assistive technology for Alzheimer's disease and other dementias: a systematic review. J. Alzheimers Dis. **56**(4), 1301–1340 (2017)

6. Coradeschi, S., Cesta, A., Cortellessa, G., Coraci, L., Gonzalez, J., Karlsson, L., Furfari, F., Loutfi, A., Orlandini, A., Palumbo, F.: Giraffplus: combining social interaction and long term monitoring for promoting independent living. In: 2013 the 6th International Conference on Human System Interaction (HSI), pp. 578–585 (2013)

7. Rashidi, P., Mihailidis, A.: A survey on ambient-assisted living tools for older adults. IEEE J. Biomed. Health Inform. **17**(3), 579–590 (2013)

8. Wada, K., Shibata, T., Saito, T., Sakamoto, K., Tanie, K.: Psychological and social effects of one year robot assisted activity on elderly people at a health service facility for the aged. In: Proceedings of the 2005 IEEE International Conference on Robotics and Automation, ICRA 2005, pp. 2785–2790 (2005)

9. McColl, D., Louie, W.Y.G., Nejat, G.: Brian 2.1: a socially assistive robot for the elderly and cognitively impaired. Robot. Autom. Mag. **20**(1), 74–83 (2013)

10. Fasola, J., Matarić, M.J.: A socially assistive robot exercise coach for the elderly. J. Hum. Robot Interact. **2**(2), 3–32 (2013)

11. Young, W., Ferguson, S., Brault, S., Craig, C.: Assessing and training standing balance in older adults: a novel approach using the 'Nintendo Wii' Balance Board. Gait Posture **33**(2), 303–305 (2011)

12. Anderson-Hanley, C., Arciero, P.J., Brickman, A.M., Nimon, J.P., Okuma, N., Westen, S.C., Merz, M.E., Pence, B.D., Woods, J.A., Kramer, A.F.: Exergaming and older adult cognition: a cluster randomized clinical trial. Am. J. Prev. Med. **42**(2), 109–119 (2012)

13. Ishii, S., Weintraub, N., Mervis, J.R.: Apathy: a common psychiatric syndrome in the elderly. J. Am. Med. Dir. Assoc. **10**(6), 381–393 (2009)

14. Matsusaka, Y., Fujii, H., Okano, T., Hara, I.: Health exercise demonstration robot TAIZO and effects of using voice command in robot-human collaborative demonstration. In: The 18th IEEE International Symposium on Robot and Human Interactive Communication, RO-MAN 2009, pp. 472–477 (2009)

15. Louie, W.Y.G., Vaquero, T., Nejat, G., Beck, J.C.: An autonomous assistive robot for planning, scheduling and facilitating multi-user activities. In: 2014 IEEE International Conference on Robotics and Automation (ICRA), pp. 5292–5298 (2014)

16. Fan, J., Beuscher, L., Newhouse, P.A., Mion, L.C., Sarkar, N.: A robotic coach architecture for multi-user human-robot interaction (RAMU) with the elderly and cognitively impaired. In: 2016 25th IEEE International Symposium on Robot and Human Interactive Communication (RO-MAN), pp. 445–450 (2016)

17. Microsoft. https://developer.microsoft.com/en-us/windows/kinect/develop. Accessed 29 Sept 2017

18. SoftBank Robotics. https://www.softbankrobotics.com/us/nao. Accessed 19 Feb 2018

19. Unity. https://unity3d.com/. Accessed 29 Sept 2017

20. Doerflinger, D.M.C.: Mental status assessment in older adults: Montreal Cognitive Assessment: MoCA Version 7.1 (original version). Clin. Neuropsychol. **25**(1), 119–126 (2012)

21. Holmin, J., Nawrot, M.: The effects of aging on the perception of depth from motion parallax. Atten. Percept. Psychophys. **78**(6), 1681–1691 (2016)

22. Lee, C.-N., Ko, D., Suh, Y.-W., Park, K.-W.: Cognitive functions and stereopsis in patients with Parkinson's disease and Alzheimer's disease using 3-dimensional television: a case controlled trial. PLoS ONE **10**(3), e0123229 (2015)

Evaluation of an English Word Look-Up Tool for Web-Browsing with Sign Language Video for Deaf Readers

Dhananjai Hariharan, Sedeeq Al-khazraji, and Matt Huenerfauth[✉]

Rochester Institute of Technology, Rochester, NY 14623, USA
{dh1723,sha6709,matt.huenerfauth}@rit.edu

Abstract. Research has shown that some people who are Deaf or Hard of Hearing (DHH) in the U.S. have lower levels of English language literacy than their hearing peers, which creates a barrier to access web content for these users. We have designed an interface to assist these users in reading English text on web pages; users can click on certain marked words to view an ASL sign video in a pop-up. A user study was conducted to evaluate this tool and compare it with web pages containing only text, as well as pages where users can click on words and see text-definitions using the Google Dictionary plug-in for browsers. The study assessed participants' subjective preference for these conditions and compared their performance in completing reading comprehension tasks with each of these tools. We found that participants preferred having support tools in their interface as opposed to none, but we did not measure a significant difference in their preferences between the two support tools provided. This paper presents the details of design and development of this proposed tool, design guidelines applied to the prototype, factors influencing the results, and directions for future work.

Keywords: American Sign Language · Reading support tools · Deaf users

1 Introduction

An estimated 28 million people in the U.S. are Deaf or Hard of Hearing (DHH) [26, 30]. While there are many DHH individuals with excellent literacy skills, research has shown that there is great diversity in the reading skills among the DHH community, and many DHH individuals exhibit lower English language literacy levels compared to their hearing peers [39]. Prior literacy research with DHH readers has found that some have effortful word recognition, lower vocabulary, slower reading rate, more limited repertoire of comprehension strategies, and some avoid reading activities [24, 27, 28, 31, 37]. When performing question-answering tasks based on a text, some DHH students rely on basic visual matching of text with words in the questions, rather than considering the meaning of the text [3, 40, 41].

Since most web content is in the form of written text, low literacy can be a barrier for information access for DHH users. Bilal and Kirby [4] found that DHH students often experience difficulties when using internet search engines. Smith [35] observed

© Springer International Publishing AG, part of Springer Nature 2018
M. Antona and C. Stephanidis (Eds.): UAHCI 2018, LNCS 10907, pp. 205–215, 2018.
https://doi.org/10.1007/978-3-319-92049-8_15

the internet search behaviors of deaf adolescents who used search engines to complete fact-based tasks, including: search query formation and modification, website identification, and selection. The researchers concluded that deaf adolescents had difficulty initiating, conducting, or validating effective internet searches in response to fact based search tasks.

For over 500,000 people in the U.S., American Sign Language (ASL) is their primary means of communication [30]: Individuals with lower English fluency may benefit from tools that can convey content in the form of ASL. Some researchers have developed websites or software that include ASL video [5, 6, 12, 15, 36] or animations [1, 2, 17, 19, 21, 22, 25] to address the issue of making the information on sites more accessible. Most of these projects address the issue of providing sign language translations for textual information or enabling website designers to author content in ASL. However, there has been relatively little research on the use of ASL video to *supplement the textual content* on web sites. In this study, we investigate providing support in the form of ASL videos that provide single-word translations of individual English words in a text. Such a tool may assist readers understand a text, and it may also improve reading vocabulary skills.

1.1 Our Approach

After examining prior research on the design and development of bilingual interfaces, we constructed design guidelines for interfaces that include text and sign language. Based on this, we implemented a web plug-in allows users to click on English words (that the user does not understand) in the text to see ASL video translations (of a single ASL sign) for that word. A user study was also conducted with DHH students to evaluate the system's usability, measure users' preferences regarding the tool, and to observe whether its use offered an improvement in reading comprehension.

1.2 Prior Work

Many researchers have studied methods for improving website accessibility for DHH users. For instance, Fajarado *et al.* [9] explored the effect of substituting graphical items (clip art images) in place of textual links on webpages during an information retrieval task, but their users (both deaf and hearing) were more successful when using the ordinary text-hypertext interface, rather than in the novel graphical one. Other researchers have examined methods for incorporating sign language into computer interfaces for DHH users [14, 16, 18], especially in the education domain, e.g., reading/writing software for deaf children [15] or e-learning systems accessible for DHH users [5, 7].

Sign-Language Only Interfaces. To produce interfaces that avoid English text use, researchers in [12, 34] explored a hyperlinked video system called "sign-linking," consisting of linking mechanisms within a video itself to take users to other sections of the video or to other pages. Fajarado *et al.* [10] found that sign language videos added to text hyperlinks improved web search efficiency for DHH users, and Reis *et al.* [33] are designing an ASL-only learning resource for STEM topics.

Combining Written Language and Sign Language Videos on Websites. Debevc *et al.* [6] embedded interactive elements in the text of a web interface that triggered video translations in sign language, and they found that providing ASL video translations of phrases or sentences increased users' interest in the content of the material. Similarly, Straetz *et al.* [36] presented an e-learning system for deaf adults who wanted to maintain and improve their math and reading/writing skills; along with text, it displayed German Sign Language videos. Our word-lookup plug-in is similar in premise to these prior projects, yet readers should note that the researchers in [6, 36] prepared all sign-language videos in advance since it is well-beyond the state-of-the-art of machine translation systems to produce automatic sign-language translations of written text. In contrast to [6, 36], we investigate a system that provides single-word translations of individual English words into videos of individual ASL words, which is much closer to being practical with current computational linguistic technology.

Combining Written Language and Sign Language Animations on Websites. Researchers have also investigated the use of sign language animations (computer generated avatars) to make web content or software more accessible to sign language users, e.g. [1, 2, 8]. Kennaway *et al.* [25] described their eSign system for generating sign language animations to accompany text, to provide access to critical web information content, such as government websites. In their system, the avatar animation was displayed on the body of the page, in the frame of the window, or as a separate pop-up.

Providing ASL Tooltips on Demand. Other researchers have investigated rapid lookup of English words in ASL dictionaries. Petrie *et al.* [32] investigated four types of tooltips (small windows that appear when the user hovers their mouse over words) for DHH users, containing: (1) sign language, (2) pictures, (3) video of a human mouth speaking the word, or (4) digital lips. Users preferred the sign-language or picture versions. Jones *et al.* [23] studied a mobile phone app to enable DHH children to look up ASL definitions by photographing printed English words using the device's camera.

Evaluating Efficacy of Sign Language Interfaces. Some researchers have tried to measure how bilingual web content influences signers' comprehension of hypertext content. Gentry *et al.* [13] conducted an experiment in which deaf participants were presented stories in four different formats: printed (text), text with pictures, text with sign language, and text with pictures and sign language. The use of signs improved performance compared to the text-only condition but not to the text with pictures condition, which yielded the highest scores. In prior work, our laboratory has presented methods for effectively measuring comprehension among DHH study participants, through the use of comprehension questions about information content [20].

Summary of Prior Work. While there has been limited work on providing sign language only interfaces on websites (due to the challenges of providing hyperlinks and other web- page structural content using a dynamic information channel like video), there has been significantly more research on finding new methods for blending written language content with sign language (either through video or animation). Further, there has been prior work investigating how pop-up tooltips could provide information in ASL on demand. While prior work has investigated the creation of easier methods for looking up ASL words in a dictionary, the specific use of pop-up tools to provide ASL translations of individual English words in web content has not previously been investigated through an experimental evaluation with DHH users.

2   Research Questions and Methods

In this study, we compare participants' subjective preferences and reading comprehension scores when using three versions of a website containing text content:

1. **Normal:** a version containing English text without any augmentations,
2. **Dictionary:** a version that enables users to click on words to see an English dictionary definition (using Google Dictionary, a plug-in for Google Chrome browsers, provided definitions for selected English words in a pop-up box, see Fig. 1), and

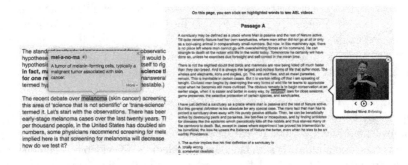

Fig. 1. On left, a screen image from the Dictionary condition in the study, which displays a pop-up English definition when an English word is clicked; on right, a screen image from our ASLPopup condition, providing pop-up ASL videos on demand, when a word is clicked.

3. **ASLPopup:** a version that allows users to click on a word to see a small video pop-up window appear in which a human performs an ASL sign that is a single-word translation of the selected English word (as shown on the right side of Fig. 1).

We investigated the following research questions (RQ1-RQ4), as DHH students were asked to use this system to perform a reading comprehension task:

1. Do DHH students show a subjective preference for having support (Dictionary or ASLPopup), as compared to no support (Normal)?
2. Do DHH students show a subjective preference for ASL video in the interface (ASLPopup), as opposed to having support from written definitions (Dictionary)?
3. Do DHH students have better performance in answering comprehension questions when provided with support (Dictionary or ASLPopup), compared to Normal?
4. Do DHH students show an improved performance in answering comprehension questions when provided with ASL video (ASLPopup), compared to Dictionary?

2.1 Prototype System Design and Implementation

To guide the design of our prototype, we consulted prior work on the design of bilingual interfaces for DHH users containing both text and sign language. For instance, DHH users of educational systems indicated a preference for videos of sign language, which would appear on demand [6, 36]. In addition, researchers in [36] found that providing sign language on-demand made content accessible to DHH users, without interfering with the usability of the system for hearing users.

Fajarado *et al.* [11] recommended that when providing sign language video translations of text content, designers should use pop-up windows with videos embedded in the same page as the text. This recommendation follows the *spatial contiguity* principle in the multimedia learning literature [29], i.e. user's understanding of the message transmitted through words and corresponding pictures will increase when they are presented near each other. However, providing multiple sources of the same information may be in conflict with the *redundancy* principle [38], which argues that users' comprehension is hampered if a multimedia system includes different sources for the same information. In addition, Richards *et al.* [34] argues that asking users to split their attention across different sources would create literacy barriers due to the continuous switching between their first and second languages. Both concerns can be mitigated if the interface allows the user to access the multimedia content *on request only*, thereby requiring the user's attention on only one part of the interface at a given moment.

Users of a sign-language animation system for websites in [25] had a preference for seeing both written text as well as signing. Participants in that study preferred animation display windows that appeared in a fixed location, rather than pop-ups, which sometimes blocked the text below. Of course, users in that study were watching sign language content with a long duration, rather than short definitions. This concern could be further mitigated by positioning a pop-up so that it does not block the text below.

Based on this prior work, we implemented a webpage for displaying text content (using HTML5, CSS3, JavaScript, and JQuery). To indicate words that users could click, a blue color font was used (and an underline appears below the word when the mouse hovers over it). A wide margin was used on the right side of the page (approximately 25% width) so that if a word is clicked, a pop-up window can appear on the right side (without blocking the text) to convey the video. When a word is clicked, it appears with highlighting background color, as shown in Fig. 1. The pop-up appears at the same vertical height as the line of text containing the word that was clicked. The window contains a single video, with media controls including a play button, and forward/backward frame controls (which were useful when watching a short video one frame at a time). The popup also contained a close button on the top-right corner. ASL videos were provided by the National Technical Institute for the Deaf (NTID) ASL Video dictionary and Inflection Guide[1] from Rochester Institute of Technology (RIT). That resource contains flash videos of 2700 ASL signs corresponding to English words.

We had to select which English words in the text should be highlighted to indicate that an ASL video was available for that word. While it is within the state-of-the-art of computational linguistic techniques to morphologically analyze words (e.g. matching

---

[1] https://www.rit.edu/ntid/dictionary/.

the dictionary entry for "absorb" with words like "absorbed" or "absorbing") or disambiguate words with multiple meanings based on their surrounding context (e.g. "can" could indicate a container or "to be able"), it was not the focus of our project to fully implement an automatic system. Instead, we were interested in how users would respond to a system like this. For this reason, we employed a Wizard-of-Oz approach, in which an ASL expert identified the appropriate ASL signs from the dictionary for individual English words in the specific texts that would be displayed during our user study. The three passages used in this study were selected from Graduate Record Exam 6 online practice resources[2], with 5 comprehension questions for each text passage. Each question was multiple choice, with a single correct answer, and the expert also identified words appearing in the questions or their answer choices that could be highlighted. In total, the expert identified approximately 51.5% of the English words in the text as corresponding to videos that we could display from the NTID dictionary.

2.2 User Study

To recruit participants for a user study comparing the three conditions (Normal, Dictionary, and ASLPopup), we posted flyers throughout the Rochester Institute of Technology campus asking potential participants if they were Deaf or Hard of Hearing and if they used ASL. Before beginning the study, participants were asked to provide some basic demographic and background information. A total of 18 participants (6 male, 12 female) were recruited, between ages 20–29. All of the participants reported having become DHH by the age of 3. Of these, 10 reported as having learned ASL by age 5, while 6 learned ASL between ages 10–18. Aside from 2 participants, all reported having used ASL at the elementary/secondary school level, and 14 participants reported that they also used English while communicating at work/school. All of the participants had experience in reading English content on a website while browsing from a computer.

Each of our three text passages was prepared in the three conditions (Normal, Dictionary, and ASLPopup), and the conditions were assigned to each passage using a Latin square schedule, and the presentation order of each passage was counterbalanced. Thus, each participant completed a total of 3 reading comprehension tasks – a participant saw each text passages only once, in one of the conditions. At the top of each webpage, brief instructions indicated if the user could click on words of the text, e.g. "On this page, you can click on highlighted words to see ASL videos." In addition, the experimenter briefly demonstrated how to click on a word before allowing the participant to begin reading the text and answering the five questions below each passage. Participants wrote their answers to each question on a paper sheet provided to them. After completing the comprehension tasks, participants assigned preference scores to each of the three conditions encountered, on a 0-to-10 scale (10 = high preference).

---

[2] http://www.ets.org/gre/.

2.3   Results for Each Research Question

One participant indicated that she did not make use of the pop-up videos in the ASLPopup condition, and she therefore refrained from providing a preference score for that condition. This participant was excluded from the analysis for RQ1-RQ2. Median 1-to-10 preference scores for the Normal condition was 6, Dictionary was 8, and ASLPopup was 9. The distributions in the three groups differed significantly (Friedman test $p < 0.001$); post-hoc Wilcoxon pairwise tests revealed significant differences ($p < 0.05$) between: Normal vs. Dictionary and Normal vs. ASLPopup.

RQ1 considered whether DHH users showed a subjective preference for having Support tools (Dictionary or ASLPopup) in the interface, as opposed to not having any support (Normal). Based on the result of the pairwise tests, we see that participants preferred each of the support conditions to the Normal condition.

RQ2 considered whether DHH users showed a subjective preference for having the ASLPopup support tool in the interface, as opposed to Dictionary support. Based on the results above, distributions in these two groups did not differ significantly. No difference in preference scores was observed between Dictionary and ASLPopup.

Participant's accuracy on reading comprehension questions was analyzed to answer RQ3 and RQ4, which considered participant performances across the three different conditions. A Shapiro-Wilks test for normalcy was performed on the collected reading comprehension data, which concluded that the data was not normally distributed (Shapiro-Wilks $W = 0.87478$, $W_{critical} = 0.95688$, $p < 0.05$). Thus, the Kruskal-Wallis non-parametric test was performed to analyze the comprehension performance data. RQ3 considered whether DHH users showed an improved performance in answering comprehension questions when provided Support tools (Dictionary or ASLPopup), as opposed to not having any support (Normal). Similarly, RQ4 considered whether participants showed an improved performance in answering comprehension questions when provided with the ASLPopup tool as opposed to while using the Dictionary tool. The Kruskal-Wallis test revealed no significant differences between groups (Kruskal-Wallis $k = 3$, $H = 1.709$, p-value > 0.05) when we consider comprehension scores.

3   Conclusions, Limitations, and Future Work

By providing sign language support in the form of ASL videos for a web interface, this project investigated methods to assist DHH users to better understand information presented as English text on websites. Our intention was to create a tool that could enable DHH users with limited English literacy skills to better understand English words in a text by identifying ASL video translations for unfamiliar English terms. This tool did not attempt to provide English-to-ASL translations of full sentences, but instead allowed users to view ASL signs of individual words. Insights and recommendations from prior relevant work informed our design of this tool, which made use of the NTID ASL Video Dictionary and Inflection Guide resource to display videos of ASL signs when the user clicked on an English word.

Our user study demonstrated that DHH users preferred to use the ASLPopup tool for sign language support, as compared to having no support provided (RQ1), and users also preferred the Google Dictionary tool for word definitions, as compared to having no support tool (RQ1). Prior research in the field has shown that DHH signers perform significantly better when provided with graphical cues or sign language support while dealing with written text. However, in this study, we did not observe any significant difference in user preferences ASLPopup and Dictionary (RQ2). We speculate that our participants recruited on a university campus may have higher levels of English literacy than the target users of a system for providing ASL translations of English words. Thus, having support in the form of ASL did not provide a significant benefit. Similarly, no significant difference was observed in participants' performance in answering reading comprehension questions across the three conditions presented (RQ3 & RQ4). Prior work had suggested that providing DHH readers with English text that is augmented with sign language or graphical content could improve comprehension [11]; we speculate that our study may have been underpowered (too few participants) to measure whether the provision of an ASLPopup tool provided any comprehension benefit.

3.1   Limitations

A possible limitation of our study design is that our reading comprehension tests were taken from Graduate Record Exam (GRE) resources, which have a high difficulty level. We speculate that the high difficulty level of the questions could have masked any influence on the participant performance scores. In particular, when designing our reading passages for this study, we found it challenging to tailor the reading difficult level of our texts to the skill level of the participants we might recruit on the university campus. Furthermore, although the NTID dictionary resource was extremely valuable for our project, it does not contain all possible ASL signs (only 2,700). Thus, it was challenging to identify English text passages that would have a high match-rate with our video dictionary resource, while at the same time being sufficiently difficult for our participants, to encourage them to make use of the word-lookup features.

Another limitation is that we asked an ASL expert to identify these English words in our text – rather than using an automatic word matching tool. Thus, our study reflects a system with a level of accuracy that may be beyond the state-of-the-art of computational linguistic tools for disambiguating the senses of individual words and accurately morphologically analyzing those words to find word matches in a dictionary.

In informal feedback comments provided by participants about their experiences with the systems, two participants provided mixed feedback regarding the ASLPopup tool. While the videos provided for some complicated words were "ok," one participant did not like amount of ASL video options that were available and felt that there were too many word on the screen that were highlighted in a blue color as click-able. Another participant commented that although she appreciated the concept of having an ASL support tool, she did not require its use during the study (since she was able to understand all of the English words on the screen).

3.2   Future Work

In future work, to address the limitation above, we intend to conduct a follow-up study using text passages at a variety of English difficulty levels and by recruiting participants with greater variation in their English literacy skill – to better explore the space of text complexity and user's literacy skills – since it is likely that tools such as the ASLPopup plugin may have particular benefits for DHH users who encounter a text includes some words that are just beyond their reading skill level.

In addition, based on user comments in our initial study, we may explore variations in the percentage of words that are marked as click-able when the text is displayed. It may be the case that too many words were visually highlighted in the current version of the system, including may easy-to-read words whose click-ability did not provide benefits to users.

Our current study used an ASL expert to label words that correspond to items in the video dictionary resource; in future work, we may experiment with implementing an automatic tool for matching English words to ASL dictionary items. Additional user studies would be necessary to determine whether errors in the output of an automatic system influence how users respond to a system like this, e.g. if an English word "right" is being used in a sentence to convey "correct" but the automatic system links it to an ASL video for the "direction opposite left."

Future studies could also investigate our speculation that an ASL video popup tool might also have an educational benefit by introducing DHH readers to additional English vocabulary terms as they read. Another potential benefit of this tool is that it may be interest to hearing students who are learning ASL, since it could further expose them to additional ASL vocabulary items. A follow-up study with hearing ASL students could investigate this additional application.

References

1. Adamo-Villani, N., Doublestein, J., Martin, Z.: Sign language for K-8 mathematics by 3D interactive animation. J. Educ. Technol. Syst. **33**(3), 241–257 (2005)
2. Bangham, J.A., Cox, S.J., Lincoln, M., Marshall, I., Tutt, M., Wells, M.: Signing for the deaf using virtual humans. In: IEEE Seminar on Speech and Language Processing for Disabled and Elderly People (Ref. No. 2000/025), pp. 4–1. IET (2000)
3. Beggs, W.D.A., Breslaw, P.I.: Reading retardation or linguistic deficit? III: a further examination of response strategies in a reading test completed by hearing impaired children. J. Res. Reading **6**(1), 19–28 (1983)
4. Bilal, D., Kirby, J.: Differences and similarities in information seeking: children and adults as Web users. Inf. Process. Manage. **38**(5), 649–670 (2002)
5. Bottoni, P., Borgia, F., Buccarella, D., Capuano, D., De Marsico, M., Labella, A.: Stories and signs in an e-learning environment for deaf people. Univ. Access Inf. Soc. **12**(4), 369–386 (2013)
6. Debevc, M., Kosec, P., Holzinger, A.: Improving multimodal web accessibility for deaf people: sign language interpreter module. Multimedia Tools Appl. **54**(1), 181–199 (2011)

7. Debevc, M., Stjepanovič, Z., Povalej, P., Verlič, M., Kokol, P.: Accessible and adaptive e-learning materials: considerations for design and development. In: Stephanidis, C. (ed.) UAHCI 2007. LNCS, vol. 4556, pp. 549–558. Springer, Heidelberg (2007). https://doi.org/10.1007/978-3-540-73283-9_61

8. Elliott, R., Glauert, J.R., Kennaway, J.R., Marshall, I., Safar, E.: Linguistic modelling and language-processing technologies for avatar-based sign language presentation. Univ. Access Inf. Soc. **6**(4), 375–391 (2008)

9. Fajardo, I., Caas, J.J., Salmern, L., Abascal, J.: Improving deaf users' accessibility in hypertext information retrieval: are graphical interfaces useful for them? Behav. Inf. Technol. **25**(6), 455–467 (2006)

10. Fajardo, I., Parra, E., Caas, J.J.: Do sign language videos improve web navigation for deaf signer users? J. Deaf Stud. Deaf Educ. **15**(3), 242–262 (2010)

11. Fajardo, I., Vigo, M., Salmern, L.: Technology for supporting web information search and learning in sign language. Interact. Comput. **21**(4), 243–256 (2009)

12. Fels, D.I., Richards, J., Hardman, J., Lee, D.G.: Sign language web pages. Am. Ann. Deaf **151**(4), 423–433 (2006)

13. Gentry, M.M., Chinn, K.M., Moulton, R.D.: Effectiveness of multimedia reading materials when used with children who are deaf. Am. Ann. Deaf **149**(5), 394–403 (2004)

14. Hanson, V.L.: Computing technologies for deaf and hard of hearing users. In: Human-Computer Interaction: Designing for Diverse Users and Domains, p. 125 (2009)

15. Hanson, V.L., Padden, C.: Handson: a multi-media program for bilingual language instruction of deaf children. In: Proceedings of the Johns Hopkins National Search for Computing Applications to Assist Persons with Disabilities, pp. 5–6. IEEE (1992)

16. Hilzensauer, M.: Information technology for deaf people. In: Ichalkaranje, N., Ichalkaranje, A., Jain, L. (eds.) Intelligent Paradigms for Assistive and Preventive Healthcare, pp. 183–206. Springer, Heidelberg (2006). https://doi.org/10.1007/11418337_7

17. Huenerfauth, M.: Generating American sign language animation: overcoming misconceptions and technical challenges. Univ. Access Inf. Soc. **6**(4), 419–434 (2008). https://doi.org/10.1007/s10209-007-0095-7

18. Huenerfauth, M., Hanson, V.L.: Sign language in the interface: access for deaf signers. In: Universal Access. Erlbaum, Handbook (2009). 38

19. Huenerfauth, M.S.: Planning models of ASL classifier predicates for machine translation. In: Proceedings of the 10th International Conference on Theoretical and Issues in Machine Translation (TMI 2004), Baltimore, MD, USA (2004). http://www.mt-archive.info/TMI-2004-Huenerfauth.pdf

20. Huenerfauth, M., Kacorri, H.: Release of experimental stimuli and questions for evaluating facial expressions in animations of American sign language. In: Proceedings of the 6th Workshop on the Representation and Processing of Sign Languages: Beyond the Manual Channel, The 9th International Conference on Language Resources and Evaluation (LREC 2014), Reykjavik, Iceland (2014)

21. Huenerfauth, M., Lu, P.: Modeling and synthesizing spatially inflected verbs for American sign language animations. In: Proceedings of the 12th International ACM SIGACCESS Conference on Computers and Accessibility (ASSETS 2010), pp. 99–106. ACM, New York (2010). http://dx.doi.org/10.1145/1878803.1878823

22. Huenerfauth, M.: Spatial and planning models of ASL classifier predicates for machine translation. In: Proceedings of the 10th International Conference on Theoretical and Issues in Machine Translation (TMI 2004), Baltimore, MD, USA (2004). http://www.mt-archive.info/TMI-2004-Huenerfauth.pdf

23. Jones, M.D., Hamilton, H., Petmecky, J.: Mobile phone access to a sign language dictionary. In: Proceedings of the 17th International ACM SIGACCESS Conference on Computers & Accessibility, pp. 331–332. ACM (2015)

24. Kelly, L.P.: Considerations for designing practice for deaf readers. J. Deaf Stud. Deaf Educ. **8**(2), 171–186 (2003)

25. Kennaway, J.R., Glauert, J.R., Zwitserlood, I.: Providing signed content on the internet by synthesized animation. ACM Trans. Comput.-Hum. Interact. (TOCHI) **14**(3), 15 (2007)

26. Lin, F.R., Niparko, J.K., Ferrucci, L.: Hearing loss prevalence in the United States. Arch. Intern. Med. **171**(20), 1851–1853 (2011)

27. Luckner, J.L., Handley, C.M.: A summary of the reading comprehension research undertaken with students who are deaf or hard of hearing. Am. Ann. Deaf **153**(1), 6–36 (2008)

28. Marschark, M., Harris, M.: Success and failure in learning to read: the special case (?) of deaf children. In: Reading Comprehension Difficulties: Processes and Intervention, pp. 279–300 (1996)

29. Mayer, R.E.: Principles for reducing extraneous processing in multimedia learning: coherence, signaling, redundancy, spatial contiguity, and temporal contiguity principles. In: The Cambridge Handbook of Multimedia Learning, pp. 183–200 (2005)

30. Mitchell, R.E., Young, T.A., Bachleda, B., Karchmer, M.A.: How many people use ASL in the United States? Why estimates need updating. Sign Lang. Stud. **6**(3), 306–335 (2006)

31. Paul, P.V.: Literacy and deafness: the development of reading, writing, and literate thought. Pearson College Division (1998)

32. Petrie, H., Fisher, W., Weimann, K., Weber, G.: Augmenting icons for deaf computer users. In: CHI 2004 Extended Abstracts on Human Factors in Computing Systems, pp. 1131–1134. ACM (2004)

33. Reis, J., Solovey, E.T., Henner, J., Johnson, K., Hoffmeister, R.: ASL CLeaR: STEM education tools for deaf students. In: Proceedings of the 17th International ACM SIGACCESS Conference on Computers & Accessibility, pp. 441–442. ACM (2015)

34. Richards, J., Fels, D., Hardman, J.: The educational potential of the signing web. In: Instructional Technology and Education of the Deaf Symposium (2005)

35. Smith, C.E.: Where is it? How deaf adolescents complete fact- based Internet search tasks. Am. Ann. Deaf **151**(5), 519–529 (2006)

36. Straetz, K., Kaibel, A., Raithel, V., Specht, M., Grote, K., Kramer, F.: An e-learning environment for deaf adults. In: Conference Proceedings 8th ERCIM Workshop User Interfaces for All (2004)

37. Strassman, B.K.: Metacognition and reading in children who are deaf: a review of the research. J. Deaf Stud. Deaf Educ. **2**, 140–149 (1997)

38. Sweller, J.: The redundancy principle in multimedia learning. In: Mayer, R.E. (ed.) The Cambridge Handbook of Multimedia Learning, pp. 183–200. Cambridge University Press, Cambridge (2005)

39. Traxler, C.B.: The Stanford achievement test: national norming and performance standards for deaf and hard-of-hearing students. J. Deaf Stud. Deaf Educ. **5**(4), 337–348 (2000)

40. Webster, A., Wood, D.J., Griffiths, A.J.: Reading retardation or linguistic deficit? I: interpreting reading test performances of hearing impaired adolescents. J. Res. Read. **4**(2), 136–147 (1981)

41. Wood, D.: Teaching and Talking with Deaf Children. Wiley, New York (1986)

Gesture-Based Vehicle Control in Partially and Highly Automated Driving for Impaired and Non-impaired Vehicle Operators: A Pilot Study

Ronald Meyer[1(✉)], Rudolf Graf von Spee[1], Eugen Altendorf[1],
and Frank O. Flemisch[1,2]

[1] Institute of Industrial Engineering and Ergonomics, RWTH Aachen University,
Aachen, Germany
{r.meyer,r.grafvonspee,e.altendorf,f.flemisch}@iaw.rwth-aachen.de
[2] Fraunhofer Institute for Communication, Information Processing and Ergonomics,
Wachtberg, Germany
frank.flemisch@fkie.fraunhofer.de
http://www.iaw.rwth-aachen.de

Abstract. A concept for shared and cooperative guidance and control based on the H-Metaphor is developed, implemented and presented in this paper. In addition, a pilot study with a small user group conducted in a static driving simulator is discussed. The concept enables communication between an automated vehicle and the driver, who is requested to take over driving in a conditional automated driving mode. The request is communicated to the driver by tactile feedback in a sidestick, which is used for control of the automated vehicle. Two different ways of take over request are investigated and later compared in a survey for "Perceived Utility", "Perceived Safety", "User Satisfaction" and "Perceived Usability". The study is a pilot study for investigating interaction paradigms that are suitable in automated vehicles used by impaired people, which frequently are operated by joysticks. The outcomes of the study are used as a basis for further research.

Keywords: Human-systems integration · Automated driving
Human-machine systems · Driver-vehicle interaction
Cooperative driving · Cooperative guidance and control

1 Introduction

Mobility serves as a key issue for many people to guarantee independence in everyday situations and to participate in social and working life. However, the ability to operate a vehicle can be limited due to high age or physical impairments caused by disease or accident. The ability to drive despite any physical limitations can be maintained by suitable modifications of the vehicle. Even if physical constraints need to be considered, the driver must remain in full control over the vehicle. Not only persons with physical difficulties find themselves confronted with several issues when driving, but also physically fit young drivers with a lack of driving experience form a risk group regarding traffic safety. The manual operation of a vehicle can be increasingly difficult depending on the vehicle operator's degree of the limiting factors, the implemented operating elements and the individual training level. Comfort, accessibility and safety in driving could therefore be increased by recent developments in automated driving and the broader availability of advanced drivers' assistant systems. In today's traffic, some vehicles are already capable of driving at least partially automated. Thus, in some vehicles drivers can choose certain maneuvers to be conducted by the automation system depending on the current driving situation. Moreover, such vehicles can, for example, intervene by initiating a braking maneuver in a dangerous driving situation. The functionality of the automation is meant to be influenced by the vehicle operator in partially and conditional automated driving, thus, the vehicle operator may execute a driving maneuver with an intuitive command or gesture. The idea of the vehicle operator controlling the automated system by gestures origins in the H(orse)-Metaphor, where the natural example of rider (or horse cart driver) and horse is used to describe the role and interaction between a driver and an automated vehicle [6]. Generally, this concept can be described as cooperative guidance and control [7], an extension of the shared control concept. To analyze different modalities for input gestures, a multimodal human vehicle interface for conducting primary driving tasks, this paper presents an experimental study. The experiment is conducted in a static driving simulator at RWTH Aachen University. The driving simulator is based on a professional driving simulation software SILAB and self developed software modules emulating a vehicle automation [1]. A concept of three different modalities was developed as input method for the activation of a maneuver under consideration that vehicle operators with different levels of impairments will be using the system throughout the research. The conducted study presented in this research considers non-impaired operators as a proof of concept. The HMI concepts in use are a haptic steering wheel operated by hand (contact), a sidestick operated by hand (contact), and a touchscreen operated by hand (contact). The research is subdivided into multiple packages where the presented results are covering an investigation of input gestures using a haptic side stick with different guidance transition methods. The automated system gives visual and audible feedback about the current state of the input and visual-only feedback about the driving state. Visual feedback was integrated as trajectories directly in the simulated world as well as feedback on a mid-console display next to the vehicle operator. The gesture-based control of the driving maneuvers was developed in an iterative design process under participation of the target group of impaired and non-impaired vehicle operators. The study was conducted with untrained non-impaired participants as a first user group to validate the consistency of the driving maneuvers where the different modalities for transition between driving modes are set as independent variables.

2   Related Work

The use of gestures for steering a vehicle is particularly eligible to be used in combination with automated driving maneuvers. For that purpose the driver should be able to intuitively give commands in automated driving while user input should intuitively be understood by the automated system without the driver having to learn circumstantial explanations. The driver's input has to be correctly interpreted by the system in critical and non-critical situations likewise. Recent studies about in-car interfaces using gestural input merely suggested to be used for secondary tasks. Secondary tasks are defined to have no relevance for the driving task i.e. are tasks that are not critical, e.g. interacting with a multimedia interface for changing the radio station or change the volume of a music player. Cairnie et al. (2000) developed a prototype finger-pointing method for operating secondary controls [5]. They replaced the physical controls by a computer interface and thus achieved to situate the interface much closer to the driver's normal line of sight. The interface is operated by pointing gestures that are processed by a computer vision system. The system implicates a gain of safety in dangerous driving situations since driver distraction through the operation of operating secondary tasks while driving is a major cause for accidents. Another system using gestural input for in-car secondary tasks was developed by Zobl et al. [12]. The system's concept allows drivers to effectively operate on a variety of multimedia and infotainment tasks with hand poses and dynamic hand gestures. The gesture inventory consisted of 22 dynamic gestures which were grouped to twelve gesture classes which were e.g. pointing, kinemimic gestures (e.g. waving to the left/right/up/down), symbolic (e.g. 'pointing' for "engage") and mimic (e.g. 'lift virtual phone'). Handposes like 'grab', 'open hand' or 'relaxed' were added to the inventory to allow additional functionality inside the user interface. These gestures enabled drivers to operate on a navigation system as well as multimedia and communication devices. The system was investigated for its recognition rate where the results show that the gesture recognition worked very well for both handposes and dynamic gesture recognition when it was adapted to a single user. [12] Zobl et al. suggest that a gesture controlled in-car human machine interface should be part of a multimodal interface, i.e. the driver should have choices on selecting the best suitable modality for an appropriate situation while driving a vehicle. Other concepts provide interaction commands to be conducted on the steering wheel. Angelini et al. developed a prototype for tangible gestures on the steering wheel for in-car natural interaction [3]. Pressure sensors in the turntable of the steering wheel are used to detect gestural input of the vehicle driver. However, no haptic feedback was given through the steering wheel for a confirming input for an input gesture since the input was used to conduct secondary tasks. Bach et al. [4] suggested not to use tactile or haptic feedback for primary and secondary tasks since tactile force is already applied on the steering wheel by the road. Thus, the tactile feedback channel is already allocated by primary tasks and should not be occupied by other tasks to distract the driver (Fig. 1).

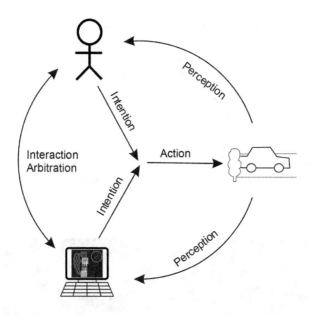

Fig. 1. (Shared and) Cooperative guidance and control [7]

Kienle et al. [9] developed a concept of automated driving to provide an active side stick for gesture input for primary driving tasks in automated driving based on the so-called H-Metaphor [6,8,10,11] (cf. Sect. 3.1). The concept suggests to establish haptic communication between the driver and the automated system which is contributing benefits that cannot be achieved through a conventional interface system. A first user study indicated that using a force feedback side stick is a promising implementation to realize the idea of the cooperative concept to be used in vehicles.

3   Method

3.1   Human Machine Interface

The human machine interface system used in the driving simulator applies a version where different levels of automation can be picked by the driver to match the desired driving experience. The H-Metaphor metaphor by [7] constitutes the basis of the gestural human machine interface to control the automated system. In this specific case the driver uses an active side stick to interact with the automated vehicle which allows to control the vehicle's automation laterally and longitudinally at the same time using the same input device. This type of input is common for altered barrier free cars to fit the requirements of drivers with impairments. The H-Metaphor's paradigm origins in nature and describes a transitive relationship between the human driver and the system in which the system behaves like a horse attached to reins. The metaphor can be interpreted to the human driver who drags the reins tighter if more control over the vehicle is desired and vice versa. This metaphor maintains different modes of control which conform with the levels of automation defined by the Society of Automotive Engineers and can be switched while driving (Figs. 2 and 3):

1. **Tight Rein.** Conforms approximately with SAE level 1: Driver Assistance e.g. with lateral or longitudinal assistance.
2. **Loose Rein.** Conforms approximately with SAE level 2: Partial Automation e.g. with lateral and longitudinal assistance.
3. **Secured Rein.** Conforms approximately with SAE level 4: Conditional Automation or autonomous driving expecting the driver to intervene in certain situations.

Fig. 2. Simulator environment: clear section example

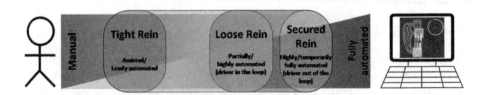

Fig. 3. Support and automation scale [1]

Interaction Modalities. The conducted study incorporates the investigation of two different interaction methods, each having a specific method for communicating a transition between different levels of automation. They both are conversed using a haptical side stick as input method and originate from the H-Metaphor. The driver is allowed to switch the modes of automation while driving but a limitation or boundary of driver control is implemented. The boundary typically occurs when driving situations become unclear and decisions have to be made or when the driver manually switches the level of automation. In case of an unclear situation the system communicates its boundaries to the driver when she or he is driving in Secured-Rein mode and switches to Tight-Rein mode in one of the two described ways (Fig. 4):

Fig. 4. Simulator environment: urban section example

1. Tactile feedback is given and the system conducts the transition automatically. The human machine interface visualizes an animation which signals the transition in between two seconds.
2. Tactile feedback is given and the system awaits input of the user to perform the transition. If no action is taken the vehicle slows down until a complete stop which only can be prevented by manually switching the mode from Loose-Rein to Tight-Rein. The allowed transition time is limited to two seconds before the vehicle slows down to zero.

The transition is carried out automatically by the system in a predefined situation in each of the specific modes. This is announced by a the described vibration of the side stick and by a short animation on the human machine interface, in which the button of the new mode is automatically stored in blue. Both interaction variants are automatically switching back to the Loose-Rein mode when the system is pulled out of the unclear situation. A subsequent change to the Loose-Rein mode is also possible at any time if the system has not exceeded the system limits. The user was allowed to perform a manual change from Loose-Rein and Tight-Rein at all times. The situations that are investigated in the study are the passing of cross road sections.

Fig. 5. Simulator environment: hardware implementation and setup

3.2   Driving Simulator

Simulation Environment. The software SILAB which is developed by the Wuerzburg Institute for Traffic Sciences (WIVW) is used as a traffic simulation environment and deployed in a static driving simulator concept with a seat box. The tools provided by the software facilitates to simulate traffic scenarios including the design of the road network, the programming of other road users and the landscaping so that a realistic riding experience can be established in any multi display setup. The simulation software was extended by a ROS interface[1] which is used for communication between the simulator software and hardware components that are installed in the seat box. The automation which conducts the conditional driving maneuvers is a software module which operates the vehicle in the simulation environment and is also connected through ROS. The simulation environment is capable of recording environmental data and driver data and allows precise statements concerning e.g. lane keeping, acceleration, distance to the car in front, capacity to react and the exact driving time (Fig. 5).

Road Structure. The applied test route is split into an urban and non-urban section. The software allows to define track layouts easily as they are written as a text file whereby very long, monotonous roads can be created quickly. A visual

---

[1] i.e. Robot Operating System, a framework providing interfaces for complex communication between platform-independent hard- and software components originally developed for communication of personal robots but grew to a multi purpose communication framework using computer network protocols.

editor can be used for complex traffic situations like they were used in the applied urban scenario. The software emulates real road courses based on satellite images and provides realistic road sign setups to emulate a preferably realistic user experience of a traffic scenario.

4 Experimental Design

A factorial design was used where the two different modalities of feedback in automated driving mode described in Sect. 3 are set as independent variables. The drivers were meant to drive the complete track manually by also using the side stick which is set as a third independent variable. A questionnaire developed by Altendorf et al. [2] was used to provide dimensions for dependent variables. The dimensions taken into account are "Perceived Utility", "Perceived Safety", "User Satisfaction" and "Perceived Usability", which later were investigated for correlations and difference of mean values. Before the test the participants gave information about demographic data, driving performance and experience with driver assistance systems. The items are evaluated used a Likert scale with up to seven evaluation steps.

4.1 Use Cases

The use-cases are intended to represent a balanced mix of realistic driving situations that automation can handle, and those that can no longer be handled by the automated system. The changes between the H-modes Loose-Rein and Tight-Rein should be forced by reaching certain points on the track. In order to achieve a comparable situation for all subjects, a forced route guidance by directory signs is necessary. To achieve a more realistic design, oncoming traffic is added on the route. In order to create confusing or complex forced situations, crossroads in particular have been selected in several variants. Thus, a takeover situation for the test persons is to be enforced in order to collect data on the functionality and user-friendliness of these transitions. In total, 17 transitions are artificially brought about on the test track of the urban scenario. The driving situation took approximately 20 min. The use cases can be divided into three groups. The first group includes crossings and bending situations. The second group can be titled obstacle. The last scenario is a two-lane roundabout.

Experimental Phase. The study was conducted in the laboratory facilities of the Institut fuer Arbeitswissenschaften (IAW) in Aachen. After the welcome and explanation of the test procedure by the study leader and the declaration of consent of the test person to participate in the study, the first questionnaire for the collection of personal data and the experiences with driver assistance systems was completed. After an explanation of the side-stick and the interface on the touch screen, the seats and side-stick were adapted to the needs of the test person. Subsequently, the participants was asked to take the test seriously and to stick as well as possible to the road traffic regulations. The driver should familiarize himself with the side-stick in the first drive, meantime no driver assistance systems have been available yet. This trip lasted between ten and fifteen minutes, depending on the speeds traveled. During the journey, the study leader logged the behavior and statements of the participants. The test was evaluated by the test person with a questionnaire afterwards. In the second ride the function and the handling of the activated driver assistance system was explained. The drive led the participant through a city center scenario, a country road and a highway. The study leader has recorded comments and the behavior of the test person while driving. This trip was evaluated with the questionnaire, which questions were arranged in a different order. Then the journey was repeated on the same route with the second test system. After the third trip, there was a short interview of the participants in which they could express subjective impressions and feelings and system improvements.

5   Results

The pilot study was conducted with twelve participants aged between 23 and 41 years (mean = 27, SD = 4.8 years). All participants owned at least a valid German driver's license for regular cars (European type B). In average, the participants had 8.7 years of driving practice with a standard distribution of 4.8 years. Their median driving distance was 6000 Km per year with nine of the twelve participants (75%) driving at least on a monthly basis. Some participants used driving assistance systems such as front collision warning systems, cruise control systems and parking assistance systems on a regular basis, while others reported only the use of GPS systems and standard features such as anti-lock brakes (ABS) and stability control systems (ESP). Due to the sample size, we conducted the statistical analysis using the Wilcoxon signed-rank test. The perceived control significantly differs between the two driving blocks ($p = .045$). For both driving conditions, the scales for "Perceived Safety", "User Satisfaction", "Perceived Usability" and "Perceived Control" correlate with "Perceived Utility". This can be interpreted as indication that the overall perception of the respective system is consistent for each individual driving block. Notably, "Perceived Safety" and "Perceived Utility" do not correlate for the manual driving block.

Table 1. Correlation of the scales for perceived safety, user satisfaction, perceived usability, and perceived control with perceived utility.

	Safety	User satisfaction	Usability	Control
Utility manual driving	-	.835**	.747**	.593**
Utility automated driving	.94**	.959**	.934**	.814**

In general, the participants reported a positive attitude towards the use of an automation system during the interviews after each driving block. This result is fully consistent with previous studies conducted with a similar automation approach [1]. All participants were able to perceive (feel) the provided haptic feedback. The feedback was individually adjusted for each participant in such a way that it could be well perceived without being too intense. Nonetheless, the automation setup with a fallback to the human driver on a two second notice received lower ratings. As a reason for this, the participants reported that the harsh fallback, even though they anticipated the situation in most cases correctly, had a negative impact on their judgment. When analyzing the actual driving data, no significant impact regarding safety between the two test conditions can be found. In this experiment, the fallback to the human driver with a warning of two seconds did have an impact only on perceived safety, not on actual safety. An explanation for this is that the participants were familiar with the system behavior and the danger of degradations in the level of automation. Thus, in real driving situations, an impact on actual safety can be expected due to the limitations in the ability of human drivers to take over control in such situations.

6   Discussion and Conclusion

Joysticks or side-sticks are among the most commonly used input devices for impaired drivers. In this paper, we focus on such interfaces and test the users' interaction with it in combination with an automation system. In a pilot study with non-impaired participants, we find that drivers who showed a positive attitude toward manual driving with an active side-stick rated the automation slightly worse in comparison to participants who were more skeptical in using an active side-stick. Most notably, the participants mentioned that controlling two degrees of freedom with one single input device led to imprecise steering actions. This indicates that degree of automation and the input device might influence each other, and that with automation, innovate input technologies might emerge. On the other hand, if these actuators also have to be used in manual conditions, they have to be designed in such a way that human drivers have a chance of taking over control when and if necessary. Especially in safety critical driving situations, such as driving through complex intersections, drivers might want to see a clear advantage in using automation technology before expressing an intention to use it. In the case of our pilot study, the participants were not used to the presented driving interface, i.e. side-stick, which might intensify a certain critical attitude towards the entire system. Future research would focus especially on the design of adequate HMI systems and user requirements regarding driving automation for people with special needs. A follow-up study will be conducted with participants who might already be more used to driving with joysticks from their driving experience in special cars. This also implies that the simulator will be equipped with the in the group of drivers with special needs more commonly known joysticks instead of sidesticks. Future research can also look into an extension of the available control gestures.

Acknowledgements. The research conducted was partly funded by the Deutsche Forschungsgemeinschaft (DFG) within the project "System ergonomics for cooperative interacting vehicles" (project number 273371579).

References

1. Altendorf, E., Baltzer, M., Heesen, M., Kienle, M., Weißgerber, T., Flemisch, F.: H-Mode. In: Winner, H., Hakuli, S., Lotz, F., Singer, C. (eds.) Handbook of Driver Assistance Systems, pp. 1499–1518. Springer, Cham (2016). https://doi.org/10.1007/978-3-319-12352-3_60
2. Altendorf, E., Schreck, C., Flemisch, F.: A new method and results for analyzing decision-making processes in automated driving on highways. In: Stanton, N., Landry, S., Di Bucchianico, G., Vallicelli, A. (eds.) Advances in Human Aspects of Transportation. Advances in Intelligent Systems and Computing, vol. 484, pp. 571–583. Springer, Cham (2017). https://doi.org/10.1007/978-3-319-41682-3_48
3. Angelini, L., Caon, M., Carrino, F., Carrino, S., Lalanne, D., Khaled, O.A., Mugellini, E.: WheelSense: enabling tangible gestures on the steering wheel for in-car natural interaction. In: Kurosu, M. (ed.) HCI 2013. LNCS, vol. 8005, pp. 531–540. Springer, Heidelberg (2013). https://doi.org/10.1007/978-3-642-39262-7_60
4. Bach, K.M., Jæger, M.G., Skov, M.B., Thomassen, N.G.: Interacting with in-vehicle systems: understanding, measuring, and evaluating attention. In: Proceedings of the 23rd British HCI Group Annual Conference on People and Computers: Celebrating People and Technology, pp. 453–462. British Computer Society (2009)
5. Cairnie, N., Ricketts, I.W., McKenna, S.J., McAllister, G.: A prototype adaptive finger-pointing interface for operating secondary controls in motor vehicles. In: 2000 IEEE International Conference on Systems, Man, and Cybernetics, vol. 2, pp. 937–942. IEEE (2000)
6. Flemisch, F.O., Adams, C.A., Conway, S.R., Goodrich, K.H., Palmer, M.T., Schutte, P.C.: The H-Metaphor as a guideline for vehicle automation and interaction (2003)
7. Flemisch, F.O., Bengler, K., Bubb, H., Winner, H., Bruder, R.: Towards cooperative guidance and control of highly automated vehicles: H-mode and conduct-by-wire. Ergonomics **57**(3), 343–360 (2014)
8. Kelsch, J., Flemisch, F., Schieben, A., Schindler, J.: Links oder rechts, schneller oder langsamer. Grundlegende Fragestellungen beim Cognitive Systems Engineering von hochautomatisierter Fahrzeugführung (2006)
9. Kienle, M., Damböck, D., Kelsch, J., Flemisch, F., Bengler, K.: Towards an H-Mode for highly automated vehicles: driving with side sticks. In: Proceedings of the 1st International Conference on Automotive User Interfaces and Interactive Vehicular Applications, pp. 19–23. ACM (2009)
10. Schieben, A., Damböck, D., Kelsch, J., Rausch, H., Flemisch, F.: Haptisches feedback im spektrum von fahrerassistenz und automation. In: 3. Tagung Aktive Sicherheit durch Fahrerassistenz (2008)

11. Schomerus, J., Flemisch, F.O., Kelsch, J., Schieben, A., Schmuntzsch, U.: Erwartungsbasierte gestaltung mit der theatersystem-/wizard-of-oz-technik am beispiel eines haptischen assistenzsystems. Tagungsband AAET 2006 Automatisierungssysteme, Assistenzsysteme und eingebettete Systeme für Transportmittel, pp. 209–225 (2006)
12. Zobl, M., Geiger, M., Schuller, B., Lang, M., Rigoll, G.: A real-time system for hand gesture controlled operation of in-car devices. In: Proceedings of 2003 International Conference on Multimedia and Expo, ICME 2003, vol. 3, pp. III–541. IEEE (2003)

Real-Time Implementation of Orientation Correction Algorithm for 3D Hand Motion Tracking Interface

Nonnarit O-larnnithipong[1]([⊠]), Armando Barreto[1],
Neeranut Ratchatanantakit[1], Sudarat Tangnimitchok[1],
and Francisco R. Ortega[2]

[1] Electrical and Computer Engineering Department, Florida International
University, Miami, FL 33199, USA
{nolar002,barretoa,nratc001,stang018}@fiu.edu
[2] School of Computer and Information Sciences, Florida International
University, Miami, FL 33199, USA
fortega@cs.fiu.edu

Abstract. This paper outlines the real-time implementation of an orientation correction algorithm using the gravity vector and the magnetic North vector for a miniature, commercial-grade Inertial Measurement Unit to improve orientation tracking in 3D hand motion tracking interface. The algorithm uses the sensor fusion approach to determine the correct orientation of the human hand motion in 3D environment. The bias offset error is the IMU's systematic error that can cause a problem in orientation tracking called drift. The algorithm is able to determine the bias offset error and update the gyroscope reading to obtain unbiased angular velocity. Furthermore, the algorithm will compare the initial estimated orientation result by using other referencing sources which are the gravity vector measured from the accelerometer and the magnetic North vector measured from the magnetometer, resulting in the improvement of the estimated orientation. The orientation correction algorithm is implemented in real-time within Unity along with position tracking, through a system of infrared cameras. To validate the performance of the real-time implementation, the orientation estimated from the algorithm and the position obtained from the infrared cameras are applied to a 3D hand model. An experiment requiring the acquisition of cubic targets within a 3D environment using the 3D hand motion tracking interface was performed 30 times. Experimental results show that the algorithm can be implemented in real-time and can eliminate the drift in orientation tracking.

Keywords: Inertial Measurement Unit · Gyroscope drift
Orientation correction algorithm · Bias offset error
Quaternion correction using gravity vector and magnetic north vector
3D hand motion tracking interface

M. Antona and C. Stephanidis (Eds.): UAHCI 2018, LNCS 10907, pp. 228–242, 2018.
https://doi.org/10.1007/978-3-319-92049-8_17

1 Introduction

The design of natural human-computer interaction interfaces is becoming increasingly important to computer manufacturers. Researchers are proposing several ideas in order to create the interaction mechanisms that are as close as possible to the natural interaction between humans. The mouse is a common device that has been used to interact with personal computers for a long time. But it is a device that is hardly close to a natural human-computer interaction. The mouse is normally used to interact with a 2D computer screen, it will eventually have a limitation when it comes to the interaction in 3D virtual environments. Several related works [1–3] tried to overcome this limitation and found alternative mechanisms to interact with computers by using computer vision to determine hand gestures or using eye tracking to interact. In the modern day, the development of the 3D User Interfaces, especially for Virtual and Augmented Reality is increasingly emphasized. In order to effectively interact with immersive VR or AR environments, the systems should provide realistic visual and acoustic output [4–7].

We have verified that our orientation correction algorithm using gravity vector and magnetic North vector compensation can effectively be used to eliminate the gyroscope drift in commercial-grade Inertial Measurement Units. The IMU we used in our research is composed of different types of sensors; for example, accelerometers, magnetometers and gyroscopes. A gyroscope measures the angular velocity, which can be used to determine orientation by performing integration through time. When the IMU has no motion, the gyroscopes are supposed to output zero values as the measurements. But, for low-cost IMUs, they can output a non-zero value even when they are not moving. This systematic error within the IMUs is called the bias offset error. In determining the orientation by means of mathematical integration, this bias offset error accumulates through time resulting in an orientation error called drift. The drift is a major problem in the navigation systems that use low-cost IMUs to measure the orientation of moving parts [8, 9].

Many studies [10–12] use Kalman filters to eliminate gyroscope drift error in inertial sensors. Other studies [13, 14], have proposed the idea of estimating the orientation using other sensor fusion methods. They combine more than one type of sensor to calculate the orientation. This is because the Kalman filter approach can be complicated and hard to implement [15, 16]. The objective of this work is to develop a system capable of determining the movement of the human hand in real-time by combining two different sources of information: orientation tracking using Inertial Measurement Units (IMUs) and position tracking using infrared cameras. To achieve that, this research also proposes an algorithm to correct gyroscope drift within the inertial measurement unit. This will be done by estimating the gyroscope bias offset error during intervals when the sensor is static and using the gravity vector measured by the accelerometers and magnetic North vector measured by the magnetometer. The goal is to monitor the movement of the human hand, in three-dimensional space including translation and rotation, in real-time.

2 Methodology and Materials

The 3D hand motion tracking interface will become aware of hand position and orientation by determining the position of an infrared marker and data from the inertial measurement unit attached on a glove, respectively. The system consists of two main parts, which are: position tracking using OptiTrack V120: Trio and orientation tracking using Yost Labs 3-Space sensors.

2.1 Position Tracking Using OptiTrack V120:Trio

OptiTrack V120: Trio is the object tracking technology that consists of three infrared sensor units. Each unit has a circular array of 26 LEDs around an infrared camera. The OptiTrack will be used to track the position of the hand moving in 3D space. OptiTrack V120: Trio was attached to a stand, above the computer screen as shown in Fig. 1. Since three IR cameras in the system have fixed distances between each other, the OptiTrack V120: Trio was pre-calibrated from the manufacturer. The hardware can be conveniently connected to the computer using a USB cable. The device comes with the licensed software called Motive:Tracker, which is an engineering-grade rigid body and marker tracking system. IR-reflective dot markers are attached around the wrist of the glove as shown in Fig. 2 to act as the referencing points for other movements of the hand beyond the wrist. The intensity of the adjustable IR LEDs is reduced within Motive:Tracker in order to eliminate unwanted spurious reflections. Each of the dot markers attached around the wrist will be visible to the three IR cameras as a single point in 3D space as shown in Fig. 3. With the combination of image processing input from three infrared cameras, Motive:Tracker can compute the position of each detected marker and will continuously provide its Cartesian coordinates (position in x, y and z) in real-time. Motive:Tracker will also display a visualization of the marker in a 3D environment, as a single point. The software allows the user to transport the marker coordinates data to other application using NatNet SDK, capable of cross-platform data streaming. With NatNet SDK, a console application written in C++ was created to stream the marker coordinates detected in Motive:Tracker. This console application establishes the connection to a NatNet server in Motive:Tracker, it receives a data stream and encodes it to an XML document. The application outputs XML locally over UDP to Unity 5 as shown in Fig. 4. In Unity, scripts written in C# were created to receive the XML document via the UDP connection. The script will be able to parse the tracking data from the streaming and apply the translation to the GameObject (3D Hand model shown in Fig. 5), which was previously prepared for the visualization of the hand motion tracking system.

2.2 Orientation Tracking Using Yost Labs 3-Space Sensors

In this work, three Yost Labs 3-Space sensors are used to determine the orientations of the hand, proximal phalange and middle phalange of the index finger. The orientation of the distal phalange of the index finger is not measured with a sensor, instead it is calculated based on the angle of middle phalange as described below. This type of low-cost Inertial Measurement Unit contains three different types of inertial sensors,

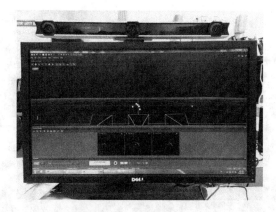

Fig. 1. The setup of OptiTrack V120: Trio with Motive:Tracker software

Fig. 2. The glove with IR-reflective dot markers attached on the wrist, one Yost Labs 3-space sensor attached on the back of the hand, and two Yost Labs 3-space sensors attached on the index finger

which are accelerometer, gyroscope and magnetometer. Each of the sensing units is able to measure in three orthogonal axes. The sensor can provide several types of information for the inertial measurement such as linear acceleration, direction of north magnetic field and gyroscope data (angular velocity). Three IMUs are connected to the host PC via USB cables and a specific command has to be sent to the sensor in order to receive the desired information. In Unity, a script written in C# was created to receive the streaming data from the Yost Labs 3-Space sensors. The script will parse the data into three sets of 3-dimensional vector: acceleration, angular velocity and direction of the magnetic field. The C# script then applies the orientation correction algorithm using gravity vector and magnetic North vector compensation to calculate an estimated output quaternion and apply the rotation to the same 3D hand model described in the

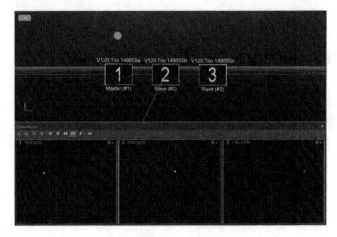

Fig. 3. Visible dot marker on three infrared cameras (white dots) and position of the marker in 3D space shown as an orange dot. (Color figure online)

```
UnitySample
[Client] Handling packet from 10.102.211.66: Command=7, nDataBytes=92
Received frame 1168129

 nOtherMarkers = 1
No.0 : x = -0.07, y = -0.02, z = 0.56
[Client] Handling packet from 10.102.211.66: Command=7, nDataBytes=92
Received frame 1168130

 nOtherMarkers = 1
No.0 : x = -0.07, y = -0.02, z = 0.56
[Client] Handling packet from 10.102.211.66: Command=7, nDataBytes=92
Received frame 1168131

 nOtherMarkers = 1
No.0 : x = -0.07, y = -0.02, z = 0.56
[Client] Handling packet from 10.102.211.66: Command=7, nDataBytes=92
Received frame 1168132

 nOtherMarkers = 1
No.0 : x = -0.07, y = -0.02, z = 0.56
```

Fig. 4. Console application to transport position marker data from Motive:Tracker to Unity

discussion of the position tracking (above). As mentioned earlier about the orientation of the distal phalange of the index finger, an empirical study and experimental observations [17] found the approximate dependency of the joint angle of the distal phalange and the joint angle of the middle phalange to be as shown in Eq. (1)

$$\theta_{Distal} = \frac{2}{3}\theta_{Middle} \tag{1}$$

Bias Offset Estimation. Bias offset error is one of the systematic errors within inertial measurement units. When the IMU is not moving or rotating, the IMU should provide the reading value of zero. But for low-cost IMUs, the bias offset error occurs and causes

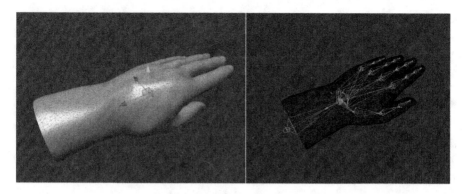

Fig. 5. 3D Hand model in Unity 5

a major problem in inertial measurement called drift. To determine the bias offset error in a real-time manner, the new bias offset error will be calculated only when the value of angular velocity is less than a predefined threshold for 5 consecutive samples (representing an interval of 250 ms). The bias offset error is calculated by determining the arithmetic mean of 5 consecutive angular velocity samples. The calculated bias offset error will be subtracted from the raw gyroscope data resulting in unbiased angular velocity as shown in Eq. (2).

$$\omega_B = \vec{\omega}_0 - \hat{b} \tag{2}$$

In this project, the quaternion notation is used to represent rotations because it is a common notation used for 3D rotation in Unity and avoids a measurement problem known as "gimbal lock". The quaternion rate ($\dot{q}$) is calculated using unbiased angular velocity as shown in Eq. (3).

$$\dot{q} = \frac{1}{2}\hat{q}_0 \otimes \omega_B \tag{3}$$

$$q_G = \exp\big((\Delta t)\dot{q} \otimes \hat{q}_0^*\big) \otimes \hat{q}_0 \tag{4}$$

In Eq. (4), the quaternion (q_G) is calculated by using quaternion rate ($\dot{q}$) obtained from Eq. (3), the previous quaternion ($\hat{q}_0$) and the sampling time (Δt). This quaternion (q_G) can be used to describe the orientation of the object in 3D space. The quaternion (q_G) will be further processed by the quaternion correction process using the gravity vector and the magnetic North vector.

Quaternion Correction
Using the Gravity Vector. When the IMU is static, each of the three axes of the accelerometer will measure only the acceleration due to gravity. The gravity vector always points towards the Earth's center in the Earth frame. If the sensor is in an oblique orientation, the acceleration due to gravity will be decomposed into three orthogonal axes resulting in gravity vector measured in the sensor's frame, which

describes the inclination of the sensor compared to the vertical gravity vector in the Earth frame. We can use quaternion (q_G) calculated in Eq. (3) to rotate [18] the initial gravity vector in the Earth frame (A_{int}) into the gravity vector in the sensor frame called *calculated gravity vector* $(\vec{a}(q_G))$ as shown in Eq. (5).

$$\vec{a}(q_G) = q_G^* \otimes A_{int} \otimes q_G \tag{5}$$

If there is no error occurred in the quaternion (q_G), the calculated gravity vector $(\vec{a}(q_G))$ will match the *measured gravity vector* $(\vec{a}_0)$ from accelerometer readings. Otherwise, the angular difference between these two vectors in quaternion form (Δq_A) will be calculated and used to correct the quaternion (q_G) as shown in Eq. (6).

$$\Delta q_A = \mathcal{H}(\vec{q}_{Av}, q_{Aw}) \tag{6}$$

$$\vec{q}_{Av} = \vec{a}_0 \times \vec{a}(q_G) \tag{7}$$

$$q_{Aw} = \|\vec{a}_0\|\|\vec{a}(q_G)\| + \vec{a}_0 \cdot \vec{a}(q_G) \tag{8}$$

$$\hat{q}_{GA} = q_G \otimes \Delta q_A \tag{9}$$

The orientation quaternion corrected the using gravity vector, denoted by $\hat{q}_{GA}$, is calculated by post-multiplying Δq_A to the quaternion (q_G) calculated from Eq. (4)

Using the Magnetic North Vector. In a way similar to the decomposition of the gravity vector measured by accelerometer described above, the magnetic North vector measured by magnetometer will be decomposed into three orthogonal axes resulting in the magnetic North vector measured in the sensor's frame. This describes the current inclination of the sensor compared to the direction of the magnetic North vector in the Earth frame. We can use quaternion (q_G) calculated in Eq. (3) to rotate the initial magnetic North vector in the Earth frame (M_{int}) into the magnetic North vector in the sensor frame called *calculated magnetic North vector* $(\vec{m}(q_G))$ as shown in Eq. (10).

$$\vec{m}(q_G) = q_G^* \otimes M_{int} \otimes q_G \tag{10}$$

If there is no error in the quaternion (q_G), the calculated magnetic North vector $(\vec{m}(q_G))$ will match the *measured magnetic North vector* $(\vec{m}_0)$ from magnetometer readings. Otherwise, the angular difference between these two vectors in quaternion form (Δq_M) will be calculated and used to correct the quaternion (q_G) as shown in Eq. (11).

$$\Delta q_M = \mathcal{H}(\vec{q}_{Mv}, q_{Mw}) \tag{11}$$

$$\vec{q}_{Mv} = \vec{m}_0 \times \vec{m}(q_G) \tag{12}$$

$$q_{Mw} = \|\vec{m}_0\|\|\vec{m}(q_G)\| + \vec{m}_0 \cdot \vec{m}(q_G) \tag{13}$$

$$\hat{q}_{GM} = q_G \otimes \Delta q_M \qquad (14)$$

The orientation quaternion corrected using the magnetic North vector, denoted by $\hat{q}_{GM}$, is calculated by post-multiplying Δq_M to the quaternion (q_G) calculated from Eq. (4). Note that regardless of the sensor's motion, the magnetometer will always measure the direction of the magnetic North vector (assuming that the magnetic field is constant in the testing area), unlike the accelerometer, which will include linear acceleration in the measurement when the sensor is in motion.

Quaternion Interpolation. Quaternion Interpolation is the parametric function that can interpolate the intermediate rotation between two quaternions by giving a control parameter that ranges from 0 to 1. In [19], even though the bias offset estimation and quaternion correction using gravity vector has been used, the resulting estimated orientation is not as expected. This is because when the sensor is in motion, the accelerometer measures not just only acceleration due to gravity but also measures the acceleration from linear motion. By using quaternion interpolation, we can control whether the output estimated orientation will be depending more on the accelerometer or magnetometer as shown in Eq. (15).

$$\hat{q}_{OUT} = \frac{\hat{q}_{GM}\sin((1-\alpha)\Omega) + \hat{q}_{GA}\sin(\alpha\Omega)}{\sin(\Omega)} \qquad (15)$$

$$\cos(\Omega) = \hat{q}_{GM} \cdot \hat{q}_{GA} \qquad (16)$$

In Eq. (15), it is one of the several types of quaternion interpolation called Spherical Linear Interpolation (SLERP) [20], which includes the control parameter (α). This parameter represents the "stillness" of the module, from 0 to 1 (1 = no movement). If α is approaching zero, it indicates that the sensor is in rapid motion and the output quaternion ($\hat{q}_{OUT}$) will tend to depend more on the quaternion correction using the magnetometer. If α is approaching one, it means that the sensor is in a static period and the output quaternion ($\hat{q}_{OUT}$) will tend to depend more on the quaternion correction using the gravity vector. The orientation correction algorithm using gravity vector and magnetic North vector is also visually described in Fig. 6.

3 Implementation

3.1 Creating the Unity Game Scene

In order to prove the concept of real-time implementation of the orientation correction algorithm using gravity vector and magnetic North vector for the hand motion tracking interface, the algorithm described in Sect. 2.2 (Orientation Tracking using Yost Lab 3-Space sensor) was adapted for real-time performance using a C# script within Unity. To evaluate the compatibility of this orientation correction algorithm on the hand motion tracking interface, a game scene in Unity has been created as shown in Fig. 7.

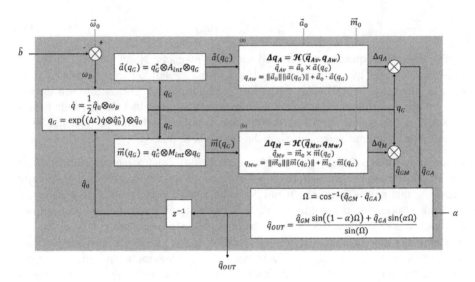

Fig. 6. Block diagram of the adopted orientation correction algorithm using gravity vector and magnetic North vector correction

Fig. 7. Unity game scene for testing real-time implementation of the orientation correction algorithm

The 3D hand model shown in Fig. 8 was attached to the C# scripts that stream the marker position in 3D space and raw accelerometer, gyroscope and magnetometer data. The marker position from OptiTrack V120:Trio were assigned as the position of the 3D hand model. The C# script that streams raw accelerometer, gyroscope and magnetometer data also implemented the orientation correction algorithm using gravity vector and magnetic North vector. For every frame of rendering, the output estimated quaternion ($\hat{q}_{OUT}$) was calculated for the hand, proximal phalange, middle phalange and distal phalange. The quaternions were assigned as the rotations for the respective

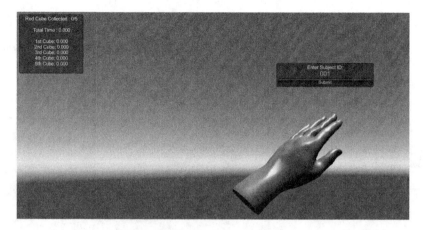

Fig. 8. Initial stage of the play mode when the subject ID is asked

parts of the hand. By combining the position tracking and orientation tracking to the 3D hand model, we can accomplish the goals of the hand motion tracking interface.

3.2   Evaluating the Hand Motion Tracking Interface Performance

To evaluate the performance of the hand motion tracking interface, a game scene with five red cubes and one blue cube was created. The experimental subject wore the glove and was asked to perform a task to "acquire" the red cubes in 3D space. A single red cube will appear in the scene after acquiring the blue cube. The acquisition of the blue cube marks the starting time for the subject to acquire the red cube. The red cubes are placed in 3D positions that are equal in distances from the origin. The time to acquire

Fig. 9. The 3D hand model will turn into green indicating the state of flexing (Color figure online)

each red cube was recorded. The blue cube appeared for the first time after the subject entered the Subject ID as shown in Fig. 8.

In order to acquire each of the cubes in this task, the subject has to flex his/her index finger while colliding with the cube. The 3D hand model will change its color into green when the flexion of the index finger is detected, as shown in Fig. 9.

Fig. 10. The red cube will appear after acquiring the blue cube (Color figure online)

In every trial, after the blue cube is acquired, the red cube will appear. The subject will try to complete the trial by moving his/her hand in 3D space to reach the red cube and flex the index finger to acquire it as shown in Fig. 10. After the subject completes a trial by acquiring each of the 5 red cubes, the trial time will be recorded. When all 5 cubes have been acquired, the total experiment time will be calculated as the sum of the 5 trial times.

4 Results and Discussion

4.1 Static Test

To perform the static test, all three inertial measurement units were fixed to a table, to prevent them from moving. The output estimated quaternions for the orientation of hand, index proximal phalange and index middle phalange were recorded for 5 min. The output estimated quaternions were recorded when the orientation correction algorithm using gravity vector and magnetic North vector are both disabled and enabled. In Fig. 11, the output estimated quaternions for hand, index proximal phalange and middle phalange recorded while the orientation correction algorithm was disabled are shown. The result indicates that the bias offset error causes the angular measurement to drift even though the sensors were placed statically on the table. It was found that the drifts occurred in different rates among the three inertial measurement

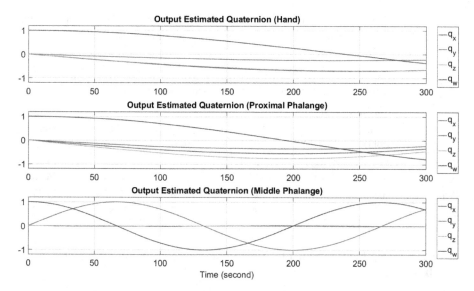

Fig. 11. Output estimated Quaternions without orientation correction algorithm

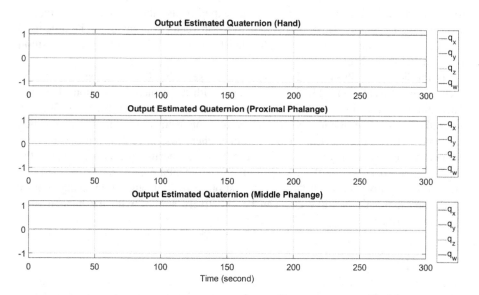

Fig. 12. Output estimated Quaternions with orientation correction algorithm

units. This is because each sensor has a different bias offset error. After enabling the orientation correction algorithm, the plots in Fig. 12 representing the orientation of $0°$ angle show that the orientation correction algorithm can improve the estimated quaternion in all three inertial measurement units. This confirmed that in the static mode (when there is no motion applied to the sensors) the orientation correction algorithm using gravity vector and magnetic North vector effectively improve the orientation measurement using the inertial measurement units in real-time.

Table 1. Statistical data of the time used to acquire red cubes

Statistic values	Time in seconds					
	1st cube (front)	2nd cube (left)	3rd cube (right)	4th cube (up)	5th cube (down)	Total time
Mean	3.34	3.44	5.04	4.60	7.33	23.75
SD	1.04	1.07	1.83	2.01	4.12	6.38
Min	2.05	1.48	2.00	1.38	2.52	15.27
Max	6.45	5.59	8.90	8.77	20.87	36.02

4.2 Performing the Experimental Task Using the Hand Motion Tracking Interface

To evaluate the performance of the hand motion tracking interface, 30 experiments (each consisting of the acquisition of 5 red cubes) were performed in the 3D environment (described above). During these experiments, the orientation correction algorithm using gravity vector and magnetic North vector was enabled. The time used to acquire each cube was recorded. The statistical characteristics of these acquisition time are shown in Table 1.

From the results shown in Table 1, it can be seen that the 5 acquisition times in each experiment added to 23.75 s on average, with the standard deviation of 6.38 s. The minimum total time was 15.27 s, whereas the maximum total time was 36.02 s. The red cube that took the longest time to acquire (on average) was the 5th cube, which appeared at the bottom of the screen. It seems, then, that the 5th red cube was more difficult to reach, compared to the other red cubes because it's almost out of the OptiTrack V120:Trio field of view. From the experimental data, it can be verified that the real-time implementation of the orientation correction algorithm using gravity vector and magnetic North vector can be effectively applied with the hand motion tracking interface.

5 Conclusion

As verified by the results, we found that we are able to implement the orientation correction algorithm using gravity vector and magnetic North vector compensation in a real-time manner. Our approach is able to correct the drift in the gyroscope measurements. This method will be one of the effective approaches for the orientation tracking in 3D hand motion tracking interface which can be an alternative way to achieve interactions between a human and a computer. This can also be a significant contribution to improvement in the realism of natural human-computer interactions.

Acknowledgment. This research was supported by National Sciences Foundation grants HRD-0833093 and CNS-1532061 and the FIU Graduate School Dissertation Year Fellowship awarded to Mr. Nonnarit O-larnnithipong.

References

1. Zhang, X., Liu, X., Yuan, S., Lin, S.: Eye tracking based control system for natural human-computer interaction. Comput. Intell. Neurosci. **2017**, 9 p. (2017). Article ID 5739301. https://doi.org/10.1155/2017/5739301
2. Roh, M., Kang, D., Huh, S., et al.: A virtual mouse interface with a two-layered Bayesian network. Multimedia Tools Appl. **76**(2), 1615–1638 (2017)
3. Pavlovic, V.I., et al.: Visual interpretation of hand gestures for human-computer interaction: a review. IEEE Trans. Pattern Anal. Mach. Intell. **19**(7), 677–695 (1997)
4. Mccall, R., et al.: Measuring presence in virtual environments. ACM (2004)
5. Slater, M., Usoh, M., Steed, A.: Depth of presence in virtual environments. Presence: Teleoper. Virtual Environ. **3**(2), 130–144 (1994)
6. Slater, M., Wilbur, S.: A framework for immersive virtual environments (FIVE). Presence: Teleoper. Virtual Environ. **6**(6), 603 (1997)
7. Heeter, C.: Being there: the subjective experience of presence. Presence: Teleoper. Virtual Environ. **1**(2), 262–271 (1992). https://doi.org/10.1162/pres.1992.1.2.262
8. Sukkarieh, S., Nebot, E.M.: A high integrity IMU/GPS navigation loop for autonomous land vehicle applications. IEEE Trans. Robot. Autom. **15**(3), 572 (1999)
9. Borenstein, J., et al.: Mobile robot positioning sensors and techniques. In: Naval Command Control and Ocean Surveillance Center RDT and E Div, San Diego, CA (1997)
10. Marins, J.L., Yun, X., Bachmann, E.R., et al.: An extended Kalman filter for quaternion-based orientation estimation using MARG sensors. In: IEEE/RSJ International Conference on Intelligent Robots and Systems, vol 4, pp. 2003–2011. IEEE (2001)
11. Yun, X., Bachmann, E.R.: Design, implementation, and experimental results of a quaternion-based Kalman filter for human body motion tracking. IEEE Trans. Robot. **22**(6), 1216–1227 (2006). https://doi.org/10.1109/TRO.2006.886270
12. Yun, X., Lizarraga, M., Bachmann, E.R., et al.: An improved quaternion-based Kalman filter for real-time tracking of rigid body orientation. In: Intelligent Robots and Systems, 2003. IEEE/RSJ International Conference, vol 2, pp. 1074–1079. IEEE (2003)
13. Bachmann, E.R., Duman, I., Usta, U.Y., et al.: Orientation tracking for humans and robots using inertial sensors. In: Proceedings of IEEE International Symposium on Computational Intelligence in Robotics and Automation, CIRA 1999, pp. 187–194. IEEE (1999)
14. Kong, X.: INS algorithm using quaternion model for low cost IMU. Robot. Auton. Syst. **46**(4), 221–246 (2004)
15. Madgwick, S.O., Harrison, A.J., Vaidyanathan, R.: Estimation of IMU and MARG orientation using a gradient descent algorithm. In: IEEE International Conference on Rehabilitation Robotics (ICORR), pp. 1–7. IEEE (2011)
16. Madgwick, S.: An efficient orientation filter for inertial and inertial/magnetic sensor arrays. Report x-io, University of Bristol (UK), p. 25 (2010)
17. Ip, H.H., Chan, C.S.: Dynamic simulation of human hand motion using an anatomically correct hierarchical approach. In: IEEE International Conference on Anonymous Systems, Man, and Cybernetics, Computational Cybernetics and Simulation, vol. 2, pp. 1307–1312. IEEE (1997)

18. Kuipers, J.B.: Quaternions and Rotation Sequences: A Primer With Applications to Orbits, Aero-Space, and Virtual Reality. Princeton University Press, Princeton (1999)
19. O-larnnithipong, N., Barreto, A.: Gyroscope drift correction algorithm for inertial measurement unit used in hand motion tracking. In: IEEE SENSORS 2016, pp. 1–3 (2016)
20. Dam, E.B., Koch, M., Lillholm, M.: Quaternions, Interpolation and Animation. Datalogisk Institut, Kbenhavns Universitet, Copenhagen (1998)

Haptic Information Access Using Touchscreen Devices: Design Guidelines for Accurate Perception of Angular Magnitude and Line Orientation

Hari Prasath Palani[1,2(✉)], G. Bernard Giudice[2(✉)],
and Nicholas A. Giudice[1,2(✉)]

[1] Spatial Informatics Program: School of Computing and Information Science,
The University of Maine, Orono, ME 04469, USA
{hariprasath.palani,nicholas.giudice}@maine.edu
[2] VEMI Lab, The University of Maine, Orono, ME 04469, USA
bernie.giudice@gmail.com

Abstract. The overarching goal of our research program is to address the long-standing issue of non-visual graphical accessibility for blind and visually-impaired (BVI) people through development of a robust, low-cost solution. This paper contributes to our research agenda aimed at studying key usability parameters governing accurate rendering and perception of haptically-accessed graphical materials via commercial touchscreen-based smart devices, such as smart phones and tablets. The current work builds on the findings from our earlier studies by empirically investigating the minimum angular magnitude that must be maintained for accurate detection and angular judgment of oriented vibrotactile lines. To assess the minimum perceivable angular magnitude (i.e., cord length) between oriented lines, a psychophysically-motivated usability experiment was conducted that compared accuracy in oriented line detection across four angles (2°, 5°, 9°, and 22°) and two radiuses (1-in. and 2-in.). Results revealed that a minimum 4 mm cord length (which corresponds to 5° at a 1-in. radius and 2° at a 2-in. radius) must be maintained between oriented lines for supporting accurate haptic perception via vibrotactile cuing. Findings provide foundational guidelines for converting/rendering oriented lines on touchscreen devices for supporting haptic information access based on vibrotactile stimuli.

Keywords: Assistive technology · Haptic information access
Haptic interaction · Multimodal interface · Design guidelines

1 Introduction

Advancements in touchscreen-based computing devices have amplified our reliance on digital information. Much of this information is based on graphical representations rather than textual content. This has resulted in a significant information access challenge for blind and visually-impaired (BVI) people as there is no commercial solution providing non-visual access to graphical materials. Several researchers and information-access

© Springer International Publishing AG, part of Springer Nature 2018
M. Antona and C. Stephanidis (Eds.): UAHCI 2018, LNCS 10907, pp. 243–255, 2018.
https://doi.org/10.1007/978-3-319-92049-8_18

technology (IAT) developers are utilizing touchscreen-based smart devices to address the non-visual graphics accessibility issue, as these solutions offer a multimodal interface based on a commercially available, inexpensive platform incorporating many native universal design and accessibility features (e.g., Voiceover for iOS or TalkBack for Android) [1]. These approaches provide access to on-screen graphical information via auditory [2, 3], vibratory [4–6], electrostatic [7], or combinations of one or more of these information sources [8–10]. While these approaches are promising, they also offer unique and novel challenges due to the limitations imposed by the touchscreen hardware as well as by the way the on-screen graphical information is accessed via non-visual haptic perception.

Perceiving digital graphical information through vibrotactile stimulation on a touchscreen display is very different from perceiving the same graphical information with vision or perceiving traditional tangible media (e.g., raised line drawings, tactile maps, etc.). With physical tangible media, users can directly touch and perceive the line stimuli with changes in force, friction, and pressure during finger/hand movement leading to skin deformation that innervates *mechanoreceptors* on the fingertip upon contact with the stimuli (see Fig. 1). Similarly, with a touchscreen-based visual interface, sighted users can perceive the stimuli using various visual cues such as the color of the line, its spatial position, its spatial structure, and angle subtended with respect to the visual axis. By contrast, with a touchscreen-based non-visual interface, the user can only perceive a flat, featureless glass screen that conveys no meaningful tactual information/cutaneous reinforcement, as the stimuli in isolation does not possess any physical attributes that are directly perceivable by the finger. Therefore, haptic interactions must rely on extrinsic feedback such as vibration to indicate contact with an on-screen graphical element. Since the device's hardware is equipped with only one vibration motor, which vibrates the entire device when triggered, users must employ only one finger to access and extract information. The result is that the focal vibration on the finger touching the display is perceived as a tactile graphical element on the screen. While the extrinsic feedback can indicate contact with on-screen elements, such feedback (in isolation) does not provide any meaningful tactual information, such as the width/height of an element. As a result, it is much more difficult to haptically distinguish fine detail and precise spatial information on a touchscreen using vibrotactile cuing that would otherwise be easily discernible from physical access using tangible graphics or from visual access to the same graphical information presented on touchscreen displays. To tackle these differences imposed by haptic information extraction and to develop truly useful touchscreen-based haptic applications, new approaches must be introduced that go beyond the naïve technique of simply trying to implement a one-to-one haptic analog of the visual graphical rendering on the touchscreen. To be successful, a principled conversion and schematization process of the underlying graphical information must be carried out to optimize effective visual to haptic sensory substitution supporting accurate vibrotactile information extraction [11]. There is an existing body of research based on traditional tangible media that has identified and established perceptual parameters and design guidelines for performing this visual-to-tactile conversion/optimization process for graphical information [12–14]. However, these results are limited to studies with tangible media and cannot be applied to extraction and perception of dynamic vibrotactile stimulation from touchscreen-based interfaces due to the previously discussed differences in haptic information extraction and the extrinsic cuing mechanism required for touchscreen-based vibrotactile stimuli. To our knowledge, there are no empirical guidelines and parameters governing the conversion of visual graphical information into haptically perceivable vibrotactile information delivered via commercial touchscreens. This paper builds on a series of studies conducted in the VEMI Lab at the University of Maine aimed at addressing this gap in the literature by developing a set of theoretically-motivated and empirically-validated guidelines for use of vibrotactile stimuli as part of a robust touchscreen-based information access solution. By extension, this work also provides foundational design guidelines that address the long-standing challenge of providing blind and visually-impaired (BVI) people with meaningful access to digital graphical materials.

Fig. 1. Perceptual differences between tangible media and touchscreen displays

2   Current Research

The current work is part of a larger corpus of research aimed at empirically evaluating and identifying a set of core nonvisual rendering parameters through a series of psychophysically-inspired usability studies. We posit that, once established, these core usability parameters will serve as a set of much-needed de-facto guidelines specifying the best techniques for accurate rendering and haptic perception of graphical materials via commercial touchscreen-based smart devices (e.g., smartphones and tablets). This paper builds on the findings from four earlier studies [15], which established four key usability parameters, namely:

(1) Graphical elements must be rendered at a width of at least 1 mm for tasks requiring simple detection of graphical elements when using vibrotactile feedback on touchscreen displays,

(2) A minimum gap width of 4 mm must be maintained for identifying each unique graphical element and accurately detecting gaps between adjacent elements. In addition to the 4 mm minimum gap width, the lines (e.g., borders of the element) must be rendered at a width greater than 2 mm for supporting discrimination of adjacent elements.

(3) For tasks requiring accurate orientation judgments of line segments (e.g., paths on a map) using vibrotactile feedback, the line elements must be rendered at a minimum width of at least 2 mm, and

(4) For tasks requiring accurate line tracing and learning of multi-line spatial patterns using vibrotactile feedback (e.g., subway maps, road networks, or corridor layouts), the line elements must be rendered at a width of at least 3 mm. (see [15] for details and discussion on the parameters)

Building on these findings, the current research was conducted to empirically identify the minimum angular magnitude that must be maintained for accurate detection and angular judgment of a range of oriented vibrotactile lines. Whether it is a simple line graph or a complex map, the ability to accurately identify an angled line and judging the angle it is subtending with respect to an adjacent line is crucial for extracting information from the graphical material. Consider, for example, a simple corridor map of a shopping mall as shown in Fig. 2. Each of the three corridors are diverging from one vertex and are oriented at different angles. Understanding this layout is a pre-requisite for developing an accurate cognitive map and being able to efficiently navigate within this environment (e.g., way-finding from Macy's to Sears). For a non-visual interface to effectively communicate this information, the rendering must support users in accurately judging the angle subtended between corridors and the angle subtended by each corridor with respect to some frame of reference (e.g., the frame of the device). As stated earlier, perceiving digital graphical information via vibrotactile feedback on touchscreen-based devices is difficult due to the sparse spatial resolution of touch as well as the extrinsic feedback mechanism. This means the corridors must not only be rendered at a width perceivable by touch but also must be separated by a minimum angular magnitude that allows users to always distinguish one corridor from another.

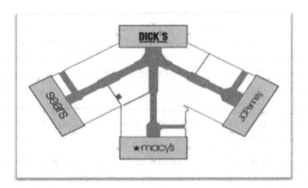

Fig. 2. Indoor corridor layout of a shopping mall.

2.1 Preliminary Studies on Angle Perception and Orientation Judgment

The importance of being able to judge line-orientations has been extensively described in the psychophysical literature with both vision and touch [16, 17]. These studies have shown that blindfolded-sighted people are more accurate when predicting vertical or horizontal orientations over obliquely oriented stimuli. Although formal research has not been conducted on orientation judgments based on active exploration of vibrotactile lines, user feedback and informal observations from earlier studies in our lab revealed that participants found it difficult to trace lines and detect their orientation when they deviated from horizontal or vertical orientations [4, 9, 18]. To investigate whether users were able to judge orientation and perceive angular magnitude between vibrotactile lines, two preliminary studies were conducted. The first study compared performance in a task where blindfolded-sighted participants had to explore and identify the angular magnitude across two touchscreen-based non-visual interfaces (i.e., vibrotactile and electrostatic). Five angle stimuli were generated for each display used in the study, covering a range from near horizontal right to near horizontal left, comprising 25°, 70°, 90°, 125°, and 155° [19]. This study showed that the vibrotactile interface exhibited superior performance over the electrostatic interface and that users were able to accurately identify the angles subtended between two vibrotactile lines with a mean signed error of 0.3° (s.e.m. 1.4°). In a second study, we investigated users' ability to judge vibrotactile line orientations across 36 angles and three different line widths. The study showed that participants were able to accurately judge vibrotactile line-orientations and that a line width of 2 mm or more must be maintained for efficient tracing and learning of vibrotactile lines [15]. While the findings from these two studies show evidence that users can accurately judge angles subtended between two vibrotactile lines, they do not provide any guidance on the perceptual limitation of detecting angular magnitude (i.e., the minimum perceivable angle between two vibrotactile lines). Identifying this angular threshold and rendering graphical material accordingly is essential for supporting accurate detection of distinct vibrotactile lines that are connected at an intersection (e.g., the intersection shown in Fig. 2). To our knowledge, there is no empirical data from the literature on the minimum angular magnitude that ensures detection of distinct vibrotactile lines. To address this gap in the literature, we designed a psychophysically-inspired usability study aimed at answering the research question: *"What is the minimum angular magnitude that best supports the detection of oriented vibrotactile lines on touchscreen interfaces?"*.

3 Evaluation of Minimum Perceivable Angular Magnitude

As stated earlier, with the extrinsic cuing mechanism employed on touchscreen devices, users can only detect whether the touched location is on or off of an on-screen graphical element but they cannot directly perceive any other meaningful information such as width/length/angle. For example, consider the triangle in Fig. 3 (right). Based on static contact, the user is able to detect whether they are touching a part of the triangle but they are not able to discern any other meaningful information such as number of edges, length of each edge, angle between two edges, etc. To extract such detailed information, users must actively explore the stimuli by employing finger movements and accurate tracking of proprioceptive information. Because of this basic difference in tactual perception between information rendered on touchscreens vs. tangible media, traditional static psychophysical methods (i.e., measuring perception via direct skin innervation) cannot be utilized for measuring the minimum perceivable angular magnitude on touchscreen-based interfaces, as the contact finger does not receive any meaningful cutaneous sensation as one would receive from tangible media.

As stated earlier, the challenge of vibrotactile exploration and tactual learning is further aggravated by technical constraints imposed by touchscreen displays, which typically limit the user to employ only one finger for exploration. This means that users cannot simply maintain static contact with the stimuli to extract meaningful information but must perform exploratory procedures (Eps), which are a stereotyped pattern of manual exploration observed when people are asked to learn about a particular object property during voluntary manual exploration without vision [20]. In contrast to traditional Eps, which generally involve use of all fingers on one or both hands, exploratory procedures with touchscreen-based vibrotactile stimuli must be done using only one finger and involve sequential apprehension/integration of the different graphical elements to develop a coherent mental representation. Germane to the current experiment, for identifying oriented lines and judging the angle subtended between them, we have found that users typically employ a 'circling' strategy, where they move their finger in a circular pattern around the intersection (see Fig. 3 (left)) as their exploratory procedure to most accurately identify the geometry and number of legs [8, 18, 21].

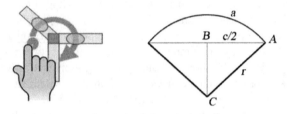

Fig. 3. (Left) Intersection circling strategy: adapted from [21], (Right) Geometric representation of cord length 'c' and radius 'r'

Based on this exploration strategy, we posit here that the arc of the circle formed between two oriented vibrotactile lines will be perceived by the user as the angular magnitude subtended between the two lines. To be recognized as a distinct vibrotactile line, each of the lines emanating from the intersection must be separated from each other by a minimum perceivable angular magnitude. As stated earlier, our previous work established that a minimum gap of 4 mm must be maintained between adjacent lines for accurate detection of parallel vibrotactile lines. From a geometric standpoint, the straight-line distance between two angled lines is the cord length (see angle-theta and cord length in Fig. 3(right)). The cord length will linearly increase with a corresponding increase in the: (1) θ – angle subtended between the lines, (2) r – the radius of the traced circle, or (3) both 1 and 2. This means that the minimum gap of 4 mm that we have previously identified for detecting two parallel lines [15] should, in theory, be translated into a 4 mm cord length for accurate detection of distinct oriented lines. However, unlike simple gap width, cord length is a variable that is directly proportional to both angle and radius (i.e., an increase in angle or radius leads to a corresponding increase in the cord length). The relation between the three variables is mathematically defined as: *cord length = 2r sin (θ/2)*. This means that the cord length is directly dependent on the radius of the circle formed by the user while performing their circling exploration strategy. For instance, an angle of 5° will lead to a 4 mm cord length with a 1-in. radius circle, and an angle of 2° will lead to a 4 mm cord length with a 2-in. radius circle. Since our interest in this experiment is on identifying the minimum perceivable angle (θ) by varying the cord length, the radius (r) will be kept constant at two levels (i.e., 1-in. and 2-in.).

3.1 Method

Participants. Eighteen blindfolded-sighted participants (nine males and nine females, ages 19–34) were recruited for the study. All gave informed consent and were paid for their participation. The study was approved by the Institutional Review Board (IRB) of the University of Maine. It is important to note that use of blindfolded-sighted participants was intentional, as although under-studied, sighted individuals can also benefit from haptic information access in eyes-free situations (e.g., Performing a secondary task while driving) and we believe that our interface has significant untapped value in such situations. With respect to traditional information-access technology design, inclusion of blindfolded-sighted participants is widely accepted in the preliminary testing of assistive technology (see [22] for discussion). Furthermore, the graphical information studied here is equally accessible to both groups, a supposition empirically corroborated by our previous studies on touchscreen-based interfaces showing no reliable differences between blindfolded-sighted and blind and visually-impaired participants [4, 23, 24].

Stimuli and Conditions. The stimulus set was designed as a simple indoor corridor layout (e.g., Shopping mall) where multiple corridors were converging to/diverging from an intersection point at the center (Fig. 4). The number of corridors in each stimuli ranged from 5 to 9 based on Miller's "The Magical Number Seven, Plus or Minus Two" [25]. To evaluate the influence of radius over perception of oriented lines, two conditions were designed and evaluated. The radius was set as a constant value of 1-in. and 2-in. for conditions 1 and 2 respectively. At a radius of 1-in. from the intersection, the minimum gap width of 4 mm (i.e., cord length in this context) was translated to an angular magnitude of ∼9°. Similarly, at a 2-in. radius, the gap width of 4 mm width was translated to a ∼5° angular magnitude. To evaluate the influence of cord length (i.e., gap) on the perception of oriented lines, two additional angles (2° and 22°) were also added to the stimuli set that approximately translated to the 4 mm gap width at a radius of 0.5-in. and 4-in. (meaning the radius of the two primary conditions increased and decreased by a factor of 2).

Apparatus. The stimuli were presented using our prototype, called a vibro-audio interface (VAI) implemented on a touchscreen equipped tablet computer - 10.1 in. Galaxy Tab 3. The interface works by allowing users to freely explore the device screen and whenever an onscreen element is touched, the device's vibration motor is triggered, creating the perception of focal vibrotactile stimulation on the users finger (more details can be found in [4]). For controlling the circle radius in each condition and for assisting users with the circling strategy, two circular paper stickers of 4 mm width (one at 1-in. from the center and the other at 2-in. from the center) were affixed

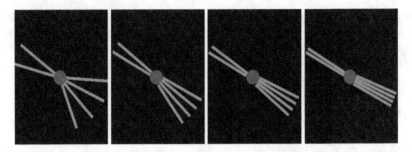

Fig. 4. Experimental angle stimuli 22°, 9°, 5°, 2° from left to right

on the screen (see Fig. 5 (right)). In addition, the intersection point (center of the screen) was also demarcated with a paper sticker of 10 mm radius. To assist participants with orienting themselves on the screen, each circle had a start point (indicated by a tactile marker at the 5 o'clock position).

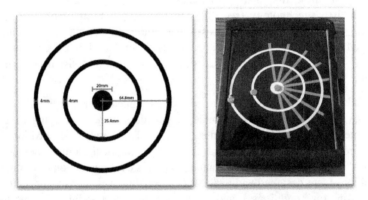

Fig. 5. (Left) Dimensions of the two conditions and their tracing radius, (right) experimental device with circular stickers for two radiuses and tactile markers for start points

Procedure and Design. The study followed a within-subjects design. A trial rendered 5, 6, 7, 8, or 9 lines on the screen (for example see Fig. 4). In each trial, the angular magnitude between adjacent lines was kept constant irrespective of line number. The order of the conditions (1-in. versus 2-in. radius) was balanced across the participants and the order of stimuli presentation in each condition was randomized within the script. In each trial, participants were asked to start at the reference start point (indicated by a tactile marker) and to count the number of lines perceived in a full 360° circuit by tracing along the circular path (either at 1-in. or 2-in. radius depending on the condition). Upon returning to the start point, they lifted their finger from the display and verbally indicated the number of lines perceived during the 360° scan. In each condition, participants began with 5 practice trials where the experimenter gave corrective feedback with respect to their tracing speed and counting accuracy. They then moved on to the 28 experimental trials in each condition (resulting in 180 observations for each tested angular magnitude). Each participant took between 20 and 40 min to complete the entire experiment.

Experimental Measures. Based on this design, two measures were compared across the four tested angular magnitudes and two circling conditions.

1. *Tracing time:* The tracing time is the time taken in each trial from the moment they first touched the reference start point until they returned to the same point after scanning along the circle.
2. *Line counting accuracy:* Accuracy in line counting was measured based on correctness of line count as self-reported by participants in each trial.

4   Results and Discussion

ANOVA results revealed that in both conditions, the tracing time did not statistically differ between the four tested angles. The f and p values are as follows,

$$\text{For the 1-inch circular path, } F(3, 500) = 1.043, \text{ } p > 0.05, \text{ } \eta^2 = 0.006$$

$$\text{For the 2-inch circular path, } F(3, 500) = 1.145, \text{ } p > 0.05, \text{ } \eta^2 = 0.006$$

A one-way ANOVA revealed that in both conditions, the accuracy in line counting was significantly different between the four tested angles. The f and p values are as follows (Fig. 6),

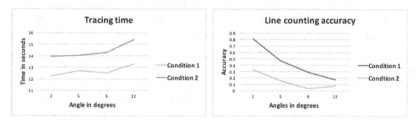

Fig. 6. (Left) Mean tracing time as a function of tested angles and two circling conditions. (Right) Mean error in line counting accuracy as a function of tested angles and two circling conditions

$$\text{For the 1-inch circular path, } F(3, 500) = 14.147, \text{ } p > 0.001, \text{ } \eta^2 = 0.019$$

$$\text{For the 2-inch circular path, } F(3, 500) = 12.559, \text{ } p > 0.001, \text{ } \eta^2 = 0.070$$

Post-hoc t-tests with Bonferroni correction revealed that the difference in line counting accuracy between observations with a 2° angle compared to the other three angles was significant (p < 0.001). But there was no significant differences between the other angles (5°, 9°, and 22°). This finding indicates that a 4 mm cord length is sufficient to accurately detect distinct oriented vibrotactile lines when using a circling strategy. This parameter is in line with our previous research that also established 4 mm as the gap width for accurate detection of distinct vibrotactile lines that are parallel to each other [15].

On comparing the tracing time between 1-in. and 2-in. circling conditions, a post-hoc paired sample t-Test revealed that the tracing time for the 1-in. radius circle was significantly faster than the tracing time for the 2-in. radius circle (T(503) = −8.060, p < 0.001). This outcome is not surprising as the tracing time is directly proportional to the perimeter of the circle (i.e., the distance they traced) and the 1-in. circle condition has half the perimeter length as the 2-in. circle condition. Similarly, the accuracy in line counting was also significantly different between the two conditions with the 2-in. radius circle condition exhibiting higher accuracy, (T(503) = 6.243, p < 0.001). This finding is also expected as the cord length increases with the corresponding increase in radius, which resulted in a higher chance of line detection for the 2-in. condition than 1-in. condition.

5 Conclusions

This paper investigated the minimum perceivable angular magnitude that is necessary for detecting oriented vibrotactile lines emanating from a common intersection. The work presented here is part of a larger research program aimed at establishing the core usability parameters and design guidelines for governing the conversion of visual graphical information into a haptically perceivable format rendered using touchscreen-based interfaces. We postulated that to accurately detect distinct oriented vibrotactile lines, the spacing between two adjacent lines (i.e., the cord length) must be maintained at a minimum length such that users can accurately detect distinct vibro-tactile lines converging or diverging from a common intersection point. As stated earlier, the cord length (and by extension the minimum perceivable angular magnitude) is a variable that is dependent on both the angle subtended between oriented lines and the radius of the circle formed by the user during their exploratory procedure when apprehending the vertex/intersection of these lines. To evaluate the minimum cord length and to assess the influence of the angle and radius on this cord length, accuracy in oriented line detection was compared across four angles (2°, 5°, 9°, and 22°) and two radiuses (1-in. and 2-in.).

The most important outcome of the study is the similarity in perceptual characteristics between parallel lines and oriented lines. The minimum value threshold of a 4 mm cord length for oriented lines established here is congruent with the minimum gap width of 4 mm we previously established for detecting parallel vibrotactile lines [15]. On comparing the two radiuses/conditions, it is evident that the line detection accuracy proportionally increases with an increase in angle magnitude (θ), and/or the radius (r). This validates our hypothesis that the cord length is a variable that depends on two other parameters (i.e., angle and radius) and that the parameters must be manipulated accordingly to maintain a minimum cord length of 4 mm. This suggests that when designing or rendering graphical materials (or converting from a corresponding visual rendering), designers must understand this dependency between angle, radius, and cord length and schematize the angular elements by calculating the minimum perceivable angle (using the formula: $\theta = 2\ arcsin\ (cord\ length/2r)$) based on the minimum 4 mm cord length. While traditional visual-to-tactile conversion methods generally adopt an 8-sector (45° interval) or 16-sector (22.5° interval) model for schematizing oriented lines [26], the results here clearly suggest that simply relying on angular magnitude will not be sufficient for ensuring accurate haptic perception of oriented vibrotactile lines on touchscreen displays when rendering graphical elements. This difference relates to the nature of haptic perception between these stimuli. That is, with tangible raised stimuli, users can directly perceive fine spatial details via skin deformation that innervates *mechanoreceptors* even with static finger contact. However, with touchscreen-based vibrotactile cuing, users must perform active exploration using just one finger to extract/perceive these attributes, movement that requires spatial extent and thus mandates incorporation of additional spacing between oriented vibrotactile lines on the display. To produce accurate and efficient vibrotactile renderings, this research demonstrates that designers must consider this difference in stimulus/perceptual coupling. Specifically, when designing/rendering oriented vibrotactile graphical elements on touchscreen-based displays, accurate haptic perception requires considering the relation between the angle (θ), the radius (r), and cord length, rather than adopting traditional parameters/models that are based only on the angular magnitude (i.e., 45°, 30°, or 22.5°).

Caveats are needed before generically adopting this 4 mm cord length threshold, as this value is based on just one exploratory procedure (i.e., circling around an intersection or vertex). Future research will address this limitation and generalize the identified value for different graphical materials (e.g., road networks, edges of a pie chart, building layout maps, etc.,) We will also investigate other exploratory strategies such as *four directional scanning*, where users start at the intersection/vertex and move their finger in cardinal directions (i.e., north, east, south, and west).

In sum, findings from this work provide foundational guidelines for converting/rendering angular elements and oriented lines on touchscreen-based interfaces for supporting vibrotactile haptic information access. Combining the cord length parameter identified here with the four parameters established from our earlier research (discussed in Sect. 2), we continue to build on our goal of developing a robust set of usability and design guidelines for rendering a wide range of haptically perceivable graphical information on touchscreen displays.

Acknowledgments. We acknowledge support from NSF grants CHS-1425337 and ECR DCL Level 2 1644471 on this project.

References

1. Grussenmeyer, W., Folmer, E.: Accessible touchscreen technology for people with visual impairments: a survey. ACM Trans. Access. Comput. **9**, 31 (2017)
2. Su, J., Rosenzweig, A., Goel, A., Lara, E. de, Truong, K.N.: Timbremap: enabling the visually-impaired to use maps on touch-enabled devices. In: Proceedings of the 12th International Conference on Human Computer Interaction with Mobile Devices and Services, pp. 17–26. ACM (2010)
3. Poppinga, B., Pielot, M., Magnusson, C., Rassmus-Grohn, K.: TouchOver map: audio-tactile exploration of interactive maps. In: Proceedings of the 12th International Conference on Human Computer Interaction with Mobile Devices and Services, pp. 545–550. ACM, Stock (2011)
4. Giudice, N.A., Palani, H.P., Brenner, E., Kramer, K.M.: Learning non-visual graphical information using a touch-based vibro-audio interface. In: Proceedings of the 14th International ACM SIGACCESS Conference on Computers and Accessibility, pp. 103–110. ACM Press, New York (2012)
5. Goncu, C., Marriott, K.: GraVVITAS: generic multi-touch presentation of accessible graphics. In: Campos, P., Graham, N., Jorge, J., Nunes, N., Palanque, P., Winckler, M. (eds.) INTERACT 2011. LNCS, vol. 6946, pp. 30–48. Springer, Heidelberg (2011). https://doi.org/10.1007/978-3-642-23774-4_5
6. Tennison, J.L., Gorlewicz, J.L.: Toward non-visual graphics representations on vibratory touchscreens: shape exploration and identification. In: Bello, F., Kajimoto, H., Visell, Y. (eds.) EuroHaptics 2016. LNCS, vol. 9775, pp. 384–395. Springer, Cham (2016). https://doi.org/10.1007/978-3-319-42324-1_38
7. Mullenbach, J., Shultz, C., Colgate, J.E., Piper, A.M.: Exploring affective communication through variable - friction surface haptics. In: Proceedings of the SIGCHI Conference on Human Factors in Computing Systems, pp. 3963–3972 (2014)
8. Palani, H.P., Giudice, N.A.: Principles for designing large-format refreshable haptic graphics using touchscreen devices. ACM Trans. Access. Comput. **9**, 1–25 (2017)
9. Klatzky, R.L., Giudice, N.A., Bennett, C.R., Loomis, J.M.: Touch-screen technology for the dynamic display of 2D spatial information without vision: promise and progress. Multisens. Res. **27**, 359–378 (2014)
10. O'Modhrain, S., Giudice, N.A., Gardner, J.A., Legge, G.E.: Designing media for visually-impaired users of refreshable touch displays: possibilities and pitfalls. Trans. Haptics **8**, 248–257 (2015)
11. Loomis, J.M., Klatzky, R.L., Giudice, N.A.: Sensory substitution of vision: importance of perceptual and cognitive processing. In: Manduchi, R., Kurniawan, S. (eds.) Assistive Technology for Blindness and Low Vision, pp. 162–191. CRC, Boca Raton (2012)
12. Johnson, K.O., Philips, J.R.: Tactile spatial resolution. I. Two-point discrimination, gap detection, grating resolution, and letter recognition. J. Neurophysiol. **46**, 1177–1192 (1981)
13. Van Boven, R.W., Johnson, K.O.: The limit of tactile spatial resolution in humans: grating orientation discrimination at the lip, tongue, and finger. Neurology **44**, 2361 (1994)
14. Craig, J.C.: Grating orientation as a measure of tactile spatial acuity. Somatosens. Mot. Res. **16**, 197–206 (1999)
15. Palani, H.P., Giudice, N.A.: Eyes-free information access on touchscreen interfaces: user evaluations and design guidelines for accurate haptic perception. ACM Trans. Appl. Percept. (2018, in review)
16. Appelle, S.: Perception and discrimination as a function of stimulus orientation: the "oblique effect" in man and animals. Psychol. Bull. **78**(4), 266–278 (1972)

17. Baud-Bovy, G., Gentaz, E.: The perception and representation of orientations: a study in the haptic modality. Acta Psychol. (AMST) **141**, 24–30 (2012)
18. Palani, H.P., Giudice, N.A.: Evaluation of non-visual panning operations using touch-screen devices. In: Proceedings of the 16th International ACM SIGACCESS Conference on Computers & Accessibility. ACM (2014)
19. Gershon, P., Klatzky, R.L., Palani, H.P., Giudice, N.A.: Visual, tangible, and touch-screen: comparison of platforms for displaying simple graphics. Assist. Technol. **28**, 1–6 (2016)
20. Lederman, S.J., Klatzky, R.L.: Hand movements: a window into haptic object recognition. Cogn. Psychol. **19**, 342–368 (1987)
21. Raja, M.K.: The development and validation of a new smartphone based non-visual spatial interface for learning indoor layouts. Unpublished Masters thesis, University of Maine (2011)
22. Sears, A., Hanson, V.L.: Representing users in accessibility research. ACM Trans. Access. Comput. **4**, 1–6 (2012)
23. Palani, H., Giudice, U., Giudice, N.A.: Evaluation of non-visual zooming operations on touchscreen devices. In: Antona, M., Stephanidis, C. (eds.) UAHCI 2016. LNCS, vol. 9738, pp. 162–174. Springer, Cham (2016). https://doi.org/10.1007/978-3-319-40244-4_16
24. Palani, H.P.: Making graphical information accessible without vision using touch-based devices. Unpublished Masters thesis, University of Maine (2013)
25. Miller, G.A.: The magical number seven, plus or minus two: some limits on our capacity for processing information. Psychol. Rev. **63**, 81 (1956)
26. Graf, C.: Schematisation in hard-copy tactile orientation maps. Unpublished Ph.D dissertation, University of Bremen, Germany (2013)

Brain Controlled Interface Log Analysis in Real Time Strategy Game Matches

Mauro C. Pichiliani[(✉)]

IBM Research, São Paulo, SP 04007-900, Brazil
mpichi@br.ibm.com

Abstract. Emotions are an important aspect that affects human interaction with systems and applications. The correlation of emotional and affective state with game interaction data is a relevant issue since it can explain player behavior and the outcome of a digital game match. In this work, we present an initial exploratory study to analyze interaction log data and its correlation with an off-the-shelf Brain Controlled Interface (BCI) that collected excitement in a RTS (Real Time Strategy game). Our results shown moderate correlations with player's preferences and amount of interactions. Additionally, we also found in the interaction and game logs that character's choice significantly impacts the time spent in data-driven levels of excitement. We did not find statistically significant differences of excitement for other factors such as player ranking and game style, map, and opponent character.

Keywords: Log analysis · Brain Controlled Interface · Video games

1 Introduction

In game analysis, the understanding of how to best use human emotions for more immersive and engaging gameplay experiences is a research topic. One of the directions explored is the detection of the player's emotional state to employ the full potential of emotions for shaping gameplay. The interpretation of emotional states traditionally relies in individual psychophysiological experiences guided by biochemical interactions and digital environmental stimuli. As they mostly occur at a subconscious level, emotions influence humans in a meaningful and critical way, often overriding rational thought.

Designing adaptive games for individual emotional experiences has many challenges mostly because the detection of player's emotional state in real time requires physiological sensing hardware and signal processing software. The potential benefits that convey player's emotions to gameplay is relevant nowadays, since the nature of video games has changed dramatically in the last decade, becoming increasingly complex, diverse, realistic and social in nature.

The motivation for the study of emotional responses includes the need to identify, quantify and better understand how the information about personal human affective condition correlate to user actions during gameplay session. These correlations can influence the user experience with the game and increase the importance of emotional affective state as a factor in the design and development of RTS games.

© Springer International Publishing AG, part of Springer Nature 2018
M. Antona and C. Stephanidis (Eds.): UAHCI 2018, LNCS 10907, pp. 256–272, 2018.
https://doi.org/10.1007/978-3-319-92049-8_19

The goal of this paper is to explore the use of an electroencephalograph system to collect information about the users' excitement in RTS games. Our research work employs a low-cost off-the-shelf electroencephalograph (EEG) system to collect excitement information experienced by the players of the RTS game StarCraft 2 [37].

The rest of this paper is organized as follows. The next section reviews existing studies in emotional digital game and characterize the RTS genre. Next, the technology behind Brain Controlled Interfaces is explained with the description of the device employed in this work. The section finishes with a review of previous research in emotions and game design. The following section describes the questions, methodology, participants, design, procedure, and results of an exploratory experiment. Afterwards, a discussion of the experiment's results is presented. The last section is the conclusion of this paper.

2 Related Work

This section briefly presents related work in general emotion game studies followed by the definition and characterization of the RTS genre and the StarCraft game.

2.1 Studies in Emotional Digital Game State

Gaming experience may be among the most efficient and effective means by which children, teenagers, and adults generate positive, neutral, or negative feelings [18]. Social, psychological, and biological scientists have been conducting studies that have shown a causal relation between playing preferred video games and improved mood, such as the works of Russoniello et al. [34] and Ryan et al. [35].

Emotion recognition while playing digital games is also addressed by previous work. For instance, Chanel et al. [6] could classify arousal using machine learning techniques from biological data, such as blood volume pressure (BVP), heart rate (HR), skin temperature and respiration (RSP) rates.

Complementary, the study presented by Drachen et al. [11] confirms that relatively simple features extracted from skin conductance (SC) and heart rate measures are highly correlated with reported affect ratings in gameplay scenarios. A more detailed study has also found proof that features extracted from HR, SC and BVP can predict higher-level concepts, such as "fun" in a game-dependent manner [38].

2.2 Real Time Strategy Games

Chan et al. [5] characterize the RTS genre as games where a player must engage in real-time actions, with the objective being to achieve military or territorial superiority over other players or the computer. Central to RTS game-play are two key problem domains: resource production and tactical battles. In resource production, the player must produce (or gather) various raw materials, buildings, civilian and military units, to improve their economic and military power. In tactical battles, a player uses military units to gain territory and defeat enemy units. A typical game usually involves an initial period where players rapidly build their economy via resource production, followed by military campaigns where those resources are exploited for offense and defense.

There are many games in the market classified as RTS and the StarCraft series is one of the most popular according to the specialized press [19] and gamer communities [17, 28]. The StarCraft series franchise has two installments: StarCraft 1 (1998) and StarCraft 2 (2010), being that the last one is the most played version made by Blizzard Entertainment [3], the game's producer, distributor, and maintainer.

In StarCraft, a futuristic multiplanetary science fiction RTS, players choose one of three existing set of characters, known as races inside the game's lore, that have exclusive units and technological/biological distinctions: Protoss, Terran, or Zerg. Each player competes in a map containing key locations where resources need to be mined so the player spent them in buildings and military units. The player's vision of the board or map is limited to his or her own units and buildings, a concept called "fog of war" that prevents them from seeing their opponent(s) or allies unless they perform reconnaissance. Worker units collect resources and build specialized buildings that can create marines, fighters, tanks, air units, and more. These units have a more elaborate version of a "rock-paper-scissors" dynamic. Some units are also better suited to certain strategies such as an armored "Blitzkrieg" through the enemy base, wave after wave of cheap disposable units, or sneak attacks behind enemy lines [8].

Following the success of its predecessor, StarCraft 2 quickly became a phenomenon with competitions, tournaments and leagues; spectators became fans and community. Dedicated e-sports television channels broadcast StarCraft 2 matches in South Korea daily and a large community of users watch replays of matches in YouTube and Twitch.tv video channels. These and other factors fostered a complex supporting infrastructure of professional leagues, teams, and superstars. We chose the StarCraft 2 game because it is popular and established as an e-sport with one of the most successful cases of RTS digital game spectating [8], with large audiences and wide appeal.

Previous research in RTS games explored resources planning [1, 5, 7], latency effects [9], cheating [4], and audience engagement [8]. From the best of our knowledge, no previous research in RTS explore excitement to understanding the player's behavior.

2.3 Brain Controlled Interfaces

In this paper, we rely on Electroencephalograph (EEG) [20], the technology most commonly used in contemporary noninvasive BCI research. EEG uses electrodes placed in the scalp to measure the weak electrical potentials generated by brain activity. The signal provided by an EEG is at best a crude representation of brain activity due to the nature of the detector. Scalp electrodes are only sensitive to macroscopic and coordinated firing of large groups of neurons near the surface of brain only when they are placed directed along a perpendicular vector relative to the scalp. Additionally, because of the fluid, bone, hair, and skin that separate the electrodes from the actual electrical activity, the already small signals are scattered and attenuated before reaching the electrodes. Nevertheless, the signal produced by these devices have been used in many applications both for control physical devices (or user interface elements) and to log brain activity [31].

Although BCIs are employed mostly in the HCI (Human Computer Interaction) area by exploring its capability to detect brain patterns to manipulate elements directly with the brain, we concentrate our attention in EEG work related to the ability to transform raw EEG data streams into emotional and affective states.

Considering the available commercial noninvasive EEG, we opted for the low-cost off-the-shelf Emotiv EEG headset [13] due to the ease of use in experimental setups and the resourceful standard SDK (Software Development Kit) that allows three event-based classification suites. The choice for the Emotiv EEG headset presents a tradeoff between limited data accuracy versus broader data collection in a naturalistic scenario.

The practical use the device SDK involves the manipulation of programming elements of the integrated software solution named EmotivePro [14]. This software provided three available suites: the Expressive suite, which tries to detect the wearer's facial expression; the Affective suite, which tries to detect mood and emotions; and the Cognitive suite, which tries to detect occurrences of user-defined cognitive events.

Since our aim is to capture of emotions, we concentrate our efforts in the Affective suite, which allows the capture of quantitative data for three affective states: excitement/ calm, engagement/disinterest and meditation. The detections provided by the Affective suite search for brainwave characteristics that are universal in nature and do not require an explicit training or signature-building step for each user.

The excitement/calm state is experienced as an awareness or feeling of physio-logical arousal with a positive value. The excitement/calm detection is tuned to provide output scores that more accurately reflect changes in excitement over times. The emotions related to the excitement/calm affective state includes titillation, nervousness, and agitation.

The Emotiv EEG headset has many differences regarding complexity, cost and operational use compared to invasive and noninvasive medical EEGs employed to exam and study the brain. However, the initial evaluation of the information it provides is adequate to the study of emotional aspects for computer interaction and emotional state by employing the many EEG concepts, techniques, models, and other resources originated for the several years of advancements that come for the medical study of the brain. Additionally, the form factor and its ergonomic wearable aspect facilitates its use in different experimental setups, such the environment described in the experiments session.

The noninvasive BCI technology that provides emotional data have been employed to evaluate human emotional response in digital games [10, 21] and other areas such as arts [16], medical [12], and marketing [22] among others. Although BCI devices are becoming affordable and used in a wide range of experiments, few research efforts are examining the possibilities of this data in games where fast paced strategy in real time is needed, which is a landmark of the RTS genre.

A notable exception of BCI exploration where strategy is at the gameplay's core is the work of Moreira [29]. This research studied the multiplayer behavior in two experiments. In the first experiment a pair of subjects wearing BCIs played a custom game where they needed to cooperate to control a spaceship in a mutual win condition.

The second experiment evaluated a game where cooperative and defective decisions should be made by the players with BCIs to defeat the adversary or maximize the group scores. Although both experiments undercover relevant player behaviors, the nature of games and the interaction characteristics are inherently different from a RTS game.

2.4 Emotions and Game Design

Nogueira et al. [32] reports several attempts by the game industry to collect and use emotional data, from early EEG tests promoted by Atari in the 1980s to recent obtrusive and unreliable gimmicks that were easily manipulated and failed to add significant depth to games.

The survey presented by Nicolas-Alonso and Gomez-Gil [31] illustrate uses of different BCI devices that employ varies modalities used for BCI gaming implementations. The survey list examples and highlights the progress in games that employs BCIs from the point of view of interaction with examples that collect and use affective states or emotions in games.

From the game design point of view, once the emotional data has been gathered, regardless of its source, modelled and made available, game designers have the option to base their designs and experiment on how a set of predetermined or dynamic game parameters (e.g., enemy and item spawning, music and lighting effects) should be adapted to convey the player's emotional state.

Examples of research studies that combine game design and emotion data include the work of Bernhaupt et al. [2] that contributed with a simple emotionally driven game that uses players' facial expressions where the goal is directly control the growth rate of virtual flowers. Using more complex mechanisms, Nacke et al. [30] explored the effects of both direct and indirect physiological control in a 2D platform shooting game, concluding that each type has its own adequate uses for shaping gameplay experience. While not physiologically driven, the works presented by Figueiredo and Paiva [15] and Pedersen et al. [33] support that complex game aspects such as storyline and gameplay parameters can be dynamically adapted to individual players to achieve a predetermined reaction. These researches present proofs of concept towards systems capable of influencing player experience.

Nogueira et al. [32] propose an approach to link emotional data with game design that avoids indirectly adapting game-specific parameters via subjective data. Their Affective Reaction Models (ARM) framework explores a direct approach through implicit biofeedback mechanisms driven by the user's own physiologically measured emotional state variations over time.

To summarize, the related work serves as proofs-of-concept for the implementation of emotion reaction mechanisms in videogames and other affective computing applications. They provide supporting evidence that this specific kind of interaction influence the player experience and can be used to benefit it by being considered by game designers [32].

3   Exploratory Experiment

While quantitative and qualitative studies of gameplay to evaluate emotional impact have been previously conducted, there is a lack of empirical evidence studying the correlation between events in a RTS game and excitement quantified data gathered from a BCI. We choose excitement as the emotional status on this experiment due to its potential impact on gameplay and the availability of this metric directly from the BCI device employed. Therefore, the goal of this exploratory experiment is to answer the following main questions:

- Q1: What game data, if any, relate to the emotional state excitement?
- Q2: Is there a noticeable player choice among the game options that correlates to excitement?

We expect that excitement data will have an impact in game decisions made by the player and that it has a significant level of correlation with game statistics.

In the following subsections, we discuss the methodology of the experiment, characterize the participants, explain the design and procedure and present the results of the study.

3.1   Methodology

An exploratory simulated design was used to observe how excitement data correlates with StarCraft 2 events raised during a game match. This study was conducted from a Naturalistic perspective [24] and guided by some aspects of Netnography [23], although our observations were made from the behavior of our individuals outside the traditional Internet use (i.e. web browsing) represented by their actions while playing the game.

We endeavored to draw theory from the data rather than to impose personal assumptions or biases on the analysis. Data-centricity required familiarity with the area as well as caution against personal biases or imposed interpretations of the data. Familiarity with the area was important in our scenario because:

1. Games defy understanding when the analysts have never played them or a similar game; and
2. The level of jargon and acronyms in the competitive communities can be nonsense to outsiders. One of the authors of this work drew on independent individual experiences as a StarCraft player in single- and multi-player contexts and as a spectator in online and live StarCraft tournaments.

We sought to protect against personal bias in how we approached the data, thus the emphasis on quantitative instead of qualitative analysis to shield personal spectating experiences as knowledge meant to aid our sensitivity ability to seek association and meaning in the data.

3.2   Participants

23 participants (2 female, 21 male), with age ranging from 15 to 32 (avg. 22.3 std. 2.4), participated in the experiments. The participants were recruited while attending the

2012 South America StarCraft II Finals event [25] that classified players for the World Championship Series, a series of events organized by or in cooperation with Blizzard where players enter and qualify individually through open tournaments starting at the national level. Professional players and event audience with at least some experience in StarCraft 2 gameplay played a match that lasted approximately 10 min and received a chocolate bar as reward. Figure 1 presents a collage of participants using the BCI during the experiment.

Fig. 1. Participants wearing the Emotiv EEG headset and playing a Starcraft 2 match during the experiment.

3.3 Design and Procedure

The exploratory study collected data while the participants played a StarCraft 2 game match. Each participant already knew how to play the game and interact with its interface elements therefore no training session was needed.

The setup of the experiment was composed of a desktop PC with Windows 7 and the StarCraft 2 Wings of Liberty version with the 1.5 Patch. Participants were free to choose any character, map, difficulty level, type of adversary (human or artificial intelligence) and number of adversaries/allies.

After a brief review of the experiment and the reading and signing of a consent form, users were asked to wear earphones to hear the game's audio and the BCI headset while playing the match. The emotional data gathered process collected excitement/calm, engagement/disinterest and meditation with the EPOC Control Paned application provide by manufacturer SDK. The BCI provided excitement, engagement and meditation levels directly based in the user's brain activity at 1 Hz.

A debrief interview with the participants was conducted by the moderator of the experiment after the participants finished the match to collect qualitative data about the participation in the experiment. The interviews were performed face to face with the subjects by one researcher using a questionnaire that asked two open ended questions about the experiment:

- Did you fell excitement while playing? If so, described how and when you fell it.
- How was your overall emotional experience while playing the match?

All the participants' and game events raised during the match were stored in the replay filed record by the StarCraft 2 game. These replay files were converted, parsed, and organized into a suitable format for analysis.

3.4 Results

Game match data was gathered from the replay files, which included the duration, events, result (win or loss) and other metrics. The excitement level collected from the BCI was normalized from 0 (calm) to 1 (excited). Table 1 presents totals and measures of central tendency separated by each race.

The game race balance is a constant issue addressed by Blizzard, however our data shows that players have a predilection by the Zerg race. The Wins-Losses values of Table 1 account for the result of the match from the player that was using the BCI. The presented time values are real-time instead of game-time values, which conversion ratio depends of the difficulty level of the game. Additionally, we list APM (Actions per Minute) [36] measurements, which is a metric of a player's load-handling capacity commonly employed for judging and comparing players skills.

The data in Table 1 shows that the average excitement level, APM, and number of events is significant higher for the Zerg race, although not statistically significant. We conjecture two possible explanations for this data variation: the predilection of players by the Zerg and the lack of lost matches in our data when this race was chosen.

The Pearson's correlation analysis shows a positive weak correlation ($r = 0.30$) of the average APM and the average excitement for all races. The correlation of average APM and average excitement for the Protoss is negative very weak ($r = -0.12$), for the Terran race is negative moderate ($r = -0.47$), and for the Zerg race is positive moderate ($r = 0.63$).

Since the APM is a relevant metric to judge skill, the Table 2 present the ranking of players classified by APM ranges (adapted from [36]) and their average excitement values.

Table 1. Totals and measures of central tendency per race.

Race	Total games	Win-loss	Avg. time (sec.)	Avg. APM	Avg. excitement	Avg. events
Protoss	8	5-3	573 ± 414	145 ± 93	0.29 ± 0.11	1,103 ± 589
Terran	5	3-2	991 ± 440	116 ± 93	0.33 ± 0.11	1,937 ± 1,1476
Zerg	10	10-0	583 ± 285	189 ± 81	0.44 ± 0.18	1,965 ± 1,343

Table 2. Player ranking and average excitement.

Player rank	APM range	Amount of players	Avg. excitement
Casual player	0–50	3	0.41 ± 0.07
Experienced player	51–75	2	0.29 ± 0.02
Proficient player	76–150	7	0.25 ± 0.1
Proficient player with high number of actions	>150	11	0.44 ± 0.17

Player ranking classification shows that in both extremes of the spectrum the average excitement is almost the double than the other ranks. One possible explanation is that excitement values for casual players are influenced by the opportunity to play the game in the environment that have an active audience observing their gameplay. For the proficient player, a reasonable assertion is that the amount of actions required an elevated level of concentration and metal coordination that influenced the excitement measures.

The dataset contains 78% victories and 22% defeats. The average excitement for players that won the match is 0.37 (std. 0.17) and for those who lost is 0.35 (std 0.09). The correlation of Wins-Losses and average excitement for all races is positive very weak ($r = 0.03$). The correction values separated by race is negative weak ($r = -0.20$) for Protoss, negative moderate for Terran ($r = -0.64$), and undefined for Zerg since the dataset contain only victories for players that chosen this race.

The excitement values for victories and defeats are within the expected values, since the subjective observed effort and other behaviors players demonstrated during the matches are similar, therefore supporting the almost symmetric average values for excitement.

The correlation of match time and average excitement for all races is negative very weak ($r = -0.04$). The correction values separated by race is positive very weak ($r = 0.16$) for Protoss, negative moderate for Terran ($r = -0.64$), and positive very weak ($r = 0.17$) for Zerg.

The correlation of the number of game events and average excitement for all races is positive very weak ($r = 0.19$). The correction values separated by race is negative moderate ($r = -0.44$) for Protoss, negative moderate for Terran ($r = -0.69$), and positive moderate ($r = 0.43$) for Zerg.

Although the data in Table 1 shows the average excitement per race, we decide to explore further this metric by clustering each participants' data individually using an unsupervised clustering algorithm, which require a distance metric and k, the number of clusters to produce, to partitions value into clusters based in the distance between them.

We evaluated existing clustering algorithms' output with two, three, and four clusters and with different metric distances. We decided by the K-means [26] to present the output in three clusters created with the median as the metric to calculate cluster membership because:

1. Visual exploratory analysis suggested that the could be separated by three levels;
2. The median produced an improved sum of the squared distance for each cluster over other metric distances; and
3. The standard deviation of one cluster was large when using two clusters.

The data from each participant was assigned to one of three clusters, namely: High, Medium, and Low excitement. After the clustering, we calculated the percentage of time participants spent in each cluster. The column graph in Fig. 1 shows the comparison of percent time spent in each excitement level for all the participants (Geral) and separated by race.

The data within the graph in Fig. 1 shows that times spent inside each excitement level have a significant increased value from high to low excitement. This is compatible with the observations from the traditional gameplay rhythm in RTS games, since there are large periods where players build structures, that intuitively lack excitement, and short attack/defenses periods associated with elevated levels of excitement.

Another observable highlight in the data shows that Zerg players have the highest value of time spent inside high excitement levels: 6.61% higher than the Geral group and 8.76% and 10.25% higher than the Protoss and Terran races, respectively.

Protoss players spent more time in medium excitement values: 5.03% more than All races, 5.83% more than Terran, and 9.85% more than Zerg players.

Matches with Terran players have the lowest level of excitement overall, which is corroborated by the highest value of time spent in the lowest level of excitement: 4.44% more than the Geral group, 7.32% above Terran and 6.22% higher than Zerg players.

We compared time spent in clusters separated by winners/losers groups, although this data is not shown in the graph of Fig. 2. The values for the high, medium and low excitement levels are within the ±1% margin of difference from the general group. The differences from the Winners and the Losers groups are 3.01%, 2.15% and 5.17% for the high, medium and low levels, respectively. This comparison highlights the small difference of excitement levels for those who won or lost the match. Similarly, we found minor differences without statistical evidence when comparing the effects of player ranking, map, opponent race and type (artificial intelligence or human player), and player style. Player style was manually classified as described in [27].

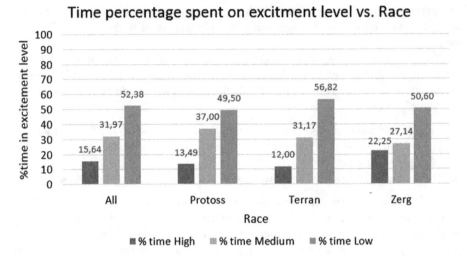

Fig. 2. Comparison of time spent in excitement levels for all participants separated by race.

Most of the extracted game events from the replay files are consequences of player commands (e.g. train an offensive unity) while others are events generated by the game engine (e.g. an event associated with the lower supply depot message). We highlight that these events represent small actions instead of a larger macro strategy, e.g. a "rush" move (a powerful attack very early in the game when the player typically sacrifices late-game stability in favor of a strong early army). Table 3 present the frequencies of the top ten events collected from the replay files regardless of race or victory/defeat.

The data from Table 3 was not separated per Race because the results are almost the same for the first five events and the distinctions are below the 1% frequency threshold without statistical significance. Due to the high APM rate and fast pacing gameplay of the RTS genre, it is expected a predominance of events that select units and commands them to move to specific locations, thus taking a large participation of the events distribution. This is the case of our dataset where the sum of the Select and RightClick, employed in tandem to move units on the map, is responsible for almost 81% of all events.

From the collected events, we calculated the ratio per minute for the periods where the excitement measure has high, medium and low provided by the levels created in the clustering analysis. We then separate these ratios by race and calculate the averages, as presented in Tables 4, 5, and 6.

Table 3. Top ten frequency of gameplay events.

Event	Description	Frequency (%)
Select	Group and select units to command them all at once	51.74
RigthClick	Free the selection of current selected game element	29.20
Train	Creates a unit	11.45
Build	Construct a building, vehicle, ship, aircraft or defensive barrier	1.54
MiniMapRightClick	A mouse button click on the map to move units to a location	1.31
HotkeyAssing	Assign a keyboard key to a group of selected units	1.21
MorphBanelingFailed	Failed event when changing a Zergling into a Baneling unit	0.86
SpawnLarva	Create a Zerg multipurpose unit	0.59
ChronoBoost	Speed up progress of Protoss upgrades	0.25
Upgrade	Improvement of tactical ability for units	0.25

Table 4. Events per minute ratio for each session and excitement level of the Protoss race.

Id	Race	Total events	Events per minute total	Events per minute high	Events per minute medium	Events per minute low
1	P	916	193.52	38.24	96.55	58.73
3	P	663	256.65	20.52	140.90	95.23
6	P	1,236	85.24	2.83	22.28	60.14
12	P	1,607	129.60	4.44	62.74	62.42
13	P	2,037	329.43	10.51	137.79	181.13
17	P	594	131.03	3.97	32.43	94.63
20	P	437	53.51	8.45	9.55	35.51
23	P	787	33.66	18.09	11.29	4.28
	Avg.	$1,034.62 \pm 552.62$	151.58 ± 102.30	13.38 ± 11.97	64.19 ± 54.64	74.01 ± 52.45

Table 5. Events per minute ratio for each session and excitement level of the Terran race.

Id	Race	Total events	Events per minute total	Events per minute high	Events per minute medium	Events per minute low
11	T	2,147	136.03	11.15	43.97	80.91
15	T	124	21.69	6.65	4.02	11.02
18	T	738	28.92	8.54	1.29	19.09
19	T	3,472	228.67	21.54	69.02	138.11
22	T	2,702	132.23	2.59	13.70	115.94
	Avg.	$1,836.6 \pm 1,383.81$	109.51 ± 86.06	10.09 ± 7.12	26.4 ± 29.23	73.01 ± 56.77

Table 6. Events per minute ratio for each session and excitement level of the Zerg.

Id	Race	Total events	Events per minute total	Events per minute high	Events per minute medium	Events per minute low
2	Z	302	98.48	3.59	32.93	61.96
4	Z	2,239	237.77	157.91	43.12	36.74
5	Z	1,003	107.66	11.06	24.36	72.24
7	Z	911	164.14	58.74	63.42	41.98
8	Z	4,443	223.45	94.65	100.54	28.26
9	Z	2,680	2,34.06	48.38	77.47	108.21
10	Z	380	55.75	13.94	15.70	26.11
14	Z	1,147	173.35	27.05	46.70	99.60
16	Z	2,588	219.32	89.24	83.14	46.95
21	Z	2,162	161.95	5.47	42.55	113.93
	Avg.	1,785.5 ± 1,283	167.59 ± 63.33	51.00 ± 50.25	52.99 ± 27.36	63.60 ± 33.36

The average ratio of events per minute for all the races is 149.40 (std 82.65). On average, players that chosen the Zerg race generated more events per minute, followed by the Protoss and Terran. However, a different pattern emerges when we analyze the ratio separated by each level of excitement (high, medium and low). Zerg players have 40.91 more events per minute than Terran and 37.62 more than Protoss in the elevated levels. For medium levels Zerg players have 26.59 more events per minute than Terran and 11.2 less than Protoss. In the low levels Protoss players have ratio values 10.41 more than Zerg and 1.00 more than Terran. All these ratios are statistically different and were checked with the Mann-Whitney test ($p < 0.05$).

The analysis of the answers from the debriefing interview indicated that players felt periods of excitement in long matches with opponents that required different strategies. P10: *"I was very excited to finally beat my opponent after a long match"*. P19: *"My attacks did not work, but when I was planning them I was very excited and hoped that they work"*. Both P10 and P19 matches took more than the average match time and player performed an elevated number of events compared to the other matches.

We also noted the excitement for specific strategies that required the long preparation of strategies with special and expensive attack units. P14: *"I was excited to see my banelings explode the enemy's buildings"*. P6: *"When my force fields worked [placed on the correct location to block the enemy moves] I was super excited"*.

Short matches with duration ranging from two to ten minutes and with a small number of events did not yield much excitement according to the subjects. P15: *"The match was easy, quick and not much interesting because the other player gg'ed [abandoned the game losing the match] early"*. P10: *"I did not fell excitement at all in any moment"*.

4 Discussion

After the presentation of the results, we return to the questions raised before our exploratory experiment (Q1 and Q2) that combined the data from the BCI and the RTS game.

To answer Q1, we showed correlations among the emotional states excitement/calm with race preference, APM, victory/defeat, gameplay time and amount of game events. We did not find any positive or negative strong correlations. However, the analysis demonstrates that there was a statistical significant relationship of excitement and game data. In particularly, the positive weak correlation between APM and excitement provide evidence that players with an elevated number of interactions with the game showed an elevated level of excitement.

The players choices during the game led us formulate an answer for Q2. Our data analyses discovered evidence that the Zerg is preferable by players, has a higher average excitement rate, generated more game events and was predominant in the highest level of excitement. The Terran race data, however, showed opposite values for the analyzed metrics. A closer look at the victory/defeat dimension did not produced evidence to support hypothesis about specific excitement variations in our dataset.

While analyzing specific game events we were not able to correlate or form a correspondence of player's actions to excitement. The reason is that most actions found in the replay files are generic movements without enough information to classify then as high-level strategies, tactics, or contextualized in-game behaviors. Nevertheless, the general and per race average events per minute ratio analysis in the three levels of excitement confirmed the association of race and excitement/calm levels.

In general, data collected from the BCI during the exploratory experiment demonstrate the device's suitability as a minimally invasive means of measuring the excitement and calm levels of a subject. The excitement and calm dataset outputted provided evidence to indicate when a subject undergoes a change in these emotions. While it was not possible to correlate isolated moments of player behavior with a precise change in either excitement or calm levels, the overall trend of the subject's emotional pattern was noticeable.

In general, player's excitement was below the average and the authors did not find impeditive barriers to infer what excitement levels players where in by analyzing the gameplay data and the output of the device for the attention metric.

Among the possibilities of StarCraft 2 game design, and in a broader sense any game of the RTS genre, the results of excitement analysis from the exploratory experiment performed leads us to share the following insight.

One naïve perspective may think that games should be designed to give as much excitement to the players as possible. In some cases, this makes sense: players will keep playing and interacting with the community (participating in tournaments, generating online content, transmitting matches) while they still fell the excitement associated with the game. One of the general rules to achieve this objective is to constantly change game mechanics and parameters to keep the balance among the races. The execution of this rule should be taken with precision to avoid underbalance while still maintaining player preferences for a specific race, difficulty level, map, or any other game setting that directly affects the gameplay experience.

However, under a closer look game designer should avoid maximize game excitement at all costs and pursue the evaluation of game options that accommodate user's predilections and prioritize a balanced experience of excitement and calm, in an analogous way of race balance. This is especially valid for game that have a campaign mode (i.e. not multiplayer) were all the race units, updates and options are gradually presented to the player as the plot unveils thorough the levels. The reasoning for this course of action is inherently from the game genre, since one of the defining characteristics of the RTS are strategies that take the form of alternating relatively calm building or exploratory phases and fast-paced battle events that define the outcome of a match.

5   Conclusion

Nowadays the understanding that emotions drive peoples' experiences in video games has becoming a key factor to guide game design. Nevertheless, understanding how they can be used to provide a targeted gameplay experience remains an unsolved issue. This work attempts to tackle this matter through an exploratory experiment to analyze the correlations between physiologically measured excitement response variations and their eliciting events.

In this paper we conducted an initial exploratory experiment to answer the following research questions, (i) What game data, if any, relate to excitement? and (ii) Is there a noticeable player preference that correlates to excitement data? The results of these analyses shown moderate correlation of excitement with player's preferences and amount of interactions, which may lead to design implications for shaping and adapting game parameters to convey the player's emotional state.

Our initial findings of can be generically applied to game design and other player-oriented behavior game mechanics to enrich the gaming experience and convey user emotions from their physiological state. In future work, we plan to expand the study of emotional states correlation besides quantitative measurement of excitement. Additionally, we are working on a classifier that detects macro strategies from a group of game events, so we can study the correlations that explore macro strategies. We also plan to study the impact of direct emotional data gathered from a BCI and its implications in dynamic game parameters changes.

References

1. Aha, D.W., Molineaux, M., Ponsen, M.: Learning to win: case-based plan selection in a real-time strategy game. In: Muñoz-Ávila, H., Ricci, F. (eds.) ICCBR 2005. LNCS (LNAI), vol. 3620, pp. 5–20. Springer, Heidelberg (2005). https://doi.org/10.1007/11536406_4
2. Bernhaupt, R., Boldt, A., Mirlacher, T.: Using emotion in games: emotional flowers. In: Proceedings of the International Conference on Advances in Computer Entertainment Technology, pp. 41–48 (2007)

3. Blizzard Entertainment. http://blizzard.com. Accessed 22 Feb 2018
4. Chambers, C., Feng, W., Feng, W., Saha, D.: Mitigating information exposure to cheaters in real-time strategy games. In: Proceedings of the International Workshop on Network and Operating Systems Support for Digital Audio and Video, pp. 7–12 (2005)
5. Chan, H., Fern, A., Ray, S., Wilson, N., Ventura, C.: Online planning for resource production in real-time strategy games. In: Proceedings of the International Conference on Automated Planning and Scheduling, pp. 65–72 (2007)
6. Chanel, G., Kronegg, J., Grandjean, D., Pun, T.: Emotion assessment: arousal evaluation using EEG's and peripheral physiological signals. In: Gunsel, B., Jain, A.K., Tekalp, A.M., Sankur, B. (eds.) MRCS 2006. LNCS, vol. 4105, pp. 530–537. Springer, Heidelberg (2006). https://doi.org/10.1007/11848035_70
7. Cheng, D., Thawonmas, R.: Case-based plan recognition for real-time strategy games. In: Proceedings of the 5th Game-On International Conference, pp. 36–40 (2004)
8. Cheung, G., Huang, J.: StarCraft from the stands: understanding the game spectator. In: Proceedings of the SIGCHI Conference on Human Factors in Computing Systems, pp. 763–772 (2011)
9. Claypool, M.: The effect of latency on user performance in real-time strategy games. J. Comput. Netw.: Spec. Issue Netw. Issues Entertain. Comput. **49**(1), 52–70 (2005)
10. Crowley, K., Sliney, A., Pitt, I., Murphy D.: Evaluating a brain-computer interface to categorize human emotional response. In: Proceedings of the 10th IEEE International Conference on Advanced Learning Technologies, pp. 276–278 (2010)
11. Drachen, A., Nacke, L.E., Yannakakis, G., Pedersen, A.L.: Correlation between heart rate, electrodermal activity and player experience in first-person shooter games. In: Proceedings of the 5th ACM SIGGRAPH Symposium on Video Games, pp. 49–54 (2010)
12. Dutta, A., Kumar, R., Malhotra, S., Chugh, S., Banerjee, A., Dutta, A.: A low-cost point-of-care-testing (POCT) system for psychomotor symptoms of depression affecting standing balance - a preliminary study in India. J. Depress. Res. Treat. **2013**, 1–8 (2013). https://doi.org/10.1155/2013/640861
13. Emotiv: Emotiv EPOC Neuro Heaset. https://www.emotiv.com/epoc/. Accessed 22 Feb 2018
14. EmotivePro. https://www.emotiv.com/emotivpro/. Accessed 22 Feb 2018
15. Figueiredo, R., Paiva, A.: "I want to slay that dragon!" - influencing choice in interactive storytelling. In: Proceedings of the Third Joint Conference on Interactive Digital Storytelling, pp. 26–37 (2010)
16. Fraga, T., Pichiliani, M.C., Louro, D.: Experimental Art with Brain Controlled Interface. In: Proceedings of the 7th International Conference on Universal Access in Human-Computer Interaction: Design Methods, Tools, and Interaction Techniques for eInclusion, vol. 1, pp. 642–651 (2013)
17. GameRankings.com: StarCraft II: Wings of Liberty. http://www.gamerankings.com/pc/939643-StarCraft-ii-wings-of-liberty/index.html. Accessed 22 Feb 2018
18. Granic, I., Lobel, A., Rutger, C.M.E.: The benefits of playing video games. J. Am. Psychol. Assoc. **69**(1), 66–78 (2014)
19. IGN: The State of the RTS. http://www.ign.com/articles/2006/04/08/the-state-of-the-rts. Accessed 22 Feb 2018
20. Jasper, H.: Report of the committee on methods of clinical examination in electroencephalography. Electroencephalogr. Clin. Neurophysiol. J. **10**, 370–375 (1958)
21. Kerous, B., Skola, F., Liarokapis, F.: EEG-based BCI and video games: a progress report. Virtual Real. J. **2017**, 1–7 (2017)

22. Khushaba, R.N., Wise, C., Kodagoda, S., Louviere, J., Kahn, B.E.: Townsend; assessing the brain response to marketing stimuli using electroencephalogram (EEG) and eye tracking. J. Expert Syst. Appl. **40**(9), 3803–3812 (2013)
23. Langer, R., Beckman, S.C.: Sensitive research topics: netnography revisited. J. Qual. Mark. Res. **8**(2), 189–203 (2005)
24. Lincoln, Y.S., Guba, E.G.: Naturalistic Inquiry. Sage Publisher, Upper Saddle River (1985)
25. Liquipedia: 2012 StarCraft 2 World Championship Series: South America Finals. http://wiki. teamliquid.net/starcraft2/2012_StarCraft_II_World_Championship_Series/South_America/ Finals. Accessed 22 Feb 2018
26. MacQueen, J.B.: Some methods for classification and analysis of multivariate observations. In: Proceedings of the 5th Berkeley Symposium on Mathematical Statistics and Probability, pp. 281–297 (1967)
27. Marcus, P., Barba, R.: Starcraft II Limited Edition Strategy Guide. BradyGames (2010)
28. Metacritic: StarCraft II: Wings of Liberty. http://www.metacritic.com/game/pc/starcraft-ii-wings-of-liberty/critic-reviews. Accessed 22 Feb 2018
29. Moreira, C.F.S.: Kessel run: exploring cooperative behaviors in a multiplayer BCI game. Master's thesis defended at the Lisboa University, Portugal (2017)
30. Nacke, L.E., Kalyn, M., Lough, C., Mandryk, R.L.: Biofeedback game design: using direct and indirect physiological control to enhance game interaction. In: Proceedings of the Annual conference on Human Factors in Computing Systems, pp. 103–112 (2011)
31. Nicolas-Alonso, L.F., Gomez-Gil, J.: Brain computer interfaces, a review. Sens. J. **12**(2), 1211–1279 (2012)
32. Nogueira, P.A., Rodrigues, R., Oliveira, E., Nacke, L.E.: Guided emotional state regulation: understanding and shaping players' affective experiences in digital games. In: Proceedings of the Ninth Artificial Intelligence and Interactive Digital Entertainment Conference (2013)
33. Pedersen, C., Togelius, J., Yannakakis, G.N.: Modeling player experience for content creation. IEEE Trans. Comput. Intell. AI Games **2**(1), 54–67 (2009)
34. Russoniello, C.V., O'Brien, K., Parks, J.M.: EEG, HRV and psychological correlates while playing Bejeweled II: a randomized controlled study. Annu. Rev. Cyberther. Telemed.: Adv. Technol. Behav. Soc. Neurosci. **7**, 189–192 (2009)
35. Ryan, R.M., Rigby, C.S., Przybylski, A.: The motivational pull of video games: a self-determination theory approach. Motiv. Emot. J. **30**(4), 344–360 (2006)
36. StarCraft Wiki: Actions Per Minute. http://StarCraft.wikia.com/wiki/Actions_per_minute. Accessed 22 Feb 2018
37. StarCraft 2. http://starcraft2.com/. Accessed 22 Feb 2018
38. Yannakakis, G.N., Hallam, J.: Entertainment modeling through physiology in physical play. Int. J. Hum.-Comput. Stud. **66**(10), 741–755 (2008)

M2TA - Mobile Mouse Touchscreen Accessible for Users with Motor Disabilities

Agebson Rocha Façanha[1](✉), Maria da Conceição Carneiro Araújo[2], Windson Viana[2],
and Jaime Sánchez[3]

[1] Federal Institute of Education, Science and Technology of Ceará (IFCE),
Fortaleza, CE, Brazil
agebson@ifce.edu.br
[2] Federal University of Ceará (UFC), Fortaleza, CE, Brazil
marianna.c85@gmail.com, windson@virtual.ufc.br
[3] Universidad de Chile (UChile), Santiago, Chile
jsanchez@dcc.uchile.cl

Abstract. This paper addresses the accessibility challenges of people with motor impairments regarding their access to the computer. Our focus is a new mouse design, which in its traditional ergonomics may affect the interaction with a computer and, consequently, with the Web. We introduce the design and development of a mobile application, the M2TA, which transforms a touchscreen mobile device into a mouse controller. The mobile application provides more flexible/customizable interfaces, it is portable, and is cheaper. Two users with motor limitations, cerebral palsy, participated in the development process of the M2TA. They used mobile interfaces interacting with computer applications of their preference freely. We aimed to observe possible bugs and receive suggestions for the M2TA improvement. We also collected their satisfaction with the use of M2TA interfaces. Preliminary results are promising and indicate a good level of acceptance. Further studies are in progress to attest the M2TA potential, such as improving the quality of life of people with neuropsychomotor sequelae caused by TBI - Traumatic Brain Injury and Stroke - Stroke.

Keywords: Motor disabilities · Ergonomics · Mouse · Mobile devices

1 Introduction

People with motor impairments are excluded from social life in many situations (e.g., school, work, and even entertainment). In fact, many daily practices are not adapted for them. Fortunately, this reality has undergone considerable changes thanks to new public policies of development and the new paradigms of social inclusion. The development of accessibility software and tools (i.e., Assistive Technologies (ATs)) has also made it increasingly possible to provide communication and access to information for people with motor disabilities independently. People with motor disabilities are closer to computers and mobile devices thanks to the emergence of assistive software and adapted devices [6].

© Springer International Publishing AG, part of Springer Nature 2018
M. Antona and C. Stephanidis (Eds.): UAHCI 2018, LNCS 10907, pp. 273–286, 2018.
https://doi.org/10.1007/978-3-319-92049-8_20

Unfortunately, web browsing on computers is still a challenging task for people with motor disabilities [1]. Keyboard and mouse are the most common input devices for computer access. In a mouse-based interface (i.e., GUI), cursor movements follow the users' hand movement in two-dimensional space. When manipulating a mouse, users obtain visual and kinesthetic information of movement and position in computer screen interactions [2, 3]. Previous research has already identified obstacles faced by people with motor disabilities when interacting with graphical user interfaces (GUIs) using these devices [1]. Some people cannot use this device independently because of their sensory-motor limitations, acquired or congenital [4, 5].

Researchers and practitioners of TA have proposed various types of adapted devices (e.g., BJOY, HeadDev, Tobii PCEye, RCT-Barban, BigTrack Trackball, Orbitrack, etc.), which provide the same functions of traditional mouse data input. These solutions make it possible for people with motor impairments the access to the computer resources (e.g., Web browsing, text editor). But, frequently, these devices have high prices. Some of them do not have a good quality of finishing and design. They also suffer from the scarcity of distribution channels, maintenance, and repair places [12, 13].

One of the little known functions that smartphones and tablets have is to enable the device to be a desktop data entry component. An application running on the device is connected as a client to an application server computer. This allows the smartphone to send data as a wireless mouse, for example. There are a wide variety of applications[1] that can be used for this, but they are not necessarily interfaces that meet the direct needs of an individual with motor impairment [22].

Following this trend, our proposal aims at the design and development of layouts that simulate an accessible mouse on the touchscreen of mobile devices. This mobile application controls the computer's cursor over wireless communication. The proposed solution, M2TA, is a more flexible and customizable tool than the adapted hardware. The M2TA has greater portability, less financial cost, and easy access. By offering several layouts, the M2TA also allows each user to choose the input interface best suited to their limitations.

People with motor disabilities and professional specialists in the area of rehabilitation have participated in the design and development process of M2TA. One of the main design challenges was the haptic feedback, such as that provided by controlling the standard mouse. For this, we use haptic devices - levers and other types of joysticks - over the smartphone touchscreens. Initial reports from users and experts indicate a good acceptance of M2TA. The diversity of mouse layouts is the M2TA more pleasured feature. Initial test results show its likely use in improving the quality of life of people with neuropsychomotor limitations [6].

---

[1] Remote Mouse (http://www.remotemouse.net/), Unifiedremote (https://www.unifiedre-mote.com/), PC Remote (http://www.monect.com/pc-remote/), WiFi Mouse (http://wifi-mouse.necta.us/).

2   Related Work

2.1   Adapted Input Devices

Input devices available on the market (e.g., mouse [7], trackball [8], joystick [9], light pen [10], touchscreen [11], etc.) differ in shape, size, mode, and control. The computer mouse requires motor skills such as the use of hands and fingers. In this context, people with motor impairments may face difficulties when using the mouse in its standard form. Some adaptations are applied based on the users' functional abilities to facilitate the interaction with computers. For instance, accessible mouses offer alternative data input modalities based on pressing, traction, blowing, blinking, and contracting of users musculature [19]. The use of the foot, mouth, or actions by the displacement of the head, and movement of the gaze are examples of new input interactions.

Each of the above solutions addresses a different strategy for decreasing the limitation that physical or motor impairment imposes for the total or partial use of the mouse in its conventional form. Some examples of Assistive Technologies are listed below. They offer better possibilities of interaction and support the process of digital inclusion of people with motor disabilities.

– **Joystick:** A pointing device in which the movement of the cursor is controlled through stick which the user can move in all directions and reproduced on the computer screen. It has two or more buttons for performing the mouse activation functions. Examples: BJOY[2], Talking Joystick Mouse[3] and Joystick - For Chin[4].
– **Mouse controlled by the movement of the head:** a resource used by people who can not use the mouse and the keyboard with the upper or lower limbs, but can move the head with some control. It is currently possible to control the mouse cursor with the movement of the head captured by a standard webcam (for example, Head-Mouse[5], HeadDev[6] and TrackerPro[7]).
– **Mouse controlled by eye movement:** suitable for users who can move their eyes and stare at specific points in the screen. No head movement is required to promote the cursor movement (e.g., Tobii PCEye[8] and Mouse Eyepiece[9]).
– **Mouse controlled by the lips movement and activated by blow or suction:** it allows the user to operate the computer entirely through mouth. Small lips movements enable the cursor movement in the computer screen movements, while left and right clicks are done by a light blow or suction, or even by an external trigger. One

---

[2] https://bjliveat.com/120-bjoy-mice.
[3] https://openassistive.org/item/talkingjoystickmouse/.
[4] http://www.anditec.pt/index.php?option=com_virtuemart&view=productdetails&virtue-mart_product_id=4&virtuemart_category_id=2.
[5] http://robotica.udl.cat/headmouse.htm.
[6] http://www.fundacionvodafone.es/proyecto/proyecto-headdev.
[7] https://www.ablenetinc.com/trackerpro.
[8] http://www2.tobiidynavox.com/pceye-go/.
[9] http://www.invencoesbrasileiras.com.br/mouse-ocular/.

of the best known mouse in this category is the Integra Mouse[10] designed for people with high spinal cord injury (quadriplegia), progressive muscular dystrophy, neuro-motor diseases and multiple sclerosis.

- **Mouse controlled by the feet:** the activation of functions and the cursor control is performed using the feet to facilitate the use, to increase the functionality and to reduce the adaptation time for users with severe motor limitations in the upper limbs (Example: Roller Mouse[11], Button Mouse[12] and RCT-Barban[13]).
- **TrackBall:** a device with a ball, of 7 cm in diameter on average that allows the cursor movement the screen requiring less motor control by the user. It has two large buttons with functions equivalent to the left and right keys of the conventional mouse with attractive looks and bright colors (e.g., Big Ball Mouse[14] and BigTrack Trackball[15]).
- **Touch sensitive:** allows the user to accurately control the cursor speed and direction on the computer with just a soft touch. It requires the minimum effort and motor coordination to use the mouse. The touchpad mouse[16] and Orbitrack[17] are examples of this type of mouse. The last one has a control ring and does not require extensive movements of the hands and wrists but only the touch of the finger.

The assistive technologies listed in Fig. 1 are the most relevant to our study. However, many other products targeting users with motor impairments are available. Frequently, the choice of the most adequate approach depends on its economic cost. In general, Assistive Technology products are expensive due to their limited market. This inconvenient, in many cases, makes them unattainable for most of the users with disabilities.

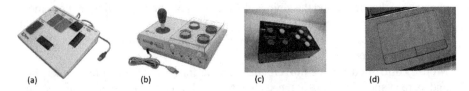

(a)   (b)   (c)   (d)

Fig. 1. Examples of adaptations: (a) RollerMouse, (b) BJoy, (c) Button Mouse, (d) Touchpad.

2.2 The Use of Smartphone as Input Devices

This subsection presents design and implementation research to turn smartphones into remote computer controllers, allowing users to use smartphones as mouse and keyboard by operating the computer remotely and wirelessly.

---

[10] https://www.integramouse.com/en/home/.
[11] http://www.terraeletronica.com.br/roller_mouse.htm.
[12] http://cta.ifrs.edu.br/manuais/visualizar/55.
[13] http://www.softmarket.com.br/?pgID=3&soft=897.
[14] http://www.terraeletronica.com.br/bigballmousefdat.html.
[15] https://www.ablenetinc.com/bigtrack-trackball-switch-adapted.
[16] https://dl.acm.org/citation.cfm?id=1120408.
[17] https://www.pretorianuk.com/orbitrack.

The advantages of using smartphones for this purpose are mainly in the ease of move because it is a small device and the possibility of use with only one hand. Also, they have a great potential for connectivity (Wi-Fi, Bluetooth and Internet access), good human-computer interface and with extensive popular use, being an excellent alternative as remote controllers for the computer.

The Accurate Air Mouse (AAMouse) [14] tracks device movement in real-time, allowing any mobile device with a microphone, such as a smartphone or a smartwatch, to serve as a mouse controlling an electronic device with speakers. In this way, low acoustic signals are emitted and the mobile device records and send to the emitter, which can estimate the position of the device based on the Doppler effect. Then the distance between the loudspeakers and the starting position of the device is calculated based on the sound frequency.

The SMTFController [15] describes how to turn smartphones into remote computer controllers. It can be used in classrooms and meeting/conference rooms for presentation and interactive discussion. It also allows users to use multiple smartphones to operate the same computer, facilitating group discussion and classroom interaction.

Some researchers present methods to control the mouse from the computer through real-time speech recognition using a smartphone [16]. The virtual mouse operation maps spoken commands using the device's microphone to the mouse computer movement command. The purpose of this method is to control different digital devices by voice. The Tongue Drive System (TDS) [17] is a wireless wearable assistive technology that allows people with severe disabilities to control their computers, wheelchairs and electronic devices using the tongue movement. TDS translates the user's language tracking to drive commands that will be read by a bluetooth module and then embedded in the smartphone. It can act as a mouse driver on other devices connected to the network with the solution.

There is also a method for using the finger movements to interact with the smartphone screen and to control the computer mouse. The application design resembles the trackball and uses scanning techniques to improve the entry speed and to reduce the user's fatigue [18].

3   M2TA Solution

This research focuses on the development of one more mouse alternatives that allow computer access by people with motor disabilities. It is a portable touchscreen version of the conventional mouse. As seen in the related works section, researchers have already proposed various hardware solutions as an alternative to the traditional mouse. In this context, our research draws on these works by adopting metaphor input interfaces similar to those input devices (e.g., RollerMouse, Touchpad, BJOY, and Button Mouse).

In our research the mobile device functions as a computer input device. The smartphone or the tablet is the support for the execution of interfaces that simulate those input device layouts. Thus, each user can choose the type of mouse that is best suited to their needs and abilities [20]. Also, the user does not need to acquire new hardware devices, which often is difficult to maintain and expensive.

3.1 Architecture

The application architecture consists of a client (Android Application) that runs on the user device and a server (Java Application) that runs on a computer. Client and server communicate via wireless technology (i.e., Bluetooth or Wifi). Thus, the server interprets the commands sent by the Android application and generates events as standard mouse commands (Fig. 2).

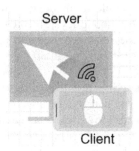

Fig. 2. M2TA main components.

3.2 Mobile Application

The application interface adapts itself according to the screen size of the device. The intention is to take advantage of the available space. The user can also switch to other input interfaces in the settings options menu. We developed four kinds of input layouts: M-Roller, Mjoy, M-Button, and MTouch. Figure 3 shows our proposal.

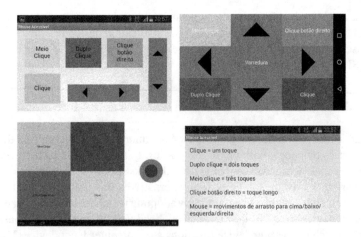

Fig. 3. M2TA layout interfaces

MTouch detects the movements and gestures of the user's finger on the mobile touchscreen. This Android application translates and transforms gestures to the cursor movement on the computer, mirroring the user's action on the computer display. For instance, one-finger touch triggers the mouse click. Two-finger touch throws double-click on the computer. Three-finger touch is equivalent to a middle-click. Finally, a long touch on the mobile screen means a right mouse click on the computer.

For the mini-joystick layout (Mjoy), the application does the translation of the torque direction and force performed by the user. For this, we define a ratio of motion to the cursor (1–100 pixels per movement). This design has the advantage of being as intuitive and easy to learn as the touchpad.

The MRoller interface has only horizontal and vertical scrolling of the cursor. It also offers four distinct buttons with click functions (Table 1). Half-click and double-click buttons are the most helpful for the user with motor disabilities.

Table 1. M2TA feature and corresponded computer event.

Action M2TA	Computer event
Click (in Portuguese, *"Clique"*)	Function equal to the conventional mouse
Right Click (in Portuguese, *"Clique Botão Direito"*)	Same as normal mouse function
Double-Click (in Portuguese, *"Duplo Clique"*)	Key for automatic double click
Half-Click (in Portuguese, *"Meio Clique"*)	Particular key for Drag & Drop function. Very useful for people who can not hold and move the directional roller at the same time

The M-Button layout is a "scan" mouse. It has four buttons to perform the cursor movement - to the right, up, down, left. It also has four buttons with distinct click functions and a centralized button to configure the scan function. The scanning on this interface works by alternating between motion and function options, varying every 5 s. Once the user has chosen one of the two options, he can switch between the four buttons every 5 s. For example, when starting MButton, the user chooses the group of directional buttons he wants to interact. Then, the application waits for the user's touch for five seconds. If the user touches anywhere on the screen, then the computer move the mouse cursor up. If not, the device waits another five seconds enabling the right arrow as the standard touch.

Users can also use these distinct M2TA layouts with their feet if they have sufficient motor control for the task. Our approach already reached the final prototyping process. Initial usability studies are in progress, some them are described in this paper.

The actions performed in the mobile application and sent to the server computer are: (1) directional cursor movements controlled by the virtual buttons or the joystick; and (2) mouse features represented by colored buttons (Table 1).

4   Initial Usability Evaluation

Four groups of specialists and two users with motor disabilities (in this case, cerebral palsy) participated in the development process of M2TA. They interacted freely with desktop applications using M2TA. Our goal was to seek for application's errors and receive suggestions for M2TA improvement. Besides, we observed their satisfaction, comfort, and the resulting impacts in the computer access experience using M2TA solutions. The evaluation was exploratory and aimed at obtaining information of qualitative nature, gathering the participants' perceptions.

4.1 Participants

Expert Users. We evaluated the proposed technology with four groups, each one composed by two or more professionals. They are from well-established health and education institutions in South America, such as: Instituto Teletón Chile (Assistive Technology Sector - Santiago Unit), SARAH Network of Rehabilitation Hospitals (Bioengineering Sector - Brasília Unit - Brazil), Federal University of Ceará - Brazil (Physiotherapy Course), and Estácio of Ceará University Center - Brazil (Physiotherapy Course).

End Users. We tested M2TA with two participants with cerebral palsy (1 male, 29 years old, graduated; and one female, 26 years old, artist). They volunteered to participate in the tests. Both users had motor disabilities and they considered smartphones and tablets as relevant devices for them to use. The inclusion criteria for participants with disabilities included a self-reported diagnosis of disability, which in both users affected the upper limbs movement function. Also, they reported difficulties in using the standard mouse. During the first interactions, we observed mainly the users' motor limitations included a lower range of hand movement, difficulty in motor coordination and body tremor.

4.2 Materials

During the evaluation sessions, the testers ran the M2TA on their own devices (mobile device and computer). The objective was to maintain the users' device preferences and to observe the M2TA performance within a real context.

4.3 Procedure

We conducted sessions involving the experts at their respective workplaces. Each session lasted up to 60 min and had four phases: (i) technology demonstration (10 min), (ii) application usage (10 min), (iii) practices of SSPT (Single Switching Performance Test) software[18] (10 min), and feedback and discussion (30 min).

With motor impaired users, we applied a free exploration test. Initially, the test observer described M2TA and installed it on the users' devices. After that, they explained to the user the test purposes (i.e., to verify satisfaction, insights, and suggestions for improving M2TA). Each user was invited to use our approach freely (e.g., access a text editor, browse the Web). Additionally, we left a tablet with them during one week to use M2TA in their houses. Finally, we conducted an unstructured interview to get their feedback and insights (Fig. 4).

---

[18] https://aacinstitute.org/sspt/.

Fig. 4. Session with an user with motor disabilities

4.4   Results

Observations and Suggestions Reported by the Experts. Experts stated that M2TA benefits from the "enchantment" factor of smartphones and tablets. These devices are far more seductive than non-digital hardware or other analogic assistive technology. Also, they confirmed that having layout options in the same software is very advantageous for this kind of users.

The experts considered the use of M2TA simple and without great cognitive efforts for their learning. They noticed users could touch on the desired feature directly. In fact, touchscreen devices are valuable to people with low muscle strength, since these users can interact with touchscreen devices without much effort. One of the experts noted that M2TA has some features similar to Augmentative and Alternative Communication (AAC)[19] tools. Although the central idea of M2TA is to replace the traditional mouse, it also becomes useful to enhance communication of people with motor disabilities. In fact, these people can use the M2TA independently, coupled to the communication software installed on the computer.

Another highlight point is the low maintenance cost of M2TA when compared to existing hardware solutions on the market. In fact, after some time of use, electromechanical materials began to get heavier. They need lubrication, and their extremities started to show signs of corrosion, originating from hands/feet sweat and users' saliva. In contrast, M2TA is only dependent on the smartphone platform, which is easier to replace and maintain.

As negative aspects, experts have reported the disadvantage of having two regions of user' visual focus (i.e., a user has to pay attention both the M2TA interface and the computer screen). This can be challenging for some users. Although, some of them may learn how to use M2TA without looking at the mobile interface over time. Experts have

---

[19] AAC englobes communication methods used to enhance or replace speech or writing for people with language impairments (e.g., the writing, speaking).

also indicated a possible fall risk of the device. In fact, interaction with the mobile device may cause it to fall when it is placed on a non-fixed surface. Another point to be studied and improved is the button sensitivity. It is common the occurrence of accidental touches, which activate unwanted functions as the devices screens are very sensitive.

We have accepted some of the experts' suggestions for implementing a new version of M2TA. For example, we standardised the colours of the various M2TA layouts to make it more comfortable to use. Another potential use is the integration of M2TA with games to improve the physical and cognitive skills of patients in rehabilitation. Another suggestion was to combine M2TA with other assistive technologies, for example, wrist weights. The goal is to help reducing the lack of motor coordination of the user. To do this, we will need to carry out a more in-depth study with patients and rehabilitation professionals.

End-User Feedback. In general, the two users were able to complete their activities on the computer (e.g., Web browsing, Facebook access, Text editing by using Windows virtual keyboard, multimedia player control, click and drag games). In the beginning, users needed the help of third parties to explain the M2TA operation. After that users performed the tasks without problems.

Overall, users enjoyed the experience of using M2TA. They stated that the four entry layouts in the same application is a great innovation. They were able to experiment all input layouts, and, thus, choose the most appropriate support for controlling the mouse cursor on the computer. The users considered that M2TA reduces the problem of access and transportation of a assistive technology, device, once it is a mobile application. They also stated that it made it possible to use our solution with their feet or even a little further away from the computer due to wireless communication.

They emphasized that the size of the buttons is relatively large, which reduced errors resulting from the interaction. Mistakes occurred, eventually, when they moved the joystick or selected an unwanted button involuntarily (e.g., the scan button on the M-Button interface). The researchers observed that the gap size between interface elements did not impact users' performance.

Regarding the MJoy interface, the two users commented on the lack of precision of the virtual joystick. They also mentioned the difficulties in controlling the joystick because, with the pressure exerted to manipulate it, the device moved over the screen. In contrast, they had no problems with the return of tactile sensation. As an improvement, one of the users suggested that the smartphones physical volume buttons could also adjust the mouse speed control.

4.5   Discussion

In general, the evaluators, experts and end users, felt confident about using the M2TA and its functions of pushing buttons and sliding the mouse cursor. They were able to perform such interactions on the mobile device touchscreens. We observed that physical and technical differences between mobile devices have impacts on the use of M2TA. We realized that users have become more aware of their possibilities and limitations in interacting with the computer. Also, the initial tests allowed us to establish the advantages and disadvantages of each of the proposed mouse layouts.

A future performance evaluation (e.g., time and accuracy) may point out to some distinctions among each M2TA layout. However, such data alone should not be critical to a user's choice of mouse design. These measurements depend on the experience of evaluators and the initial performance of their motor skills. For continuous and long-term use, users with motor impairments must choose the more appropriated assistive technologies resource in conjunction with a team of experts.

The evaluators pointed out that the financial cost of M2TA is not a significant barrier to its adoption since the average price of the mobile device is similar or lower than those of several accessible mouses on the market. Besides, smartphones and tablets are general purpose devices, and users can benefit of other features when they are not on the computer.

As a relevant result, we realize how people with motor disabilities interact with touchscreens and how this can allow designers and engineers to improve the usability of this type of interface.

Concerning the threats to validity, our initial analysis cannot yet be generalized, since the number of users was limited. However, the results provided new ideas and suggestions that will allow the improvement of our approach. The study examined only the interaction of users during the prototyping process of M2TA. This study also did not measure the impact of additional and unwanted touches (i.e., a rate of unintentional errors). In this sense, we need to implement more specific assessments of usability and performance of M2TA.

Due to sampling limitations, the results do not provide a definitive interpretation of the advantages and disadvantages of each M2TA mouse layout. Also, we can not say that the M2TA outperforms other accessible mouses devices regarding their comfort and input data rate.

5   M2TA Improvements

After this initial analysis we sought to use other haptic devices coupled to the mobile device screens. We combine other models of joysticks with M2TA. A new feature adapts the mobile application interface according to the place the user connects the physical joystick on the screen. Figure 5 shows some of the new supported joysticks.

We began planning M2TA usability assessment sessions based on Fitts's law [21] - commonly referred as the paradigm in input device ergonomics. We have developed a tracking application to facilitate the analysis of the interface versus mouse cursor path. This will allow to identify which mouse layouts get the best performance results for each evaluator. Figure 6 shows an example of the execution of the tracking software that we developed. The evaluator has to select in the software ten objects of different sizes that appear in distinct positions on the screen. We define the distribution of points on display based on the use of a Website.

Fig. 5. New supported joysticks

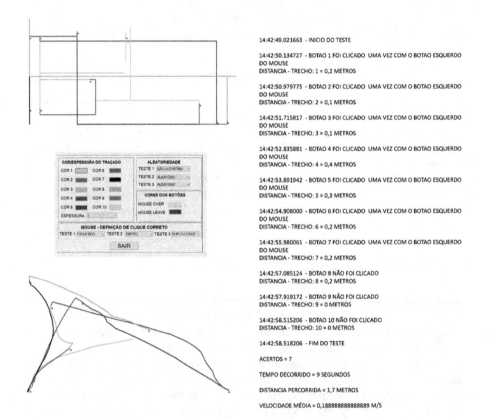

14:42:49.021663 - INICIO DO TESTE

14:42:50.134727 - BOTAO 1 FOI CLICADO UMA VEZ COM O BOTAO ESQUERDO DO MOUSE
DISTANCIA - TRECHO: 1 = 0,2 METROS

14:42:50.979775 - BOTAO 2 FOI CLICADO UMA VEZ COM O BOTAO ESQUERDO DO MOUSE
DISTANCIA - TRECHO: 2 = 0,1 METROS

14:42:51.715817 - BOTAO 3 FOI CLICADO UMA VEZ COM O BOTAO ESQUERDO DO MOUSE
DISTANCIA - TRECHO: 3 = 0,1 METROS

14:42:52.835881 - BOTAO 4 FOI CLICADO UMA VEZ COM O BOTAO ESQUERDO DO MOUSE
DISTANCIA - TRECHO: 4 = 0,4 METROS

14:42:53.891942 - BOTAO 5 FOI CLICADO UMA VEZ COM O BOTAO ESQUERDO DO MOUSE
DISTANCIA - TRECHO: 5 = 0,3 METROS

14:42:54.908000 - BOTAO 6 FOI CLICADO UMA VEZ COM O BOTAO ESQUERDO DO MOUSE
DISTANCIA - TRECHO: 6 = 0,2 METROS

14:42:55.980061 - BOTAO 7 FOI CLICADO UMA VEZ COM O BOTAO ESQUERDO DO MOUSE
DISTANCIA - TRECHO: 7 = 0,2 METROS

14:42:57.085124 - BOTAO 8 NÃO FOI CLICADO
DISTANCIA - TRECHO: 8 = 0,2 METROS

14:42:57.919172 - BOTAO 9 NÃO FOI CLICADO
DISTANCIA - TRECHO: 9 = 0 METROS

14:42:58.515206 - BOTAO 10 NÃO FOI CLICADO
DISTANCIA - TRECHO: 10 = 0 METROS

14:42:58.518206 - FIM DO TESTE

ACERTOS = 7

TEMPO DECORRIDO = 9 SEGUNDOS

DISTANCIA PERCORRIDA = 1,7 METROS

VELOCIDADE MÉDIA = 0,188888888888889 M/S

Fig. 6. Examples of track and logging developed for future evaluation sessions

Our tracking software represents a typical demand of those who interact with the computer, that is, select objects in different screen places by pointing and clicking. If the participant hits the target correctly, the software provides positive visual feedback. After that, it displays the next objective. If the click fails, the software also shows the next point to be clicked on the screen. Timestamp, spatial information of cursor movements (x, y coordinates in pixels), and the button actions are recorded in a textual log. In the end, the software generates an image with the cursor tracking lines traversed during the navigation (Fig. 6).

6   Final Considerations and Future Work

The preliminary results obtained in this study suggest a high acceptance by the users and experts in motor disabilities. The two users with motor disabilities indicated a good satisfaction with the M2TA use and they presented an initial acceptable performance for their routine adoption. They also have caveats and suggestions for improvements that are in progress. Within this context, the proposed system is promising and still has many features to improve.

Our first future work is to implement the improvements highlighted using artificial intelligence techniques to learn how to use the system. Also, we are planning a usability assessment with a significative number of participants. The goal is to measure the performances of each layout and captures the new feedbacks and suggestions. For that, we will use the tracking software showed in Sect. 5. The sessions will also use the SSPT (Single Switching Performance Test) software.

In the long run, we plan to use M2TA in the rehabilitation of people with neuropsychomotor sequelae caused by TBI - Brain Injury and Stroke - Stroke. The idea is to combine the M2TA with games that only use the mouse[20].

Acknowledgements. This research is funded by Chilean FONDECYT #1150898; Basal Funds for Centers of Excellence, Project FB0003 - CONICYT.

References

1. Hastings, S., et al.: Interviews and observation to investigate health effects from using non-keyboard input devices (NKID). In: Proceedings of the Human Factors and Ergonomics Society Annual Meeting, vol. 44, no. 30. SAGE Publications, Los Angeles (2000)
2. Akamatsu, M., MacKenzie, I.S., Hasbroucq, T.: A comparison of tactile, auditory, and visual feedback in a pointing task using a mouse-type device. Ergonomics **38**(4), 816–827 (1995)
3. Atkinson, S., et al.: Using non-keyboard input devices: interviews with users in the workplace. Int. J. Ind. Ergon. **33**(6), 571–579 (2004)
4. Sutter, C., Ziefle, M.: Interacting with notebook input devices: an analysis of motor performance and users' expertise. Hum. Fact. **47**(1), 169–187 (2005)
5. Belatar, M., Poirier, F.: Text entry for mobile devices and users with severe motor impairments: handiglyph, a primitive shapes based onscreen keyboard. In: Proceedings of the 10th International ACM SIGACCESS Conference on Computers and Accessibility (Assets 2008), pp. 209–216. ACM, New York (2008). http://dx.doi.org/ 10.1145/1414471.1414510

---

[20] http://www.oneswitch.org.uk/art.php?id=28.

6. Shakespeare, T., Officer, A.: World report on disability. Disabil. Rehabil. **33**(17–18), 1491 (2011)
7. Kaneko, S.T.: Computer mouse. USPatent D349, 280, 2 August 1994
8. Meriaz, R.: Trackball mouse. US PatentApp. 09/790,354.35, 22 August 2002
9. Cordes, S.A., Leach, D.C., Loussedes, D.A., Obszamy, C.E.: Joystick type computer input device withmouse. US Patent 8,576,170.37, 5 November 2013
10. Basnett, R.J., Gregory, M.A., Cowell, S.L.: CRT lightpen interface for flat panel displays. US Patent 8,963,893.38, 24 February 2015
11. Gralewski, W.A., Massaro, K.L., On, P.M.: Touchpad input device. US Patent App. 13/125,084.36, 11 August 2011
12. Dhingra, S., Entwisle, J., Lopez-Garcia, L., Center, U.W., Gilkison, S., Martin, J.K., Michels, M., Shin, Y.J.: Current practices in maintenance and repair of mobility assistive technology
13. Section 508: Buy Accessible Technology. U.S. General Services Administration Federal Government-wide Section508 Accessibility Program (2017). https://www.section508.gov/content/buy. Accessed 12 Dec 2017
14. Yun, S., Chen, Y.-C., Qiu, L.: Turning a mobile device into a mouse in the air. In: Proceedings of the 13th Annual International Conference on Mobile Systems, Applications, and Services, pp. 15–29. ACM (2015)
15. Yang, Y., Li, L.: Turn smartphones into computer remote controllers. Int. J. Comput. Theory Eng. **4**(4), 561 (2012)
16. Jang, T., et al.: Implementation of real-time vowel recognition mouse based on smartphone. KIISE Trans. Comput. Pract. **21**(8), 531–536 (2015)
17. Kim, J., Park, H., Ghovanloo, M.: Tongue-operated assistive technology with access to common smartphone applications via Bluetooth link. In: 2012 Annual International Conference of the IEEE Engineering in Medicine and Biology Society (EMBC), pp. 4054–4057. IEEE (2012)
18. Kim, C.G., Jang, U.H., Song, B.-S.: Development of a portable alternative computer access APP for the physically disabled in Korea. In: Proceedings of the 7th International Convention on Rehabilitation Engineering and Assistive Technology (i-CREATe 2013), Singapore Therapeutic, Assistive & Rehabilitative Technologies (START) Centre, Kaki Bukit TechPark II, Singapore, 4 p. (2013). Article 18
19. Trewin, S., Swart, C., Pettick, D.: Physical accessibility of touchscreen smartphones. In: Proceedings of the 15th International ACM SIGACCESS Conference on Computers and Accessibility (ASSETS 2013), 8 p. ACM, New York (2013). Article 19. http://dx.doi.org/10.1145/2513383.2513446
20. Do Nascimento Maia, F., De Freitas, S.F.: Proposal of a flowchart for the development process of assistive technology products. Cadernos de Terapia Ocupacional da UFSCar, vol. 22, no. 3 (2014)
21. Soukoreff, R.W., Mackenzie, I.S.: Towards a standard for pointing device evaluation, perspectives on 27 years of Fitts' law research in HCI. Int. J. Hum.-Comput. Stud. **61**(6), 751–789 (2004)
22. Trewin, S., Swart, C., Pettick, D.: Physical accessibility of touchscreen smartphones. In: Proceedings of the 15th International ACM SIGACCESS Conference on Computers and Accessibility (ASSETS 2013), Article 19, 8 pages. ACM, New York (2013). http://dx.doi.org/10.1145/2513383.2513446

Multi-switch Scanning Keyboards: A Theoretical Study of Simultaneous Parallel Scans with QWERTY Layout

Frode Eika Sandnes[1,2(✉)], Evelyn Eika[1], and Fausto Orsi Medola[3]

[1] Department of Computer Science, Faculty of Technology, Art and Design,
OsloMet – Oslo Metropolitan University, Oslo, Norway
{frodes,Evelyn.Eika}@hioa.no

[2] Faculty of Technology, Westerdals Oslo School of Art, Communication and Technology,
Oslo, Norway

[3] School of Architecture, Arts and Communication, São Paulo State University (UNESP),
Bauru, Brazil
fausto.medola@faac.unesp.br

Abstract. Scanning keyboards can be useful aids for individuals with reduced motor function. However, scanning input techniques are known for being very slow to use because they require waiting for the right cell to be highlighted during each character input cycle. This study explores the idea of parallel scanning keyboards controlled with multiple switches and their theoretical effects on performance. The designs explored assume that the keyboard layouts are familiar to users and that the mapping between the switches and the keyboards are natural and direct. The results show that the theoretical performance increases linearly with the number of switches used. Future work should perform user tests with parallel scans to assess the practicality of this approach.

Keywords: Scanning keyboards · Text entry · Joystick · Parallel scans
Reduced motor function

1 Introduction

Individuals with reduced motor function may be unable to use a regular keyboard. It may be due to tremor, stiffness, missing hand or arm, or the total inability to use arms or hands. One solution is to control computers with a switch, either controlled with the hand, the head, gaze, eye blink, or a brain-computer interface. Much research effort has gone into the use of single switches to perform text entry by the means of scanning keyboards [1].

Scanning keyboards are time-consuming to use since most of the time is involved in waiting for the target to be highlighted. Therefore, most studies into scanning keyboards have focused on layout optimizations [2–4], word prediction [5], ambiguous keyboards [6], and reducing errors [7, 8].

This study explores the concept of using several switches in parallel to improve text entry performance. By using several switches, multiple scanning sequences can be performed in parallel. One can thereby possibly achieve performance improvements.

© Springer International Publishing AG, part of Springer Nature 2018
M. Antona and C. Stephanidis (Eds.): UAHCI 2018, LNCS 10907, pp. 287–298, 2018.
https://doi.org/10.1007/978-3-319-92049-8_21

2 Background

The literature on scanning keyboards is vast; see, for instance, the survey by Polacek [1]. A typical scanning keyboard is usually implemented by displaying a virtual keyboard where the rows are displayed in a sequential order. Once the row with the desired character is displayed, it can be selected by activating the switch. Next, the cells of the selected row are shown one-by-one for a certain dwell-time. Once the desired cell is highlighted, it is selected by activating the switch. Research into scanning keyboards has attempted to reorganize the virtual keyboards into more efficient layouts with shorter distances to the more frequent characters [2–4]. Word prediction is also commonly used to help users speed up the text entry [5]. Keyboards with multiple characters assigned to each cell combined with dictionaries to resolve ambiguities were also attempted [6].

A number of studies have also explored error patterns that are specific to scanning-based text entry [7–9].

Alternatives to scanning keyboards include Morse code [10], which can be input using a single switch with long and short presses and tapping [11, 12] by the means of two-dimensional tapping codes. Another different area of research includes chording [13, 14] where a finger is only assigned one key, but several keys are often pressed simultaneously. Chording also allows for certain error correction mechanisms [15, 16]. Other approaches include menu-based systems [17, 18] where the user finds the desired character by going through some menu structure, gestures [19, 20], prefix-based prediction [21], and abbreviations expansion [22] where the user could just enter key consonants to save effort and these abbreviations are expanded using dictionaries. In addition to simplifying text entry, text prediction [21] and other query building aids have also shown to be beneficial for users with dyslexia [23, 24]. Indirect information input based on proximity is another totally different approach suitable for specialized applications [25, 26].

It has been pointed out that scanning keyboard research is challenging due to the difficulties of recruiting participants from the target group and several researchers have therefore proposed various performance models [9, 27, 28]. Of interest herein are the scan steps per character [28] which is the sum of the number of scan steps to reach a character multiplied by the frequency of that particular character.

3 Input Methods

This section describes the multi-switch input techniques explored in this study. Common to all the techniques is that they are based on the QWERTY layout since users are more likely to accept new input techniques if they can reuse existing skills and are exposed to familiar elements [29, 30]. One important principle is that there should be a direct mapping between the controls and the virtual keyboard such that learning time is minimized.

3.1 Double Switch

A simple enhancement of a simple switch is a double switch, which is a spring-loaded device that can be moved left or right and that will return to its original position once it is released. It would typically be operated by an individual with very limited motor function who can perform very coarse-grained motions. A double switch can, for instance, be implemented using a single joystick where all leftwards motions are interpreted as West and all rightwards motions interpreted as East.

Unlike the other designs described herein, the double switch requires characters to be selected in two steps: first the group, then the cell. Two designs are explored: column-cell and row-cell. The Column-cell-design first scans the five columns on each side of the keyboard in parallel during the first step. The user then selects the left or right side when the desired column is determined. During the second step the three cells within the selected column is selected by any motion with the joystick. This gives the user

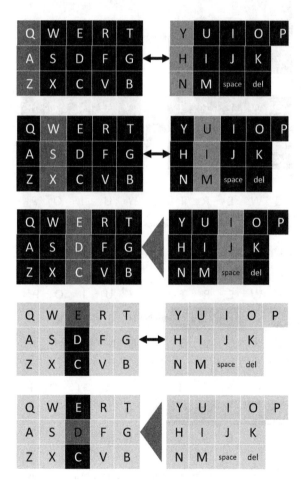

Fig. 1. Two-level scanning keyboards with double switch (column-cell).

freedom in the direction of the second motion allowing the user to make a more natural continuous motion, that is, left-to-right, instead of left-release-left.

With the second variation, the user first selects the desired row on the left or right side when it is highlighted. During the second step the user selects the desired cell within the group with either a left or right motion with the switch. Figure 1 illustrates the character grouping and switch mapping using the row-cell and Fig. 2 column-cell strategies. In both cases, it is simulated that the user wants to input the character D. With the column-cell strategy, the five columns for each hand are scanned in parallel. Once the third column on each side is reached, the user moves the joystick left to select the left column (EDC) and not the right column (I, J, SPACE). Next, the three cells EDC of the column are scanned and the user selects the second one (D) once it is highlighted by moving the joystick in any direction. In total, the user needs to make two decisions and two actions and wait for five scan steps.

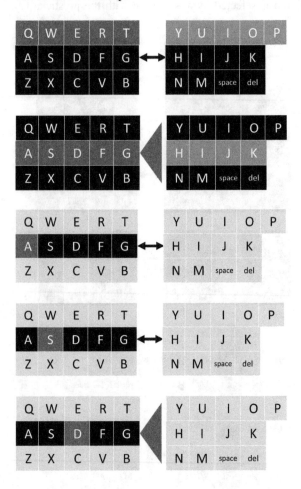

Fig. 2. Two-level scanning keyboard with double switch (row-cell).

The procedure is similar with the row-cell strategy, with the difference that the entire rows are scanned first. Once the second row is displayed, the left part of the row (ASDFG) is selected by moving the joystick left.

Next, the cells of the row ASDFG are scanned and the user selects the third cell D once it is highlighted. Again, the user needs to make two decisions and take two actions and have to wait five scanning steps in total.

3.2 Double Joystick

The double joystick, or game controller, comprises two joysticks where each joystick can be moved in one of eight directions, or 16 directions for the two joysticks. Previously, text input for joysticks has been proposed by the means of an ambiguous keyboard where users would imagine each joystick being placed in the middle of each side of the keyboard and the joystick moved in the direction of the desired characters [29].

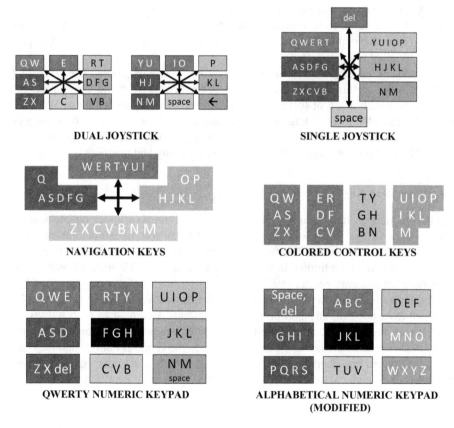

Fig. 3. Multi-switch input methods: (a) dual joystick, (b) single joystick, (c) navigation keys, (d) four colored control keys, (e) QWERTY numeric keypad, and (f) alphabetical numeric keypad. Colors are used to highlight direction.

The double joystick input technique proposed herein comprises dividing the keyboard into two halves and with the joysticks virtually located between the S and D keys and between the J and K keys (see Fig. 3a). For each hand, a selection is made by moving the joystick in the direction of the desired group once the desired character of that group is highlighted.

An advantage of this input strategy is that each group is relatively small comprising 1 to 3 characters. Therefore, the penalty of missing a character during a scan is not too large.

Obviously, a double joystick requires the operation of both hands, and may therefore not be usable for people who are unable to use the hands in this way. However, in situations that allow for bimanual input, the double joystick may host the possibility of more efficient text input because of the 16 unique directions.

3.3   Single Joystick

Single joystick text input may be used for individuals who perhaps may only use one hand or may use some alternative input device such as a mouth-controlled switch. The most noteworthy research into single joystick text entry is by the means of gestures. The proposed approach requires much simpler single strokes compared to the more complex motions required to input gestures.

The single joystick allows the user to select one of eight directions. The QWERTY keyboard was therefore divided into six groups, comprising a left and a right part with three rows in each. Each of these six groups was accessed by North-West, West and South-West and North-East, East and South-East. Most of the groups are thus assigned five cells or characters. Space is assigned South and backspace is assigned North. Figure 3b illustrates the single joystick character grouping and mapping.

3.4   Navigation Keys

The navigation keys design could be applicable to individuals who are unable to accurately control a single joystick in eight directions but can control the four easiest directions North, East, South, and West. Alternatively, it could be non-disabled users who need to input text with a limited input device such as a Smart TV remote control or an in-flight entertainment system controller.

The navigation maps directly to North, East, South, and West. Clearly, the QWERTY keyboard does not naturally partition into four groups according to such a division. However, an attempt is illustrated in Fig. 3c. The idea behind the partitioning is that the origin is the center of the keyboard located between the G and H buttons and the characters are divided into characters above, below, to the left, and to the right. Moreover, the group sizes were balanced such that no groups have more than seven cells or less than six cells.

3.5   Colored Control Buttons

Four colored control keys can be found on SmartTV remote controls and on some in-flight entertainment systems. Clearly, entertainment for individuals with limited input device characteristics is the intended application area.

With this design, the keyboard is partitioned into four groups along vertical lines of division comprising three groups of six cells and one group with eight cells at the right. The design is illustrated in Fig. 3d.

3.6   Numeric Keypad

Numeric keypads as text input devices have been explored in the text entry literature in terms of mobile text entry. The main strategies include multi-tap and ambiguous text entry. In this study, a parallel scan pattern is assigned to each key of the numeric keypad, where the desired letter is selected by pressing the assigned keypad button once the character is highlighted.

Two keypad assignments are made, namely to evenly distribute the characters across all the keys and to reuse the familiar numeric keypad character assignments as found on mobile phone keypads. The two key assignments are illustrated in Fig. 3e and f, respectively.

3.7   Scanning Sequence

For each of the designs described in the previous sections, three variations are explored: left-to-right, highest-frequency-letter-first, and decreasing-frequency. The left-to-right scanning sequence starts with the left-most character and goes towards the right. When the rightmost character is reached, the scan starts over again at the left. In cultures with left-to-right writing systems, it is believed that there is a preferential bias to go from left to right [31]. In the example in Fig. 4(left) the scan goes via the sequence Q, W, E, R, T and start over with Q.

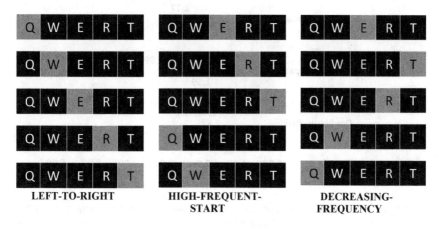

Fig. 4. Scanning sequences

The second variation also goes from left to right, but starts with the most frequent character. This is illustrated in Fig. 4(middle) where the scan starts with the most frequent character E and continues with R, T, Q, W.

The third variation involves scanning the character in decreasing order of frequency. For the sequence in Fig. 4(right) this is E, T, R, W and Q.

4   Results

Figure 5 shows the effort required for each of the designs in terms of scanning steps per character [28]. A single-switch input strategy is provided as a baseline [32]. Each of the

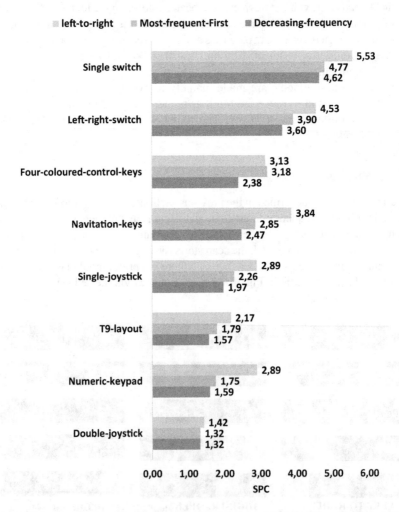

Fig. 5. SPC for the scanning keyboard designs with left-to-right scanning sequences (yellow), left-to-right-starting with the highest frequency letter scanning sequence (orange) and decreasing order of frequency (brown) (Color figure online)

strategies is evaluated under three scanning sequence conditions, namely: from left-to-right, from-left-to-right but starting with the highest frequency character in the group, and scanning sequence according to decreasing frequency of occurrence (see Fig. 4). For each instance, it is assumed that the scanning pattern is repeated if the user does not act during a scan.

As expected, the single key strategy requires the most scan steps per character (5.53), while the double joystick requires the fewest (1.42 SPC). By replacing the single switch with a double switch, the saving is about one scan step per character. Further, the single joystick reduces the number of scan steps by 1.5 in comparison to the double switch, and it is nearly half the number of scan steps required with a single switch. The single joystick is obviously more complex to control, requiring more accurate motor control than the double switch. The number of scan steps with the dual joystick is only a small fraction of what is required with the single switch. However, the dual joystick required bimanual operation and quite detailed motor operations.

Several keyboard-based input strategies were included. These are not necessarily optimal for individuals with reduced motor function but may be suitable for individuals with limited input hardware such as text entry via remote controls or simple entertainment system controllers. The results show that the four-button design (3.13 SPC) performs better than the navigation key design (3.84 SPC). The reason for this is probably partially chance, that is, it happens that the division of the keyboard is more beneficial with the four colored keys than the navigation keys. Moreover, four navigation directions (north, east, south, and west) do not naturally map onto the QWERTY layout. However, the trend is reversed when scanning from left-to-right starting with the most frequent character, and the two techniques are nearly similar when scanning the characters in decreasing order of frequency.

Two numeric keypads are also included for reference, one based on the QWERTY layout (nonstandard mapping) and the other an alphabetical mapping (standard mapping). The results show that both numeric keypad-based techniques give fewer scan steps per character compared to the other techniques based on fewer switches. Note that the QWERTY based mapping uses nine switches while the alphabetical (standard) mapping only uses eight as the 1-key is not used. Surprisingly, the alphabetical layout yields a lower number of scan steps per character when each group is scanned from left-to-right.

Although the numeric keypad yields fewer scan steps per character, it may be more challenging to use compared to control keys or especially navigation keys. This is because the user probably will have to perform a visual search for the right key before pressing the key. With navigation keys the mapping may be more intuitive.

Another interesting observation is that the alphabetical numeric keypad only uses eight switches for characters. Yet, its performance (2.17 SPC) is much better than the QWERTY-based method for single joysticks (2.89), which also have eight switches. However, the single joystick-based method uses the familiar QWERTY layout and two of the directions are assigned to backspace and space. Simply, by assigning the characters of the alphabetical numeric keypad to the eight joystick directions the scan steps per character could be reduced quite significantly. However, this assignment would come at the expense of being unfamiliar and more complex access to the space and backspace characters.

To explore the effects of switch quantity, the results obtained with the techniques discussed herein were visualized. Figure 6 shows a scatterplot of the number of switches plotted against a theoretical measure of words per minute. The plot shows that the techniques explored approximately follow a line. However, it is important to note that the measures of words per minute are theoretical and not based on actual measurements.

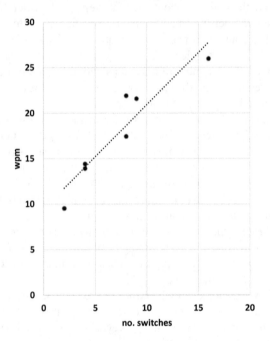

Fig. 6.   Theoretic upper bound of wpm as a function of number of switches.

An important difference between the double switch technique and the other techniques discussed herein is that the former requires two scanning levels, while the latter only requires one scanning level. One may expect that it is more tolerable to use a scanning keyboard with just one scanning level as it should be cognitively less demanding requiring only one action per character.

5   Conclusions

This study explored the effects of using multiple switches with parallel scanning keyboards based on a theoretical model. The results show that that it is theoretically possible to achieve an approximate linear increase in text entry rates with the number of switches. This study has explored this phenomenon under the assumptions that the letters must have a familiar layout (QWERTY) and a natural and direct mapping. Several configurations were explored, opening up for the possibility to tailor a particular design according to the characteristics of a user's motor abilities. It is also possible that scanning keyboards may be beneficial for non-disabled users in resource constrained systems that only allowprimitive input devices such as entertainment systems. This study is a theoretical back-of-the envelope evaluation of several text entry designs. Theoretical evaluations are by no means a valid substitute for performing measurements with real users, however, theoretical models can sometimes help identify interesting designs worth further study [33]. Future work will explore how users respond to parallel scanning keyboard designs.

References

1. Polacek, O., Sporka, A.J., Slavik, P.: Text input for motor-impaired people. Univers. Access Inf. Soc. **16**, 51–72 (2017)
2. Abascal, J., Gardeazabal, L., Garay, N.: Optimisation of the selection set features for scanning text input. In: Miesenberger, K., Klaus, J., Zagler, W.L., Burger, D. (eds.) ICCHP 2004. LNCS, vol. 3118, pp. 788–795. Springer, Heidelberg (2004). https://doi.org/ 10.1007/978-3-540-27817-7_117
3. Higger, M., Moghadamfalahi, M., Quivira, F., Erdogmus, D.: Fast switch scanning keyboards: minimal expected query decision trees. arXiv preprint arXiv:1606.02552 (2016)
4. Zhang, X.C., Fang, K., Francis, G.: Optimization of switch keyboards. In: Proceedings of the 15th International ACM SIGACCESS Conference on Computers and Accessibility. ACM (2013)
5. Jones, P.E.: Virtual keyboard with scanning and augmented by prediction. In: Proceedings of the 2nd European Conference on Disability, Virtual Reality and Associated Technologies, pp. 45–51 (1998)
6. Mackenzie, I.S., Felzer, T.: SAK: scanning ambiguous keyboard for efficient one-key text entry. ACM Trans. Comput.-Hum. Interact. (TOCHI) **17**, (2010)
7. Zhang, X., Fang, K., Francis, G.: How to optimize switch virtual keyboards to trade off speed and accuracy. Cogn. Res.: Princ. Implic. **1**, 6 (2016)
8. Simpson, R.C., Mankowski, R., Koester, H.H.: Modeling one-switch row-column scanning with errors and error correction methods. Open Rehabil. J. **4**, 1–12 (2011)
9. Francis, G., Johnson, E.: Speed–accuracy tradeoffs in specialized keyboards. Int. J. Hum.-Comput. Stud. **69**, 526–538 (2011)
10. Levine, S., Gauger, J., Bowers, L., Khan, K.: A comparison of mouthstick and morse code text inputs. Augment. Altern. Commun. **2**, 51–55 (1986)
11. Sandnes, F.E., Medola, F.O.: Exploring Russian tap-code text entry adaptions for users with reduced target hitting accuracy. In: Proceedings of the 7th International Conference on Software Development and Technologies for Enhancing Accessibility and Fighting Info-exclusion, pp. 33–38. ACM (2016)
12. Gong, J., Haggerty, B., Tarasewich, P.: An enhanced multitap text entry method with predictive next-letter highlighting. In: CHI 2005 Extended Abstracts on Human Factors in Computing Systems, pp. 1399–1402. ACM (2005)
13. Sandnes, F.E.: Can spatial mnemonics accelerate the learning of text input chords? In: Proceedings of the Working Conference on Advanced Visual Interfaces, pp. 245–249. ACM (2006)
14. Sandnes, F.E.: Human performance characteristics of three-finger chord sequences. Procedia Manuf. **3**, 4228–4235 (2015)

15. Sandnes, F.E., Huang, Y.P.: Chording with spatial mnemonics: automatic error correction for eyes-free text entry. J. Inf. Sci. Eng. **22**, 1015–1031 (2006)

16. Sandnes, F.E., Huang, Y.P.: Chord level error correction for portable Braille devices. Electron. Lett. **42**, 82–83 (2006)

17. Sandnes, F.E., Thorkildssen, H.W., Arvei, A., Buverad, J.O.: Techniques for fast and easy mobile text-entry with three-keys. In: Proceedings of the 37th Annual Hawaii International Conference on System Sciences. IEEE (2004)

18. Sandnes, F.E., Jian, H.-L.: Pair-wise variability index: evaluating the cognitive difficulty of using mobile text entry systems. In: Brewster, S., Dunlop, M. (eds.) Mobile HCI 2004. LNCS, vol. 3160, pp. 347–350. Springer, Heidelberg (2004). https://doi.org/10.1007/978-3-540-28637-0_35

19. Sandnes, F.E., Tan, T.B., Johansen, A., Sulic, E., Vesterhus, E., Iversen, E.R.: Making touch-based kiosks accessible to blind users through simple gestures. Univers. Access Inf. Soc. **11**, 421–431 (2012)

20. Perlin, K.: Quikwriting: continuous stylus-based text entry. In: Proceedings of the 11th Annual ACM Symposium on User Interface Software and Technology, pp. 215–216. ACM (1998)

21. Darragh, J.J., Witten, I.H., James, M.L.: The reactive keyboard: a predictive typing aid. Computer **23**, 41–49 (1990)

22. Sandnes, F.E.: Reflective text entry: a simple low effort predictive input method based on flexible abbreviations. Procedia Comput. Sci. **67**, 105–112 (2015)

23. Berget, G., Sandnes, F.E.: Do autocomplete functions reduce the impact of dyslexia on information searching behaviour? A case of Google. J. Am. Soc. Inf. Sci. Technol. **67**, 2320–2328 (2016)

24. Berget, G., Sandnes, F.E.: Searching databases without query-building aids: implications for dyslexic users. Inf. Res. **20**, n4 (2015)

25. Huang, Y.P., Chang, Y.T., Sandnes, F.E.: Ubiquitous information transfer across different platforms by QR codes. J. Mob. Multimed. **6**, 3–13 (2010)

26. Sandnes, F.E., Herstad, J., Stangeland, A.M., Orsi Medola, F.: UbiWheel: a simple context-aware universal control concept for smart home appliances that encourages active living. In: Proceedings of Smartworld 2017, pp. 446–451. IEEE (2017)

27. Bhattacharya, S., Samanta, D., Basu, A.: Performance models for automatic evaluation of virtual scanning keyboards. IEEE Trans. Neural Syst. Rehabil. Eng. **16**, 510–519 (2008)

28. MacKenzie, I.S.: Modeling text input for single-switch scanning. In: Miesenberger, K., Karshmer, A., Penaz, P., Zagler, W. (eds.) ICCHP 2012. LNCS, vol. 7383, pp. 423–430. Springer, Heidelberg (2012). https://doi.org/10.1007/978-3-642-31534-3_63

29. Sandnes, F.E., Aubert, A.: Bimanual text entry using game controllers: relying on users' spatial familiarity with QWERTY. Interact. Comput. **19**, 140–150 (2007)

30. Sandnes, F.E.: Effects of common keyboard layouts on physical effort: implications for kiosks and Internet banking. In: Sandnes, F.E., Lunde, M. Tollefsen, M., Hauge, A.M., Øverby, E., Brynn, R. (eds.) Proceedings of Unitech2010: International Conference on Universal Technologies, pp. 91–100. Tapir Academic Publishers (2010)

31. Sandnes, F.E.: Directional bias in scrolling tasks: a study of users' scrolling behaviour using a mobile text-entry strategy. Behav. Inf. Technol. **27**, 387–393 (2008)

32. Sandnes, F.E., Medola, F.O.: Effects of optimizing the scan-path on scanning keyboards with QWERTY-layout for English text. Stud. Health Technol. Inform. **242**, 930–938 (2017)

33. Sandnes, F.E.: Evaluating mobile text entry strategies with finite state automata. In: Proceedings of the 7th International Conference on Human Computer Interaction with Mobile Devices & Services, pp. 115–121. ACM (2005)

Towards Multi-modal Interaction
with Interactive Paint

Nicholas Torres, Francisco R. Ortega$^{(\boxtimes)}$, Jonathan Bernal, Armando Barreto,
and Naphtali D. Rishe

Florida International University, Miami, FL 33196, USA
{ntorr054,fortega,jber006,barretoa,rishen}@fiu.edu,
fortega@cs.fiu.edu

Abstract. We present a Multi-Modal Interactive Paint application. Our
work is intended to illustrate shortcomings in current multi-modal interaction and to present design strategies to address and alleviate these
issues. In particular, from an input perspective use in a regular desktop
environment. A serious of challenges are listed and addressed individually with their corresponding strategies in our discussion of design practices for multi-modality. We also identify areas which we will improve for
future iterations of similar multi-modal interaction applications due to
the findings identified in this paper. These improvements should alleviate
shortcomings with our current design and provide further opportunities
to research multi-modal interaction.

Keywords: Multi-modal · Interaction · Multi-touch · Modality

1 Introduction

New input devices (e.g., Leap Motion, Intel RealSense, Microsoft Kinect, Tobii
EyeX) are changing the 3D user interface landscape [1], by enabling more intuitive (or "natural") interaction. This interaction is more intuitive as social action
and interaction is inherently multi-modal and represents a significant portion of
human activity. For example, Stivers et al. defined face-to-face interaction as
multi-modal through the composition of the vocal and visuospatial modalities
[2]. However, combining various modern input devices has created many challenges for user interaction research. Many of these devices enable unimodal interaction (vision-based, touch-based, speech recognition, etc.) as such the difficulty
comes from attempting to combine the disparate modalities that typically are
ignorant of one another.

Regardless of the difficulty, multi-modality has been the focus of a continuous
research effort by the Human-Computer Interaction (HCI) community due to the
promising improvements to user interaction. For example, Jourde et al. created
an editor using their Collaborative and Multimodal (COMM) notation, allowing users to identify relationships between them and their devices [3]. In another

© Springer International Publishing AG, part of Springer Nature 2018
M. Antona and C. Stephanidis (Eds.): UAHCI 2018, LNCS 10907, pp. 299–308, 2018.
https://doi.org/10.1007/978-3-319-92049-8_22

study, Prammanee et al. proposed an architecture to discern the modalities of different devices [4]. In this paper, we present design strategies for multi-modal interaction and the challenges faced during the construction of Multi-Modal Interactive Paint (MIP).

2   Background

Modality can be defined as the mode in which something is experience, expressed or exists but is also used in the context of sensory perception. In this paper, we use both because each definition is applicable to our uses. For example, a touch gesture is an expression which is also a modality, but touch is also a sensory perception. With this definition, we can state that multi-modality is a combination of two or more modalities that can be a composition of touch, vision, speech recognition, etc. For example, there may be the utilization of touch and vision when identifying attributes of an object such as shape, color, and texture. The set of modalities that we discuss are those who mainly have the capability for active interaction such as touch and vision. Others are also useful for interaction even though they do not provide direct input to an application but we will not discuss those at any length in this document as our primary focus is on input devices and the previously discussed modalities.

This area interests us because multi-modal interaction is the default state of social interactions. In social situations, we incorporate various modalities when engaging others. The two central modalities in social situations such as face-to-face as discussed previously in the introduction are vocal and visuospatial. Stivers et al. define visuospatial as consisting of manual gestures, facial expressions, and body posture [2]. These elements of the visuospatial modality may be culturally dependent. For example, a hand with the index and middle finger forming a "V" shape has a significant difference in American and British culture. However, regardless of differences in the precise details of these elements all social actions and interactions are comprised of the visuospatial modality and the vast majority incorporate the vocal modality when face-to-face. This multi-modal interaction is regardless of cultural, racial or national background. Such a universal, inherent and instinctual form of interaction is why multi-modal interaction shall be a significant and critical area of research in the field of HCI.

3   Motivation

The motivation of MIP is to create a fun application that can be used to test multi-modal interaction (from an input perspective) while developing strategies to lessen the challenges in this type of interaction. Most importantly, we are interested in improving user interaction towards a more intuitive experience.

4   Multi-modal Interactive Paint

This section provides information about MIP.

4.1   An Overview

In the quest for multi-modal interaction, we asked ourselves what will be the best application that can demonstrate true multi-modal interaction? We concluded that a painting application would be the best demonstration of true multi-modal interaction. This conclusion was due to a painting application providing a complex environment for testing real-time interaction while being a fun application to use, and most importantly, it has demonstrable benefits in aiding children by helping to identify their psychological profiles [5], which can also help research in multi-modal interaction for education. In addition to the complexities inherent in multi-modal interaction, studying children's interactions provide an additional layer of complexity. This additional complexity is due to the developmental differences between adults and children with regards to cognition. The difference necessitates recognition algorithms which can account for the increase in complexity. The aforementioned helps to make the case that multi-modal interaction design strategies will be different if used by children versus adults [6].

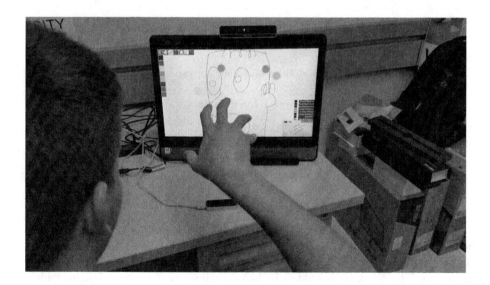

Fig. 1. Leap-motion and real-sense demo

This desire to create a proper demonstration of true multi-modal interaction lead to the creation of MIP. This application is a painting (drawing) application with multi-modal support, as shown in Figs. 1 and 2. The motivation to create MIP was due to the previous benefits discussed with regards to aiding children, among others. For example, painting in general not only helps develop a board psychological profile but can assist in identifying psychopathologies [5]. Currently supported modalities and their corresponding input device can be seen in Table 1.

Fig. 2. Multi-touch demo

Table 1. Supported modalities and their corresponding input device

Modality	Input device
Touch	Multi-touch display
Visual	Tobii EyeX
Manual gesture	Leap motion
Facial gesture	Intel RealSense

Users can use any the modalities provided by the input devices as well as any of the built-in tools. Currently, built-in MIP toolset is a composition of basic shapes, random color selection, save and undo operations, layers, and image mirroring. The set of basic shapes includes circles, squares, and triangles which each support activities such as filling and transparency Additionally, the modalities described previously add additional functionality which can trigger upon performing a specific set of gestures. For example, the Intel RealSense camera has support for facial gestures, such as smile and puffy face. The former gesture allows shapeshifting, and the latter changes shape color. The Leap Motion device is capable of triggering the *Save* feature upon performing a double-tap gesture; performing rotation gestures as well as left and right swipes triggers the shape selection capability. The Tobii EyeX tracker enables the capability of drawing using the gaze of the user. The Tobii EyeX tracks the user's point of gaze on the computer screen and draws at the position where the user is looking. Perhaps, the most important feature is the coordination of the input devices enabled by MIP. For example, if the user has a multi-touch display and a Leap Motion, the latter will be used only for specific functions in the system by default. However, these functions can be overridden by the user as they may also decide to turn it into a drawing device. This flexibility allows for a rich set of interaction options for which can provide a tailor-made experience for the user matching their exact preferences if they so choose. Moreover, the number of responsibilities of a device may decrease if more devices become available to the system.

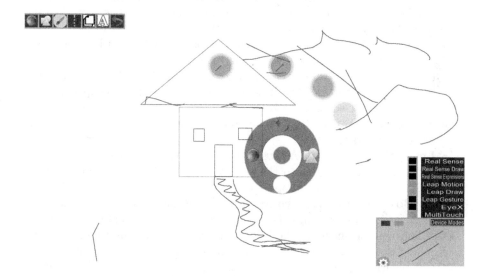

Fig. 3. Multi-modal canvas

Currently, MIP restricts all of the modalities provided by the input devices to 2D painting. However, the application makes use of LibCinder and OpenGL as core components. These components provide the possibility of adapting MIP for 3D painting. MIP for 3D painting would enable other industrial applications in addition to the benefits to psychologists that 2D painting brings. The industrial applications may include graphics professionals who paint onto 3D models, architects who create 3D drafts and other professionals. Also, the same therapeutic benefits from MIP for 2D painting should hold in a 3D painting environment.

MIP is also useful as a baseline for future device enablement and will serve as a testbed for new input devices. This testbed will allow us to tune new input devices for modalities that we have previously used since we will already have previous experience with user interaction with that specific modality. Having this ability enables rapid enablement for other projects.

4.2 User Interface

The MIP application's user interface consists of two major and ever-present components: (i) the Mode Buttons, (ii) the Mode Box. Both of these can are present in Fig. 3 as well as a couple of contextual menus.

- **Mode Buttons** – Top left corner of the User Interface (buttons from left to right). Enables the user to specify their input and organize their painting.
  - **Color Change Button** – Allows the user to make a color selection in the same manner they make in unimodal applications such as Microsoft Paint.
  - **Change Button** – Allows the user to make a shape selection, where users can choose from Lines, Circles, Rectangles or Triangles. A shape is filled (with the color selection) or unfilled (transparent) based on the user inputted value of the Toggle Fill Button.
  - **Buttons** – This button has several buttons nested which become available to the user upon selection. The buttons are: (i) Toggle Fill Button (enable or disable transparency), (ii) Line Size Increase Button, (iii) Line Size Decrease Button, (iv) Transparency Increase (increase opacity), (v) Transparency Decrease (decrease opacity).
  - **Toggle Symmetry** – Enforces symmetric input by reflecting input over a user selected axis.
  - **Layer Visualization** – Allows users to select different layers for painting. This function is similar to those found in popular applications such as Krita and Adobe Photoshop.
- **Mode Box** – Bottom right corner of the User Interface. Informs the user of currently selected settings. For example, if the user is entering a line, a set of lines will be shown in the box in the color that the user currently has selected. Also, the box display information of devices at the beginning of the MIP application's execution (launch) and allows the user to select devices that they would like to enable or disable. Finally, there is a cog icon in the bottom left corner of the Mode Box that allows diagnostic information to be displayed in MIP such as Frames Per a Second (FPS). All of these present in Fig. 3.

5 Design Practices for Multi-modality

During the design of MIP, we were able to find many challenges that provide insight into the design and research directions for multi-modal interaction. Some of these challenges are more apparent than others which are only found while conducting live testing of a multi-modal application and even then only with some modalities. The following list summarizes some of those challenges and their suggested solutions or areas of further research interest:

- **InfraRed (IR) technology** – having multiple devices with infrared emitters creates a problem if their respective fields of view (of the camera) intersect their counter emitters. The best solution is to use at most one IR device (e.g., Leap Motion) and provide other means of recognition – in particular, the use of optical tracking. For example, Hu et al. accomplished gesture recognition by using two optical cameras, achieving accuracies of 90% when detecting the position of fingers and hands [7].

- **Gestures and Children** – As previously discussed children provide a unique challenge when trying to form an interactive experience in not only multi-modal interactive experiences but even unimodal interactions. Lisa Anthony and Colleagues have advanced the field in this area. They provide the following recommendations, which have been useful in our application [6]:
  - It is essential to prevent unintended touch interactions
  - Use platform-recommended sizes (and larger whenever possible)
  - Increase the area for the widgets
  - Align targets to the edges
  - Use tailored gesture recognition for children

- **Gesture Discovery** – it is best to keep gestures simple whenever possible and the total number small. One option for finding the best gestures is to use a Wizard-of-oz experiment, such as the one done by Wobbrock et al. [8]. However, there is a divide in the 3D User Interface community in their acceptance of this approach. Differences in gesture discovery can also be seen when a set of gesture is developed by users as seen in Balcazar et al. [9].

- **Paper Prototyping:** Paper prototyping may be beneficial at the early stages of development to showcase different ideas as shown in Figs. 4 and 5. Paper prototypes allow for rapid iteration and feedback when creating a user interface as in the figures. This rapid iteration allows less development time to be spent refactoring boundary class code and more time spent improving code quality. Also, having this provides materials which can be shown during the requirements elicitation phase of development.

- **Modes** – What role does each input device undertake for user interaction and how do the input devices cooperate? This question is fundamental when devising a multi-modal application that relies on several unimodal input devices, and a solid plan of action must be developed to coordinate the devices to provide meaningful user interaction. To address this question, we created different modes depending on the available devices and the preferences of the user. Having different modes allows for more dynamic modality as devices can come online or offline at any time, as such the responsibility of a device at these events is a crucial component of multi-modal interaction. However, this is only one question, and there are others that must be addressed and answered (see examples in the previous section). We believe that the discovery of the right combination of responsibilities between input devices and the interaction they drive will be an important research direction.

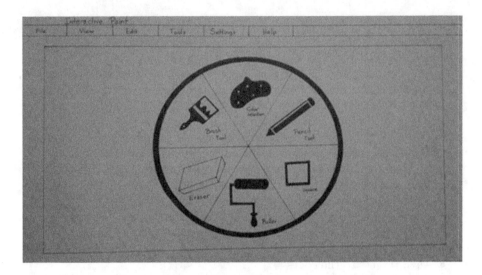

Fig. 4. Radial menu

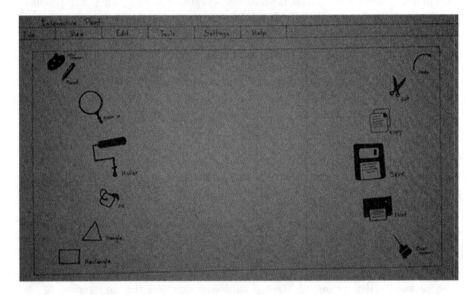

Fig. 5. Double-sided menu

6   Conclusion and Future Work

We have presented the Multi-Modal Interactive Paint application which combines several unimodal input devices to present the user with a cohesive multimodal interactive experience. As discussed previously the MIP application has the possibility of assisting children by helping psychologists develop psychological profiles and identify psychopathologies. MIP helps psychologists by providing an interactive painting experience for children with an intuitive form of input. By accepting that children are one of the targeted audiences MIP can prepare for interaction by more general audiences because children are a more difficult audience for multi-modal interaction because their level of cognitive development is vastly different from adults. There is an increased challenge because it is difficult to extract meaningful information modalities of touch and manual gestures when children interact with the application.

We have also identified software design and research problems for multi-modal interaction with our painting application. The simplest among these for others to test when designing software is the paper prototyping as the tools for doing so are widely available across the globe. This rapid and iterative process should have the capability to provide improved multi-modal interactions as it helps developers consider their ideas in a more tangible medium. The problem with IR cameras that we identified should allow other developers to avoid similar mistakes by avoiding multiple IR cameras and instead sticking to a single IR camera, such as the Leap Motion. While this may be a well-known problem, it is imperative to keep it in mind when developing multi-modal technologies with IR cameras. In particular, the need for non-IR cameras are critical in multi-modal interaction. One of the most intriguing research problems we have identified is finding the most appropriate combination of input device responsibility. A finer tuned set of responsibilities will enhance user interaction.

6.1 Future Directions

Future work includes addressing essential questions, such as the mode-switching of devices, how devices interact with each other, and the best approach for user interfaces when dealing with multi-modal applications. Our highest priority is to conduct formal user studies to identify any issues with the interaction in MIP further and record notable observations to drive an more intuitive form of interaction. Formal studies will be conducted similarly to other OpenHID studies such as those found in CircGR [9] The next version of an improved MIP is at https://goo.gl/3oxWv0. In the next version of MIP, we shall improve the user interface of the application. Also, we shall expand the list of input devices to include the Microsoft Kinect, MicroChip 3D multi-touch, active pen and motion sensors. Furthermore, the use of more stereo-vision (i.e., without IR technology) is critical. Another intriguing avenue of exploration is exploiting the vocal modality as discussed in [2] it is a commonly utilized modality that leads to natural and intuitive interaction. Techniques can be adapted from Adler et al. where the ASSIST system is defined in detail and enables natural conversation with the system [10]. This modality is significant as it can allow users with disabilities to benefit from the multi-modal interaction if other modalities are unavailable.

Acknowledgments. We acknowledge the support by the National Science Foundation under Grant Nos. I/UCRC IIP-1338922, AIR IIP-1237818, SBIR IIP-1330943, III-Large IIS-1213026, MRI CNS-1532061, OISE 1541472, MRI CNS-1532061,

MRI CNS-1429345, MRI CNS-0821345, MRI CNS-1126619, CREST HRD-0833093, I/UCRC IIP-0829576, MRI CNS-0959985, RAPID CNS- 1507611. Also, we acknowledge Garrett Lemieux and Andrew Mitchell for their help with the first prototype.

References

1. Ortega, F.R., Abyarjoo, F., Barreto, A., Rishe, N., Adjouadi, M.: Interaction Design for 3D User Interfaces. The World of Modern Input Devices for Research Applications, and Game Development. CRC Press, Boca Raton (2016)
2. Stivers, T., Sidnell, J.: Introduction: multimodal interaction. Semiotica **156**, 1–20 (2005)
3. Jourde, F., Laurillau, Y., Nigay, L.: COMM notation for specifying collaborative and multimodal interactive systems. In: Proceedings of the 2nd ACM SIGCHI (2010)
4. Prammanee, S., Moessner, K., Tafazolli, R.: Discovering modalities for adaptive multimodal interfaces. Interactions **13**, 66–70 (2006)
5. Khorshidi, S., Mohammadipour, M.: Children's drawing: a way to discover their psychological disorders and problems. Int. J. Ment. Disord. **14**, 31–36 (2016)
6. Anthony, L., Brown, Q., Tate, B., Nias, J., Brewer, R., Irwin, G.: Designing smarter touch-based interfaces for educational contexts. Pers. Ubiquit. Comput. **18**, 1471–1483 (2013)
7. Hu, K., Canavan, S., Yin, L.: Hand pointing estimation for human computer interaction based on two orthogonal-views. In: Pattern Recognition (ICPR), pp. 3760–3763 (2010)
8. Wobbrock, J.O., Morris, M.R., Wilson, A.D.: User-defined gestures for surface computing. In: The SIGCHI Conference, pp. 1083–1092. ACM Press, New York (2009)
9. Balcazar, R., Ortega, F.R., Tarre, K., Barreto, A., Weiss, M., Rishe, N.D.: CircGR: interactive multi-touch gesture recognition using circular measurements. In: Proceedings of the 2017 ACM International Conference on Interactive Surfaces and Spaces, ISS 2017, pp. 12–21. ACM, New York (2017)
10. Adler, A., Davis, R.: Speech and sketching for multimodal design. In: ACM SIGGRAPH 2007 Courses, SIGGRAPH 2007. ACM, New York (2007)

Non Visual Interaction

Nateq Reading Arabic Text for Visually Impaired People

Omaimah Bamasag[1(✉)], Muna Tayeb[2], Maha Alsaggaf[2], and Fatimah Shams[2]

[1] Faculty of Computing and Information Technology, Computer Science Department, University of Jeddah, P.O. Box 80221, Jeddah 21589, Saudi Arabia
obamasag@uj.edu.sa
[2] Faculty of Computing and Information Technology, Information Technology Department, Computer Science Department, King Abdulaziz University, P.O. Box 42808, Jeddah 21551, Saudi Arabia
{mtayeb0007,malsaggaf0009,fshamsulalam9}@stu.kau.edu.sa

Abstract. Nateq is a system developed to aid visually impaired people in their daily life tasks. Nateq allows blind users to read text written on papers and labels using their mobile phones. It uses two sources to read text from, either from camera or photo gallery. In the camera mode, the system will automatically capture the image once the object is sufficiently detected along with an option to capture the image of the object manually. To increase the accuracy, a novel approach was implemented to ensure the correctness of the extracted text, by adding rectangular boundaries detection to the system. It helps the user to avoid partial capturing of the object which may lead to extracting incomplete sentences. Testing on target users showed high level of satisfaction on the improvement made in the field of assistive application with an overall process being faster in comparison to similar applications in the market.

Keywords: Visual impairment · Image processing · Text extraction
Boundaries detection · OCR · Accessibility · Reader assistant

1 Introduction

The decrease in vision ability that cannot be fixed by usual means, such as glasses is called Visual impairment and also known as vision impairment or vision loss [5]. The term blindness is used for complete or nearly complete vision loss. Visual impairment may cause difficulties for people to carry on their normal daily activities such as driving, reading, socializing and walking.

The World Health Organization (WHO) estimates that the number of visually impaired people in the world is 285 million, 39 million of them are blind and 246 million having low vision; 65% of visually impaired people and 82% of the complete blind are at the age of 50 years and older [11].

In the world of advanced technology, many tools have been invented to ease our lives. Disabilities field is one of the most significant aspects that attracted

© Springer International Publishing AG, part of Springer Nature 2018
M. Antona and C. Stephanidis (Eds.): UAHCI 2018, LNCS 10907, pp. 311–326, 2018.
https://doi.org/10.1007/978-3-319-92049-8_23

the attention of the researchers. It should conform to the development of current technology and meet the requirements of this digital age. To accomplish this goal, many technologies have emerged to improve the daily lives of people suffering from this impairment. One type of technology that is available nearly to everyone, is the use of mobile applications. In this project, we aim at developing a mobile application to assist blind people and improve the quality of their lives. This paper will illustrate and clarify the problems faced by people with this specific disability and the suggested solutions that our work will propose to address these problems. The rest of the paper is structured as follows: Sect. 2 presents the methodology followed for data collection and analysis. Section 3 describes the specifications of the system requirements. Section 4 demonstrates the implementation process. Section 5 presents the evaluation of the implemented system. Finally, Sect. 6 concludes the paper and outlines future work (Fig. 1).

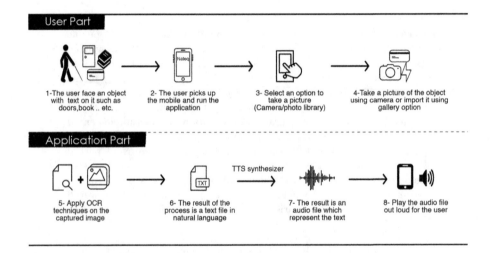

Fig. 1. Proposed process of the system

2   Related Systems Analysis

This section reviews well-known software solutions that are most related to the proposed project.

2.1   KNFB Reader

The KNFB Reader [10] is capable of reading different types of documents that one might face in daily life. The application uses VoiceOver on iOS and Google TalkBack on android to assist visually impaired users and guide them vocally while using the application.

2.2   Amedia Live Reader

Amedia Live Reader [12] takes the scan of a captured live image and reads any texts in it in real-time. It is designed for visually impaired users. it uses the VoiceOver on iOS platform as a guidance.

2.3   Google Translate

Google translate [7] is a mobile application running on both iOS and Android that translates between many languages. It provides instant camera translation using phone camera and for higher-quality translations, it takes picture of text.

2.4   Acapela TTS Voices

Acapela TTS [1] turns written text into speech and gives you the advantage of buying and installing voices as well as integrating them in your Android device in order to be used with the system or any TTS compatible applications such as Google TalkBack.

2.5   Adel TTS Voice

The Best-of-Vox [14] the application gives you the advantage of typing or pasting text and having it read out loudly by the sound that you have chosen.

2.6   Text Fairy (OCR Text Scanner)

TextFairy [15] turns a scanned image of a document to text and correct the viewpoint of the image. It has the facility to edit extracted text and copy it into the clipboard for utilization in other apps. It can also transform the scanned page into a PDF form.

2.7   CamScanner

CamScanner [6] helps in scanning, storing, syncing and collaborating on numerous contents across smartphones and computers. It uses the phone camera to scan documents and provides text extraction from Image with OCR (optical character recognition) for further editing or text sharing (Table 1).

KNFB Reader is a good multi language OCR reader, however, it does not support Arabic language as Amedia Live Reader. Amedia Live Reader has a real-time OCR feature but difficult to use because it repeats reading the captured text when the phone camera moves. Text Fairy and CamScanner perform the OCR without the TTS feature and both do not support the Arabic language. CamScanner has the feature of edge detection which is an important feature for our proposed app. Google Translate has a good OCR that supports Arabic language and its API is available in the Google Cloud Platform services.

Table 1. Summary comparison between related systems

Systems	Cost	Provide OCR	Provide TTS	Platform	Support Arabic Language	Supports Blind User
KNFB Reader	Not free	Yes	Yes	iOS and Android	No	Yes
Amedia Live Reader	Not free	Yes	Yes	iOS only	No	Yes
Google Translate	Free	Yes	Yes	iOS and Android	Yes	No
Acapela TTS voices	Free	No	Yes	Android only	Yes	Yes
Adel TTS voice	Not free	No	Yes	Android only	Yes	Yes
Text Fairy	Free	No	No	Android only	No	Yes
CamScanner	Free with licensed	Yes	No	iOS and Android	No	No
Nateq System	Free	Yes	Yes	iOS	Yes	Yes

3 Data Collection and Analysis

This section describes the data collection process to identify the needs of the potential users. The data was collected from 30 visually impaired persons in both genders. Their ages range from 18 to over 50 years old.

3.1 Data Collection Methods

Questioners and interviews have been conducted with visually impaired people and heads of departments from the Governmental foundation for rehabilitation and visual impairment in Jeddah, Saudi Arabia and Special Needs Center in students affairs of King Abdulaziz University.

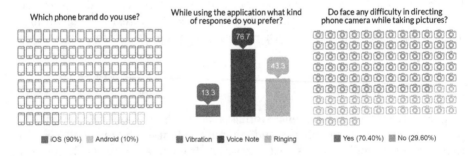

Fig. 2. Main questionnaires results

3.2 Questionnaires Results

Questionnaires results (Fig. 2) show that 90% of the volunteers use iPhone. Most volunteers prefer voice note feedback and about 70% have a problem in directing camera toward objects. The gathered data from the volunteers is considered as the main requirements of the system.

3.3   Interview Results

The interviews highlighted some findings supported by the questionnaire results, which will be considered in the requirements specification:

1. There are no good existing quality apps that support reading Arabic text through the phone camera. Also, there are inaccuracy issue in extracting the Arabic text from scanned PDF documents.
2. The reason for the domination of the iOS platform for the hand-held over all other platforms is that there is a good quality built-in accessibility features.
3. The visually impaired people are very good in using hand-held devices.
4. There are some levels of visual impairment where people can see using special techniques and devices.
5. The difficulty of learning braille system results in resistant to use this system especially for those who lost their vision in late ages.

4   Requirement Specification

Functional non-functional requirements for the proposed system were specified by using the data gathering methods illustrated in Data Collection and Analysis section.

4.1   Functional Requirements

The systems functional requirements have been categorized as User Manual, Input, Processing, Output, Feedback and Help.

User Manual

1. The system shall play the audio user manual file automatically the first time the user opens the application.
2. The system shall allow the user to replay the audio user manual upon user request.
3. The system shall allow the user to navigate through the application.

Input

1. The system shall allow the user to automatically take a picture by the hand-held device camera.
2. The system shall allow the user to manually take a picture by the hand-held device camera.
3. The system shall allow the user to import a selected photo from the mobile gallery.

Processing

1. The system shall be able to detect the edges of the object in real time in order to auto capture the required object.
2. The system shall be able to detect and extract the printed Arabic text in the captured image.
3. The system shall keep the user aware of the progress while extracting the image by voice notes.

Output

1. The system shall be able to play the extracted text using VoiceOver iOS built-in Screen reader.
2. The system shall allow the user to replay the extracted text.

Feedback and Help

1. The system shall allow the user to read a new object after a task completion.
2. The system shall allow the user to change the speed of the reading inside the application.

4.2   Non-functional Requirements

This section illustrates the non-functional, i.e. quality, requirements of the proposed system, which are categorized into response time and usability.

Quality Requirements

1. Response time:
   The System OCR gives the desired response within a reasonable time.
2. Usability:
   (a) The system shall be easy to use for the visually impaired after listening to the user manual.
   (b) All functions of the system shall have audio responses to facilitate the app usage.
   (c) The system interfaces shall be minimized and support accessibility for visually impaired.

5   Implementation

This section presents the algorithms developed to implement the required functionalities of the proposed system. This is followed by listing the technologies used in the implementation and a walk-through the system.

5.1   Developed Algorithms

Several algorithms were developed to implement the requirements gathered from end users. Three main algorithms were used for text extraction, frame extraction and boundaries detection, explained in the following subsections.

Text Extraction

Algorithm 1. Extracting Text from a Given Image

Input: Image.
Output: Plain text.

1: Convert the JPEG image to PNG
2: Check the size of the picked image before sending it to the API server.
3: **if** the image is larger than the server's request limit 4MB **then**
4:     Shrink the image size to fit the request limits.
5: **end if**
6: Encode the PNG image to base-64 string.
7: Use the Alamofire library to:
    1. Specify the request parameters and embed the converted image string within the request.
    2. Create a custom HTTP header.
    3. Send the POST HTTP request to the Google API server included with the API key to authenticate the request plus the customized HTTP header.
8: Get the server response and check
9: **if** the returned response is an empty message **then**
10:     Play a voice over a message that there is no text has been detected from the picked image.
11:     End the call and return to the main application screen.
12: **end if**
13: Use the SwiftyJSON library to serialize the JSON server response and put it in Swift array.
14: Iterate the response array and get the extracted text.
15: open a new screen that displays the extracted text centered and large formatted.

Boundaries Detection Identifying rectangular objects within an image captured by the user camera was the core of our project. Below is the approach we followed to implement this feature.

Figure 3 shows the intermediate results generated from the algorithms mentioned in the pseudocode, while Fig. 4 shows the final result.

Frame Extraction. Camera Auto Capture captures the frames in real time through the mobile camera. These frames are the input for Boundaries Detection algorithm. The boundaries algorithm processes the captured frames to find the rectangular boundaries of the object, which triggers the auto capture event. To implement this functionality, several packages and algorithms were used as illustrated in the following.

Algorithm 2. Detecting Rectangular objects Algorithm

Input: Image frame.

Output: Image with border around the rectangle if any.

1: Convert the image frame to matrix.
2: Convert matrix's color space to grayScale.
3: Apply median filter on the grayscale matrix.
4: Apply Canny algorithm on the blurred image.
5: Apply morphological transformations for lines closing.
6: find contours and return in 2D array.
7: Sort contours descending by area.
8: **for** each contour **do**
9:     Approximate the contour to a polygon by Douglas-Peucker algorithm.
10:    **if** (approximated polygon has 4 points and it's Convex) **then**
11:        Draw a border around the rectangle detected.
12:        **break**
13:    **end if**
14: **end for**
15: Convert matrix back to image.
16: Return image.

Algorithm 3. Capture Frames in Real Time

Input: Camera permission Granted.

Output: Camera frame.

1: Choose the video capture device.
2: Set the device camera to backward facing camera.
3: Set focus mode to continuous Auto Focus.
4: Create a capture session to coordinate the data flow from the input to the output.
5: Preset the capture session with quality 1024*760.
6: Use Capture Inputs to provide input data to a capture session.
7: Use Capture Outputs to Get Output from a Session.
8: Set capture output's buffer as serial queue for the transmitted video frames.
9: Add both Capture Inputs and Capture Outputs to the capture session.
10: Start the capture session.
11: **while** The session is running **do**
12:    Add The captured data to the buffer.
13:    Convert the data to an image.
14:    Return the image as a camera frame.
15: **end while**

5.2   Technologies Used

Google Cloud Vision API provides powerful Image Analytics capabilities as easy to use APIs. It enables application developers to build applications that can see and understand the content within the images. The service enables customers to detect a broad set of entities within an image from everyday objects to faces and product logos [8].

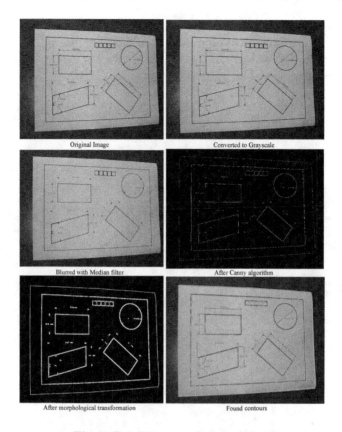

Fig. 3. Detecting paper's boundaries

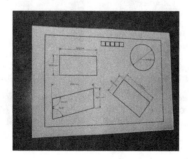

Fig. 4. Detecting boundaries final result

OpenCV is an open source computer vision and machine learning software library mainly aimed at real-time computer vision applications and its originally developed by Intels research center [13].

Voice Over is a screen reader built into Apple Inc.s macOS, iOS, tvOS, watchOS operating systems. By using VoiceOver, the user can access their Macintosh or iOS device based on spoken descriptions. The feature is designed to increase accessibility for blind and low-vision users [4].

5.3   Walk-Through the System

See Fig. 5.

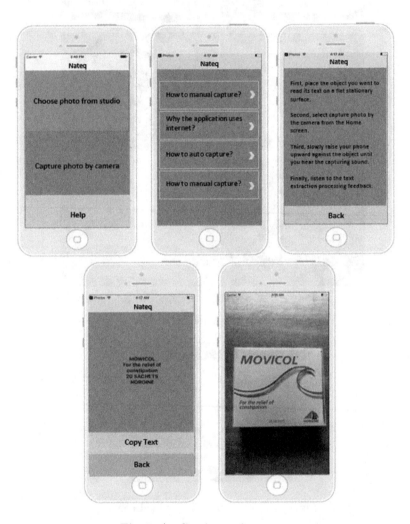

Fig. 5. Application main screens

6   Evaluation

The components of Nateq system are tested by applying different measures and testing approaches. The testing process is divided into two sub-tests: System test which is conducted on the application itself to examine the resources and time consumption, and the usability test which is conducted on the applications end users to observe and record their interaction with it. The data gathered from both sub-tests are considered for the applications reliability and satisfaction in terms of functions and user experience.

6.1 System Testing

The system testing examines the applications consumption levels of resources, the efficiency of the boundaries detection algorithm, the speed and accuracy of the text extraction operation.

Resources Consumption Test. Table 2 shows the applications resources consumption according to different applications status.

Table 2. Resources consumption

	Idle state	Edge detection state	Text extraction state
CPU	0%	46%	1%
Memory	5.2 MB	7.7 MB	15.1 MB
Energy	0	Low	High
Network	-	-	Up less than 2 MB
			Down depends to text in the image

When the application launches, it takes about 5.2 MB of the phones memory. When camera works, it processes the frames which results in an increase in the apps memory allocation to 7.7 MB while the CPU usage is about 46%. When the captured image is sent to the text extraction server, the application requires a network connection to upload the image to the server where the image size should not exceed 2 MB and the downloading amount depends on the text written in the captured image. Regarding the battery consumption, the energy required will be high because of the network overhead required to establish the connection [2].

Boundaries Detection Test. Two testing approaches were applied on Boundaries Detection algorithm, performance and speed testing.

Performance Testing: The ability to identify and detect the boundaries of rectangular objects were tested with different background situations (modes) Includes:

1. Test detection in solid color background with high contrast between the background and the object colors.
2. Test detection in solid color background with low contrast between the background and the object colors.
3. Test detection with wobbly (Textured) background.

The evaluation is performed by applying 30 different sample images. Table 3 shows the testing results and success rate along the previously mentioned three cases.

Table 3. Boundaries performance testing results

Background mode	Expected result	Success rate	Performance
Solid - high contrast	Detect	100%	Excellent
Solid - low contrast	Detect	40%	Not accepted
Textured	Detect	60%	Needs enhancement

According to the results shown above, following is the constraints on the boundaries detection:

1. The contrast between the background and the object must be high for better detection.
2. Solid color backgrounds provides better detection rate.
3. Reflected light on the object surface decreases the detection rate.

Speed Testing: The average execution time for the algorithm is **0.05** s, which is considered good compared to Apples CIDetector API [3], which detects rectangles in **0.03** s. The execution time for our algorithm is calculated by running the algorithm in real time and taking the average of 500 different readings.

OCR Test

Response Time Testing: The speed of the OCR provided in the application is tested under different Internet speed. Table 4 shows (in seconds) the effect of the Internet provided on the device in the OCR processing speed.

Table 4. OCR response time in seconds

Measure	3G	4G	Fiber optics
Short text/cover page	16	6	4
Long text/full page	36	25	16

Extraction Accuracy Testing: The accuracy is tested by applying the OCR on 40 images as a sample size with different fonts styles. The testing is divided into to categories; Testing on document fonts (books, papers, etc) and products fonts (food products, cleaning products, medicines, etc). Table 5 shows the results in each category.
Observations:

1. Google OCR gives the best results when applied to documents/Books fonts.
2. It cannot detect stretched Arabic words.

Table 5. Accuracy testing results

Font type	Word count	Wrong words	Undetected words	Success percent
Documents fonts	550	32	16	91%
Products fonts	150	26	32	61%

6.2 Usability Testing

The goal of conducting the usability test is to evaluate Nateqs interface and its functions on real users. The test will help to determine whether the application design is usable for the user who uses it for the first time. The users feedback which will be gathered during the test will help the team to improve the application.

Tasks to be Evaluated. Six tasks were chosen to test Nateq functionality. Each of which was piloted to determine the suitable performance measures used for each task. An iPhone- expert visually impaired user was timed when doing these tasks and provided us with a baseline to judge the times that participants would take.

1. **Task 1:** Access the user manual and navigate through the questions.
2. **Task 2:** Get Text from a photo saved in photo gallery.
3. **Task 3:** Repeat reading the extracted text.
4. **Task 4:** Reach copy text button.
5. **Task 5:** Get text from a photo captured using Manual Capture
6. **Task 6:** Get text from a photo captured using Auto Capture

In addition to task completion time, the number of navigation clicks and the number of (action) clicks were added as a measurement. On accessibility mode, users flick (swipe) to the left or right to move to the next item on screen and single-tap to hear a description of what is tapped, these counts as navigation clicks. On the other hand, users double-tap on an item to open or activate it, these counts as action clicks.

The following tables (Tables 6, 7 and Table 8) indicates the tasks performed and measurement levels used for each task.

Testing Results for five participants (Tables 9, 10, 11, 12, 13 and 14).

Table 6. Excellent performance

Measure	Task 1	Task 2	Task 3	Task 4	Task 5	Task 6
Time to complete the task	<23 s	<45 s	-	-	<26 s	<40 s
Number of navigation clicks	<13 clicks	<25 clicks	1 click	1 click	<5 clicks	<6 clicks
Number of clicks	<4 clicks	<4 clicks	-	-	<3 clicks	<3 clicks

Table 7. Acceptable performance

Measure	Task 1	Task 2	Task 3	Task 4	Task 5	Task 6
Time to complete the task	23–31 s	45–55 s	-	-	<26–34 s	<40–60 s
Number of navigation clicks	13–21 clicks	25–34 clicks	2–3 clicks	2–3 clicks	<5–12 clicks	<6–9 clicks
Number of clicks	4–6 clicks	4–6 clicks	-	-	3–5 clicks	<3–5 clicks

Table 8. Unacceptable performance

Measure	Task 1	Task 2	Task 3	Task 4	Task 5	Task 6
Time to complete the task	>31 s	>55 s	-	-	>34 s	>60 s
Number of navigation clicks	>21 clicks	>34 clicks	>3 clicks	>3 clicks	>12 clicks	>9 clicks
Number of clicks	>6 clicks	>6 clicks	-	-	>5 clicks	>7 clicks

Table 9. Task 1: Access the user manual and navigate through the questions

Measure	1	2	3	4	5	Performance
Time to complete the task	21	37	25	16	23	Accepted
Number of navigation clicks	9	15	12	10	12	Excellent
Number of clicks	2	2	2	2	3	Excellent

Table 10. Task 2: Get text from a photo saved in the studio

Measure	1	2	3	4	5	Performance
Time to complete the task	53	40	77	53	55	Accepted
Number of navigation clicks	23	33	90	30	19	Accepted
Number of clicks	4	2	3	2	3	Excellent

Table 11. Task 3: Repeat reading the extracted text

Measure	1	2	3	4	5	Performance
Number of navigation clicks	1	1	1	1	2	Excellent

Table 12. Task 4: Reach copy text button

Measure	1	2	3	4	5	Performance
Number of navigation clicks	2	1	2	2	2	Accepted

Table 13. Task 5: Get text from a photo captured using manual capture

Measure	1	2	3	4	5	Performance
Time to complete the task	20	25	19	30	24	Excellent
Number of navigation clicks	7	9	15	10	12	Accepted
Number of clicks	2	4	2	1	2	Excellent

Table 14. Task 6: Get text from a photo captured using auto capture

Measure	1	2	3	4	5	Performance
Time to complete the task	56	6	120	120	94	Not accepted
Number of navigation clicks	7	9	3	10	11	Accepted
Number of clicks	1	2	1	1	2	Excellent

According to the previous tables, task 1 to task 5 present acceptable results by taking all participants average performance per each task. While task 6 demonstrated some difficulties faced when using the camera. As per users feedback, more instructions were needed to explain how auto capture works.

7   Conclusion

The paper is concluded by listing the findings of project work and testing on the target users:

1. There is no adequate software that guide blind people in directing the camera toward objects while taking photos.
2. The need of descriptive photo gallery, as blind people face difficulties in finding photos, which are currently labeled only by the date of creation.

These could be future research directions in the field of special needs aid.

References

1. Acapela TTS. http://www.acapela-group.com/. Accessed 15 Nov 2016
2. Apple Inc.: General Battery Information. https://www.apple.com/sa/iphone/battery.html
3. Apple Inc.: CIDetector. https://developer.apple.com/reference/coreimage/cidetector. Accessed 20 May 2017
4. Apple Inc.: Apple VoiceOver. http://www.apple.com/accessibility/mac/vision/. Accessed 20 Nov 2016
5. Blindness and Vision Impairment, 8 February 2011. http://www.cdc.gov/healthcommunication/ToolsTemplates/EntertainmentEd/Tips/Blindness.html. Accessed 10 Nov 2016
6. CamScanner. https://www.camscanner.com. Accessed 15 Nov 2016

7. Google corp. Google Translate. https://play.google.com/. Accessed 20 Nov 2016
8. Google Cloud Platform. cloud.google.com/vision/docs. Accessed 17 Mar 2017
9. Canny, J.: A computational approach to edge detection. IEEE Trans. Pattern Anal. Mach. Intell. **8**(6), 679–698 (1986)
10. Sensotec: KNFB Reader. http://www.knfbreader.com/. Accessed 15 Nov 2016
11. World Health Organization: Global Data on Visual Impairments. Silvio P. Mariotti, Geneva (2010)
12. Mochizuki, Y., Mochizuki, T.: Amedia Live Reader. http://www.amedia.co.jp/english/product/iphone/livereader. Accessed 15 Nov 2016
13. OpenCV: OpenCV Library (2011). docs.opencv.org/2.4/doc/. Accessed 16 Mar 2017
14. VOXYGEN: Adel TTS. https://best-of-vox.com/android (n.d.)
15. Wellnitz, R.: Text Fairy (OCR Text Scanner). https://play.google.com/. Accessed 15 Nov 2016.

Designing a 2 × 2 Spatial Vibrotactile Interface for Tactile Letter Reading on a Smartphone

Shaowei Chu[(✉)] and Mei Peng

Zhejiang University of Media and Communications, Hangzhou, China
chu@zjicm.edu.cn

Abstract. In this paper, an eyes-free tactile reading system on a smartphone is proposed. This system adopts 2 × 2 flat vibration motors that are attached to the back of a smartphone, and a spatial tactile feedback will be generated and applied to the palm while the user holds the device. The tactile reading of 26 English letters was designed using spatial vibration codes. The hieroglyphs of English letters and their order of writing strokes were borrowed to minimize the tactile code learning curve for users. Numerous user experiments were conducted to tune important design parameters, such as distance between motors and vibration times. Results showed that a 3-cm distance between motors and a 200-ms vibration time are appropriate for designing an efficient system. The accuracy of tactile letter reading was 84.6%, time was 976.9 ms per letter, and the system can provide an efficient tactile reading technique for users in an eyes-free interaction.

Keywords: Spatial vibrotactile · Tactile interface
Empirical studies in interaction design · Tactile reading

1 Introduction

Smartphones are becoming an important computing platform in our daily life. However, smartphone touchscreens inherently lack tactile feedback compared with the conventional physical keyboard; hence, the interaction is generally susceptible to high errors and hardly supports eyes-free interactions [1]. The vibration motor provides linear tactile feedback and vibrates the entire device although this vibration motor inside the smartphone can provide tactile feedback to enhance interaction on a smartphone. The single vibration motor only supports a vibration on/off scheme to convey tactile codes; therefore, the dimensions of tactile coding design are limited [2].

In this paper, we propose a multiple vibration motor system that provides spatial vibrotactile feedback for a smartphone. The system adopts 2 × 2 flat vibration motors that are attached to the back of a smartphone. The spatial tactile feedback will be generated and applied to the palm while the user holds the device, as illustrated in Fig. 1.

M. Antona and C. Stephanidis (Eds.): UAHCI 2018, LNCS 10907, pp. 327–336, 2018.
https://doi.org/10.1007/978-3-319-92049-8_24

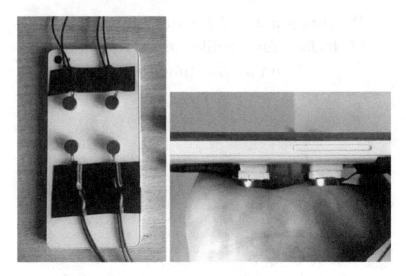

Fig. 1. System prototype. Four flat vibration motors attached to the back of the smartphone. The motors contact with palm while holding the device.

Order: • start → direction						
Spatial: •1 •2 •3 •4			m	) (	31024	4
			n	⊓	3124	4
a	∠	234	3	o	⊔	13421	5
b	L	134	3	p	⌐	213	3
c	⊏	2134	4	q	⌐	124	3
d	⌐	243	3	r	γ	132	3
e	⊠	32134	5	s	⊃	2143	4
f	⌐	21312	5	t	⊏	12134	5
g	⊐	1243	4	u	⊔	1342	4
h	⋈	1324	4	v	⌄	142	3
i	◊	242	3	w	) (	13042	4
j	⊿	2432	4	x	⋈	1423	4
k	⊭	13234	5	y	⋎	14243	5
l	)	13	2	z	7	1234	4

Fig. 2. Tactile codes of the 26 English letters.

We empirically investigated the parameter design in terms of efficient motor distance, appropriate vibration time, and vibration switching time between actuators to improve the usability of the prototype. These factors are important in designing an effective tactile interface with time efficiency and high user perception accuracy [3]. Moreover, we implemented a tactile letter code system for tactile reading of English letters based on the prototype design. The hieroglyphs of English letters and their order of writing strokes were borrowed to minimize the learning curve, as depicted in Fig. 2. A user experiment with nine participants was conducted to evaluate the performance of the tactile reading system. The results showed that the overall perception accuracy of tactile letter codes is 84.6%, and the mean time for presenting a letter is 976.9 ms. The system can provide an efficient tactile reading system for users in an eyes-free interaction.

2 Related Works

2.1 Single Vibrator Tactile Design

A single vibrator was widely used for designing non-visual tactile message on smartphones. The different vibration on/off patterns can be encoded to convey tactile codes and carry Morse or braille codes to deliver character information. For example, Rentala et al. [4] achieved the tactile reading method on a touchscreen mobile device, which expresses the raised and lowered information of six braille dots consequently through the tactile feedback in processing "rhythmic" patterns to be able to read tactile braille. Al-Qudah et al. [5] improved the design by encoding the braille with the vibration rhythm and Morse code to increase the tactile reading performance. These authors showed that the average reading speed can reach up to 855 ms per character, and the reading accuracy is approximately 71%.

However, the problem with these methods was that the linear tactile feedback with single vibrator only supports a vibration on/off scheme to convey tactile codes. Therefore, the dimensions of tactile coding design are limited to code vibration on/off intervals in the different patterns. In addition, the linearity of tactile feedback in the timeline is typically difficult for users to catch up, thereby resulting in low perception accuracy. The user experience on tactile information acquisition using a single vibrator is frequently reduced because of these problems.

2.2 Spatial Vibrotactile Design

To enhance expressiveness, previous studies have adopted multiple vibrators to deliver spatial vibrotactile information. For example, SemFeel [2] designed a five-vibration motor system in a cross shape attached to the backside of a smartphone. The system could generate different spatial patterns of vibration, such as position notification, linear, and circular messages. The experimental results showed that users can distinguish 11 patterns with 65.8%–93.3% accuracy in 2.19–2.95 s per pattern. The parameter design was not discussed in their work, although the system can generate different spatial patterns. For example, the physical distance between vibrators and the sensory saltation times between vibrators were not given. However, these parameters are important in designing an efficient tactile reading system.

In EdgeVib [3], a wrist-worn smartwatch with 3 × 3 and 2 × 2 multiple vibration motors was implemented; the distance of the vibrators were 1.5 and 3 cm, respectively. The vibration periods of a running vibration were 500 ms, and the interval between vibrators was 100 ms. The user experimental results showed that the 2 × 2 layout of vibration motors outperform the 3 × 3 layout in terms of recognition rate and time efficiency. Therefore, a spatiotemporal vibration pattern that uses a 2 × 2 layout and unistroke patterns that represent characters were adopted to implement tactile reading. The user experiment results showed that the system recognition rate is 85.8%. The results of wrist perception can hardly be generalized to a palm in a smartphone-holding situation because different body positions demonstrate distinct sensitivities to tactile feedback, although the design parameters have been considered in this study [6]. For example, Lee [7] revealed that the sensory saltation and locus of stimuli can affect the performance of information transfer.

Therefore, carefully tuning the design parameters related to the distance and vibration time of motors remains crucial. This open question motivated us to design an efficient spatial vibrotactile interface for implementing tactile reading on a smartphone.

3   Prototype Design

The prototype system is exhibited in Fig. 3. Four flat XY1027L vibration motors were attached to the back of a smartphone. The working voltage of the vibration motors was 3 V, and the current was 100 mA. The diameter and thickness of the motor are 10 and 2.7 mm, correspondingly. The Arduino Uno was used to control the vibrations.

The vibration motors were elevated with a spongy for approximately 5 mm raise that easily contacts with the palm while the user holds the device, as presented in Fig. 4. The spongy can reduce the vibration noise and cache the knock with the solid surface of the smartphone.

4   Parameter Tuning

The design has two important parameters, that is, the distance between vibration motors and the appropriate timing for vibration stimuli and switching between vibration motors. These parameters are crucial to user recognition for tactile codes.

We conducted a user experiment on six university students who were majoring in digital media technology to refine these parameters. Their mean age was 20.3 (19–21), and three respondents were male.

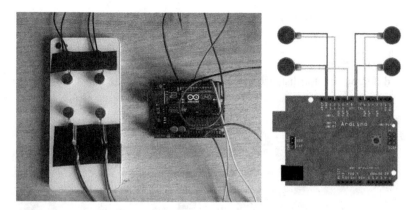

Fig. 3. Prototype designs. Four flat vibration motors were attached to the back of a smartphone. The Arduino was used to control the vibrations.

4.1 Vibrator Distance

The experiment was conducted in the laboratory. A PC was used to send a control command to the Arduino and generate vibration patterns to the vibrators.

The apparatus and experimental environment are presented in Fig. 5.

Fig. 4. Size of the vibration motor and spongy was used to raise the motors.

Procedure: The experimenter explained the system function and allowed the participants to hold the device on the right hand to perceive the different vibrations generated by each vibrator. The experimenter will change the vibrators in different distances, that is, 2, 2.5, 3, and 3.5 cm, and explain to participants that the experiment was aimed at examining the appropriate distance for obtaining a favorable recognition accuracy. The formal experiment started after approximately 10 min of familiarizing themselves with the system.

The experimenter provided the participant with the device, which was set to a predefined vibrator distance (2, 2.5, 3, or 3.5 cm). The experimenter then sent a random position (up–left, up–right, down–left, and down–right) of vibration stimuli to the device using the PC. The participants perceived the stimuli and reported to the experimenter the relative position of the vibrator that generated the vibration. The perception correctness of the participant was recorded to calculate the accuracy of the various vibrator distances.

Each different vibrator distance had six random stimuli. The total test trails were as

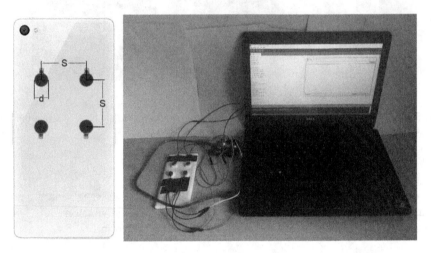

Fig. 5. Experiment apparatus. The PC was used to control the experiment procedure.

follows: 6 stimuli × 4 distances × 6 participants = 144.

Result: The experiment result is displayed in Fig. 6. The perception accuracy increases when the distance between vibration motors is large. The 3-cm distance is appropriate for users to obtain a high perception accuracy because no significant difference exists between 3 and 3.5 cm; the t-test is p = 0.182. The t-tests on other distances are: 2 cm versus 2.5 cm, p = 0.013; 2.5 cm versus 3 cm, p = 0.038.

4.2 Vibration Times

In this user experiment, we tested different vibration times and combined various intervals between the motors to find the appropriate parameters for achieving a high perception accuracy. We aimed to find the minimal vibration time T and vibration interval I that user can perceive and simultaneously guarantee a favorable perception accuracy.

The apparatus and participants are respondents in the previous experiment session.

Procedure: The participants were encouraged to join this experiment after the previous experimental session. The combinations of T = 75, 100, 125 ms; and I = 150, 175, 200 ms conditions were tested. In each condition, six random sequences of stimuli were generated by the device. These sequences, which were e, f, k, o, t, and y, were

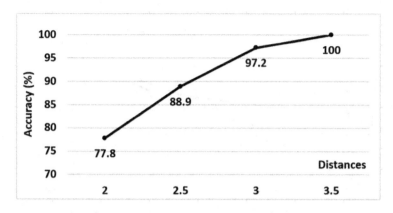

Fig. 6. Result of perception accuracy for different vibration motor distances.

letter codes that are illustrated in Fig. 2. These stimuli were selected because they had five strokes and were the most complex stimuli in our letter code design.

Participants were allowed to familiarize themselves with the six stimuli in different T and I conditions for 10 min. In the formal test, the experimenter sent a vibration code to the device, and the participants perceived and reported to the experimenter the exact sequence of the vibrations generated by the device. The result was recorded as correct if the participant reported the same vibration code to the code the experimenter sent.

The total test trails are as follows: 3 vibration times T × 3 intervals I × 6 stimuli × 6 participants = 324.

Result: The results are depicted in Fig. 7. The perception accuracy reached the highest value with mean = 91.7% when the vibration time $T > = 100$ ms and interval $I = 200$ ms. The t-test exhibited a significant difference between $I = 175$ and $I = 200$ ms when p = 0.001.

5 Tactile Letter Code Perception

We designed tactile letter codes after tuning the appropriate parameters to implement tactile reading on a smartphone (Fig. 2). The codes were designed based on the strokes while writing the lowercase letter. The number of vibrations and their switches was reduced as much as possible. The minimum number of vibrations is two (such as letter l), and the maximum vibrations (i.e., letters e, f, k, o, t, and y) are five. A user experiment was conducted to evaluate the performance of the tactile letter perception.

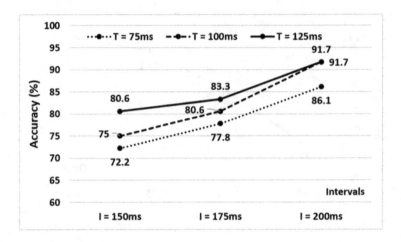

Fig. 7. Result of the perception accuracy for different vibration times and intervals.

5.1   Experiment

Nine university students were invited to participate in the experiment. Their mean age was 20.5 (19–22), and four were male. In the experiment, the 26 letters were presented to the nine participants randomly, and they reported their perceived letters to the experimenter for correctness check. The participants were allowed to familiarize themselves with the system for 5 min, and the formal experiment lasted for approximately 10 min.

5.2   Result

The final results are presented in Fig. 8. The overall accuracy of perception on the 26 letter codes is 84.6%.

   We calculated the accuracy of the different numbers of vibrations. Figure 9 illustrates that the accuracy was higher than 88.9% when the number of vibrations is less than five. The accuracy dropped to 57.4% on 5 times of vibrations (the letter codes of e, f, k, o, t, and y). The ANOVA (Analysis of Variance) indicated no significant difference on 2, 3, and 4 times of vibrations, but a significant difference was found between 4 and 5 vibrations.

6   Discussion

In the tactile display design, we adopted the 2 × 2 shape of vibrators and tuned the parameter design. However, other shapes of a tactile display, that is, cross shape design, should also be considered [2]. In the future, we will compare the current design with other tactile displays and explore their differences.

   In the letter code perception experiment, 2, 3, and 4 vibration codes showed a higher recognition performance than the 5 vibration codes. Thus, we will optimize the

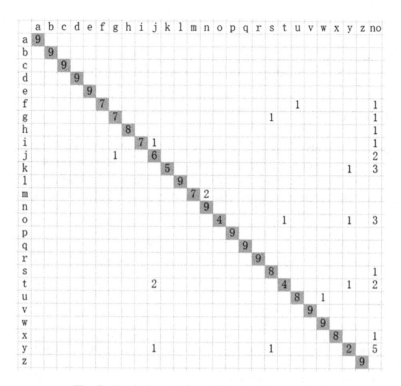

Fig. 8. Confusion matrices of letter code perception.

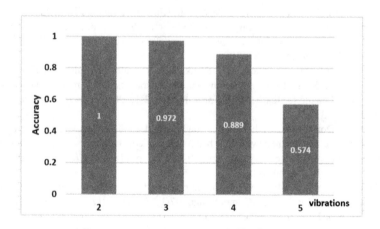

Fig. 9. Accuracy of the different numbers of vibrations.

low-accuracy letter code design, that is, e, f, k, o, t, and y, and avoid using 5 or more vibrations in the future work.

In the tactile code design, we only adopted a single vibration at a time; future work should also consider the simultaneous vibrations generated on the multiple vibrators [7].

7   Conclusion

We learned that the relative locus of vibrators and the number of sensory saltation can affect the performance of a tactile display through a series of experiments. Based on our findings, our recommendation for an efficient tactile reading system on a 2×2 tactile display is to use temporal patterns with sensory saltation and limit the number of saltations to less than five.

Acknowledgments. This paper is supported by National Natural Science Foundation of China (NSFC) (No. 61502415) and Public Projects of Zhejiang Province (No. 2016C31G2240012).

References

1. Grussenmeyer, W., Folmer, E.: Accessible touchscreen technology for people with visual impairments: a survey. Acm Trans. Access. Comput. **9**(2), 1–31 (2017). https://doi.org/10.1145/3022701
2. Yatani, K., Truong, K.N.: SemFeel: a user interface with semantic tactile feedback for mobile touch-screen devices. In: Proceedings of the 22nd Annual ACM Symposium on User Interface Software and Technology, pp. 111–120 (2009). http://dx.doi.org/10.1145/1622176.1622198
3. Liao, Y.-C., Chen, Y.-L., Lo, J.-Y., Liang, R.-H., Chan, L., Chen, B.-Y.: EdgeVib: effective alphanumeric character output using a wrist-worn tactile display. In: Proceedings of the 29th Annual Symposium on User Interface Software and Technology, pp. 595–601 (2016). http://dx.doi.org/10.1145/2984511.2984522
4. Rantala, J., Raisamo, R., Lylykangas, J., Surakka, V., Raisamo, J., Salminen, K., Pakkanen, T., Hippula, A.: Methods for presenting braille characters on a mobile device with a touchscreen and tactile feedback. IEEE Trans. Haptics **2**(1), 28–39 (2009). https://doi.org/10.1109/TOH.2009.3
5. Al-Qudahj, Z., Doush, I.A., Alkhateeb, F., Maghayreh, E., Al-Khaleel, O.: Reading braille on mobile phones: a fast method with low battery power consumption. In: 2011 International Conference on User Science and Engineering (i-USEr), pp. 118–123 (2011). http://dx.doi.org/10.1109/iUSEr.2011.6150549
6. Dim, N.K., Ren, X.: Investigation of suitable body parts for wearable vibration feedback in walking navigation. Int. J. Hum.-Comput. Stud. **97**(1), 34–44 (2017). https://doi.org/10.1016/j.ijhcs.2016.08.002
7. Lee, J., Han, J., Lee, G.: Investigating the information transfer efficiency of a 3×3 watch-back tactile display. In: Proceedings of the 33rd Annual ACM Conference on Human Factors in Computing Systems, pp. 1229–1232 (2015). http://dx.doi.org/10.1145/2702123.2702530

LêRótulos: A Mobile Application Based on Text Recognition in Images to Assist Visually Impaired People

Juliana Damasio Oliveira[✉], Olimar Teixeira Borges[✉],
Vanessa Stangherlin Machado Paixão-Cortes[✉], Marcia de Borba Campos[✉],
and Rafael Mendes Damasceno[✉]

School of Technology, Pontifical Catholic University of Rio Grande do Sul (PUCRS),
Porto Alegre, Brazil
{juliana.damasio,olimar.borges,vanessa.stangherlin,
rafael.damasceno}@acad.pucrs.br, marciabcampos@hotmail.com

Abstract. The autonomy of the visual impaired person can be evaluated in day to day activities like recognizing objects, identifying textual information, among others. This paper features the OCR technology-based LêRótulos application, with the objective of helping visually impaired users to identify textual object information that is captured by the camera of an smartphone. The design of the prototype followed guidelines and recommendations for usability and accessibility, aiming for greater user autonomy. There was an evaluation with specialists and end users, in real situations of use. The results indicated that the application has good usability and meets accessibility criteria for blind and low vision users. However, some improvements were indicated. Related work is presented, the LêRótulos design process, the results of usability and accessibility assessments, and lessons learned for the development of assistive technology aimed at visually impaired users.

Keywords: Accessibility · Assistive technology · Evaluation
Mobile devices · OCR · Usability · Visually impaired people

1 Introduction

A person's autonomy with visual impairment (VI) can be evaluated in daily activities, such as recognizing objects, identifying textual information, among others. Interaction design is about designing interactive products to support the way people communicate and interact in their daily lives, whether at home or work [12]. In these circumstances, it is essential that interactive products are developed to overcome barriers faced by VI in their daily tasks. Shilkro et al. [15,16] state that blind users are interested in reading text fragments, such as restaurant menus, screen texts, business cards and canned labels. It is worth mentioning that these simple tasks, such as reading text fragments, can be a significant challenge to be overcome by a person with VI [11].

© Springer International Publishing AG, part of Springer Nature 2018
M. Antona and C. Stephanidis (Eds.): UAHCI 2018, LNCS 10907, pp. 337–354, 2018.
https://doi.org/10.1007/978-3-319-92049-8_25

Assistive technology (AT) emerged as a way to help people with VI. In addition to screen readers, lenses and electronic magnifiers, braille printers, sticks with obstacle sensors, there are applications available on smartphones that become essential allies since it is possible to focus on a single device with different resources, reducing costs and portability [6]. However, despite these several advantages derived from mobile devices, people with VI still face difficulties on using them due to the lack of integration with applications and screen readers, problems related to handling, use requirements and device's physical characteristics, which tends to have fewer and fewer physical buttons.

Additionally, there are applications that propose to read small text fragments, through the recognition of photographs taken from these objects, e.g., Be my eyes[1], Taptapsee[2], Abbyy[3], Knfbreader[4]. However, these applications are usually complex to use, paid and/or are in English, which becomes a barrier for the Brazilian public.

In order to address this issue, we present and discuss the development and evaluation of an Android application, which recognizes texts from images captured by the smartphone's camera, intended for the Brazilian public. Called LêRótulos, this application uses OCR technology (Optical Character Recognition) available from Microsoft Cognitive Services[5] and screen reader Talkback[6], native to Android platform. Our prototype design followed guidelines and recommendations for user's usability and accessibility aiming for greater user autonomy.

The contributions for this paper are: (i) LêRótulos application design, with an accessible and usability interface for identifying texts in objects, (ii) usability studies to evaluate the application's use, (iii) that LêRótulos can be used in real-world situations and demonstrate some of the foremost problems that people with VI faces while using text-reading applications, and (iv) lessons learned with LêRótulos creation process and evaluation.

2   Related Work

Bigham et al. [2] argue the use of the VizWiz[7] application, which allows users who are blind to capture images from the environment, send them and receive information about it in real time. For this, there is a network of collaborators, which is formed by Web workers and services (software of object recognition, e-mail and Twitter), for example. The study describes that the network of collaborators has increased as there are more questions to be answered, while there

---

[1] http://bemyeyes.com/.

[2] http://taptapseeapp.com/.

[3] http://www.abbyy.com/textgrabber.

[4] http://www.knfbreader.com.

[5] https://azure.microsoft.com/pt-br/services/cognitive-services/computer-vision/.

[6] https://play.google.com/store/apps/details?id=com.google.android.marvin.talkback.

[7] http://www.vizwiz.org/.

is a small financial return for those who collaborate. This app is available on Android and iOS systems.

Jayant et al. [7] described the use of EasySnap, which assists a blind person to take pictures. In this way, the application provides real-time feedback on the image quality the camera is aiming at, also considering informations like frame adjustment, zoom level and lighting. This app is available on the iOS system.

Saleous et al. [14] research developed the software Read2Me[8], which uses OCR-based technology and text to audio conversion through Text-to-Speech (TTS). Two prototypes are presented: RPi-based Platform and Android Application. The first uses a Raspberry Pi 2 Model B (RPi) microcomputer and a camera, which can be attached to a pair of glasses, for example. Thus, the camera module, which is in the RPi, captures the image and executes the OCR that is in a service in the cloud, and then executes the TTS. The other prototype was developed as an Android application. In the comparison between the prototypes, users stated that it was easier to use the RPi, however, the accuracy of the smartphone's camera was better than that used in the RBi.

Shilkrot et al. [15] presents FingerReader, an index-finger wearable device, which makes real-time reading of printed texts as the user swipes the text. Thus, the device makes a local sequential reading, of linear and non-linear texts, from a close-up camera view. Performs on Mac and Windows machine.

The Be My Eyes application connects by video call the user with VI to a sighted volunteers network, who are able to describe what is being captured by the smartphone's camera. To access the network, the user and volunteer need to be registered on the platform. The app is available for Android and IOS.

The TapTapSee application has the most similarities with LêRótulos. Among the strengths, it has the ease of use, identification of different types of objects based on images and possibility to share the recognized text. However, it does not yet have an interface and sound system in Portuguese. Although TalkBack text is read in the configured language, all menus and device usage guidelines do not have customization for other languages. Another point to note is that the camera was customized without the inclusion of autofocus, which could make it difficult to read OCR.

3   LêRótulos Application

LêRótulos application aims to convert textual information from images captured by the camera's smartphone to audio description. The application development was based on interactive design process proposed by Preece et al. [12], which has 4 basic activities: establish requirements, (Re) design, build an interactive version and evaluate. These activities should complement each other and repeat themselves, until the end product becomes available to users. The following is a description of what was done in each step.

---

[8] https://read2me.online/.

3.1   Establish Requirements and (Re) Design

The application requirements were identified through usability goals based on [13] and accessibility. These goals were essential for the development of the application and for the evaluation with later users:

– Metas de usabilidade
  - *Be easy to remember how to use:* it should be easy to remember how to use the system. The application should be well organized, intuitive and the sequence of steps required for label recognition should be easy so the user will not forget how to perform them. Questions: Does the user make too many errors when using the system? Is a previous training phase necessary? What types of interface support are provided to help users remember how to perform tasks? Can the user perform the activities easily? Is it easy to remember how to use the application? Is the user able to use the application without needing help?
  - *Be efficient in use:* the application should allow to recognize the object label through the camera's phone. Questions: Is the user able to use efficiently the application and quickly recognizing objects? Does the user find suitable the number of clicks needed to detect an object? Is the application efficient for users to achieve their goals?
  - *Be safe to use:* the application should disable buttons that are not needed. In addition, it must protect the user from dangerous and undesirable situations. Questions: How was the occurrence of false positives in the text recognition? Does the application disable unnecessary buttons?
  - *Be useful:* the application must have commands that allow to identify object labels. In addition, it must provide the necessary functionality so that users can do what they need or want. Questions: Is it better to recognize texts through the application than through third-party help or reading Braille labels?
  - *User satisfaction:* the application should promote a good user experience for users. Questions: Does the user feel good while using the app? Does the user feel confident when using the application?
– Accessibility goals
  - *Accessibility:* the application should be well integrated with accessibility resources. Questions: Was the application well integrated with accessibility features? Has the user encountered any barriers using the application?

3.2   Build an Interactive Version

LêRótulos was developed for the Android platform, chosen for being an open source platform that brings cheaper and innovative products to customers and better development platforms for programmers [9]. The official Android website[9] has a developer area where it explains, which are the best practices in the use

---

[9] https://developer.android.com/guide/topics/ui/accessibility/apps.html.

of accessibility for both native and implemented components. These tips have been observed in LéRótulos development.

For text recognition we used an API called Computer Vision provided by Microsoft[10].This API provides image analysis services to obtain information about the visual content of an image using OCR technology, which is used to extract text from images, in a way that allows the manipulation of these texts in digital form. To use this API, one must generate a key that allows 5 thousand transactions monthly or choose to pay the service and have unlimited access.

From the usability and accessibility goals, and the mentioned technologies, the LêRótulos application was developed as it can be visualized in the Fig. 1. The operation is simple and can basically be used as follows:

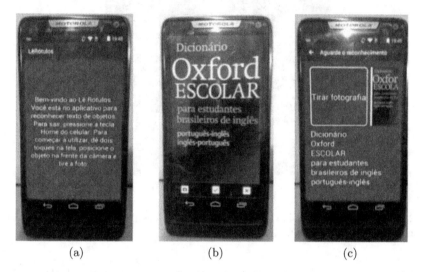

(a)   (b)   (c)

Fig. 1. LêRótulos screens. (a) Initial screen with instructions for use. (b) Photography of an object. (c) Recognized photo data.

– When the application opens, a screen with instructions appears and are narrated to the user as shown: "Welcome to LêRótulos. You are in the application to recognize text from objects. To exit, press the Home key on your phone. To get started, double-tap the screen, position the subject in front of the camera, and take the picture." (Fig. 1a), and to open the device's default camera the user only need to press this screen.
– The user must position the camera in the direction of the object at a distance of approximately 20 cm and take the picture (Fig. 1b).
– Depending to the device's camera, the user may need to select the photo confirmation button for the application to start recognizing.

---

[10] https://www.microsoft.com/cognitive-services.

- In the recognition screen, the time for finalizing recognition may be influenced by internet speed.
- If the device loses its connectivity to the Internet, a message will appear informing the connection lost.
- If the image does not have text, or if it has been unreadable, a message appears stating that the text was not recognized.
- As long as there is no recognition, the user can continue shooting.
- When the caption of the object is recognized, it is spoken to the user narrated to the user (Fig. 1c).

(a)   (b)

Fig. 2. Resource for low vision. (a) Contrast and colors patterns for low vision. (b) Screen magnification (Zoom).

To facilitate its use by people with low vision, it has a graphic interface, which follows recommendations of Kulpa et al. [8]. Also, the border color of the button responsible for opening the camera for capturing the photo, and scrolling text in the box with the text identified were enabled. In addition, the "Magnifier" function can be enabled on the Smartphone (Fig. 2).

3.3   Evaluated

Two evaluations were used to evaluate LêRótulos: evaluation by inspection with Human-Computer Interaction (HCI) specialists (Study 1) and evaluation with end users by observation of use and questionnaires (Study 2), described in the continuity.

Study 1 - Evaluation by Inspection. LêRótulos was evaluated by HCI and application experts, who used the inspection evaluation method, called heuristic evaluation (HE). This method is based on the 10 heuristics of Nielsen [10] to evaluate usability problems. Table 1 details the profile of these evaluators.

Table 1. Specialist profile

Specialist	Time experience	Experience in heuristic evaluation
E1	4 years	1 year and 6 months
E2	2 years and 5 months	1 year
E3	10 years	10 years

Results. We identified 19 usability problems, with some related to more than one heuristic. There are no problems associated with the "Recognition rather than memorization" heuristic. Table 2 reports the number of errors pointed out by the evaluators for each Nielsen's heuristic. Table 3 check the amount of problems encountered for each severity.

Table 2. Heuristic errors

Nielsen's 10 heuristics	Amount of errors
Visibility of system status	4
Match between system and real world	4
Consistency and standards	5
User control and freedom	3
Error prevention	7
Recognition rather than recall	0
Flexibility and efficiency of use	4
Aesthetic and minimalistic design	2
Help user s recognizes, diagnose and recover from errors	2
Help and documentation	1

We chose to present the results as [4,5]. In this way, the main identified problems grouped by violated heuristics will be presented.

1. **Visibility of system status:** the application displays sound information on the home screen, instructions, screen capture (photo) and results. However, while the app is recognizing the photo text, no feedback is given to the user. The suggestion would be to include a beep to inform that the image is being processed. Additionally, the user must be informed that he can use the camera of the phone, in the capture of the photo, in both portrait and landscape mode. It was also pointed out a violation in the use of the back button of the camera, which, instead of returning to the previous screen, remained in the image text recognition screen. Thus, even if the image was "approved", the application continued to issue the information to await recognition.
2. **Match between system and the real world:** in general, the terms and vocabularies used in the Labels were considered to be familiar. However, in

Table 3. Severity errors

Severity	Amount of errors
0 - there is no consensus on the usability problem	0
1 - cosmetic problem	1
2 - minor problem	6
3 - important usability problem to fix	10
4 - Usability catastrophe - imperative to correct!	2
Amount	19

the results screen was being issued the label "oral box", which is not intuitive. Refers to the box in which the text that is recognized at the end of the photo processing is found. Experts suggested changing to "image reading" or "text resulting from capture". Also, in the recognition screen, the back button was being read as "navigate up" button, which is not related to its function. The suggestion was to change to "back". Other buttons were unmarked and tagged.

3. **Consistency and standards:** some button-related violations have been detected. The camera button was not coming back and the label was not being identified correctly. Also, in the image recognition screen, it was informed "To take a new photo, double-tap the take photo button that is located in the upper left corner or touch the back button of the mobile". Again, the back button of the application was returning to the previous screen and did not stay on the same screen as the application.

4. **User control and freedom:** was not found a way to pause the execution of the informative text of the initial screen, being that the user needs to listen to the whole dialogue. If the user touches this screen again, the text restarts and there is no control over this feature. It was suggested that the user be able to control the progress of the text presentation, being able to pause, restart or finish its execution. Taking into account the problems already presented on the camera back button, the user should also be able to choose whether to return to the home screen, take a new photo, or wait until processing is complete.

5. **Flexibility and efficiency of use:** there is repeated information on the home screen and the photo recognition screen, which can make it tedious to the user with more experience in using the Label. Another suggestion was to be able to capture images with a click anywhere on the device screen. The application allows the photo to be obtained only with the standard camera button. Another point mentioned is when the correct recognition of the characters of the photograph does not occur. The system could inform and ask the user to rephrase the photo without having to change the screen, increasing the efficiency in the use of the application.

6. **Aesthetic and minimalist design:** the dialogs should contain necessary and relevant information, with an access point for more information if the user wishes to obtain them. Repeated use instructions have also been identified.
7. **Error prevention:** there were cases of false positives and the suggestion was that LêRótulos informs when an image was not clear. Another suggestion was to include a filter or dim the image. As for the messages in the photo recognition screen, the following instruction is given "To listen to the message again, move your finger in the lower half of the screen", but does not inform the type of slide and in which direction the movement should be performed. When the finger move right or left, all objects on the screen are reset, not the message. Additionally, errors may occur due to a missing photo history, such as if the user accidentally clicks to make a new photo, the previous one is not saved. Since it is difficult to repeat the same photo, it was suggested that it could keep the previous photo for consultation.
8. **Recognize, diagnose, and recover from errors:** there was a suggestion that when the characters were not correctly identified, a clear and informative error message could be presented to help the user understand what had happened and repair the problem.
9. **Help and documentation:** it was suggested to include a faster help option in addition to the instructions that are reported when the application is initialized.

The results of the heuristic evaluation allowed to identify problems in the interface and in some non-precise ways of using the Labels. This evaluation was complemented by the evaluation with real users, described in Study 2, and will be considered in the next version of the application.

Study 2 - Evaluation with End Users. In order to evaluate the accessibility and usability of our application and to verify if LêRótulos assists the user in the identification of text objects, Study 2 was carried out with the target audience of the application. This evaluation involved 6 main steps, which were based on [17]:

Table 4. Sample

Id	Age group	Gender	Visual impairment	Platform used
P1	18–28	Male	Totally blind (congenital)	Android
P2	51–61	Male	Low vision (acquired)	Android
P3	29–39	Male	Totally blind (congenital)	Android and IOS
P4	40–50	Male	Totally blind (acquired)	Android and IOS
P5	18–28	Female	Totally blind (congenital)	IOS
P6	29–39	Female	Low vision (acquired)	Android

1. Definition of the target audience and selection of participants: as a selection criterion, participants should already be smartphone and screen readers users. Thus, 6 participants participated, being 4 people blind and 2 with low vision, who were recruited through friends nominations (snow ball sampling technique [20]). The profile of the users can be verified in the Table 4.

2. Definition of the platform to be used: a Motorola RAZR i device with Android 4.0 operating system and native Talkback reader enabled, depending on the availability of the resource in the research group's lab. However, participants P3 and P4 preferred to use their own handsets, with Talkback enabled and with their usage preferences. LêRótulos has been installed on these devices.

3. Definition of usability and accessibility evaluation methods: the evaluation occurred with real users. The level of experience in using the *TalkBack* screen reader has been checked and demonstrated how the LêRótulos worked. Afterwards, tasks were performed to be performed with the use of the LêRótulos. To evaluate the usability of the application was used the System Usability Scale (SUS) [3], which has 10 closed questions with a 5-point Likert scale with a range from Strongly Agree to Strongly Disagree. In order to evaluate questions related to application accessibility and satisfaction of use, a questionnaire containing 13 questions was elaborated. These issues were based on the usability and accessibility goals used in the application design and in [18]. There are 8 open issues related to accessibility and 5 questions related to use satisfaction. Of these, 4 were open questions.

4. Preparation of the test: 4 tasks were developed to test the accessibility and usability of the Labels (Fig. 3).
   - Task 1 - Classification of objects of the same size: six packs of instant noodles containing three different flavors were supplied: 2 meat, 2 chicken and 2 tomatoes. The task was to identify the flavor of each of them and to group them according to the flavor (Fig. 3a).
   - Task 2 - Identification of objects of equal size: Three packages of identical drugs were made available in size and shape and needed to identify the name of the drug and chemical compound present in each (Fig. 3b).
   - Task 3 - Identification of objects of different sizes: similar to task 2, however, using three drug packages with different sizes and text fonts. The participant needed to identify the name and compound of the drug (Fig. 3c).
   - Task 4 - Identification of text of business cards: three business cards with different texts and fonts were made available. The objective was to identify the text of these cards (Fig. 3d).

5. Evaluation: it was done individually and in the place of preference of each participant. Initially, a questionnaire was filled out that contained 11 questions to identify the profile and register the user experience with smartphones. After completing the tasks, the participants answered the SUS questionnaires and the questionnaire of accessibility and satisfaction of use. There was video recording, audio and photos of the tasks being performed, with the informed consent of the participants. The execution time and errors committed in each task were recorded.

6. Results analysis: the videos, the evaluators notes related to the observations of use and the participants answers to the evaluation questionnaires were analyzed. The length of trial sessions varied depending on the level of user experience on smartphone usage, Android operating system, and TalkBack reader. The results are described below.

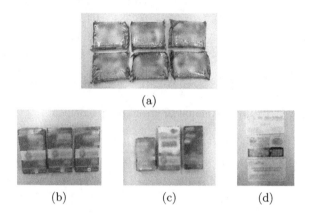

(a)

(b)   (c)   (d)

Fig. 3. Tasks (a) Task 1, (b) Task 2, (c) Task 3, and (d) Task 4

Results. The profile questionnaire allowed to verify the experience of the participants with the use of Smartphones. Among the uses were: phone calls, social networks, e-mail, clock, contacts, text messages, weather, Youtube, games and calendar. Participant P4 has already used sound recorder and musical instrument tuner. Additionally to these applications, users were asked about the use of more specific applications where they reported using audiobooks, ballot readers, barcode readers, homebank applications, color identifiers. Participants P4 and P5 had already tried other applications to read texts in objects. P4 was quoted as Be my eyes, Docscanner, TestGraber and Prizmo applications. Already the participant P5 quoted the KNFB Reader. Participant P6 reported that it uses the digital loupe feature instead of screen reader. User P3 has already used the Talks screen reader of the Symbian platform and the user P4 the screen reader ShanePlus.

After completing the profile questionnaire, the participants started the Tasks. The execution time of the tasks was counted from when the participant started the task until its completion (Table 5). The total participation of each user lasted on average 1 h and 30 min, including the time of the training and to respond to the questionnaires. One of the requirements for the application to work is that the user is connected to the Internet. In the case of the participant P4, access to the internet was made by mobile cellular network (3G), unlike the other participants, who used Wi-Fi connection. This reflected in the execution time of the tasks, because when the connection failed, it was not possible to recognize the text.

Table 5. Execution time per participant

Id	Task 1[a]	Task 2[a]	Task 3[a]	Task 4[a]	Amount of time[a]
P1	09:22	05:03	03:48	03:57	21,30
P2	19:39	03:34	02:18	10:26	35,17
P3	11:31	02:59	02:08	07:44	23,42
P4	11:13	15:51	03:32	15:43	45,39
P5	08:15	08:05	03:58	04:13	23,91
P6	08:16	04:24	01:45	03:09	16,94
Amount	67,36	38,76	16,09	43,92	166,13
Average run time	11,22	6,46	02,68	7,32	27,68

[a]in minutes

Table 6. Amount of errors per participant

Id	Task 1	Task 2	Task 3	Task 4
P1	6	0	0	2
P2	8	0	0	1
P3	17	1	0	8
P4	2	5	0	–
P5	4	2	1	3
P6	5	1	0	0

The Table 6 informs the number of times that each participant had to repeat the image capture, which is being described as a read error, or only as an error. Despite the errors, the tests demonstrated that the application is effective in identifying the labels of the tested objects, because all the users were able to complete the tasks successfully. Considering the time for carrying out the activities and the number of errors, it can be concluded that the use of LêRótulos was more efficient in Task 3, in which packs of medicines of different sizes were compared. During the execution of Task 4 by participant P4, there was a problem in the recording that prevented the counting of errors during the activity.

The Fig. 4 illustrates two participants performing the tasks. At Fig. 4a, the participant P1, who is blind from birth, performing Task 1 and in Fig. 4b we have the participant P6, who has low vision performing Task 2.

After completing the tasks, the participants answered the questionnaire SUS and accessibility and satisfaction of use. The SUS questionnaire score was 90 points. According to the satisfaction scale of Bangor et al. [1], means that LêRótulos has been rated as excellent and with a high level of user satisfaction. Still, according to Tenório et al. [19], it is possible to recognize the usability principles indicated by Nielsen [10] in SUS issues. In this way, we have:

– Ease of learning: Questions 3, 4, 7 and 10 of the SUS questionnaire. One of the questions to be answered with the evaluation was to see if it is easy to learn

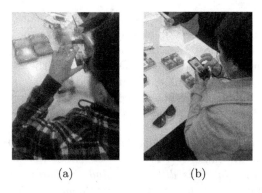

(a)   (b)

Fig. 4. Participants performing the tasks (a) user who are blind and (b) user with low vision.

how to use the application. All participants agreed that the application was easy to use (question 3) and they figured that people will learn how to use it quickly (question 7). With regard to learning, there was a suggestion that it was necessary to learn more about moving the phone and the screen reader to better use the application (question 10). P1 justified that he had never used the smartphone camera and needed to learn how to take pictures and the P5, who was a user only of the IOS platform, had not yet used Talkback. Only P1 reported that he would need the help of a person with technical knowledge to use the application (question 4).

- Efficiency: Questions 5, 6, 8 of the SUS questionnaire. All participants disagreed that the application was confusing to use (question 8). Only the participant P5 disagreed with the statement of question 5. The reason the participant described was that the application should use a camera of its own and not the standard camera of the smartphone because it considers it difficult to use. Three participants stated that they partially agree that the application presents a lot of inconsistency (question 6), since the text recognition had flaws that were described in the execution of the tasks. Additionally, P3 reported that failure in recognition is a common error that occurs with OCR:
  - (...) I think only the recognition of letters, but this is a problem that has in all screen readers. It is not really a barrier of yours, but a barrier of materials. (P3)
- Ease of memorization: Question 2 of the SUS questionnaire. All participants disagreed that the application was unnecessarily complex, suggesting that the system could be easily memorized and that users could easily remember how to use it.
- Minimization of errors: In the SUS questionnaire is represented by the same question 6 answered in the previous item Efficiency.
- Satisfaction: Questions 1, 4, 9 of the SUS questionnaire. All questions regarding usage satisfaction were ranked with full agreement by participants, which meant that participants were satisfied with their use.

In addition to the responses of the SUS questionnaire, the participants answered the instrument of accessibility and usability. In the accessibility questionnaire, participants report that the Talkback accessibility feature does not work properly with the Android camera. Depending on the model of the device, there are buttons that make it difficult to use, and there are applications where the button description labels are not correctly identified. Here are excerpts from testimonials:

- *I just think it needs someone to give the initial tricks of how to position the object in front of the camera.* (P1)
- *Only with the camera, it is difficult to find the button to take photo. My suggestion is to enter direct with the take photo button selected and only have this option on the camera."* (P2)
- *I found no barrier. Because the application is ok. The limitation is not the application but the camera. Does not apply to the application. Maybe I could take the picture straight away.* (P3)
- *The camera could have names on the buttons. (...) I had a bit of trouble with using the camera, but the problem was with Talkback not the application. I did not know the commands to take a photo.* (P4)

Participants with low vision (P2 and P6) answered questions about screen contrast. The participant P2 validated the contrast as appropriate, but preferred to use the audio to avoid straining the eyes. P6 stated that the contrast is adequate.

As far as audio information is concerned, participants report that the audio information was appropriate, well-crafted, creative, simple, and easy to understand. All participants agreed that they were able to manipulate sound information as to whether to repeat and stop the audios and that the application responded well to the Talkback reader. P3 made suggestions for improvement in audio information:

- *Maybe he could have a little help button that had all that information, or just take it out. Because people who have more advanced usability, the less they talk the better (...) I suggest a button on the screen that could activate. A button setting that becomes customizable. This is to see if you want the information or what you do not want. (...) <sound> information will be unnecessary for those more accustomed users. Low vision, for example, accustoms him to run the screen to read, and the blind man gets used to the information by listening once or twice (...) Usually applications have a help button.* (P3)

In the questions related to use satisfaction, suggestions for improvement were requested for application, and again, the camera issue was highlighted:

- *Just the question of the camera, my suggestion is that you enter direct with take photo button selected and you only have that option in the camera.* (P2)
- *Integration with the camera decreases the number of clicks. Greater integration with the camera.* (P3)

- *The camera might not request confirmation when taking the picture and go straight to recognition. The buttons on the camera are also labeled. And it would be interesting to copy the recognized text. (P4)*
- *It was very simple, very easy for me. Adapt the touch sensitivity a bit more. If I were to wear this, it would be perfect. My only difficulty was sensitivity. (P5)*
- *Let the application recognize people and larger objects as books. (P1)*

Also, with respect to the satisfaction of use, were cited:

- *Was able to take pictures and see the things I have. It is easy to use, to handle. It's not boring to deal with. (...) I found it very accessible, very calm to use. (P1)*
- *I found it excellent, makes it easy for the handicapped. It's very objective. (P2)*
- *Facility it provides to independence. We have not even tested this with money, but I think he'll read it too. I think you are to be congratulated both for the initiative and for the effectiveness of the project. It's a project that works, it's working well, so that's it. (P3)*
- *I found the recognition very good. The OCR used has a very good quality of recognition. (P4)*
- *It's a practical application, it does not have to come in many screens, there are some that are more complex, sometimes other applications have to keep fighting to recognize the text, and the amount paid is not worth it. That he has the option to repeat the reading of the text, and I think that the fact that he is good from day to day, I am sure that I will use direct. (...) He is very simple. (P5)*
- *That he is quick, that he is easy, that he is complete. (P6)*

Finally, the participants were asked if they would indicate the use of the application to other people, they all answered yes. Here are some testimonials:

- *Yes. And I also want to, because the application is very useful. (P1)*
- *For everyone, the application facilitates a lot. I even got confused when I took medicine because the boxes were the same. (P2)*
- *Would indicate. Because it has great utility to identify labels. Of all the applications I've tested in this regard, I think it's pretty cool. (P4)*

4 Lessons Learned

The development and evaluation process of LêRótulos has brought lessons learned, which are expected to assist other researchers in the area of assistive technology for visually impaired users. Among these, some are mentioned:

- Experienced participants suggested having an option to access the instructions for use instead of automatically making them available at each start of the system.

- The use of cellular resources, such as the camera, was not well accepted. When the LêRótulos application was started, it was decided to use the camera native to the cell phone. This decision was made believing that it would be easier for people with VI to use their own camera, which they had more familiarity with. In view of the problems encountered by specialists and people with VI, it is believed that this decision presented more problems than advantages. In this way, it is suggested to implement a camera, in which one can have friendly labels on the buttons, reduce the amount of these and customize their options and way of presenting the information on the screen.
- In the evaluation with people with VI it was possible to verify the interaction of the user with the cell phone. For example, it was possible to observe that instead of using the finger at each corner of the screen searching for information and identifying the buttons, most of the users touched only in the middle of the phone, traversing all the components of the screen. This highlights the importance of performing evaluations with the target audience of the application to understand the form of interaction and their needs.
- The Talkback speed used by participants with VI is superior to human speech. For this reason, each user must set the speed according to their preference.
- There was difficulty in the composition of the sample of the end users, even using the technique of snowball.
- The impact of choosing the location where the assessment will take place in controlled environments or natural environments should be checked, as the need for internet access or environmental characteristics (such as brightness) may interfere with the results of the evaluation.

5   Conclusion

The research aimed to introduce the application LêRótulos and evaluate if it meets its main objective, which is to help people who are visual impairment to recognize texts that are in images that are captured by the Android smartphone camera.

Inspection assessments were carried out with HCI and application specialists (Study 1), and evaluation with application end users, in real situations of use (Study 2). The results indicated that the application fulfills its function with good usability and accessibility, but indicated improvements for the same, which were described in the sections of this work. As future work, we intend to make the usability and accessibility corrections indicated in the evaluations as well as incorporate improvements, mainly, related to the camera.

Last, but not least, it should be noted that the P3, who has congenital blindness, used LêRótulos to assist him in the enrollment process at a university. The usage situation was that he needed to select different documents and there were no monitors to assist him. Through the application, you can recognize the documents, and separate the ones you needed to present. He thus exercised his right to access information and autonomy.

Acknowledgments. We also thank the PDTI Program, financed by Dell Computers of Brazil Ltd (Law 8.248/91). JDO and VSMPC are supported by CAPES/PROSUP PhD scholarships. Thank you to all participants in this study.

References

1. Bangor, A., Kortum, P., Miller, J.: Determining what individual sus scores mean: adding an adjective rating scale. J. Usability Stud. **4**(3), 114–123 (2009)
2. Bigham, J.P., Jayant, C., Ji, H., Little, G., Miller, A., Miller, R.C., Miller, R., Tatarowicz, A., White, B., White, S., Yeh, T.: Vizwiz: nearly real-time answers to visual questions. In: Proceedings of the 23nd Annual ACM Symposium on User Interface Software and Technology, UIST 2010, pp. 333–342. ACM, New York (2010). http://doi.acm.org/10.1145/1866029.1866080
3. Brooke, J., et al.: SUS-a quick and dirty usability scale. Usability Eval. Ind. **189**(194), 4–7 (1996)
4. Cortes, W.R.P., Zanin, A., Soletti, L.V., Machado, V.S., Silveira, M.S., da Silva, P.H.L.: Zumbis vs sedentários: Quem irá vencer? avaliando a usabilidade do aplicativo zombie's, run! In: Companion Proceedings of the 13th Brazilian Symposium on Human Factors in Computing Systems, IHC 2014, pp. 143–157. Sociedade Brasileira de Computação, Porto Alegre (2014). http://dl.acm.org/citation.cfm?id=2738165.2738206
5. Cunha, B.C.R., Machado Neto, O.J., Pimentel, M.D.G.C.: A heuristic evaluation of a mobile annotation tool. In: Proceedings of the 19th Brazilian Symposium on Multimedia and the Web, WebMedia 2013, pp. 89–92. ACM, New York (2013). http://doi.acm.org/10.1145/2526188.2526232
6. Damaceno, R.J.P., Braga, J.C., Chalco, J.P.M.: Mobile device accessibility for the visually impaired: problems mapping and empirical study of touch screen gestures. In: Proceedings of the 15th Brazilian Symposium on Human Factors in Computer Systems, IHC 2016, pp. 2:1–2:10. ACM, New York (2016). http://doi.acm.org/10.1145/3033701.3033703
7. Jayant, C., Ji, H., White, S., Bigham, J.P.: Supporting blind photography. In: The Proceedings of the 13th International ACM SIGACCESS Conference on Computers and Accessibility, ASSETS 2011, pp. 203–210. ACM, New York (2011). http://doi.acm.org/10.1145/2049536.2049573
8. Kulpa, C.C., Teixeira, F.G., da Silva, R.P.: Um modelo de cores na usabilidade das interfaces computacionais para os deficientes de baixa visão. Des. Tecnologia **1**(01), 66–78 (2010)
9. Maasalmi, E., Pitkänen, P.: Comparing Google's Android and Apple's iOS mobile software development environments (2008)
10. Nielsen, J.: Usability Engineering. Morgan Kaufmann Publishers Inc., San Francisco (1993)
11. Prates, D.: Acessibilidade Atitudinal. Gramma, Rio de Janeiro (2015)
12. Rogers, Y., Sharp, H., Preece, J.: Design de interação: além da interação humano-computador. Bookman (2013)
13. Rogers, Y., Sharp, H., Preece, J.: Interaction Design: Beyond Human-Computer Interaction. Wiley, New York (2011)
14. Saleous, H., Shaikh, A., Gupta, R., Sagahyroon, A.: Read2me: a cloud-based reading aid for the visually impaired. In: 2016 International Conference on Industrial Informatics and Computer Systems (CIICS), pp. 1–6. IEEE (2016). https://doi.org/10.1109/ICCSII.2016.7462446

15. Shilkrot, R., Huber, J., Liu, C., Maes, P., Nanayakkara, S.C.: Fingerreader: a wearable device to support text reading on the go. In: CHI 2014 Extended Abstracts on Human Factors in Computing Systems, CHI EA 2014, pp. 2359–2364. ACM, New York (2014). http://doi.acm.org/10.1145/2559206.2581220
16. Shilkrot, R., Huber, J., Meng Ee, W., Maes, P., Nanayakkara, S.C.: Fingerreader: a wearable device to explore printed text on the go. In: Proceedings of the 33rd Annual ACM Conference on Human Factors in Computing Systems, CHI 2015, pp. 2363–2372. ACM, New York (2015). http://doi.acm.org/10.1145/2702123.2702421
17. da Silva, C.F., Ferreira, S.B.L., Ramos, J.F.M.: Whatsapp accessibility from the perspective of visually impaired people. In: Proceedings of the 15th Brazilian Symposium on Human Factors in Computer Systems, IHC 2016, pp. 11:1–11:10. ACM, New York (2016). http://doi.acm.org/10.1145/3033701.3033712
18. Sonza, A.P., et al.: Acessibilidade e tecnologia assistiva: pensando a inclusão sociodigital de pessoas com necessidades especiais. BBB, Bento Gonçalves (2013)
19. Tenório, J.M., Cohrs, F.M., Sdepanian, V.L., Pisa, I.T., de Fátima Marin, H.: Desenvolvimento e avaliação de um protocolo eletrônico para atendimento e monitoramento do paciente com doença celíaca. Revista de Informática Teórica e Aplicada 17(2), 210–220 (2010)
20. Weiss, R.S.: Learning from Strangers: The Art and Method of Qualitative Interview Studies. Simon and Schuster, New York (1995)

Information Design on the Adaptation of Evaluation Processes' Images to People with Visual Impairment

Fernanda Domingues[✉], Emilia Christie Picelli Sanches,
and Claudia Mara Scudelari de Macedo

Federal University of Paraná, UFPR, Curitiba, PR 80060-150, Brazil
fernanda.fdomingues@gmail.com

Abstract. It is a right for people with visual impairment to have access to tests and evaluation processes of various kinds. That way, adapted tests must present themselves in a way that visually impaired candidates can demonstrate their knowledge in the same way as the others. In this context, the importance of adapting images and complex information to an adequate comprehension of the questions is highlighted. The aim of this present paper is to explore the adaptation processes of tests for people with visual impairment, as well as to explore the role of information design on the production of tactile images to assist the evaluation process. Through a literature review, this paper presents five examples of tests applied to visually impaired candidates, focusing on the way tactile images were presented and how the candidates participated on the process. As a result, the importance of the adapted image as well as the need of evaluation processes that explore diversified means of comprehension is verified.

Keywords: Information design · Evaluation processes · Images
Visual impairment

1   Introduction

According to Masini [1], from the educational point of view, people with visual impairment are divided in two groups: blind and subnormal vision. This classification is made according to visual acuity, being blind the individual that has 20/200 vision on the better-seeing eye, with best correction, and subnormal vision or low vision the one that has 20/70 vision on the same condition.

Blindness can be characterized as congenital or acquired. The first happens before or during birth, and the second is acquired at any other life stage, due to health complications or accidents, for example [1].

For many years, people with visual impairment were considered incapable of any physical or intellectual activity. Only after the end of the 1950 decade that blind people inclusion became a public policy. In 1990, inclusive education arises, where each individual's peculiarities are considered in the pedagogical process. From this, an increase in the admission of visually impaired people at schools, universities and public office jobs was verified [2].

© Springer International Publishing AG, part of Springer Nature 2018
M. Antona and C. Stephanidis (Eds.): UAHCI 2018, LNCS 10907, pp. 355–364, 2018.
https://doi.org/10.1007/978-3-319-92049-8_26

Brazilian law n°. 8.112, dated December 11th, 1990, describes in the 5th article §2nd the right of disabled people to apply for public office jobs, guaranteeing up to 20% of the positions exclusively to these people [3]. Each official notice establishes how these people will be placed and which devices will be available during the test, a right to the blind candidate, for example, is a Braille test and a reader (person who reads the test). The reader is also a right supported by the law, according to decree 5.296, subsection 59 dated December 2nd, 2002.

The regulations on selective processes that include people with disabilities are important mainly for college entrance exams. Decree No. 2998 of December 20, 1999, regulating Law No. 7,853, dated October 24, 1989, provides the National Policy for the integration of people with disabilities in universities. The Article 27 establishes, in addition to Braille and reader, additional time for test execution and adaptations previously requested by the student, according to the degree of disability.

It is important to think, however, about the interpretation problem when the reader faces images in the tests. Borges [4] explains the context of the college entrance exam for UFRJ, in which the Braille test and reader were used. According to the author, the application formula was not particularly effective for issues with graphs and maps, with mathematical and/or chemical formulas and showed other types of representation which verbalization by the reader is difficult, such as cartoons and comics.

As Thurlow et al. [5] point out, adapted tests should be designed to enable students with disabilities to fully demonstrate their knowledge in academic tests, minimizing obstacles or disorders arising from their disabilities. This way, the importance of considering accessibility of images and complex representations in the evaluation processes, besides the process of text adaptations for the correct interpretation by the visually impaired candidate, where the information design becomes fundamental.

Information design, as its name suggests, can be seen as a design process for the purpose of informing people, involving both the communicator and the recipient of those messages [6]. Information, Waller [6] argues, comes up during this design process, through the need to explain something to the recipient.

As a complement, the International Institute for Information Design (IIID) exposes information design as 'defining, planning, and modeling the contents of a message and the environments in which they are presented, with the intention of satisfying the information needs of the recipient' In the original: 'defining, planning, and shaping of the contents of a message and the environments in which it is presented, with the intention to satisfy the information needs of the intended recipients' [7].

In these definitions of Waller [6] and IIID [7], a visually impaired recipient, for example, should be taken into account in the elaboration and manipulation of the information so that the goal is fulfilled and the recipient understands the message. This means presenting the visual information in an accessible way, through touch or audio, for example. Considering the limitations of visually impaired people, their rights, the role of information design as a process for efficient communication, Gruenwald [8] argues that complex images and concepts demand features such as tactile images, for example.

This paper aims to bring up how the images in evaluative processes are being adapted for this public.

As a way of exploring the problem, this paper is a review of the literature, exploring the process of adaptation of evidence for people with visual impairment, as well as the role of information design in the production of tactile images that assist in the evaluation process.

Five examples of test applied to visually impaired candidates were analyzed, observing how the images were translated to the tactile and how the candidates participated in the process. Adapted tests were considered both for students with acquired or congenital blindness and for students with low vision, even if tactile images are used more often by blind people. This article begins by discussing definitions of image in information design and the role in the evaluation process, followed by visual information access by people with visual impairment, presenting examples of adapted tests and concluding with a brief discussion and final considerations.

2 Image

There are several ways to define image, taking into account the study focus. [9] define image as 'a term we commonly use to designate graphic or verbal representations of something that exists or could exist'. The image is part of the visual and graphic language and appears as a way of transmitting certain information to the receiver of the message.

Horn [10] comments on the emergence of visual language because of the human's difficulty in expressing complex and abstract information, and subdivides it into primitive and property levels. Primitive level consists of words, shapes and images. Words are defined through the linguistic approach. Forms are characterized as abstract representations that stand out as units but do not resemble objects in the natural world, such as points, lines and arrows. Finally, images present themselves as a visible form that resemble objects of the natural world. Property level consists of primitive elements such as value, texture, color, orientation, size, location of two-dimensional and three-dimensional space, movement, thickness and illumination.

Considering the graphic language, Twyman [11] defines as 'graphic' what is drawn or made visible in response to conscious decisions, and as 'language' what serves as a vehicle for communication. For the author, the graphic language is divided into three levels: verbal, pictorial and schematic. In addition, Twyman [11] observes the possibility of representing visual information in different ways, such as tables, lists, maps, diagrams, etc.

Engelhardt [12] defines a graphical representation as "a visible artifact on a more or less flat surface, that was created in order to express information". From this definition, the author classifies the visual representations into ten primary types and six hybrid types. In the first, maps, illustrations, statistical graphs, time charts, link diagrams, grouping diagrams, tables, symbol compositions and written texts are inserted. In the second one there are statistical maps, route maps, statistical route maps, statistical time graphs, statistical link charts, and chronological link diagrams.

In the evaluation processes, Da Silveira [13] emphasizes the importance of the image mainly because it allows an immediate understanding and a faster reading than written text. According to the author, the image increases aesthetic and communicative pleasure, helping spontaneous understanding of the information.

In these processes, there are numerous categories of images used to compose the questions and assist the candidate in the understanding process. In a college entrance test, for example, there are graphs, photos, geometric figures, cartoons, illustrations, among others. The role of these representations in evaluative processes is often crucial to solve a question.

Thus, it is necessary to reflect on the process of image interpretation by visually impaired candidates, so that the understanding of the adapted images allow equality comparing to sighted candidates.

3   Access to Visual Information by the Visually Impaired

Visual impairment is a classification that "encompasses people who have weak vision (or low vision), those who can distinguish lights but not shapes, and those who cannot distinguish even light" [14]. In this way, with the visual field compromised, the reception of visual information must be adapted.

The adaptation differs between people with low vision and blind people. For those with low vision, the aid comes with expansion of the information, guaranteeing sharpness and clarity in texts and images. It should follow accessibility recommendations such as high contrast and use of matte paper, for example [15]. In addition, when visual information cannot be magnified directly, the use of Assistive Technology (AT) is necessary, using magnifying glasses for example.

For blind people, the perception of what is visual is happens through other senses. According to Sacks [16], with the visual cortex not being used for the action of seeing, it becomes "hypersensitive to all kinds of internal stimuli: its own autonomous activity, signals from other brain areas - auditory, tactile, and verbal areas - and thoughts, memories, and emotions." Thus, it is possible to understand that the blind is stimulated by the body itself to receive visual information through audio and touch. The adaptation of materials that use visual information should be done for audio or touch, such as audio description of images, use of lenses, translation for Braille, creation of tactile images, among others. As AT, blind people use, for example, screen reader software and Braille printers.

In adapted evaluative processes, it is necessary to take into account the need to transpose the test to the tactile medium, for both texts (Braille) and for images (tactile images) and, for this, understanding how tactile perception works is fundamental.

Touch is a proximal perception, performed in a sequential-temporal way, that is, it is done at a short distance from the receiver of the message, unlike hearing and vision, where recognition is allowed at a distance, and is performed at the time when hands touch the object [17, 18]. In this way, the tactile reading is fragmented and sequenced, and early stimulation from childhood (or from the acquisition of blindness) is recommended, so that there is no overload in attention or memory [17, 18].

In the case of tactile images, the adaptation can be made by various means of production, for example:

- Craft process: process that allows the use of the largest number of materials, such as string, cork, wood, clay, paper, among others. Does not focus on just one specific technique for production, and does not demand skilled labor.
- Embossed printing: printing of microencapsulated paper (alcohol microcapsules), made in two stages. First, print on special paper with black ink and, later, warming this paper, causing the alcohol to react with black ink and form the relief of the image.
- Temperature: uses plastic material, and is done by pressing a thin layer of plastic against a previously built mold.
- 3D printing: rapid prototyping technology that allows both two-dimensional and three-dimensional printing, differing from embossing and thermoforming [19]. The most commonly used materials for 3D printing are plastic filaments.

Regardless of how images are used in evaluative processes, adaptation must be carried out in a rigorous manner, taking into account the difficulties of disabled people, their particularities, the way they understand information, as well as principles of information design.

4   Adaptation of Images in Evaluative Tests

As previously mentioned, it is a right of the visually impaired candidate to have a reader (a professional who assists in reading the test and completing the answers), as well as a Braille test or magnified for people with low vision.

The National Curricular Parameters (PCNs in Portuguese) highlight the selection of Assistive Technology instruments for candidate evaluation, as well as presentation of accessible images that facilitate the understanding of the questions by the candidates [20].

Hereafter, five examples of evaluation processes that include candidates with visual impairment, applied in different countries, are presented. In these examples, the role of the image and its interpretation, the use of Assistive Technology, as well as the adaptation process used are highlighted.

4.1   SARESP (School Performance Evaluation System of the State of São Paulo)

Fernandes and Healy [21], evaluated the process of adaptation and application of tests belonging to the School Performance Evaluation System of the State of São Paulo (SARESP). The tests, applied in the public and private network of the state, focus on the assessment of cognitive skills of reading, writing, and math acquired by students throughout elementary and high school. For students with visual impairment, the process consists of a Braille test and a reader (to assist when necessary reading the test).

In this context, the authors identified and described a series of problems faced by blind or low vision students, especially regarding the interpretation of images.

As an example, the authors cite questions 24 and 25 of the Literature test of the 7th grade applied in the year of 2005. In its elaboration, a comic strip of the "Menino Maluquinho" presented in colors in the printed test as in Fig. 1.

ZIRALDO. As melhores tiradas do menino Maluquinho. São Paulo: Melhoramentos, 2000. p.5.

Fig. 1. "Menino Maluquinho" comic strip used in a SARESP 2005 test. Source: Fernandes and Healy [21]

The questions are proposed as follows:

24 - In the penultimate box, the girl's expression reveals that she was:
(A) scared.
(B) upset.
(C) cheerful.
(D) desperate.

25 - Among the resources used to tell the story of the boy Maluquinho, it is highlighted:
(A) The background colors of each box.
(B) The gestures and physiognomy of the characters.
(C) The thoughts of the characters in balloons.
(D) The noises of the environment where the story takes place [21].

According to the authors, the Braille test in analysis did not present any type of tactile image, using only subtitles to describe the representations. For the story referring to Fig. 1, the first comic is thus described, according to Fernandes and Healy [21]: "Girl talking to boy Maluquinho and says: I'm going to make a cake! Help me? Maluquinho replies cheerfully: only if you let me break the eggs!".

Firstly, the inviability of question 24 requiring a detailed interpretation of facial expressions is stated: even if the reader describes them in great detail, the impartiality due to the professional personal interpretation would be lost. Likewise, question 25 requires reflection on colors used, gestures and physiognomy of the characters, thoughts and noises presented. For these concepts, just the description is not enough. Therefore, the need for image adaptations that are effective for the reader with disabilities and that transmit the information properly are stressed.

4.2   University of Brasília (UnB)

Soares and Rabelo [22] show the perspective of the University of Brasilia (UnB) in the application of the college entrance exam for disabled people. People with visual impairment can use a special room, and have access to resources such as magnified and super magnified tests, Braille tests, reader and aid to fill in the answer sheet and transcribe discursive tests.

According to the authors, in the case of magnified or super magnified tests, no modification of the original test is performed. However, for those who need the test in Braille or a reader, the university procedure is to remove figures, tables, references to texts, graphics, among others.

4.3   Comprehensive Adult Student Assessment Systems (CASAS - United States of America)

Posey and Henderson [23], through a focus group with 75 participants, between teachers and students with visual impairment, evaluated the adapted test from Comprehensive Adult Student Assessment Systems (CASAS). The test, intended for adults and widely applied in the United States, measures the literacy and basic skills required to enter the job market through 90 objective questions.

In this analysis, the authors verified the difficulty of Braille reading of some participants, mainly because they are used to a screen reader. There was also too much effort needed to interpret tactile maps produced with a 3D printer, since the adult audience in question was not familiar with the new technology. For a better applicability of the test with blind adults, the authors conclude the research recommending the test application in two distinct days for a new schedule, the inclusion of more detailed instructions for reading the tactile maps, as well as the elaboration of questions that are close to the blind adult's daily life.

4.4   Evaluation in the UK

Woods, Parkinson and Lewis [24] review the process of adapting and applying assessments for visually impaired people in the United Kingdom[1]

During the evaluations, students may request the following items: a person to read the exam (reader), electronic reading devices; extra time; a laptop to complete the exam, rest periods during the test, a person to transcribe the answers and a person to encourage the candidate and help them focus, known as 'prompter'.

---

[1] In this context, refers to three of the four United Kingdom countries: England, Wales and Northern Ireland.

4.5   Adaptive Content with Evidence-Based Diagnosis (ACED)

Hansen et al. [25] discuss the usability of the assessment system called Adaptive Content with Evidence-based Diagnosis (ACED), which provides audio-tactile graphs to assess algebra learning by visually impaired people. The system provides three different interfaces or modes: normal mode, low vision mode, and blind mode.

Normal mode uses regular-sized fonts and does not provide voice output. Works on a computer monitor with an optional keyboard and mouse. The low vision mode provides text and image magnification, descriptive audio on the content and speech synthesis used only to reproduce the typed characters in open response questions. Finally, the blind mode resembles the low vision, except for also using a tactile device known as Talking Tactile Tablet (TTT).

The tactile tablet is a digital input device that uses paper to create 3D overlays and connects audio files to describe overlays. The device, connected to a computer that uses the ACED, allows through its tactile surface that students with visual deficiency interpret diagrams, graphs and maps, producing a tactile image with description in audio. When a student touches the tablet, the location of the touch is sent to the computer, which then plays the contents or instructions. Blind mode also plays characters and words as they are typed to guide the user to input their answers.

5   Discussion

Sitlington [26] states that adapting a test is effective when scores of students with special needs increase, while those who do not require special aid keep the same score on the test.

In the examples collected, there are adaptations that aim at the total integration of the visually impaired person, as well as evaluations that disregard the importance of the tactile image, thus harming the candidate's score. As the example of SARESP and UnB, which simply describe the images or discard them, deprive the visually impaired candidate of the same information as the others. In these cases, only the Braille test and the learner are not enough, considering the difficulty of verbalization or transcription of complex information, such as graphs or chemical and mathematical formulas, for example.

The role of Assistive Technology in image interpretation is emphasized in UK-based assessments as well as in the ACED system. In both cases, the availability of technological resources put the candidate with visual impairment at the same level as the others, giving full conditions for the interpretation of images and complex information. However, the context of the candidates who will make use of these resources should be considered. Taking CASAS as an example, some candidates had difficulties in interpreting tactile maps produced by 3D printers because they were not familiar with the new technology.

According to the role of information design, the need for evaluation processes that elaborate the content is reinforced so that the receiver fully understands the message. Within the universe of the visually impaired person, this study brought up the importance of the tactile image as well as technologies that aid in its interpretation.

This article has raised five examples, Brazilian and foreign, to understand the context in which the problem is embedded. However, to draw further conclusions, it is necessary to consider the wide range of existing evaluative processes and their peculiarities: in each location the tests for candidates with special needs will be applied in different ways and using various resources.

6   Final Considerations

The present study sought to demonstrate the image role in evaluative processes for people with visual impairment, and to point out information design as essential in these processes. The literature review provided examples of assessments that almost completely disregarded the role of image comprehension by visually impaired candidates, as well as examples that have used several alternatives to provide equal conditions of interpretation.

Being an article of exploration of the literature to point out examples of evaluative processes for people with visual impairment, it does not intend to exhaust the discussion about the subject, but rather to open the range of research possibilities.

Therefore, it is necessary to carry out new studies that will explore the various possibilities of adapting tests and images through guidelines and information design concepts that collaborate with the presentation of content comprehensible by all visually impaired candidates, in evaluative contexts.

References

1. Masini, E.F.S.: A educação do portador de deficiência visual–as perspectivas do vidente e do não vidente. Em Aberto **13**(60), 615–634 (2008)
2. Castro, S.F.: Ingresso e permanência de alunos com deficiência em universidades públicas brasileiras. In: Tese (Doutorado em Educação Especial)-Centro de Educação e Ciências Humanas. Universidade Federal de São Carlos, São Carlos (2011)
3. Brasil: Lei nº 8.112, de 11 de dezembro de 1990. Dispõe sobre o regime jurídico dos servidores públicos civis da União, das autarquias e das fundações públicas federais. Diário Oficial da União, Brasília, DF, no. 227, Seção 1, p. 1, 22 December 1990. http://www.planalto.gov.br/ccivil_03/leis/L8112cons.htm. Accessed 27 May 2017
4. Borges, J.A.S.: Será "correto" o uso de um computador por um estudante cego no vestibular?. In: VII Esocite Jornadas Latino-Americanas de Estudos Sociais das Ciências e das Tecnologias, pp. 1–19 (2008)
5. Thurlow, M.L., Elliott, J.L., Ysseldyke, J.E.: Testing Students with Disabilities: Practical Strategies for Complying with District and State Requirements. Corwin Press, Thousand Oaks (2003)
6. Waller, R.: Transformational information design. In: Oven, P.Č., Požar, C. (eds.) On Information Design. The Museum of Architecture and Design, Ljubljana (2016)
7. IIID Definitions: What is information design? http://www.iiid.net/home/definitions/. Accessed 28 May 2017
8. Gruenwald, L.: Impressão 3D: lendo imagens através do tato. Um recurso a mais para estudantes com deficiência visual. Revista nacional de reabilitação – reação (98) (2014)
9. Contrera, M.S., Hattori, O.T.: Publicidade e Cia. Thompson, São Paulo (2003)

10. Horn, R.E.: Visual Language: Global Communication for the 21st Century. MacroVU, Incorporated, Washington, D.C. (1998)
11. Twyman, M.: The Graphic Presentation of Language. Information Design Journal 3(1), 2–22 (1982). Grillford Ltd, Stony Stratford
12. Engelhardt, Y.: The Language of Graphics: A Framework for the Analysis of Syntax and Meaning in Maps, Charts and Diagrams. University of Amsterdam, Amsterdam (2002)
13. Da Silveira, J.R.C.: A imagem: interpretação e comunicação. Linguagem em (Dis) curso 5, 113–128 (2010)
14. Sonza, A.P. (org.): Acessibilidade e tecnologia assistiva: pensando a inclusão sociodigital de PNEs. IFRS, Bento Gonçalves (2013)
15. Meürer, M.V., Gonçalves, B.S., Correio, V.J.B.: Tipografia e baixa visão: uma discussão sobre a legibilidade. Projética 5(2), 33–46 (2014). Londrina
16. Sacks, O.: O olhar da mente. Companhia das Letras, São Paulo (2010)
17. Kastrup, V.: A invenção na ponta dos dedos: a reversão da atenção em pessoas com deficiência visual. Psicologia em Revista 13(1), 69–90 (2007). Belo Horizonte
18. Duarte, M.L.B.: Desenho infantil e seu ensino a crianças cegas: razões e métodos. Insight, Curitiba (2011)
19. Gual, J., Puyuelo, M., Lloveras, J.: Three-dimensional tactile symbols produced by 3D printing: improving the process of memorizing a tactile map key. Br. J. Vis. Impair. 32(3), 263–278 (2014)
20. Brasil: Secretaria de Educação Fundamental. Parâmetros curriculares nacionais: Adaptações Curriculares/Secretaria de Educação Fundamental. Secretaria de Educação Especial. MEC/SEF/SEESP, Brasília, 62 p. (1998)
21. Fernandes, S.H.A.A., Healy, L.: Desafios associados à inclusão de alunos cegos e com baixa visão nas avaliações escolares. Escritos Pedagógicos 4, 119–139 (2009)
22. Soares, M.V.A., Rabelo, M.L.: Atendimento a candidatos com necessidades especiais em processos seletivos da Universidade de Brasília. Linhas Críticas 9(16), 127–139 (2003). Brasília
23. Posey, V.K., Henderson, B.W.: Comprehensive adult student assessment systems braille reading assessment: an exploratory study. J. Vis. Impair. Blind. 106(8), 488 (2012)
24. Woods, K., Parkinson, G., Lewis, S.: Investigating access to educational assessment for students with disabilities. Sch. Psychol. Int. 31(1), 21–41 (2010)
25. Hansen, E.G., Shute, V.J., Landau, S.: An assessment-for-learning system in mathematics for individuals with visual impairments. J. Vis. Impair. Blind. 104(5), 275 (2010)
26. Sitlington, S.G., Scarpati, S.: The effects of test accommodations on test performance: a review of literature, Report no. 485. Center for Educational Assessment Research, University of Massachusetts, Amherst (2000)

Cognitive Impact Evaluation of Multimodal Interfaces for Blind People: Towards a Systematic Review

Lana Mesquita[1]([⊠]), Jaime Sánchez[2], and Rossana M. C. Andrade[1]

[1] Department of Computer Science, Universidade Federal do Ceará (UFC),
Fortaleza, CE, Brazil
lanamesquita@great.ufc.br, rossana@ufc.br
[2] Department of Computer Science, Universidad de Chile, Santiago, Chile
jsanchez@dcc.uchile.cl

Abstract. Visual disability has a major impact on people's quality of life. Although there are many technologies to assist people who are blind, most of them do not necessarily guarantee the effectiveness of the intended use. Then, we have conducted a systematic literature review concerning the cognitive impact evaluation of multimodal interfaces for blind people. We report in this paper the preliminary results of the systematic literature review with the purpose of understanding how the cognitive impact is currently evaluated when using multimodal interfaces for blind people. Among twenty-five papers retrieved from the systematic review, we found a high diversity of experiments. Some of them do not present the data clearly and do not apply a statistical method to guarantee the results. Besides this, other points related to the experiments are analyzed. We conclude that there is a need to better plan and present data from experiments on technologies for cognition of blind people. Moreover, as the next step in this research, we will investigate these preliminary results with a qualitative analysis.

Keywords: Impact evaluation · Cognitive evaluation · Multimodal interfaces
Blind people

1 Introduction

Visual disability has a major impact on the quality of life of people who has it, including their ability to study, work and to develop personal relationships [1]. In this aspect, technologies, such as serious games [2], have been designed to assist people who are blind to support daily life activities. These technologies work as aids to facilitate their independence, autonomy, and safety. Thus, such technologies improve the quality of life of people with visual disabilities and could stimulate and develop several skills, such as cognitive skills [3].

Even though there is technology specialized for blind people (i.e., visually impaired), they are still using applications that are similar to older applications for the sighted population. For example, Battleship was one of the earliest games to be produced as a computer game with its release in 1979 [4]. AudioBattleShip, a version for

© Springer International Publishing AG, part of Springer Nature 2018
M. Antona and C. Stephanidis (Eds.): UAHCI 2018, LNCS 10907, pp. 365–384, 2018.
https://doi.org/10.1007/978-3-319-92049-8_27

both blind children and sighted playing together came many years later [5]. In general, blind people have particular human-computer interaction needs, and the user interface should be suitable for them.

There are many efforts towards to develop accessible multimodal interfaces for visually impaired, especially in multimodal games [6, 7]. Despite this effort and in contrast to the visual interface evolutions of games and applications for sighted people, interfaces for people who are blind explore other ways to interact with the user. In general, technologies for people with visual disabilities combine different sources of perceptual inputs and outputs. The modes (sources of perceptual inputs and outputs) combined, typically audio and haptics [5, 8], provide multimodal interfaces that enable multimode channels for the combination of different user senses [2]. Although multimodal interfaces could help to improve the learning skills of people with visual disabilities, most of these technologies have been not completely validated; mostly, they remain in the prototype phase without being integrated into the people's everyday life [9].

In relation to the quality of applications, the No Child Left Behind (NCLB) Act defined that research in inclusive education must (a) utilize the scientific method, (b) be replicated in more than one set by more than one investigator, and, (c) result in findings that converge to a clear conclusion [10]. Thus, some studies in this area use Evidence-Based Practice [5, 11], which meets prescribed criteria related to the research design, quality, quantity, and effect size of supporting research [12, 13]. Thus, this method provides the measurement of the effectiveness of using technology.

Considering these multimodal interactions with interfaces for blind people, it is necessary to verify if the technologies thought for them are effective and how they impact users in cognitive dimensions [14]. Effective impact evaluation, which has been used as evidence-based in other domains for users with and without disabilities, should, therefore, be able to assess precisely the mechanisms by which people with visual disabilities are developing or enhancing cognitive skills [3]. According to Darin et al. (2015), there is a gap of studies proposing instruments and methods for evaluating the cognitive impact in the context of multimodal video games for cognitive enhancement of people who are blind. In general, the literature studies do not follow guidelines to support cognitive impact evaluation of multimodal interfaces for blind people.

In pursuing to shed some light concerning this, our work presents the state-of-the-art study on cognitive impact evaluation of multimodal interfaces for blind people with profound inability to distinguish light from dark, or the total inability to see [15]. This state-of-the-art study consists of a systematic review to analyze how studies evaluate the cognitive impact in this context. The systematic review is part of an ongoing work on the design of guidelines for evaluating the cognitive impact development and enhancement in multimodal interfaces for blind people. As related literatures, some works also propose guidelines for other concepts in the context of accessibility. As an example, the study [16] defines games accessibility guidelines helping developers to design their products with the interface and the parameters adapted to the needs of users with disabilities.

The remainder of this paper is organized as follows: Sect. 2 includes the Theoretical Background; Sect. 3 presents the methodology used in this work; Sect. 4 covers the results of the systematic review; Sect. 5 discusses the results; and, finally, Sect. 6 concludes the study.

2 Background

2.1 Cognitive Impact Evaluation

There are technological aspects to these systems which are investigated from the perspective of how they affect use [17]. Cognitive impact concerns the interaction between humans and systems. The field of human-computer interaction has pioneered in the formal study of the cognitive relationship between a person's activities, the artifact of the computer, and the task [18]. The technologies could enhance human cognitive capabilities.

Darin et al.'s (2015) literature mapping study shows the cognitive process analyze applications according to a four-dimensional classification (Interface, Interaction, Cognition, and Evaluation). The evaluation dimension includes two main aspects: usability and cognitive impact. This last one assures that an application can develop or enhance any cognitive skills for people with visual disabilities.

Still on this study, the cognition dimension comprises six skills: mental models, mental maps, spatial structures, Orientation and Mobility (O&M), problem-solving, and social collaboration. Such approach addresses the main cognitive skills developed and enhanced for impact evaluation purposes. These dimensions could provide directions to define tasks in an experiment to measure the cognitive impact as detection of some obstacles, a useful data for evaluating O&M [19].

The study also shows that most papers classified in main cognitive skills are about Mental Map and O&M. The O&M skill is a broad concept that is also related to wayfinding and navigation. According to Pissaloux and Velázquez (2018, p. 1), "Human mobility is one of the most important cognitive tasks. Indeed, independent and secure mobility in real physical space has a direct impact on the quality of life, on well-being, and on integration in the numeric society."

Darin et al. [19] define mobility in a four-dimensional problem: *walking*, *wayfinding* (or orientation), *space awareness* (or space knowledge) and *navigation*. According to this definition, walking is a low conscious cognitive task and involves displacement in the near space. It takes in account obstacle detection and localization. The wayfinding is a set of processes to know one's current position in space to reach one's target. The space awareness requires a high consciousness level. It includes forming mental maps, e.g., know the name of the street on a plan. The navigation, the highest level cognitive task, is a result of the implementation of all listed above functions while traveling.

2.2 Experiment in Software Engineering

The impact evaluation of a software is an experiment process and includes several steps: Scoping; Planning; Operation; Analysis and interpretation; Presentation and package [20]. This provides a high level of control, using a formal, rigorous and controlled investigation.

The main concepts involved in the experiment, shown in Table 1, are used to understand how the cognitive impact is evaluated and to conduct the designing of the guidelines. Figure 1 shows how these concepts are related to the experimental process.

Table 1. The main concepts of experimental design [20]

Concepts	Description
Measure	A mapping from the attribute of an entity to a measurement value
Instrumentation	The instruments for an experiment are of three types, namely objects, guidelines and measurement instruments
Dependent variables	The dependent variables are those we want to see the effect; the independent variables are those controlled and manipulated
Independent variables	The independent variables are those controlled and manipulated
Factors	The independent variables which the experiment changes to verify the effect. Treatment is one value of a factor

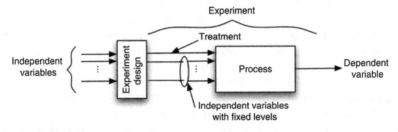

Fig. 1. Variable relationship in the experiment process (Source: [20]).

As an example of experiment process, we consider the measurements, instrumentation, and variables from the experiment conducted in [21]. In this study, the authors evaluate the navigational performance the of virtual environment called Audio-based Environment Simulator (AbES) that can be explored for the purposes of learning the layout of an unfamiliar, complex indoor environment. The dependent variable evaluated was the navigation performance (Orientation & Mobility, O&M).

Some information about the participants is controlled and works as independent variables such as etiology of blindness, age, gender, hand preference, and verbal memory (assessed by using the Wechsler Memory Scale). These variables are controlled and fixed to ensure the correct measurement. The factors in the experiment are the age of blindness onset and the interaction condition with AbES. The factors are randomly distributed into groups: early blind and late blind; and gamers, directed navigators, and control group. The measurements variables used are task success, navigation time, and shortest possible path score.

3 Methodology

The methodology consists in a Systematic Review [22], which aims to review the existing evidence concerning the impact evaluation of multimodal interfaces and also seeks to summarize the empirical evidence concerning the strengths and limitations of a specific evaluation method [22]. In contrast to an ad hoc literature review, the systematic review is a methodologically rigorous analysis and study of research results.

To achieve our goal, the main research question for this first part of the proposal was "How is the cognitive impact evaluated on multimodal interfaces for people who are blind?" For a better understanding, as a second goal question, we aim to learn the challenges regarding impact evaluation on this scenario.

The process of a systematic review includes three main phases: *planning the review*; *conducting the review* and *reporting the review* [22]. During all process of the systematic review, we used the tool StArt [23] and the software Microsoft Excel[1] as a support to create the protocol, apply the filters, select the papers and show the results. We organize all references on software Mendeley[2]. As the papers retrieved from PubMed Central are in MEDLINE format, we developed the tool Medline2bibtex[3]. It works as a parser to permit the list to be read by both StArt and Mendeley.

The next subsections describe the planning (the study selection criteria, the research sources selected) and the conducting phase (the search Process, the data extraction form fields and the studies quality evaluation). The entire process was stored in an excel worksheet available online[4].

3.1   Planning: Definition of the Protocol

In the planning phase, we define a review protocol that specifies the research question being addressed and the methods that will be used to perform the review [22]. Based on the goal of systematic review we define the search string as shown in the Fig. 2.

```
(  ((evaluat* OR assessment)
       AND (cognitive NEAR (impact or effectiveness)))
   AND (design OR development)
   AND (blind* OR "visually impaired" OR "visual disability")
   AND (multimodal OR haptic OR audio OR auditory OR vibrotactile)
   AND (interface OR "user interact*")   )
```

Fig. 2.   Search string

Study Selection Criteria. We define the search criteria as studies that present technology for people who are blind or visually impaired and has applied a cognitive impact evaluation. The inclusion and exclusion criteria are according to the goal of the systematic review. These requirements comply the general objective of this study, but also aim to have a broader view of the assessment in various technologies in the area.

---

[1] Microsoft Excel - https://products.office.com/pt-br/excel

[2] Mendeley - https://www.mendeley.com/

[3] Medline2Bibtex - https://github.com/lanabia/Medline2Bibtex

[4] https://www.dropbox.com/s/4wiiqnwqyd3cquw/Systematic%20Review%20v5.xlsm?dl=0

Table 2 presents the inclusion (*I*) and exclusion (*E*) selection criteria. To be accepted, a scientific paper must cover all inclusion criteria and none exclusion criterion.

Table 2. Inclusion and exclusion criteria

Code	Inclusion criteria
I.01	The study must be published after 1998 and written in English
I.02	The study has a technology for people who are blind or visually impaired according to the search criteria
I.03	The study evaluates the technology by using some approach that involves the user
I.04	The study evaluates the technology by using a method to evaluate the impact the cognitive impact
Code	Exclusion Criteria
E.01	Title and abstract out the search criteria (*I.02, I.03, I.04*)
E.02	Entire text out the search criteria (*I.02, I.03, I.04*)
E.03	The document is a book, a congress' abstract, an extended abstract, a poster, an oral communication, proceedings of a conference, a seminar, a research plenary, a dictionary or an encyclopedia

The *I.01* criterion defines the scientific articles must be in English, because it is the mandatory language for the main events and scientific journals in the search area. And they must be published between 1st January 1998 and 2nd August 2017. The year 1998 was a milestone due to the paper Lumbreras et Sánchez (1998) which works with 3D acoustic interfaces for blind children and is the last study known [24].

The technologies defined in the *I.02* criterion include mobile application, computer software, IoT systems, virtual environments or a video game with multimodal interfaces. Also, we accept technologies that are not specifically for people who are blind or visually impaired with the goal of expanding the results, but the studies present the technology focused on users with visual disabilities. We exclude from all technologies that uses Sensory Substitution Devices [19], which substitutes a sense. The device SSD (Sensory Substitution Devices), out of our scope, includes sensory replacement, haptics as sensory augmentation, bionic eyes, retinal visual prosthesis, cortical implants and others. This definition is important to plan the methodology proposed and to delimit the focus.

We define the studies type in the *E.03*. This criterion excludes all studies type different from primary studies that present technology for people who are blind and its evaluation. We accept articles, conference papers, short papers, and book chapters. This criterion includes documents that have the minimum information to understand the evaluation. We did not cover books because the information is dispersed inside them.

3.2   Conducting

In the conducting phase, firstly, we identify and select studies. To identify, we did a manual string research in five scientific bases: Scopus, Springer Link, PubMed, PubMed Central, and Web of Science. We chose the main research bases in the research area or the bases that index them [25]. Other bases were not included because they are indexed by the bases considered.

Search Process. The conducting phase starts with the initial search in the scientific bases proposed. The string was applied on the metadata of papers, which includes abstract, index terms, and bibliographic citation data (such as document title, publication title, etc.). It was retrieved 2136 papers. Figure 3 resumes the conducting phase process.

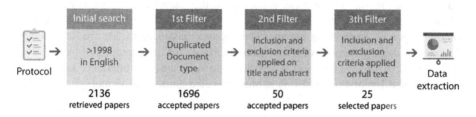

Fig. 3. Filters in the conducting phase

The first filter excluded papers duplicated and document types out the scope due their format (*E.03*). The second filter identifies which paper is in and out the scope by reading their titles and abstracts (*E.01*). A lot of papers were excluded in the first filter because the scientific base PubMed Central (PMC) brings a lot of medical papers focused on disease effectiveness and specific medical statements. Even though the area of this study is computer science, we decided to insert the PMC in the bases' list due to the nature of the subject.

Next, in the third filter, we evaluated each retrieved paper in its entirety (*E.02*). If necessary, besides the entire text, we search more about the technologies and processes described, as project and institutional websites, videos, newspaper articles and others.

Once we have chosen the select papers, we extract all data required (detailed in the protocol) to achieve the objective. The organization of the data generates data synthesis, which will be shown in the Sect. 5.1. It remains to be done the study quality assessment of each paper retrieved. Table 3 shows the quantity of papers selected in each filter per scientific bases. The main reason for withdrawing papers in the last filter was the evaluation performed is out the search and at most times related to the system performance, e.g., sensor performance evaluation.

Table 3. Quantity of papers accepted per filter

	Initial search	*Filter 1*	*Filter 2*	*Filter 3*	*Acceptance rate*
Scopus	217 (10,2%)	135	9	5 (20%)	2,3%
Springer	424 (19,85%)	235	16	9 (36%)	2,1%
WoS	1 (0,05%)	1	1	1 (4%)	100,0%
VIB	7 (0,33%)	7	2	1 (4%)	14,3%
PMC	1486 (69,57%)	1317	21	8 (32%)	0,5%
Manual	1 (0,05%)	1	1	1 (4%)	100,0%
Total	**2136**	**1696**	**50**	**25**	–

Data Extraction Form Fields. The data extraction was designed to answer the main and second questions and to understand the context in which each paper is inserted. We divide the data collected into three categories: *(i)* General, *(ii)* Research and *(iii)* Empirical. The general category comprises bibliographic information.

The research category comprises the attributes of the research and the technology present in the paper. In this category we appraise the scientific paper into two classifications. The first one fit the paper according to the research type [26], which can be validation research, evaluation research, solution research, philosophical research, opinion paper or experience papers. The second classification fits the technology presented in the key features of multimodal interfaces for the cognition of people who are blind [3]. This classification is divided into 4-dimension: Interface, Interaction, Cognition, and Evaluation; and it is applied to video games and virtual environments (Fig. 4).

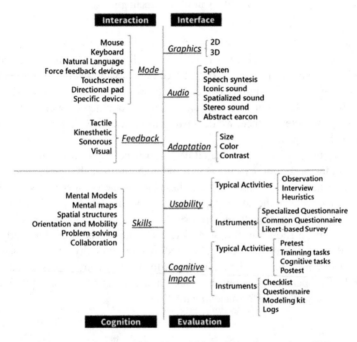

Fig. 4. Key features in multimodal interfaces (Image from [3])

For our purpose, we classify only in the interaction, interface and cognition dimensions; and we cover, in the classification, more than video games and virtual environments, since we also found these features present in the technologies selected. These features provide necessary insights for the practical understanding of the issues involved in their design and evaluation [3]. They are useful in our research for giving a comprehensive overview of technologies and evaluations regarding the multimodal interfaces. The research category still shows more information about the research, as other strategies used to evaluate.

The *empirical category* provides information specifically about how the empirical method evaluates the impact of the cognitive impact. The empirical method classification [27], which is retrieved in this category, classifies the empirical method in three types: Experiment, Survey and Case Study.

To conclude the achievements, all data pass by a manual analysis for acquiring qualitative and quantitative results. The Sect. 4 of this paper brings the compilation of data extraction.

Studies Quality Evaluation. Study quality assessment. The quality evaluation was based on [28]. Although the areas are different, we apply adaptation that resulted in the quality checklist of Table 4. The checklist assesses the studies and measures the weight of each study found in the final results. Each question subtracts or adds points that give a general score to the empirical method. This score was defined according to the importance of the requested data and they are all linked to the data extraction form fields.

Table 4. Quality assessment form

ID	Question
Q1	Was it possible to extract all data regarding the data the Key features in multimodal interfaces (Classification category from extraction form? (−0.1 pts per missing input; min value: −4.1 pts)
Q2	Is there a complete description of how the evaluation has been applied? (1.0 pt per complete input in Empirical category; max value: 8,0 pts)
Q3	Are the groups of participants in the experiment randomly assigned? (0.5 pts)
Q4	Is the description of the impact evaluation understandable? (0.5 pts)
Q5	How many steps does the experiment take (e.g., Pretest, Training Tasks, Main Tasks and Posttest)? (0.08 pts per step)
Q6	Does the article present different evaluation types of the proposal? (0.25 pts x number of evaluations types)
Q7	How many experiments does the paper present? (0.5 pts per experiment, if more than two experiments)
Q8	Is the goal of the evaluation cleared defined? (0.5 pts)
Q9	Is the hypothesis (null and alternative) explicitly described in the study? (1 pt)

4   First Results of the Systematic Review

The systematic review brought 25 papers that have 28 experiments because three papers have two experiments per paper [19, 29, 30]. Among these 25 papers, some of them do a cognitive impact evaluation in the same technology. Then the papers present 23 technologies for people who are blind or visually impaired as shown in Table 5. The next subsections explain all results obtained in each category of data.

Table 5. Technologies encountered

Technology	Technology description
AbES [21, 31, 32]	An environment to be explored for the purposes of learning the layout of an unfamiliar and complex indoor environment
aMFS [29]	Audible Mobility Feedback System
ATM machine [33]	ATM usage fees are the fees that many banks and interbank networks charge for the use of their automated teller machines (ATMs)
Audio Haptic Maze (AHM) [34]	AHM allows a school-age blind learner to be able to navigate through a series of mazes from a first-person perspective.
AudioBattleShip [5]	A sound-based interactive and collaborative environment for blind children. This system is a similar version of the traditional battleship game for sighted people but including both a graphical interface for sighted users and an audio-based interface for blind people
AudioGene [35]	A game that uses mobile and audio-based technology to assist the interaction between blind and sighted children and to learn genetic concepts
AudioLink [36]	An interactive audio-based virtual environment for children with visual disabilities to support their learning of science
AudioMath [37]	An interactive virtual environment based on audio to develop and use short-term memory, and to assist mathematics learning of children
AudioNature [38]	An audio-based virtual simulator for science learning implemented in a mobile device (PocketPC) platform
Audiopolis [8, 39, 40]	A video game designed for developing orientation and mobility
AudioStoryTeller [11]	A tool for PocketPCto support the development of reading and writing skills in learners with visual disabilities (LWVD) through storytelling, providing diverse evaluation tools to measure those skills
AudioTransantiago [41]	A handheld application that allows users to plan trips and provide contextual information during the journey through the use of synthesized voices
BlindAid [42]	The system allows the user to explore a virtual environment
Building Navigator [43]	A digital-map software with synthetic speech installed on a cell phone or PDA
EyeCane [44]	A hand-held device which instantaneously transforms distance information via sound and vibration
Métro	A software solution for blind users that represents a subway system
Métro Mobile (mBN)	A software solution for blind users that represents a subway system in a mobile version
Mobile devices	Mobile devices in general
R-MAP	Reconfigured Mobile Android Phone is a fully integrated, stand-alone system, that has an easy-to-use interface to reconfigure an Android mobile phone

(continued)

Table 5. (*continued*)

Technology	Technology description
TactiPad	An academic prototype of a tangible refreshable multimodal interface that has an interface similar to a Braille matrix
Tower defense	A video game that allows users who are blind to gradually build up a mental model based on references between different points on a Cartesian plane, in a way that is both didactic and entertaining
UnrealEd	A 3D virtual environment
vMFS	A vibrotactile mobility feedback system

General Data. Among all papers, 14 are conference papers [5, 8, 11, 30, 33, 34, 36, 38–40, 45–48], 1 paper [19] is a book chapter and the others (10 papers) are from scientific journals. Figure 5 shows the papers selected regarding the timeline that started in 2004 and has peaked in 2011 and 2014. The affiliation most present is University of Chile with 15 papers.

Research Data. The papers selected present two types of research [26]: one paper is validation research [19], and 24 papers are evaluation research. The only validation research paper is defined in this way due to the technology presented is novel and have not yet been implemented in practice.

The interfaces, interactions and cognition skills of technologies presented in the papers are classified according to their key features of multimodal interfaces [3]. These characteristics are important to understand which type of interfaces are assessed and how the impact is evaluated on them. Figure 6 shows that the most notable mode of interaction is the keyboard and the least used is the mouse. The keyboard does not generate more complexity and expenses as the Novint Falcon device, used in [34]. The Novint Falcon is one of the Force Feedback Device that promotes a Tactile and Kinesthetic Feedback. Mouse and Natural language are less used. The mouse is replaced by buttons or other specific devices for better interaction as shown in [33]. The most common Feedback is the Sonorous and the main Audio Interface used is the Iconic Sound, which are sounds associated with each available object and action in the environment [8].

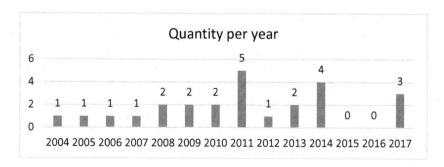

Fig. 5. Timeline papers

Many papers apply another approach to evaluate other criteria not covered in the cognitive evaluation. Concerning other strategies used to evaluate the interface, 14 papers [5, 11, 29, 30, 34–39, 41, 42, 47, 48] applied a usability evaluation together with cognitive evaluation. Other strategies used were: evaluation of a tactile perception [19, 46], system performance [38] that tested the hardware used, evaluation based on HCI heuristics [33], recognition of pattern [19], obstacle awareness goal [19], homing and obstacle avoidance [19] and iconic evaluation [39]. Eight papers do not apply other strategy to evaluate the system or user interaction.

Usability evaluation is the most used assessment besides cognition impact evaluation. The usability evaluation is mainly used to obtain information about the user's acceptance of the software and the match between his or her mental model and the representation included in the software [36].

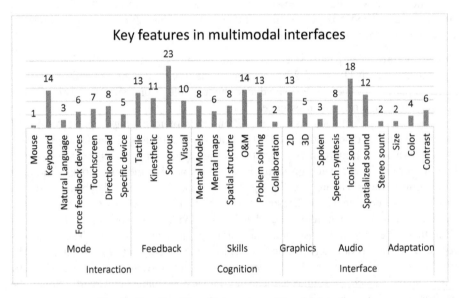

Fig. 6. Results of key features in multimodal interfaces

Empirical Data. Concerning the 28 empirical strategies that evaluate the cognitive impact, most papers applied experiments and only one applied a case study [38] due to the small number of participants. As our focus is the experiments, we treat in both types only the experiment criteria. Due to this fact, we call all empirical methods as experiments. The data that came from the Empirical category gave a substantial part of the comprehension of this research. Figure 7 presents all data extracted from each experiment. It is important to note that not all the papers presented the data sought. These faults were included in the quality criteria and then considered in the discussions and conclusions. The empirical data is counted according to the number of experiments (28 experiments), and not papers.

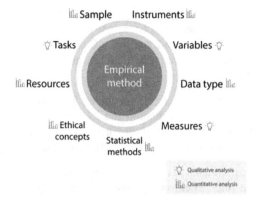

Fig. 7. Data extracted in Empirical category

Instruments. The instruments are means for data collection in the cognitive impact evaluation with the objective of identifying some user ability controlled on the Experiment (as an independent variable), e.g., the mathematics knowledge test in [37] or is used to guide the evaluation process, e.g., observation guideline to assess O&M skills in [39]. Among them, there are 15 checklists [5, 8, 11, 32, 34, 37, 39–41, 45, 46] which include guidelines and specific tests, 11 questionnaires [11, 29, 32, 35, 36, 38, 42, 43, 46, 47], 7 interviews [8, 29, 33, 39, 41, 42], 6 modeling kits [5, 19, 30, 32, 37, 42] and 9 logs [5, 21, 29–33, 36, 42, 48] which include, in addition to the system log, the video and audio logs. Many studies produce their instruments (7 experiments), others work with instruments found in scientific literature.

Statistical Methods. Figure 8 shows the statistical methods used in the experiment data analysis. Neither we take account of simple statistical methods as averages and gain percent, that is the only method used by 11 experiments [19, 30–33, 35, 37, 38, 42].

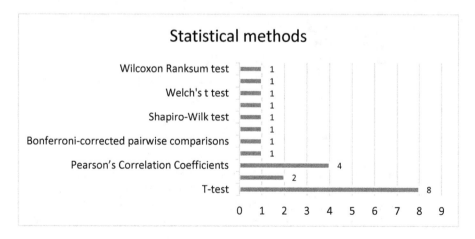

Fig. 8. Statistical methods

Three experiments [36, 39, 45] do not specify the statistical method used, neither in the references. T-test, which uses statistical concepts to reject or not a null hypothesis is the most used, followed by ANOVA and Pearson's Correlation Coefficients. These two methods are used to analyze the variation between groups. ANOVA procedure was applied in one, two and three-way.

Resources. Concerning the resources, 7 experiments [11, 30, 36–38, 41] give information about the time spent in the evaluation and 2 experiments in the same paper [29] specify the human resource. The mean of the time among these is 3.4 months and the longest time spent is 6 months. None of them talk about financial resources.

Ethical Concepts. 5 experiments [21, 29, 43, 44] mentioned signing consents. One of them also applies stop rules to enforcing ethical concept [21] and present the ethics council that it approved.

Sample. From the number of users to the onset age of blindness, there are many sample combinations in the selected experiments. The sample choice could be based on level of experience required to do the task, age or level of blindness. Some characteristic controlled in the sample are related to the disabilities, as the onset of blindness, the etiology of a visual impairment or the presence of another disability. The quantity of users varies as shown in Fig. 9. Most of the experiments (75%) are applied to 3 to 12 users. About the range of age, the most of experiments (9 experiments) are applied in teenagers (10 to 15 years old). The range and ages are shown in Fig. 10.

The gender distribution in samples is equilibrated in most cases, but we not count the 11 experiments which do not describe this information. The mean of gender proportion is 50% for women and men, with 2% of variance.

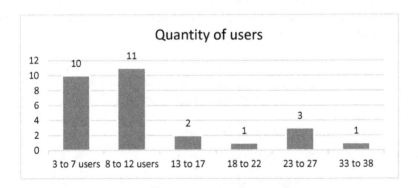

Fig. 9. Quantity of users in the samples

The distribution between the blindness level is varied. There are experiments where the sample is all formed by people who are blind [49] and there are samples formed only by people who are blindfolded, as the experiments in [19]. Figure 10 shows the user age range. Figure 11 shows the blindness level distribution between the samples.

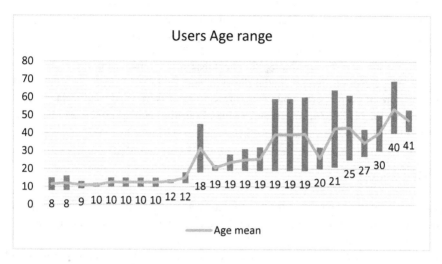

Fig. 10. Users age range per experiment

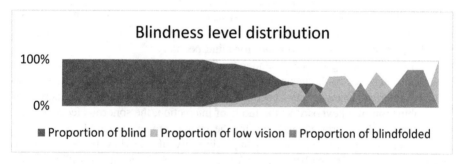

Fig. 11. Blindness level distribution

Tasks. The tasks explored in the experiments are related to the technology assessed. The tasks to assess the development of O&M skills are based on virtual and real environments [30, 34]. Some of them use modeling kits to represent the virtual environment in the real world and to analyze the space awareness of each participant and the cognition improvement [30]. Another example of cognitive task is to read of a text with the guidance of virtual sounds. Some works have used levels of complexity in the tasks to quantify the cognition impact, for example, the work [45] estimates the task performance in 5 levels.

Variables. The most current independent variables, which are controlled in the experiment, are related to the sample choice, the characteristics defined as etiology of blindness, age, blindness level and gender [41]. The dependent variables, in which we want to see the effect, are related to the measures and the impact. The factor, which is a type of variable controlled is modified in the experiment to see the cognitive effect. For example, the experiment proposed in [8] uses as factor different outputs of the multimodal interface (audio group, haptic group, and haptic-audio groups).

Measures. The measure to evaluate the cognitive impact focuses on the performance to compare before and after the use of the technology assessed, e.g., [37], or between two groups with and without the technology, e.g. [21]. The measures are strongly related to the instruments used. For example, the checklists of [34] assess the task using scores for sensory perception, tempo-spatial development, and O&M skills. In some works, each measure has a property scale or options, as the Likert scale used in [41]. Eleven experiments [8, 11, 30, 34, 37–40, 42, 48] apply instruments as pretest and posttest to measure the impact.

5 Discussion

As shown in the previous section there is consistent research that evaluates the cognition impact since 2004, showing the importance of this type of study on technologies for blind people. Among all papers retrieved from initial search in the systematic review, we could see in general, that the papers do not evaluate the cognition impact. The preference of evaluation lies to the system, be it hardware or software. The same result is seen in papers that are retrieved in the third filter, one of the most used strategies to evaluate the technologies is the system evaluation besides cognitive evaluation. Despite this finding, the leading role of these technologies is often to help a user's cognitive activity. Thus, assessing if the cognitive purpose was achieved is an important part of constructing software for blind people.

The research data give us an understanding of how the interaction works on multimodal interfaces of the technologies for blind people. The interaction, cognition skills, and interface characteristics encountered model the planning of the experiment. The combination of a keyboard as the mode of interaction, the sonorous feedback and iconic sound to the interface stands out for the interactions encountered.

In the empirical data, we found a huge diversity of experiments. Although we understand these differences between the experiments, we come across differences in the process of planning and presenting the experiment and data acquired. Instruments, tasks, variables, and measures are strongly related to the technology assessed and the cognitive purpose. Almost no work presented the variables explicitly according to the classification of dependent variables, independent variables, and factors. To understand the experiments, we define these three kinds of variables in each experiment. However, this adds a cost to fully understand the experiment.

From the number of users to the onset age of blindness, there are many sample combinations in the selected experiments. One point that stands out in the selection of the sample is the number of blind users who perform the experiments and how these data are computed. There is, for example, one work that uses the only blindfolded sample, which refocus the conclusion of the experiment.

Statistical power is an inherent part of empirical studies that ensure the results found and to the study conclusions [50]. However, 11 experiments analyzed only the percentage of the gain or the average. Wohlin et al. [20] mention that one of the advantages of an experiment is the ability to perform statistical analysis using hypothesis testing methods and opportunities for replication.

Almost no experiment dealt with the resources and ethical concepts. Although there is information about the resources in some papers, in general, this information is not clear in the text and is often incomplete. The missing information makes difficult to repeat the experiment. The ethical concepts also are not well covered in the papers; even it is an essential step to produce an experiment with people who have disabilities [20].

6 Conclusion

The goal of a state-of-the-art is to review the existing evidence concerning the impact evaluation of multimodal interfaces and also seeks to summarize the empirical evidence concerning the strengths and limitations of a specific evaluation method [22]. With this work, we expected to have created a bibliographic review on the cognitive impact evaluation based on the steps of the systematic review approach. Our scope was bounded by multimodal interfaces for people who are blind (in this paper a synonym of visually impaired).

The technologies for people who are blind have many needs due to the target audience and special characteristics with multimodal interfaces, moreover, lots of applications for blind people aims to improve cognitive skills, such as enhancement in O&M, wayfinding, and navigation skills, and thus supporting the user in daily lives. As so, it is important to point out that the use of evidence-based is essential to measure the real impact of the technologies.

After compiling the data from the systematic review and analyzing theoretical foundations, we conclude that there is a need to better plan and present data from experiments on technologies for blind people. With this, we guarantee the quality of the experiment itself and the interaction of the technology with respect to the cognitive objective. Faced with this nego, we propose as future work to better explore the preliminary results found to improve the data analysis using Grounded Theory and create a set of guidelines that appropriately guide experiments to evaluate tools for blind people. These guidelines will provide a way to evaluate the cognitive impact to development and enhancement in blind people or visually impaired, considering the main aspects of multimodal interfaces.

Acknowledgments. This research is funded by Chilean FONDECYT #1150898; Basal Funds for Centers of Excellence, Project FB0003 - CONICYT. We would like to thank FUNCAP for sponsoring a master scholarship (MDCC/DC/UFC) for the author Lana Mesquita.

References

1. Bamac, B., Aydin, M., Ozbek, A.: Physical fitness levels of blind and visually impaired goalball team players. Isokinet. Exerc. Sci. **12**, 247–252 (2004)
2. Sánchez, J., Darin, T., Andrade, R., Viana, W., Gensel, J.: Multimodal interfaces for improving the intellect of the blind. In: XX Congresso de Informática Educativa – TISE, vol. 1, pp. 404–413 (2015)
3. Darin, T., Andrade, R., Sánchez, J.: Dimensions to analyze the design of multimodal videogames for the cognition of people who are blind dimensions (2015)

4. Hinebaugh, J.P.: A Board Game Education. Rowman & Littlefield Education, Lanham (2009)
5. Sánchez, J., Baloian, N., Hassler, T.: Blind to sighted children interaction through collaborative environments. In: de Vreede, G.-J., Guerrero, L.A., Marín Raventós, G. (eds.) CRIWG 2004. LNCS, vol. 3198, pp. 192–205. Springer, Heidelberg (2004). https://doi.org/10.1007/978-3-540-30112-7_16
6. Buaud, A., Svensson, H., Archambault, D., Burger, D.: Multimedia games for visually impaired children. In: Miesenberger, K., Klaus, J., Zagler, W. (eds.) ICCHP 2002. LNCS, vol. 2398, pp. 173–180. Springer, Heidelberg (2002). https://doi.org/10.1007/3-540-45491-8_38
7. Grammenos, D., Savidis, A., Georgalis, Y., Stephanidis, C.: Access invaders: developing a universally accessible action game. In: Miesenberger, K., Klaus, J., Zagler, W.L., Karshmer, A.I. (eds.) ICCHP 2006. LNCS, vol. 4061, pp. 388–395. Springer, Heidelberg (2006). https://doi.org/10.1007/11788713_58
8. Sánchez, J., De Borba Campos, M., Espinoza, M., Merabet, L.B.: Audio haptic videogaming for developing wayfinding skills in learners who are blind (2014)
9. Goria, M., Cappaglia, G., Tonellia, A., Baud-Bovyb, G., Finocchietti, S.: Devices for visually impaired people: high technological devices with low user acceptance and no adaptability for children. Neurosci. Biobehav. Rev. 69, 79–88 (2016)
10. Alicyn Ferrell, K.A.: Evidence-based practices for students with visual disabilities. Commun. Disord. Q. 28, 42–48 (2006)
11. Sánchez, J., Galáz, I.: AudioStoryTeller: enforcing blind children reading skills. In: Stephanidis, C. (ed.) UAHCI 2007. LNCS, vol. 4556, pp. 786–795. Springer, Heidelberg (2007). https://doi.org/10.1007/978-3-540-73283-9_85
12. Weber, A.: Credentialing in assistive technology. Technol. Disabil. 9, 59–63 (1998)
13. Dalton, E.M.: Assistive technology standards and evidence-based practice: early practice and current needs, 10 June 2015
14. Dumas, B., Lalanne, D., Oviatt, S.: Multimodal interfaces: a survey of principles, models and frameworks. In: Lalanne, D., Kohlas, J. (eds.) Human Machine Interaction. LNCS, vol. 5440, pp. 3–26. Springer, Heidelberg (2009). https://doi.org/10.1007/978-3-642-00437-7_1
15. World Health Organization: The prevention of blindness. Report of a WHO Study Group. Technical report series, no. 518, pp. 1–18 (1973)
16. Ossmann, R., Miesenberger, K.: Guidelines for the development of accessible computer games. In: Miesenberger, K., Klaus, J., Zagler, W.L., Karshmer, A.I. (eds.) ICCHP 2006. LNCS, vol. 4061, pp. 403–406. Springer, Heidelberg (2006). https://doi.org/10.1007/11788713_60
17. Ritter, F.E., Baxter, G.D., Churchill, E.F.: Foundations for Designing User-Centered Systems. Springer, London (2014). https://doi.org/10.1007/978-1-4471-5134-0
18. Norman, D.A., Donald, A., Carroll, M.: Cognitive artifacts. Des. Interact. Psychol. Hum.-Comput. Interface 1, 17–38 (1991). Cambridge
19. Pissaloux, E., Velázquez, R.: Model of cognitive mobility for visually impaired and its experimental validation. In: Pissaloux, E., Velázquez, R. (eds.) Mobility of Visually Impaired People. LNCS, pp. 311–352. Springer, Cham (2018). https://doi.org/10.1007/978-3-319-54446-5_11
20. Wohlin, C., Runeson, P., Höst, M., Ohlsson, M.C., Regnell, B., Wesslén, A., Anders, W.: Experimentation in Software Engineering. Kluwer Academic Publishers, Norwell (2000)
21. Connors, E., Chrastil, E., Sánchez, J., Merabet, L.: Virtual environments for the transfer of navigation skills in the blind: a comparison of directed instruction vs. video game based learning approaches. Front. Hum. Neurosci. 8, 223 (2014)

22. Kitchenham, B., Charters, S.: Guidelines for performing systematic literature reviews in software engineering version 2.3. Engineering **45**, 1051 (2007)
23. StArt. http://lapes.dc.ufscar.br/tools/start_tool (2016)
24. Lumbreras, M., Sánchez, J.: 3D aural interactive hyperstories for blind children. Virtual Real. 119–128 (1998)
25. Harzing, A.-W., Alakangas, S.: Google scholar, scopus and the web of science: a longitudinal and cross-disciplinary comparison. Scientometrics **106**, 787–804 (2016)
26. Petersen, K., Feldt, R., Mujtaba, S., Mattsson, M.: Systematic mapping studies in software engineering. In: 12th International Conference on Evaluation and Assessment in Software Engineering, pp. 1–10 (2008)
27. Ampatzoglou, A., Stamelos, I.: Software engineering research for computer games: a systematic review. Inf. Softw. Technol. **52**, 888–901 (2010)
28. de Sousa Santos, I., de Castro Andrade, R.M., Rocha, L.S., Matalonga, S., de Oliveira, K.M., Travassos, G.H.: Test case design for context-aware applications: are we there yet? Inf. Softw. Technol. **88**, 1–16 (2017)
29. Adebiyi, A., Sorrentino, P., Bohlool, S., Zhang, C., Arditti, M., Goodrich, G., Weiland, J.D.: Assessment of feedback modalities for wearable visual aids in blind mobility, 1–17 (2017)
30. Sánchez, J., Maureira, E.: Subway mobility assistance tools for blind users. In: Stephanidis, C., Pieper, M. (eds.) UI4ALL 2006. LNCS, vol. 4397, pp. 386–404. Springer, Heidelberg (2007). https://doi.org/10.1007/978-3-540-71025-7_25
31. Connors, E.C., Yazzolino, L.A., Sánchez, J., Merabet, L.B.: Development of an audio-based virtual gaming environment to assist with navigation skills in the blind, 1–7 (2013)
32. Sánchez, J., Sáenz, M.: Enhancing navigation skills through audio gaming (2014)
33. Shafiq, M., Choi, J.-G., Iqbal, M., Faheem, M., Ahmad, M., Ashraf, I., Irshad, A.: Skill specific spoken dialogues based personalized ATM design to maximize effective interaction for visually impaired persona. In: Marcus, A. (ed.) DUXU 2014. LNCS, vol. 8520, pp. 446–457. Springer, Cham (2014). https://doi.org/10.1007/978-3-319-07638-6_43
34. Sánchez, J., Espinoza, M.M., Sanchez, J., Espinoza, M.M.: Audio haptic videogaming for navigation skills in learners who are blind. In: ASSETS 11: Proceedings of the 13th International ACM SIGACCESS Conference on Computers and Accessibility, pp. 227–228. Association for Computing Machinery, New York (2011)
35. Sánchez, J., Aguayo, F.: *AudioGene*: mobile learning genetics through audio by blind learners. In: Kendall, M., Samways, B. (eds.) Learning to Live in the Knowledge Society. ITIFIP, vol. 281, pp. 79–86. Springer, Boston, MA (2008). https://doi.org/10.1007/978-0-387-09729-9_10
36. Sánchez, J., Elías, M.: Science learning in blind children through audio-based games. In: Redondo, M., Bravo, C., Ortega, M. (eds.) Engineering the User Interface. Springer, London (2008). https://doi.org/10.1007/978-1-84800-136-7_7
37. Sánchez, J., Flores, H., Sánchez, J.: AudioMath: blind children learning mathematics through audio. Int. J. Disabil. Hum. Dev. **4**, 311–316 (2005)
38. Sánchez, J., Flores, H., Sáenz, M.: Mobile science learning for the blind (2008)
39. Sánchez, J., Mascaró, J.: Audiopolis, navigation through a virtual city using audio and haptic interfaces for people who are blind. In: Stephanidis, C. (ed.) UAHCI 2011. LNCS, vol. 6766, pp. 362–371. Springer, Heidelberg (2011). https://doi.org/10.1007/978-3-642-21663-3_39
40. Sánchez, J., Espinoza, M., De, B., Merabet, L.: Enhancing orientation and mobility skills in learners who are blind through video gaming. In: Conference on Creativity & Cognition, 2013, pp. 353–356 (2013)
41. Sánchez, J., Oyarzún, C.: Mobile audio assistance in bus transportation for the blind (2008)
42. Lahav, O., Schloerb, D., Kumar, S., Srinivasan, M.: A virtual environment for people who are blind – a usability study. J. Assist. Technol. **6**, 38–52 (2012)

43. Kalia, A., Legge, G., Roy, R., Ogale, A.: Assessment of indoor route-finding technology for people with visual impairment. J. Vis. Impair. Blind. **104**, 135–147 (2010)
44. Buchs, G., Simon, N., Maidenbaum, S., Amedi, A.: Waist-up protection for blind individuals using the EyeCane as a primary and secondary mobility aid. Restor. Neurol. Neurosci. **35**, 225–235 (2017)
45. Villane, J., Sánchez, J.: 3D virtual environments for the rehabilitation of the blind. In: Stephanidis, C. (ed.) UAHCI 2009. LNCS, vol. 5616, pp. 246–255. Springer, Heidelberg (2009). https://doi.org/10.1007/978-3-642-02713-0_26
46. Guerreiro, T., Oliveira, J., Benedito, J., Nicolau, H., Jorge, J., Gonçalves, D.: Blind people and mobile keypads: accounting for individual differences. In: Campos, P., Graham, N., Jorge, J., Nunes, N., Palanque, P., Winckler, M. (eds.) INTERACT 2011. LNCS, vol. 6946, pp. 65–82. Springer, Heidelberg (2011). https://doi.org/10.1007/978-3-642-23774-4_8
47. Hossain, G., Shaik, A.S., Yeasin, M.: Cognitive load and usability analysis of R-MAP for the people who are blind or visual impaired (2011)
48. Espinoza, M., Sánchez, J., de Borba Campos, M.: Videogaming interaction for mental model construction in learners who are blind. In: Stephanidis, C., Antona, M. (eds.) UAHCI 2014. LNCS, vol. 8514, pp. 525–536. Springer, Cham (2014). https://doi.org/10.1007/978-3-319-07440-5_48
49. Lahav, O., Mioduser, D., Lahav, O.: Blind persons' acquisition of spatial cognitive mapping and orientation skills supported by virtual environment. Int. J. Disabil. Hum. Dev. **4**, 231–238 (2005)
50. Dybå, T., Kampenes, V.B., Sjøberg, D.I.K.: A systematic review of statistical power in software engineering experiments. Inf. Softw. Technol. **48**, 745–755 (2006)

Keyboard and Screen Reader Accessibility in Complex Interactive Science Simulations: Design Challenges and Elegant Solutions

Emily B. Moore[✉], Taliesin L. Smith, and Jesse Greenberg

University of Colorado Boulder, Boulder, USA
{emily.moore,taliesin.smith,jesse.greenberg}@colorado.edu

Abstract. Interactive science simulations are commonly used educational tools that, unfortunately, present many challenges for robust accessibility. The PhET Interactive Simulations project creates a suite of widely used HTML5 interactive science simulations and has been working to advance the accessibility of these simulations for users of alternative input devices (including keyboards) and screen reader software. To provide a highly interactive experience for students, science simulations are often designed to encourage interaction with real-world or otherwise physical objects, resulting in user interface elements being implemented in ways either unrecognizable as native HTML elements, or that require fully custom implementation and interactions. Here, we highlight three examples of simulation design scenarios that presented challenges for keyboard and screen reader access. For each scenario, we describe our initial approach, challenges encountered, and what we have found to be the most elegant solution to address these challenges to date. By sharing our approaches to design and implementation, we aim to contribute to the general knowledge base of effective strategies to support the advancement of accessibility for all educational interactives.

Keywords: Web accessibility · Usability · Inclusive design
Keyboard navigation · Alternative input · Text description
Interactive science simulation

1 Introduction

Interactive simulations are effective tools used to support teaching and learning of science content around the world (e.g., [1]). Unfortunately, the vast majority of interactive simulations are not accessible to many students. A reliance on highly visual representations and the use of mouse, trackpad, or touch interfaces limits the accessibility of these learning resources for students with certain sensory, mobility, or cognitive impairments. While there has been progress in the development of standards and guidelines to support the accessibility of interactive scientific graphics [2], and digital games [3], many of these resources do not address the specific design and implementation challenges encountered within the context of creating accessible complex interactives for learning [4, 5].

© Springer International Publishing AG, part of Springer Nature 2018
M. Antona and C. Stephanidis (Eds.): UAHCI 2018, LNCS 10907, pp. 385–400, 2018.
https://doi.org/10.1007/978-3-319-92049-8_28

The PhET Interactive Simulations project [6] at the University of Colorado Boulder, a resource that includes more than 50 popular free HTML5 science and mathematics simulations, has been designing and implementing multiple new accessibility features into simulations to support access for students with disabilities [7]. These accessibility features include auditory description (verbalized text), sonification (non-speech sound), and alternative input. PhET simulations are complex from an accessibility perspective for multiple reasons and require innovative approaches to provide the most inclusive outcome. Here, we focus on three design challenges that arise when creating accessible complex interactive science simulations, and some of the more elegant solutions we have found to address these challenges. All solutions can simultaneously support visual and non-visual access, consistent with a goal of inclusion and the practical need to support collaborative learning opportunities for students with diverse needs.

2   PhET Interactive Simulations

PhET simulations (sims) are designed to be playful, intuitive to use without instructions, and flexible for use in many different teaching contexts (lecture, group activities, online, etc.). The sims are designed to provide strong visual cues to support effective use. Interactive objects, layout, and colors are chosen to create an inviting environment for students of all ages. The sims do not contain explicit instructions, which allows for tremendous flexibility of use – each sim can be used to meet a range of learning goals across different grade levels and topics. Each sim's design supports initial exploration, which results in pedagogically relevant changes and encourages further investigation.

As an example, we introduce the sim *Balloons and Static Electricity* (Fig. 1). This sim is used from elementary school through introductory college level to introduce the topic of static electricity, charge transfer, attraction, repulsion, and induced charge. The

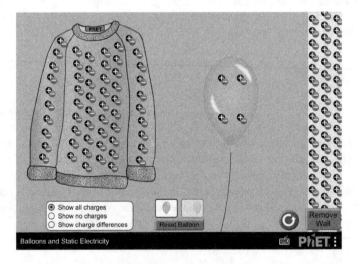

Fig. 1. Screenshot of the PhET simulation *Balloons and Static Electricity*. Reproduced with permission from the PhET Interactive Simulations project (Color figure online).

sim opens with a Yellow Balloon in the center of the screen, a Sweater to the left and a Wall on the right. On each object are pairs of positive charges (red circles with "+" on them) and negative charges (blue circles with "−" on them). Near the bottom of the screen, there are options to change the view (to show all charges, show no charges, or show only the charge differences), to add/remove a second (green) Balloon, to reset the Balloon to its starting location, to remove/return the Wall, and to reset the entire sim screen.

The Balloon can be moved around the sim screen in all directions, including rubbing on the Sweater (resulting in a transfer of negative charges from the Sweater to the Balloon), and rubbing against the Wall (resulting in no transfer of charges). When the Balloon is negatively charged, releasing the Balloon will result in it being attracted to the Sweater or the Wall, depending on the amount of charge and its proximity to these other objects – the more negatively charged the Balloon is and the closer to an object, the faster it moves.

The *Balloons and Static Electricity* sim is one example of many PhET sims available. Each PhET sim is unique and tailored to encourage productive exploration of a specific science or mathematics topic. The result is a suite of simulations that support learning [8, 9], utilizing many different interactive objects (balloons, sweaters, and walls, as well as arms, planets, wire, atoms and more), through many different interactions.

2.1 PhET Simulation Architecture

Each sim's graphical representations are organized and rendered using the custom scene graph, Scenery. With Scenery, rendering of a PhET sim is done graphically with multiple renderers, including SVG, Canvas, and WebGL. Use of a scene graph provides a logical data structure, but does not contain – or provide a straightforward way to associate – the semantic structure typical of HTML. Graphics created with a single renderer (e.g., SVG), such as chemical diagrams and data charts, have been made accessible through the addition of descriptions and simple hierarchical navigation [10, 11]. However, in the case of PhET sims, where multiple graphics renderers are used and frequent interaction is paramount, the challenge of adding accessible descriptions and interactivity is more complex. To address this challenge, we advanced Scenery to now generate a parallel document object model (PDOM) alongside the graphical representations [12]. The result is a robust accessible – and dynamic – document which contains the semantically rich interactive content (e.g., regions, headings, labels, help text, object descriptions, and alerts) and interfaces with common assistive devices with appropriate use of HTML and WAI-ARIA [13–15]. The PDOM solution avoids current shortcomings of accessibility solutions specific to each graphics renderer and provides a wide range of native interactions. Significant use of native interactions allows us to limit the use of custom approaches that require the use of the ARIA application role which can result in unintuitive interactions – and present a potential barrier to access – for users.

2.2   Accessibility Challenge

The inclusive design of navigation and interaction capabilities for alternative input (such as keyboard input) for highly interactive and highly dynamic sims involves addressing visual and non-visual accessibility needs simultaneously. Alternative input may be used to directly interface with a sim or may be used to control software – such as screen reader software, that is providing access. Screen reader software is used to navigate applications, interact with interactive elements, and read aloud text content – including onscreen text presented visually, as well as content provided non-visually, e.g., alternative text, HTML element labels, and help text.

Complex interactive simulations present many challenges for alternative input capabilities and for screen reader compatibility. Elegant solutions that simultaneously support visual and non-visual access within complex interactives can be challenging to design and implement. In this work we present three design challenges and the solutions we arrived at. These solutions leverage native HTML enhanced with WAI-ARIA to design and implement complex accessibility features for interactive graphics objects.

2.3   PhET's Design Process

The PhET project conducts all design and development work through an iterative process involving user interviews (e.g., [5, 16]). In the development of the accessibility features presented in this work, we refined our approaches through user interviews with visually impaired users, and consultation with expert screen reader users. User interviews are conducted in a think-aloud style, where an accessible sim is provided to a user not familiar with a particular sim and they are prompted to think-aloud while using the sim. The interviewer may ask clarifying questions as the user engages with the sim, but the primary goal of the interviewer is to observe and listen. Once the user is done exploring the sim – the bulk of the interview time – the interviewer will ask further clarifying questions and may ask the user to attempt specific tasks with the sim to gain further insight into the design of particularly challenging interactions or representations. When consulting with screen reader experts, we gain insight from users knowledgeable about PhET sims and typical interactions, which provides an opportunity to ensure that the navigation and description choices we make are perceived as consistent across sims and screen reader software.

3   Design Challenges and Solutions

This work presents design challenges we have encountered and our implemented solutions – focusing on scenarios that highlight design to support visual and non-visual access. For each challenge we summarize the specific goals of a desired interaction sequence, the challenges we sought to address, and our implemented solution. All challenges and solutions take into consideration interviews with users with and without visual impairments, discussions with expert screen reader users, as well as the general expertise of PhET's design team and pedagogical expertise of PhET's science content and pedagogy experts. The result is that some design decisions and aspects of the resulting solutions stem from unique pedagogical needs of the sims and may not be a direct result from interpreted or stated user needs or preferences from interviews.

3.1 Custom Slider Features to Support Content Learning

The sim *Resistance in a Wire* (Fig. 2) is used in high school and introductory college physics courses to teach the relationship between the resistance of a wire and its resistivity, length, and area. The sim consists of an equation ($R = \rho L/A$) and a piece of a wire, with three sliders with various input ranges to adjust the values of resistivity (ρ), length (L), and area (A). Incrementing or decrementing the slider range values results in a change to the size of the variables in the equation and parameters of the piece of wire. For example, increasing the length slider value results in an increase in size of the variable L in the equation and a corresponding increase in size of the variable R, while simultaneously increasing the length of the piece of wire. Decrementing the resistivity slider value results in a decrease in the size of the variables ρ and R in the equation, and decreasing the number of small black dots in the piece of wire, which represent impurities.

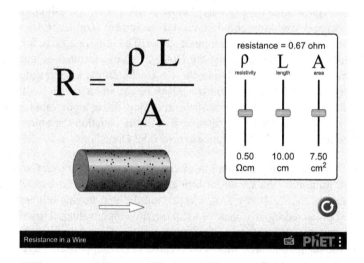

Fig. 2. Screenshot of the PhET sim *Resistance in a Wire*. Reproduced with permission from the PhET Interactive Simulations project.

The desired interaction sequence with this sim is for students to initially explore by changing the sliders' input values with a qualitative focus, changing the input values to extremes (e.g., the maximum, minimum, and median values) and observing how the variables and the piece of wire change. Then, as students continue manipulating the sliders, to compare changes across the mathematical and physical representations, building connections between the mathematical equation and a real-world example (the physical piece of wire). Another useful interaction sequence would be for students to make quantitative comparisons, using the numerical slider values to set up comparisons convenient for simple mental calculations – typically doubling or halving values. For example, comparing two scenarios with the same resistivity, but one scenario having double the length and area as the other scenario (both scenarios result in the same resistance). Attending to the quantitative slider values can also be utilized by teachers in the classroom to direct students to specific scenarios for exploration, calculations, or discussions.

When implementing alternative input capabilities and descriptions, we wanted to ensure we provided access to the sliders, and that this included intuitive and efficient access to: (1) the extreme values of each input range, with description highlighting the extreme size differences in the equation variables that result, (2) "double" and "halve" slider values, and (3) all values in the input range.

Initial Implementation. All interactive objects in the sim were instrumented to support alternative input access and descriptions were designed and implemented to support non-visual access. Here we focus on the navigation and description capabilities associated with the sliders.

We initially implemented each slider with the standard and recommended native HTML slider attributes to support access to the input type range. Users could press *Tab,* or other common navigation approaches, to move focus to each of the three sliders. Once a slider had focus, Arrow keys could be used to increment (*Up/Right Arrow keys*), or decrement (*Down/Left Arrow keys*) the input values. The initial step size for each slider was 1/100th of the slider range. Using the *Home/End* keys resulted in jumping to the maximum/minimum input range. Using the *Pg Up/Pg Down* keys resulted in incrementing/decrementing the input value by 1/10th of the slider range. As the slider is adjusted by the student, a description of the resulting slider input value is provided, followed by an alert describing the relative size of the equation variables – e.g., "As letter ρ grows, letter R grows. Resistance is now 0.82 Ohms."

Challenges. The initial implementation effectively supported efficient access to the maximum and minimum slider values (through the use of *Home/End*, or alternatively, multiple presses of the *Pg Up/Pg Down* keys), but did not provide efficient access to easily doubled or halved input values, or to all possible input values. These issues are a result of the extreme differences in the input range for the ρ (resistivity) slider as compared to the length and area sliders (see Table 1). To support effective qualitative comparisons, the range must span values that students perceive as physically small to large (e.g., length ranging from 0.10 cm to 20.00 cm). Minimum values must be non-zero to avoid zero or undefined resistance.

Table 1. Initial input range parameters for sliders in *Resistance in a Wire*

	Resistance	Length	Area
Input range	[0.01, 1.00]	[0.10, 20.00]	[0.01, 15.00]
Median value	0.5	10.00	7.5
1/10 range	0.099	1.99	1.49
Min step size	0.01	0.01	0.01
Total number of input values	99	1990	1499

In the initial implementation, using the arrow keys to adjust the input values would result in default step sizes of 0.0099 for ρ, 0.199 for Length, and 0.149 for Area, as typical HTML range inputs require the range to be evenly divisible by the step size for the whole range of values to be accessible. These are not intuitive numbers for comparisons, or mental mathematical manipulation like double or halving. Figure 3 compares the slider panel in *Resistance in a Wire* with quantitative values not rounded (Fig. 3, left panel), and rounded (Fig. 3, right panel). Such a small default step size could also have the undesirable outcome of initial changes to the input value resulting in very small changes to the equation and piece of wire, obscuring important qualitative comparisons readily apparent with larger changes to the input values.

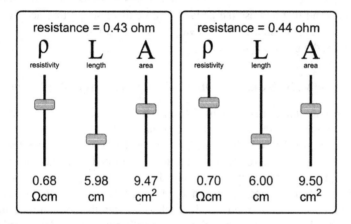

Fig. 3. Slider panel from the PhET simulation *Resistance in a Wire* showing (left panel) quantitative values that are not rounded and (right panel) quantitative values that are rounded.

Solution. To address these challenges, we first implemented the sliders with the standard native HTML features, and then added two additional new features: a modifier key and a custom variable step size. The new modifier key is the *Shift* key. Used in combination with the Arrow keys, i.e., *Shift* + Arrow key, increments/decrements the input value by the smallest allowable step size. For this sim, across all sliders, this is 0.01. Using standard ways of adjusting the input value of a slider – Arrow keys, *Home/End*, *Pg Up/Pg Down* – allow the user to efficiently span the range of input values, and use of the *Shift* + Arrow keys allows fine control when targeting a specific input value. We will implement this modifier key for all sliders in PhET sims, for consistency.

A variable step size was also implemented, to support more efficient access to input values that support simple mental calculations. There is a base step size used through most of the input range. This base step size is varied to address two specific scenarios – ensuring the minimum and maximum values of the sliders can always be reached, and ensuring that rounded input values (easier for mental mathematical calculations) are reached when transitioning between different slider navigation approaches. For the ρ slider, with a range of 0.01–1.00, the base step size is used across the range 0.05–1.00. When decrementing with an Arrow key from an input value of 0.05, the input value changes to 0.01 the minimum input value (a step size of 0.04) – ensuring the Arrow keys support navigation to the extreme ends of the input range. When using the *Pg Up/Pg Down* keys, or the *Shift* modifier key to access an input value not an increment of 0.05, incrementing/decrementing with an Arrow key will result in an input value that is the nearest increment of 0.05. Similarly, the Length and Area sliders have a base step size of 1.00. When decrementing by Arrow key from an input value of 1.00, the input value changes to the minimum value – 0.10 (Length) and 0.01 (Area). When an input value is accessed that is not an increment of 1.00, incrementing/decrementing by Arrow keys results in the nearest input value that is an increment of 1.00.

The result of this implementation are sliders that can be accessed in all of the typical ways – meeting expectations of interaction with sliders for users with and without visual impairments – and that address the pedagogical goals of supporting access to (1) the extreme values of each input range, (2) values easy to "double" and "halve", and also (3) all values in the input range.

3.2   Interacting with Uncommon Objects Using Native HTML Elements

The sim *John Travoltage* (Fig. 4) is used from elementary school through introductory college level to introduce the topic of static electricity. The sim opens with the character John, standing in a room, on a rug, next to a door. He has a moveable leg and arm. Rubbing his foot on the rug results in electrons, represented as blue circles with a "–" sign on them, transferring from the rug onto John's body. John's arm can be moved closer, or farther, from the nearby doorknob. Moving John's arm closer to the doorknob can result in the electrons on John's body discharging into the doorknob, resulting in a shock. A productive exploration of this sim typically includes students exploring the relationship between the amount of charge on John's body, and the distance between

Fig. 4.   Screenshot of PhET sim *John Travoltage*. Reproduced with permission from the PhET Interactive Simulations project.

his hand and the doorknob that result in a discharge. The more charge on John's body the farther his hand can be from the doorknob while still getting shocked.

When implementing alternative input capabilities and descriptions, we wanted to ensure (1) leg and arm interaction is intuitive – since these are the primary interactive objects in the sim, (2) efficient access to electron transfer and discharge scenarios, and (3) descriptions support users in knowing the relative location of the arm/leg.

Initial Implementation. In collaboration with the Inclusive Design Research Centre at OCAD University, all interactive objects in the sim were instrumented to support alternative input access and to provide description. Here we focus on the navigation and description capabilities associated with the arm and leg. When the sim was first developed, the arm and leg objects were not implemented as HTML elements. The arm and leg each spanned a range of locations – 180° of a circle for the leg, and 360° of circle for the arm. We investigated implementing the arm and leg as sliders, number spinners, and in an application mode. Upon consideration, we concluded sliders would likely provide the most intuitive experience to the desired interaction pattern [17].

Our initial implementation of these objects as sliders had the arm implemented with a range of 0–60, and the leg with a range of 0–30, each with a step size of 1. Descriptions indicated 12 different regions of the slider (Fig. 5, left panel), with each region spanning

Initial Implementation		Current Implementation	
Position Number	Region Descriptions	Position Number	Landmark & Region Descriptions [RD]
0	Farthest from the doorknob.	-15	**Farthest from the doorknob. Last stop.**
1 - 5	Very far from the doorknob.	-14	Very far from the doorknob.
		-13	**Hand pointing away from door**, [RD].
		-12	Very far from the doorknob.
6 - 10	Far from the doorknob.	-11	
		-10	Far from the doorknob.
		-9	
11 - 15	Neither far or close to the doorknob.	-8	**Hand pointing straight up.**
		-7	Not so close to doorknob.
16 - 20	Somewhat close to the doorknob.	-6	Not so close to doorknob.
		-5	Close to doorknob.
21 - 25	Close to the doorknob.	-4	**Hand pointing at upper door**, [RD].
		-3	Close to doorknob.
		-2	Very close to doorknob.
26 - 29	Very close to the doorknob.	-1	Just above doorknob.
30	Closest to the doorknob.	0	**At doorknob.**
31 - 34	Very close to the doorknob.	1	Just below doorknob.
		2	Very close to doorknob.
35 - 39	Close to the doorknob.	3	Close to doorknob.
		4	**Hand pointing at lower door**, [RD].
		5	Close to doorknob.
40 - 44	Somewhat close to the doorknob.	6	Not so close to doorknob.
		7	**Hand pointing straight down.**
45 - 49	Neither far or close to the doorknob.	8	Not so close to doorknob.
		9	
50 - 54	Far from the doorknob.	10	Far from doorknob.
		11	
55 - 59	Very far from the doorknob.	12	Very far from doorknob.
		13	**Hand pointing away from door**, [RD].
		14	Very far from doorknob.
60	Farthest from the doorknob.	15	**Farthest from the doorknob. Last stop.**

Fig. 5. Position, region, and landmark descriptions for the initial implementation (left) and current implementation (right) of the arm slider in the PhET simulation *John Travoltage*.

five input values. Eleven of these regions had one description that would be read aloud, indicating proximity to the doorknob, e.g., "Position 12, Close to the doorknob" and "Position 55, Far from the doorknob." In the region nearest the doorknob, additional descriptions were provided, indicating "Close to doorknob," "Very close to doorknob," and "Closest to doorknob." Descriptions for the leg, which moves 180° of a circle, had three regions – each indicating whether foot was off (e.g., "Position 2, Foot is off the rug"), or on the rug (e.g., "Position 15, Foot is on the rug").

Challenges. The slider implementation successfully supported access to incrementing and decrementing arm and leg position values. The interaction did not support efficient access to charge transfer or discharge behavior, and the descriptions were not always meaningful during interaction. A common complaint from users was that it took too many keypresses to reach a new description region, resulting in repetitive descriptions and an overall feeling that the arm/leg was moving too slowly. Also, each object has a 'target' area, a location that has unique consequences for the slider interaction. For the arm, this is typically the region where the hand is nearest the doorknob; for the leg this is the region where the foot is on the rug.

Additionally, there are two challenges inherent in using a linear slider to represent a circular interaction. First, there is no way to continuously increment the input values to result in multiple same-direction (e.g., clockwise) passes around the circle. For example, incrementing the slider from input value 0 to 60 results in moving the arm clockwise around the circle. Once the maximum input value of 60 is reached, the user must stop, or decrement through decreasing input values (moving arm counterclockwise) to continue moving the arm. The second challenge is that at some point in traversing the slider input values, using the *Up/Right (or Down/Left) Arrow* key to increment (or decrement) the input value will actually result in decrementing (or incrementing) the position value.

Solution. To address these challenges, we decreased the input value ranges for the arm and leg, and made significant changes to the description approach. For the arm, the input value range is now −15 to 15; the leg has an input range of half that, −7 to 7. This results in requiring fewer keypresses to span the full range, and more object movement with each keypress.

To improve the descriptions of the arm position, three description types were created (Fig. 5, right panel) the region (e.g., "Close to doorknob," "Not so close to doorknob," "Far from doorknob"), landmark (e.g., "Hand pointing straight up" and "At doorknob"), and direction change descriptions (i.e., "Away from doorknob" or "Towards doorknob"). Upon change of position for the arm, the slider value is announced as well as one of the following: If change of direction, direction is announced; if arm enters landmark location, landmark is announced; otherwise, region is announced. The leg descriptions were also improved. For the leg, one of two regions are announced in addition to slider value: "Foot rubbing on rug" or "Foot off rug".

The resulting sim interaction provides efficient access to the leg and arm as well as the important electron discharge scenarios, while the descriptions provide new information on relative position with each move of the leg or arm. The result is an interaction that highlights the significance of the location of the arm with respect to the doorknob, supporting the user to create and explore electron discharge events.

3.3   Providing Custom Control and Using Visual and Non-visual Cues

The sim *Balloons and Static Electricity* (described in Sect. 2, shown in Fig. 1) allows students to investigate static electricity, charge transfer, attraction, repulsion, and induced charge through free range movement of a Balloon. The Balloon can be rubbed on a Sweater or a Wall, resulting in different charge transfer or induced charge behavior. The Balloon can be moved by the user, and can also move independently upon release – with the Balloon location, state (more or less negatively charged), and release location all being significant for the free-movement velocity of the Balloon, and the final resting position of the Balloon.

When implementing alternative input capabilities and descriptions, we wanted to ensure students could (1) intuitively pick up, move, and release the Balloon, (2) easily understand the specific location of the Balloon, and (3) understand when a transfer of negative charge occurs.

Initial Implementations. The *Balloons and Static Electricity* sim presented numerous challenges for implementing accessibility features. The Balloon in the sim needs to have a four-way, drag and drop-like, behavior – with any location in the sim being a possible release location. Upon release the Balloon may move to other locations based on the current state of charge differences in the sim. This behavior is unlike any native HTML elements [13]. Additionally, while the Balloon is in motion (either controlled by the user or moving independently) the user needs to be kept up-to-date on various state changes, including the Balloon's current location, any occurrence of charge transfer and the resulting net charge, any occurrence of an induced charge at the wall (which occurs when the negatively charged Balloon is near the Wall), and current location and relative speed (when in motion) of Balloon release. The amount of dynamic information that happens outside the user's keyboard focus that must be conveyed to the user is far beyond what might be conveyed by alerts in a typical web page.

The *Balloons and Static Electricity* sim underwent far more implementation iterations than the sims previously described. An example of an early implementation included: the Balloon implemented as a custom element using the ARIA application role with associated instructions on how to move it read out automatically, followed by the Remove Wall button, Two-balloon Experiments checkbox, and the Reset All button. The radio button group controlling charge views was not made accessible until later in the design process. In this early implementation, interaction with the Balloon involved moving focus to the Balloon and then hearing not only its label, "Yellow Balloon", but hearing its role "Application", its technical interactive state, "draggable", and finally a description of how to move it, "Grab and drag Balloon up, left, down, or right with the *W, A, S,* or *D* key." Once users moved the Balloon, they would hear alerts that would guide them towards an object (Sweater or Wall), simultaneously providing direction, progress, and actual location. They would hear the following five alerts as they progressed towards the sweater with successive presses of the *A* key: "Left. Towards sweater", "Left. Closer to sweater", "Left. On left side of Play Area", "Left. Near sweater", "Yellow Balloon has a few more negative charges than positive charges. Sweater has a few more positive charges than negative charges."

Challenges. These early implementation approaches resulted in multiple challenges, particularly for users with visual impairments. These challenges included difficulty recognizing the Balloon as the most important sim object, difficulty understanding how to interact with the Balloon, and difficulty recognizing the location of the Balloon during interaction.

When interactive HTML elements are accessed while using screen reader software, the user hears both the label of the interactive element (i.e., its accessible name) and the elements functional role. Ideally, the label describes what an element is or does in context, and the role reveals to the user how they will interact with the interactive object. Exploring an early prototype for the accessible *Balloons and Static Electricity* sim using only the *Tab* key (keypress indicated by *[Tab]*), would sound like the following, with some variation depending on screen reader software used: *[Tab]* "Application, Yellow Balloon, draggable", *[Tab]* "Remove Wall, button", *[Tab]* "Two-Balloon Experiments, checkbox, not checked" and *[Tab]* "Reset Balloon, button." If the user did not move on after hearing the label and role, further descriptive content (e.g., help text for how to move the Yellow Balloon) may be read out, depending on the screen reader software in use.

Initial implementations of the Balloon resulted in users not recognizing the Balloon as an important object to interact with, and not understanding how to interact with the Balloon. The interaction required users to hear the Yellow Balloon element's role and state first (i.e., "Application, draggable"), which does not indicate to the user how to interact with the Balloon. The more useful information, the help text indicating how to grab and move the Balloon, followed this role and state information. Most users chose to move focus to the next interactive element, rather than taking the actions described in the help text. The more inviting interaction, based on its description, was the "Two-Balloon Experiments" checkbox, resulting in most users selecting the checkbox before interacting with the Yellow Balloon. This choice is undesirable for multiple reasons as this selection made the sim screen and potential interactions more complex (with two Balloons to interact with) before users had a chance to explore and make sense of a simpler (single Balloon) scenario.

Once users successfully began interacting with the Yellow Balloon, users often ran into challenges understanding the location of the Balloon, due to the original structure of the location alerts. Initially, each keypress used to move the Balloon resulted in an indicator of the Balloon's direction of motion. For example, when repeatedly pressing the *A* key to move the Balloon to the left, the initial word of the alert read out was always the word "Left." If the user made successive soft keypresses (pressing lightly), the Balloon would not change in position enough to get a full change in location description, and would hear only the direction indicator, for example "Left. Left. Left.". If users made harder keys presses (advancing further) and also did so quickly, the alerts would interrupt themselves, reading out, "Left. .... Left. ..... Left. ..." In both cases, soft keypresses or quick successive key presses, users did not get a sense of progress or a sense of where the Balloon actually was in relation to the Sweater or Wall.

Solutions. To address the challenge of users having difficulty interacting with the Balloon, we implemented a two-step process for Balloon interaction. Users first "grab" the Balloon through selection of the "Grab Yellow Balloon" button, a native HTML interaction. Once the Balloon is "grabbed," the user receives the information that it is an "Application" and the following help text "Press W, A, S, or D key to move Balloon up, left, down, or right". While this two-step interaction has been more intuitive for non-visual users who access the description content, this interaction is less intuitive for those relying solely on the visual representations in the sim. We added visual cues (Fig. 6) that appear during initial interaction with the Balloon to provide visual guidance for this two-step interaction. With carefully designed auditory description as well as visual cues, the two-step interaction with the Balloon simultaneously supports visual and non-visual access.

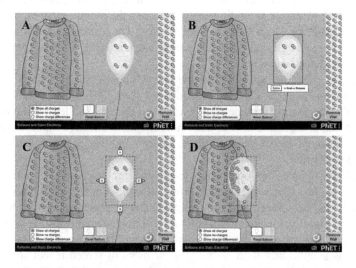

Fig. 6. Screenshots of initial interaction with Balloon in the PhET Simulation *Balloons and Static Electricity.* (A) Sim at opening, (B) focus on Balloon, not yet grabbed; (C) focus on Balloon, grabbed, showing letter and arrow key options for four-way movement; (D) moving Balloon on sweater (Color figure online).

To cue users with visual impairments that the Balloon is the most important object to interact with, we added two interaction hints to the PDOM description. The first is placed at the end of the Scene Summary that describes the sim on page load, "Grab balloon to play.", and the second, "Look for grab button to play." is placed at the end the Balloon's description, just before the "Grab Yellow Balloon, button".

To ensure users are kept up-to-date on the location of the Balloon during user-controlled motion and upon release, we implemented a sophisticated alert structure that still provides the user with directional information, a sense of progress and actual location, but does so more efficiently and ensures that the start of most alert text is unique to avoid repetition. After the Balloon is grabbed, a series of moving alerts that occur with successive presses of the *A* key now sounds like this, "Left. Closer to sweater", "On left side of Play Area", "On left side of Play Area", "Near sweater", "On sweater. Yellow Balloon picks up negative charges from sweater", and finally, "Yellow Balloon has a few more negative charges than positive charges. Sweater has a few more positive charges than negative charges."

4   Conclusions

In this work, we presented three design scenarios. For each scenario, we described our initial approach to implementation of accessibility features, challenges encountered, and the resulting – more successful – design. In our first example, we implemented sliders with all typical slider features, as well as enhanced features to support access to the specific pedagogical goals of the simulation *Resistance in a Wire*. The resulting sliders provide more efficient access to immediately useful numerical values than our initial implementation, while still providing access (through the use of a custom variable step size and a modifier key) to all possible input values. The resulting simulation provides improved access to the desired user interactions when utilizing keyboard input with or without screen reader software.

Our second example expands upon the use of sliders, this time implemented to provide access to unique arm and leg motion in the *John Travoltage* simulation. Use of sliders for this interaction provides direct access to the arm and leg via the keyboard, though required some refinement to determine the most effective input range, and to improve the descriptions of the location of the arm and the leg when accessed using screen reader software.

In our final example, we describe the design and implementation of a fully custom interaction to support four-way Balloon movement in the simulation *Balloons and Static Electricity*. In this design scenario, initial implementation presented significant usability challenges for visually impaired users utilizing screen reader software. To address this, we implemented a two-step process to first grab and then move the Balloon. This approach was significantly more successful for users of screen reader software, but introduced a new challenge for sighted keyboard users – as the two-step process was less intuitive without auditory descriptions. To address this challenge, we designed visual cues that appear during initial balloon interaction, resulting in similar guidance being provided for both visual and non-visual access. The result is a relatively intuitive user experience for a fully custom interaction.

4.1   Limitations

Throughout the design of these solutions, we incorporated analysis of user interviews and direct feedback from assistive technology users, as well as expert pedagogical and interface design expertise. This approach provided many insights that guided our designs, but is not an exhaustive representation of potential needs and preferences of the many users of keyboard and screen reader accessible content. We wholeheartedly acknowledge that more feedback from students, parents, and teachers will benefit our design approach, and may result in future improvements to the solutions described in this work. We expect to receive more feedback and to continue refining our design ideas and solutions once more accessible PhET simulations are publicly available and there is broader awareness and use of their accessibility-related features.

4.2 Looking Forward

In the presentation of these design scenarios, challenges encountered, and our solutions, we aim to contribute to the knowledge base for general strategies to the design and development of accessible interactive learning resources. These example scenarios were selected from the many design challenges we have encountered while implementing accessibility features into a subset of the PhET simulations. As we work with each new simulation, we add new strategies to our toolbox of approaches, and become better able to address challenges in PhET's more complex simulations. We welcome opportunities for further discussion, sharing of insights, and generalization of solutions with the broader accessibility community.

Acknowledgments. We would like to thank the PhET team, our collaborators at the Inclusive Design Research Centre at OCAD University and the Sonification Lab at the Georgia Institute of Technology, and research participants for their contributions to the design and development of the accessibility features for the three simulations discussed in this work. This material is based upon work supported by the William and Flora Hewlett Foundation, the University of Colorado Boulder, and the National Science Foundation under DRL-1503439 and DRL-1621363.

References

1. D'Angelo, C., Rutstein, D., Harrison, S., Bernard, R., Borokhovski, E., Haertel, G.: Simulations for STEM learning: systematic review and meta-analysis. Technical report, SRI International (2014)
2. Keane, K., Laverent, C.: Interactive scientific graphics recommended practices for verbal description. Technical report, Wolfram Research (2014)
3. Ellis, B., Ford-Williams, G., Graham, L., Grammenos, D., Hamilton, I., Lee, E., Manion, J., Westin, T.: Game accessibility guidelines (2017). http://gameaccessibilityguidelines.com
4. Smith, T.L., Lewis, C., Moore, E.B.: Description strategies to make an interactive science simulation accessible. J. Technol. Pers. Disabil. 5, 225–238 (2017)
5. Smith, T.L., Lewis, C., Moore, E.B.: A balloon, a sweater, and a wall: developing design strategies for accessible user experiences with a science simulation. In: Antona, M., Stephanidis, C. (eds.) UAHCI 2016. LNCS, vol. 9739, pp. 147–158. Springer, Cham (2016). https://doi.org/10.1007/978-3-319-40238-3_15
6. PhET Interactive Simulations (2018). http://phet.colorado.edu/
7. Accessible PhET Interactive Simulations (2018). http://phet.colorado.edu/en/about/accessibility
8. Wieman, C., Adams, W.K., Perkins, K.K.: PhET: simulations that enhance learning. Science 322, 682–683 (2008)

9. Perkins, K.K., Moore, E.B., Chasteen, S.V.: Examining the use of PhET interactive simulations in US college and high school classrooms. In: Proceedings of the 2014 Physics Education Research Conference, pp 207–210 (2015). https://doi.org/10.1119/perc.2014.pr.048

10. Sorge, V., Lee, M., Wilkinson, S.: End-to-end solution for accessible chemical diagrams. In: Proceedings of the 12th Web for all Conference, Article no. 6 (2015). https://doi.org/10.1145/2745555.2746667

11. Fitzpatrick, D.R., Godfrey, J.A., Sorge, V.: Producing accessible statistics diagrams in R. In: Proceedings of the 14th Web for all Conference, Article no. 22 (2017). https://doi.org/10.1145/3058555.3058564

12. Smith, T.L., Moore, E.B., Greenberg, J.: Parallel DOM architecture for accessible interactive simulations. In: proceedings of the 15th web for all conference (2018) (in Press)

13. King, M., Nurthen, J., Bijl, M., Cooper, M., Scheuhammer, J., Pappas, L., Schwerdtfeger, R.: WAI-ARIA authoring Practices 1.1 (2017). https://www.w3.org/TR/wai-aria-practices-1.1/

14. Faulkner, S., Eicholz, A., Leithead, T., Danilo, A., Moon, S.: HTML 5.2 (2017). https://www.w3.org/TR/html52/

15. Diggs, J., McCarron, S., Cooper, M., Schwerdtfeger, R., James Craig, J.: Accessible rich internet applications (WAI-ARIA) 1.1 (2017). https://www.w3.org/TR/wai-aria-1.1/

16. Moore, E.B., Smith, T.L., Randall, E.: Exploring the relationship between implicit scaffolding and inclusive design in interactive science simulations. In: Antona, M., Stephanidis, C. (eds.) UAHCI 2016. LNCS, vol. 9739, pp. 112–123. Springer, Cham (2016). https://doi.org/10.1007/978-3-319-40238-3_12

17. Hung, J.: PhET John Travoltage simulation design (2016). https://wiki.fluidproject.org/display/fluid/PhET+John+Travoltage+Simulation+Design

Fair Play: A Guidelines Proposal for the Development of Accessible Audiogames for Visually Impaired Users

Olimar Teixeira Borges[(✉)], Juliana Damasio Oliveira[(✉)],
Marcia de Borba Campos[(✉)], and Sabrina Marczak[(✉)]

School of Technology, Pontifical Catholic University of Rio Grande do Sul (PUCRS),
Porto Alegre, Brazil
{olimar.borges,juliana.damasio}@acad.pucrs.br,
marciabcampos@hotmail.com, sabrina.marczak@pucrs.br

Abstract. The area of games, digital entertainment, and development of assistive technologies is constantly growing. However, there are still groups of users who face barriers to using games, such as visually impaired people. Audiogames defined as games based on sound interface, have been an initiative for the inclusion of this audience. Conversely, these are not always games with good accessibility. In order to address this issue, this study presents Fair Play, a set of 33 guidelines for audiogames design. Fair Play aims, aiming to promote good accessibility, gameplay, and usability in audiogames. Fair Play was proposed based on the results of a literature review. The guidelines were validated following 6 steps, detailed in this study. Also available online for the use of the community.

Keywords: Accessible games · Audiogames · Usability
Accessibility · Visually impaired users

1 Introduction

There is still a way to be followed in relation to the inclusion of the visually impaired (VI) public in the game entertainment universe. Garcia e Almeida [15], define the games usually use graphical interface to transmit information to the player. This limits visually impaired people given that the gameplay characteristic of a game can be understood as the nature of interactivity. That is, how and how much the player can interact with the game world, and how this world reacts to the choices the player makes [22]. Therefore, it is necessary that the users can have access to all the information so that they can better interact and make their decisions to face the challenges of the game.

Thus, the design and development of audiogames can be seen as an initiative to include people with VI, considering those they are games based mainly on a sound interface. These games may or may not contain the graphical interface,

© Springer International Publishing AG, part of Springer Nature 2018
M. Antona and C. Stephanidis (Eds.): UAHCI 2018, LNCS 10907, pp. 401–419, 2018.
https://doi.org/10.1007/978-3-319-92049-8_29

which in this context is an irrelevant requirement to understand the game, the sound interface should be sufficient for the VI user to play the game. To enhance the user experience, some audiogames use 3D sounds. This kind of sound promotes that the user can perceive various dimensions through the sound interface, creating an immersion environment. Some audiogames use screen reader software, while others develop their own voice synthesizer. There are also those that include the use of haptic interface adapted to the mouse or make use of more specialized features such as the vibration of mobile devices. In any case, audiogames should follow accessibility criteria, which unfortunately is not always the case [2].

Some studies propose the use of heuristics/guidelines for game evaluation and development [2,12,13]. However, these do not fully cover the criteria needed to promote accessibility, gameplay, and usability required by audio-based games. In this context, Campos and Oliveira [7], proposed a set of 12 heuristics for the evaluation of audiogames. The study by Borges and Campos [8] presents an initial set of 31 guidelines for audiogames design. These studies were related so that it is possible to carry out evaluations during the development of audiogame. Guidelines are guidance that helps the designer build interfaces with a greater degree of usability [9]. Guidelines have as their main advantage, offering flexible guidelines and assisting in setting project goals and decisions. Guidelines to address a variety of issues, one of the ways companies disclose rules, standards or style guides for the development of their products [9].

Based on these studies, this papers presents Fair Play, a (final) guidelines for the design of audiogames. The guidelines proposed here will serve as an instrument to assist in the design of an audiogame, following good development practices for better usability, accessibility, and gameplay of the game. This proposal was elaborated and validated through diverse research studies, presented in this paper in details.

Therefore, the remainder of the paper is organized as follows: Sect. 2 presents the papers related to this study, Sect. 3 shows the steps taken to consolidate the Fair Play guidelines, Sect. 4 presents Fair Play which is the final set of guidelines already consolidated. Section 5 concludes the paper with lessons learned and final consolidation.

2   Related Work

Although there are studies that propose the use of guidelines for the development of accessible games, these do not focus on the development of games for visually impaired users. Therefore, the related work we present in this section mostly are guidelines proposal for the development/evaluation of accessible games in general, these work served as a reference for the proposal of Fair Play.

Desurvire et al. [12] proposed a set of game evaluation heuristics (HEP) organized into 4 categories, namely gameplay, history, game mechanics, and usability. Heuristics were proposed to be used early in the game design to facilitate design thinking from the user's point of view. Later, the same authors [13], adapted these heuristics, resulting in a new list (PLAY) that was created to help game developers throughout the design process, particularly at the beginning of the concept phase, when design changes are less costly. The new list of heuristics was grouped into the following categories: gameplay, fun factors/Entertainment/Humor/Immersion, usability and game mechanics. One of the advantages described by the authors is that the PLAY proposal is modular [13]. For example, if a game does not have a history, questions related to this heuristic should be taken from the evaluation instrument.

Yuan et al. [23] reviewed the state of the art in the research and practice of accessibility in video games and pointed out relevant areas for future research. As a disability can affect a player's ability to use different games, a generic interaction model for games has been defined, allowing identification of the types of barriers faced. A large number of games accessible and research for different types of disabilities and with different genders. They were then classified into a series of accessibility strategies according to their degree of severity between high and low. This helps developers identify accessibility issues in their game design.

A large number of studies (e.g. [1,3–6,10,11,14–21,23,24]) proposed recommendations for the development of accessible games in general. However, there is no standardization of how they are categorized. Some studies organize the guidelines by level or progression, data entry, graphics, sound and installation/configuration [20,21]. Others organize by disability, being a user with motor, cognitive, visual, hearing and speech disabilities [18,23]. Others organize by the severity of accessibility violations [3], while others suggested guidelines based on the of WCAG 2.0 structure [10,19], being these perceptible, operable, comprehensible and compatible. There are also studies that did not present any kind of categorization [6,16].

The guidelines proposed in this paper differs from previous studies by, specifically to assist the development of audiogames for visually impaired users and still have principles of usability, gameplay, and accessibility, different from others.

3   Fair Play Creation Method

Fair Play was proposed based on a technique of reviewing the literature called Snowballing, in which studies were identified that have recommendations for games generally accessible. From these, recommendations were selected that could also be applied to audiogames, resulting in an initial set published by Borges and Campos [8]. For the consolidation of this set, 6 stages were carried out, the last two being related to their availability and which are described in this section.

3.1   Stage 1: Data Collected

In order to evaluate the 31 guidelines proposed in a previous study by Borges e Campos [8] (initial proposal) we first carried out two studies (A and B). The goal of these two studies was to verify whether the 31 guidelines would be used to guide the implementation in audiogames projects and the relevance during the development process. Additionally, it was necessary to verify if the guidelines were identified in existing audiogames.

Study A - Evaluation with Audiogames Developers. To assist in this process, an online questionnaire was developed to verify if the proposed set of guidelines could be used by audiogames developers during the construction of their projects. To do this, the questionnaire was organized into 6 sections, which sought to identify the profile of the respondent, verify information about the developed audiogame, to analyze the implementation priority of each of the 31 proposed items, to identify which of the items had been implemented in them projects, to analyze if the items were clear or if there were suggestions for changes, and finally, to understand what lessons were learned during the development of their audiogames.

At the beginning of the questionnaire, it was explicitly described that the respondent should be an audiogame developer. This restriction was due to the fact that the study is interested only in the development of audiogames. The questionnaire was made available in Portuguese and in English.

Results. We collected 8 responses, 6 from Brazil and 2 from abroad. To ensure the confidentiality of the responses, the participants were named from R1 to R8. The average experience of audiogames development reported by respondents was 1 to 3 years, and only two respondents (R4 and R5) had experience in developing games accessible to people with visually impaired of 7 years or older. The audiogames gender varied, from the adventure (R2, R3, R6, R7 and R8), action (R4), experimental (R1), and simulations and strategy (R5). As for the care that was considered to facilitate and allow use by people with visually impaired, most participants reported using diverse audio resources, such as 3D sound localization and sound feedback throughout the game. In addiction, respondents also reported that they use the provision of shortcut keys to facilitate the player's actions and choices, and other sound resources that aid in the orientation of the player.

We also asked the respondents to prioritize the importance of enhance of the 31 guidelines. The 5 points likert scaled was: "High priority", "Medium priority", "Low priority", "Not important" and "no comment". Among all the guidelines, some have stood out because they have been considered as "high priority" by at least half of the respondents, such guidelines are: D3, D5, D8, D9, D10, D11, D15, D17, D19, D22, D26, D27, D28, D29, and D30. The guidelines D1, D2, D12, D20, D23, D24, D25, and D31 have been marked as a "Medium priority", also by the same number of respondents, which still maintains them at a high acceptance level. None of the guidelines were labeled "Not important" by more than 50% of respondents. And for the "no comment" option, guidelines D12, D15, D16, D21, and D27 have had one to two markings. The respondents with more experience in the development of audiogames, had very different results. While R4 considered that 48.4% of the guidelines can be considered as "High priority" and 41.9% of "Medium priority", R5 considered that 35.5% of the guidelines could be classified as "Not important" and 22.6% as "High Priority". Thus, taking into account the next most experienced respondent, R1 considered that 48.4% of the guidelines are "High priority" and 41.9% are "Medium priority". The responses of the other respondents were also analyzed and their highest percentages remained as of "High priority" and "Medium priority".

Another question asked was to verify if the proposed guidelines were considered during the development of audiogames projects. Of all the guidelines, more than half were "fully implemented" by more than half the respondents. The "Partially Implemented" option was the most used by respondents. In contrast, 13 guidelines (D3, D4, D6, D11, D12, D13, D14, D20, D21, D23, D25, D27, D31) were marked as "Not implemented", also by at least half of the respondents. For this question, we emphasize that the implementation or not of the guidelines is very variable, since factors such as scope, gender, available platform and experience of the developer, directly influence the execution of some criteria defined in the set of guidelines. For example, experimental games, as in the case of R1, may have a few functionalities and therefore the game do not implement many of the proposed guidelines. In the case of R1, 51.6% of the guidelines were marked "Not implemented". Of the five respondents who reported having participated in the creation of an adventure game-type audiogame, the average of "fully implemented" guidelines was 56.77% versus 36.77% of "Not implemented" guidelines and 29.03% of "Partially Implemented". For the other respondents, the average "fully implemented" of the guidelines was 11.6%, against 10.3% of "Not implemented" guidelines and 6.6% "Partially Implemented".

And finally, the importance of audio in the game, emphasizing that all graphics should be represented, such as soundtracks, sound effects, locutions, and environment were the most lessons learned reported. Sounds should be clearly implemented so that the player has as much information as possible, such as where he is, where he should go, what he should do, and how he can feel the emotions of the characters. Otherwise, the immersion can be broken and the gaming experience becomes understandable for all audiences, whether or not VI. Another well-quoted point was the testing of people with visual impairment during the development of audiogame. It was also mentioned the importance of creating a tutorial and following development guidelines for the creation of audiogames.

Our results indicate that the set of proposed guidelines was well accepted by the respondents, always maintaining an average of acceptance above 50%. However, some of the guidelines should be re-examined to be better described and clearer.

Study B - Evaluation with Blind User with Experience in the Use of Audiogames. The set of guidelines for the development of audiogames was used to verify if audiogames already developed implemented the items of the proposed guidelines. To that end, a user who is blind and who has experience in the use of audiogame was invited to carry out the evaluation of 8 different audiogames. The tested audiogames were: Dark Destroyer[1], Last Crusade[2], *Segredo do mosteiro*[3], Tic Tac Toi[4], Duck Blaster[5], *Cobras e escadas*[6], Snakes and ladders[7], and Super Mario Brothers[8]. All audiogames used in the analysis are available for desktop only. The Audiogames vary greatly in their game categories they go from adventure to RPG, board, shooting, and action.

After playing each audiogame, the user received the online questionnaire with the 31 guidelines and for each of them, was asked to the mark on a Likert Scale, verifying that each of the 31 items were observed in the audiogame, with the scale of 5 points ranging from: "Strongly Disagree", "Partially Disagree", "No comment", "Partially Agree" and "Strongly Agree".

Results. For the analysis of the data, a descriptive statistic was used, using the most frequent response for each item of the 31 guidelines. After the calculation of modal, the answer most used for each item was "Strongly disagree", obtaining a percentage of 62.9%. That is, most of the proposed guidelines were not identified during game use, which is of concern since in that many of them are basic items needed in an audiogame, such as D31, which provides mechanisms to configure the audios and sounds of the game. This guideline was only observed in one of the games, in the Last Crusade. The most guideline identified in the audiogames was the D15, which proposes for games in desktop, that the player can do all the operations of the game by means of the keyboard. Note that all audiogames tested in this step are for desktop and even so, some of them do not provide all their functionality accessible by the keyboard.

Lastly, it is observed how much it is necessary to include in the process of development of audiogames, guidelines, and recommendations for the development because only then, will be generated audiogames with greater gameplay, accessibility, and attractiveness for users with VI.

3.2   Stage 2: Data Analysis

The guidelines needed to be refined based on the results of the assessments conducted in Step 1. In this way, the authors of discussed them in person and modified those that had changes applied for clarity (i.e., D2, D6, D11, D14, D15, D17, D21, D23, D25, D27, D29, D30), grouped by being similar (D3 with D4) and divided to become more specific (D9, D24). Additionally, initially, the guidelines were directed only to blind people and, therefore, items related to the GUI had been disregarded. However, for a better experience of use by people with low vision, items related to the graphics interface were inserted in the present

---

[1] http://www.audiogames.com.br/jogos/dark-destroyer/.

[2] http://www.audiogames.com.br/jogos/last-crusade/.

[3] http://www.audiogames.com.br/jogos/o-segredo-do-mosteiro/.

[4] http://www.audiogames.com.br/jogos/tic-tac-toi/.

[5] http://www.audiogames.com.br/jogos/duck-blaster/.

[6] http://www.audiogames.com.br/jogos/cobras-e-escadas/.

[7] http://www.monkeytalk.com/chutes%20and%20ladders.zip.

[8] http://www.audiogames.com.br/jogos/super-mario-brothers/.

study, for a new analysis. Thus, we analyzed another 51 items that apply to the graphical interface and that generated another category called Graphic Elements with 4 linked guidelines, which were added to the original set, resulting in 35 guidelines (Proposal preliminary).

3.3   Stage 3: Heuristic Relationship of Guidelines

In the study of Borba Campos, Oliveira [7], in which a set of 12 heuristics for evaluation of audiogames was elaborated, it was defined and explained how each heuristic can be applied in an audiogame evaluation. Heuristics contained examples of evaluation issues, which needed to be generalized to make them applicable to a wider variety of games and regardless of the used platforms (e.g. desktop, mobile, and console). Additionally, it was necessary to confirm the association between the examples of questions with the heuristics.

To do this, we performed a process of modification of the evaluation questions, which consisted of the re-evaluation of the 50 examples of initial questions, presented in the 12 evaluation heuristics [7], and in the addition of new questions, with the aim to make them more comprehensive, totaling in 81 questions. From these modifications, we individually, in possession of the definitions of the 12 heuristics, carried out in a first moment, the relation of the heuristics with the 81 examples of questions of evaluation of audiogames. Afterward, we as a group, analyzed and discussed the individual relationships.

Following the same process, we performed the relationship between the 35 development guidelines and the 12 evaluation heuristics. In a group, it was verified that one of the guidelines (D35- Allowing the interfaces and texts to be resized, allowing the player to zoom and pan the screen) was already being considered as part of another guideline (D18). For this reason, directive D35 was unified with D18, resulting in 34 guidelines. Additionally, following the template of WCAG 1.0[9] the naming of "evaluation questions" has been changed to "checkpoints". The changed heuristics are described below.

- **H1 - System state visibility**: The audiogame should keep the user informed by audio about the relevant actions of the game. **Checkpoints:** Does audiogame keep the user informed about what's happening? Can the user know your score/status at any time?
- **H2 - Correspondence between the system and the real world**: The audiogame should use a more natural language possible for the user. **Checkpoints:** Are the concepts used in audiogame comprehensible? Does the game follow trends established by the community of players facilitating their learning?
- **H3 - Control and user freedom**: The user must feel in control of the audiogame. **Checkpoints:** Do you feel that you are in control of the application? Can you save the game? Can you go back to an earlier point in the game? Can you forward audio? Can you rewind audios? Can you adjust the

---

[9] https://www.w3.org/TR/WAI-WEBCONTENT/.

audio speed? Is it possible to adjust the audio volume? Is it easy to return to the beginning of the game?

- **H4 - Consistency and standardization**: audiogames should be performed through consistent and standardized actions. **Checkpoints:** Is there consistency between the control of the game and what do it do? Shortcut keys follow a gaming industry standard, when there? Are the controls the same throughout the game? Is there standardization in the navigation of the menu options? Is there consistency in setting shortcut keys? Is there standardization in audio volume? Does the audio type of the elements remain the same throughout the game? Is the sound interface consistent? Is the graphical interface consistent? Are the vibration features consistent?

- **H5 - Error prevention**: Audiogame should prevent the user from making mistakes. **Checkpoints:** Can the user identify when a menu option is disabled? Does Audiogame disable keyboard keys that are not used during the game? When the user selects the option to quit the game is requested confirmation? Is the user prompted to save the game? Does the game disable options that should not be used by the user in certain parts and moments of the game?

- **H6 - Recognition rather than memorization**: The user must recognize what to do while using the audiogame instead of memorizing it. **Checkpoints:** Are the sounds understandable? Are the effects of vibration understandable? Are the concepts used in the game understandable? Are the sequences of actions to complete the tasks of the game occur properly? Is the menu easy to use? Is it easy to learn how to use the game? Is the information presented easy to understand? Are the controls intuitive? Is it easy to use the game? Does the navigation follow a logic? Is the information presented to the user relevant? Is the menu easy to understand? Are shortcut keys easy to remember? Do the sounds of objects remind you of what they mean?

- **H7 - Flexibility and efficiency in use** Audiogame must be flexible and efficient so that it can be used by different user profiles. **Checkpoints:** Are the game controls customizable? Is the shortcut key sequence easy to use? Are all controls necessary? Is the combination of keys used simultaneously appropriate? Allows efficient use by different user profiles?

- **H8 - Aesthetic and minimalist design**: Audiogame should have an aesthetic and minimalist design. **Checkpoints:** Is the sound interface consistent? Is the graphical interface consistent? Are the vibration features consistent? Are the sounds easily identifiable? Are the effects of vibration easily identifiable? Is the information presented to the user relevant? Is sound quality adequate? Is the amount of sounds adequate? Is the use of the haptic interface adequate? Is the intensity of the vibration adequate?

- **H9 - Recognition, diagnosis and recovery of errors**: The user must understand when an error occurs and succeed in re-establishing. **Checkpoints:** Can the user redo an error? Does audiogame tell you how to get out of an unwanted state? Is it easy to know when an error occurs? Is it easy to know why an error occurred?

- **H10 - Help and documentation**: The audiogame should provide help and documentation to the user. **Checkpoints:** When starting the game, does the user have enough information to understand the game? Does the user receive help information according to the context in which he is in the game? Are the most important options presented first?
- **H11 - Gameplay**: The audiogame must have gameplay. **Checkpoints:** Do audio effects generate interest? Do vibration effects generate interest? Does the game introduces its goals? Does the game have different levels of difficulty? Does the game offer different ways to achieve its goals? Does the game present challenges to the user? Does the game privilege the experience, that is, the character gets stronger as the levels and secondary objectives are conquered? Does the game allow the user to exercise any ability, be it physical, mental or social? Is the user involved quickly and easily? Is the game enjoyable to play again? Overall, the user is satisfied with this game? Does the user feel enthusiastic about the game?
- **H12 - Accessibility**: The audiogame must be accessible to the user. **Checkpoints:** Can the controls be customized? Are the most important options presented first? Can the user access the options quickly? Does the game allow the use of a screen reader? Is the information accessible? In case of using a screen reader, can the information be accessed?

It is expected that an instrument with the relationships between guidelines and heuristics can be used by the developer during the process of developing an audiogame, thus identifying the guidelines to be implemented, and then, confirming in the related heuristics, through the verification, if the implementation is in agreement. When conducting the evaluation during development, it is believed that it is possible to avoid future rework. Additionally, this set of guidelines is modular, that is, if the audiogame to be created does not have a graphical interface, for example, the guidelines of the category of Graphic elements can be disregarded. The final result of this study, with the related heuristic relations, according to the new numbering of the guidelines, follows in the next Sect. 4.

3.4   Stage 4: Focus Group and Development of Audiogame

Development of Audiogame Applying the Guidelines. In order to verify the applicability of the proposed guidelines in a real development project, an audiogame was developed, named "The Campus of Shadows: A Game Based on Development Guidelines for Audiogames", as a course completion work by 2 undergraduates[10]. The audiogame has the RPG genre and the game scene is a part of the PUCRS university map, using the buildings, routes, parking lots and setting. The game uses 2D graphics and information in the form of audio. During development, a report was drawn up which described which guidelines

---

[10] Matheus Plautz Prestes and Elton Nogueira de Matos are the authors of the audiogame "The Campus of Shadows: A Game Based on Development Guidelines for Audiogames". The audiogame is available for download in: https://github.com/MatheusPrestes/O-CAMPUS-DAS-SOMBRAS.

were applied in the game and which were not used in the development due to development time or did not apply to the style of game proposed during the project.

Results. Out the 34 guidelines, a 15 guidelines were applied during the development of audiogame (D1, D2, D3, D6, D8, D9, D10, D16, D17, D19, D25, D26, D27, D28, D34). Out of these, 7 guidelines (D11, D15, D22, D23, D29, D30, D31) were partially applied, needs to be improved its application in the audiogame, so that it reaches completely. While 9 guidelines (D4, D5, D7, D13, D18, D20, D24, D32, D33), although developers deem it important, were not applied due to the short development time. There was a consensus among developers that 3 guidelines (D12, D14, D21) did not apply to game style. Additionally, the group described that the guidelines served as support for the implementation of audiogame in a way that made the game more interesting to users with visually impaired and that meet the synthesis in which the set of guidelines is proposed, in proposing a game with usability, gameplay, and accessibility.

Focus Group. A focus group was developed with game developers to answer the following question: *Is the set of guidelines proposed in this study suitable for use in an audiogame development project?*. In this sense, the guidelines were analyzed to verify their clarity, understanding, importance, and applicability in an audiogame development project.

Prior to the focus group, a pre-questionnaire was sent to the participants for a better understanding of each participant on the purpose of this research. This questionnaire was composed of questions about the profile of the participant and brought the 34 guidelines for the respondent to assign a degree of clarity and another of importance, within a Likert scale of 5 points for each one. There was a field for the participant to write observations on the guidelines. This questionnaire was completed online before to the focus group.

The procedure used in the focus group session was as follows:

- **Presentation of the research:** Moment to contextualize the research, outline how the study was carried out so far, present the moderators who will assist and/or conduct the activities and explain the objective for the Focus Group.
- **Presentation among group members:** Each member of the group was asked to introduce herself, stating her name, profession, experience with games and/or accessible games and other information relevant to the group.
- **Task 01 - Greater relevance:** This activity consisted of two stages, the first, individually, the participants listed and justified the five guidelines, which in their opinions, were the most relevant to be implemented in an audiogame project. In the second step, after all, participants justified their choices in the previous step, the participants chose the seven most relevant guidelines in the group consensus.
- **Task 02 - Clarity and Importance:** From the answers obtained in the pre-questionnaire, the guidelines with the lowest clarity and importance scale and/or that had some observation related to their understanding were listed.

Each selected guideline was discussed with the group to suggest changes in its description and to verify if the guideline really is important to be maintained in the final set of guidelines.

- **General comments:** At this point, participants were invited to comment on the set of guidelines in general, allowing them to discuss guidelines that were not highlighted in the pre-questionnaire, for example.

Results. The focus group session lasted 2 hours. There were 5 game developers who were identified in this study from P1 to P5, as presented in Table 1. Participants are between 18–44 years old, with an average experience of 1 to 3 years in game development and three of them had the same amount (1–3 years) of experience in the development of accessible games, including audiogames.

Table 1. Profile of the participants

Id	Experience in game development	Experience in the audiogames development
P1	4–6 years	No
P2	1–3 years	1–3 years
P3	1–3 years	1–3 years
P4	1–3 years	No
P5	1–3 years	1–3 years

Each participant presented herself to the group, informing her name, profession, experience with games and/or games accessible, among others. Afterward, we proceeded as follows for Task 1:

- Part 1: participants individually selected the top 5 guidelines they considered to be most relevant to audiogames implementation. The guidelines chosen by participants were: P1 (D10, D19, D30, D17, D11), P2 (D29, D30, D9, D26 e D2), P3 (D10, D30, D9, D27 e D26), P4 (D19, D30, D9, D13 e D6) and P5 (D30, D19, D26, D22, D9). After the selection, each participant presented to the group the chosen guidelines, justifying her choice. During this phase, the moderator-researcher was collecting the guidelines informed by each participant in a spreadsheet, generating, in the end, a short summary with the most cited guidelines to assist in the second part of Task 01. The most cited guidelines were: D9 e D30 (4 votes), D19 (3 votes), D10 (2 votes), D26 (2 votes) e D2, D4, D6, D11, D13, D17, D22, D27, D28, D29 (1 vote).
- Part 2: the researcher showed the spreadsheet with the result ordered by the most voted guidelines by the group. Based on the summary of the most cited guidelines, participants were asked to choose the top 7 most important guidelines in the group consensus. For that, a paper was given, with 7 fields and a space to describe the indications. Participants defined the most important guidelines in the group's opinion, reaching a slightly different consensus from

the top 5 listed in the spreadsheet. The following guidelines were indicated: D9 - Navigation patterns, D19 - Conflict between sounds, D26 - Tutorial, D27 - Shortcut keys, D28 - Accessibility features, D29 - Interactive sound mechanisms and D30 - Different sounds. Namely, such guidelines were also cited in Study A by audiogames developers.

For Task 02 the moderator-researcher brought to the discussion some of the guidelines that were evaluated in the pre-questionnaire as less clear (D4, D26, D7, D34), less important (D16) or less clear and minor importance (D5, D17). For the guidelines that were considered less clear, there were problems of understanding about them, participants were asked to make a suggestion of a new description of the guidelines. Observations and suggestions for improvements in the descriptions of the guidelines can be observed in Table 2.

Table 2. Result of observations and suggestions for descriptions of Task 02.

Guideline	Suggestion/note	Focus group
D4	Suggestion of description	Provide a safe and penalty-free environment so that the user to practice the mechanics freely
D5	Note	It depends a lot on the design of the game, but it does not accessibility
D7	Note	Reinforce that the environment to be exploited is virtual and remove the item "GPS"
D16	Suggestion of description	The use of keys, buttons or gestures should be used in a cohesive way, avoiding little used combinations
D17	Note	It will depend on the game-design and the purpose of the game
D26	Suggestion of description	Initial presentation of a game mechanic in a didactic way
D34	Suggestion of description	Avoid using visual information as the only source of information. Diverse visual and sound alerts

Guidelines D5 and D17 were considered less clear and less important. The group reported that D5 (Include auxiliary game modes, with direct access to secret areas and challenges) is unrelated to the original guidelines and a game design decision that does not interfere with gameplay. While D17 (Avoiding actions that require user's precision to interact in the game scenario), they argued that it depends on the game design and goal proposed by the game.

To conclude the Focus group, a space for discussion of the guidelines was opened in a general way. P5 suggested examples of the use of the guidelines. P2 reported on the importance of including a user test guideline, with testing the mechanics in isolation and then together. P3 commented on D12 (including features of haptic interfaces such as vibration and touch capabilities), stating that it depends on the hardware - it was a consensus in the group - and it should be possible to explore the possible resources of available hardware.

3.5   Consolidation of the Results

Based on the results obtained in this section, some guidelines have undergone changes in their descriptions (D4, D7, D16, D26, and D34) in order to provide a better understanding of what they are proposing. Additionally, one was excluded (D5) because its priority since Study A has always remained low and the Focus Group has confirmed this issue.

According to the results of Study A, some of the guidelines stood out because they were considered high priority by at least half of the respondents in that study. A total of 15 guidelines were related, and all 7 guidelines considered to be basic to implementation by the Focal Group were also related in that group of selected guidelines. Similarly, we verified which guidelines were implemented as fully implemented by at least half of the respondents and only the basic guideline "Shortcut Keys" did not appear in this second relation, among the 18 guidelines listed. Table 3 presents these relationships between the guidelines. In this way, it is clear that such basic guidelines are really essential to the implementation, by the opinion of different experts in the development of audiogames.

Table 3. Comparison between the results of Study A, Audiogame developed and the Focus Group, regarding the basic guidelines

Study A _(Numbering of Proposal initial [8])_		Audiogame Developed _(Numbering of Proposal preliminary (3.2))_			Focus Group _(Fair Play numbering)_
Priority High	_Implemented Fully_	_Implemented Fully_	_Implemented Partially_		_7 basic guidelines_
D3	D1	D1	D11		D9
D5	D2	D2	D15		D18
D8	D5	D3	D22		D25
D9	D7	D6	D23		D26
D10	D8	D8	D29		D27
D11	D9	D9	D30		D28
D15	D10	D10	D31		D29
D17	D12	D16			
D19	D15	D17			
D22	D16	D19			
D26	D17	D25			
D27	D18	D26			
D28	D19	D27			
D29	D22	D28			
D30	D26	D34			
	D28				
	D29				
	D30				

4   Fair Play: A Proposal Guidelines

Based on the previous steps, 33 guidelines were consolidated that take into account criteria of accessibility, usability, and gameplay. The following steps, which are related to its presentation, provide an instrument to be followed during the process of developing an audiogame and a web environment for the public consultation of the results of this study.

4.1   Stage 5: Elaboration of the Instrument

As a final result, an instrument/guide was developed to be used by the developer during the audiogame development process. Thus, it is possible to identify the guidelines to be implemented and then confirm with the checkpoints of the heuristics if the implementation of the guideline is in agreement. The complete tool with the guidelines, their relations to the evaluation heuristics and checkpoints, can be seen below.

- Category: GAME EXPERIENCE, LEVEL, AND PROGRESSION
  - **D01. Clear Language:** Use simpler and clear dialogues so that the instructions in the game become easy to understand. [5, 10, 14, 17, 18, 20, 21]
    Related evaluation heuristics: H2
  - **D02. Game experience:** Offer predictable and expected information, making game content, challenges and functionality consistent with the mechanics of the game, while avoiding escaping your gameplay pattern. [17–20]
    Related evaluation heuristics: H4
  - **D03. Levels of difficulty:** Offer varying levels of difficulty and allow them to be adjusted during the game. [4, 14, 17, 18, 20, 21]
    Related evaluation heuristics: H3, H11
  - **D04. Training:** Provide a safe environment so that the player can practice the penalty mechanics of play. [1, 10, 18]
    Related evaluation heuristics: H10
  - **D05. Quick start:** Enable the game to start quickly, without the need to navigate through several menus. [17–21]
    Related evaluation heuristics: H3, H7
  - **D06. Exploitation of the environment:** Provide means to help players explore the virtual environment of the game by accessing content and interactive elements through easy orientation, moving through cardinal points and/or degrees, to determine where they are in the game. [6, 10, 18, 23]
    Related evaluation heuristics: H2, H11
  - **D07. Logical sequence:** Provide menus that follow a logical sequence. [3, 5]
    Related evaluation heuristics: H6, H12
  - **D08. Navigation patterns:** Use screen navigation navigation patterns for easy navigation. [3, 5, 14, 15, 19]
    (*Basic guideline for implementation*)
    Related evaluation heuristics: H4, H12
  - **D09. Keep context:** Keep the player informed of what is happening in the game, avoiding loss of context. [3]
    Related evaluation heuristics: H1

- **D10. Progress Summaries:** Allow the player to visualize their progress summaries during the different phases of a game, such as punctuation, lives and challenges. [3,18,20,21]
  Related evaluation heuristics: H1
- **D11. Vibrating and touch features** Include haptic interfaces features such as vibration and touch features. [6,23,24]
  Related evaluation heuristics: H12
- Category: **DATA ENTRY/SOFTWARE AND HARDWARE**
  - **D12. Sensitivity and time of action:** Provide a means of setting time-dependent characteristics such as sensitivity and speed of events, movements, and game actions. [3,4,14,17,18,20,21,24]
    Related evaluation heuristics: H3, H7
  - **D13. Auto save:** Enable mechanisms to automatically save the current state of the game. [18,19]
    Related evaluation heuristics: H3
  - **D14. Input Devices:** Allow the use of different input devices. [3–6,10]
    Related evaluation heuristics: H3, H7, H12
  - **D15. Simultaneous and special keys:** Provide the use of keys, buttons or gestures cohesively, avoiding combinations rarely used in game patterns. [5,17,18,20]
    Related evaluation heuristics: H7, H12
  - **D16. Accuracy of actions:** Take care of the actions that require the player's precision to interact in the game scenario, verifying if its use makes sense to the context of the game. [3–5,15,18,23]
    Related evaluation heuristics: H12
  - **D17. Assistive Technology Assets:** Predict the use of assistive technology features, such as voice control, extended keyboards, brain-computer interface, screen reader, virtual loupes, and so on. [4,10,14,16–19,23,24]
    Related evaluation heuristics: H3, H7, H12
  - **D18. Conflict between sounds:** Avoid conflicts in the sound information that is emitted by the game and those that are transmitted by screen reader. [3,6,16,23]
    (***Basic guideline for implementation***)
    Related evaluation heuristics: H12
  - **D19. Configuring controls and commands:** Enable game controls and commands to be changed/reconfigured, making sure they are as simple as possible. [4,10,11,14–18,23]
    Related evaluation heuristics: H3, H7
  - **D20. Voice Commands:** When using voice commands, use individual words from a small vocabulary, for example: "Yes", "No", "Exit", "Open", "Skip", "Save" and so on. [11,18,24]
    Related evaluation heuristics: H3, H7
- Category: **INSTALLATION/CONFIGURATION/HELP**
  - **D21. Issuing immediate feedbacks:** Send immediate feedbacks according to the player's actions, so that he can know that his actions are

being processed, such as reporting to the player about the data entries, need to close the dialog window, and so on. [3,4,6,15,18–21]
Related evaluation heuristics: H12

- **D22. Tips and reminders to the player:** Send tips and reminders to the player, depending on the context in the game, to assist you in cases of difficulty, including mechanisms to reduce the occurrence of errors, such as disabling menu items that are not available to use, close dialog dialog after user action, and so on. [3,10,19]
  Related evaluation heuristics: H10

- **D23. Bug fix:** Include mechanisms that provide error correction, such as allowing the player to return to a safe point in the game, providing messages clearly indicating the reason for the error, and so on. [10]
  Related evaluation heuristics: H5, H9

- **D24. Manual and documentation:** Provide manuals and installation instructions and game setup mechanisms. [3,10,15,18–21]
  Related evaluation heuristics: H10

- **D25. Tutorial:** Provide information on how to play and interact in the game through an initial presentation of a game mechanic in a didactic way. [15,18,20]
  (*Basic guideline for implementation*)
  Related evaluation heuristics: H10

- **D26. Hotkeys:** Provide shortcut keys to interact in the game options and to access information, such as to save, exit, pause, access help, and so on. [3,18]
  (*Basic guideline for implementation*)
  Related evaluation heuristics: H3, H7

- **D27. Accessibility features:** Inform in the descriptions of the game explicitly that it provides for use by people with visual impairment. [14,16,18]
  (*Basic guideline for implementation*)
  Related evaluation heuristics: H10

– Category: **SOUND ELEMENTS**
  - **D28. Interactive sound mechanisms:** Use fun sounds, audio tracks and sound effects such as 3D sound, binaural recording, surround sound, sonar style audio map and etc. in a fun and entertaining way. [3,6,14,17,18,20,23]
    (*Basic guideline for implementation*)
    Related evaluation heuristics: H11

  - **D29. Different sound for each event:** Allow the objects and scenery of the game to be recognized by sound, providing sonic feedback for the actions of the player. [3,10,15,18]
    (*Basic guideline for implementation*)
    Related evaluation heuristics: H12

  - **D30. Sound and Audio Settings:** Provide mechanisms to configure the audios and sounds of the game, such as narratives and ambient noises, including the ability to mute and/or turn them off, toggle them,

controlling their duration, voices and volume of sounds, individually. [3–5, 11, 14, 15, 17–21]
Related evaluation heuristics: H3, H7
- Category: **GRAPHIC ELEMENTS**
  - **D31. Graphics Configuration:** Provide graphic settings options, such as disable 3D graphics, enable color customization, brightness, contrast and text and font size. [1, 4–6, 11, 16–21, 23, 24]
  Related evaluation heuristics: H12
  - **D32. Interactive Elements:** Clearly indicate the existence of interactive visual elements, using sound elements to describe them. [18, 23]
  Related evaluation heuristics: H12
  - **D33. Repetitive Elements:** Avoid repetitive animations and visual elements as the only source of information, diversifying visual and sound alerts. [5, 10, 18, 19]
  Related evaluation heuristics: H8, H12.

4.2   Stage 6: Web Environment

In order for this set of guidelines to be consulted by a greater number of developers interested in the development of audiogames, a web environment was developed[11], with the relation of the guidelines and linked evaluation heuristics, in order to bring the research work closer to the stakeholders and directly involve them in order to achieve continuous improvement. Initially, the environment was only available in the Portuguese language, but an English version is provided.

The environment was developed in a static way, that is, without the need for a server and was hosted publicly in on GitHub. This way, anyone interested in the topic could reuse the code and even suggest changes. The environment was organized into five sections, and in the Categories section, all 33 guidelines of the final set of guidelines, named in this study by Fair Play, are listed and organized into their 5 main categories. In the Basic Guidelines section are presented the 7 minimum implementation guidelines for an audiogame project. The Test section presents a reminder of the importance of performing tests during all phases of an audiogame project, to further ensure the accessibility and usability of the game to a player with visually impaired. In the About section, a brief explanation of the project developed in this research is described. And finally, the Contact section brings information to the communication, with the objective of generating interaction and possible evolutions of this project.

5   Conclusion

The final proposal of guidelines presented in this study was elaborated taking into account the existing literature on recommendations for the development of

---

[11] https://olimarborges.github.io/FairPlay/.

games accessible in general. Because it is a study focused on the development of games for the visually impaired, there was a constant follow-up by blind users throughout the creation of the guidelines, aiming to consolidate a more concise set with the target audience of this study. It is important to emphasize that the audiogame project must, besides following good development recommendations, include during all the processes of elaboration of the game, tests with players with visual deficiency so that the users can grant important feedbacks, aiming at a more accessible and immersive game.

The present work made possible the consolidation of the initial study proposed by Campos and Borges [8]. For this, it involved a process for evaluating the guidelines with accessible and end-user game developers. With developers, there was the application of an online questionnaire, the development of an audiogame and a focus group. With the end user, there was the evaluation of audiogames already available to verify which guidelines were applied. In addition, there was the linkage of the guidelines with heuristics of evaluation of audiogames, by the authors of this work, in which an instrument was created.

This will enable a more concise development with recommendations based on the literature. Fair play guidelines have been made available for community use through a web environment. It should be noted that by not applying guidelines, during the development of an audiogame, it can lead to a decrease in the interest of a user with VI in the use of the game. Also, when given audiogame does not have a focus on the end user, the player's experience can become discouraging. It is not enough to predict the use of different audios if they do not create the feeling of immersion and do not guide the player in an easy and interactive way.

Acknowledgments. OTB thank the PDTI Program, financed by Dell Computers of Brazil Ltd (Law 8.248/91) and ThoughtWorks. JDO also are supported by CAPES/PROSUP Ph.D. scholarships. To the developers and the blind user who agreed to participate in this study.

References

1. Abenójar, A.V.: Buenas prácticas de accesibilidad en videojuegos. http://www.ceapat.es/InterPresent1/groups/imserso/documents/binario/accesvideojuegos.pdf. Accessed 2016
2. Araújo, M.C.C., Façanha, A.R., Darin, T.G.R., Sánchez, J., Andrade, R.M.C., Viana, W.: Um estudo das recomendações de acessibilidade para audiogames móveis. In: Simpósio Brasileiro de Jogos e Entretenimento Digital. pp. 2179–2259. SBC, Teresina (2015)
3. Bannick, J.: Blind computer games: guidelines for building blind-accessible computer games. http://www.blindcomputergames.com/guidelines/guidelines.html. Accessed 2016
4. Barlet, M.C., Spohn, S.D.: Includification: A Practical Guide to Game Accessibility. The Ablegamers Foundation, Charles Town (2012)
5. BBC: Future media standards and guidelines. http://www.bbc.co.uk/guidelines/futuremedia/accessibility/games.shtml. Accessed 2016

6. Bierre, K., Hinn, M., Martin, T., McIntosh, M., Snider, T., Stone, K., Westin, T.: Accessibility in Games: Motivations and Approaches. IGDA, Toronto (2004)
7. de Borba Campos, M., Damasio Oliveira, J.: Usability, accessibility and gameplay heuristics to evaluate audiogames for users who are blind. In: Antona, M., Stephanidis, C. (eds.) UAHCI 2016. LNCS, vol. 9737, pp. 38–48. Springer, Cham (2016). https://doi.org/10.1007/978-3-319-40250-5_4
8. Teixeira Borges, O., de Borba Campos, M.: "I'm blind, can i play?" recommendations for the development of audiogames. In: Antona, M., Stephanidis, C. (eds.) UAHCI 2017. LNCS, vol. 10278, pp. 351–365. Springer, Cham (2017). https://doi.org/10.1007/978-3-319-58703-5_26
9. Carvalho, J.O.F.: Referenciais para projetistas e usuários de interfaces de computadores destinadas aos deficientes visuais. Master's thesis, Faculdade de Engenharia Eletrica - UNICAMP (1994)
10. Cheiran, J.F.P.: Jogos inclusivos : diretrizes de acessibilidade para jogos digitais. Master's thesis, Instituto de Informática - UFRGS (2013)
11. Microsoft Corporation: The need for accessible games. https://msdn.microsoft.com/en-us/library/windows/desktop/ee415219(v=vs.85).aspx. Accessed 2016
12. Desurvire, H., Caplan, M., Toth, J.A.: Using heuristics to evaluate the playability of games. In: International Conference on Human Factors in Computing Systems, pp. 1509–1512. ACM, Vienna (2004)
13. Desurvire, H., Wiberg, C.: Game usability heuristics (PLAY) for evaluating and designing better games: the next iteration. In: Ozok, A.A., Zaphiris, P. (eds.) OCSC 2009. LNCS, vol. 5621, pp. 557–566. Springer, Heidelberg (2009). https://doi.org/10.1007/978-3-642-02774-1_60
14. Special effect: Wish list for accessible game design. http://www.gamebase.info/magazine/read/wish-list-for-accessible-game-design_531.html. Accessed 2016
15. Garcia, F.E., de Almeida Neris, V.P.: Design guidelines for audio games. In: Kurosu, M. (ed.) HCI 2013. LNCS, vol. 8005, pp. 229–238. Springer, Heidelberg (2013). https://doi.org/10.1007/978-3-642-39262-7_26
16. GASIG I.G.D.A.G.A.: Game accessibility topten. https://igda-gasig.org/about-game-accessibility/game-accessibility-top-ten. Accessed 2016
17. Grammenos, D.: Game over: learning by dying. In: International Conference on Human Factors in Computing Systems, pp. 1443–1452. ACM (2008)
18. Game Accessibility Guidelines: Game accessibility guidelines full list. http://gameaccessibilityguidelines.com/full-list. Accessed 2016
19. Moura, E.J.R., Cheiran, J.F.P.M.A.M.: Diretrizes de Acessibilidade para Jogos em Dispositivos Móveis. Trabalho de conclusão de curso, Universidade Federal do Pampa - UNIPAMPA (2015), http://dspace.unipampa.edu.br:8080/bitstream/riu/887/1/Diretrizes%20de%20acessibilidade%20para%20jogos%20em%20dispositivos%20m%C3%B3veis.pdf
20. Ossman, R., Miesenberger, K.: Guidelines for the development of accessible computer games. http://ucdmanager.net/heuristics/68. Accessed 2016
21. UPS Project: Guidelines for the development of entertaining software for people with multiple learning disabilities. http://www.medialt.no/rapport/entertainment_guidelines. Accessed 2016
22. Rouse III, R.: Game design: Theory and practice. Jones & Bartlett Learning, Texas (2010)
23. Yuan, B., Folmer, E., Harris Jr., F.C.: Game accessibility: a survey. Univ. Access Inf. Soc. 10, 81–100 (2011)
24. Zahand, B.: Developing for different types of disabilities. http://www.brannonz.com/accessibility/disabilities.html. Accessed Out 2016

Comparison of Feedback Modes
for the Visually Impaired: Vibration vs. Audio

Sibu Varghese Jacob$^{(\boxtimes)}$ and I. Scott MacKenzie

Department of Electrical Engineering and Computer Science, York University,
Toronto, ON, Canada
sibuvjacob@gmail.com, mack@cse.yorku.ca

Abstract. Mobile computing has brought a shift from physical keyboards to touch screens. This has created challenges for the visually impaired. Touch screen devices exacerbate the sense of touch for the visually impaired, thus requiring alternative ways to improve accessibility. In this paper, we examine the use of vibration and audio as alternative ways to provide location guidance when interacting with touch screen devices. The goal was to create an interface where users can press on the touch screen and take corrective actions based on non-visual feedback. With vibration feedback, different types of vibration and with audio feedback different tones indicated the proximity to the goal. Based on the feedback users were required to find a set of predetermined buttons. User performance in terms of speed and efficiency was gathered. It was determined that vibration feedback took on average 41.3% longer than audio in terms of time to reach the end goal. Vibration feedback was also less efficient than audio taking on average 35.2% more taps to reach the end goal. Even though the empirical evidence favored audio, six out of 10 participants preferred vibration feedback due to its benefits and usability in real life.

Keywords: Mobile user interface · Feedback mode · Vibration
Audio · Visually impaired

1 Introduction

Technology plays a significant role in most people's lives. An example is the constantly evolving field of computing. Over the years, computing has shifted towards mobility, with mobile computing arguably one of the greatest innovations of our time. From being stuck on a desktop computer and confined to a desk, we are now *on the move* and using ever-smaller devices.

In mobile computing, user interface (UI) design is of interest as it directly involves the user's satisfaction and ability to complete tasks. Designing a user interface is challenging since it requires optimizing the interface to be aesthetically pleasing while at the same time maintaining the desired functionality, without hindrances.

Mobile user interfaces are especially challenging due to the added constraints to support mobility. For example, there is a need to fit considerable information onto a small screen. Mobile user interfaces should also enable the user to perform the tasks with minimal effort in diverse environments.

© Springer International Publishing AG, part of Springer Nature 2018
M. Antona and C. Stephanidis (Eds.): UAHCI 2018, LNCS 10907, pp. 420–432, 2018.
https://doi.org/10.1007/978-3-319-92049-8_30

As much as mobile user interfaces have evolved, there are still improvements needed. One field of interest is improving the accessibility features of mobile user interface to accommodate different characteristics of humans, including those with special needs. One of the most essential pillars of achieving accessibility is providing quality feedback to the user. Feedback can be provided using auditory, visual, and tactile forms where each has advantages and disadvantages. This is particularly important for accessibility since appropriate feedback can guide users with extra information or even act as a form of alert.

Android mobile devices increase accessibility at the system level. As seen in Fig. 1, Android has a built-in feature called TalkBack, which provides spoken feedback. Spoken feedback is meant to assist blind and low-vision users who are unable to look at the screen. In general, this might be a good idea and should work most of the time, but issues arise when the user is in a crowded area where the noise level is higher than usual. Another situation where TalkBack is not effective is for users who are hearing impaired. These types of scenarios highlight the need to provide feedback through other means.

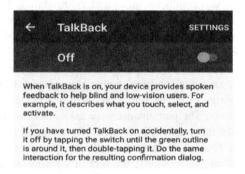

Fig. 1. Android TalkBack feature.

Since visually impaired users are unable to look at the screen, they are challenged in utilizing device functions such as navigation, data entry, accepting/declining actions, etc. The topic of this paper is to explore methods to assist the visually impaired in achieving tasks without looking at the screen. The goal of the user study presented herein is to examine a task that avoids visual feedback and instead relies on vibration or audio feedback. To achieve this, various forms of vibratory and audio feedback will be used to guide the user towards a goal. The feedback should enable the user to perform variety of tasks in different types of applications.

The methodology used to guide a visually impaired user is as follows. A visually impaired user wishes to press a button on the screen to proceed. Since the user is unaware of where the button is located s/he would press the screen at various locations. For each press the user interface determines if a goal button is pressed. If the user presses the wrong location (an alternative button), different variations of vibratory or audio feedback are provided. As the user gets closer to the goal, the vibratory/audio feedback differs, thus informing the user that s/he is getting closer to the goal. The functionality can also be implemented at the operating system or application level. This would be beneficial when the user's goal is unknown. In these forms of implementation all the possible actions that can be performed by the interface would be given variations of vibration/audio feedback and would be used to guide the user to the desired end goal. The user can determine if s/he wants to perform the action that was guided by the user interface.

2 Related Work

An examination of tactile feedback for mobile interaction was conducted by Brewster et al. [1]. They were interested in mitigating the difficulty in using touch-screen keyboards on personal digital assistants (PDAs). Their research was conducted in situations where users were mobile, motivated by the observation that users make more errors when subjected to external factors such as shaking. The first phase of the study was conducted in a lab setting, where participants entered poems into a PDA device. With tactile feedback added, users were able to enter greater amount of text with less errors. The second phase was conducted on an underground train. With tactile feedback present, participants were better able to detect errors and take corrective actions. Qualitative responses strongly favored the presence of tactile feedback.

A study by Shin et al. [5] examined tactile feedback for graphical buttons on touch devices. Different tactile patterns were designed and evaluated. The goal was to provide a sensation of pressing an actual physical button on a device that only has a touch screen. To extend the range of tactile sensations, new hardware was designed implementing six tactile patterns. The participants were asked to rank the different patterns based on which provided the most realistic sense of touching a physical button. From the different patterns, a Touch + Release pattern scored the highest, with participants ranking it the most realistic in providing the feel of clicking a real button. The participants also stated that using vibration reminded them of a warning.

Chang and O'Sullivan [2] conducted a study on audio-haptic feedback in mobile phones aiming to improve the user interface through audio-haptic feedback. The study presented ways to create different types of audio-haptic feedback. In order to test the theory, 30 participants were given a haptic phone and a non-haptic phone and were asked to play ring tones as well as navigate using the menu keys. Participant ranking indicated a preference for the feel of the interaction in the presence of audio-haptic feedback. The study also found audio-haptic feedback improved the "perception of audio quality".

A set of audio-based multi-touch interaction techniques for blind users to properly interact with touch screens was studied by Kane et al. [3]. The motivation for the study arose from the fact that touch-screen devices are hard to use for the visually impaired since they must look at the screen to determine the location of UI elements. Elements in a touch screen cannot be felt to degree of physical elements such as buttons. To improve the accessibility for visually-impaired users, Slide Rule was designed. Slide Rule works by creating a touch surface that talks, and therefore in practice transforms the surface to a "non-visual interface". Slide Rule achieves this by using several basic gesture interactions such as a "one-finger scan" for browsing a list, "second-finger tap" for selection, a "flick gesture" for additional actions and "L-select gesture" which provides hierarchical information. To perform the test, 10 blind users were asked to perform tasks on two devices, one enabled with Slide Rule. The tasks included making a phone call, using email, etc. Accuracy and speed were measured. The study determined that Slide Rule reduced task completion time, compared to a device with physical buttons. But, there was a corresponding increase in errors. The study concluded that touch screens could be used as a form of "input technology for blind users".

Yatani and Truong [6] studied the use of tactile feedback to provide visually impaired users with "semantic information". The motivation arose from the fact that mobile touch-screen devices do not have tactile feedback and thus users are unable to understand the information presented without looking at the screen. To alleviate this problem, a new type of tactile feedback called SemFeel was developed. SemFeel uses different vibratory patterns to convey meaningful information on the location of user touch points. The system uses five vibration motors. SemFeel used vibratory feedback instead of audio feedback so the device could operate quietly and without interrupting others. Two experiments were conducted. The first asked the user to match the vibration pattern produced with a pattern shown on a screen. The goal was to gauge the accuracy of distinguishing patterns. The results indicated that participants had difficulty with counter-clockwise patterns. The second experiment focused on user performance, namely input accuracy, and compared SemFeel with a UI without tactile feedback and a UI with tactile feedback provided by one source. The task consisted of entering a set of numbers using a numeric keyboard. Three types of feedback were compared: no tactile feedback, single tactile feedback (using a single vibration motor), and multiple tactile feedback (SemFeel). The results demonstrated that SemFeel had higher accuracy when compared to no tactile feedback and single-motor tactile feedback. It was also concluded that using SemFeel shows promise for interacting without looking at a display, thus aiding visually-impaired users.

Li et al. [4] conducted a study to determine the effects of replacing a visual interface with auditory feedback. A prototype called BlindSight was developed. The aim was to eliminate the need to look at the screen for accessing a phone's functions and personal information during a phone conversation, thus eliminating interruptions. Two experiments were conducted. In the first phase, 12 participants were asked to enter a 10-digit number on the device. Users were provided with auditory feedback to acknowledge the correct input as well as input errors. Three interfaces were compared: ear, flip, and visual. It was determined that the ear interface was the best option. The second phase of the experiment used eight participants who performed tasks such as adding contacts during a phone conversation. Six of the eight participants preferred the BlindSight interface.

3   Method

An experiment was conducted in which users were asked to determine the effects of vibratory feedback vs. audio feedback. The results were then analyzed on the basis of efficiency as well as the speed in which users were able to complete the task.

3.1 Participants

Twelve participants were recruited. Of the twelve, the data for two of the participants were discarded since they did not seem to fully understand the task. The remaining 10 participants consisted of five male and five female participants. All of the participants who participated were not visually impaired, as this is instead being simulated in the application. Participants were between 19–25 years. All participants use mobile devices daily. The participants received a $10 remuneration for their assistance.

3.2 Apparatus

The test was conducted on an ZTE *Grand X4* mobile phone running Google *Android 6.0.1 Marshmallow*. See Fig. 2. The device has a 5.5" (139.7 mm) display with a resolution of 720 × 180 pixels and a 16:9 screen ratio. The display was an in-plane switching (IPS) liquid-crystal display (LCD) capacitive touchscreen with a 267 ppi pixel density. The device has a vibration actuator as well as a speaker.

Fig. 2. ZTE Grand X4.

A custom application was built using *Android Studio* version 2.3.3.

The application was written in Java for the functionality and used extensible markup language (XML) for the graphical user interface.

The setup screen and results screen of the application are seen in Fig. 3a and b. The application included two modes. In mode 1, the application relied on vibration feedback. In mode 2, the application used audio feedback. The UI for each mode is in Fig. 4a and b. Fifteen buttons appear in each mode.

In mode 1, the vibration features of the device were accessed using the Vibrator class. Varying types of vibrational feedback were created by increasing the duration of vibration and changing the vibration pattern. The correct "end goal" for each of the five trials were buttons 15, 10, 3, 9 and 4. One button in each of the four directions around the end goal used a vibration pattern of three 100-ms pulses indicating one button away

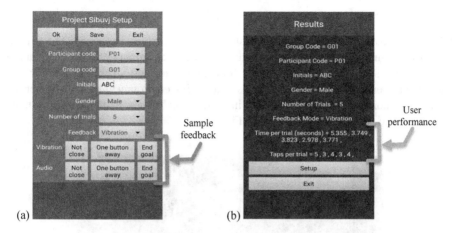

Fig. 3. Various parts of the application (a) setup and (b) result screen.

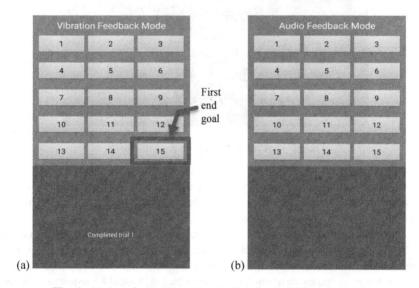

Fig. 4. Various feedback modes (a) vibration and (b) audio mode.

from goal. The other buttons had a single 100-ms vibration pulse indicating the end goal was more than a button away, and finally the end goal was a single 500-ms pulse indicating the correct button.

In mode 2, audio-feedback features were implemented using the `ToneGenerator` class. Different sounds were used to represent user's proximity to the goal. From the `ToneGenerator` class, TONE_CDMA_SOFT_ERROR_LITE for 300 ms indicated one button away from goal, TONE_PROP_BEEP for 100 ms indicate more than one button away from goal, and TONE_CDMA_HIGH_L for 500 ms indicate the end goal has been reached.

3.3   Procedure

When participants arrived, the purpose of the experiment was explained. The experimenter then summarized the tasks to participants. Participants used the demonstration buttons in the setup screen to sample the different sounds and vibrations. See Fig. 3a. Participants were then given practice trials. The testing environment had mostly normal background noise. The device was held in participants' hands, as they liked, as trials were performed. An example is seen in Fig. 5.

Fig. 5. Participant performing the experiment.

To offset order effects, the participants were divided into two groups. One group did the audio-feedback trials first, followed by the vibration feedback trials. The other group did the trials in the reverse order.

In the vibration feedback mode, participants were asked to press the buttons that they desire. They were asked to reach the end goal by finding and pressing a predetermined finish button. In order to simulate a situation that visually impaired users encounter, the participants were not aware which buttons would be required to press in order to finish the test. Instead, they were asked to reach the end goal by relying on the feedback provided from the device's vibration. Each button press had varying types of vibrational feedback, as noted earlier. When the participants pressed buttons closer to the end goal, a pattern-based vibrational feedback was provided indicating they are getting closer to the end goal. Once the participant pressed the correct end-goal button, a lengthy vibration was produced to notify the user and terminate the trial.

Users were also provided with a text on the display indicating the completion of the different trials. This is seen in Fig. 4a. After the completion of the first trial, the second trial started with different predetermined finish button. For each trial, the predetermined buttons changed. After the completion of the trials the members of group 1 were given access to the feedback mode 2 which utilizes the audio feedback.

Similar to mode 1, before the test for mode 2 was conducted participants were allowed to sample the demonstration buttons to understand the different tones that indicated the correct direction. Participants were then given access to the test and completed each trial upon pressing the predetermined finish button.

The test concluded when all of the trials were completed using both of the feedback modes and the user was brought to the result screen as seen in Fig. 3b. The experiment took less than five minutes to complete. After the test was completed participants were given an open-ended questionnaire to solicit information and provide feedback on which mode they preferred. The questionnaire also invited participants to provide suggestions for improvement.

3.4 Design

The user study employed a 2×5 within-subjects design. The independent variables (and levels) were as follows:

- Feedback mode (vibration, audio)
- Trial (1, 2, 3, 4, 5)

Similarly, there were two dependent variables, time per trial and efficiency. Efficiency was quantified as the number of taps required to complete a trial. In all, there were 10 Participants $\times$ 2 Feedback Modes $\times$ 5 Trials = 100 Trials.

4 Results and Discussion

There were 100 trials in total, where each participant performed five trials for each of two feedback modes. In general, participants completed tasks faster with audio feedback compared to vibration feedback, thus making audio feedback a viable choice in terms of speed. Audio feedback was also better in terms of efficiency, as vibration feedback took more taps per trial than audio feedback. Although audio feedback performed better in both speed and efficiency, users generally preferred vibration feedback for social reasons.

4.1 Speed - Time Per Trial

The mean time per trial was 10.5 s over the 100 trials in the experiment. The mean for the audio feedback trials was 8.7 s. Vibration feedback took 41.3% longer with a mean time per trial of 12.3 s. See Fig. 6. The difference was statistically significant ($F_{1,9} = 7.57$, $p < .05$).

Reducing the time as much as possible in order to reach the goal faster is paramount and audio feedback provides a promising start. This difference could be possibly due to the need to wait and feel the vibration. Audio feedback on the other hand is easily distinguishable allowing participants to quickly realize that they have not reached the end goal yet. The feedback result aligns with Yatani and Truong's findings [6] in which the interface with tactile feedback was slower than an interface without tactile feedback.

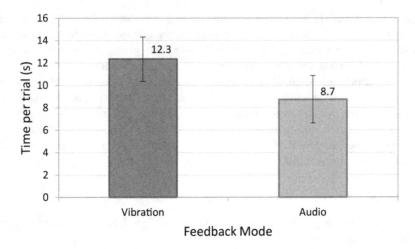

Fig. 6. Mean time per trial (s) by feedback mode. Error bars represent ±1 *SD*.

A comparison of the mean times per trial between the feedback modes is presented in Fig. 7. Of the five trials, the highest mean completion time for vibration feedback was 14.7 s thus making trial 4 the slowest for vibration. On the other hand, audio feedback experienced its slowest mean completion time in trial 1 which was 11.4 s. It can be observed that the highest mean completion time for vibration observed in trial 4 was 3.3 s or 28.9% slower than the highest time audio feedback experienced in trial 1. The promising finding is how audio feedback shows steady improvement from trial 1 to trial 5, with each trial decreasing in the time to complete the task.

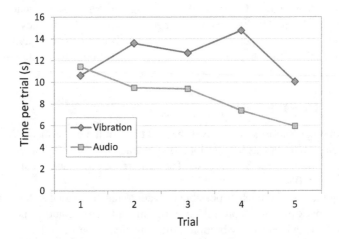

Fig. 7. Mean time per trial (s) by feedback mode and trial.

This demonstrates promise for the future since as the users get familiar with the various audio feedback tones, the possibility to reduce completion time improves.

Surprisingly, vibration feedback showed increase in time after trial 1, except for trial 3, peaking at trial 4 after which it reaches its lowest time in trial 5. The considerable delay for vibration could be attributed to participants familiarizing themselves with the interface to properly understand the different variations and meanings.

As users became familiar with the vibration forms, we can see a significant improvement in trial 5 for vibration feedback. This could suggest an even lower completion time for vibration feedback with continued practice. However, the effect of trial on time per trial was not statistically significant ($F_{4,36} = 0.71$, ns). These findings therefore show participants were able to learn audio feedback faster and thus performed better than with vibration feedback.

4.2   Efficiency - Number of Button Taps Per Trial

The second dependent variable was efficiency, which was measured as the number of button taps required before reaching the desired end goal. Obviously, lower scores are better. The grand mean was 5.9 taps per trial. The mean for audio feedback was 5.1 taps per trial. Vibration feedback took 35.2% more taps per trial with a mean of 6.9 taps. See Fig. 8. However, the difference was not statistically significant ($F_{1,9} = 1.76$, $p > .05$). This demonstrates another area where audio feedback performed better than vibration feedback (although the difference was not statistically significant).

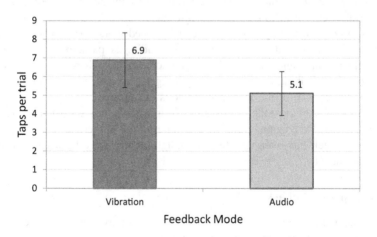

Fig. 8. Number of button taps per trial by feedback mode. Error bars represent ±1 SD.

The breakdown by trial paints an interesting picture. As seen in Fig. 9, the mean for vibration feedback was 5.2 taps in trial 1 which was lower than the rest of the trials afterward. As the trials went on, the number of taps for vibration feedback increased, reaching the highest at trial 4 requiring a mean of 8.9 button taps.

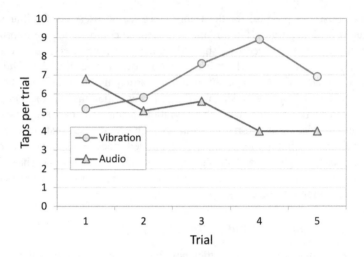

Fig. 9. Number of button taps by trial and feedback mode.

After trial 4, vibration improved, reaching 6.9 taps in trial 5 which was again higher than trial 1 at 5.2 taps. On the other hand, audio feedback had its highest number of taps in trial 1 at 6.8 taps. Comparing the two highest means, namely trial 4 for vibration and trial 1 for audio, we see that audio feedback was 2.1 taps lower or 30.8% less compared to vibration. Audio feedback demonstrated considerable improvement from trial 1 to trial 5, except in trial 3 with a slight increase.

This is in contrast to vibration which demonstrated worse performance over time, except trial 5. Understandably, in the case of audio, as participants became more familiar with the task and the meaning of audio feedback, there was improvement, unlike in the case of vibration. These findings suggest that with continued practice there is a possibility for both of the feedback methods to improve.

The effect of trial on efficiency (taps per trial) was not statistically significant ($F_{4,36} = 0.21$, ns). This, again, gives an indication in the higher efficiency capabilities that audio feedback has over vibration (although, again, the difference was not statistically significant).

4.3   Participant Feedback

An open-ended questionnaire was used to gather the participants preference of the feedback modes and the reasoning behind them. The results from the questionnaire were surprising. The majority of the participants preferred vibration feedback over the audio feedback. Of the 10 participants, six preferred vibration feedback while four participants preferred audio feedback. This is in contrast to the empirical evidence that was gathered which demonstrated audio feedback was faster and more efficient. There are several possible reasons for why participants preferred vibration.

One reason for preferring vibration is the annoyance of using audio in some environments. On vibration feedback, one of the participant said the following:

You can use it anywhere, anytime without interrupting others.

There are many places such as libraries which are meant to be quiet. In these places, unnecessary noise is an annoyance to others.

Another preference for vibration feedback was due to the effects of a noisy environment on an audio-based feedback. As mentioned by one participant,

If the user is in a noisy environment, then the audio is harder to hear.

In noisy environments such as public places it may not be possible to hear audio feedback. Vibration feedback would not have this issue since it is based entirely on feel.

On the other side, for users preferring audio they mentioned the ability to distinguish audio feedback better as opposed to vibration. One participant mentioned the following:

Vibrations are often more similar to each other, not as easy to distinguish, compared to different auditory signals.

Finally, participants also provided suggestions on improving the applications used for the user study. One participant mentioned using better audio feedback for the buttons "one button away" and "not close". The other improvement suggested by one of the participant was to add more rows in the application.

5 Limitations and Future Work

One of the most profound limitations in this study was the lack of visually impaired participants. The results are based on visually-abled users; results could differ if the trials were performed by visually-impaired users.

Another limitation is that the end-goal button was known in the experiment software. In real use, the end goal is often not known, but simply exists according to a user's intention. However, in some situations, such as games, the end goal may be known; so, the methodology employed here has some applications in practical use.

A possibility for future work is to use swipe gestures, rather than button taps. The user touches and moves their finger on the display. Feedback (audio or vibration) is generated repeatedly, and changes according to the distance from the goal, until the desired contact location is reached. Even if visually-abled participants were used, the talk could be done eyes-free – without looking at the display.

Additional future work could focus on the type of tones that are easier for users to understand as well as their effects on user performance. This also applies to vibration with the goal of improving speed, efficiency, and user satisfaction.

6 Conclusion

In conclusion, this user study compared two types of feedback, namely vibration and audio. The goal was to reduce the hindrances that are faced by visually-impaired users, since the transformation to touch-screen devices. The aim was to identify the ideal form of feedback that guides the user to a goal without the need for visual feedback.

To conduct the study, an application providing two different forms of feedback was designed. From the user study, it was determined that audio feedback performed better both in terms of speed as well as efficiency. Vibration feedback took 41.3% longer to complete and, as well, took 35.2% more taps than audio feedback. In terms of participants preference, six out of 10 participants preferred vibration feedback making it the preferred feedback mode as a practical issue in day-to-day life.

References

1. Brewster, S., Chohan, F., Brown, L.: Tactile feedback for mobile interactions. In: Proceedings of the ACM SIGCHI Conference on Human-Factors in Computing Systems - CHI 2007, pp. 159–162. ACM, New York (2007)
2. Chang, A., O'Sullivan, C.: Audio-haptic feedback in mobile phones. In: Extended Abstracts of the ACM SIGCHI Conference on Human Factors in Computing Systems - CHI 2005, pp. 1264–1267. ACM, New York (2005)
3. Kane, S.K., Bigham, J.P., Wobbrock, J.O.: Slide rule: making touch screens accessible to blind people using multi-touch interaction techniques. In: Proceedings of the ACM SIGACCESS Conference on Computers and Accessibility - ASSETS 2008, pp. 73–80. ACM, New York (2008)
4. Li, K.A., Baudisch, P., Hinckley, K.: BlindSight: eyes-free access to mobile phones. In: Proceedings of the ACM SIGCHI Conference on Human Factors in Computing Systems - CHI 2008, pp. 1389–1398. ACM, New York (2008)
5. Shin, H., Lim, J., Lee, J., Kyung, K., Lee, G.: Tactile feedback for button GUI on touch devices. In: Extended Abstracts of the ACM SIGCHI Conference on Human Factors in Computing Systems - CHI 2012, pp. 2633–2636. ACM, New York (2012)
6. Yatani, K., Truong, K.N.: SemFeel: a user interface with semantic tactile feedback for mobile touch-screen devices. In: Proceedings of the ACM SIGCHI Symposium on User Interface Software and Technology - UIST 2009, pp. 111–120. ACM, New York (2009)

Ultrasonic Waves to Support Human Echolocation

Florian von Zabiensky[✉], Michael Kreutzer[✉], and Diethelm Bienhaus[✉]

Technische Hochschule Mittelhessen, University of Applied Sciences,
Wiesenstr. 14, 35390 Gießen, Germany
Michael.Kreutzer@mni.thm.de

Abstract. In this paper a new device and methods to get an acoustic image of the environment is proposed. It can be used as an electronic aid for people who are visual impaired or blind. The paper presents current methods on human echolocation and current research in electronic aids. It also describes the technical basics and implementation of the audible high resolution ultrasonic sonar followed by a first evaluation of the device. The paper concludes with a discussion and a comparison to classical methods on active human echolocation.

Keywords: Human echo localization · Audible ultrasound sonar
Blind People · Spatial hearing · Obstacle detection

1 Introduction

The human echolocation is used by people who are visual impaired or blind to help build a mental spatial map of their environment. Echolocation is often enabled by creating a clicking sound with their tongue. Objects in the environment reflect discernible sounds to the human ear. The human brain can construct a structured image of the environment to build a mental spatial map. With this method, trained users reach enormous perception performances. Position, size or density of objects could be determined. In the brain of people who are blind, the visual cortex supports this kind of construction.

Unlike bats, which perceive structures in submillimeter range by ultrasonic echolocation, the human perception is restricted by the large wavelength of acoustic waves. Ultrasonic waves are reflected back by little, finely structured or soft objects where acoustic waves pass through objects like fences, bushes or thin piles without any considerable reflection because of their stronger diffraction. Another problem is smooth surfaces which normal don't point in the direction of the user. As light will be spread back at finely structured surfaces even roughly structured surfaces act like a mirror for acoustic waves. As a result, transversal sound waves from the user to the objects are not reflected to the user (stealth effect). This way it is not possible by the user to detect such objects. Ultrasonic

© Springer International Publishing AG, part of Springer Nature 2018
M. Antona and C. Stephanidis (Eds.): UAHCI 2018, LNCS 10907, pp. 433–449, 2018.
https://doi.org/10.1007/978-3-319-92049-8_31

waves with high frequencies or short wavelengths, conversely, are reflected to the sound source at smaller structures as soon as the wavelength reaches the order of magnitude of the structure size.

Experiments in creating electronic aids to hear ultrasonic waves and perceive special environmental information are very difficult. The cause lies in the complexity of hearing. Stereo microphones can only measure time differences of an ultrasonic signal. Only the azimuth angle can be derived at this time difference. The information if the object is in front, behind, on top or under the user is normally derived of complex direction-dependent filters which are formed among others by the pinna (outer ear) of the user. Without such a mechanical filter this information could not be derived. The digital clone of this filter, the Head Related Transfer Function, often fails in terms of functionality (forward backward confusion) and complexity (long record sessions).

Nevertheless, a way to use ultrasonic waves in combination with the human ear is enabled by nonlinear acoustics. In presence of high sound pressure levels, the air behaves in a nonlinear manner. This enables the transformation of ultrasonic to acoustic waves in the air itself by special signal modulation. During the process of transformation, the physical features of the ultrasonic signal retains in the acoustic signal. This auto conversion from ultrasonic to acoustic waves enables the user at perceiving ultrasonic signals with their own ears.

With this method a directed ultrasonic wave could be oriented to an object. The object reflects the ultrasonic waves. In the journey, from the source via the object back to the source, the ultrasonic waves will be transformed to acoustic waves. To the listener it behaves as if the object itself is the sound source.

A device which creates exactly the effects described above has been developed by the authors and will be described in the proposed paper. With this device it is possible for the user to hear objects and obstacles and determine their position. We tested the audible high resolution ultrasonic sonar (AHRUS) with four participants to get first insights about the possibilities that the system offers.

The device introduced brings a completely new application of ultrasonic waves in the case of electronic aids for people who are visual impaired and blind. The approach uses the ears of the user, with existing skills knowing how to interpret acoustic stimuli (like a falling coin), without additional help. The interpretation of the generated signals, however, needs to be trained, just like interpretation of normal acoustic signals was trained in childhood. But the advantages of the device are very promising and improve the perception of the environment as an extension to the white cane.

The proposed paper first comes up with a discussion on related work. Next the basics of spatial hearing are covered to give an insight about human hearing. A current strong related method is the human echolocation that is used by trained people to build an acoustic image of the environment. Different methods for human echolocation are explained in Sect. 4. The following section describes the AHRUS device itself. After a discussion of different promising signal shapes and methods to use the AHRUS device, a first evaluation of AHRUS is presented.

Conclusively a comparison of the results to classical methods of active human echolocation is drawn up followed by a conclusion.

2   Related Work

In research there are several aids that use ultrasonic signals. The existing aids share the commonality that they use the ultrasonic signals to measure characteristics about the environment and interpret echoes by a computer. This differs from the approach of using a parametric ultrasonic speaker and letting the ear and brain do the rest.

To name a view projects that use ultrasonic sensors for aiding people who are visual impaired, an early project was "The People Sonar" described in [3]. It uses ultrasonic sensors to get information about obstacles in the environment. It measures if there are living or non-living obstacles near the user and presents the information by vibrotactile feedback. Another project takes a greater advantage in the field of robotics. In [9] a robot is used as guide dog. The user pushes the robot and it recognizes and bypasses obstacles providing guidance around the obstacle.

There is also research related to the sonification aspect of AHRUS. AHRUS sonifies the environment physically but there is the possibility to do this in a virtual manner. The environment is recorded with 3D cameras. These images are processed and relevant obstacles can be presented by playing a 3D sound to the user that mimics the objects position. This topic, with others is researched in the "Sound of Vision" project [7].

The contribution of AHRUS in comparison to related work is a direct perception of the environment by the own ears and brain. There is no digital signal processing and presentation layer between the physical environment and the user.

3   Spatial Hearing

The human ear is very precise. It is possible to find a fallen object like keys just by hearing their sound as they land on the ground. The possibility of hearing stereo sounds is one key in the process of locating a sound source. Figure 1 on the left side illustrates a sound source that is moving on a horizontal plane where the azimuth angle changes. The brain can resolve direction by interpreting the time delay between the sound arriving each ear [10]. If the brain used only this method, it be impossible to differentiate sounds from the front and sounds from the back. To give a plain example Fig. 1 shows on the right side a sound source that is moving exactly in the middle between the ears. There is no delay between the sounds arriving at each ear. Determining the different directions is also done by introducing the shape of the ears and the head. They build a directional signal filter that enables the brain to determine the direction of a sound. Since childhood the brain is trained to make such calculations. By combining both

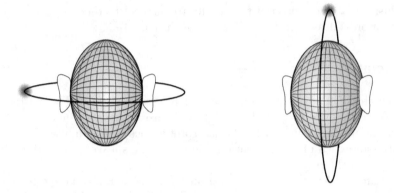

Fig. 1. Sound source that is moving in azimuth (left) or elevation (right).

signal interpretations humans can distinguish between directions in azimuth by 5° and in elevation by 13° [5].

Because of the uniqueness of the shape of a human ear in combination with the shape of the head the directional manipulation of sounds is different from person to person. So Spatial Listening is a learned, subconscious perception of the phenomena.

4   State of the Art in Human Echolocation

The term human echolocation describes a group of methods that enable people who are visual impaired to gather an acoustic image of their environment. To learn the skills for such an environmental perception there are orientation and mobility (O&M) trainings as well as traveling skills using the white cane. The goal of human echolocation is to improve the orientation and navigation skills but also to get structural information about the environment nearly like an image provides.

Passive Methods

The methods are differentiated into active and passive methods. Passive echolocation is done by casual sounds made by a practitioner, e.g. sounds from steps or the white cane. The sound waves are thrown back by objects in the environment like walls. The audio impressions of such reflected sounds are dependent on specific features of the objects like height or hardness. Those impressions allow conclusions about the environment. Such an acoustic image is fuzzy, but it provides enough information to find doors or cars. Despite the inadequacy this method is often used even if it is used subconsciously [1].

Active Methods

By generating a striking acoustic signal a practitioner gets a much more detailed acoustic image of the environment. Such techniques are called active echolocation. The generated signals are adapted to the current situation. A kind of dialog between the practitioner and its environment arises in which the practitioner systematically scans its environment. This is realized by changing the practitioners position relative to the object or in changing the loudness or waveform of the signal. A tongue click, or a finger flick are common used signals in human echolocation. The duration of an impulse and the echoes of the environment give only a short acoustic image. Because of these characteristics this technique is also called flash sonar [1,4].

Daniel Kish, a pioneer of flash sonar, says that a suitable signal is as sharp as the bursting bubble of a bubble gum as well as discreet and only as loud as needed. Otherwise multiple echoes emerge and disturb the perception of the environment. Aids as hand clicker are in certain circumstances to loud e.g. for indoor environments. Other acoustic signals like the noise of a long cane are in unfavourable orientation to the practitioner's ears. A disadvantageous angle between sound source, object and ear causes a wrong acoustic image. So, a tongue klick seems to be the best method for a controlled signal to get an acoustic image. In comparison to passive echolocation characteristics of surrounding structures and objects are much more detailed in flash sonar if the technique is learned and applied the right way. An intentional produced sound signal can be identified quite good even in noisy backdrops [1,2].

Brain-scan research has shown that hearing offers the ability to analyze scenes. This analysis of scenes describes the ability of recognizing and imagining different events in a dynamic changing room [6,8].

Possibilities and Limits

Practitioners, even with exercise, can discern object sizes, shapes of rooms, courses of buildings or holes in objects. Advanced practitioners can analyze complex scenes with different shapes and objects. They are also able to recognize complex environmental characteristics. Even little objects and fine details can be discerned. Some advanced practitioners can ski or go biking [1].

Subgroups of flash sonar are differentiated between localizing, shape and texture recognition. Localizing describes the task of recognizing different objects and their relative position to the practitioner. In shape recognition by finding edges or corners of an object the size and shape is determined. Texture recognition allows the classification of different surfaces like hard or soft, fine structured or rough structured, smooth or porous.

The maximum resolution that a practitioner without any aid can reach is in the case of a freestanding object, under calm circumstances an area of about $0.2\,m^2$ ($8\,in^2$) at a distance of about $45\,cm$ ($18\,in$). The range depends on the ambient noise, the object's size and hardness. By using a tongue click the range is about $10\,m$ ($33\,ft$). By using clapping hands and big objects like buildings the range can be extended up to $50\,m$ ($164\,ft$) or greater [1,2].

5   The AHRUS System

AHRUS, is defined as an ultrasonic sonar whose echoes can be perceived directly with the human ear. The concept was developed to make the positive properties of ultrasonic waves, known from bats or dolphins, usable for the orientation and navigation by people who are blind. Hearing aids for the translation of ultrasound in auditory sound are deliberately omitted, since they generally cannot reproduce the precise directional perception of natural human hearing.

Working Principles

The AHRUS-System is based on "parametric speakers". This special form of ultrasonic speakers uses effects of nonlinear acoustics to achieve a self demodulation of an ultrasound beam after a reflection on an object to a strongly directed audible sound which can be perceived directly with the human ear, but having ultrasound-like properties. The principle of a so-called parametric ultrasonic loudspeaker has been known for many years and is usually used for highly directed audio spotlights, e.g. for a playback of sharply demarcated audio information in a museum.

A strongly directed ultrasonic beam with a very high sound pressure level is generated with an array of ultrasonic transducers. This beam is modulated in its amplitude by an audio signal, which remains initially inaudible. At a very high pressure level the air as "sound transmitting medium" can no longer be considered as linear. Instead, characteristics and behavior occur that are described by the laws of nonlinear acoustics. One of these characteristics is the gradual transformation (demodulation) of the modulated ultrasonic beam. On journey through the air, the ultrasonic beam is converted into a sharply focused audible signal which is detected with the natural ear. The resulting generation zone can extend up to about 10 m (33 ft). Beyond this zone the demodulation stops because of decreasing ultrasound pressure level due attenuation in air and beam expansion [9].

Figure 2 illustrates the principle of the audible ultrasonic sonar. An object in front of the user is illuminated with the modulated ultrasound beam. Because of diffraction effects the ultrasound component of the beam is preferred reflected at the object and returns as echo. On their return, these echoes are de-modulated to audible sound and then processed over the natural sense of hearing. This results in an optimal spatial perception of the reflecting object.

Device Design

Figure 3 shows the prototype of the AHRUS system. The transducer is composed of 19 piezo ultrasound emitters, producing an ultrasound pressure level up to 135 dB at a frequency of 40 kHz. The beam is very focused with an aperture angle of about 5°. The short wavelength of the ultrasonic waves of 8 mm (0.3 in) results in well audible echoes, also from finely structured or small obstacles like wire fences or twigs.

The beam is harmless for humans and animals. A guide dog, for example, is only able to hear frequencies up to 25 kHz and therefore not able to hear the sound of the AHRUS device at all. The intensity of the beam decreases rapidly with distance due to strong attenuation of ultrasound in the air. So the reach of the ultrasound is strongly limited and animals using ultrasound for navigation like bats are not disturbed.

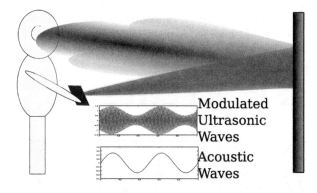

Fig. 2. Principle of ultrasound demodulation in air.

Figure 4 illustrates a design scheme of the AHRUS system. In addition to the battery and power management, the device includes an amplifier for powering the transducers, a Bluetooth Low Energy (BLE) Module for configuration via a smart-phone and an Inertial-Measurement-Unit (IMU). The user interface is implemented by an audio menu using a mini speaker and seven tactile buttons. The menu allows the configuration of the device parameters, the selection of the operating mode and the modulation-signal form.

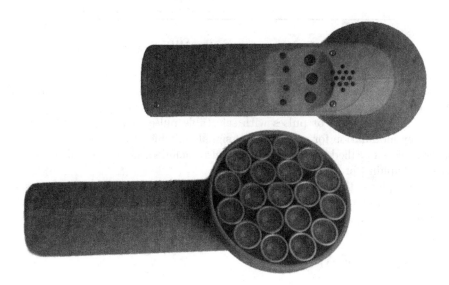

Fig. 3. AHRUS prototype Implementation

The IMU is used to support the user in spatial orientation and includes a 3D-compass, -gyroscope and -accelerometer. Silent, haptic hints to the user are given by an integrated multistage vibration motor. The heart of the whole system is an ARM Cortex-M4 microcontroller, which provides sufficient computing power with despite low energy consumption due to its integrated digital signal processor.

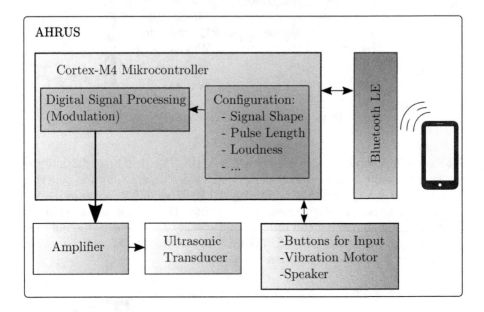

Fig. 4. Design overview of the AHRUS system.

A configurable synthesizer for signal generation has been implemented on the signal processor. It allows the generation of click, noise or sound signals, as a continuous signal or pulses with selectable pulse frequency and width. A frequency modulation for generation of signals in which the frequency increases or decreases, so called "chirp-signals", is also included. Chirps are also used by bats or dolphins for echo localization.

Future plans, to integrate a community platform to allow users to create their own modulation signals and share them with others. This, to promote the exchange and improve the experience with the new technology.

6   Methods of Application

Based on the different signal shapes some methods for practical use of the AHRUS-System were considered. We distinguish the following disciplines: Localization of objects, perception of outlines, obstacles detection, estimation of distances and the recognition of different structures and their roughness.

Localization

For people using AHRUS the first time, a continuous white-noise-like sound was most suitable. Irradiated objects are easily audible and localizable. The auditory impression is as if the object itself is emitting the sound. The signal sounds like a wind gust and is not intrusive. Other people, in proximity, are not disturbed. This modus can be used as a kind of "acoustic white cane". The user who is blind scans the environment with the focused beam while for example discernible edges or obstacles in distances up to about 10 m (33 ft), depending on size and reflecting surface, will get audible and localizable.

Because of a diffuse backscattering of the ultrasonic waves, also structured grounds like grassland or gravel in a shallow angle to the beam are audibly discerned in most cases. This can be used to localize the border of a sideway going along for example. Also fine structured objects like bushes or fences usually are audible. This is a significant difference to the classical flash sonar method, which (due to the directed reflection) depends on relatively large surfaces with an orthogonal alignment to the listener.

Distance Estimation

For distance estimation of objects or obstacles based on the time span, a signal needs to travel its way from the AHRUS device to a reflector and back to the ear of the user, continuous sounds are not usable. Instead short staccato tone or noise bursts with a clear beginning and ending are best suited. The human sense of hearing is able to perceive the delay of an echo very exactly. Very short distances are perceived as an increasing reverb while larger distances sound like a more or less time shifted impulse [10]. Experienced users (e.g. one of the authors of this paper) are able to estimate object distances up to 10 m (33 ft) with an accuracy of about 0.5–1.5 m (1.6–5 ft).

A variation of this method for less experienced persons is achieved by an adjustment of the pulse frequency on the AHRUS device for a certain reference distance. Therefore a duty cycle between sound and silence of 50 % is chosen. In the next step a reference object in a certain distance (e.g. 10 m or 33 ft) is targeted. Now the pulse frequency is adjusted in a way that an echo of a broadcast burst exactly hits the silent phase of the cycle. So the user hears a continuous tone. For a reference distance of 10 m (33 ft) a sonic speed of 340 m (1100 ft) per second we get a delay of about 60 ms, so if we choose a burst duration of 60 ms the echo fills the space between two bursts.

A variation of the distance leads to significant gaps between signal and echo again. For an unexperienced user it is much easier to assign the gap duration to a difference in distance than the first method based on the estimation of the absolute echo delay.

Structures and Their Roughness

The methods presented so far dealt with the localization of objects and obstacles and the estimation of distances. The next method is used to distinguish different surface roughness and structures. Objects with a surface roughness with a magnitude below the ultrasonic wavelength (8 mm or 315 mil in case of AHRUS) can be described as "almost smooth", e.g. walls or smooth road surfaces. Echoes from such a reflector are very directed and clear in the sense that the echo has the same signal shape as the original. Rough objects, on the other hand, deliver diffuse (non directed) echoes. Structured objects even deliver multiple echoes from different parts of the structure in various distances of the user.

A good approach to make this effect detectable is the use of "chirps". A chirp is a signal in which the frequency increases (up-chirp) or decreases (down-chirp) with time. Structured objects change a clear chirp-echo to a blurred noise-like sound. Because of the frequency modulation of the chirp the frequency of an individual echo corresponds with its flight time. In the end the listener hears a mixture of echoes having slightly different distances and delay, depending on the depth distribution of the structure parts. A mixture of many different frequencies is perceived as noise. The strength and spectral distribution of the noisy sound corresponds with the surface structure of the reflector, so the user can differentiate surface textures like a smooth wall, grass or bushes.

Handling Considerations

In addition to the signal shape there are different ways to carry the device. AHRUS can be mounted on a hood or hand held. The advantage of Head-mounting is that the hands stay free for holding a white cane. Also the audio-beam has a fixed position related to the ears and the beam follows the line of vision. So the user is able to scan his environment by turning the head. This method is described as very intuitive and similar to the classical flash sonar technique where the clicks are produced with the mouth.

If the device is carried on a necklace at the height of the solar plexus, the user has to turn their torso to influence the direction of the audio-beam. But compared to head-mounting this way is less conspicuous and may be preferred by some users.

If AHRUS is hold in the hand, fast periodic scanning moves are possible by turning the device off the wrist. In this way an angle of about 45 o degrees can be scanned continuously. The method is similar to the use of a white cane of a blind person walking. The white cane is moved periodically from the left to the right edge of the foot walk and vice versa. So obstacles in the complete width of the walkway are detected. In case of AHRUS this scanning is done with the audio-beam with the advantage that the beam also detects obstacles above the ground level (e.g. letter boxes or branches sticking out of the way). Also the scanning range is up to 10 m (33 ft) and more, so the device can also be used for orientation purposes by detecting known objects in the near environment.

A last method is holding AHRUS at the outstretched arm for finding the position and distance of objects or obstacles. The method is based on two steps. In the first step the direction of an object is piled by holding the device in the center and turning the whole body until the echo magnitude reaches its peak. Now the body of the user is aligned to the object. In the second step the arm is stretched out while the wrist and AHRUS is slowly turned to the inside until the beam hits the object again and the echo magnitude reaches its peak. The angle of the rotation corresponds to the distance of the object. This method is generally called triangulation and works fine for localization of near objects.

7   Evaluation of AHRUS

To get a first insight about the acceptance and the usefulness of the AHRUS system, we evaluated it with four subjects. All of them were in an age between 25 and 27. Two subjects are blind (Subject 1, Subject 2). One from birth and the other for about ten years. The other two subjects were blindfolded (Subject 3, Subject 4). The subjects had to use the AHRUS system in five situations which are explained and evaluated below.

Directional Perception

An obstacle was placed in a distance of five meters around the subject. The subjects had to point to the obstacle. The results of this experiment are outlined in Fig. 5. Most of the subjects, especially the subjects who are blind, found every obstacle. Only one subject made a mistake by recognizing a bush as obstacle which was not the desired obstacle to find.

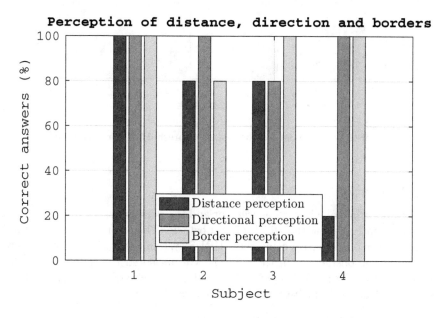

Fig. 5. Perception of distances and directions to obstacles and also the borders between different surfaces.

Distance Perception Threshold

We tested two different obstacles that had to be perceived, a car and a pillar. The subject was placed 15 m (49 ft) from the car and 10 m (33 ft) from the pillar. The subject was led to the obstacle and gave a signal when they heard the obstacle. The distance to the obstacle was measured. The results are nearly the same. The car is a big obstacle that the subjects heard directly. The pillar gave more information about the accuracy of AHRUS. Both subjects who are blind heard it in a higher distance than the blindfolded subjects. Figure 6 illustrates the results of this experiment.

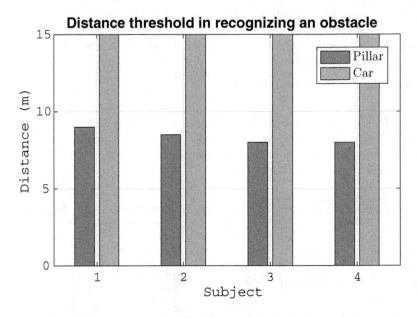

Fig. 6. Results of the experiment for the distance threshold of perceiving an obstacle.

Width Estimation

To test the accuracy of width measurement and the perception of object borders, the subjects had to show the width of an obstacle. They were positioned three meters from the obstacle. By using the AHRUS system the subjects had to show the width of the obstacle with their hands. We measured the difference to the obstacle's width. Figure 7 illustrates the results for each subject. It shows that a user can get a rough impression about the size of an object.

Perception of Borders between Surfaces

To test the possibility of hearing boarders between two surfaces, in this case between grass and crushed stone, the subjects had to point to the border between both surfaces. Figure 5 illustrates that all subjects recognized the border by using the AHRUS system.

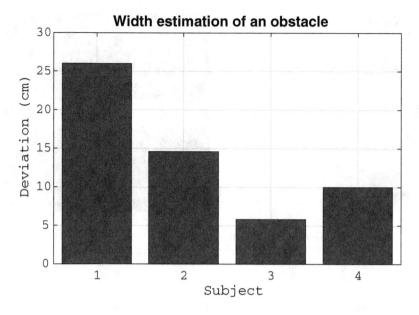

Fig. 7. Results of the experiment for width estimation of an obstacle.

Distance Perception

We also tested the perception of the distance. We positioned an obstacle in 1 m, 2 m and 5 m (3 ft, 7 ft and 16 ft) distance to the subject. The subject had to differentiate between near, middle and far away. Figure 5 illustrates promising results. Three of four subjects did this very well. One subject had problems with this technique but told us that he thinks it would be better with more than five minutes training for the distance perception.

8 Comparison to Flash Sonar

The classical flash sonar with tongue click and the AHRUS differ in several essential points. The reason is the different wavelength of audible sound and ultrasound. Flash sonar uses a large wavelength λ between 80–800 mm or 3–31 in (0.4–4 kHz). AHRUS, on the other hand, works with a wavelength λ of only 8 mm or 0.30 in (40 kHz) what is about 10–100 times smaller.

Directivity

The small wavelength allows sharp focusing of the ultrasound beam with an aperture angle of about 6°. In the case a tongue click, the aperture angle is in a magnitude of about 45–90° depending on the frequency and the mouth opening. Figure 8 shows the difference based on a point source synthesis of the two sound sources in Matlab.

Fig. 8. Matlab simulation - Comparison of sound intensity and directivity of a tongue click (left) and the AHRUS system (right). Red for a high and blue for a low sound intensity. (Color figure online)

A sharp focused sound source like AHRUS has many advantages. It allows the user a selective scanning of his environment while an echo only comes from a small target area. On the opposite site an unfocused tongue click causes multiple simultaneous and unidirectional echoes from many different reflectors. The simultaneous echoes overwhelm the user while less powerful echoes from smaller objects cannot be heard anymore.

Loudness

In order for a listener to hear the echoes reflected by an object, these have to be sufficiently louder than the environment noise. This is a problem especially in traffic situations or other noisy places. The echo volume depends on the intensity of the sound wave, on the sonar cross section and in case of fine structured or small objects also from the wavelength.

In case of a less focused sound source the sound intensity decreases quickly with increasing distance. While a tongue click rapidly degenerates with distance due the fast growing area on which the sound energy is distributed. The sharp focused beam of AHRUS keeps its intensity over a long distance. This is an important prerequisite for audible echoes from far away or small objects [10].

The sonar cross section describes the ability of an object to reflect a soundwave in the direction of its source. On the one hand, it depends on the size and surface characteristics of an object. On the other hand it depends on the relation between structure size and wavelength.

While the properties of a reflecting object are given, the wavelength can be affected. If the structure size in the magnitude is of the wavelength or even smaller, diffraction effects can be observed. This directs the sound wave around the object and the echo volume decreases rapidly. In the case of audible sound, this limit is already reached at structure sizes of about 0.1 m (4 in), thus small or finely structured objects such as fences or bushes hardly produce any echoes.

With the small ultrasound waves, on the other hand, much smaller structures can be perceived by the user.

The Stealth Problem

The reflection law states that the angle of incidence and emergent angle of a wave entering a reflector have to be the same. This effect is known from the billiards game. When a ball hits a gang at an angle it bounces back in exactly the same angle. The same thing happens with a soundwave bouncing at a smooth surface. When the surface is perpendicular to the user, it sends back a loud echo. On the other hand, when the reflecting surface is at a flat angle to the user the sound energy is reflected away from him and only weak or no echoes can be heard. Similar effects are used in technology to hide ships or airplanes from radar waves (Stealthtechnology).

This effect is one of the biggest problems for human echolocation because smooth surfaces with unfavorable angle cannot be perceived in some cases. For flash sonar users the world sometimes appears like a kind of mirror cabinet. For example a smooth wall in walking direction is nearly imperceptible.

A solution of the "stelth problem" is the use of so called diffuse reflection. It occurs when the roughness or structure of a surface is greater than the sound wave length. In this case the wave is scattered diffusely in every direction. In relation to the small wavelength of visible light, almost all surfaces, with the exception of mirrors, are very rough. The seeing person is therefore unaware of this problem of the acoustic world. Only the short wavelengths of ultrasound can at least partially eliminate this condition. Due to the diffuse reflection with the AHRUS system, structured surfaces at an unfavorable angle to the listener are audible even from a roughness of about 4–8 mm (0.15–0.30 in), for example rough road surfaces or a meadow [10].

Comparison Cases

Table 1 shows a comparison between the classical active human echo localization (e.g. in form of flash sonar with tongue click) and the AHRUS system using some practical examples. In summary the AHRUS system has serious advantages. The sharply focused beam is very selective and delivers loud echoes also from smaller objects. The small wavelength reduces the stealth-problem and allows distinction of surface structures and floor coverings. Special methods like triangulation support the estimation of object distances. In result AHRUS delivers better results in the four considered disciplines Localization, Shape Recognition, Overlapping Objects and also Distance Recognition.

The main disadvantage is that the user has to carry an electronic device with him/her. Here, the developers have the task of making the device as small, reliable and user-friendly as possible to increase user acceptance.

Table 1. Comparison of AHRUS and classical active echolocation (flash sonar)

Discipline	Classical active echolocation	AHRUS
Localization	A mast of 5 cm (2 in) diameter can be perceived in a distance of aprox. 0.6 m (24 in). A car in 3–4 m (118–157 in). - objects with structures smaller than 3–10 cm (1–4 in) barely perceptible. - multiple echoes, as many objects may be illuminated at the same time.	A mast of 5 cm (2 in) diameter can be perceived in a distance of aprox. 6–8 m (236–315 in). A car in 8–15 m (315–591 in) + small or finely structured objects still perceptible in a few meters + selective echoes, good scanning resolution and directional perception
Shape recognition	Is possible but requires: - very short object distance - many position changes of the user	+ very easy by scanning the object with the sound beam + also from a distance
Separate perception of overlapping objects	- separation of overlapping objects or objects before a background is generally not possible	+ possible if the overlapping objects have different surface structures (e.g. a bush in front of a wall)
Distance recognition	+ basically possible because the human sense of hearing is able to detect very small differences in sound propagation time depending on the object distance - very unselective (only large and free-standing objects) - for larger distances, louder signals (hand claps) necessary	+ different methods for distance estimation + long range with high selectivity and echo volume

9   Conclusion

Methods of the active echolocation support users in the tasks of orientation, localization and perception of forms. Methods to support such tasks are systematically developed like different tongue clicks. The long wavelength of acoustic signals only allows a very low resolution of the acoustic image gathered by tongue clicks. A big problem is based on the long wavelengths that are often longer than an object structure of interest. Therefor only echoes of surfaces with vertical alignment to the user are reflected. The user only hears these echoes whereby many objects or parts of them cannot be perceived.

The proposed audible high resolution ultrasonic sonar (AHRUS) eliminates the significant disadvantages of classic active echolocation techniques. By using self-demodulating ultrasonic waves, it enables the perception of much smaller object structures. Even little surface roughness, e.g. at surfaces of roads, reflects ultrasonic waves in a diffuse manner. This enables the user to take notice of surfaces even by beaming the ultrasonic waves in a low angle at it. While a tongue click creates an undirected signal the ultrasonic beam of AHRUS is bundled up so that the signal is strongly directed to a point a user focuses. By this behaviour a user can scan the environment precisely.

The technology is very small. This enables the user to wear it close to the body or in the hands. Special signal forms enable new application methods for the environment perception, e.g. chirp signals. One example is the perception of surfaces and depth structures. In contrast to electronic aids that use headphones with special signal processing as an audio interface to the user, AHRUS uses the individual and efficient ears of the user himself. Furthermore, the ears stay free to hear the normal information of the environment.

By using soft but striking signals e.g. noisy clicks, the signals are easy to hear but not disturbing during travel. Because of the advantages of ultrasonic waves and configurable signals AHRUS is an efficient extension to classical flash sonar. Nonetheless the full potential of AHRUS will be discovered after more persons who are blind use this technology to discover its pros and cons.

References

1. Kish, D.: Flash sonar program: learning a new way to see. World Access for the Blind, Copyright (2013)
2. Kish, D.: Bilder im Kopf: Klick-Echoortung für blinde Menschen, 1 edn. edition bentheim, Würzburg (2015)
3. Ram, S., Sharf, J.: The people sensor: a mobility aid for the visually impaired. In: Second International Symposium on Wearable Computers, Digest of Papers, pp. 166–167. IEEE (1998)
4. Rojas, J.A.M., Hermosilla, J.A., Montero, R.S., Esp, P.L.L.: Physical analysis of several organic signals for human echolocation: oral vacuum pulses. Acta acustica united with acustica **95**(2), 325–330 (2009)
5. Romigh, G.D., Brungart, D.S., Simpson, B.D.: Free-field localization performance with a head-tracked virtual auditory display. IEEE J. Selected Topics Sig. Process. **9**(5), 943–954 (2015)
6. Sinne: Klickblitze im Dunkeln. http://www.spektrum.de/news/klickblitze-im-dunkeln/1130592. Accessed 29 Jan 2018
7. Sound of Vision. https://soundofvision.net/. Accessed 29 Jan 2018
8. Thaler, L., Wilson, R.C., Gee, B.K.: Correlation between vividness of visual imagery and echolocation ability in sighted, echo-naive people. Exp. Brain Res. **232**(6), 1915–1925 (2014)
9. Ulrich, I., Borenstein, J.: The guidecane-applying mobile robot technologies to assist the visually impaired. IEEE Trans. Syst. Man Cybern. Part A: Syst. Hum. **31**(2), 131–136 (2001)
10. Weinzierl, S.: Handbuch der Audiotechnik, 2008th edn. Springer, Berlin (2008). https://doi.org/10.1007/978-3-540-34301-1

Wayfinding Board Design for the Visually Impaired Based on Service Design Theory

Wanru Wang[✉] and Xinxiong Liu

Huazhong University of Science and Technology,
No. 1037, Luoyu Road, Wuhan, Hubei, China
m201570705@hust.edu.cn, xxliu@mail.hust.edu.cn

Abstract. The visually impaired people have difficulty in finding positions in public places. Current wayfinding systems usually neglect the demand of the visually impaired people. Many studies have focused on designing the wayfinding system for the visually impaired people. But current researches have some disadvantages when applying. In this paper, a color related and QR code enhanced wayfinding system is proposed to provide wayfinding service for the visually impaired people. The design of the proposed system is based on the service design theory. The proposed system has the advantage of low cost, smooth update and high level of effect.

1 Introduction

Wayfinding system is crucial for people to familiarize a strange environment. Wayfinding systems have been generally utilized inside of buildings, traffic roads and other public places. Traditional wayfinding systems rely on users' visual ability, which means that users with normal visual ability will have great advantage of using traditional wayfinding systems. However, traditional systems are unfriendly to the visually impaired people since the visually impaired people are difficult to recognize the character and the pattern on the board. The design of traditional wayfinding board usually ignores the need of the visually impaired people. So there is an urgent need for designing wayfinding system specifically for the visually impaired people.

Nowadays, many studies have been done about the wayfinding system design for the visually impaired people. These studies can be classified as indoor systems and outdoor systems according to the application scenario. In order to compensate for the visual ability reduction of the visually impaired people, some supplementary devices are needed, like GPS [1,2], camera [3,4] and robots [5–7]. GPS provides position service for the visually impaired people. Combined with digital map, GPS has been used as a method for helping the visually impaired people. Camera-aided methods mainly utilize the mechanism of image processing. The camera of smart phones takes the picture of current environment and by image processing the location of the user can be obtained. Some studies chose the specially designed

© Springer International Publishing AG, part of Springer Nature 2018
M. Antona and C. Stephanidis (Eds.): UAHCI 2018, LNCS 10907, pp. 450–460, 2018.
https://doi.org/10.1007/978-3-319-92049-8_32

image related to current environment, which reduces the complexity of computation. Robot-aided methods utilize robots to guide the visually impaired people. The robot gets the position information of the destination by smart algorithms.

However, all these methods have some disadvantages under the circumstance of indoor wayfinding. Firstly, indoor wayfinding requires high level precision of positioning since a small error of positioning will lead to a different place considering the small size of indoor environment. The precision of GPS in indoor scenario needs to be improved, thus limiting its application potential in the indoor environment. Secondly, camera-aided methods usually require installing additive APPs on the smart phone. In addition, the management department of the indoor space needs to develop the backstage program of the APP and maintain its operation. The overall procedures are too complex and the cost is high. At last, robot-aided method is expensive and the design of robot is relatively complex. In conclusion, a low cost, easily maintained and effective wayfinding system for the visually impaired people is extremely urgent under current circumstances.

The design of a system or a service needs principle. Service design theory not only considers the service process but also supporting resources like human resources and technical challenges [8]. Currently service design theory has been applied in many fields like APP design [10], Web design [11] and O2O design [12]. Tools of service design theory include service blueprint [9,13] and quality function deployment [14,15].

In this paper, a color related and QR code enhanced wayfinding system is proposed to meet the demand of the visually impaired people. The proposed system is designed based on the service design theory and has the advantage of low cost, easily upgraded and high added value. Main innovations of this system can be listed in the following aspects:

1. The proposed system is designed based on service design theory. It fully utilized the information contained on the traditional wayfinding board. Detailedly speaking, the relation of background color and destination is established in this system. Moreover, the QR code is added on the wayfinding board to transfer information from the wayfinding board to the smart phone. The system fully utilizes the residual visual ability and hearing ability of the visually impaired people.
2. The proposed system can be upgraded smoothly from current wayfinding system. This characteristic saves the time of developing and deploying new system. Current infrastructure could be fully utilized.
3. The proposed system is of low cost. No other additive devices are needed except for the commonly used smart phones. In addition, no other specifically APPs need to be developed. And the backstage maintain is easy to be conducted.

2   Visual Ability Experiment

The visually impaired people are not fully blind. The target group of people in this system is not blind people. Even though the visually impaired people may not distinguish the detail of a pattern, they can still recognize some visual elements. An experiment was conducted by our group to find the visual ability of the visually impaired people in order to guide our design. 104 volunteers were invited to participate in this experiment including 85 nearsighted people and 12 people who have cataracts and 7 people who have glaucoma. Since visual impairment is a decreased ability to see to a degree, the invited volunteers were asked to take off their glasses or aided devices when participating in the experiment.

Volunteers of nearsighted people were mainly from college students. Cataract patients and glaucoma patients were invited from the blind massage company, who were hired by the blind massage company. Average age of volunteers is 24.8 and the average visual acuity level is 4.13, measured by the International standard vision chart.

2.1   Recognition Ability Experiment of the Visually Impaired People

In this experiment, different recognition abilities for the wayfinding board pattern detail and boundary were tested. Although the content of the wayfinding board is relatively difficult for the visually impaired people to recognize, the shape of the pattern boundary seems distinguishable.

The experiment was conducted in separate places. 85 nearsighted volunteers were mainly colleague students. They could be easily gathered and the experiment could be conducted in one specific place. 19 cataracts and glaucoma people were separated in different places and their experiment was conducted by visiting them face to face.

During the experiment, the volunteer was asked to clarify both the content and the boundary of the pattern on the wayfinding board at a distance of 0.5 m, 1 m and 1.5 m. The provided wayfinding board is designed with the size of 10 cm * 30 cm. The content was designed with different content complexities, as shown in first line of Fig. 1. The characteristic of these wayfinding boards is that the boundary is relatively simple when the content is complex.

The complexity of the content could be quantificationally described using the principle in the field of image processing. The complexity of a image could be calculated using the ratio R_{edge}. R_{edge} is the ratio of boundary pixel amount to the amount of all pixels, which is shown in Eq. (1).

$$R_{edge} = P_{edge}/(m * n), \tag{1}$$

P_{edge} is the number of pixel in the content boundary, m is the number of pixels on the column and n is the number of pixels on the row. Higher R_{edge} represents higher level of content complexity. From the Eq. (1), the boundary of the content should be detected first. The Sobel operator was used as the method to detect image boundary. By MATLAB simulation, the detected boundary was shown in the second line of the Fig. 1. From left to the right, R_{edge} of these images is 0.0369, 0.0175, 0.0206 and 0.0314, which basically suits the experience of visual eyesight. During the experiment, the wayfinding board was placed at different heights in order to match the volunteers' height. The volunteer was asked to recognize different wayfinding boards at different distances, 0.5 m, 1 m and 1.5 m. A successful recognition of pattern content and boundary was recorded. After experimenting with 104 volunteers, the result was listed in Table 1.

Fig. 1. Experiment material and boundary detection results

Table 1. First part experiment results

Content of the pattern	Ratio of the edge	Success rate of content recognition			Success rate of boundary recognition		
		0.5 m	1 m	1.5 m	0.5 m	1 m	1.5 m
'AA'	0.0369	18.27%	15.38%	11.54%	79.81%	67.31%	56.73%
'-'	0.0175	94.23%	76.92%	61.54%	95.19%	83.65%	75.96%
'X'	0.0206	79.81%	59.62%	43.27%	93.27%	80.77%	65.38%
'U'	0.0314	35.58%	26.92%	21.15%	88.46%	71.15%	48.08%
'P'	0.0287	56.73%	46.15%	35.58%	97.12%	79.81%	59.62%

From Table 1, the success rate of content recognition is basically lower than the boundary. The success rate of content and boundary is increasing with the decreasing of the distance between the volunteer and the wayfinding board, since smaller distance can help the volunteer clarify the pattern on the wayfinding board more clearly. With the increase of the ratio of the edge, the success rate of content is decreasing. However, the success rate of boundary recognition is nearly the same when at different ratios of the edge. This is because that the shape of the boundary is almost regular and is not related to the content of the pattern.

From the experiment, it can be concluded that the visually impaired people still have some visual abilities. Although the visually impaired people have difficulty in distinguishing the content of the pattern on the wayfinding board, they can still clarify the boundary of the pattern. This means that the visually impaired people can locate where the image is if provided with a frame in a regular shape. This conclusion can be utilized for guiding the design of the wayfinding board for the visually impaired people.

2.2   Visual Learning Ability Experiment

People have abilities for learning from the experiment. When facing a strange environment, they may learn from the visual elements contained in the environment. We can all imagine the situation that when we are in a strange situation and provided with a new wayfinding system with different patterns, an adaptation process is progressed. When a pattern on a wayfinding board is witnessed for a second time, the time needed for us to recognize it reduces in a large extent. The visual learning ability experiment is aimed at testing people's learning ability of the strange wayfinding board.

In this experiment, different patterns with different background colors were prepared as experiment material. The experiment contained two parts. For the first part, the volunteer were asked to clarify the content on the wayfinding board. Each volunteer was asked to take 3 rounds of experiment, each round is equipped with a specific kind of wayfinding boards with the same background color. The background color of the wayfinding board in different rounds is different. In this experiment, three colors were taken as the three rounds' color. In each round of the experiment, 3 wayfinding boards were prepared with different content on the board. And the testing sequence of the 3 boards in the same background color is their permutation sequence, which means that each experiment board was shown 6 times. All the testing boards' patterns and characters are shown in Fig. 2. During the first part of the experiment, when the volunteer gave the wrong answer about the content of the board, the correct answer would be given to the volunteer. And a successful recognition of content would be recorded. For the second part of the experiment, each volunteer was provided with 20 wayfinding boards with different background colors and contents to recognize. The sequence of the experimenting materials was not predefined. All the 20 wayfinding boards were contained in the first part of the experiment. At this part, the correct answer would not be given if a wrong answer was shown. Through this two steps experiment, we aim to test the visually impaired people's ability to establish the relation between content and background color.

The result of first step experiment is shown in Fig. 3. From Fig. 3, it can seen that the success rate of recognition is increasing with the increasing rounds of experiment. This is because the volunteer gradually adapted to the new system

Fig. 2. Experiment material of the second round experiment

through the correct answer. After average 3 rounds of experiment, the success rate reached over 70%. At the second step of the experiment, the overall success rate remained around 65%. Compared with the first round test in the first round experiment, the success rate of recognition improved a lot. Whats more, the wrong answer of the volunteer was also recorded. It can be found that around 89% of the wrong answer lied in the set of the rest wayfinding boards in the same background color. Through this experiment, it can be concluded that the visually impaired people have the ability to adapt to the new wayfinding system. And the relation of color and content can be gradually established by several rounds of training.

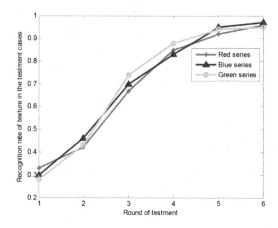

Fig. 3. The success rate of recognition increases with the round of the experiment

2.3 Button Size Experiment for the Visually Impaired People

The visually impaired people still use smart phones. From our observation of the our invited volunteers, cataracts and glaucoma people also use smart phones but their face is much closer to the screen than the normal eyesight people. Since our design consider using the smart phone as the platform, the ability for the visually impaired people to use smart phones needs to be verified. In this experiment, the visually impaired peoples ability to correctly press a button is experimented.

During the experiment, the volunteer was asked to press the button on the screen on the smart phone in a distance of normal eyesight button. If the button is correctly pressed, an indication voice will be provided. Different sizes of patterns were designed as experiment materials. The result of the experiment was shown in Table. From Table 2, it can be shown that the success rate of pressing the button is increasing with the increase of the pressing number. And the shape of the button is not a decisive reason for the success rate. It can be found that the success rate reached around 90% when the experiment time reached 5. Thus, it can be concluded that the visually impaired people could still have the ability to use smart phone UI with a relatively large size button.

Table 2. Second part experiment results

Shape of the button	Ratio of button size to screen size	Round of experiment				
		1	2	3	4	5
Rectangular	1:4	94.23%	97.12%	98.08%	98.08%	99.04%
	1:9	62.50%	68.27%	85.58%	95.19%	98.08%
	1:16	32.69%	44.23%	69.23%	76.92%	87.50%
Circle	1:4	86.54%	91.35%	95.19%	99.04%	99.04%
	1:9	69.23%	75.96%	82.69%	88.46%	93.27%
	1:16	32.69%	40.38%	59.62%	75.96%	83.65%

3 Proposed Design

Based on the conclusion obtained from the experiment, we propose a new wayfinding system. The proposed system contains color related system and the QR code enhanced system. The color related system utilizes the potential relationship between the pattern and the color, which makes it convenient for the visually impaired people to search information for the destination. The QR code enhanced system is the extension for the color related system. The QR code enhanced system provide vocal guidance for the visually impaired people and by using the smart phone, the information can be heard repeatedly. The proposed system utilized the residual visual ability of the visually impaired people and provide more service through hearing sense.

3.1   Service Touchpoint Analysis of the Wayfinding System

When designing the wayfinding system, the wayfinding board could not just be viewed as a product, but as a service. The service is to provide wayfinding information the visually impaired people. By applying the service design theory, the optimization of service touchpoint is conducted to optimize the service experience and improve service quality. In traditional wayfinding service, the service touchpoint mainly relies on the visual sense. The background color is to make the character and pattern more visible. The character is to illustrate the information about the destination. The pattern is to give a vivid illustration about the destination. For the backstage operation, the backstage maintaining is simple and only needs regular clearance. However, from the view of service design, traditional service has some disadvantages. The visual service touchpoint is not fully utilized since the background color is not fully utilized. In addition, the pattern and character is not easy for the visually people to recognize. What's more, the update about the destination information is difficult. Rebuilt of the wayfinding board is inevitable. The service blueprint of traditional wayfinding system is shown in Fig. 4.

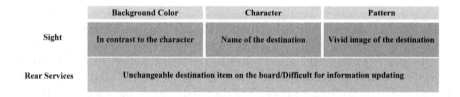

Fig. 4. Service blueprint of traditional wayfinding system

3.2   Color Related Wayfinding System

Traditional wayfinding system utilizes the background color to make the character and pattern more visible. However, this mechanism has little effect among the visually impaired people since they have low ability to distinguish the detail. According to the service design theory, this phenomenon indicates that visual service touchpoint is not fully utilized. In the color related system, the relationship between the background color and destination pattern is established. One background color relates to one specific destination. According to our experiment, the visually impaired people has the ability to establish the relationship. An illustration of the proposed color related system is shown in Fig. 5. The color related system has several advantages. The relationship of color and destination reduces the level of needed visual ability. The user only needs to differentiate the color to find which item of the wayfinding board is needed. In addition, the sequence of items on the wayfinding board may be different at different places. The user has to recognize all the items on the board to find the needed one in the traditional system. In the proposed system, this problem could be easily solved. What's more, the proposed system is both helpful for the normal eyesight people and the visually impaired people. And the colorful wayfinding board is environmentally friendly.

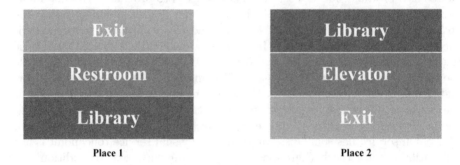

Fig. 5. Color related wayfinding system

3.3 QR Code Enhanced Wayfinding System

QR code has been widely used in current society. In China, thanks to the development of smart phones, the QR scanner APP has been an integrated APP. In the QR code enhanced system, the QR code is used as a channel for transferring the user from the wayfinding board to the smart phone. One QR code is placed on one item of the wayfinding board. The user could scan the QR code and get an UI on the smart phone. The user could press the button on the UI to get vocal guidance to the destination. An illustration of the proposed QR code enhanced system is shown in Fig. 6. According to the conclusion obtained from our experiment, the visually impaired people has residual visually ability to recognize the boundary of the pattern and press the button. This conclusion makes the QR code enhanced system feasible. The proposed QR code enhanced system has several advantages. The hearing service touchpoint is exploited to provide additional channel for the information transportation. In addition, the proposed system suits the visual ability of the visually impaired people. Whats more, extension of the smart phone UI is easy to conduct and the backstage maintenance is convenient.

3.4 Service Blueprint

The proposed service blueprint is illustrated in Fig. 7. From the Fig. 7, it can be found that the proposed service has more service touchpoints and the utilization of the service touchpoint is improving.

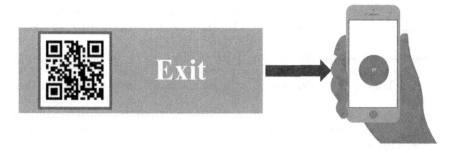

Fig. 6. QR code enhanced wayfinding system

	Traditional Services			**Proposed Services**	
	Background Color	Character	Pattern	QR Code	Smart phones
Sight	In contrast to the character	Name of the destination	Vivid image of the destination	Channel for smart phones	Button to press
	Related to the destination	Related to the color			Interface to the user
Hearing					Sound of information about the destination
Touch					Screen of smart phones
Rear Services	Changeable destination item on the board			Information could be maintained online	

Fig. 7. Comparison of traditional and proposed service blueprint of wayfinding systems

4   Conclusion

A new wayfinding system was proposed in this paper. The system used the color to carry more information about the destination and a sound guidance is constructed using QR code. All the devices needed is a smart phone with QR scanning function. So the implementation is low cost and easy to update. The future work of this direction is that the UI interface could be updated. For example, the AR/VR could be used to guide the direction of the destination.

References

1. Ishikawa, T., Fujiwara, H., Imai, O., Okabe, A.: Wayfinding with a GPS-based mobile navigation system: a comparison with maps and direct experience. J. Environ. Psychol. **28**(1), 74–82 (2008)
2. Li, B., Zhu, K., Zhang, W., Wu, A., Zhang, X.: A comparative study of two wayfinding aids for simulated driving tasks C single-scale and dual-scale GPS aids. Behav. Inf. Technol. **33**(4), 361–371 (2014)
3. Manduchi, R., Coughlan, J., Ivanchenko, V.: Search strategies of visually impaired persons using a camera phone wayfinding system. In: Miesenberger, K., Klaus, J., Zagler, W., Karshmer, A. (eds.) ICCHP 2008. LNCS, vol. 5105, pp. 1135–1140. Springer, Heidelberg (2008). https://doi.org/10.1007/978-3-540-70540-6_170

4. Arditi, A., Tian, Y.L.: User interface preferences in the design of a camera-based navigation and wayfinding aid. J. Vis. Impairment Blindness **107**(2), 118–129 (2013)
5. Kulyukin, V., Gharpure, C., Sute, P., De Graw, N., Nicholson, J.: A robotic wayfinding system for the visually impaired. In: Proceedings of the 16th Conference on Innovative Applications of Artifical Intelligence, pp. 864–869. AAAI Press (2002)
6. Kulyukin, V., Gharpure, C., Nicholson, J., Osborne, G.: Robot-assisted wayfinding for the visually impaired in structured indoor environments. Auton. Rob. **21**(1), 29–41 (2006)
7. Kulyukin, V., Gharpure, C., Nicholson, J., Pavithran, S.: RFID in robot-assisted indoor navigation for the visually impaired. In: Proceedings 2004 IEEE/RSJ International Conference on Intelligent Robots and Systems, vol. 2, pp. 1979–1984. IEEE (2004)
8. Edvardsson, B., Gustafsson, A., Johnson, M.D., Sanden, B.: New Service Development and Innovation in the New Economy. Studentlitteratur AB, Lund (2000)
9. Shostack, G.L.: How to design a service. Eur. J. Mark. **16**(1), 49–63 (2013)
10. Peng, L.H., Huang, Z.T.: Study on the universality of the service design of the "friendly restaurant app". In: International Conference on Applied System Innovation, pp. 1–3 (2016)
11. Lin, D., Ishida, T.: Participatory service design based on user-centered QoS. In: International Joint Conferences on Web Intelligence, vol. 1, pp. 465–472. IEEE (2013)
12. Zhou, M.Y., Xu, P., Liang, P.L.: The innovation research of takeaway O2O based on the concept of service design. In: Rau, P.-L.P. (ed.) CCD 2016. LNCS, vol. 9741, pp. 816–823. Springer, Cham (2016). https://doi.org/10.1007/978-3-319-40093-8_81
13. Zhou, Q., Tan, K.C.: The application of tools and techniques in a unified service design theory. In: IEEE International Conference on Industrial Engineering and Engineering Management, pp. 930–934. IEEE (2009)
14. Chan, L.K., Wu, M.L.: Quality function deployment: a literature review. Eur. J. Oper. Res. **143**(3), 463–497 (2002)
15. Dijkstra, L., Bij, H.V.D.: Quality function deployment in healthcare: methods for meeting customer requirements in redesign and renewal. Int. J. Qual. Reliab. Manage. **19**(1), 67–89 (2002)

Designing for Cognitive Disabilities

Design of an Assistive Avatar in Improving Eye Gaze Perception in Children with ASD During Virtual Interaction

Ashwaq Zaini Amat[1(✉)], Amy Swanson[3,4], Amy Weitlauf[3,4], Zachary Warren[3,4], and Nilanjan Sarkar[1,2]

[1] Electrical Engineering and Computer Science,
Vanderbilt University, Nashville, TN 37212, USA
`ashwaq.zaini.amat.haji.anwar@vanderbilt.du`
[2] Mechanical Engineering, Vanderbilt University, Nashville, TN 37212, USA
[3] Treatment and Research Institute for Autism Spectrum Disorders (TRIAD),
Vanderbilt University, Nashville, TN 37212, USA
[4] Pediatrics, Psychiatry and Special Education, Vanderbilt University, Nashville, TN 37212, USA

Abstract. Children diagnosed with autism spectrum disorder (ASD) usually experience impairment in social interaction and often display reduced gaze sharing when interacting with another person. The lack of gaze sharing or joint attention early in the children's developmental stage may create a delay in their ability to learn new things and share information with others. The presented study involved the design of a novel virtual reality (VR)-based training game with an avatar and eye tracker aimed to eventually address the joint attention impairment in children with ASD. The assistive avatar provides necessary cues and hints based on both the eye tracking data recorded by the VR system and the task performance of the participant. The system uses the task performance to adaptively change the difficulty level of the game. We believe that the training game will be able to improve participant's gaze following skill. A usability study was carried out to validate the system design. The result showed that the system was feasible and able to obtain the expected gaze performance from the participants. The details of the system architecture and result of system validation are presented in this paper.

Keywords: Virtual reality · Eye gaze · Joint attention · Autism spectrum disorder
Children with ASD

1 Introduction

Autism spectrum disorder (ASD) is a range of disorder that affects social communication and interaction. As of 2014, 1 in every 68 children in the USA are diagnosed with ASD [1]. Individuals within the ASD spectrum usually have atypical gaze patterns [2] and often display reduced gaze when interacting with another person [3]. Research shows that individuals with ASD spend less time looking at facial features especially the eye region compared to other non-facial areas. This atypical gaze behavior contributes to

© Springer International Publishing AG, part of Springer Nature 2018
M. Antona and C. Stephanidis (Eds.): UAHCI 2018, LNCS 10907, pp. 463–474, 2018.
https://doi.org/10.1007/978-3-319-92049-8_33

impairment in language development, facial expression processing and sharing of information during social interaction [4].

The human gaze plays an important role as a mechanism for information sharing in addition to emotional cues. This form of information sharing is also known as joint attention, which can be defined as one's ability to coordinate one's attention with another person [5], which is a fundamental social skill that is impaired in many children with ASD [6–8].

Children with ASD, in general, show more affinity towards computer and machine interaction than human interaction [9]. In particular, advancement in virtual reality technology has contributed towards significant boost in the use of virtual systems for children with ASD. Virtual systems have the added advantage that they can record quantitative measures and track performance in real-time. As a result, several important virtual systems have been explored in the context of social games [10–12]. While there have been several studies on robot-assisted joint attention [13], studies on joint attention for individual with ASD using virtual systems are limited. Caruana et al. introduced an interactive VR-based joint attention social task that is focused on adult with ASD and found that joint attention difficulties are still present even in adult with ASD [14]. Courgen et al. conducted studies with adult and adolescent with ASD on gaze awareness and a pilot study on joint attention with adult with ASD participants only [15]. Researches have shown that early intervention of joint attention in children with ASD can significantly improve the children's ability to develop their communication skills [16–18].

The current study presents the design and development of a novel VR-based gaze training paradigm with an avatar. The aim of the design is to address the joint attention impairment and reduced eye contact in many children with ASD through the gaze-based interaction paradigm with the avatar. In this paradigm, a children with ASD participant and the avatar play a puzzle game in VR where the participant will be required to look at the avatar's eye region in order for the avatar to cue which puzzle piece the participant has to move. The system is capable of providing: (1) different gaze configurations for the avatar, (2) real-time computation of game performance, (3) game hints by the avatar when the participant is unable to get the correct piece and 4) an adaptive difficulty level adjustment based on the participant's performance. We present this new framework with system architecture, initial system validation and conclusion together with future works in this paper.

2   System Design

The system provides an environment that aims to improve gaze sharing and gaze perception in children with ASD. The virtual system is set up with an avatar at the center of the screen, seven pieces of tangram puzzle is spread around the avatar and a target image placed in front of the avatar at the lower part of the screen as shown in Fig. 1. An eye tracker is used to track the participant's gaze position on the screen and as an input device that interacts with the avatar and puzzle pieces in the virtual system. Participant is required to share their gaze with the avatar in order to know which puzzle piece to move to complete the target image. The participant uses the mouse to move the puzzle pieces.

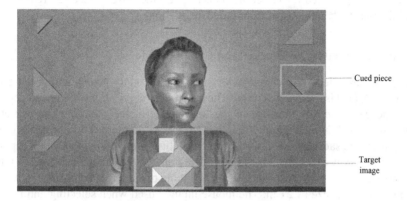

Cued piece

Target image

Fig. 1. The view of the training game. Avatar is at the center of the screen with tangram puzzle pieces spread around it. In this figure, the avatar is currently cueing the piece on the right. The target image is placed at the bottom in front of the avatar.

The system calculates the participant's performance based on the eye gaze inputs and response time. There are three different gaze configurations in the avatar that is used in the system. The different configuration is used to train gaze perception of the participant. An adaptive change and assistive hints are introduced in the system to optimize the system further. Figure 2 illustrates the block diagram of the eye tracking training system. Details of each of these configuration and game components are discussed in the subsequent sub-sections.

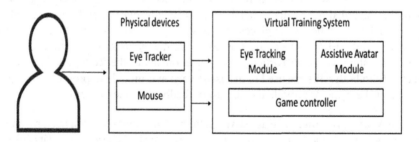

Fig. 2. Block diagram of the eye tracking training system

At the beginning of the training game, all the colors of the puzzle pieces were removed (zero color saturation). The avatar waits for the participant to make eye contact before it cues the piece to move. Participant will then look for the correct piece and when a correct piece is selected (through participant's gaze), the color of the puzzle piece is revealed and the participant is allowed to move the piece using the mouse to the corresponding slot on the target image. The interaction with the avatar is repeated for the remaining six puzzle pieces to complete the target image. The adaptive difficulty level is applied at the beginning of every game. When a participant is not making eye contact or unable to select the correct piece in time, the avatar will provide necessary hints. Participants are provided with three attempts to select the correct piece before the avatar moves the piece when the participant failed all attempts.

2.1 Physical Inputs: Eye Tracker and Computer Mouse

The eye tracker collects participant's eye gaze position on the screen during the game. A Tobii EyeX [19] is used in this study. The eye tracker is very lightweight and portable to use and can be easily attached to the lower edge of the monitor. The operating frequency is 50 Hz which is quite low, but since we are interested in at fixation data points rather than saccadic and fast-moving gaze, this sampling frequency is acceptable [20]. Tobii EyeX uses a USB 3.0 cable for data transfer with a rate of 20 MB/s. Other specifications of the eye tracker include an operating distance between 50–90 cm and a maximum monitor size of 27 in. The mouse input is used when selecting and moving puzzle pieces. A typical USB connected mouse is used in this experiment.

2.2 Virtual Training System

The virtual system is a platform for the participant to interact with the assistive avatar throughout the game. The system was developed using Unity v5.6.1f1 [21] and the games were modeled as finite state machines as shown in Fig. 3. The finite state machine provides a clean and organized way of tracking the state of the game. In each state, the corresponding adaptive response can be provided based on the performance level.

Eye Tracking Module. The eye tracking module is the interface between the physical world and the virtual world. A set of regions of interest (ROIs) were defined in the virtual system that included the avatar's facial features such as eyes, mouth, nose, forehead, and ears, and each of the puzzle pieces. The module uses a Tobii-Unity library [22] that has a gaze point API to collect gaze position from the eye tracker and another API to inform the system whenever participant's gaze is on any of the ROIs. The information collected from both APIs are used in the assistive avatar module to progress to the next sequence of the game or provide the necessary feedback to the participant.

Assistive Avatar Module. The assistive avatar module consists of the avatar, controls of the animation and other configurations related to the avatar. The avatar and its different animations were created using Autodesk Maya [23]. Seven different gaze directions were created for the avatar for the different positions of the puzzle pieces on the screen. For each of the gaze directions, three different gaze configurations were created for the avatar to create different level of gaze perception in the cues: (1) head movement together with eye movement (HE), (2) only eye movement (E), and (3) minimal eye movement (ME). There were a total of 22 animations (21 moving animations and 1 static animation) stored in the system. Figure 4 shows the difference in the gaze configurations between HE and E. These different configurations were implemented to increase the difficulty

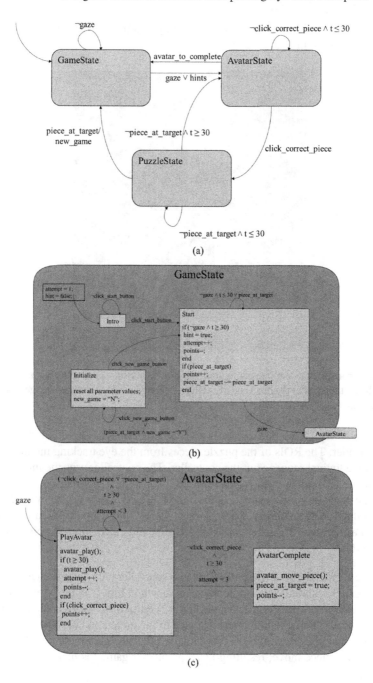

Fig. 3. (a) State machine of the training system (b) state machine for the puzzle pieces, PuzzleState (c) state machine for the virtual avatar, AvatarState

level of the gaze perception, where the region of gaze cue reduces from the whole head movement to very minimal eye movement.

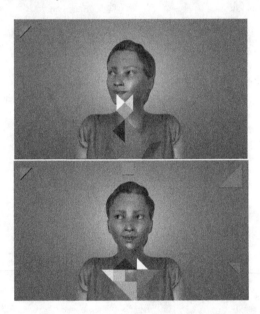

Fig. 4. Comparison of avatar cue configurations. Both avatars are cueing the piece at the top left corner. The first image has the head and eye (HE) movement while the bottom image has eye only (E) movement.

Game Controller. Each puzzle pieces and the target image is configured through the game controller. The ROIs of the puzzle pieces from the eye tracking module are used as part of the logical sequence in the controller. The controller uses the input to enable or disable the movement of the puzzle pieces and also the color display settings of the pieces. The target location and angle of the puzzle pieces are determined by the controller using information of the target image in each game. Other game configuration parameters such as number of games, game progression and calculation of points are in the game controller.

Real-Time Game Points Calculation. Game controller calculates the game points at four different checkpoints in a single move as shown in Fig. 5. Points are gained when: (1) Participant makes eye contact with avatar; (2) Participant chooses the correct piece that was cued; (3) Participant moves the piece to the target; and (4) The piece is at the target within the response time. Based on this settings, the maximum points achievable is 4 per puzzle piece move, resulting in 28 points per game (as there are 7 pieces per game).

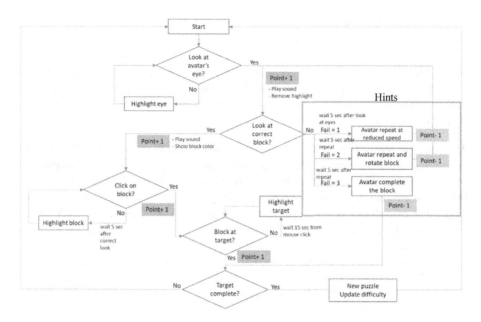

Fig. 5. Flow chart of game protocol

Assistive Hints. Figure 5 also shows the algorithm designed for point reduction and assistive hints provided by the avatar for the participant. Hints are system prompts that

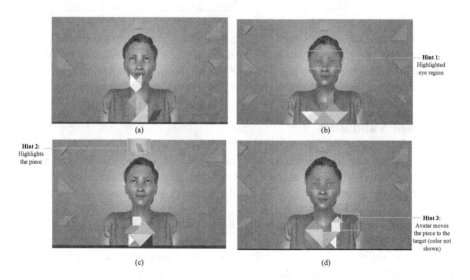

Fig. 6. (a) Avatar cues the piece at the top of the screen. (b) Highlighted eye region as a hint to make eye contact. (c) Avatar cues the piece at the top of the screen and a hint that highlights the piece it is looking at. (d) Avatar moves the piece to the target on its own when participant failed to select and move the correct piece three times.

are performed when participant fails to do certain tasks. In this training game, on the first failed attempt, the avatar will repeat the same gaze direction cue with its eye region highlighted as a hint. On the second failed attempt, the hint highlights and rotates the correct piece. On the last attempt, if the participant is still unable to choose the correct piece, the avatar will move the piece to the target on its own. Points are reduced in each failed attempt. Figure 6 shows an example of a hint where a piece is highlighted with a spotlight while the avatar cues it.

Adaptive Difficulty Level. The algorithm for adaptive difficulty level is designed by integrating the components of the system and evaluating the overall task performance of the participant. The adaptive changes in the avatar's speed and the participant's time to respond are shown in Table 1. When a participant earns between 7 to 14 points per game, it is considered as low performance category and no changes are made to the avatar's speed and time to respond in the consecutive game. For points earned between 15 to 21 points, medium performance category, only the avatar's speed is increased and time to respond remain the same in the next game. For highest points ranging between 22 and 28 points, the avatar's speed is increased and time to respond is reduced. High performers are challenged to respond in shorter time and at higher avatar's speed.

Table 1. Adaptive difficulty level matrix

Points earn in each puzzle game	Performance category	Avatar's speed	Time to respond
7–14	Low	Remain the same	Remain the same
15–21	Medium	Increase speed	Remain the same
22–28	High	Increase speed	Reduce time

By configuring the avatar to wait for the participant to make eye contact before it cues any puzzle piece, it is hoped that it will encourage the participant to make more frequent eye contact to progress in the game. Overall, the data collected from the system can be used to provide a comprehensive view of the participant's training performance.

3   System Validation

Usability study and system validation were conducted with the training. The system was tested for its feasibility, validity and reliability of the data collected and reliability of the algorithms. Three typically developing (TD) volunteers were recruited and tested the system.

The volunteers provided positive feedback after completing the test. They commonly agreed that: (1) the objective of the game was easy to understand; (2) all the gaze directions from the different gaze configurations correspond correctly to the location of the puzzle pieces; and (3) the eye tracker was responsive and sensitive to the gaze direction even when volunteers' head moved around a little bit.

To calculate the validity and accuracy of the eye tracker, we used eye gaze data and the ROIs that were defined in the training game. We selected three ROIs, highlighted in

Fig. 7, to be analyzed with gaze data from all three volunteers. The position of the ROIs on the screen were known, and data collected by the eye tracker includes gaze location on the screen and also identify if the eyes are on the ROIs. Based on these information, we calculated the distance between the gaze position to the actual position of the ROIs. We found that the accuracy were 0.88 cm in the y-direction ($0.95°$ angle deviation in vertical direction) and 1.23 cm in the x-direction ($1.33°$ angle deviation in the horizontal direction). These angles are acceptable for the application in this training game since the pieces and their ROIs are arranged far apart from each other.

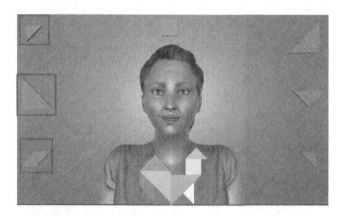

Fig. 7. The ROIs marked in the red boxes used for the accuracy calculation. (Color figure online)

In order to validate the algorithm used in the training game, a graph of events against game time progression was created for the volunteers for a single game. Based on the graphs in Fig. 8, each graph was unique and represents the performance of the volunteers. In Fig. 8(a), data from volunteer 1 (V1) showed multiple pauses in between movement of pieces to the target due to the volunteer having motor skill issues with using the mouse and had to take short breaks for each piece. But as the game progressed, the volunteer's performance improved but was not consistent as can be seen in the time interval for piece 3 which is shortest but then increased again for piece 4. The total time to complete one game for V1 was 226 s. As for volunteer 2 (V2), as can be seen in Fig. 8(b), it shows that the volunteer was able to progress quite well on average, except for the second puzzle piece where the avatar had to provide all three hints to the volunteer and completed the piece for the volunteer. The rest of the game progressed well with a smooth progression and shorter interval. The total time to complete one game for V2 was 106 s. For volunteer 3 (V3) as shown in Fig. 8(c), the graph showed a steady progression from the first piece to the seventh piece and also the first piece of the second game. The volunteer did not use any hints and was able to proceed with each trial successfully. The total time to complete one game for V3 was 59 s. These data show that the algorithm designed for the training game is working and that data analysis for this training game can show the level of performance for each participant and provide a good comparison of performance progress for the participant over the period of training sessions.

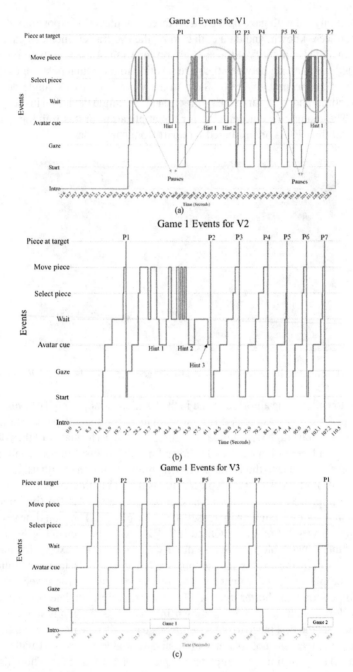

Fig. 8. Volunteers' performance during system validation test. (P1–P7 indicates Piece 1 until Piece 7)

4   Conclusion and Future Work

Autism spectrum disorder (ASD) affects the social and communication skills of 1 in 68 children in the USA. Therapies and intervention sessions are known to be financially costly and time-consuming. Advancement in virtual reality and human-computer technology have provided a platform to further explore the application of virtual systems in the intervention and training for children with ASD.

One area of interest for intervention for children with ASD is in gaze sharing and joint attention. Children with ASD are known to have reduced gaze during social interaction and have poor joint attention skills. The training game discussed in this paper introduced a novel virtual reality-based game designed for joint attention training for children with ASD. The design and architecture were explained in detail. Results from system validation showed that the system is feasible, reliable and can provide the sufficient view of the performance of each participant.

Future work will include running clinical experiment with children with ASD and typically developing (TD) children and compare the difference in gaze pattern and visual information processing during such social interaction.

Acknowledgment. We are grateful for the support provided by NIH grants 1R21MH111548-01 for this research. The authors are solely responsible for the contents and opinions expressed in this manuscript.

References

1. Centers for Disease Control (CDC): Facts About ASD (2014)
2. Van Der Geest, J.N., Kemner, C., Verbaten, M.N., Van Engeland, H.: Gaze behavior of children with pervasive developmental disorder toward human faces: a fixation time study. J. Child Psychol. Psychiatry **43**, 669–678 (2002). https://doi.org/10.1111/1469-7610.00055
3. Pelphrey, K.A., Sasson, N.J., Reznick, J.S., et al.: J. Autism Dev. Disord. **32**, 249 (2002). https://doi.org/10.1023/A:1016374617369
4. Dawson, G., et al.: Early social attention impairments in autism: social orienting, joint attention, and attention to distress. Dev. Psychol. **40**(2), 271 (2004)
5. Mundy, P., Newell, L.: Attention, joint attention, and social cognition. Curr. Dir. Psychol. Sci. **16**(5), 269–274 (2007). https://doi.org/10.1111/j.1467-8721.2007.00518.x
6. Charman, T., Swettenham, J., Baron-Cohen, S., Cox, A., Baird, G., Drew, A.: Infants with autism: an investigation of empathy, pretend play, joint attention, and imitation. Dev. Psychol. **33**(5), 781–789 (1997). https://doi.org/10.1037/0012-1649.33.5.781
7. Mundy, P., Sigman, M., Kasari, C.: A longitudinal study of joint attention and language development in autistic children. J. Autism Dev. Disord. **20**(1), 115–128 (1990)
8. Dawson, G., et al.: Early social attention impairments in autism: social orienting, joint attention, and attention to distress. Dev. Psychol. **40**(2), 271 (1990)
9. Moore, M., Calvert, S.: J. Autism Dev. Disord. **30**, 359 (2000). https://doi.org/10.1023/A:1005535602064

10. Bian, D., Wade, J.W., Zhang, L., Bekele, E., Swanson, A., Crittendon, J.A., Sarkar, M., Warren, Z., Sarkar, N.: A novel virtual reality driving environment for autism intervention. In: Stephanidis, C., Antona, M. (eds.) UAHCI 2013 Part II. LNCS, vol. 8010, pp. 474–483. Springer, Heidelberg (2013). https://doi.org/10.1007/978-3-642-39191-0_52

11. Zhang, L., et al.: Design of a mobile collaborative virtual environment for autism intervention. In: Antona, M., Stephanidis, C. (eds.) UAHCI 2016 Part III. LNCS, vol. 9739, pp. 265–275. Springer, Cham (2016). https://doi.org/10.1007/978-3-319-40238-3_26

12. Bekele, E., et al.: Understanding how adolescents with autism respond to facial expressions in virtual reality environments. IEEE Trans. Vis. Comput. Graph. **19**(4), 711–720 (2013)

13. Zheng, Z., Zhao, H., Swanson, A.R., Weitlauf, A.S., Warren, Z.E., Sarkar, N.: Design, development, and evaluation of a noninvasive autonomous robot-mediated joint attention intervention system for young children with ASD. IEEE Trans. Hum.-Mach. Syst. **48**, 125–135 (2017)

14. Caruana, N., et al.: Joint attention difficulties in autistic adults: an interactive eye-tracking study. Autism (2017). https://doi.org/10.1177/1362361316676204

15. Courgeon, M., et al.: Joint attention simulation using eye-tracking and virtual humans. IEEE Trans. Affect. Comput. **5**(3), 238–250 (2014)

16. Mundy, P., Crowson, M.: Joint attention and early social communication: implications for research on intervention with autism. J. Autism Dev. Dis. **27**, 653 (1997)

17. Kasari, C., Freeman, S., Paparella, T.: Joint attention and symbolic play in young children with autism: a randomized controlled intervention study. J. Child Psychol. Psychiatry **47**, 611–620 (2006)

18. Zheng, Z., Nie, G., Swanson, A., Weitlauf, A., Warren, Z., Sarkar, N.: Longitudinal impact of autonomous robot-mediated joint attention intervention for young children with ASD. In: Agah, A., Cabibihan, J.-J., Howard, A.M., Salichs, M.A., He, H. (eds.) ICSR 2016. LNCS (LNAI), vol. 9979, pp. 581–590. Springer, Cham (2016). https://doi.org/10.1007/978-3-319-47437-3_57

19. Tobii Eyetracking EyeX. https://help.tobii.com/hc/en-us/categories/201185405-EyeX

20. Gibaldi, A., Vanegas, M., Bex, P.J., Maiello, G.: Evaluation of the Tobii EyeX Eye tracking controller and Matlab toolkit for research. Behav. Res. Methods **49**(3), 923–946 (2017)

21. Unity. https://unity3d.com/unity

22. Tobii Unity SDK. http://developer.tobii.com/tobii-unity-sdk/

23. Maya, 3D animation software. https://www.autodesk.com/education/free-software/maya

ICT to Support Dental Care of Children with Autism: An Exploratory Study

Mariasole Bondioli[1], Maria Claudia Buzzi[2], Marina Buzzi[2], Susanna Pelagatti[1], and Caterina Senette[2(✉)]

[1] University of Pisa, Lungarno Pacinotti 43, 56124 Pisa, Italy
{mariasole.bondioli,susanna.pelagatti}@di.unipi.it
[2] IIT-CNR, via Moruzzi 1, 56124 Pisa, Italy
{claudia.buzzi,marina.buzzi,caterina.senette}@iit.cnr.it

Abstract. The dental health of children with autism presents many challenges, since they usually perceive sensory experiences differently and have problems accepting unknown social contexts. In a dental care setting, there are many strong sound-visual stimulations that are not experienced in any other setting. This usually upsets a patient with autism, often forcing dentists to administer chemical sedation in order to carry out dental work. Recently, many technology-enhanced systems and apps have been proposed to help people with autism adapt and cope with distressing situations. However, few studies have attempted to exploit ICT to simplify dental care in people with autism. This study explores the potential of personalized digital tools to help children with autism become familiar with dental care procedures and environments and to learn how to perform proper oral hygiene at home. To this aim, we carried out a 3-month exploratory study involving a multidisciplinary team of researchers, developers, dentists, psychologist, parents and ten children with autism observed under natural conditions during their first dental care cycle. The results appear to confirm the potential of technology for reducing anxiety in professional settings, increasing children's wellbeing and safety. The main contribution of this paper is the detailed account of this exploratory study and the discussion of the results obtained. Moreover, we outline the user requirements of an accessible and customizable multimodal platform to help dentists and families facilitate ADS children's dental care according to the methodology described here.

Keywords: Autism · Dental care · ICT tools

1 Introduction

Autism spectrum disorder (ASD) usually manifests in children before 3 years of age, affecting three main areas: (a) social interaction, (b) communication and language, (c) symbolic or imaginative play. The severity of symptoms varies significantly from individual to individual, so it is very important to deliver a personalized training intervention tuned to the child's needs, preferences, pace and abilities. Accessible training is delivered through trials and games based on Augmentative and Alternative Communication (AAC), an assistive technology allowing people with autism to take advantage of their

© Springer International Publishing AG, part of Springer Nature 2018
M. Antona and C. Stephanidis (Eds.): UAHCI 2018, LNCS 10907, pp. 475–492, 2018.
https://doi.org/10.1007/978-3-319-92049-8_34

visual channel, usually the most effective of the senses [23]. In fact, hearing and touch are often altered, so unfamiliar voices and noises (such as that of dental tools), touch sensations in the mouth and unknown social contexts are challenging situations that must be gradually introduced to the subject to avoid provoking anxiety, stress and pain. Communication and comprehension are the basis for enabling child interaction. In addition, rewards and motivations are fundamental for modeling adequate behaviors and encouraging collaboration. The peculiarity of the syndrome (each person with autism is different and has specific special needs) suggests adopting a personalized holistic intervention involving behavior, skills and social abilities. The use of visual stimuli (familiar images and objects) as well as the massive use of reinforcement are motivating elements.

Oral hygiene is very important for everyone, since prevention reduces the need for invasive interventions in the mouth. Indeed, for a child with autism, accepting the unknown sound-visual stimulations typical of a dental care setting is very difficult task: the sounds of suction or dental drills can be intolerable, as can be the bright light above the dentist's chair. The main obstacle is the previously unknown context, which produces anxiety and unexpected behaviors in nearly all people with autism, often forcing dentists to administer anesthesia in order to complete dental work.

In recent years, ICT has been used to teach people with autism how to adapt to new contexts and cope with distressing social situations [13, 17]. However, to the best of our knowledge, using ICT to familiarize these children with dental care procedures and environments in a personalized way is still a largely unexplored topic.

In this paper, we describe an exploratory study to evaluate the potential of ICT to facilitate dental care of children with autism by lowering anxiety and avoiding sedation. Previous studies have reported successful experiences, suggesting that digital resources and ICT tools could facilitate dental care for children with autism [4, 15]. Starting from this, we investigated how to take advantage of the every child's interest in gaming and multimedia content, to design an assistive educational methodology enhanced by ICT, to facilitate the dental care of children with autism. The flexible and dynamically programmable technology is able to adapt to the specific needs and preferences of each child. Moreover, we collected the user requirements for an assistive application able to help dentists and parents/caregivers organize and deliver personalized ICT activities to each child. In the rest of this paper, we use the term "caregivers" to indicate anyone (including parents and other family members) who cares for a patient with autism.

To better identify the most usable and useful digital resources and ICT tools for children and dentists, we applied a participatory design approach [26] with a multidisciplinary team (researchers, developers, dentists, a psychologist and parents). Furthermore, in order to better refine the user requirements, investigate and prove their acceptability in a real dental setting, also collecting feedback from final users, we performed a 3-month exploratory qualitative study with ten children with autism observed under natural conditions during their first dental care cycle. Children performed personalized pleasant ICT activities, such as multimedia games, to lighten the tension and familiarize themselves with the dentist's environment and oral procedures. Furthermore, during dental visits they used a tablet to take photos and videos of the dental setting and procedures. The multimedia content was recorded on a server and made available to the children together with other interactive ICT tools (games, interactive pdf files, didactic videos, etc.) to be (re)viewed at home. The results appear to confirm the potential of technology for reducing anxiety and increasing the children's wellbeing and safety, while making the procedure more pleasant and encouraging oral hygiene as part of their daily routine.

The contributions of this paper are (1) a general methodology using ICT to simplify dental care for children with autism, (2) results of a 3-month exploratory qualitative study involving ten children and their caregivers; and (3) the user requirements for the design of a customizable web application to facilitate ADS children's dental care according to the proposed methodology.

The paper is organized into five sections. Section 2 introduces related work and Sect. 3 introduces the study design, detailing our methodology and what procedures were identified and followed during the 3-month observational study carried out with ten children with autism undergoing dental care in the clinical environment. Section 4 discusses the results of our study, highlighting lessons learnt and introducing the requirements for supporting software as well as some general guidelines for designing software tools to support children with autism in a dental setting environment. Section 5 concludes and discusses some future work.

2   Related Works

2.1   Autism Challenges in Dental Care

The dental health of children with ASD has been investigated in several recent medical studies. The behavior of patients with ASD makes the delivery of oral hygiene and dental treatment a serious problem [27]. The link between the patient's sensory sensitivity, related to the autism spectrum, and their refusal of the dentist's interventions appears clear, considering the specific setting where the dentist receives patients [5, 6]. Thus, since the 1990s physical restraints and chemical sedation have been commonly implemented in dental sessions to control disruptive behaviors caused by the reaction to a stressful situation [12]. In addition, recent studies acknowledge the child's difficulty approaching dental visits and performing daily oral care as the most significant factor in their poor oral health [9, 15, 16]. A recent study showed that due to poor oral care, children with autism exhibited a higher prevalence of caries (tooth decay), poor oral hygiene and extensive unmet needs for dental treatment than did a non-autistic healthy control group [16]. Analogously, the predisposition of ASD subjects toward oral issues was studied by Cagetti, who observed that the increased number of dentistry issues is not connected to a peculiar predisposition of ASD subjects (a sample of 35 children between 6 and 16 years of age). The higher rate of pathologies can be related to a lack of prevention in oral care, which usually is not appropriately delivered to meet their special needs [6]. Unfortunately, the professional training offered by most university programs does not include dealing with ASD children, so it is necessary to teach dental professionals how to treat them correctly [14, 29]. ASD children need to be supported and guided during her/his visit by an interdisciplinary plan of action that takes into account his/her specific needs to promote better dental health [15]. Therefore, to increase the probability of successful dental treatment of ASD patients, the dentist should have an in-depth interdisciplinary understanding of the autism syndrome as well as of behavioral principles for therapeutic intervention.

Difficulties dealing with the dental care of ASD children are documented in literature but are also experienced every day by many dentists who are unprepared to deal with these patients. Anxiety, lack of collaboration, stereotypes and disruptive behaviors can scare dentists, who often bypass these difficulties by delivering patients to the hospital to undergo the procedure under chemical sedation. In this setting, a simple dental disease will nearly always become a serious health problem. Families too are painfully tried by their child's suffering. Therefore, ASD children have few chances to learn how to perform and maintain good oral hygiene autonomously. Barry [4] examined the issues encountered by children with ASD accessing dental care, using a questionnaire completed by 112 parents. This research provided insight into potential barriers to dental care for children with ASD from the perspective of their parents, and suggestions to help to overcome some of them. Some of the strategies proposed involved photos and social stories, which are a subset of the ICT activities attempted in our study.

2.2   ICT in Dental Care for People with Autism

The use of ICT to facilitate dental care delivered to patients with ASD is a relatively unexplored field. Medical research clearly supports the need to apply behavioral approaches to model ASD people's actions appropriate for the context, especially under stressful conditions, [18, 25, 30]. Several studies underline the positive effect of daily use of ICT on people with ASD, in both learning contexts and social situations, such as a dental visit [8, 10, 20, 22, 29]. The effectiveness of ICT in teaching different skills has been studied by many authors. Several studies have proved the advantages of using video modeling techniques [8, 11, 30], augmented reality [7], and software to facilitate communication (such as Picture Exchange Communication Systems) [13] and develop social skills [3]. All these studies report that people with ASD like the innovative educational approach introduced by ICT. Using technology, they could avoid typical issues involved in human interaction, such as impatience, feelings of inadequacy, unpredictability of people's behavior, and poor recognition of emotions, irony, and figurative language.

The literature mainly reports the use of video materials to create favorable conditions for obtaining the cooperation of children with ASD in a dental visit. For instance, a sequence of images showing how to perform tooth brushing was proposed to fourteen children for a period of 18 months, demonstrating the potential of this tool for improving the oral hygiene of people with ASD [23]. Visual scheduling has also been very useful for making the child understand and accept sequences of activities [17, 24]. Conyers et al. carried out desensitization using video modeling to encourage collaboration in persons with mental retardation, observing the best results with in vivo desensitization [9]. However, this cognitive impairment differs greatly from autistic syndrome, for which video modeling has proved to be very successful in different educational and social contexts [3, 8, 30].

A study closer to ours is the work of Isong et al. [15] in which the authors tested two types of electronic screen media – a Google glass (sun-glass-style video eyewear) and a DVD reader – showing that their use helped reduce fear and uncooperative behaviors in children with ASD undergoing dental visits. They performed a randomized study to verify whether visual materials could facilitate the dental operation. Results showed that the anxiety decreased in children when they were approached by the dentist with visual tools. Although the goal of this study is similar to ours, there are some important differences. Isong et al. used tools and content not strictly related to the specific context. We believe personalization may increase the intervention's usability and efficacy so we use videos and pictures made during the child's own dental sessions; in our approach the child is an active actor in content creation. Isong et al. only used video content, while we used various kinds of multimedia content (images, audio, interactive games, etc.) that most likely can better meet different users' needs. Finally, Isong et al. tested the effectiveness of some ICT tools for anxiety reduction but did not indicate a way to reproduce its approach. Barry [4] describes a potential strategy mediated by photographs of the dental clinic and staff, social stories made by picture cards and an Apple application as a means of distraction, in order to enhance communication with the patients. In this study, the ICT tools were not personalized and the children were passive users not involved in content creation.

Summarizing, only a few studies have attempted to explore the full potential of ICT to teach useful skills for improving ASD people's dental care. Positive results have been achieved using video modeling, helping patients reduce their anxiety, but to the best of the authors' knowledge, other tools such as cognitive games or the active involvement of children in content creation have not yet been investigated.

3 Study Design

3.1 User Recruitment

Users were recruited from among young patients with autism seeking access to dental care at a public hospital in Pisa (Clinica Odontoiatrica Universitaria). The no-profit association Autismo Pisa Onlus (part of Autism Europe), facilitated the identification of a group of ten children in need of dental care or interested in a preventive course of dental treatment. We recruited them as our user group. Only one child fell within the category of high-functioning autism while nine were low-functioning; three of them were non-verbal and non-receptive, three non-verbal but receptive, and three were both verbal and receptive. The only recruitment criterion was age, accepting children 6-12 years old in the study because this age range covers the permanent dentition process.

We describe the protocol followed in Sect. 3.2 and give a detailed characterization of the user sample in Sect. 3.3.

3.2 Protocol

The protocol of the study was defined in collaboration with two dental professionals and one neuro-psychiatric expert enrolled in the project. Procedures and rules of protocol included: (i) identification of all the figures to involve and their role in the study (Sect. 3.2.1); (ii) the number and frequency of the visits for each user

(Sect. 3.2.2 and 3.2.3); (iii) the amount, type, and collection of data needed to characterize the users (see Sect. 3.3); (iv) activities to perform with the children during dental sessions (see Sect. 3.4); (v) definition of the materials to be used during the study (see Sect. 3.2.4).

3.2.1 Planning Actors and Roles

The multidisciplinary team enrolled in this study comprised clinical professionals (dentists and neuropsychiatrist) and ICT researchers. Parents played a crucial role, especially in assisting and supervising recommended activities at home. The team member roles were specified: two dentists performed the activities in the clinical room in collaboration with a hygienist and a researcher; one of them supervised the overall procedures and interacted mainly with parents especially during data collection, the other dentist (the operative dentist) was directly involved with medical procedures with children, assisted by the hygienist if necessary. Activities regarding technical and research aspects such as preparing tools (hardware and software), management and collection of digital resources, included in materials (see Sect. 3.2), and collection of observational data regarding children's behavior, were carried out by an ICT researcher on the team. Children were naturally brought to interact mostly with the operative dentist, the hygienist and the ICT researcher. The presence of all these three figures was guaranteed in each session.

3.2.2 Planning Visits with Users

First Visit: The first meeting helped the dentist to get to know each child (and his/her parents) and to test their reactions to simple requests such as to sit down on the dental chair or to open his/her mouth. During the visit, a questionnaire was administered to the caregivers in order to collect data related to the child's oral condition, dental hygiene habits, child's autism condition, the presence of any sensory disturbances and the usage of technological devices such as tablets, smartphones and video cameras.

Other Appointments: A series of weekly appointments (each lasting around 45 min) for each patient over a period of 3 months was scheduled. All the appointments took place in the same clinical room, in order to avoid confusion and ease familiarization. During these appointments, thanks to the parents' cooperation, we offered a kit of digital tools to the child to help him/her become familiar with the dentist and the clinical environment, before carrying out the medical intervention. The dentist (helped by the ICT researcher) personalized the kit's components in all the intervention phases depending on the child's needs. At the end of each appointment, a set of tools for the kit was selected to be used at home to introduce the activities scheduled for the next appointment.

3.2.3 Planning Activities

The children's training was structured to include three different types of activities, as detailed in Fig. 1.

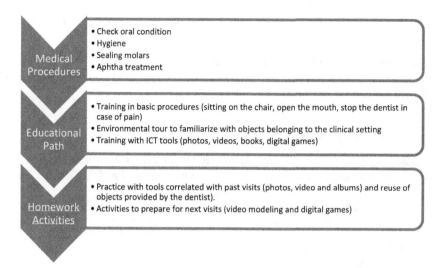

Fig. 1. Proposed activities

3.2.4 Defining Materials to Use

Materials used during the study included hardware and software tools, together with common objects that are part of the clinical setting. Two tablets were used by the children, usually as a camera, in order to create a personal multimedia archive of resources constantly updated with materials from the dental sessions. Tablets were selected since they are familiar to most of the children and are a source of great interest regardless of the context. A kit of software resources was provided to the children starting from his/her second appointment. The kit included customizable digital games and multimedia materials narrating in a simple way what is present (such as dentist mirror, probe, toothbrush, gloves and sunglasses) and what happens in a dental clinic. Specifically:

- Cognitive learning games (memories, puzzles, sequences and matching exercises) to familiarize the patient with dental procedures and environment in an amusing way. The use of games for educating people with cognitive needs has been widely investigated in literature. In children with autism, games are used to stimulate learning through imitation (since subjects with autism usually lack this skill [1, 2, 30] and to capture user attention and collaboration for performing specific tasks, taking advantage of AAC (Augmentative Alternative Communication).
- Interactive PDFs (pdf files equipped with sound effects): particularly useful for narrating procedures and/or dental objects. This allows associating positive elements with a stressful event and can help reduce resistance to the change.
- Audio, video and photos indexed by visit date, to keep track of the important phases of the visit. The child can navigate their resources and show them to caregivers.
- Videos reproducing all actions from the arrival at the clinic to the child sitting in the dentist's chair. The videos are essential for activating the imitation of a targeted behavior functional to the context. Seeing familiar people performing target actions can help the child's imitation process [21]. Crucial attention is devoted to technical

details such as freeze frame, zoom, audio-visual aids, and graphics that transform the footage into a powerful educational tool.

The resources are partly created using the tablet's camera (photos and videos) and partly (games, interactive PDFs and video-modeling sequences) specifically prepared by ICT researchers on the team.

3.3   User Group Characterization

Data collected via the questionnaire administered to the caregivers during the first visit allowed us to characterize the user group, as shown in Tables 1 and 2.

Table 1. Demographic information and autism condition

User	Gender	Age	Verbal	Receptive	Age of diagnosis
U1	M	10	No	Yes	3
U2	M	9	Yes	Yes	6
U3	M	6	Yes	Yes	2
U4	F	8	No	Yes	2
U5	M	12	Yes	Yes	5
U6	M	12	Yes	Yes	2
U7	M	8	No	No	5
U8	M	7	No	Yes	3
U9	F	9	No	Yes	3
U10	M	11	Yes	Yes	3

Regarding children's familiarity with the use of electronic devices (smartphone and tablets), data collected highlighted that all of them have some experience. The most common use of the tablet included watching YouTube videos, using the camera, searching elements in the archive of photos and video. Some of the users, (specifically U2 and U8) also used the tablet during other autism intervention programs external to the dental care context, U1 used the tablet with his/her parents at home for entertainment and educational activities. In the latter cases, children were also familiar with digital games such as puzzles and sequences. U3 and U4 manifested compulsivity in the use of tablet. In U3, that fact made it impossible to propose the approach described herein; instead, with U4, the work was possible after overcoming some initial difficulties.

Table 2. Clinical information and dental habits

User	Dental hygiene habits	Dental care need	Previous dental visits	Sensory disturbance
U1	Regularly brush teeth with parent	Oral hygiene Oral education	Yes	Noise of water of the tap
U2	Regularly brush teeth alone	Oral hygiene Sealing molars	Yes	Dazzling lights
U3	Regularly brush teeth with parents	Oral education	No	High tactile sensitivity
U4	Irregularly brush teeth alone	Basic oral education Caries care	No	Acute Noises
U5	Regularly brush teeth with parents	Oral hygiene Sealing molars	Yes	Dazzling lights
U6	Irregularly brush teeth alone	Oral hygiene	Yes	Dental chair noises and movements
U7	Irregularly brush teeth with parents	Basic oral education Caries care	No	Acute noises High tactile sensitivity
U8	Irregularly brush teeth with parents	Basic oral education	No	Noise of dental aspirator
U9	Regularly brush teeth with parents	Oral education Oral hygiene	No	Environmental noises
U10	Regularly brush teeth with parents	Oral hygiene Sealing molars	Yes	Dental chair noises

3.4 Sessions with Users

Sessions with children were structured to include activities that relate to the current visit and activities to prepare for next visit. Each activity was planned and performed taking into account a specific subdivision of goals in distal outcomes and proximal outcomes. The latter in turn was divided into elementary units. The distal outcome is the process of familiarization of the medical environment and the dental procedures and it was pursued during all the study. This familiarization process was then applied to a list of medical activities represented by proximal outcomes.

For instance, if the proximal outcome is oral hygiene, the child has to be prepared for this activity and in parallel he/she has to work toward familiarization with the general environment: (i) go to the dentist; (ii) access the clinic; (iii) wait for his/her turn; (iv) sitting in the dentist chair; (v) open their mouth; (vi) halt the dentist; (vii) ask for help. If this familiarization process fails somewhere, the proximal activity cannot be performed or needs to be proposed in a lighter form; for instance, it would be a great result even to clean only one tooth.

Given this subdivision, depending on the objectives to achieve, as illustrated in Sect. 3.2, the proposed activities were the same for all the children but adapted to the circumstances and to the children's needs. For instance, for the proximal outcome requiring the patient to "open your mouth" the dentist planned to achieve the goal in two steps, in order to allow the child to rehearse in the clinic with practice activities (first time) and at home with video-modeling sessions (second time). If one child was more receptive than others were and he/she was able to perform the task quickly, the two-step procedure was equally respected but in a different form, trying to allow the child to generalize the task. Likewise, if the child manifested some disturbance regarding one of the phases' procedures, the task was re-modulated.

We proposed to the patients a general schema including medical and ICT activities at the clinic and at home. Obviously, the medical activity is the main goal for each patient; the activities with ICT tools are only an aid toward reaching this goal. During the first visit, the dentist tries to ascertain the child's oral situation and he/she uses the tablet to record photos, videos and selfies aided by the child. The ICT activity is mainly carried out by the dentist and serves to collect resources for future visits. On this occasion, the child learns preliminary strategies to familiarize themselves with the environment, acting there (if he/she wants) in first person. Moreover, he/she becomes familiar with the tablet as a part of the clinical setting. In that sense, the pleasure offered by the tablet's use acts as reinforcement for the child, helping mitigate the aversion to the medical environment. From the second appointment onward, the order of activities is as follows:

1. **ICT activity at home:** learning games, review of photos and video modeling sessions with materials collected in the previous visit, to prepare for the next visit.
2. **Medical activity at clinic:** different for each child depending on his/her need.
3. **ICT activity at clinic:** depending on the success of 2. Medical activity:
   a. If the medical task failed: 20 min of activity using the tablet performed away from the dentist's chair in a dedicated room including activities to familiarize themselves with the failed medical task and familiarization activity in general
   b. If the medical task is successful: 20 min of activity using the tablet performed away from the dentist's chair in a dedicated room including review of activities already mastered and positive rewards for activities well completed.

Each activity respected the general approach used in behavioral intervention with subjects with autism [19]: short and diversified activities are performed quickly in order to avoid problem behaviors and reduce self-stimulations in children. Moreover, each "theoretical" activity should have a correspondent in practice. For instance, a desensitization task of noisy sounds using digital games is followed by a direct experience (touching it) with the medical devices that produces those sounds. This practice is already efficiently used in children's dentistry to control the source of disturbance in order to reduce the pain but in this case the novelty is the combination of these good practices with ICT tools.

Regarding appropriateness of tools during the dental session, the following summarizes the main observations:

- *Familiarization with objects*: a **matching program** using images (photos) of dental setting objects was proposed with efficacy.
- *Familiarization with procedures*: digital games such as "**sorting sequence**" of the intervention were usually considered the default best tool since they provide an

effective way to learn the sequence of steps of the procedure. For example: "the child has a toothache, (s)he goes to the dentist, then the pain goes away".

- *Child "control" over his/her environment to relax him/her*: a suitable activity was the **collection of digital photos and videos**: (i) take photos and videos of everything that might be of interest in the dental environment and of procedures, to create the child's digital toolbox; (ii) reassure the child during an intervention using the camera's selfie mode (some children became more cooperative knowing what the dentist was doing inside their mouth).

Regarding what specific tool could be the best choice for homework assisted by parents, we observed that:

- Customized video-modeling resources and photos or videos reproducing memories of the dental visit in the clinic are useful for learning procedures. In this case, customization mainly relates to photograms with the child's caregivers and the child himself, as actors.
- Logical sequences about dental procedures and interactive digital stories had introduced main concepts that helped develop the child's conditioning process to facilitate the procedures.
- Most of the parents helped their children do their homework, especially in tasks requiring imitation of the procedure of the mouth inspection. The simulation of the visits in a familiar context, repeated many times, in most cases was decisive in overcoming the dentist's otherwise common difficulties completing the child's mouth evaluation

4 Results and Discussion

4.1 Children's Responses

Children performed didactic activities, using the tablet attentively and collaboratively. Its use facilitated the initial contact with the dentist and the other figures who were present during sessions, capturing their interest and reducing any pain resulting from the unknown environment and dentist's intervention procedures. Nearly all the children used the tablet carefully and followed the rules. Younger children unfamiliar with the tablet needed to be physically guided initially, but they quickly learned how to use it.

Regardless of disability, no technological aid can be valid for all. In our study, two children used the tablet in a compulsive way. Specifically, with one child, U3 (6 years old, non-verbal) that fact impeded the training. Stereotypies are a frequent symptom in autism so we must contemplate this scenario, managing the compulsion before the intervention, or abandon this approach to identify the more suitable strategies.

Most of all, the other children greatly appreciated the opportunity to take and collect photos and videos of their visits. Some of them wanted to see themselves during the dental intervention (using the camera in selfie-mode) to better understand what was happening. In some cases, the tablet camera had a very positive distraction effect, especially during invasive dental procedures. At home, all the children wanted to explore their personal archive and share it with parents. Photos and videos are also a great resource for the parents and the dentist, allowing customization of stories and games.

After two visits, one child (U9) abandoned the study for family reasons. Of the remaining eight children (not considering U9 and U3), most of them began to perceive the tablet as a part of the clinical environment: (i) they expected to see the assistant taking photos during the dental operation (in some cases no photos meant no visit); (ii) they were motivated to play with the tablet, considering it a reward (iii) at home, they asked to see all the material collected during the visits again.

For three children (U5, U7, U10) the time scheduled for the intervention protocol was not enough to implement and verify all the familiarization steps, planned to achieve the previously mentioned distal outcomes. This is mainly because caregivers were not steadily present in the weekly visits, affecting the results. Participants in the whole (3-month) experimental phase (four children) respecting scheduled appointments changed their attitude radically; they started with a total rejection of the intervention, refusing even to sit in the dentist's chair, but at the end of the intervention accepted a dental hygiene procedure collaboratively and without a sedative.

One child also accepted sealing molars, revealing high confidence in the environment and the people who took care of him during the experimental period. Those children, for whom systematic frequency had sustained the intervention, even when the dentist's requests increased, such as for invasive procedures, showed an increased willingness to accept them, reflecting a successful desensitization process and decreased level of anxiety. Those children started to learn how to ask for help or pause, and how to wait to complete the activity even if they wished to escape.

The educational activities performed during the visits as well as at home motivate children to tolerate the fear and pain associated with the unfamiliar, noisy, multi-stimulating clinical environment that without personalized training is quite stressful (often children accepted sitting in the chair after having a relaxing time using the tablet). Positive results achieved in this exploratory study seems to confirm the potential of ICT technology in a dental care context with subjects with autism, already suggested by previous studies. However, the approach, in the form described here, has some limits affecting its replicability: (i) It required considerable time and effort, and the children needed to be constantly guided and monitored during the proposed activities; (ii) Each visit produced a great deal of digital material, growing exponentially visit-by-visit. It seems unrealistic to propose a similar setting every time a child needs a dental intervention. However, it seems possible that proceeding in the familiarization process with dental procedures, the child will require less and less support; (iii) During the observational phase in the real context, children did not use the tablet completely on their own; an adult (dentist, parents, assistant, etc.) constantly monitored each activity since the use of the Internet connection lacked system protection for the child; (iv) As confirmed in literature [19], we observed that caregiver and family involvement was a crucial key to the success of an intervention, guaranteeing continuity of intervention at home/clinic. Moreover, it also seems to influence correct or incorrect usage of technology.

From this exploratory study, it is clear that following this approach requires effectively managing a large volume of data, games and personalized material. Thus, there is a clear need for an accessible digital platform able to effectively support dentists and patients during the process. In the following sections, we turn our observation to global software requirements for a Web application supporting dentists and patients and to a few guidelines that could drive the next phase of our project and benefit other researchers working in this field.

4.2 Software Requirements

Platform Requirements

Functional and non-functional requirements of the ICT platform have three main objectives: (i) Providing children with ASD and their caregivers with an accessible and usable digital resource toolkit to familiarize them with dental tools and settings, and deliver a structured dental hygiene educational course; (ii) Facilitating patient management and make easier for the dentist personalizing patients profiles and assigning preparatory activities, according their personal and medical profile; (iii) Improving the organization and management of resources for ease of use by professionals, patients and caregivers.

Global requirements incorporate the Web Content Accessibility Guidelines (WCAG 2.0): the platform should promote inclusion and satisfy usability principles: easy to learn, easy to remember (control elements), and satisfying to use [28].

Domain-related requirements involving technical aspects aimed at optimizing the platform in flexibility, scalability and performance. Selecting a Web platform offers some advantages: multi-device availability, ease of deployment and update, rapid and efficient data exchange, multimedia dimension, privacy and security treated carefully, so health information should be stored in a remote database (anonymized data, and secured transfer sessions).

User requirements could be instantiated differently depending on the user's role (dentist or patient) as illustrated in the next sections.

User Requirements: The Dentist's Nees

User requirements emerged from the direct observation of the dentist's work during the 3 months of the study, and from participatory design sessions:

- Environmental: this requirement is crucial for the interface's design. Our main constraints were to simplify interaction, ensure robustness and minimize errors while engaging children with ASD. The dentist needs to easily manage everyday activities and gain more time to win the patients' cooperation.
- Usability and User Experience: (i) Efficiency – goals need to be easily and rapidly accomplished, minimizing possible user errors; (ii) Intuitiveness – UIs must be easy to learn and navigate; buttons, headings, and help/error messages should be simple and easy to understand (iii) Natural interaction – with clear UIs and recognizable elements and functions; the interaction should not require much cognitive effort and should satisfy the user.
- Functional: The activities identified during the study have to be reproduced in the system (collecting user data, organizing current and future visits, preparing and showing games and materials, personalizing the intervention, etc.).

Above all, functional requirements demand appropriate UI design and a suitable navigation flow of UIs. We identified three main activities carried out by the dentist that need attention:

(a) To record and manage the child's information, i.e., personal details, neuropsychiatric diagnosis and dental care diagnoses.
(b) To manage materials related to personal visits as well as other resources to share among patients. Manage, in this context means: (i) collect and redistribute primary resources (photos, video, audio files and other documents); (ii) use these primary resources to generate other resources, especially personalized learning games.
(c) To schedule the next visit and prepare tasks and materials for the child, selecting them from the available resources (public repository or the child's personal repository)

Interaction mechanisms and time are decisive aspects in this special context; UI visual elements should be preferred to textual elements, and the (inter)actions to accomplish a task have to be minimized, exploiting natural paradigms (e.g., exploiting drag-and-drop). Globally, the proposed approach should be efficient and not time-consuming.

User Requirements: The Child's Needs

Careful design is required for the user experience of children with ASD since each individual has his/her own peculiarities. Observational data coming from contextual task analysis during sessions with users (see Sect. 3.4) showed how our young participants used a tablet and performed proposed tasks. Children should access a personal section in the platform offering:

– Extremely simplified UIs (minimal), with only a few elements clearly linked to the available activities, to avoid anxiety and confusion during user interaction
– Accessible stimuli: soft colors, sounds only where necessary
– An errorless system: no possibility of error in performing the activities that lead to unexpected system behavior
– Timely feedback from the system to reinforce or discourage certain behavior
– A safe environment for the child: (i) inability to quit the application and move to the Web; (ii) screen control, available on the mobile platform to avoid zoom-in/out, scroll, etc., which might trigger problem behaviors in ASD children.

The platform should facilitate the child when performing activities of the intervention protocol. We propose a main interface organized in three sections, reproducing activities that have been observed to be effective in a real context.

Play: This section would promote the child's acceptance of dental procedures by allowing access to interactive learning games and video-modeling created by the dentist.

Explore: In this section the child can access all materials collected or selected by the dentist: explore photos and interactive pdf files, and play videos or audio. Menus should be minimal and visually oriented so that the child can move among different types of resources correctly oriented in the platform structure.

Remember: This section should be a sort of a digital Personal Visual Diary[1] where the child is invited to remember and "refresh" previous dental visits. At the same time, it offers a memorandum on what (s)he will do during the next visit. The child should move between past and future experiences using clear and accessible elements linked to the history of past experiences, or to a preview of future appointments. In this case, an interactive calendar page would be the best choice to give the child a description of what he/she will do and provides a collection of materials and tools (pre-selected by the dentist) for facilitating the familiarization process with new situations.

4.3 General Guidelines

The experience of participatory design was extremely valuable and help us to better understand the needs and preferences of people with autism. We have summarized a few guidelines to help researchers offer a pleasant and accessible experience for this target. Since every individual is different, some guidelines might not be suitable for everyone and must be adapted to a specific subject. Probing the target subject on the first visit as well as previously collecting information and preferences with their parents can help to correctly evaluate the child's needs and preferences. In the following, the guidelines are listed and marked as software design (s) or behavioral principles (b):

Familiarization with the Context

Show pictures of dental setting (s)
Show pictures and videos of dental tools and procedures (s)
Introduce the subject slowly, with one or more sessions solely for familiarization with environment and dental tools (b)

Personalization

Incorporate pictures/videos showing the child's previous activities (s)
Enable the addition of familiar preferred images (s)
Enable customization of preferred games (sequence, matching, puzzle, …) (s)

Awareness of Next Action

Offer visual scheduling, to make children aware of and ready for the visit time (s)
Incorporate video showing next activities (s)

Time Adaptation

During the visit offer a visual tool for Request to Pause (provide a plasticized card to require a pause) (b)
The same functions might be activated using technology, for example with one click of a wireless mouse activating an audio alert for the dentist (s)

---

[1] In autism it is common to keep a notebook with transparent envelopes where the child harvests the "memories" of meaningful life experiences (trips, parties, activities, etc.). It can contain objects or fragments (sand, shells, glitter, photos, etc.) and is frequently used as a means of communicating about any change in the child's life-contexts (home, school, etc.).

Control of Current Actions

Offer a mirror to see what dentist is doing in the child's mouth (b).

5   Conclusion

Children with autism find it very hard to accept dental treatment due to the unfamiliar people and context with new sounds, lights and tactile stimulation; this provokes high levels of anxiety and stress that can degenerate into inadequate behaviors. Unfortunately, many dentists are still unprepared to deal with these special needs patients, and often chemical sedation is administered even for simple interventions, with a potential negative impact on children's health.

This research investigates whether technology can make dental care more efficient, effective and pleasant for children with autism. To address this challenge, a multidisciplinary team composed of professionals and researchers worked together for 3 months. Since co-design is hard to carry out with people with autism, an observational protocol was applied to gain information in an operative environment, probing the use of digital resources as an emotional balancer. Specifically, a clinical protocol also using digital resources was tested with ten children with autism who had a weekly dental visit for 3 months, in order to implement desensitization and anxiety control in a real dental care setting using a kit of digital resources as assistive technology.

Results seem to confirm the feasibility of the proposed approach and the positive role of technology support. Eight out of ten children responded to this approach positively, overcoming their initial diffidence, modeling their behavior and becoming increasingly collaborative, visit-by-visit. Almost all caregivers manifested satisfaction with the approach due to their active involvement. Furthermore, caregivers strongly committed to the protocol and respecting the weekly schedule felt the child-parent relationship was reinforced, and five children successfully completed the dental protocol in the time scheduled. In contrast, three children who missed half or more of the scheduled sessions due to caregiver issues were also unable to complete the familiarization protocol. This result confirmed the importance, already highlighted in literature, of active parent involvement in the care of children with autism [19].

Results obtained from this exploratory study enabled the definition of user requirements for the collaborative design of a Web platform for easy creation, management and fruition of digital resources for children with autism and dentists in a more accessible structured framework. Furthermore, to exploit the valuable insights collected, we have formulated some general guidelines for designing accessible multimodal tools for reducing anxiety during dental care sessions that could be useful cues for other researchers and developers approaching this research field.

Future work will apply participative design and early prototyping to create the platform. This digital environment will be rigorously experimented with testing protocols and the software tool (with a control group) in order to evaluate both its efficacy and efficiency. Lastly, additional effort will be devoted to raising awareness of local healthcare and educational organizations regarding the need to create dental care protocols for patients with special needs, using ICT technology as a valid support for the medical intervention.

Acknowledgements. We thank Prof. Maria Rita Giuca and Dr. Francesca Pardossi for their scientific contribution to the project. We also thank all the children with autism and their caregivers who took part of this study.

References

1. Aresti-Bartolome, N., Garcia-Zapirain, B.: Technologies as support tools for persons with autistic spectrum disorder: a systematic review. Int. J. Environ. Res. Public Health **11**(8), 7767–7802 (2014)
2. Artoni, S., Pelagatti, S., Buzzi, M.C., Buzzi, M., Senette, C.: Technology-enhanced discriminative programs for children with autism. In: Proceedings of the 8th International Conference on Pervasive Computing Technologies for Healthcare, pp. 331–334 (2014)
3. Ayres, K.M., Maguire, A., McClimon, D.: Acquisition and generalization of chained tasks taught with computer based video instruction to children with autism. Educ. Train. Dev. Disabil. **44**, 493–508 (2009)
4. Barry, S.M.: Improving access and reducing barriers to dental care for children with autism spectrum disorder. University of Leeds (2012)
5. Bertness, J., Holt, K.: Oral Health Services for Children and Adolescents with Special Health Care Needs: A Resource Guide, 2nd edn. National Maternal and Child Oral Health Resource Center, Washington, DC (2011)
6. Cagetti, M.G.: Un progetto di prevenzione e terapia odontoiatrica su pazienti autistici in età evolutiva. Prev. odontostomatologica **1**, 5–11 (2008)
7. Casas, X., Herrera, G., Coma, I., Fernández, M.: A Kinect-based augmented reality system for individuals with autism spectrum disorders. In: GRAPP/IVAPP, pp. 440–446 (2012)
8. Charlop, M.H., Milstein, J.P.: Teaching autistic children conversational speech using video modeling. J. Appl. Behav. Anal. **22**(3), 275–285 (1989)
9. Conyers, C., Miltenberger, R.G., Peterson, B., Gubin, A., Jurgens, M., Selders, A., Barenz, R.: An evaluation of in vivo desensitization and video modeling to increase compliance with dental procedures in persons with mental retardation. J. Appl. Behav. Anal. **37**(2), 233–238 (2004)
10. Da Silva, M.L., Gonçalves, D., Guerreiro, T., Silva, H.: A web-based application to address individual interests of children with autism spectrum disorders. Procedia Comput. Sci. **14**, 20–27 (2012)
11. D'Ateno, P., Mangiapanello, K., Taylor, B.A.: Using video modeling to teach complex play sequences to a preschooler with autism. J. Posit. Behav. Interv. **5**(1), 5–11 (2003)
12. Davila, J.M.: Restraint and sedation of the dental patient with developmental disabilities. Spec. Care Dentist. **10**(6), 210–212 (1990)
13. De Leo, G., Leroy, G.: Smartphones to facilitate communication and improve social skills of children with severe autism spectrum disorder: special education teachers as proxies. In: Proceedings of the 7th International Conference on Interaction Design and Children, pp. 45–48). ACM, June 2008
14. Delli, K., Reichart, P.A., Bornstein, M., Livas, C.: Management of children with autism spectrum disorder in the dental setting: concerns, behavioural approaches and recommendations. Med. Oral Patol. Oral Cir. Bucal **18**(6), e862–e868 (2013)

15. Isong, I.A., Rao, S.R., Holifield, C., Iannuzzi, D., Hanson, E., Ware, J., Nelson, L.P.: Addressing dental fear in children with autism spectrum disorders: a randomized controlled pilot study using electronic screen media. Clin. Pediatr. 53(3), 230–237 (2014)
16. Jaber, M.A.: Dental caries experience, oral health status and treatment needs of dental patients with autism. J. Appl. Oral Sci. 19(3), 212–217 (2011)
17. Kientz, J.A., Hayes, G.R., Westeyn, T.L., Starner, T., Abowd, G.D.: Pervasive computing and autism: assisting caregivers of children with special needs. IEEE Pervasive Comput. 6(1), 28–35 (2007)
18. Konstantinidis, E.I., Luneski, A., Frantzidis, C.A., Nikolaidou, M., Hitoglou-Antoniadou, M., Bamidis, P.D.: Information and communication technologies (ICT) for enhanced education of children with autism spectrum disorders. J. Inf. Technol. Healthc. 7(5), 284–292 (2009)
19. Lovaas, O.I.: Behavioral treatment and normal educational and intellectual functioning in young autistic children. J. Consult. Clin. Psychol. 55(1), 3 (1987)
20. Moore, D., Cheng, Y., McGrath, P., Powell, N.J.: Collaborative virtual environment technology for people with autism. Focus Autism Other Dev. Disabil. 20(4), 231–243 (2005)
21. Oberman, L.M., Ramachandran, V.S., Pineda, J.A.: Modulation of mu suppression in children with autism spectrum disorders in response to familiar or unfamiliar stimuli: the mirror neuron hypothesis. Neuropsychologia 46(5), 1558–1565 (2008)
22. Passerino, L.M., Santarosa, L.M.C.: Autism and digital learning environments: processes of interaction and mediation. Comput. Educ. 51(1), 385–402 (2008)
23. Pilebro, C., Bäckman, B.: Teaching oral hygiene to children with autism. Int. J. Pediatr. Dent. 15(1), 1–9 (2005)
24. Rao, S.M., Gagie, B.: Learning through seeing and doing: visual supports for children with autism. Teach. Except. Child. 38(6), 26–33 (2006)
25. Reed, F.D.D., Hyman, S.R., Hirst, J.M.: Applications of technology to teach social skills to children with autism. Res. Autism Spectr. Disord. 5(3), 1003–1010 (2011)
26. Sanders, E.B.N., Stappers, P.J.: Co-creation and the new landscapes of design. Co-Des. 4(1), 5–18 (2008)
27. Shapira, J., Mann, J., Tamari, I., Mester, R., Knobler, H., Yoeli, Y., Newbrun, E.: Oral health status and dental needs of an autistic population of children and young adults. Spec. Care Dent. 9(2), 38–41 (1989)
28. Shneiderman, B.: Universal usability. Commun. ACM 43(5), 84–91 (2000). https://doi.org/10.1145/332833.332843
29. Stiefel, D.J.: Dental care considerations for disabled adults. Spec. Care Dent. 22(3 Suppl.), 26S (2002). Official publication of the American Association of Hospital Dentists, the Academy of Dentistry for the Handicapped, and the American Society for Geriatric Dentistry
30. Tereshko, L., MacDonald, R., Ahearn, W.H.: Strategies for teaching children with autism to imitate response chains using video modeling. Res. Autism Spectr. Disord. 4(3), 479–489 (2010)

Design of an Interactive Gesture Measurement System for Down Syndrome People

Marta del Rio Guerra[1($\boxtimes$)], Jorge Martin Gutierrez[2,3],
and Luis Aceves[1]

[1] Departamento de Ciencias Computacionales, Universidad de Monterrey,
Monterrey, Mexico
{marta.delrio,luis.carlos.aceves}@udem.edu
[2] Departamento de Técnicas y Proyectos en Ingeniería y Arquitectura,
Universidad de La Laguna, Tenerife, Spain
jmargu@ull.edu.es
[3] Universidad La Laguna, Tenerife, Spain

Abstract. Usability and accessibility are perhaps the most important issues when using software. In our research, we propose measuring the type of movements that may affect the interactions of Down syndrome people when using touch gestures in devices, body gestures in console games, and eye gestures in glasses or other devices. In this research work we present our approach and a process description for the acquisition of empirical data whereby we shall observe the differences among interaction gestures performed in different devices by people with trisomy 21.

Keywords: Interaction design · Gesture design · Down-syndrome interaction
Accessibility for cognitive impaired

1 Introduction

As Kumin et al. indicate [1], there is an emerging research field regarding Down Syndrome (DS) persons' computer skills. Using games [2, 3], looking for jobs [1], using numerical applications [4] and mathematical learning [5], authentication in software [6], comprehension of mobile requirements [7], work-related tasks using a tablet [8], the use of computer skills [9] and the use of their musculoskeletal system during tablet interactions [10].

There are three main skills that influence computer usage: cognitive, motor and perceptual [6, 11]. DS people's cognitive skills struggle with abstract thinking, short-term memory and have attention spans [6]. Their visual and spatial memory is better than their hearing and verbal skills [12]. As Brandão et al. [13] pointed out, they have poor imitation skills. And, because children with DS don't develop spontaneous learning strategies, they find problem-solving very difficult. They also have a problem with decision-making, action-initiative and mental calculation [14]. Another limitation is the association and task composition/decomposition [15].

© Springer International Publishing AG, part of Springer Nature 2018
M. Antona and C. Stephanidis (Eds.): UAHCI 2018, LNCS 10907, pp. 493–502, 2018.
https://doi.org/10.1007/978-3-319-92049-8_35

In a research carried out by Feng and Lazar [6], parents of SD children reported that their offspring had trouble answering who, where, when, what and why questions. In addition to that, authors mention that their perceptual skills are also affected by disability and, in general, they need extra time to complete any task. Most of DS people have limited language communication and memory skills. They acquire fine and gross motor skills at a later age even though most of them have visual and hearing problems; their main strength is that they are highly visual [16].

Their low-reading level impacts their computer usage. The basic-reading performance that those people have, influences their use of the computer. In a research paper parents reported their children had trouble following instructions on websites and apps; they suggested the use of verbal instructions, because spelling is another problem [6].

Nevertheless, the use of technology has increased tremendously, including people with cognitive and physical disabilities, because of the benefits that it represents to them [17, 18]. With enough practice, DS people can acquire the same skills and become as dexterous as anyone. Accessible IoT devices will be a future solution for interaction, so studying them is important. In this paper we propose a methodology to measure what kind of movements are easier to use and determine which ones should be included in a software in order to make it more accessible. Thus, we intend to study the touch, eye movement and body gestures that will be suitable for the design of applications accessible for people with DS.

2 Purpose of this Research

The Web Accessibility Initiative (WAI) [19] has guidelines that are regarded as international standards for Web accessibility. We would like to extend those guidelines to include Down-Syndrome people and to design better interactions for touch, body and eye gestures. We expect to design guidelines for those gestures that are more adequate for all kind of tasks.

We consider that not all gestures are equal, so by measuring their friendliness, we can suggest which ones would simplify those interactions for common software DS people use, such as Spotify, Angry Birds, or Netflix. At the same time, we can suggest difficult actions that would ensure no accidental enabling for app configuring or shut down functions.

3 Work in Progress

The proposed methodology is described here, including an explanation on how to measure the different types of gestures, and the validation of those measurements with empirical observations.

3.1 Gesture Selection

Since we have had little experience with DS users, we began with empirical observations. First, we observed what type of apps they preferred and how often did they use a smartphone. Results varied greatly, but some users were extremely proficient with smartphone use. We decided games would be the best option for measuring gesture use.

A list of the main actions used in touching is shown in Figs. 1, 2, 3 and 4 and body and eye movements in Figs. 5 and 6 was produced. We devised a small game for each task which is explained with greater detail in the gestures sections.

Fig. 1. One hand touch gestures using fingers, selected for measurement.

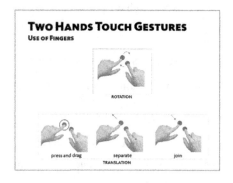

Fig. 2. Two hands touch gestures using fingers, selected for measurement.

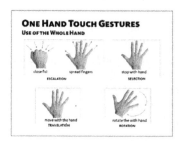

Fig. 3. Whole hand touch gestures, selected for measurement.

Fig. 4. Two whole hands touch gestures, selected for measurement.

Instructions for each game will have to be verbal, since we noted in our empirical observations, most of the users had little or no reading skills.

The games will measure their number of attempts, the number of completed gestures, time employed to complete them, and if a gesture was not completed, the percentage of completeness. To identify if Fitt's law [20] determines those results, each movement will be measured by presenting images used on touch and eye measurements in five different sizes and shown in a random order. All data collected will be analyzed to determine whether there is a correlation between successful gestures and the person's age, gender, target size and gesture type.

3.2   Participants

This research is qualitative and theoretical. We are following Sampieri et al. [21] who suggest that 20 to 30 cases should be observed in each study. We intend to contact several independent institutions that help people with Down syndrome, thus ensuring a wider socio-economical range. By doing this, we will be sure that the ease of movement is not deviated by their familiarity with the technology used.

We expect to have participants ranging from 10 to 40 years of age, of both genders, and with no restrictions on technology skills.

3.3   Touch Gestures Measurement

In order to determine which of the touch gestures is easier to use, we first listed the most popular ones. Table 1 shows all of them. We divided them according to use of one or two hands, and observed if the person was using several fingers or the whole

Table 1. Gestures and games associated to their measurement.

Touch involved	Gesture	Instruction of game
One hand, using fingers only	Tap	Tap on the mole's head when it pops up
	Double tap	Double tap on the bomb to deactivate it
	Hold and press	Use your finger to stop the sun for ten seconds
	Rotate	Use two fingers to rotate the starfish to its outline
	Pinch	Using one hand, join the baby with his mother
	Spread	Using the finger of one of your hands, separate the dog and cat so they won't fight
	Swipe	With your finger, take the bee to the flower
	Drag	Drag the ball towards the goal
One hand, use of the whole hand	Close fist	Crumble the paper with your hand
	Open hand	Enlarge the starfish by spreading it with your hand
	Stop	Stop the butterfly with your whole hand
	Drag	Use your hand to drag the mouse towards the cheese
	Rotate	Using your hand, rotate the hand to say goodbye
Two hands, only fingers	Rotate	Use one finger of each hand to rotate the starfish to its outline
	Press and drag	Stop the wolf with one finger and drag Little Red Riding Hood to the house with another one
	Spread	Separate the dog and cat so they won't fight using one finger of each hand
	Pinch	Using only your fingers, join the baby and his mother
Both whole hands	Separate or expand	Unroll the map using both hands
	Join or collapse	Using your hands, join the coins in one pile
	Rotate	Rotate the book with your hands, so the girl can read it

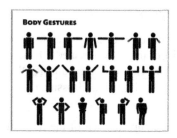

Fig. 5. Body gestures selected for measurement.

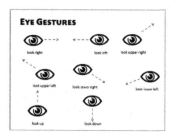

Fig. 6. Eye gestures selected for measurement.

hand to complete the gesture. Then, we devised a small game to ensure the user would be applying that gesture. as shown on Table 1. We programmed all these for a tablet app which measured the gestures.

Grossman et al. [22] suggested task metrics based on task performance which Mendoza et al. [23] adapted to measure task completion by Down Syndrome users:

(1) Percentage of users that have completed the task optimally.
(2) Percentage of users who completed the task without any help.
(3) Ability to complete a task optimally after certain time frame.
(4) Decrease in task errors made during a certain period of time
(5) Time employed until the user completes a certain task successfully.

We adapted these metrics considering a one-time observation only and also taking into account Fitt's Law [20] regarding the size of the target. All images will be randomly presented in five sizes in order to determine the minimum target size required to achieve success.

Thus, the same individual would not be using the software several times in order to increase his/her learnability. The metrics that were defined are:

(1) Percentage of users who completed the task.
(2) Time used to complete de task.
(3) Minimum target size for completed tasks.

3.4 Body Gestures Measurement

To determine which body movements are easier to use, we listed the main ones. Table 2 offers a complete list of them. We created a Kinect "dancing game" where the user will copy the gestures presented by the console. We provided three choices of music to increase its appeal. Again, using Grossman's [22] suggestion, we included these measurements:

(1) Percentage of users that complete each of the movements,
(2) Time taken to complete each task.

In this case, all gestures will be presented in the same order, and chosen to be executed with a fluent movement.

Table 2. Interviews to be conducted to DS caretakers.

Question	Purpose of question
What is your professional background?	Used to determine if the person has a college degree in psychology, or studies in computer science, for example
For how long have you worked with DS people?	Used to determine experience
What percentage of the DS people that you work with use technology (tablet/smartphone/computer)?	We observed all of the subjects had a smartphone, but we have to validate if this observation was only a coincidence
Describe the DS person that you consider has the most advanced technological skills and how does he/she use it	Used to discover if there are outstanding skills we had not considered
Have you witnessed someone who discovered techno- logy? How was this process?	If possible, we want to learn about the process. We expect most people will have prior experience with technology when arriving at the institutions
Are there any restricting aspects that prevent DS people from interacting easily with technology?	Discover if there are special aspects we need to take into account in our study
Have you observed any differences between smartphones and tablets? Which one do they prefer?	Determine if iPhone/Android/Windows phones have better accessibility
Do the more skilled persons have a bigger screen or larger keyboard keys?	Determine if Fitt's Law has any relation with hardware
What is technology used for? (communication, entertainment, socializing, watching videos, hearing music, looking for information, organization of pending tasks)	Discover what is the main motivation for their use of technology

3.5   Eye Gestures Measurement

To measure if there are some eye movements easier than others, an eye tracking test was designed. This game is called "follow the butterfly" and begins by presenting a blank screen with a butterfly in each of the four corners and one in the center, as shown in Fig. 7. After this, in Fig. 8, a butterfly was presented "hidden" among flowers, but still being visible. Immediately afterwards, butterflies appeared in different parts of the screen; sometimes they appeared in the same location as the previous one, and others were hidden in different parts of the screen. Butterflies were hidden by using the same color as the flowers, as in Figs. 9 and 10. We also included images that are very evident distractors, as the cat in Fig. 11, in order to observe if users concentrate on the task or are distracted by other elements in the pictures. The size of the butterflies varied to measure the ease of use according Fitt's law [20].

Fig. 7. An example of a highly visible butterfly in white background used as instructions for "Spot the Butterfly". Variations of this image include the same butterfly in all four corners and in the center.

Fig. 8. A highly visible butterfly hidden among flowers from a different color

Fig. 9. An orange butterfly (circled in yellow) hidden among flowers of the same color (Color figure online)

Fig. 10. A red butterfly (circled in yellow) hidden among red, white and purple flowers, on a different part of the screen (Color figure online)

Fig. 11. A cat used as distraction where the butterfly to be found is circled in red (Color figure online)

Finally, the Eye tracking study will produce gaze plots and heat maps that can be reviewed individually and grouped by all users.

3.6 Interviews

Other inputs for our research are the empirical observations of DS people and the use of technology. For example, we have observed that they can be quite proficient when using Spotify. Even though one person could not read, he was able to find his favorite music by looking at the images of albums. And we noticed he used his smartphone with amazing speed. Thus, we expect to conduct interviews with teachers and staff, working in DS institutions.

The script for these interviews is shown in Table 2.

4 Conclusions

Many Graphical User Interface design guidelines exist, but they tend to be too general and do not take into account specific adaptations for specific users with certain disabilities. This can have a negative impact in the user's interface design. We expect these measurements will enlighten us to decide if some movements are easier than others. With this in mind, we may be able to create a guideline of best practices for usability and accessibility of interfaces designed for DS users. We should remember difficult gestures are the best designed options when we want to be sure users want to perform a drastic action with their device, for example, shutting it down. Therefore, the mentioned guidelines can help determine which gestures should be programmed, and in which situations. We believe there is still much to be done concerning software and hardware inclusive design to improve experiences for cognitive disabilities. We hope this can be a small step to improve this trend.

Acknowledgments. We would like to thank the Universidad de Monterrey in Mexico and the Universidad de La Laguna in Spain for their support in this research.

References

1. Kumin, L., Lazar, J., Feng, J.H.: Expanding job options. In: ACM SIGACCESS Accessibility Computers, pp. 14–23 (2012)
2. Durango, I., Carrascosa, A., Gallud, J.A., Penichet, V.M.R.: Using serious games to improve therapeutic goals in children with special needs. In: Proceedings of the 17th International Conference on Human-Computer Interaction with Mobile Devices and Services, Copenhagen, Denmark, pp. 743–749. ACM Press, New York (2015)
3. Macedo, I., Trevisan, D.G., Vasconcelos, C.N., Clua, E.: Observed interaction in games for Down syndrome children. In: Proceedings of the Annual Hawaii International Conference on System Sciences, pp. 662–671, March 2015
4. Abdul Aziz, N.S., Ahmad, W.F.W., Zulkifli, N.J.B.: User experience on numerical application between children with Down syndrome and autism. In: Proceedings of the International HCI and UX Conference in Indonesia on - CHIuXiD 2015, pp. 26–31. ACM Press, New York (2015)
5. Ortega-Tudela, J.M., Gómez-Ariza, C.J.: Computer-assisted teaching and mathematical learning in Down syndrome children. J. Comput. Assist. Learn. **22**, 298–307 (2006)
6. Feng, J., Lazar, J., Kumin, L.: Computer usage by children with Down syndrome: challenges and future research. Comput. (Long Beach Calif.) **2**, 12 (2010)
7. Dawe, M.: Understanding mobile phone requirements for young adults with cognitive disabilities. In: Proceedings of 9th International ACM SIGACCESS Conference on Computers and Accessibility, pp. 179–186 (2007)
8. Kumin, L., Lazar, J., Feng, J.H., Wentz, B., Ekedebe, N.: A usability evaluation of workplace-related tasks on a multi-touch tablet computer by adults with Down syndrome. J. Usability Stud. **7**, 118–142 (2012)
9. Lazar, J., Kumin, L., Feng, J.H.: Understanding the computer skills of adult expert users with Down syndrome. In: The Proceedings of the 13th International ACM SIGACCESS Conference 2010
10. Lozano, C., Jindrich, D., Kahol, K.: The impact on musculoskeletal system during multitouch tablet interactions. In: Proceedings of the 2011 Annual Conference on Human Factors in Computing Systems - CHI 2011, p. 825. ACM Press, New York (2011)
11. Alfredo, M.G., Francisco, J.A.R., Ricardo, M.G., Francisco, A.E., Jaime, M.A.: Analyzing learnability of common mobile gestures used by Down syndrome users In: Proceedings of XVI International Conference Human Computer Interaction, pp. 1:1–1:8 (2015)
12. Bird, E.K.-R., Chapman, R.S.: Sequential recall in individuals with Down syndrome. J. Speech Lang. Hear. Res. **37**, 1369 (1994)
13. Brandão, A., Brandão, L., Nascimento, G., Moreira, B., Vasconcelos, C.N., Clua, E.: JECRIPE. In: Proceedings of the 7th International Conference on Advances in Computer Entertainment Technology - ACE 2010, p. 15. ACM Press, New York (2010)
14. Kirijian, A., Myers, M., Charland, S.: Web fun central: online learning tools for individuals with Down syndrome (2007)

15. Afonseca C., i Badia, S.B.: Supporting collective learning experiences in special education. In: 2013 IEEE 2nd International Conference on Serious Games and Applications for Health (SeGAH), pp. 1–7. IEEE (2013)
16. Wuang, Y.-P., Chiang, C.-S., Su, C.-Y., Wang, C.-C.: Effectiveness of virtual reality using Wii gaming technology in children with Down syndrome. Res. Dev. Disabil. **32**, 312–321 (2011)
17. Black, B., Wood, A.: Utilising information communication technology to assist the education of individuals with Down syndrome. Down Syndrome Issues and Information (2003)
18. Haro, B.P.M., Santana, P.C., Magaña, M.A.: Developing reading skills in children with Down syndrome through tangible interfaces In: ACM International Conference Proceeding Series (2012)
19. Web Accessibility Initiative (WAI) | Web Accessibility Initiative (WAI) | W3C. https://www.w3.org/WAI/
20. Ramcharitar, A., Teather, R.J.: A Fitts' Law evaluation of video game controllers. In: Proceedings of the 2017 CHI Conference Extended Abstracts on Human Factors in Computing Systems - CHI EA 2017, pp. 2860–2866. ACM Press, New York (2017)
21. Sampieri, R., Fernandez, C., Baptista, P.: Metodología de la Investigación Cuantitativa. Mc Graw Hill, Mexico (2006)
22. Grossman, T., Fitzmaurice G., Attar, R.: A survey of software learnability: metrics, methodologies and guidelines In: Conference on Human Factors in Computing Systems - Proceedings (2009)
23. Mendoza, A., Alvarez, F., Mendoza, R., Acosta, F., Muñoz, J.: Analyzing learnability of common mobile gestures used by Down syndrome users. In: Proceedings of the XVI International Conference on Human Computer Interaction - Interacción 2015, 07–09 September 2012, pp. 1–8 (2015)

Assistive Technologies for People with Cognitive Impairments – Which Factors Influence Technology Acceptance?

Susanne Dirks[(✉)] and Christian Bühler

Rehabilitation Technology, School of Rehabilitation Sciences,
TU Dortmund University, Emil-Figge-Str. 50, 44227 Dortmund, Germany
susanne.dirks@udo.edu

Abstract. While in the general field of acceptance research convincing and empirically well-tested models for the acceptance of technical systems exist, only a few studies have been carried out in the area of acceptance of assistive software systems. Appropriate acceptance models play an important role, especially for user-centered and participative software development and quality assurance. In this article, the most important models from general acceptance research are briefly introduced. Based on the results of an acceptance study of an app for independent media access for users with cognitive impairments, a proposal for an acceptance model of assistive technology was developed, in which personal and environmental factors are considered more strongly than in the classical acceptance models.

Keywords: Assistive technology · Cognitive accessibility
Technology acceptance · Acquired brain injury · Participation
Independent media use

1 Introduction

Since the mid-1980s, technology acceptance models have been an essential part of sociological, economic and media research. Technology acceptance models describe the subject-, object- and context-related factors that influence the acceptance of technology in general. Although technology acceptance research is nowadays an important part of economic research, it is still not very widespread in the field of assistive technologies. Based on the theoretical models of acceptance research, only a few empirical studies have been carried with different user groups and for different areas of application, e.g. for users with cognitive impairments, with multiple sclerosis, for students with frequently occurring impairments, users with traumatic brain damage and dementia [1–3]. Particularly for complex aids, e.g. software to support cognitive functions, inadequate instruction and training in the use of the aid constitute major barriers to successful use. Often the training does not only fail due to time and financial resources, but also due to the lack of technical competence of the experts involved in the supply process [4].

While motor and sensory impairments can usually be well compensated for by the use of assistive technologies, cognitive impairments often negatively influence the

© Springer International Publishing AG, part of Springer Nature 2018
M. Antona and C. Stephanidis (Eds.): UAHCI 2018, LNCS 10907, pp. 503–516, 2018.
https://doi.org/10.1007/978-3-319-92049-8_36

possibilities for participation and a self-determined lifestyle. People with cognitive impairments after acquired brain damage are usually affected by disorders of memory, attention, action and affect control. As a result, such persons are dependent on the support and care of family members and nursing staff in many aspects of their lives.

The UN Convention on the Rights of Persons with Disabilities, which came into power in 2008, provides for all people to have full participation in public and social life and the right to a self-determined lifestyle. The availability of suitable assistive devices is an important mean to enable people to participate as fully as possible in public and social life after having suffered from brain damage. As part of the rehabilitation process, the supply of aids, which also includes demand-oriented access to assistive computer technologies, is of particular importance.

In the subsequent sections, the most important models of acceptance research will be presented and their applicability to the acceptance of assistive technologies for people with cognitive impairments will be discussed. Based on the results of a user acceptance study for a cognitive support app for the use of web applications, a proposal for an extended model of assistive technology acceptance will be developed.

1.1   Technology Acceptance Research

Technology acceptance is generally defined as the 'positive adoption or transfer of an idea, an issue or a product, in the sense of active willingness and not only in the sense of reactive acquiescence' [5, 6].

Over the last 30 years, many different models have been developed that have aimed at describing and correlating the subject-, object- and context-related factors that influence technology acceptance. The following section presents the most influential models for the acceptance of IT technologies that are considered relevant for the acceptance of assistive software systems.

TAM, TAM3. The Technology Acceptance Model (TAM) was first developed by Davis [7] and is regarded as the initial model of technology acceptance in international research. Davis defines acceptance as the actual use of the respective technology by its (potential) users based on perceived usefulness (PU) and perceived ease of use (PEOU). Perceived usefulness (PU) refers to a user's estimation of how the use of a specific IT application improves the completion of work tasks within a specific organizational (acceptance) context. Perceived ease of use (PEOU) refers to the estimation of the user whether the use of the IT system can be learned and handled effortlessly. In Davis' model, the interaction of these two factors results in an intention to use the technology in question (intention of use, BI). This intention of use may then lead to an actual use of the respective technology (actual use). Figure 2 illustrates the relationships between the mentioned factors of the TAM model.

In various empirical studies it has been shown that the factors PU and PEOU postulated by Davis are valid indicators for the acceptance (intention to use) and actual use of a technical systems [8, 9] (Fig. 1).

However, other empirical studies revealed that the factors postulated by Davis are not sufficient to explain the acceptance and subsequent use of technical systems completely. In subsequent research, Davis' original technology acceptance model was

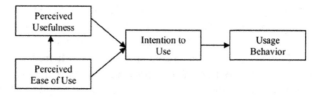

Fig. 1. TAM – technology acceptance model [7]

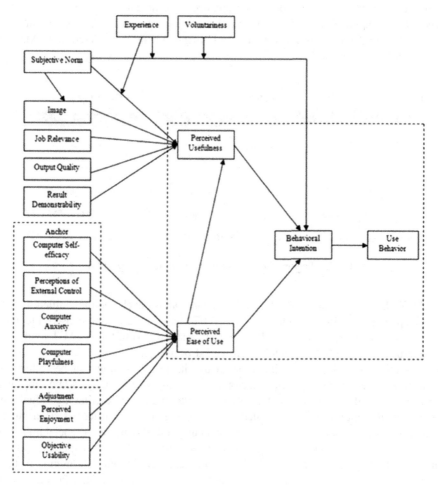

Fig. 2. TAM 3 [11]

modified in numerous adaptations. In particular, the influence of external variables such as demographic factors or personality traits of the potential user, as well as the influence of subjective norms on the acceptance of technical systems, have been taken into account in different models, e.g. in the extended technology acceptance model of

Davis and Venkatesh [10]. In their research on changes in acceptance of technical systems over a longer period of use, the authors found that, in addition to the known factors 'perceived usefulness' and 'perceived ease of use', social influences such as the subjective norm, voluntariness and self-image significantly influence the acceptance of technical systems. Further important factors for acceptance are the importance of the tool for the professional development and the quality and visibility of the achieved results. In a further revision of the original model, TAM3 [11], some intrinsic factors, like computer self-efficacy and playfulness of use and extrinsic factors, like objective usefulness and their influence on the acceptance of technical systems were taken into account. The applicability of TAM3 has been demonstrated in several longitudinal studies. Figure 3 shows an overview of the influence factors considered in TAM3 and their interdependencies.

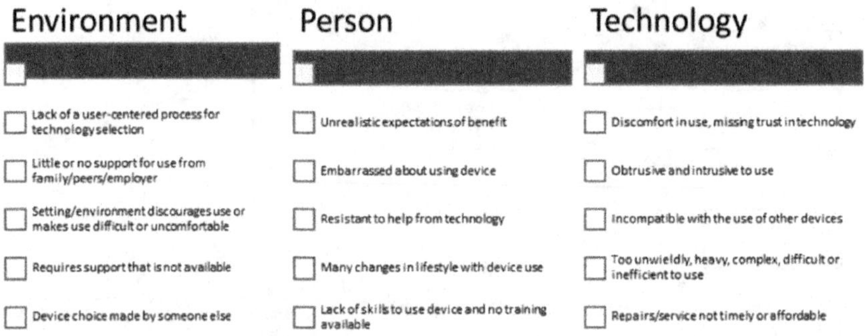

Environment	Person	Technology
Lack of a user-centered process for technology selection	Unrealistic expectations of benefit	Discomfort in use, missing trust in technology
Little or no support for use from family/peers/employer	Embarrassed about using device	Obtrusive and intrusive to use
Setting/environment discourages use or makes use difficult or uncomfortable	Resistant to help from technology	Incompatible with the use of other devices
Requires support that is not available	Many changes in lifestyle with device use	Too unwieldly, heavy, complex, difficult or inefficient to use
Device choice made by someone else	Lack of skills to use device and no training available	Repairs/service not timely or affordable

Fig. 3. Factors for non-use of assistive technology [24]

UTAUT. In 2003, Venkatesh, Morris, Davis and Davis developed the Unified Theory of Acceptance and Use of Technology (UTAUT) based on a comprehensive literature analysis of acceptance research [12]. The basic assumptions of the UTAUT model are closely based on the TAM model, again based on the premise that the actual use of technology is preceded by an intention to use it. That intention can be influenced positively or negatively by certain factors. As a result of the analysis and empirical comparison of different theoretical models for explaining and predicting individual user behaviour, the authors have identified the following four constructs as determining factors for user acceptance: performance expectancy, effort expectancy, social influence and facilitating conditions. Other factors, such as social gender, age, experience of use and the voluntary nature of use moderate the influence of the four determining factors. Various empirical studies have demonstrated that the four determining factors have a significant influence on the user's intention to use a technical system in different contexts and for different user groups. Furthermore, a positive influence of behavioral intent on actual use could be empirically confirmed.

Additional Theories. In parallel to the development of the technology acceptance models described in the previous sections, user satisfaction research has been focusing on the levels of contentment among users of IT systems. In psychological research, user satisfaction is seen as an important prerequisite for performance in work and everyday situations. Important determinants of user satisfaction included the usefulness, simplicity of use, usage results, user expectations, operational factors, service quality, system quality and information quality [13].

Contrary to the technology acceptance models, which focus on the user with their characteristics and environmental impacts, the Technology Task-Fit Model (TTF) focuses on the nature of the task to be solved and the support the user receives from the technology used in the given task [14]. The more technology is used to support the user in solving the tasks, the more the IT system is used in real life and therefore contributes to an improvement of the work performance.

Limitations of Existing Models. All models and theoretical approaches of acceptance research presented so far have been tested to varying degrees in many empirical studies. Due to their great popularity and good applicability, the TAM-based models provide a highly utilized theoretical basis for empirical studies on user acceptance. Other approaches could also be validated for specific kinds of applications and user groups. Nevertheless, there are contradictory results for some of the proposed constructs. For example, the influence of social norm on the intention to use technology depends strongly on factors such as user experience, gender and type of task (obligatory or voluntary task) [12]. The influence of PEOU, which is a central construct of the TAM-based models, could be demonstrated in some empirical studies, but only for some user groups and task types [15].

A further relevant limitation for the applicability of the presented models for the general acceptance of technical systems lies in the prevailing limitation to the use of IT systems in work processes. Although there are some studies on the acceptance of eHealth and telemedicine systems, there is currently only one known publication available on the acceptance of assistive technologies based on the described acceptance models [16].

1.2 Acceptance of Assistive Technology

A closer look at resource directories for medical aids shows that there is no shortage of all types of technical aids. Nevertheless, in their regularly published reports the health insurance companies complain about an insufficient supply and use of these aids. International studies on acceptance of medical aids report that approx. 30% of the prescribed aids are insufficiently used or abandoned [17].

One reason for this unsatisfactory situation lies in the fact that, despite best efforts, there is often a one-sided view of patients' needs. The doctors and therapists involved in the care process have excellent specialist knowledge, but they often focus only on the functional aspects of the prescribed aids. The personal preferences of the user, the psychosocial conditions and the available support, which play an important role for the actual use of an aid, are often not sufficiently considered in the provision process. Another reason for the high proportion of unutilized devices is the lack of supervision and aftercare for the user. The standard regulatory processes usually include a verification of the sustainability of the provisions, but in reality, this step is often omitted due to a lack of time and financial resources. Furthermore, neither patients nor doctors are currently obliged to pass information about the success of treatment on to the insurance providers.

Looking at assistive technology more specifically, the concepts of environmental factors, accessibility and universal design [18–21] come into focus. This relates also to the process of development and service provision of assistive technology rather than the mere outcome of the provision. Participative processes in the provision of assistive technologies can be considered as one prospective avenue to better and more acceptable products and services.

Matching Person and Technology Model. There are few approaches in scientific research that deal with the acceptance and sustainable use of assistive computer technologies. Scherer's 'Matching Person and Technology Model' [22] is a theoretical framework for the application of assistive technologies, which can also be applied to software systems for cognitive support. The framework consists of a set of person-centered measures to assess the subjective judgements of the users' abilities, needs, goals, expectations, preferences and psychosocial characteristics. A good agreement between person and technology takes into account the interaction of the environmental conditions in which the technology is used, the needs and preferences of potential user and the functions and characteristics of the applied assistive technologies [23]. The proposed measures are grounded in the author's research on the underlying reasons for the abandonment of prescribed assistive technologies. These studies have shown that the abandonment of assistive technologies is generally based on a negative interaction of environmental factors, user characteristics and characteristics of the technology. Figure 5 gives an overview of the most important factors for non-use of assisted technologies [24].

Empirical Studies on the Acceptance of Assistive Technologies. Based on theoretical models of acceptance research, various empirical studies have been carried out with different user groups and for different areas of application, e.g. for users with cognitive impairments, with multiple sclerosis, for students with frequently occurring impairments, users with traumatic brain damage and dementia [1–4, 10]. These studies demonstrate that similar factors are relevant to the acceptance and use of assistive technologies for all investigated user groups and areas of use. The more individual needs and living conditions of potential users are integrated into the provision process, the better the individual counselling is in the provision process and the better the users are supported and advised during use, the greater are the acceptance, the intention to use and finally the actual use of a technical aid. Particularly for complex aids like software to support cognitive functions, inadequate instruction and training in the use of the aid constitute major barriers to successful use. Often the training does not only fail due to time and financial resources, but also due to the lack of technical competence of the experts involved in the supply process [4].

In relation to the acceptance concept PEOU the accessibility and user-friendly design of software, electronic documents and internet resources become important elements [25]. Unlimited accessibility is an essential prerequisite for the perceived ease of use and the acceptance of a technical aid, especially for handicapped users.

2 Study

Various empirical studies in the context of general technology acceptance research have shown that certain psychological constructs, in particular the constructs of 'perceived ease of use' (PEOU) and 'perceived usability' (PU), have a strong influence on technology acceptance. To date, there are only a few studies on the acceptance of assistive technologies. However, since acceptance is an important prerequisite for the continuous use of the provided aids, there is an ethical and economically motivated necessity to carry out further studies on this topic.

The acceptance study described here was carried out as part of the Mediata project. The goal of the media project was to develop an app that enables people with cognitive impairments or learning disabilities to use Internet and social media resources independently [26]. The developed app supports people with cognitive impairment through an easy and consistent interface design, a single sign-on approach, support for various input modalities, direct linking of popular apps and a configurable user profile. The functional scope and design of the user interface was determined in a user-centered requirements analysis in close cooperation with a group of users with cognitive impairments in order to ensure the development of an assistive device tailored to the needs of potential users [27]. Figure 5 shows an overview of the cognitively accessible login options in the app (Fig. 4).

Fig. 4. Picture based and pattern based login into the Mediata-App

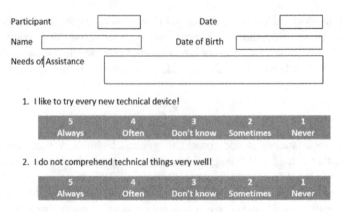

Fig. 5. Starting section of acceptance questionnaire

2.1 Method

In order to continuously monitor the usability of the app, intensive test phases were already carried out during the development phase. Once the development was completed so far that a stable prototype of the app was available, a final usability test and an acceptance test were carried out. The results of the usability tests can be found in Dirks and Bühler [27, 28] here the focus of the presentation is on the results of the acceptance test.

The items of the acceptance questionnaire have been adapted to the structure of the 'Matching Person and Technology Assessment' form and have been formulated according to the rules of easy language. Due to their cognitive limitations, the user of the respective user group have specific requirements to formal and verbal design of questionnaires. Therefore, the study did not use a standardized questionnaire but developed a proprietary format. In addition to the personal contentment in different areas of life, various questions were asked about the satisfaction with the application. Acceptance was evaluated using a 5-step Likert questionnaire. Figure 6 shows the starting section of the acceptance questionnaire.

The following hypotheses have been formulated to examine the acceptance of the Mediata App:

- Hypothesis 1: Perceived Usefulness (PU)
  - The Mediata app helps users with cognitive impairments to use Internet and social media services independently.

- Hypothesis 2: Perceived Ease of Use (PEOU)
  - The user interfaces are easy to use for users with cognitive impairments.

- Hypothesis 3: Behavioural Intention (BI)
  - Users with cognitive impairments want to use the Mediata app because it increases their sense of participation and independence.

2.2 Participants

Altogether 17 people participated in the acceptance test. Of the 17 persons, 13 people suffered from acquired damage and four persons had cognitive impairments of different origins. As part of the participatory requirements analysis for the Mediata app, the preferences of potential users were assessed. The functional requirements for the Mediata app were compiled based on the indicated user preferences. Table 1 shows an exemplified overview of the gathered user information.

2.3 Results

For reliability analysis, a Cronbach's alpha was calculated to assess the internal consistency of the subscale for positive affect, which consists of ten questions. The internal consistency of the questionnaire is satisfying, with Cronbach's alpha for positive affect = .95.

Table 1. User profile examples

User	Age	Diagnosis	Deficits	ICT interests
1	54	Cerebral haemorrhage	Memory deficits, reduced attention span, mood swings	YouTube, email, messenger
2	56	Cerebral haemorrhage	Hemiparesis, short term memory deficits, reduced drive	Games, news, reading, google search
3	36	Alcohol intoxocation	Dysarthria, reduced attention span	Office, facebook, google search
4	57	Traumatic Brain Injury	Memory deficits, reduced impulse control	YouTube, games, travel, languages

In order to check whether the psychological constructs PU, PEOU and BI have an influence on the acceptance of assistive technologies, the questionnaire items were assigned to the corresponding acceptance constructs of TAM3. Table 2 shows the assignments of the questionnaire items to the TAM3 constructs.

Table 2. Mappings of questionnaire items to TAM3 constructs

TAM3 construct	Questionnaire items
Experience	newTech_like, newTech_knowGood, newTechSeldom_insecure
Output Quality	appUse_quicker, appUse_feelGood, appUse_withoutHelp
Result Demonstrability	appUse_independence, appUse_likeOthers, appUse_ownAfraid
Perception of External Control	friends_help
Image	friends_interest, friends_disapprove
Computer Anxiety	newTech_diff, newTech_insecure, newTech_afraidToBreak
Computer Playfulness	newTech_likeToPlay, appUse_fun
Perceived Usefulness	appUse_important
Perceived Ease of Use	appUse_easy

Correlations between the items were calculated and high positive correlations were found between items that influence the constructs PU and PEOU in the TAM3 model, e.g. experience, computer playfulness, result demonstrability. The influence of the PU and PEOU constructs on the BI construct postulated in the TAM3 model could also be demonstrated for the examined app. Table 3 shows the most important results of the descriptive data analysis.

As can be seen in the data in Table 3, the questionnaire items that correspond to the TAM3 constructs' Computer Playfulness',' Result Demonstrability',' Perceptions of External Control' and' Output Quality' have been consistently rated as highly beneficial.

Table 3. Descriptive data analysis

Item	N	$\bar{x}$	σ^2	σ
newTech_like	17	3,18	3,15	1,78
newTech_difficulties	17	2,76	2,69	1,64
newTech_likeToPlay	17	3,88	2,36	1,54
newTech_knowGood	17	4,00	2,62	1,62
newTech_insecure	17	3,06	3,31	1,82
appUse_fun	17	4,47	1,64	1,28
appUse_independence	17	3,70	3,10	1,76
appUse_likeOthers	17	4,00	2,25	1,50
appUse_feelGood	17	4,41	1,51	1,23
appUse_withoutHelp	17	3,82	2,53	1,59
appUse_easy	17	4,35	1,62	1,27
appUse_important	17	3,94	2,68	1,64
appUse_quicker	17	3,47	4,02	2,00
appUse_likeToUse	17	4,29	1,60	1,26
newTech_afraidToBreak	17	4,06	2,43	1,56
newTechSeldom_insecure	17	3,71	2,97	1,72
appUseOwn_afraid	17	3,59	4,13	2,03
friends_help	17	4,35	1,87	1,37
friends_interest	17	3,18	2,78	1,67
friends_noInterest	17	3,00	6,12	2,48

In order to determine the influence of the constructs 'Perceived Ease of Use', 'Perceived Usefulness' and 'Behavioural Intention to Use' postulated in the acceptance models, correlations between the questionnaire items were calculated. For an overview of the calculated values, see Table 4.

High positive correlations could be found between the item' appUse_important' (Perceived Usefulness) and the following items: newTech_knowGood (Experience), friends_interest (Image), appUse_likeOthers (Result Demonstrability), new-TechLikeToPlay (Computer Playfulness), appUse_fun (Computer Playfulness) and appUse_wantToUse (Behavioural Intention).

For the item 'appUse_easy' (Perceived Ease of Use) positive correlations to the following items could be found: appUse_feelGood (Output Quality), appUse_-likeOthers (Result Demonstrability), friends_help (Perception of External Control), newTech_afraidToBreak (Computer Anxiety), newTech_liketoPlay (Computer Playfulness) and appUse_fun (Computer Playfulness).

Moreover, positive correlations for the item' appUse_wantToUse' (Behavioural Intention) could be found to the following items: newTech_knowGood (Experience), appUse_feelGood (Output Quality), friends_help (Perception of External Control), appUse_fun (Computer Playfulness), appUse_easy (Perceived Ease of Use) and appUse_important (Perceived Usefulness).

Table 4. Correlations between questionnaire items

Variablen	newTech_ likeToPlay	newTech_ knowGood	appUse_ fun	appUse_like Others	appUse_ feelGood	appUse_ easy	appUse_ important	appUse_ wantToUse	newTech_ afraidToBreak	friends_ help	friends_ interest
newTech_like	0,70	0,65	0,48	0,77	0,42	0,41	0,58	0,42	0,45	0,36	0,37
newTech_difficulties	0,46	0,24	0,35	0,51	0,36	0,43	0,27	0,28	0,13	0,29	0,06
newTech_likeToPlay	1,00	0,80	0,54	0,76	0,52	0,63	0,67	0,57	0,37	0,47	0,64
newTech_knowGood	0,80	1,00	0,54	0,69	0,57	0,58	0,80	0,64	0,54	0,48	0,60
newTech_insecure	0,63	0,68	0,36	0,48	0,35	0,40	0,59	0,40	0,46	0,32	0,43
appUse_fun	0,54	0,54	1,00	0,59	0,94	0,81	0,64	0,88	0,55	0,76	0,57
appUse_independence	0,75	0,79	0,43	0,73	0,44	0,44	0,51	0,46	0,58	0,36	0,36
appUse_likeOthers	0,76	0,69	0,59	1,00	0,58	0,66	0,71	0,59	0,48	0,49	0,27
appUse_feelGood	0,52	0,57	0,94	0,58	1,00	0,86	0,60	0,96	0,61	0,88	0,54
appUse_withoutHelp	0,71	0,70	0,50	0,79	0,55	0,47	0,57	0,59	0,58	0,49	0,34
appUse_easy	0,63	0,58	0,81	0,66	0,86	1,00	0,46	0,79	0,68	0,71	0,41
appUse_important	0,67	0,80	0,64	0,71	0,60	0,46	1,00	0,70	0,32	0,51	0,62
appUse_quicker	0,38	0,37	0,54	0,48	0,55	0,40	0,35	0,51	0,23	0,30	0,42
appUse_WantToUse	0,57	0,64	0,88	0,59	0,96	0,79	0,70	1,00	0,53	0,91	0,60
newTech_afraidTo Break	0,37	0,54	0,55	0,48	0,61	0,68	0,32	0,53	1,00	0,46	0,26
newTechSeldom_ insecure	0,69	0,85	0,49	0,65	0,53	0,54	0,57	0,56	0,68	0,39	0,39
appUseOwn_afraid	0,80	0,68	0,44	0,45	0,42	0,47	0,57	0,46	0,11	0,44	0,71
friends_help	0,47	0,48	0,76	0,49	0,88	0,71	0,51	0,91	0,46	1,00	0,46
friends_interest	0,64	0,60	0,57	0,27	0,54	0,41	0,62	0,60	0,26	0,46	1,00
friends_noInterest	0,43	0,55	0,34	0,35	0,31	0,16	0,37	0,32	0,37	0,13	0,53

Values in red bold are different from zero with a significance level of alpha=0.01

2.4   Discussion

Based on the three postulated research hypotheses, it can be stated that the Mediata app helps users with cognitive impairments to use Internet and social media services independently (hypothesis 1). Moreover, the user interfaces are easy to use for the user group (hypothesis 2) and users with cognitive impairments want to use the Mediata app because it increases their sense of participation and independence (hypothesis 3).

It can further be assumed, that the psychological constructs of 'Perceived Usefulness' (PU) and 'Perceived Ease of Use' (PEOU) postulated in the TAM models also play an essential role for the acceptance of assistive technologies. There is evidence that they are influenced by the same intrinsic and extrinsic factors as described in the TAM3 model for general acceptance of technology. Similarly, an influence of 'Perceived Usefulness' (PU) and 'Perceived Ease of Use' (PEOU) on the 'Behavioral Intention' (BI) to use the Mediata app as an example for assistive technology for cognition could be found in the data.

3   Conclusions

The influencing factors PU and PEOU postulated in the TAM models also seem to apply to the acceptance of assistive technologies for cognitive support and are mediated by at least some of the psychological constructs postulated in the TAM3 model.

Experience, result demonstrability, computer playfulness and perception of external control play an important role in the technical acceptance of assistive technologies for people with cognitive impairments. From the results of the presented study, it can be deduced that the TAM 3 model seems to be suitable for the assessment of the acceptance of assistive technologies for cognitive support. Figure 6 shows the factors of the TAM3 model that seem to be particularly relevant for the acceptance of assistive technology for cognition and their relationships to each other. However, more focus need to be given to the relevance of accessibility and environmental factors in the context of TAM3. While accessibility seems to be closely connected to 'perceived ease of use' environmental factors relate to social and other external facilitation factors.

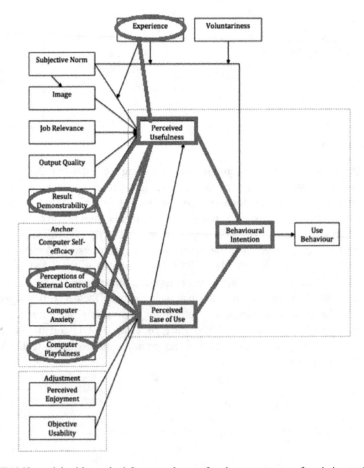

Fig. 6. TAM3 model with marked factors relevant for the acceptance of assistive technologies

Since only a small group of users was analyzed in the presented study, the results can be generalized only to a limited extent. It is intended to conduct further studies to investigate the acceptance of assistive technologies for cognitive support in various fields and to explore the relation of technology acceptance to accessibility and environmental factors in this context. In times of increasing need for support in the use of internet and media services by various user groups (seniors, immigrants with limited language skills), the development of highly acceptable and cognitively accessible support technology is of particular importance and requires special social and scientific attention.

As there is still limited research on the acceptance of assistive technologies, the relationship between accessibility, ICF-based context factors and technology acceptance has not been clarified yet. There is still much to be done in this area of research.

Acknowledgements. The authors would like to thank all participants of the study for their helpful feedback and good spirits during the interviews. Special thanks go to the v. Bodelschwingh Foundation Bethel, Bethel.regional office Dortmund, and gGmbH In der Gemeinde Leben, Düsseldorf, for their financial and practical support of the Mediata project.

References

1. Adolfsson, P., Lindsedt, H., Janeslätt, G.: How persons with cognitive disabilities experience electronic planning devices. NeuroRehabilitation **37**(3), 379–392 (2015)
2. Squires, L.A., Williams, N., Morrison, V.L.: Matching and accepting assistive technology in multiple sclerosis: a focus group study with people with multiple sclerosis, carers and occupational therapists. J. Health Psychol. (2016). https://doi.org/10.1177/1359105316 677293. Accessed 14 Aug 2017
3. Poudel, B.P.: Acceptance and use of assistive technology: perspective of high school and college students with high incidence disabilities. University of Deleware, School of Education (2014). http://udspace.udel.edu/handle-/19716/16818. Accessed 14 Aug 2017
4. Wang, J., Ding, D., Teodorski, E., Mahajan, H.P., Cooper, R.: Use of assistive technology for cognition among people with traumatic brain injury: a survey study. Mil. Med. **181**, 560–566 (2016)
5. Schäfer, M., Keppler, D.: Modelle der technikorientierten Akzeptanzforschung Überblick und Reflexion am Beispiel eines Forschungsprojekts zur Implementierung innovativer technischer Energieeffizienz-Maßnahmen. Technische Universität Berlin (2013)
6. Dethloff, C.: Akzeptanz und Nicht-Akzeptanz von technischen Produktinnovationen. Pabst, Lengerich (2004)
7. Davis, F.: Perceived usefulness, perceived ease of use, and user acceptance. MIS Q. **13**(3), 319 (1989)
8. Venkatesh, V., Davis, F.D.: A model of the antecedents of perceived ease of use: development and test. Decis. Sci. **27**, 451–481 (1996)
9. Arning, K., Ziefle, M.: Understanding age differences in PDA acceptance and performance. Comput. Hum. Behav. **23**(6), 2904–2927 (2007)
10. Venkatesh, V., Davis, F.D.: A theoretical extension of the technology acceptance model: four longitudinal filed studies. Manag. Sci. **46**, 186–204 (2000)
11. Venkatesh, V., Bala, H.: Technology acceptance model 3 and a research agenda on interventions. Decis. Sci. **39**(2), 273–312 (2008)

12. Venkatesh, V., Morris, M.G., Davis, G.B., Davis, F.D.: User acceptance of information technology: toward a unified view. MIS Q. **27**(3), 425–478 (2003)
13. DeLone, W.H., McLean, E.R.: Information systems success: the quest for the dependent variable. Inf. Syst. Res. **3**(1), 60–95 (1992)
14. Goodhue, D.L.: Development and measurement validity of a task-technology fit instrument for user evaluations of information systems. Decis. Sci. **29**(1), 105–138 (1998)
15. Gefen, D., Straub, D.W.: The relative importance of perceived ease of use in IS adoption: a study of ecommerce adoption. MIS Q. **21**(4), 389–400 (1997)
16. Kaleshtari, M.H., Ciobanu, I., Seiciu, P.L., Marin, A.G., Berteanu, M.: Towards a model of rehabilitation technology acceptance and usability. Int. J. Soc. Sci. Hum. **6**(8), 612–616 (2016)
17. Scherer, M.J.: From people-centered to person-centered services, and back again. Disabil. Rehabil.: Assist. Technol. **9**(1), 1–2 (2014)
18. Bühler, C.: Universal design – computer. In: Stone, J., Blouin, M. (eds.) Center for International Rehabilitation Research Information and Exchange (CIRRIE) Internation Encyclopedia of Rehabilitation (2010)
19. Bühler, C.: Management of design for all. In: Stephanidis, C. (ed.) The Universal Access handbook, Human Factors and Ergonomics. CCRC Press Taylor & Francis Group, Boca Raton, 56-1-12 (2009)
20. Bühler, C., Pelka, B.: Empowerment by digital media of people with disabilities. In: Miesenberger, K., Fels, D., Archambault, D., Peňáz, P., Zagler, W. (eds.) ICCHP 2014. LNCS, vol. 8547, pp. 17–24. Springer, Cham (2014). https://doi.org/10.1007/978-3-319-08596-8_4
21. Bühler, C.: Empowered participation of users with disabilities in R&D projects. Int. J. Hum.-Comput. Stud. **55**(4), 645–659 (2001)
22. Scherer, M.J.: Assessing the benefits of using assistive technologies and other supports for thinking, remembering and learning. Disabil. Rehabil. **27**(13), 731–739 (2005)
23. Scherer, M.J., Craddock, G.: Matching person and technology assessment process. Technol. Disabil. **14**, 125–131 (2016)
24. Scherer, M.J., Federici, S.: Why people use and don't use technologies. NeuroRehabilitation **37**, 315–319 (2015)
25. ISO/IEC Guide 71:2014 (E): Guide for addressing accessibility in standards, 2014. http://www.iec.ch/webstore/freepubs/isoiecguide71%7Bed2.0%7Den.pdf. Accessed 27 Jan 2018
26. Bühler, C., Dirks, S., Nietzio, A.: Easy access to social media: introducing the mediata-app. In: Miesenberger, K., Bühler, C., Penaz, P. (eds.) ICCHP 2016. LNCS, vol. 9759, pp. 227–233. Springer, Cham (2016). https://doi.org/10.1007/978-3-319-41267-2_31
27. Dirks, S., Bühler, C.: Partizipation and autonomy for users with ABI through easy social media access. In: Cudd, P., de Witte, L. (eds.) Harnessing the Power of Technology to Improve Lives. Studies in Health Technologies and Informatics, vol. 242, pp. 813–819 (2017)
28. Dirks, S., Bühler, C.: Akzeptanz von assistiven softwaresystemen für Menschen mit kognitiven Beeinträchtigungen. In: Eibl, M., Gaedke, M. (eds.) Informatik 2017, pp. 345–359. Gesellschaft für Informatik, Bonn (2017)

Designing Wearable Immersive "Social Stories" for Persons with Neurodevelopmental Disorder

Franca Garzotto[✉], Mirko Gelsomini, Vito Matarazzo, Nicolo' Messina, and Daniele Occhiuto

Innovative Interactive Interfaces (I3) Lab, Department of Electronics, Information and Bio-Engineering, Politecnico di Milano, Milan, Italy
{franca.garzotto,mirko.gelsomini,vito.matarazzo,nicolo.messina, daniele.occhiuto}@polimi.it

Abstract. "Social stories" are used in educational interventions for subjects with Neurodevelopmental Disorder (NDD) to help them gain an accurate understanding of social situations, develop autonomy and learn appropriate behavior. Traditionally, a Social Story is a short narrative that uses paper sheets, animations, or videos to describe a social situation of every day life (e.g., "going to school", "visiting a museum", "shopping at the supermarket"). In our research, we exploit Wearable Immersive Virtual Reality (WIVR) technology to create a novel form of social story called *Wearable Immersive Social Story (WISS)*. The paper describes the design process, performed in collaboration with NDD experts, leading to the definition of WISS. We also describe an authoring tool that enables therapists to develop WISSes and to personalize them for the specific needs of each person with NDD.

Keywords: Storytelling · Social Story · Neurodevelopmental Disorder Wearable Immersive · Virtual Reality · 360° videos

1 Introduction

"Social stories" are a storytelling approach used in educational and therapeutic interventions for persons with Neurodevelopmental Disorder (NDD)[1], particularly autism. A social story is a short narrative that uses visuals and in most cases also written text to describe a particular social situation, event, or activity in a clear and reassuring manner that is easily understood by the individual with disability. Social stories are used as learning material to promote the development of autonomy and appropriate behaviors, and to teach particular social skills, such as identifying important cues in a given situation, understanding rules, routines, and expectation, or taking another's point of view.

---

[1] NDD is an umbrella term for a group of disabilities that appear during the developmental period and are characterized by deficits and limitations in the cognitive, emotional, motor and intellectual spheres. Examples of NDD are ADHD - Attention Deficit/Hyperactivity Disorder, ASD - Autism Spectrum Disorder, Learning Disability, and Intellectual Disability.

© Springer International Publishing AG, part of Springer Nature 2018
M. Antona and C. Stephanidis (Eds.): UAHCI 2018, LNCS 10907, pp. 517–529, 2018.
https://doi.org/10.1007/978-3-319-92049-8_37

We exploit Wearable Immersive Virtual Reality (WIVR) technology to create a novel form of Social Story, i.e., Wearable Immersive Social Story (WISS).

The digital content of a WISS are 360° videos that reproduce real environments of everyday life and the social situations taking place there (e.g., "taking the metro", "visiting a museum", "shopping at the supermarket"). These videos are executed on a smartphone and viewed through a low-cost Head-Mounted Display (Google Cardboard) that makes the user feel inside the virtual space. Interaction is achieved through head movements, gaze pointing, or gaze focus. In a WISS, videos are organized into a hypertextual structure. They are enriched with visual clues, which help users gain a better understanding of the social situation, and with interactive elements. The latter make the virtual experience more fun and engaging, while the action-feedback mechanism of interaction enforces cause-effect understanding and promotes a sense of purpose and of active control over the stimulation.

The paper discusses the design process - 4 workshops with NDD experts interplayed with prototyping activities – which was performed in cooperation with 6 NDD specialists leading to the definition of WISS and to the creation of two examples of Wearable Immersive Social Stories. We briefly describe the technological framework (called XOOM) that enables the authoring and personalization of a WISS and its execution at run-time. We finally discuss the highlights emerged from the final workshop concerning the usability of XOOM and the benefits and drawbacks of Wearable Immersive Social Stories for persons with Neurodevelopmental Disorder.

2   Related Work

Social stories have been proposed as an effective intervention for persons with (Autism Spectrum Disorders) ASD since the early 1990s. The term "Social Story" has been trademarked by its original creator to denote a narrative characterised by 10 detailed criteria [7] that define and guide the story creation in order to help the individual with disability understanding the entirety of a situation - who, what, when, where, and why. In most of the existing literature [1, 3, 5, 10, 20, 21, 22] the term is used in a broader sense according to the definition given at the beginning of this paper. The research on the effectiveness of this instrument is limited and highlights highly variable effects in the learning process [13, 15]. Still, social stories remain widely used in therapeutic and educational interventions for subjects with ASD as well as with other forms of disability in the NDD spectrum.

Originally based on paper-based visual and textual materials only, in today's practices the social stories often use digital media, e.g., images, animations and videos on computer displays [8, 16]. In the research arena of Virtual Reality (VR) and Wearable Immersive Virtual Reality (WIVR), there are some examples of applications created for subjects with NDD that focus on social situations and can be regared as transpositions of social stories. Strickland et al. [19] developed desktop 2D virtual environments to teach fire safety skills to young (3–6 years old) children with ASD. Josman et al. [9] used 2D VR to teach students on the autism spectrum aged 8–16 years to cross the road safely. In [12], participants with autisms used a WIVR application for Oculus Rift[2] that aims at preparing individuals with ASD to use public transportation by placing them in a 3D city and setting tasks that involve taking the bus to reach specific destinations. Cheng et al. [4] presents a system that employs a 3D virtual environment in I-Glasses PC 3D Pro to help children concentrate on social situations and to learn non-verbal communication and social behavior. VR is thought appropriate for this target group to help learning about real life situations because in the virtual space behaviors and responses can be practiced in a safe and repeatable environment while interactivity promotes engagement and cause-effect understanding [2, 11].

WIVR applications have been found to improve attention skill because the head monuted display (HMD) removes the distractions of the outside world, a feature that is important for subjects with NDD who often have severe attention deficits. Benefits in this area have been observed in the study reported in [5], with low-medium functioning children with NDD using a low cost viewer to interact with the immersive digital transpositions of paper-based fantasy tales. Two important concerns related to the use of WIVR in interventions for persons with NDD are the acceptability of the headset and the risk of physical side-effects that are typical of experiences with wearable VR environments [17]: Motion sickness (due to a disagreement between visually perceived movement in the simulated world and the vestibular system's sense of movement our body), double-vision (a particular condition under which the virtual elements are seen twice as overlapping copies instead of being perceived as one as they should) and eye fatigue (the feeling that our eyes are burning, itchy, and tired). The first-generation VR headsets were characterized by poor viewing angles, high latency, and weight. In 1996 Strickland et al. [18] explored the acceptability of WIVR in a study with two autistic children, aged 7.5 and 9 years, aimed at teaching them to recognize the colors of cars and cross the street safely. The authors defined the HMD as "heavy and awkward": eventually the children accepted to wear it, but they manifested dizziness and eye fatigue during the experience. Today HMDs are much more comfortable, including those commercially available at an affordable cost (e.g., Samsung Gear VR[3] and Google Cardboard[4]). In [5] the majority of study participants using WIVR on Google Cardboard had an enjoyable experience, were fascinated by the immersive experience, and manifested the willingness to play with it again.

VR headsets are increasingly being used to view 360° videos, e.g., in tourism, cultural heritage, and professional training. There are examples of the use of wearable immersive 360° videos in regular education, e.g., the Google Expeditions Program[5] and the Immersive Education Initiative[6]. To our knowledge, the VR environments adopted in existing studies on WIVR for subjects with NDD are created in computer graphics, and the use of wearable 360° videos has not yet been explored in learning interventions for persons with NDD. In our research, we use Google Cardboard, the cheapest WIVR

---

[2] https://www.oculus.com/rift/.

[3] http://www.samsung.com/us/explore/gear-vr/.

[4] https://www.google.com/intl/en/get/cardboard/.

[5] https://www.google.com/edu/expeditions/#about.

[6] http://immersiveeducation.org/.

solution in the market (5€ for the paper version, 30€ for more resistant plastic variants). The VR viewer is composed of two biconvex lenses mounted on a plastic or cardboard structure available in different colors and shapes. The smartphone positioned inside the visor displays the visual contents, splitting them into two near-identical bi-dimensional images (Fig. 1 – left). The illusion of space depth and immersion in the virtual environment is created by the stereoscopic effect generated by the viewer lenses (Fig. 1 – right). The interaction is achieved through gaze pointing and focus, assuming that the direction of the gaze focus is defined by head orientation (detected by smartphone sensors), and is always at the center of the screen. Users can navigate the virtual world by rotating their head, which will consequently rotate the virtual scene projected in the display.

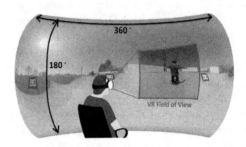

Fig. 1. Google cardboard viewer (top-left), view on the smartphone screen (bottom-left) and conceptual view during the experience (right)

3   Designing and Developing Wearable Immersive Social Stories

The design of Wearable Immersive Social Stories was a collaborative process among our university group (4 computer engineers and 1 designer, hereinafter referred to as "technical team") and a team of 6 NDD specialists (special educators, neuro-psychiatric doctors, therapists, hereinafter referred to as "experts") from two local care centers. We did not involve subjects with NDD in the design activities because of the nature and severity of the disability of the persons attending the centers. The experts and their patients had participated in an empirical study to evaluate of our previous applications for WIVR. They were enthusiast of this technology and had the idea of using it for the purposes of their "M4A - Museum4All" project, an initiative devoted to improving accessibility of museums for persons with NDD. In this project they created a set of social stories about the visit to different museums (see example in Fig. 2 – left) and they wanted to transpose them in WIVR environments. The iterative co-design process comprised 4 workshops interplayed with the development of progressive prototypes.

3.1   Workshop 1

The first workshop was devoted to identifying the contents and the technology for the social stories to be rendered in a virtual environment. We discussed the tradeoffs between computer graphic contents and 360° videos, and between the different VR devices. We selected some examples of 360° videos available on the Internet in various museum websites (e.g., Louvre) and the experts experienced them on different devices (HTC Vive[7], Samsung Gear VR and Google Cardboard). We agreed to use 360° videos and Google Cardboard, for several reasons. Story contents based on 360° videos can be created at low cost, by recording real-life situations (using commercial and cheap 360° cameras) or retrieving existing videos from the web.

Fig. 2. Left: paper-based social story about the museum visit; Right: script for the 360° video (scenes 1 and 2) defined during workshop 1

In principle, caregivers (specialists and parents) can create these contents autonomously, without learning any particular technical skill except video editing, and without the need of involving technology experts. 360° videos were perceived as more immersive and realistic than computer graphic applications, and enable the person with NDD to experience a naturalistic setting and to have the visual stimuli of the social space "as it really is". Inside the immersive digital space, the user is required to build and process a representation of the virtual environment "as a location" in order to successfully

---

[7] https://www.vive.com/eu/.

navigate it. Outside the virtual experience, the user is expected to capitalize on this generalization construct, linking his/her mental representation of the virtual environment to the real world in order to understand the physical environment and the social situation in it. Subjects with NDD have limited capability of generalization, and this process may require long exposure with the virtual environment to take place; 360° videos of real contexts would facilitate this mapping. Finally, high-end headsets (e.g. HTC Vive) offer better quality VR experiences in terms of accuracy of head movement detection and screen resolution. Still, the very low cost of Google Cardboard increases its potential for adoption of WIVR experiences at care centers and facilitates its use at home. After this discussion, we selected a specific social story as case study, and the rest of the workshop was devoted to design the videos for its WIVR transposition. We decided to record different situations, one for each scene of the paper-based social story. We explored pros and cons of recording each scene with a fixed camera or a mobile camera. In the first case, the camera is placed in a specific point of the environment and remains fixed, so that the user of the 360° video would perceive to stand in the scene. Instead, producing a video with a mobile camera would suggest to the user the idea of walking through the scene, following the movement of the camera. In the end, we generated a detailed video script, defining what the camera should record and in which mode (fixed or mobile) for each scene (Fig. 2 – right.)

3.2   First Prototype and Workshop 2

During the 3 weeks between workshop 1 and workshop 2, two members of the technical team and one therapist went to the museum and, using a Samsung Gear 360[8] camera, shot the videos for each scene according to the script. In doing so, we followed existing guidelines on how to correctly record 360° videos[9]. For example, in order to make the viewer feel present in first person in the story, the camera should be mounted at almost 150 cm from the floor to simulate an average person's height, and all the key elements in the scene must be kept roughly 1 to 1.5 meters away from the camera. In fact, if they are too close, they look distorted, while if they are too far they may be indistinguishable. Other important suggestions are to avoid unexpected and fast movements with the camera and to keep camera's front side in the movement direction in case of mobile camera videos, otherwise the vision of the final product can cause dizziness or nausea in the users. To reduce vibrations the camera was mounted on a bike helmet and was worn by the smallest team member (1.55 m) to meet at the best the height criterion.

After merging the single scenes, the resulting 360° video was experienced and discussed among experts in workshop 2 to identify requirements for improvements and extensions.

Some of the videos we recorded had quality issues: in some cases, the camera was not steady enough to guarantee a smooth VR experience in a few others the camera was not on focus, resulting in a blurred fragment. Low quality video fragments could induce

---

[8] http://www.samsung.com/it/galaxy/gear-360/.

[9] http://www.samsung.com/ae/discover/how-to/how-to-film-the-best-360-videos;
     http://vrscout.com/news/avoid-motion-sickness-developing-for-vr/.

possible sense of sickness; we identified the problematic fragments and decided to re-shoot them with greater care after the workshop.

The therapists pinpointed the need for *facilitators*, i.e., visual cues superimposed on the video that attract the user's attention and help users focusing on those elements in the virtual that are more appropriate for understanding the current situation or explaining the behavior in a given context. To make the experience more engaging and fun some facilitators should be interactive, i.e., they generate visual (animated) effects when the user focuses the eye gaze on them. We defined the following facilitators:

- *Geometric shape* (e.g., arrow or circle): it draws the user's attention with clear visual signals contrasting with the realistic background.
- *Highlight*: it lights up a specific area in a scene "shading" the rest of the environment, to drive the user's attention on relevant details of the scene removing the surrounding stimuli.
- *PCS* (Picture Communication Symbols): widely used in Augmentative and Alternative Communication (AAC), PCSs are color or black & white picture cards that represent objects, actions, activities, people, events, or more abstract concepts like feelings (e.g., happiness, sadness, disappointment).
- *Sound*: it adds more realism to the scene or provides voice instructions and details in a specific situation.
- *Textual popup*: it contains textual instructions, social cues, or comments for subjects who can read.

The experts also recommended to introduce *"pause points"* in which the video is suspended. Pause points would give the user some time to explore the surrounding environment, to discover "facilitators" and to understand their meaning; they would facilitate interaction with the interactive facilitator (which would be difficult while the video is running). Pauses can have a fixed duration, or the video would restart when the user focuses his/her gaze on an interactive element.

Workshop 2 led to the design of a new script for the videos of the "museum" WISS extending the initial one with the allocation of pause points at specific times and the specification of facilitators (type, content, space and time characteristics, i.e., when they had to appear, where, and for how long).

3.3 Second Prototype and Workshop 3

Between workshop 2 and 3 (4 weeks), the technical team re-shooted the low-quality video fragments and implemented the second version the Wearable Immersive Social Story, adding facilitators (Fig. 3) and pause points according to the specifications defined in Workshop 2.

Fig. 3. Examples of facilitators: an interactive sphere (left) and a highlight (right)

In workshop 3, the therapists brought an additional social story, "going to the supermarket", which they normally use to teach persons with NDD to search and buy specific products in a large store. This story was used as second case study. As a group activity, we defined the script for a second WISS based on this story in order to validate the overall approach and to elicit additional requirements. Four new ideas emerged: "Distractor", "Hyper-story", "Caregiver's Monitoring and Control", and "Personalization".

Distractor. Reexamining the role of the stimuli associated to "facilitators", we realized that depending on the user, the contexts, and the learning goal, the same stimulus could have different meanings, and trigger different reactions. For instance, the noise of a car in a city environment would act as facilitator, since users expect it as they see cars in the video: not having it would somehow break the immersion. Still, the same car roaring in a video showing a nature landscape would probably distract the user attention. A graphic element such as an arrow pointing to a door could indicate that the door should be opened and the user should interact with it; but in case of an emergency door, the user should ignore it or at least avoid interaction. So we came out with the idea of "distractor", i.e., visual elements (of the same type as facilitators) that could be introduced in advanced sessions to train selective attention and improve understanding of a social situation.

Hyper-story. The experience of a real situation is intrinsically sequential in the time dimension but is not always linear in terms of the space. The physical environment (e.g., a large supermarket with main aisles) may have a "hyper" structure with different paths available from a given position. To help persons with NDD master the complexity of "hyper" physical spaces, the experts suggest creating hyper-stories, in which at some moments the users must choose among alternative directions to take, i.e., alternative videos to play in order to continue the experience. In these situations, some interactive elements on the videos are "links" and act like "portals" towards different physical contexts. For instance, in the supermarket scenario, choosing an interactive element on a specific aisle would correspond to activating the video fragment that "moves along" the selected aisle. Hyper-stories increase the "realism" of the experience and stimulate some basic skills that are often impaired in subjects with NDD: the capability of "making choices" and the sense of "agency" (the subjective awareness of initiating, executing, and controlling one's own volitional actions in the world).

Caregiver's Real-Time Monitoring and Control. To monitor, give support to, and stimulate the user during the WISS experience, the therapist should be enabled to see what the person is currently watching in the head mounted display, and in some cases to control the video execution (i.e., pausing the video because a person needs more time to explore the space or to use facilitators, or restarting the video when the subject is unable to proceed after a pause point).

Personalization. Each person with NDD is unique, and the value of any interactive technology for this target is directly related to its ability to meet the specific characteristics and the needs of each single person [14]. Hence the expert's final requirement was about a tool enabling them to personalize stories for each patient.

3.4 Technological Tools and Workshop 4

In the four months between workshop 3 and 4 an intense development activity took place, involving the implementation of a software platform for WISS creation, personalization and execution, and the construction of a tele-operated mobile robot for video shooting. The workshop then focused on the experimentation of the authoring tool and on the evaluation and discussion of the overall results of the project.

Software Platform. The software platform - called XOOM [6] – is *web-based* and integrates two main components: *Creator* and *Runtime Controller*. The Creator is an authoring tool for Wearable Immersive Social Stories. It enables therapists to create a new WISS starting from a set of 360° videos, and to personalize an existing WISS (Fig. 4). The authoring functionalities include: allocation of videos on a timeline; definition of visual elements (facilitators and distractors) in terms of graphic and interactive properties and positioning on the videos; definition of pause points. The *Runtime Controller* manages the interaction with and the execution of fully featured Wearable Interactive Social Stories on smartphones. This component also enables the visualization of the running WISS on an external PC and the manual control of its flow (launching a WISS, pausing/starting a video, launching a different WISS).

Fig. 4. The creator component of the technological platform XOOM

The Robot. Our simple remotely operated mobile robot – called Bob (Fig. 5). - has been created to shoot 360° videos with a better quality than the ones recorded manually. Bob's body is composed by plastic pipe inserted in a hard plastic cone and a "hat" on top of the pipe. The cone has a movement stabilization purpose and is mounted on a mobile base that exploits the commercial iRobot iCreate programmable platform. A Samsung Gear 360° camera is placed on the hat. The body height can be adjusted based on specific needs (e.g., if we want to record video with a child's eyes or from an adult perspective). A therapist and two members of our team used Bob at a local supermarket (outside opening hours) to record the videos for the WISS "shopping in the supermarket" (Fig. 5 - left), the specifications of which were defined in Workshop 3.

Fig. 5. Left side: Bob video-recording outside and inside the supermarket; Right side: resulting WISS with a superimposed PCS card as facilitator

Activities During Workshop 4. During the workshop, we used the videos recorded by Bob and the complete script of the "shopping at supermarket" WISS as testbed materials for a final evaluation and brainstorming session. Each expert was required to use XOOM and to create a new WISS according to the "shopping at supermarket" specifications.

At the end of this work, the experts were asked to write down their opinions about the usability of the system, the benefits of Wearable Immersive Social Stories for specific target groups in the NDD spectrum, and the potential drawbacks of this instrument. We discussed these results in a final brainstorming session.

4 Discussion

A number of interesting themes emerged from the answers collected in the form and the following discussion. Only 50% of the experts could complete the creation of all features of the WISS in the required timeframe (20 min). Some of them omitted to do the most complex task. This concerned the creation of an interactive visual element to simulate the "placing a box in the shopping chart" (by creating a pause point, defining a 3D interactive shape that disappears when pointed and appears on top of the shopping chart). Still, all experts expressed a global positive judgment about the usability of the authoring tool and the control functionalities. All participants understood the structure and the different functionalities offered by XOOM, considered them intuitive, and managed to use them with a progressively increasing autonomy.

Concerning the WISS, all therapists and educators claimed the intention to adopt the two wearable immersive social stories as a complement of their current learning practices for NDD individuals. All experts confirmed the initial impression emerged since workshop 1, i.e., that they expect to be easy for a subject with NDD to navigate the 360° videos and interact with interactive elements. Still, they also pinpointed some potential drawbacks in this technological approach. Individuals with NDD may have an initial resistance to wear the HMD and to explore a WISS, as in general these persons feel a strong need for routine and tend to get distressed when a situation or a pattern of behavior changes. Some educators suggested some preliminary familiarization activities without the viewer that would mitigate the risk of resistance to use a WISS, e.g., wearing a hand-crafted cardboard-based mask like the ones used in some physical games and look at the 360° videos on a regular PC screen. The experts also argued that a WISS, and WIVR technology in general, may be not suitable for patients that suffer of psychosis or hallucinations, since they already live situations of detachment from the reality and the immersion in a virtual environment could worsen their condition.

With the above caveat, the expert highlighted the *motivational* benefit that a WISS can have among the persons with NDD, particularly children and young adults. Once the "distress" originated from novelty is overcome, a WISS offers a playful and enjoyable experience that can promote learning. It would be particularly useful for patients that need to develop autonomy, such as taking the metro and other public transport means alone, or learning new street paths. The virtual experience can act as a preparation to the reality, helping users in driving attention towards the relevant elements and teaching them to overcome unexpected events and distractions. They experts also pinpointed that Wearable Immersive Social Stories should be offered also at school, and in non-structured learning environments, e.g., at home or in the social contexts that are the subjects of the social story. Finally, the experts were convinced that the combination of Wearable Immersive Social Stories with a tool like XOOM have many advantages with respect to traditional social stories. XOOM makes it possible to create and control visual stimuli inside a WISS in a way that is appropriate for each specific subject, and to create becoming a progressively more complex story with the addition of new facilitators and distractions at each repetition. XOOM offers a simple and smooth way to play the same story as many times as one wills, or to change it when the subject is bored. It was hypothesized that subjects that suffer of anxiety would particularly benefit of the possibility of repeating the experience again and again in order to familiarize with it.

5   Conclusions

The main contribution of our work is in the definition of the concept of Wearable Immersive Social Story for persons with NDD and in the presentation of a co-design process for these learning tools that can guide designers of WIVR experiences for this target group. The next step in our research agenda is to validate all the considerations emerged during the co-design process reported in this paper. Concerning XOOM, we will perform a more systematic usability study involving a wider number of NDD experts who never experienced WIVR before. Concerning WISS, we have planned a long term empirical study involving 40 subjects with NDD at the 2 centers participating in our research. The research is designed as a controlled study to investigate the learning benefits of Wearable Immersive Social Stories also compared to more traditional forms of social stories.

References

1. Adams, L., Gouvousis, A., VanLue, M., Waldron, C.: Social story intervention. Focus Autism Other Dev. Disabil. **19**(2), 87–94 (2016)
2. Andersson, U., Josefsson, P., Pareto, L.: Challenges in designing virtual environments: training social skills for children with autism. Int. J. Disabil. Hum. Dev. **5**(2), 105–111 (2006)
3. Barry, L., Burlew, S.B.: Using social stories to teach choice and play skills to children with autism. Focus Autism Dev. Disabil. **19**(1), 45–51 (2016)
4. Cheng, Y., Huang, C., Yang, C.: Using a 3D immersive virtual environment system to enhance social understanding and social skills for children with autism spectrum disorders. Focus Autism Other Dev. Disabil. **30**(4), 222–236 (2015)
5. Garzotto, F., Gelsomini, M., Clasadonte, F., Montesano, D., Occhiuto, D.: Wearable immersive storytelling for disabled children. In: Proceedings of the International Working Conference on Advanced Visual Interfaces, pp. 196–203 (2016)
6. Garzotto, F., Gelsomini, M., Matarazzo, V., Messina, N., Occhiuto, D.: XOOM: an end-user development tool for web-based wearable immersive virtual tours. In: Cabot, J., De Virgilio, R. (eds.) ICWE 2017. LNCS, vol. 10360, pp. 507–519. Springer, Cham (2017). https://doi.org/10.1007/978-3-319-60131-1_36
7. Gray, C.A.: The New Social Story Book. Future Horizons Inc., Arlington (2010)
8. Hagiwara, T., Smith Myles, B.: A multimedia social story intervention. Focus Autism Other Dev. Disabil. **14**(2), 82–95 (1999)
9. Josman, N., Ben-Chaim, H.M., Friedrich, S., Weiss, P.L.: Effectiveness of virtual reality for teaching street-crossing skills to children and adolescents with autism. Int. J. Disabil. Hum. Dev. **7**, 49–56 (2008)

10. Kuoch, H., Mirenda, P.: Social story interventions for young children with autism spectrum disorders. Focus Autism Other Dev. Disabil. **18**(4), 219–227 (2003)

11. Lányi, C.S., Tilinger, Á.: Multimedia and virtual reality in the rehabilitation of autistic children. In: Miesenberger, K., Klaus, J., Zagler, W.L. (eds.) ICCHP 2004. LNCS, vol. 3118, pp. 22–28. Springer, Heidelberg (2004). https://doi.org/10.1007/978-3-540-27817-7_4

12. Newbutt, N., Sung, C., Kuo, H.J., Leahy, M.J., Lin, C.C., Tong, B.: Brief report: a pilot study of the use of a virtual reality headset in autism populations. J. Autism Dev. Disord. **46**, 1–11 (2016)

13. Nichols, S.L., Hupp, S.D., Jewell, J.D., Zeigler, C.S.: Review of social story interventions for children diagnosed with autism spectrum disorders. J. Evid. Based Pract. Sch. **6**(1), 90–120 (2005)

14. Phillips, B., Zhao, H.: Predictors of assistive technology abandonment. Assist. Technol. **5**(1), 36–45 (1993)

15. Reynhout, G., Carter, M.J.: Social stories for children with disability. Autism Dev. Disord. **36**, 445–469 (2006)

16. Sansosti, F., Powell-Smith, K.A.: Using computer-presented social stories and video models to increase the social communication skills of children with high-functioning autism spectrum disorders. J. Posit. Behav. Interv. **10**(3), 162–178 (2008)

17. Sharples, S., Cobb, S., Moody, A., Wilson, J.R.: Virtual reality induced symptoms and effects (VRISE): comparison of head mounted display (HMD), desktop and projection display systems. Displays **29**(2), 58–69 (2008)

18. Strickland, D.C., Marcus, L.M., Mesibov, G.B., Hogan, K.: Brief report: two case studies using virtual reality as a learning tool for autistic children. J. Autism Dev. Disord. **26**(6), 651–659 (1996)

19. Strickland, D., McAllister, D., Coles, C.D., Osborne, S.: An evolution of virtual reality training designs for children with autism and fetal alcohol spectrum disorders. Top. Lang. Disord. **27**, 226–241 (2007)

20. Swaggart, B.L., Gagnon, E., Bock, S., Earles, T.L., Quinn, C., Smith Myles, B., Simpson, R.L.: Using social stories to teach social and behavioral skills to children with autism. Focus Autism Other Dev. Disabil. **10**(1), 1–16 (1995)

21. Test, D.W., Richter, S., Knight, V., Spooner, F.: A comprehensive review and meta-analysis of the social stories literature. Focus Autism Other Dev. Disabil. **26**(1), 49–62 (2010)

22. Thiemann, K.S., Goldstein, H.: Social stories, written text cues, and video feedback: effects on social communication of children with autism. J. Appl. Behav. Anal. **34**(4), 425–446 (2001)

An AAC System Designed for Improving Behaviors and Attitudes in Communication Between Children with CCN and Their Peers

Tetsuya Hirotomi[(✉)]

Interdisciplinary Graduate School of Science and Engineering,
Shimane University, 1060 Nishikawatsu-cho, Matsue, Japan
hirotomi@cis.shimane-u.ac.jp

Abstract. Visual aids are widely used in augmentative and alternative communication (AAC) for individuals with pervasive developmental and intellectual disabilities. To satisfy their complex communication needs, a variety of AAC systems have been developed as mobile applications (apps). The effectiveness of these apps mainly relies on the abilities of communication peers. Persuasive technology is aimed at changing behaviors and attitudes. In order to increase the frequency of presenting visual aids with verbal messages, we applied persuasive principles in designing the mobile AAC app named "STalk2." The app is capable of recognizing voice and presenting visual aids stored in a local database and/or retrieved by image search on the web; it also monitors communication activities. In this study, we examined the effects of using STalk2 on the behaviors and attitudes of five children with CCN and eleven of their peers. Special attention was paid to analyzing questionnaires, diaries, and video recordings obtained from peers. The results suggest that persuasive technology in AAC systems may be effective in improving communication behaviors and attitudes.

Keywords: Adaptive and augmented interaction
Design for quality of life technologies
Augmentative and alternative communication
Complex communication needs · Persuasive technology

1 Introduction

Children with complex communication needs (CCN), including pervasive developmental and intellectual disabilities, often present with difficulties in expressing and/or understanding verbal messages. Augmentative and alternative communication (AAC) interventions can promote positive peer interactions of children with CCN [21]. For example, visual aids, such as pictorial symbols and photographs, are widely used for exchanging messages between the children and their communication peers [3]. A variety of AAC systems have been developed and used as assistive products to communicate by presenting visual aids on a screen and generating speech in daily activities [2]. In many cases, the vocabulary used in such systems should be selected by speech-language pathologists (SLPs), occupational therapists (OTs), educators, parents, and manufacturers prior to exposing them to children [22]. Although several research have been conducted to build core vocabulary lists for AAC systems [1,10], vocabulary selection is still a challenging process. On the one hand, additional vocabularies are required to support communications in diverse settings by collecting communication samples in each context [18]. On the other hand, paradoxically, if the vocabulary becomes too large, the access to each word becomes overloaded. As a result, the selected vocabularies are often insufficient to respond to children's interests, needs, and actions as they arise during interactions.

However, few studies have focused on "just-in-time" language acquisition for daily interactions through AAC systems [4,17]. Hirotomi et al. developed the PC-based communication aid called "STalk" system [13]. Its principal objective was to augment the understanding of verbal messages. It is capable of recognizing voices, extracting words and chunks from verbal messages, and presenting visual aids stored in a local database and/or retrieved via image search on the web. In this study, we examined the change in the behaviors and attitudes of children with CCN and their communication peers when communication is mediated by the mobile application (app) version of STalk, named "STalk2."

2   AAC and Persuasive Technology

The behavior and attitudes of the peers are one of the most crucial determinants of successful communication with individuals using AAC. Instructions for communication peers are highly effective because knowledge on how to facilitate interactions is not intuitive for most peers [15].

Interactive information technology designed to change the user's behavior and attitude is known as "persuasive technology" [7]. The target behavior can be hindered by a combination of three factors: lack of motivation, lack of ability, and lack of a well-timed trigger to perform the behavior [9]. That is, increasing ability by providing appropriate instructions to the communication peer is not always the solution. The AAC system designer should consider ways to simplify behavior and increase motivation. Oinas-Kukkonen and Harjumaa [19] classified the principles used in persuasive technology. We adopted two principles for our system design:

- The "reduction" principle is a system that helps users perform the target behavior by reducing complex behavior into simple tasks.
- The "self-monitoring" principle is a system that supports users in achieving their goals by helping them track their performance or status.

3   STalk2 Mobile App

The STalk2 mobile app runs on Android OS; the "S" stands for Smart Assistive Technology (SAT). Hirotomi et al. [13] proposed SAT as an ICT-based assistive technology (product) that provides smarter services for individuals with special needs to improve their quality of life; reduce the heavy burden on caregivers, therapists, and other assistive technology practitioners in installing and maintaining assistive products through their smart functions; and record evidence for rehabilitation and further improvement of assistive products. To achieve these goals, STalk2 was designed to increase the use of visual aids in the dynamic process of interaction between children and their peers.

We gathered requirements for the design of STalk2 from SLPs, OTs, educators, parents, and other caregivers from February 2011 to August 2012. We conducted focus groups with 39 caregivers, while 49 caregivers answered an open-ended questionnaire after the demonstration of STalk and/or a prototype of STalk2. Consequently, we focused on reducing the efforts that users have to make in creating, finding, editing, and presenting visual aids; and providing visual feedback on the usage of the system. These are based on the "reduction" and "self-monitoring" principles of persuasive technology. Additionally, we decided to implement functions for synchronizing multiple devices, backing up data, and providing web access to the data.

Figure 1 shows the process flow. In STalk2, a message is represented in a "multimedia hieroglyph" format [11,12,14]. In this format, a set of visual aids, i.e., images with captions, are allocated into five columns for answering the following questions: when (time), where (place), who (subject), how (feeling, language, method, tool, transportation, or material), and what (action). Originally, this format had one more question, why (reason). However, this question was omitted as a result of the requirement gathering process because the potential user groups may have difficulty answering the question.

Each column has twelve cells. The user can input visual aids in these cells in three ways, as shown in Step 1:

- The user can touch the title of the specific column and select visual aids from the most recently used list.
- The user can touch an empty cell and search for a visual aid by speech recognition. First, STalk2 will try to retrieve it from a fringe vocabulary database containing visual aids created or edited by the user. If no results match, STalk2 will retrieve it from a core vocabulary database containing approximately 1700 droplet symbols (http://droplet.ddo.jp/). If no results match again, STalk2 will finally try to obtain the corresponding image from a web image search.
- The user can perform a long press on an empty cell and create a new visual aid by taking a photograph or selecting an image from the gallery app.

If necessary, the user can edit or delete a visual aid by making a long press on the cell. As shown in Step 2, the user can edit the caption, replace the image, and place a question mark or slash symbol over it.

In Step 3, the user can touch a visual aid and present it to the peer with an enlarged image, caption, and synthesized speech of the caption. N2 Text-To-Speech engine (KDDI Research, Inc.) is used for speech synthesis. STalk2 also has a special presentation panel designed for choosing among several visual

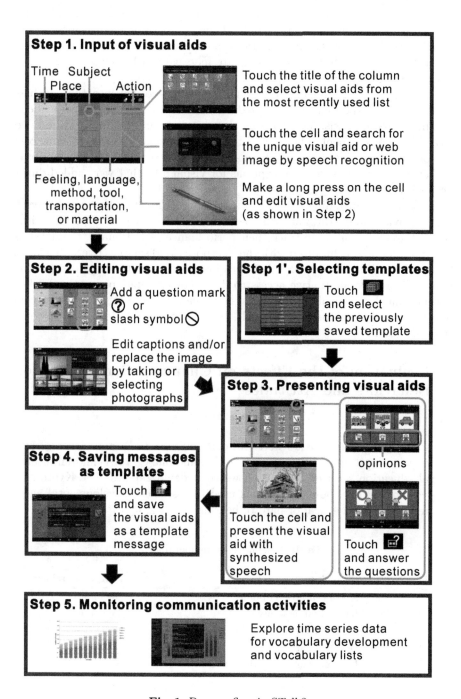

Fig. 1. Process flow in STalk2

aids with a question mark. In this panel, three visual aids are also displayed to express the following opinions: "I don't know," "None of them," and "I don't want to answer." After the presentation, the user can save these visual aids as a template message in Step 4. The template message can be selected and reused quickly, as shown in Step 1'.

User activities, messages, and visual aids are recorded into the database. In Step 5, these data can be analyzed and presented as quantitative evidence of communication assistance, such as the visualization of time series data for vocabulary development. The stacked bar chart segments the bars to show comparisons between the message columns. The user can touch the bar to obtain further details, such as a set of captions for visual aids that were added during a certain time period.

Steps 1 to 4, including Step 1', aim to reduce the effort that users have to make to create, find, edit, and present visual aids. Step 5 aims to provide visual feedback to enable users to track their performance. Additionally, the database of STalk2 can be synchronized with the Evernote cloud service (Evernote Corp.). The service will synchronize STalk2 apps installed in multiple devices, back up data, and provide alternative access to data. For example, parents and school teachers can share visual aids and messages. They can also create low-tech communication aids, such as picture cards, by printing visual aids using Evernote web pages and apps.

4   Evaluation of the Effects on Changing Communication Behaviors and Attitudes

4.1   Participants

In our study, the participants were five children with CCN and eleven of their peers, including three parents, seven teachers, and one OT. All children received special education services. Table 1 shows their demographics. The Kyoto scale of psychological development [20] was used to assess the developmental age of children who were not deaf or hard of hearing (P1, P2, and P3).

Table 1. Children's demographics

ID	Age	Sex	Eligibility	Developmental age
P1	7	M	Autism spectrum disorder	569 days
P2	7	F	Intellectual disability	35 months
P3	7	M	Autism spectrum disorder	41 months
P4	9	M	Deaf and hard of hearing	N/A
P5	18	M	Deaf and hard of hearing, intellectual disability	N/A

Pictorial symbols, freehand drawings, and/or photographs were actively used for communication. Simple text messages were used in combination with visual aids for communication with P3, P4, and P5 children. P4 and P5 children have been able to exchange simple messages in sign language but often need visual aids to compensate for insufficient hand signing skills for expressing and understanding messages.

4.2 Procedure

We conducted the longitudinal study to evaluate the effects on changing communication behaviors and attitudes by using STalk2 in real world situations. Peers used STalk2 with the children at schools, home, dormitory, and child development support centers from November or December 2012 to March 2013. Prior to interacting with children using STalk2, we provided all peers with an approximately 30-min tutorial on STalk2. They were able to explore all the features of STalk2 within the tutorial.

At the end of the study, the communication peers completed the questionnaire shown in Table 2. All statements were originally in Japanese, the native language of all participants. The questionnaire consists of ten statements, and a five-point scale ranging from "strongly disagree" to "strongly agree" was used for each. Q1 focused on the changes in the frequency of the target behavior; Q2–Q5 are related to the children's behaviors and attitudes; and Q6–Q10 are related to the peers' impressions about the use of STalk2.

Table 2. A list of statements in a questionnaire on changing behaviors

ID	Statements
Q1	I thought the opportunities to present visual aids with verbal messages to the child were increased
Q2	I thought the vocabulary used in the communication with the child was increased
Q3	I thought the communication on which the child focused his/her attention was increased
Q4	I thought the frequency of the child exhibiting problem behavior was reduced because he/she understood messages better
Q5	I thought the child enjoyed communication with you better
Q6	I felt that the burden of communicating with the child was reduced
Q7	I thought that I found the new side of the child
Q8	I want to use STalk2 in conversations with the child in the future
Q9	I want other individuals to use STalk2 in conversations with the child
Q10	Overall, STalk2 satisfied our needs

The peers were also asked to record in a diary or video actual instances of communication, regardless of the presence or absence of STalk2, and their impressions about each instance during the study. Recordings of 93 and 56 instances with and without STalk2 were obtained, respectively. These recordings were made to verify the results of the questionnaire.

5   Results and Discussion

Figure 2 shows the results of the questionnaire. The percentage of top-two-box scores, which refer to those who agreed with the statement, was 91%, 64%, 55%, 64%, 91%, 82%, 91%, 91%, 91% and 73% for Q1–Q10, respectively.

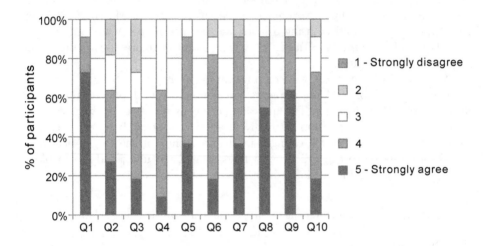

Fig. 2. Stacked bar chart showing different levels of agreement for each statement

5.1   The Frequency of Presenting Visual Aids with Verbal Messages

STalk2 was designed to increase the opportunities to present visual aids with verbal messages to children with CCN. In Q1, all peers except one answered that the frequency of the target behavior increased. The peer who answered "3" actively used visual aids during class; for example, showing presentation slides prepared in advance or communicating with the child by drawing. In this case, the peer substituted the use of STalk2 with these behaviors.

The following are actual instances from the diaries and video recordings of peers who used STalk2 to communicate to the child:

- Providing an assortment of potentially reinforcing items (photographs of toys, food, drinks, places to go, and play activities) for self-selection
- Confirming daily schedules with/without changes
- Providing class instructions
- Teaching good/bad behaviors
- Orienting a person with whom the child will perform activities with (taking a bath, driving to school, etc.)

- Confirming a driving route
- Confirming details of occasional events
- Explaining the current situation to ease the child's anxiety and confusion
- Collecting and organizing information in the form of STalk2 messages with the child with explanations.

5.2   Children's Behaviors and Attitudes

The opportunities to present visual aids with verbal messages were increased during the study. This peer's behavior may affect children's behaviors and attitudes. Q2–Q5 examined these effects from the aspects of vocabulary development, focus of attention, reduction of problem behaviors, and enjoyment. The results were interpreted based on the opinions expressed by peers in their diaries and video recordings.

Vocabulary Development. Seven out of eleven peers positively evaluated the effects of STalk2 on vocabulary development in Q2. Other peers used STalk2 within conventional communication contexts. In such cases, they simply attached visual aids to words that were already expressed in verbal messages. They commented that the children understood words more precisely but the vocabulary size did not increase.

Attentional Focus. In Q3, six peers positively evaluated the effects of both STalk2 and the tablet computer on the attentional focus of children. STalk2 and the tablet computer attracted the attention of the children. Some children focused on the messages presented by the device and achieved successful communication. However, other children were sometimes too excited to operate the device.

Problem Behavior. Improved communication skills occurred in conjunction with decreased problem behaviors [5,6]. Increasing the frequency of presenting visual aids may improve such behaviors. In Q4, seven peers positively evaluated the effects on STalk2 on reducing problem behaviors. Five of them were peers of P1, P3, and P5–children who exhibited problem behaviors in the recordings.

P1 often engaged in self-injury behavior, such as hitting the head and lower limbs, as well as biting. P1 practiced self-selection using a set of printed cards prior to using STalk2. The interval between incidents of self-injury ranged from 10 to 18 s. Once the self-injury behavior started, P1 could not stop at will. The teacher often had to snuggle with P1 until P1 calmed down. After using STalk2, P1 could select desired items, events, and places to go more successfully. The self-injury behavior persisted but P1 sometimes selected items and places by himself in order to keep calm.

P3 often exhibited high levels of anxiety when unexpected events occur; for example, when P3's brother caught the flu, when the dog barked at night, or when P3 had no classes because it was the Foundation Day of the school. P3 often brought the tablet STalk2 installed to the parent and requested an explanation with visual aids. P3 tried to understand the events that happened and kept calm by repeatedly touching the visual aids and hearing synthesized speech.

P5 frequently stands up, spins around, and slaps his head when he is unable to understand class instructions and the rescheduling of daily activities. P5 concentrated on using STalk2 and teachers provided these information on STalk2; for example, the cancellation of some activities was represented by the slash symbol. The frequency of these problem behaviors was decreased by presenting information via STalk2 instead of printed materials.

Enjoyment. In Q5, all peers except one said that the child found communication much more enjoyable using STalk2. The opinions relating to enjoyment include the following:

- When peers presented visual aids more frequently, the child had better understanding of the messages. Consequently, the child's anxiety and confusion were alleviated.
- The peers could quickly and easily add new visual aids and/or edit them to suit different communication contexts. The children enjoyed opportunities to express their thoughts, including self-selection, by using these visual aids in combination with synthesized speech.
- Two of the children were very eager to use STalk2 and the tablet computer. Their enthusiasm was sometimes too great, which made communications difficult, as discussed in Q3.

5.3   Peers' Impressions About the Use of STalk2

Q6–Q10 examined peers' impressions about the use of STalk2 from in terms of reducing the burden of communication, discovering new sides of children, continuous use, recommendation to others, and overall satisfaction.

Reducing the Burden of Communication. Nine peers answered that STalk2 reduced the burden of communicating with the child in Q6. The implementation of the reduction principle ensured that the visual aids were simple to search, create, edit, and present. However, a few peers reported that STalk2 slowed down in cases of poor network connectivity. As STalk2 uses cloud services, a caching mechanism should be implemented for the updated version.

Discovering the New Side of the Child. Ten peers answered that STalk2 was useful in finding the new side of the child in Q7. P1's peers felt that P1's requests, which they previously could not understand, were revealed in the study. The peers of P2 understood P2's story better; for example, how school was that day. The peers of P3 and P5 observed their flexible actions while accommodating anxiety and changes. The peers of P4 realized that they could communicate with P4 in detail.

Continuous Use, Recommendation to Others and Overall Satisfaction.
Ten peers answered that they will continue to use STalk2 in Q8. Ten peers also
answered that they want others to use STalk2 in Q9. One peer answered "3"
in Q8 and another also answered in Q9. They commented that literacy skills to
use tablet computers were the key determinants of acceptability, especially if the
child could interact by using nonaided communication on some level. Finally, all
except for these peers answered that STalk2 satisfied their needs.

5.4 Implications

In this study, we examined the effects of applying persuasive technology to the
mobile AAC app, STalk2. The frequency of presenting visual aids with verbal
messages was increased as intended. The simple steps for creating, searching,
editing, and presenting visual aids reduced the burden of peers. Additionally,
the problem behaviors of a few children were decreased. The reduction of such
behaviors made the abilities required for AAC easier. STalk2 also motivated
peers by helping them discover new sides of the child; the children also enjoyed
using the app. These results suggest that behaviors and attitudes in AAC may
be modeled by the dimensions of abilities and motivation as Fogg proposed [8].
Future AAC apps should take into account the principles of persuasive technologies facilitating communication through better design.

5.5 Limitations

This study was conducted on eleven communication peers and five children with
CCN. Although it is generally acceptable to have 5–10 participants in research
focusing on individuals with disabilities [16], our participants used STalk2 within
a limited range of communication needs and settings. Thus, the results may not
be generalized to other cases. Future research should replicate this study; for
example, with a larger number of participants and/or over an extended period,
to cover diverse needs and settings.

We have implemented functions to support the self-monitoring principle.
However, these functions were rarely used in this study. Evaluations should be
conducted to examine the effects of these functions.

6 Conclusion

The results suggest that persuasive technology in AAC systems may be effective
in improving communication behaviors and attitudes. Our future work will be to
conduct in-depth observations and/or distributed research [16] to provide more
substantial evidence for our results or findings.

Acknowledgements. This work was supported by JSPS KAKENHI Grant Number
JP16K01553.

References

1. Beukelman, D., Jones, R., Rowan, M.: Frequency of word usage by nondisabled peers in integrated preschool classrooms. Augment. Altern. Commun. **5**(4), 243–248 (1989)
2. Beukelman, D.R., Mirenda, P.: Augmentative and Alternative Communication Management of Severe Communication Disorders, 2nd edn. Paul H. Brookes Publishing Co., Baltimore (1998)
3. Bondy, A.S., Frost, L.A.: The picture exchange communication system. Focus Autism Other Dev. Disabil. **9**, 1–19 (1994)
4. Caron, J., Light, J., Drager, K.: Operational demands of AAC mobile technology applications on programming vocabulary and engagement during professional and child interactions. Augment. Altern. Commun. **32**(1), 12–24 (2016)
5. Carr, E.G., Durand, V.M.: Reducing behavior problems through functional communication training. J. Appl. Behav. Anal. **18**(2), 111–126 (1985)
6. Charlop-Christy, M., Carpenter, M., Le, L., LeBlanc, L., Kellet, K.: Using the picture exchange communication system (PECS) with children with autism: assessment of PECS acquisition, speech. Soc.-Commun. Behav. **35**(3), 213–231 (2002)
7. Fogg, B.J.: Persuasive Technology: Using Computers to Change What We Think and Do. Interactive Technologies. Elsevier Science, New York (2003)
8. Fogg, B.: A behavior model for persuasive design. In: Proceedings of the 4th International Conference on Persuasive Technology, Article no. 40, 7 p. (2009)
9. Fogg, B.J.: Creating persuasive technologies : an eight-step design process. In: Technology, vol. 91, pp. 1–6 (2009)
10. Fried-Oken, M., More, L.: An initial vocabulary for nonspeaking preschool children based on developmental and environmental language sources. Augment. Altern. Commun. **8**(1), 41–56 (1992)
11. Hirotomi, T., Mirenkov, N.N.: Self-explanatory components: a basis for new communicators. J. Vis. Lang. Comput. **14**(3), 215–232 (2003)
12. Hirotomi, T., Mirenkov, N.N.: Augmentative and alternative communication based on multimedia hieroglyphs. J. Jpn. Soc. Wellbeing Sci. Assist. Technol. **3**(2), 40–50 (2004)
13. Hirotomi, T., Tanaka, K., Inamura, S.: A communication aid for people with developmental disorders to augment the understanding of messages. IEICE Trans. Inf. Syst. **J97-D**(1), 117–125 (2014)
14. Hirotomi, T., Zhang, Y.: Multilingual and multicultural message presentations to enhance communication capabilities of people with special needs. Int. J. Comput. Appl. Technol. **33**(2/3), 190–198 (2008)
15. Kent-Walsh, J., Murza, K.A., Malani, M.D., Binger, C.: Effects of communication partner instruction on the communication of individuals using AAC: a meta-analysis. Augment. Altern. Commun. **31**(4), 271–284 (2015)
16. Lazar, J., Feng, J.H., Hochheiser, H.: Research Methods in Human-Computer Interaction. Wiley, Hoboken (2010)
17. Light, J., McNaughton, D.: Communicative competence for individuals who require augmentative and alternative communication: a new definition for a new era of communication? Augment. Altern. Commun. **30**(1), 1–18 (2014)
18. Marvin, C., Beukelman, D., Bilyeu, D.: Vocabulary-use patterns in preschool children: effects of context and time sampling. Augment. Altern. Commun. **10**(4), 224–236 (1994)

19. Oinas-Kukkonen, H., Harjumaa, M.: A systematic framework for designing and evaluating persuasive systems. In: Oinas-Kukkonen, H., Hasle, P., Harjumaa, M., Segerståhl, K., Øhrstrøm, P. (eds.) PERSUASIVE 2008. LNCS, vol. 5033, pp. 164–176. Springer, Heidelberg (2008). https://doi.org/10.1007/978-3-540-68504-3_15
20. Society for the Kyoto Scale of Psychological Development Test: The Kyoto scale of psychological development test 2001. Nakanishiya Shuppan, Kyoto (2008). (in Japanese)
21. Therrien, M.C., Light, J., Pope, L.: Systematic review of the effects of interventions to promote peer interactions for children who use aided AAC. Augment. Altern. Commun. 32(2), 81–93 (2016)
22. Thistle, J.J., Wilkinson, K.M.: Building evidence-based practice in AAC display design for young children: current practices and future directions. Augment. Altern. Commun. 31(2), 124–136 (2015)

Teaching Concepts with Wearable Technology: Learning Internal Body Organs

Ersin Kara[✉], Mustafa Güleç, and Kürşat Çağıltay

Middle East Technical University, Ankara, Turkey
{ekara,mgulec,kursat}@metu.edu.tr

Abstract. In this study, a wearable smart cloth was designed and developed for children with intellectual disabilities (IDs) to help them learn name and position of internal body organs. In this regard, five plush organs (heart, lungs, stomach, liver and intestines) that can interact with a smart cloth were designed. Additionally, an application that provides animated characters, feedback, visual cues, and sounds and also interacts with the smart cloth by controlling the sensors on the smart cloth were developed and utilized during the implementation. Participants of the study were four students from a private Special Education School in Turkey. As a research methodology, a single-subject research method was employed and the data were collected via field notes and video recordings. Results of the study showed that students with IDs can use smart cloth and it can help them to learn names and positions of internal body organs. Moreover, animated character can get their attention and students with IDs can complete instructions on their own.

Keywords: Smart clothes · Wearable technology · Internal body organs
Plush organs

1 Introduction

We are witnessing far-reaching technological advances every day; however, not all people have chance to access and use them. One of these disadvantageous groups is people with intellectual disabilities. People with IDs have problems accessing and the using technology [2, 3, 5, 6]. As Mechling [3] stated, creative use of new technologies and their capabilities to assist individuals with IDs should be explored.

An appropriate device to support individuals with IDs should be simple and intuitive. Wearable technologies, when designed to be used intuitively can remove the barrier of human-computer interaction complexity, which has been possible by relatively few interaction means. Students with low cognitive abilities can benefit from wearable learning tools developed to assist them in learning settings [2]. Current technologies predominantly address visual sense of human and new ways to create interactions between physical and digital world may change our perception of things [4]. Addressing various dimensions of human sensory (i.e., feeling, hearing, seeing) in learning settings may help learners having stimulate-rich experiences and long-lasting learning. In this regard, designing and developing well-organized, developmentally

© Springer International Publishing AG, part of Springer Nature 2018
M. Antona and C. Stephanidis (Eds.): UAHCI 2018, LNCS 10907, pp. 542–550, 2018.
https://doi.org/10.1007/978-3-319-92049-8_39

appropriate materials that meet students with IDs' needs and help them in various learning settings seems to be significant.

In this study, a wearable smart cloth was designed and developed to help children with IDs to learn name and position of internal body organs. In this regard, five plush organs (heart, lungs, stomach, liver and intestines) that can interact with the cloth and an application to assist in the instruction were developed. The application provides on-screen agents, feedbacks, visual cues, sounds and can interact with the smart cloth to detect whether an organ is located properly by controlling sensors on the cloth.

2 Purpose

This study aims to design and develop a computer-based interactive smart cloth to help students with IDs to learn names and locations of internal body organs and to determine effectiveness of the developed material.

3 Method

Under single-subject research methodology the A-B-A design (baseline-treatment-baseline) was employed in the study. Single-subject research methodology has been used in special education mostly and is especially useful when the observation is the inevitable method of data collection [1]. In this type of research, generally intensive data are collected from few participants [1]. Therefore, both qualitative and quantitative data were collected for the study. Qualitative data include field notes and video recordings which were done before, during and after treatment to reveal inter-actions between the smart cloth and students and their knowledge of internal body organs. Quantitative data such as correct/wrong attempts and completion time were obtained by analyzing video recordings to support qualitative findings of the study.

3.1 Participants

Four students in a private special education school participated in the study. The necessary permissions were taken from the institution before the study. Participants were selected from students who are identified as having mild or moderate ID, need to learn internal body organs and don't have any feature that threads internal validity (e.g., physical disabilities and severe ID). Detailed information about participants is given in Table 1.

3.2 Procedure

The researcher asked participants locations and names of aforementioned internal body organs for the first baseline (A condition). After that session, participants attached the interactive cloth with the help of researcher and connection between computer and the smart cloth was checked. Implementation was completed in three stages. The first and the second stages are part of the intervention and corresponds the B condition in the design. The third stage corresponds to the second baseline (A condition) in the design.

Table 1. Characteristics of participants

Participant	Age	Gender	Disability	Other information
A	16	Female	Mild ID	Has speech problem, good attention, difficulty in perception
B	17	Male	Down Syndrome – Moderate ID	Has speech problem, weak attention, good motivation
C	26	Male	Moderate ID	Has speech problem, good attention
D	10	Male	Mild ID	Literate, knows left-right concepts

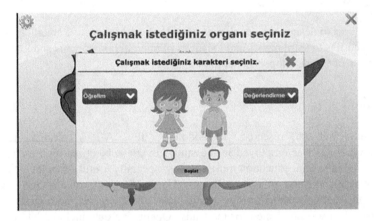

Fig. 1. An example screenshot from the application

In the first stage, instruction, which has two levels, was provided. In the first level of the first stage, a plush organ was put on a table and part of the application introducing that organ's position and name was started (see Fig. 1). In the application, an animated character articulates that organ's name, describes its basic functions and shows its place on his/her body. Next, in Level 1 of the first stage, the character asks students to mount plush organ to the smart cloth by saying "It's your turn now. Mount the toy (organ name) on the cloth". According to student's attempt, application gives positive or negative feedback. If s/he failed to complete the task (when there was no attempt), the researcher showed correct place and if s/he placed on a wrong location, animated character showed correct location. In the Level 2 of the first stage, the character does not show the organ's position and again asks for mounting related plush organ. These activities were done for all five internal organs (see Fig. 2).

In the second stage, randomly chosen three plush organs were put on the table and the character on the screen asked students to choose and mount the right one to the smart cloth. After the second stage, the researcher showed each organ's place and name to students by the help of the smart cloth and plush organs for 7–8 min. This was done to make sure that students were not left confused after the second stage.

After a week, the third stage was completed. In this stage, the researcher asked students to show each organ's location on their body. Next, researcher showed each

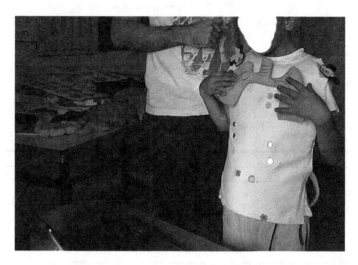

Fig. 2. A participant mounting plush lungs

plush organ and asked its name and place again. All these stages were recorded by a video camera.

3.3 Analysis of Data

The recordings were analyzed by researchers and coded by help of a form. The form has three sections to code: Stages 1, 2 and 3 (one week later assessment). Three categories were defined to explain interaction type and four categories were defined to explain participants' behavior. Interaction type categories are as follow:

1: Student did not listen to character and did nothing
2: Student listened to character but waited for researcher's instruction
3: Student listened to character and completed the task by himself/herself

The categories stating participants' behavior:

- Correct: Placed plush organ on correct part of the smart cloth
- Partially Correct: Placed plush organ on correct part of the smart cloth but upside down
- Wrong: Placed plush organ on wrong part of the smart cloth
- Fail to complete: Did nothing and could not complete the task

4 Results

First baseline results showed that almost all participants had not known name and place of these five internal body organs. Only Participant A had already known the position of heart.

As Table 2 shows, Participant A placed heart correctly in all levels but Level 2. During Level 2, she placed heart upside down (partially correct). Lungs were the organs that she was best at locating. She could not find right place for stomach in Level 1 and could not complete the task in Level 2. Both in Level 1 and Level 2, she mounted liver on wrong places.

Table 2. Results for Participant A

| Organ | Stage 1 | | | | | | Stage 2 | | | |
| | Level 1 | | | Level 2 | | | | | | |
	Interaction Type	Completion Time (sec)	Placement	Interaction Type	Completion Time(sec)	Placement	Completion Time (sec)	Picking Right Organ	Showing Right Place	6–7 min Practice
Heart	3	8	Correct	3	6	Partially Correct	8.5	Correct	Correct	
Lungs	3	8.5	Correct	3	7.5	Correct	12.5	Correct	Correct	
Stomach	3	7	Wrong	3	-	Fail to complete	22	Correct	Wrong	
Liver	3	10	Wrong	3	6	Wrong	12	Correct	Wrong	
Intestines	3	9	Correct	3	6	Correct	7	Correct	Correct	

In the second stage, each time she chose the right organ but could not place stomach and liver correctly. According to results, participant A always listened the animated character and attempted to complete the task by herself. In the case of participant A, stomach and liver were the organs that she found difficult to locate. A week later in Stage 3, she could articulate only name of heart. Her speaking problems probably made it difficult to say name of some organs. However, when the researcher gave a plush organ and asked the position, she showed place of heart, lungs and intestines correctly. These results are indicated in Table 6.

According to Table 3 Participant B listened the animated character; however, most of the time he had waited researcher's instructions. He could not place stomach and liver on the smart cloth. When the animated character asked him to place the organ without showing location of the organ on body (Level 2), he mounted stomach, liver and intestines upside down. As Stage 2 data shows, most of the time he picked right organ from three random organs but mounted them on a wrong part of the smart cloth or failed to complete the task. However, he placed heart and intestines correctly.

A week later, when he was asked to show each organ's place, he could only show place of heart correctly. After that researcher showed each plush organ and asked him to say organ's name and place. He showed all organs' place correctly but could not say their names aside from heart. His speaking problems might lead such a result as shown in Table 6.

Table 3. Results for Participant B

Organ	Stage 1						Stage 2			
	Level 1			Level 2						
	Interaction Type	Time to complete task	Placement	Interaction Type	Completion Time	Placement	Completion Time	Picking Right Organ	Showing Right Place	
Heart	2	15	Correct	2	6	Correct	8	Correct	Correct	6-7 min Practice
Lungs	2	17	Correct	3	9	Correct	-	Correct	Fail to complete	
Stomach	3	-	Fail to complete	2	9	Partially Correct	-	Correct	Fail to complete	
Liver	2	-	Fail to complete	2	7	Partially Correct	29	Wrong	Wrong	
Intestines	3	4	Partially Correct	2	6	Partially Correct	23	Correct	Correct	

According to Table 4, Participant C listened the animated character but most of the time had waited researcher's instructions. He failed to locate liver, and mounted stomach on a different part of body in Level 1. However, he was mainly successful at determining location of organs at Level 2 and most of the time he was able to pick right organs at Stage 2. An interesting result is that although he picked wrong organ at Stage 2 instead of lungs, she always located them correctly meaning that she could not recall name of lungs.

A week later, he showed place of heart, lungs and liver correctly without seeing plush organ. Because he could not speak, the researcher put three organs on table and asked him to show a specific organ. He only correctly picked heart and lungs and only placed them correctly when plush organs were showed Table 6 shows number of the correct answers he gave.

As shown in Table 5 Participant D was very good at listening the animated character and attempting to complete task. In Level 1, he only mounted stomach wrongly. Although he was very good at picking right organ at Stage 2, he could not show location of heart, lungs, and stomach correctly.

A week later, he showed place of all organs correctly but stomach without seeing plush organs. As Table 6 shows, when plush organs were showed, he said all of their names correctly and placed on the smart cloth without error.

According to results, in Level 2, students were able to complete instructions in a shorter time with higher number of correct answers. Moreover, students needed more time to complete Stage 2, which means picking right organ among three choices took their time.

Table 4. Results for Participant C

| Organ | Stage 1 | | | | | | Stage 2 | | | 6-7 min Practice |
| | Level 1 | | | Level 2 | | | | | | |
	Interaction Type	Completion Time	Placement	Interaction Type	Completion Time	Placement	Completion Time	Picking Right Organ	Showing Right Place	
Heart	2	7	Partially Correct	2	5	Correct	18	Correct	Wrong	
Lungs	2	6.5	Correct	2	5.5	Correct	8	Wrong*	Correct	
Stomach	3	10	Wrong	2	10	Wrong	38	Correct	Partially Correct	
Liver	2	-	Fail to complete	2	4	Correct	16	Correct	Wrong	
Intestines	3	5	Partially Correct	2	4	Partially Correct	38	Wrong	Wrong	

*Researcher showed correct organ after wrong attempt

According to Table 6, students could remember locations of internal body organs even a week later and for some students using plush organs as clues helped them to give more answers that are correct. Recalling name of the organs was difficult for Participant A, B, and C as they only managed to give one or two correct answers during second baseline.

Table 5. Results for Participant D

| Organ | Stage 1 | | | | | | Stage 2 | | | 6-7 min Practice |
| | Level 1 | | | Level 2 | | | | | | |
	Interaction Type	Completion Time	Placement	Interaction Type	Completion Time	Placement	Completion Time	Picking Right Organ	Showing Right Place	
Heart	3	14	Correct	3	3.5	Correct	25	Correct	Wrong	
Lungs	3	7	Correct	3	6	Correct	23	Correct	Wrong	
Stomach	3	4	Wrong	3	6	Correct	13	Correct	Wrong	
Liver	3	12	Correct	3	6	Correct	11	Correct	Correct	
Intestines	3	3	Correct	3	3	Correct	13	Correct	Correct	

Table 6. Summary of second baseline

Participant	Number of correct answers		
	Showing right place without plush organ	Showing right place with plush organ	Recalling name of organ
A	Not collected	3	1
B	1	5	1
C	3	2	2
D	4	4	5

5 Conclusions

According to results, participants' performances vary considerably depending on their ID type, personal characteristics and learning capacity.

The study showed that all students carefully listened to characters and most of the time they completed the tasks on their own after one or two trials. In this example, animated character could get attention of students with ID and students could follow the instructions the character gave. However, in this case, most of the participants were confused when it comes to place stomach and liver on the smart cloth. This is because in the animation, character's left side corresponds to students' right side and this makes students confused. They already have limited cognitive abilities and this situation posing them as extra cognitive load. A demonstration from a different angle may help students to comprehend on which side of body the organ mounted.

Another important point is that participants who have speaking problems could not recall name of some organs. They need to match visual and auditory stimuli to be successful and results show that they need more time and more practice to do this. In addition, results indicated that visual cues (using plush organs and showing their places on their own bodies) helped them to remember place of a specific organ even though they could not recall its name. For example, almost all participants guessed location of lungs correctly during intervention. Second baseline results showed that some students were better at using visual cues than auditory cues. Researchers' field notes showed that some students used color of an organ to recall name/place of it and for some of them shape of an organ served as a clue.

Another interesting finding is that most of the time students did not pay attention to organs' vertical positions on the body. Three of the participants placed an organ at least once upside down (partially correct).

Results showed that six to seven minutes of practice also might had positive effect on learning of the students. For example, in the case of participant D, although he could not show right locations for three organs at Stage 2, one week later he only made one mistake at Stage 3.

Although they need to make more practice for learning names of these five internal body organs, interactive smart cloth and plush organs as educational materials can be used to help students with IDs while learning internal body organs' names and locations. They can pick the right organ and mount it to the smart cloth in a very short time and according to Level 1 results, practice enabled them to complete tasks in a shorter time. Smart cloth and interactive application can help students practicing a topic several times by themselves. Furthermore, they can follow instructions given by an animated character. This interaction may go further as researchers noticed that some students tried to speak with the character during implementations.

Second baseline results showed that even a week later students can remember some of organs' places. It should be noted that most of participants had speaking problems and to teach them name of the organs, further practices would give better results.

6 Future Studies

In this study, the researchers tried to teach five internal organs' names and positions by handling them one by one. However, it would help students to do better if they see all five internal body organs at the same time on their bodies. Some teachers noticed and specified this as a suggestion.

The researchers only investigated whether they can learn name of five internal organs and whether they can show right places on their own body. Future research may investigate whether they can transfer this knowledge by showing organs' places on another person's body.

An improved version of the interactive cloth and the application can be designed and then similar studies can be conducted.

References

1. Fraenkel, J.R., Wallen, N.E., Hyun, H.H.: How to Design and Evaluate Research in Education, 8th edn. McGraw-Hill, New York (2012)
2. Braddock, D., Rizzolo, M.C., Thompson, M., Bell, R.: Emerging technologies and cognitive disability. J. Spec. Educ. Technol. 19(4), 49–56 (2004)
3. Mechling, L.M.: Assistive technology as a self-management tool for prompting students with intellectual disabilities to initiate and complete daily tasks: a literature review. Educ. Train. Dev. Disabil. 42(3), 252–269 (2007)
4. Uğur, S.: Wearing Embodied Emotions: A Practice Based Design Research on Wearable Technology. Springer Science & Business Media, Milan (2013). https://doi.org/10.1007/978-88-470-5247-5
5. Wehmeyer, M.L., Smith, S.J., Palmer, S.B., Davies, D.K.: Technology use by students with intellectual disabilities: an overview. J. Spec. Educ. Technol. 19(4), 7–22 (2004)
6. Lewis, C.: HCI and cognitive disabilities. Interactions 13(3), 14–15 (2006)

The Utility of the Virtual Reality
in Autistic Disorder Treatment

Sicong Liu[✉], Yan Xi, and Hui Wang

Nanjing College of Information Technology, Nanjing, People's Republic of China
liusc@njcit.cn

Abstract. Autistic disorder patients lack the social communication abilities and need interventional therapy to alleviate such symptoms. The cost of health care and treatment across the lifespan of patients were up to $3.2 million which places a crushing burden on the poor patients and their families. To relieve the symptoms of disease and reduce the financial pressure of the patients, many methods were proposed. The normal therapy is proceeding under the instruction of professional doctors in the hospital. Each person need to spend 6–8 h in the specialized institutions. Given the cost of treatment and time, the treatment could not carry out continually which could lead to reducing the curative effectiveness. The current study explores the utility of the virtual reality interventions to the autistic disorder patients. In the virtual environment, the patients could be receiving treatment continually and practice their social communication abilities in different social scenes. To generate immersive virtual social environment, a VR engine (Unity3D 5.0) were used. Some typical social communication scenes were also established which include the classroom, shopping mall and hospital. In these virtual scenes, the ASD patients were required to communicate with artificial intelligence (AI) players and finish some tasks. The coach which played by the researcher or expert would send appropriate instructions to help the patient when they encounter the difficulties. Two different statistic tables will be collected twice: one is before the training, the other one is after the training. The two checklists are Autism Behavior Scale (ABS) table and Childhood Autism Rating Scale (CARS) table. By comparing the scores which achieved in different time, researchers could assess the result of treatment and changing the content of the treatment in time. Four ASD children who had confirmed ASD diagnoses from a clinical doctor take part in this experiment. Informed consent was obtained from the parents before participation. The average age of the subjects is 6 ($\pm$1). These volunteers were asked to execute nine tasks in different social scenes, which include communicate with strange teachers, sellers and doctors. All these tasks have three levels: in lv1, only one AI player in the scenes, in lv2, two AI players in scenes, in lv3, no less than three AI players will in the scenes. The patients in which scenes at which levels is controlled by researchers. According to the results, we find that after the training that the scores of the ASD patients are raised. Such results suggest that the VR technology could very helpful for the adjuvant therapy of the ASD.

Keywords: Virtual reality · Autism · Assistant training system

© Springer International Publishing AG, part of Springer Nature 2018
M. Antona and C. Stephanidis (Eds.): UAHCI 2018, LNCS 10907, pp. 551–559, 2018.
https://doi.org/10.1007/978-3-319-92049-8_40

1   Introduction

Autism as a pervasive developmental disorder it could lead the patients' social, communicative and behavioral functions impaired seriously. For adult patients of ASD, nearly two thirds of persons remain unable to provide basic personal care (Dorothy et al. 1998). The cost of health care and treatment across the lifespan of patients was up to $3.2 million (Ganz 2007; Peacock et al. 2012). It also would place a crushing burden on the poor patients and their families. For the adolescent patients, the lack of basic social and living skills could cause the difficulty to integrate themselves into the society. From the 1990s the prevalence of autism spectrum disorders increased rapidly (Mathew et al. 2014). The autism spectrum disorder (ASD) is now more and more focused by the psychologists and doctors. Many therapies appeared to address or relieve the symptoms which were caused by the ASD. The purpose of these methods is to help the patients possess basic social or living skills.

Previous intervention studies had utilized observational techniques, such as make a conversation during a simulated social party or a job interview (Howlin and Yates 1999). Self-rated questionnaires were also used by doctors (Hillier et al. 2007). These interventional therapies could improve the social communication skills of the adult patients of ASD significantly (Hillier et al. 2007). Although these methods were of power to relieve the symptoms of the ASD, but there are still some disadvantages of these therapies: (1) the simulation environment is the lack of immersion, the effectiveness of these methods was limited by the patients' imagination. (2) could not control the input stimuli, although the environment of the intervention was carefully designed but considered the uncontrollable in the real-world, the stimuli of the input was still not fully controlled. (3) safety of the learning situation, for the normal training methods, patients were forced to learn the social communication skills in a real environment which means it is not friendly to the ASD patients when they make mistakes.

With the rapid development of the technology, the virtual reality technology was utilized to overcome these disadvantages which could offer an immersion, fully controllable and friendly to the patients virtual training environment. The VR system can generate a special stimulation according to the training task and allow the experts to monitor the whole process and change the stimulation in time. Given the features of the VR system, it could offer fully immersed environment by using a helmet-mounted displays (HMD). Synthesize all of above characters, such system establishes a virtual but realistic enough training environment which allows the ASD patients to practice repeatedly and no need to be concerned about the mistakes.

Based further advantages of the VR system, psychologist and doctors could design more individualized training plans: the ASD patients may vary widely in their strength and weakness between different days. For a better treatment effect, doctors need to make more individualized treatment plan. To achieve the aim, experts will analyze the behavior data of the patient which is record by the training system or the experts themselves and make some change to the personal training plan properly. Such process also very slow and inefficient while with the help of the VR training system which based on computer system, it will be very efficient. The VR system stresses the response of visual and auditory rather than touch. For the ASD patients, the visual and sight stimulation has been more helpful to teach them the abstract concepts, such as social skills.

2   Methods

2.1   Participants

Four volunteers took part in the experiment. (mean age 6 ± 1 year) which includes 1 female child. All participants had confirmed ASD diagnoses from a clinical doctor. Informed consent was obtained from the parents before participation. Each subject was required to complete two different checklists: (i) the Autism Behavior Scale table; (ii) the Childhood Autism Rating Scale table. The score of these two tables will be regarded as the baseline to the participant (Table 1).

Table 1. The basic scores achieved from the volunteers before the experiment.

Scores of baseline			
Subject ID	Sex	Scores of ABS	Scores of CARS
NJASD01	Male	75	45
NJASD02	Female	72	39
NJASD03	Male	78	46
NJASD04	Male	71	38

2.2   Experiment Paradigm

In this research, we establish an immersive virtual environment for children with ASD to improve their social communication skills.

The whole training paradigm is composite of three subsets which have different difficulty levels: in the 1st level, volunteers will communicate with single artificial intelligence actor which generated by the VR system. In the 2nd level, volunteers need interact with two AI actors with the same environment. In the 3rd level, participants will try to communicate with no less than three actors (Fig. 1). In each training task, the subjects must be finished such tasks: (1) tell the name, age to the AI actors; (2) do some daily communication with the AI actors; (3) follow the instruction given by the coach to have a rest (Fig. 2).

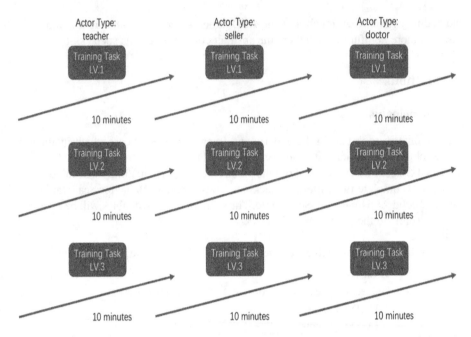

Fig. 1. Three levels in the training session. Each training task will be last 10 min and the task with different levels but has the same actor type will be executed sequentially.

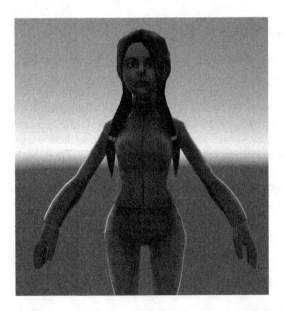

Fig. 2. A female coach which is displayed in the training task. Given that the female is more approachable and easy to be accepted by children with ASD, so in this study, we utilized a female avatar to act as the coach.

For all three levels, there are three different AI actor types: teacher, seller and doctor. Each training session will last 10 min. The coach will change the contents of the instruction which decide by the behavior of the volunteers. Before the formal experiment, a preliminary test will be executed first to make sure the participants will follow the instruction which is gave by the coach. The whole training process will last for 8 weeks.

2.3 Composition of Training System

The training system is composited by three components: application software; helmet-mounted-display device; a high-performance desktop computer (Fig. 3).

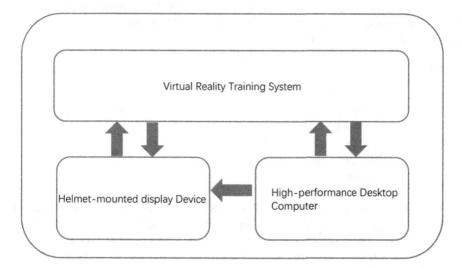

Fig. 3. The virtual reality training system was generated by using Unity3D software, when the subject training in the VR system researchers could monitor the situation of the patients and give the appropriate instructions.

The VR experiment system is generated by the Unity3D software (version 5.0). The whole VR system is running in a VR HMD system (HTC Vive).

3   Results

After each training session, participants were required to complete a rating scale which is used to assess the effectiveness of the task. The range of the checklist score is from 0 to 5 which 0 means difficult to accomplish and 5 represents easy to finish. The score of the task effectiveness listed in the Table 2.

Table 2. In order to assess the effectiveness of training tasks, after each task, participant will be required to answer a checklist.

Task effectiveness assessment										
ID	Sex	Teacher			Seller			Doctor		
		L1	L2	L3	L1	L2	L3	L1	L2	L3
NJASD01	Male	3	2	1	3	1	0	4	3	1
NJASD02	Female	4	3	2	3	3	2	5	3	2
NJASD03	Male	5	4	2	4	4	2	5	4	2
NJASD04	Male	4	3	2	4	3	3	5	3	2

Two checklists which the subjects were required to finish before the training sessions were graded again when the training process finished. The score of the two ASD diagnose checklists listed in the Table 3.

Table 3. Scores of the two checklists which obtained from the subjects after the training.

Scores of checklists			
Subject ID	Sex	Scores of ABS	Scores of CARS
NJASD01	Male	70	34
NJASD02	Female	68	32
NJASD03	Male	69	41
NJASD04	Male	64	30

Compared to the average scores of the ABS scale before and after the training, it shows that the scores of the ASD patients reduced. The former average score is 74 and the later average score is 67.75. According to the result of the independent t test analysis, the difference between two types was significant ($p < 0.05$). For the CARS scale, the

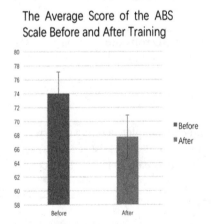

Fig. 4. The average scores of the two checklists (ABS, CARS) which obtained from the subjects before and after the training sessions.

former average score is 42 and the later score is 34.25. The difference between two types was significant (p < 0.05) (Fig. 4).

4 Discussion

Social communication as a very important skill, the lack of it would impaired the living quality of the ASD patients seriously. To improve the communication ability of the ASD patients, many methods were proposed by researchers. For example, Howlin et al. (1999). Proposed that utilized the observational techniques to improve the conversation skills of the adult ASD patients by establishing scenes of simulated job interview and social party. Hillier et al. (2007) make the ASD patients to observe the different types of conversation frequently. These methods could improve the communication skills of the ASD patients. But there are still some disadvantages for these methods: (1) uncontrollable stimuli; (2) could not change the training scenes in time; (3) the training time is not last too long.

Considering the rapid evolution of the VR technology, it has much powerful abilities to generate an immersive virtual world and has been considered as an effective tool to improve the social and life skills of ASD patients. A growing number of studies have examined applications of advanced interactive technologies to social and communication related intervention (Park et al. 2011; Rus-Calafell et al. 2014; Blocher and Picard 2002; Kozima et al. 2005; Parsons et al. 2004; Uttama et al. 2014). According to the results of this study, it shows that VR technology would helpful to raise the communication ability of the ASD patients, especially for the young children. Comparing the scores of two checklists which are obtained before and after the training tasks, it shows that the social communication skills of ASD children improved significantly by using the virtual reality training system. The VR training system not only allow the doctors to monitor the training process but also make the switching the training tasks in time possible. The VR system offers a safety and friendly virtual environment to ASD patients to practice their social and living communication skills.

Although the results of this study support the views that the VR training system could relieve the symptoms of the ASD patients, but there are still some disadvantages be founded during the experiment: considering the weight of the helmet-mounted display device, the time of the training task could not continue too long. During the training days, participants need come to the library on time which raise the cost of time. For some ASD patients who also suffered from the claustrophobia, they refused to take the helmet which lead the training interrupt. In the current version of the VR training system, the helmet-mounted-display device was used the HTC Vive which is a high-performance device. Although the display effect was good, but the portability of it was bad because it has to be connected to the computer by some cables. Considering the treatment which patients need to utilize the training system at home and practice for a long time that the whole system should be robust and easy to maintaining.

For future research, we plan to import the eye-tracking and facial-tracking technologies into our training system. This would promise the human-computer interaction of VR training system more naturalistic and flexible. For the HMD device, it is planning to add a wireless suite to the HTC Vive which could allow the device connects to the computer without using the cables. Considering the similarity degree between AI actors and human beings could affect the training effectiveness, further research paradigm will be design.

References

Aksan, N., Anderson, S.W., Dawson, J.D., Johnson, A.M., Uc, E.Y., Rizzo, M.: Cognitive functioning predicts driver safety on road tests 1 and 2 years later. J. Am. Geriatr. Soc. **60**, 99–105 (2012). https://doi.org/10.1111/j.1532-5415.2011.03739.x

Johnson, J.: Designing with the Mind in Mind. Morgan Kaufman Publisher, Burlington (2010)

Brooks, J.O., Mossey, E.M., Collins, J.C., Tyler, P.: An exploratory investigation: are driving simulators appropriate to teach pre-driving skills to young adults with intellectual disabilities? Br. J. Learn. Disabil. **42**(2), 204–213 (2013)

Cassavaugh, N.D., Kramer, A.F.: Transfer of computer-based training to simulated driving in older adults. Appl. Ergono. **40**(5), 943–952 (2009)

Cox, D.J., Merkel, R.L., Kovatchev, B., Seward, R.: Effect of stimulant medication on driving performance of young adults with attention-deficit hyperactivity disorder: a preliminary double-blind placebo controlled trial. J. Nerv. Ment. Dis. **188**(4), 230–234 (2000)

Parsons, S., Mitchell, P., Leonard, A.: The use and understanding of virtual environments by adolescents with autistic spectrum disorders. J. Autism Dev. Disord. **34**(4), 449–466 (2004)

Daly, B.P., Nicholls, E.G., Patrick, K.E., Brinckman, D.D., Schultheis, M.T.: Driving behaviors in adults with autism spectrum disorders. J. Autism Dev. Disord. **44**(12), 3119–3128 (2014). https://doi.org/10.1007/s10803-014-2166-y

Dickerson, A.E., Bédard, M.: Decision tool for clients with medical issues: a framework for identifying driving risk and potential to return to driving. Occup. Ther. Health Care **28**(2), 94–202 (2014). https://doi.org/10.3109/07380577.2014.903357

Sheppard, E., Van Loon, E., Underwood, G., Ropar, D.: Attentional differences in a driving hazard perception task in adults with autism spectrum disorders. J. Autism Dev. Disord. **47**, 405–414 (2016)

Wade, J., Bian, D., Zhang, L., Swanson, A., Sarkar, M., Warren, Z., Sarkar, N.: Design of a virtual reality driving environment to assess performance of teenagers with ASD. In: Stephanidis, C., Antona, M. (eds.) UAHCI 2014. LNCS, vol. 8514, pp. 466–474. Springer, Cham (2014). https://doi.org/10.1007/978-3-319-07440-5_43

Bell, M., Bryson, G., Lysaker, P.: Positive and negative affect recognition in schizophrenia: a comparison with substance abuse and normal control subjects. Psychiatry Res. **73**, 73–82 (1997)

Taylor, J.L., Seltzer, M.M.: Employment and post- secondary educational activities for young adults with autism spectrum disorders during the transition to adulthood. J. Autism Dev. Disord. **41**, 566–574 (2011). https://doi.org/10.1007/s10803-010-1070-3

Wing, L., Gould, J.: Severe impairments of social interaction and associated abnormalities in children: epidemiology and classification. J. Autism Dev. Disord. **9**, 11–29 (1979)

Huang, P., Kao, T., Curry, A.E., Durbin, D.R.: Factors associated with driving in teens with autism spectrum disorders. J. Dev. Behav. Pediatr. **33**, 70–74 (2012)

Hillier, A., Fish, T., Cloppert, P., Beversdorf, D.Q.: Outcomes of a social and vocational skills support group for adolescents and young adults on the autism spectrum. Focus Autism Other Dev. Disabil. **22**(2), 107–115 (2007)

Cox, D.J., Moncrief, M., Rizzo, M., Fisher, D., Lambert, A., Thomas, S., et al.: Low hanging fruit: use of virtual reality simulation in Department of Motor Vehicles to assess minimal competence of novice drivers. Paper Presented at International Driving Symposium on Human Factors in Driving Assessment, Training, and Vehicle Design, Salt Lake City, UT (2015)

Gregory, R.L.: Seeing by exploring. In: Ellis, S.R. (ed.) Pictorial Communications in Virtual and Real Environments, pp. 328–337. Taylor and Francil, London (1991)

Grandin, T.: An inside view of autism. In: Schopler, E., Mesibov, G.B. (eds.) High-Functioning Individuals with Autism, pp. 105–126. Plenum Press, New York (1992)

Blocher, K., Picard, R.W.: Affective social quest: emotion recognition therapy for autistic children. In: Canamero, L., Edmonds, B., Dautenhahn, K., Bond, A.H. (eds.) Socially Intelligent Agents: Creating Relationships with Computers and Robots. Kluwer, Dordrecht (2002)

Park, K.M., Ku, J., Choi, S.H., Jang, H.J., Park, J.Y., Kim, S.I., et al.: A virtual reality application in role-plays of social skills training for schizophrenia: a randomized, controlled trial. Psychiatry Res. 189(2), 166–172 (2011)

Parsons, S., Mitchell, P.: The potential of virtual reality in social skills training for people with autistic spectrum disorders. J. Intellect. Disabil. Res. 46(Pt 5), 430–443 (2002)

A Data-Driven Mobile Application for Efficient, Engaging, and Accurate Screening of ASD in Toddlers

Arpan Sarkar[1], Joshua Wade[2(✉)], Amy Swanson[3], Amy Weitlauf[3], Zachary Warren[4], and Nilanjan Sarkar[2]

[1] Statistics, Harvard University, Cambridge, MA 02138, USA
[2] Mechanical Engineering, Vanderbilt University, Nashville, TN 37212, USA
joshua.w.wade@vanderbilt.edu
[3] Treatment and Research Institute for Autism Spectrum Disorders (TRIAD),
Vanderbilt University, Nashville, TN 37212, USA
[4] Pediatrics, Psychiatry and Special Education, Vanderbilt University, Nashville, TN 37212, USA

Abstract. Early detection of Autism Spectrum Disorder (ASD) followed by targeted intervention has been shown to yield meaningful improvements in outcomes for individuals with ASD. However, despite the potential to curtail developmental delays, constrained clinical resources and barriers to access for some populations prevent many families from obtaining these services. In response, we have developed a tablet-based ASD screening tool called Autoscreen that uses machine learning methods and a data-driven design with the ultimate goal of efficiently triaging toddlers with ASD concerns based on an engaging and non-technical administration procedure. The current paper describes the design of Autoscreen as well as a pilot evaluation to assess the feasibility of the novel approach. Preliminary results suggest the potential for robust risk classification (i.e., F1 score = 0.94), adequate levels of usability based on the System Usability Scale (M = 87.19, 100 point scale), and adequate levels of acceptability based on a novel instrument called ALFA-Q (M = 85.94, 100 point scale). These results, combined with participant feedback, will be used to improve Autoscreen prior to evaluation with the target population of toddlers with concerns for ASD.

Keywords: Autism screening · Autism Spectrum Disorder · Machine learning

1 Introduction

Autism Spectrum Disorder (ASD) is a lifelong neurodevelopmental disorder that is routinely screened for in children as young as 18 months using gold-standard clinical instruments such as the Autism Diagnostic Observation Schedule, Second Edition (ADOS-2) [1]. Early detection followed by targeted intervention has been shown to yield meaningful improvements in outcomes for individuals with ASD [2–4]. Despite the potential of early intervention to curtail developmental delays, constrained clinical resources and barriers to access for some populations prevent many families from

© Springer International Publishing AG, part of Springer Nature 2018
M. Antona and C. Stephanidis (Eds.): UAHCI 2018, LNCS 10907, pp. 560–570, 2018.
https://doi.org/10.1007/978-3-319-92049-8_41

obtaining these services [5, 6]. For example, evidence from the CDC indicates dispro-
portionate identification of ASD along racial and ethnic lines with non-Hispanic white
children being more likely to access early screening than both non-Hispanic black children (by 30%) and Hispanic children (by 50%) [7]. Even when diagnostic services are
available, constrained clinical resources can lead to substantial delays in diagnosis
resulting in lost opportunities for early intervention [8].

Attempts to address this issue of accessibility have produced a rich body of research
on approaches to clinical screening as well as commercial products for early detection.
A number of screening and diagnostic instruments have been developed, including the
Modified Checklist for Autism in Toddlers (M-CHAT; [5]), the Autism Diagnostic
Interview-Revised (ADI-R; [9]), and the previously mentioned ADOS-2 [1]. Recent
commercial products have also been developed with aims of broadening access to early
screening (e.g., Cognoa; [10]) and translating paper-based instruments to an easier-to-
use digital platform (e.g., CHADIS; [11]). While each of these solutions directly
addresses a number of the barriers to early screening and diagnosis, existing methods
may not fully optimize analytical and technological utilities that can be used to conduct
brief, simple, and accurate screening procedures for use by expert and non-expert
administrators alike.

In response to the limitations of existing approaches, we have developed a tablet-
based ASD screening tool called Autoscreen that uses machine learning (ML) methods
and a data-driven design to effectively triage toddlers with ASD concerns based on an
engaging and non-technical administration procedure. In this paper, we present the
design of the novel system as well as preliminary evaluations of usability and acceptability by expert clinicians. We hypothesized that (a) ML algorithms could be developed
to stratify risk according to binary labels with acceptable accuracy and (b) the novel
system would be judged favorably on measures of usability and acceptability. The
remainder of this paper is structured in the following manner: Sect. 2 discusses related
work, Sect. 3 details the design of the software including the user interface and analytics
modules, Sect. 4 presents the design of a preliminary evaluation of the novel application
with expert clinical users, Sect. 5 gives preliminary evaluation data, and Sect. 6 provides
a discussion of the results and concludes with a summary of the current work's contributions, limitations, and planned future work.

2   Related Work

Some of the literature has highlighted the effects of age on completion of an autism
screening test, such as the M-CHAT [5]; higher failure rates for M-CHAT tasks are more
likely to be due to developmental immaturity rather than due to the presence of ASD
symptoms [11]. Another study found that a two-tiered screening process, using both the
M-CHAT and the Screening Tool for Autism in Toddlers and Young Children (STAT),
improved early identification of young children who were at risk for ASD [12]. ML
techniques have also been used to both broaden the reach of ASD evaluation of at-risk
populations and to improve upon widely-used ASD screening and diagnostic tools [13–
15]. Specifically, the use of ML algorithms has played a great role in identifying a small

number of attributes (or "features") of the tested items in ASD screening tools, such as ADOS-2, and making diagnoses with a high degree of accuracy [13, 14]. However, when applying ML algorithms to autism diagnostics, it is necessary to avoid certain pitfalls such as assuming the ready availability of numerous features from gold-standard instruments [14]. Indeed, this was an important consideration in the current work to use ML to identify a minimal feature set.

In addition to sophisticated paper-based instruments, digital applications have been developed to assess ASD risk. The previously mentioned Child Health and Development Interactive System (CHADIS) is a web-based platform for administering commonly used paper-based screeners and assessments in a digital format to a variety of populations, such as children with ASD and adolescents with eating disorders [11]. Although CHADIS supports an extensive catalog of ASD-centric instruments, it does not have the specific focus on ASD risk assessment in toddlers based on a very brief (i.e., 10–15 min) interaction with minimal training which is available in the current work. Another related application is Cognoa which consists of a mobile application that provides a variety of screening and assessment utilities for individuals with concerns related to ASD and ADHD, among others [10]. While the technical elements of Cognoa are novel (e.g., child behavior analysis through uploaded video), like CHADIS, it may not facilitate rapid administration in constrained clinical settings. Furthermore, the availability of these tools does not guarantee uptake in clinical practices. Thus, there remains a need for a tool capable of providing ASD risk assessment in a manner that is brief, easy to learn and use, and accurate in its labelling of risk categories.

3   Autoscreen Software Design

Autoscreen, the system presented in this paper, is a tablet-based mobile application for ASD screening that uses ML algorithms to effectively separate toddlers into two categories of risk for ASD: namely, *high* and *low*. This system is designed to guide non-expert test administrators—who may be clinicians, primary care providers, or parents—through a series of play-like procedures intended to reveal characteristics of toddlers that are indicative of ASD risk. Two distinct software modules—a simple user interface and an analytics module for data processing—were designed to achieve this goal and are described in detail in Subsects. 3.1 and 3.2, respectively. The Autoscreen system was developed initially for Android devices (version 4.1 "Jelly Bean" and higher) using Unity 2017.3.0f3, a cross-platform 3D game engine, and the C♯ programming language, but Unity also supports seamless deployment to other environments including desktop operating systems.

3.1   User Interface Design

The Autoscreen system is intended to be an easy-to-use, accessible, and understandable screening tool for non-therapists or other untrained users. In order to create such a system, a wide range of design features needed to be considered, primarily application complexity, navigation, display arrangement, and intuitive interaction. The entire

Autoscreen application can be logically divided into five subsections: landing page, tutorial, screening activities, scoring form, and risk assessment. The "screening activities" subsection can be further expanded into subject information entry, materials checklist, and tasks administration. Using the application, from start to finish, is largely a linear process.

Autoscreen is intended to run primarily on mobile devices, and each of the application pages must adhere to design choices that facilitate such use. Although pages in Autoscreen may have different purposes, according to their respective subsection, they each build off of the same template (see Fig. 1). Each page displays informative features such as a descriptive header, buttons for playing audio tips, buttons for page navigation, and a navigation pane. The header and the audio tips buttons serve both to inform the user of the purpose of each page of the application and to offer an aural walkthrough of each task presented. The navigation buttons allow the user to move between neighboring pages while the navigation pane provides the user with a convenient reference to the present stage of task completion. The navigation pane is presented vertically on the left-hand side of the screen; each of the subsections is represented by a small representative

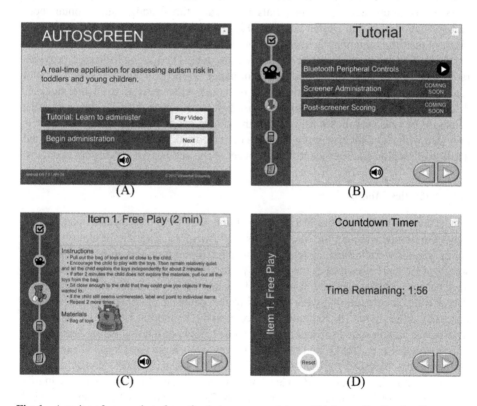

Fig. 1. A series of screenshots from the Autoscreen prototype: (A) the application landing page; (B) a page providing a list of video materials for training; (C) a page showing the instructions for a "Free Play" activity designed to elicit social behaviors over a period of two minutes; and (D) a page showing a timer associated with the "Free Play" activity.

icon. For example, a checkbox was used to represent the material checklist page, and a cinema camera was used to represent the tutorial page, which features descriptive videos.

While the aforementioned design layout is highly consistent throughout the application, each of the specific subsections make use of different features. The tutorial page features video guides on application use, where touching a specific play button icon presents the user with detailed video examples of various application functionalities. The screening activities subsection is the most intensive portion of the Autoscreen application. In the first step of screening activities, subject information is entered by the user. In an effort to make data entry on a mobile device as convenient as possible, conventional widgets such dropdown menus, radio buttons, and text fields were used. For example, the subject's date of birth is fully selectable through dropdown menus and a unique subject ID can be specified via a text field. The next stage of the screening activities process involves the material checklist. The user is provided with a list of materials that must be acquired before continuing with the tasks; relevant items include a ball, matchbox cars, dolls, and snacks. The final segment of the screening activities subsection is the task page. Tasks are defined as either one-step or two-step. One-step tasks are untimed and display instructions and materials involved in the task. Two-step tasks consist of instructions and materials, but are also timed, and, as such, contain both an information page and a timer page (see Fig. 1C and D). The timer page prominently displays the time remaining across the middle of the screen. The two final subsections are the scoring form page and the risk assessment pages. The scoring form page provides radio buttons for evaluating a child's performance on the previous tasks on a 3-point scale. The attributes on which the child is scored were derived from the analyses discussed in the next section. Finally, the risk assessment page provides the user with a summary of risk classification based on the scores entered by the user. The user is provided with a quantitative score of risk, a classified risk status (i.e., high or low), and a listing of specific qualities identified as concerns and another list identifying strengths.

3.2   Analytics Module

Autoscreen embeds machine learning algorithms that were developed outside of the Unity environment. Using the ML toolkit *scikit-learn* [16], a variety of binary classification models were trained and evaluated using a 70–30 train-test split approach. The weighted F1 score was used as the primary metric for the evaluation of model performance because, unlike accuracy, it is robust to issues arising from imbalanced data. The data used for model training were obtained from a database of clinically-verified diagnoses of toddlers (aged 18–30 months) collected at the Vanderbilt Kennedy Center. This dataset was ideally suited for supervised ML due to its high-quality feature set, labelled binary structure (i.e., "ASD" and "Non ASD"), relatively large size ($N = 737$ examples), and relatively balanced makeup (i.e., 69.74% ASD versus 30.26% Non ASD). The *features* of this dataset included codes from a variety of clinical instruments including the ADOS-2 (Toddler Module), Mullen Scales of Early Learning (MSEL), and Vineland Adaptive Behavior Scales, Second Edition (Vineland-II). As in related work [14], we chose to explore model development focusing on features derived from ADOS-2; exploration of MSEL and Vineland-II features will be pursued in future work. Analysis of

ADOS-2 codes contributed to the identification of the key dimensions of child behaviors that could potentially be teased out using short and engaging procedures designed in our novel screener.

It is important to draw a clear distinction between the features used in the ML analyses and the features ultimately used by Autoscreen in the prediction of ASD risk. The features in the ML analyses were originally derived from long, formal diagnostic interviews conducted by expert clinical administrators and it is not possible to obtain precisely equivalent features during a brief assessment. The input parameters obtained within Autoscreen, on the other hand, were designed to quantify a minimal set of characteristics indicative of ASD risk through a brief but efficient interaction. This minimal set of characteristics was selected through a process of feature selection conducted on the ADOS-2 codes using a variety of ranking methods which included information gain and the χ^2 measure of fitness. This process revealed a common subset of seven core attributes—two related to communication, two related to reciprocal social interaction, and three related to restricted and repetitive behaviors—which were used to devise the screening activities and a new set of coded attributes in Autoscreen. Using the previously described 70–30 split design, predictive models were trained using a variety of simple supervised classification models. The Naïve Bayes model using default parameters yielded the strongest performance with an F1 score of 0.94 (accuracy = 91.4%). The k-Nearest Neighbors ($k = 5$, uniformly weighted) model demonstrated comparable performance with an F1 score of 0.93 (accuracy = 91.0%), as did the Logistic Regression model using default parameters with an F1 score of 0.93 (accuracy = 90.0%). From these results, it was clear that even a simple model comprised of only a handful of features could produce a strong ASD risk classification algorithm for practical screening. However, future work will be required to properly determine the accuracy of Autoscreen's risk assessment algorithm.

4 Preliminary Evaluation of Usability and Acceptability

While accuracy of risk assessment will be critical to the success of Autoscreen, other major aspects of the application must also be carefully considered in order to maximize adoption likelihood. Two other major considerations described here are *usability* and *acceptability*. While these terms are somewhat subjective and task-specific, a wide range of researchers have found use in quantifying users' perspectives of technologies along these dimensions [17–19]. In the context of this work, usability is intended to quantify users' impressions of the general likability of the application with respect to user interface design, report content, and task presentation. The measure of acceptability, on the other hand, is intended to quantify users' attitudes concerning the appropriateness, likely effectiveness, and feasibility of the proposed application. Stated simply, usability is about the mechanics of the user experience while acceptability gets at the broader question of whether this technology will be useful in the real world. In this paper, usability is measured using the 10-item System Usability Scale (SUS) which employs a 5-point Likert-type scale [17], while acceptability is measured using a new instrument devised for this study which we have dubbed the Acceptability, Likely Effectiveness, Feasibility, and Appropriateness Questionnaire (ALFA-Q). The 10 items of the ALFA-Q were adapted from two different questionnaires from the literature on acceptability of intervention protocols; specifically, items were adapted from the Intervention Rating Profile for Teachers (IRP-15; [19, 20]) and the Treatment Acceptability Rating Form—Revised (TARF-R; [18, 21]). Although both the IRP-15 and TARF-R use a 6-point Likert-type scale, for consistency with the SUS, ALFA-Q also employs a 5-point scale with rating labels equivalent to those of the SUS. Table 1 provides the details of the ALFA-Q.

Table 1. Acceptability, likely effectiveness, feasibility, and appropriateness questionnaire (ALFA-Q)

Item no.	Item description	Derived from
1	Autoscreen would be an acceptable method for the assessment of ASD risk in toddlers (12–36 months)	IRP-15: 1 TARF-R: 2
2	Autoscreen would be an appropriate assessment for children across a spectrum of impairment (i.e., low vs. high)	IRP-15: 9
3	The problem of limited availability of assessment services is an important problem and is large enough to justify the use of Autoscreen	IRP-15: 5
4	**Clinicians** in a diagnostic or intervention setting would find Autoscreen to be an appropriate method for the assessment of ASD risk in toddlers	IRP-15: 6
5	**Primary care providers** in a community practice setting would find Autoscreen to be an appropriate method for the assessment of ASD risk in toddlers	IRP-15: 6
6	**Parents** would find Autoscreen to be an appropriate method for the assessment of ASD risk in toddlers	IRP-15: 6
7	(*Circle appropriate user category*) As a **Clinician/Primary Care Provider/Parent**, I would be willing to use Autoscreen in the **Clinical/Primary Care/Home** setting	IRP-15: 7 TARF-R: 3
8	The use of Autoscreen is unlikely to result in serious negative outcomes for the child	IRP-15: 8 TARF-R: 6, 16
9	I like the methods used in the Autoscreen application	IRP-15: 13 TARF-R: 14
10	I would recommend the use of Autoscreen to others	IRP-15: 4

ALFA-Q instructions for the user: "*Please indicate your level of agreement with the following statements by circling the number above each label that most accurately represents your opinions.*" Scoring of each item follows a 5-point Likert-type scale where 1 = "Strongly Disagree", 3 = "Neutral" and 5 = "Strongly Agree". This scheme was used to maintain consistency with the SUS.

4.1 Participants

Eight volunteers provided feedback concerning elements of usability and acceptability with regards to the Autoscreen application. Because the primary goal of this study was to identify weaknesses of the application that could be corrected prior to later evaluation with the target cohort (i.e., toddlers and screener administrators), a small convenience sample of volunteers was recruited. This sample included two individuals with expertise in ASD diagnostic procedures and six individuals without such expertise, but with at least some awareness of common diagnostic tools such as ADOS-2 or STAT. All participants provided informed consent prior to engaging in study procedures, and these procedures were approved by the university's Institutional Review Board.

4.2 Procedures

The Autoscreen application was loaded onto two ASUS ZenPad S 8.0 tablets running Android 6.0 ("Marshmallow") and a shortcut to the application was placed on the first tablets' home screens. Participants were asked to use Autoscreen to walk through the procedures of a simulated assessment. As stated above, the focus of this initial study was to identify areas for improvement with regards to measures of usability and acceptability. As such, the application was not used to evaluate ASD risk among children at this stage. Once launched, Autoscreen automatically guides the user through the steps of task administration including entry of subject information (i.e., regarding the child being assessed), assessment activities, scoring the internal form, and reviewing the system-generated risk report. After completing the task procedures, participants provided anonymous responses on both the SUS and ALFA-Q while Autoscreen internally logged user inputs and event data. Once each of the participants had completed the task procedures, the researchers compiled all of the data for analysis.

4.3 Measures

The primary study measures for this work were the composite scores of the SUS and ALFA-Q. The SUS composite score is computed on a scale ranging from 0 (i.e., lowest rating of usability) to 100 (i.e., highest rating of usability). The ALFA-Q composite score also ranges from a minimum of 0 (i.e., lowest rating of acceptability) and a maximum of 100 (i.e., highest rating of acceptability), and is computed using Eq. (1)

$$score = -25 + \frac{5}{2} \sum_{i=1}^{10} a_i \tag{1}$$

where, a_i is the value of the ith item of the ALFA-Q. Because the ALFA-Q score is introduced in this paper as an exploratory measure of acceptability, its interpretation should be considered cautiously within the context of this paper; future work is required to refine the ALFA-Q instrument. A secondary measure of interest was the task completion time because it provides an indication of the time demand of task procedures. Because a primary goal of Autoscreen is to make ASD risk screening both fast and convenient, task completion time should be as low as possible. Lastly, some participants also provided open-ended feedback, which is discussed in the following sections.

5 Results

Participant responses to survey items are given in Table 2. Responses were largely favorable on both the SUS (M = 87.19, SD = 12.28) and ALFA-Q (M = 85.94, SD = 13.02), although the variation in scores across participants suggests areas for improvement. An item-level analysis of the SUS revealed that the lowest rated item was item two, which describes the degree to which the system is "unnecessarily complex" [17]. The item with the poorest performance on the ALFA-Q was also item two, which describes the appropriateness of the application for individuals at a variety of positions on the autism spectrum, perhaps suggesting that Autoscreen—in its current form—may be best suited for comparatively higher-functioning individuals. With regards to task completion time, participants completed the entire set of administration tasks with a mean time of 8.72 min (SD = 4.16). Although promising, the reader is reminded that this represents only an approximation of a lower bound on task administration time. Participants also provided open-ended feedback with regards to aesthetic elements of the application, including content layout, button sizes, font selection, etc. The data obtained in this preliminary work will be used to improve Autoscreen prior to its evaluation with children. The reader is reminded that the results observed in this preliminary study are based on use of the application outside of the use case ultimately intended (i.e., to assess ASD risk of a child via the administration of a structured interaction). Again, the purpose of the current study was to evaluate the feasibility of the proposed system by measuring aspects of usability and acceptability.

Table 2. Participant responses on the SUS and ALFA-Q

Participant ID	SUS composite (0 to 100)	ALFA-Q composite (0 to 100)
1	82.5	97.5
2	97.5	97.5
3	67.5	75
4	95	92.5
5	70	62.5
6	95	77.5
7	95	87.5
8	95	97.5
Mean	87.19	85.94
SD	12.28	13.02

6 Discussion and Conclusion

The feasibility of Autoscreen appears to be supported by the feedback received from participants. With regards to usability, the application was rated favorably with scores on the high end of the scale (i.e., 87.19). However, this score was obtained from users who were not actively administering study procedures with a child, and thus should be interpreted conservatively. Despite this limitation, however, Autoscreen can be improved using the information obtained on the SUS; specifically, noted user concerns about system complexity can now be addressed before the application is used in actual therapist-child evaluations. Similarly, ALFA-Q scores indicate favorability of the system (i.e., 85.94), and also bring to light areas in which Autoscreen may be improved or extended. For instance, the applicability of Autoscreen across the autism spectrum may be achieved by constructing a dynamic set of assessment activities according to child ability, rather than using a one-size-fits-all approach as in the current iteration. The brevity of administration procedures (i.e., 8.72 min) is in line with our goal of delivering a 10–15 min interaction, but requires evaluation of the target population for confirmation. Additionally, open-ended feedback concerning specific UI elements—such as size, color, and style of font as well as location of buttons and text on the page—will be used to refine Autoscreen prior to evaluation with children. Future work with Autoscreen will include the evaluation of the system in a cohort of toddlers with and without concerns for ASD to gauge the accuracy of the predictive models.

References

1. Lord, C., Rutter, M., DiLavore, P., Risi, S., Gotham, K., Bishop, S.: Autism Diagnostic Observation Schedule (ADOS-2), 2nd edn. Western Psychological Corporation, Los Angeles (2012)
2. Dawson, G., Jones, E.J., Merkle, K., Venema, K., Lowy, R., Faja, S., Kamara, D., Murias, M., Greenson, J., Winter, J.: Early behavioral intervention is associated with normalized brain activity in young children with autism. J. Am. Acad. Child Adolesc. Psychiatry **51**(11), 1150–1159 (2012)
3. Dawson, G., Rogers, S., Munson, J., Smith, M., Winter, J., Greenson, J., Donaldson, A., Varley, J.: Randomized, controlled trial of an intervention for toddlers with autism: the early start denver model. Pediatrics **125**(1), e17–e23 (2010)
4. Warren, Z., McPheeters, M.L., Sathe, N., Foss-Feig, J.H., Glasser, A., Veenstra-VanderWeele, J.: A systematic review of early intensive intervention for autism spectrum disorders. Pediatrics **127**(5), e1303–e1311 (2011)
5. Robins, D.L., Casagrande, K., Barton, M., Chen, C.-M.A., Dumont-Mathieu, T., Fein, D.: Validation of the modified checklist for autism in toddlers, revised with follow-up (M-CHAT-R/F). Pediatrics **133**(1), 37–45 (2014)
6. Chlebowski, C., Robins, D.L., Barton, M.L., Fein, D.: Large-scale use of the modified checklist for autism in low-risk toddlers. Pediatrics **131**(4), e1121–e1127 (2013)
7. Baio, J.: Prevalence of autism spectrum disorders: autism and developmental disabilities monitoring network, 14 sites, United States, 2008. Morb. Mortal. Wkly. Rep. Surveill. Summ. **61**(3), 1–19 (2012). Centers for Disease Control and Prevention
8. Wiggins, L.D., Baio, J., Rice, C.: Examination of the time between first evaluation and first autism spectrum diagnosis in a population-based sample. J. Dev. Behav. Pediatr. **27**(2), S79–S87 (2006)
9. Lord, C., Rutter, M., Le Couteur, A.: Autism diagnostic interview-revised: a revised version of a diagnostic interview for caregivers of individuals with possible pervasive developmental disorders. J. Autism Dev. Disord. **24**(5), 659–685 (1994)
10. Cognoa for Child Development, Cognoa, Inc., Palo Alto, Mobile application, 30 Aug 2017
11. Sturner, R., Howard, B., Bergmann, P., Stewart, L., Afarian, T.E.: Comparison of autism screening in younger and older toddlers. J. Autism Dev. Disord. **47**, 3180–3188 (2017)

12. Rotholz, D.A., Kinsman, A.M., Lacy, K.K., Charles, J.: Improving early identification and intervention for children at risk for autism spectrum disorder. Pediatrics **139**, e20161061 (2017)
13. Bone, D., Bishop, S.L., Black, M.P., Goodwin, M.S., Lord, C., Narayanan, S.S.: Use of machine learning to improve autism screening and diagnostic instruments: effectiveness, efficiency, and multi-instrument fusion. J. Child Psychol. Psychiatry **57**(8), 927–937 (2016)
14. Bone, D., Goodwin, M.S., Black, M.P., Lee, C.-C., Audhkhasi, K., Narayanan, S.: Applying machine learning to facilitate autism diagnostics: pitfalls and promises. J. Autism Dev. Disord. **45**(5), 1121–1136 (2015)
15. Wall, D., Kosmicki, J., Deluca, T., Harstad, E., Fusaro, V.: Use of machine learning to shorten observation-based screening and diagnosis of autism. Transl. Psychiatry **2**(4), e100 (2012)
16. Pedregosa, F., Varoquaux, G., Gramfort, A., Michel, V., Thirion, B., Grisel, O., Blondel, M., Prettenhofer, P., Weiss, R., Dubourg, V.: Scikit-learn: machine learning in Python. J. Mach. Learn. Res. **12**(Oct), 2825–2830 (2011)
17. Brooke, J.: SUS-a quick and dirty usability scale. Usability Eval. Ind. **189**(194), 4–7 (1996)
18. Reimers, T.M., Lee, J.: Parental acceptability of treatments for children's hypercholesterolemia. J. Behav. Med. **14**(3), 225–239 (1991)
19. Martens, B.K., Witt, J.C., Elliott, S.N., Darveaux, D.X.: Teacher judgments concerning the acceptability of school-based interventions. Prof. Psychol.: Res. Pract. **16**(2), 191 (1985)
20. Witt, J.C., Martens, B., Elliott, S.N.: Factors affecting teachers' judgments of the acceptability of behavioral interventions: time involvement, behavior problem severity, and type of intervention. Behav. Ther. **15**(2), 204–209 (1984)
21. Kazdin, A.E.: Acceptability of alternative treatments for deviant child behavior. J. Appl. Behav. Anal. **13**(2), 259–273 (1980)

An Interactive Cognitive-Motor Training System for Children with Intellectual Disability

Caterina Senette[1(✉)], Amaury Trujillo[1], Erico Perrone[1], Stefania Bargagna[3],
Maria Claudia Buzzi[1], Marina Buzzi[1], Barbara Leporini[2], and Alice Elena Piatti[3]

[1] IIT-CNR, via G. Moruzzi 1, 56124 Pisa, Italy
{caterina.senette,amaury.trujillo,erico.perrone,claudia.buzzi,
marina.buzzi}@iit.cnr.it
[2] ISTI-CNR, via G. Moruzzi 1, 56124 Pisa, Italy
barbara.leporini@isti.cnr.it
[3] Fondazione Stella Maris, Viale del Tirreno 331, Calambrone-Pisa, Italy
{stefania.bargagna,aliceelena.piatti}@fsm.unipi.it

Abstract. It is increasingly evident that engaging in regular physical activity is important for people's health and well-being. However, physical training is still a big challenge for individuals with cognitive disabilities since it is difficult to motivate them and provide them with sustained pleasant training experiences over time. Active Video Games and Exergames may help achieve this, especially in the younger population. This paper describes an accessible Interactive Cognitive-Motor Training system (ICMT) created to encourage physical activity in children with cognitive disabilities by combining cognitive and gross motor training. The system was developed at a low cost, on top of an open source rhythm game, which has built-in support for dance pads and large video screens. The application employs user profiling in order to deliver personalized training. Performance data are recorded for further analysis to verify the training's efficacy and if needed, to tune the intervention. A pilot study showed the effectiveness of the proposed system, which by taking advantage of the positive effects of playing videogames, appears to encourage cognitively impaired people's physical activity.

Keywords: Cognitive impairment · Physical activity · Video game

1 Introduction

The term Intellectual Disability (ID) refers to a disorder that evolves during the development period and includes intellectual deficits in the three areas of conceptualization, socialization and practical abilities, as reported in the Diagnostic and Statistical manual of Mental disorder DSM-5.[1] Functional aspects of ID include: deficits in attention, memory, executive function and problem-solving other than linguistic and verbal comprehension. As confirmed in literature, some of these factors, especially executive functions that control and integrate other cognitive activities, have great impact on

---

[1] American Psychiatric Association (2013). Diagnostic and statistical manual of mental disorders (DSM-5®). American Psychiatric Pub.

© Springer International Publishing AG, part of Springer Nature 2018
M. Antona and C. Stephanidis (Eds.): UAHCI 2018, LNCS 10907, pp. 571–582, 2018.
https://doi.org/10.1007/978-3-319-92049-8_42

common tasks in daily life requiring attention, rapid motor planning process, and effective inhibition of irrelevant or inappropriate details [24]. Consequently, people with ID often have difficulty maintaining a physically active lifestyle. Moreover, many of them have very low levels of cardiovascular endurance, compared to typical peers [5]. Besides the inherent cognitive and physiological conditions of subjects with ID that limit their physical fitness, several other intrinsic and extrinsic aspects have been put forward as contributing factors. Among these we find barriers in the physical environment, lack of social and family support, lack of awareness of the positive health effects of physical exercise, lack of motivation to perform any motor activity, economic/logistic difficulties in fruition of physical intervention programs, and need for supervision, especially in cases of severe disability [7–9].

Nevertheless, increasing physical activity is even more important in the case of individuals with cognitive disabilities, since these persons tend to have more health concerns than their peers [1, 25]. Moreover, for people with a cognitive disability, inactivity could cause additional cognitive decline, isolation and worsening of the symptoms.

The project Carpet Diem aims at providing an Interactive Cognitive-Motor Training system (ICMT) that supports physical activity in children with a mild or moderate cognitive disability, by combining cognitive tasks and gross motor movements for a simultaneous co-training. Exploiting the positive results shown in literature, the study proposes a novel system to attempt to overcome some of the limitations observed in previous research. More specifically, a combination of motion monitoring, visual instructions and musical sources (properly adapted) has been utilized to propose a suitable system for cognitively impaired subjects. The methodology and the system are described herein.

The paper is organized as follows: after an overview on the related work, the proposed ICMT is described in Sect. 3. Section 4 describes a pilot test conducted with six children with mild or moderate cognitive impairment, aimed at prompting the efficacy of the system, especially in term of motivation. Conclusions and future work end the paper.

2   Related Work

In recent years, many researchers have focused on how to promote physical activity among people with ID. Most of these attempts involve encouraging a healthy lifestyle to lower their cardiovascular and diabetes risk [10, 12]. However, the main issue is to identify the best strategies for fitness intervention, since traditional techniques have been inadequate for motivating this population [9]. The best approach should be the result of a coherent, complex and coordinated series of interventions in different areas, considering the social, emotional and cognitive development of individuals as well as their areas of interest [21]. In this regard, the use of technology-enhanced interventions could be a viable option, and as such, it has been the subject of several research efforts.

For instance, Virtual Reality (VR) allows users to interact within computer-simulated environments and has been extensively used over the past decade in a variety of rehabilitation and educational interventions for people with cognitive impairment. Many studies confirm its positive effect in: (i) encouraging and motivating individuals [14]; (ii) adapting the treatment to allow personalization and control of the stimuli provided [13]; (iii) effectively enhancing the physical fitness of individuals. Unfortunately, often the use of VR appears to be impractical in a non-research context due to the need for special (and frequently expensive) equipment or extensive supervision, especially when disability symptoms are severe. Considering the potential and limitations of current research, it is a challenge to design fitness programs that: (i) improve subjects' motivation and participation, overcoming the limits of traditional interventions; (ii) make these alternatives reproducible in real-life contexts (home, school, gym) without entailing unaffordable expenses; (iii) propose early-age intervention in order to prevent the risk of obesity and diabetes, highly correlated to the population with cognitive disabilities [10, 12].

Solutions based on ICMTs are an effective and more affordable alternative to expensive VR systems. ICMT systems require participants to interact with a computer interface via gross motor movements such as stepping, receiving immediate visual feedback from the projection screen [11, 19]. For example, the use of ICMTs has been tested positively, especially for cognitive or motor-cognitive interventions, as a way to improve physical functioning in older adults with mild cognitive impairment (due to aging) to prevent falls [3, 11, 16, 17]. Results from literature show that continual training, through well-timed and directed stepping under cognitive load, improves step performance in real life [2]. Aside from being relatively inexpensive, such systems combine physical and cognitive training, allowing task-specific training of cognitive function while performing physical exercises. Several studies confirm the potential of this combination for reciprocal improvement in both cognitive and motor areas [11, 16, 22].

For these reasons, our study aims to provide an accessible ICMT system for children with cognitive disabilities to promote physical activity while improving cognitive skills, using a serious game as a motivational trigger. The system's expected benefits are motor coordination, visual-motor coordination, sustained attention, inhibition capacity, visual-space memory, equilibrium and processing speed. Incidentally, all these factors may also affect mood and the individual's general quality of life.

3   Methodology

To develop the proposed system, existing software (Stepmania) has been adapted according to the users' requirements as well as the specifics stated for the user interface. More specifically, the requirements for the motion monitoring, for the instructions as well as for the music characteristics have been identified. To design the Cognitive-Motor Training Programs, we took into account the suggestions proposed by [20]. In addition, the songs used were selected according to the desired training goals.

4   The Cognitive-Motor System

Our target group includes children expressing mild to moderate cognitive disabilities and without any motor impairment. Literature reports positive cognitive and behavioural effects of adequate physical activity beginning at a young age, when neural plasticity is especially active [18, 23]. Even with certain differences, similar and (in some cases) amplified bene-fits have also been found in children with cognitive disabilities [4, 8, 9]. The major chal-lenge in addressing this population concerns how to motivate them and obtain cooperation when proposing cognitive-motor training programs. Lotan et al. [9] highlighted the impor-tance of respecting individual preferences, proposing enjoyable activities, guaranteeing flexibility and allowing sharing of activities between peers and friends.

4.1 Key System Components

Carpet Diem provides a controlled environment for supported training enjoyed through dance using a rhythm video game, called Stepmania, an open source application.[2] The proposed system has five components:

(1) A tutor's laptop running several software tools (as described in Sect. 4.4)
(2) A dance pad where the children perform the exercises
(3) A large-size monitor where the game is shown
(4) Speakers to amplify the music (optional)
(5) A Fitbit tracker, worn by the child, to record calorie consumption during playtime.

The tutor supervises the training session via a desktop application implemented in Java that allows recording and managing the users' data, controlling Stepmania execu-tion while collecting data derived from performance of the training programs.

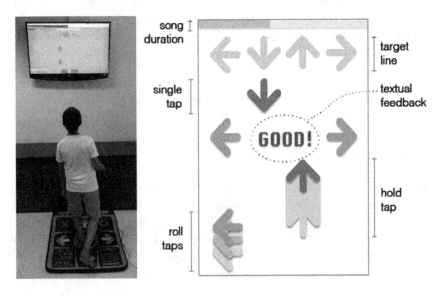

Fig. 1. (a) A room equipped with the training system, (b) game screen, detail of elements

---

[2] https://www.stepmania.com/.

The child interacts via the dance pad while looking at the monitor for game instructions. We chose dance pads with high-density foam inserts for their noiselessness, ability to absorb the shock from leg joints, and low height, avoiding the risk of falls as could occur using thicker dance mats with a metal surface.

4.2   Technical Overview of the System

The system conceptual model is depicted in Fig. 2. It includes two main components: the Stepmania Software and the Carpet Diem application.

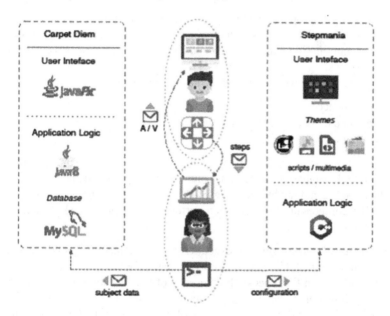

Fig. 2.   System conceptual model

Stepmania Software: An open source video game-engine, whose core source code is released under the MIT License. The application logic is made on C++ and the user interface operations are implemented through Lua[3] scripts managing different multimedia files. The game-engine is the result of an ongoing community effort, which has been involving many developers all over the world for more than 10 years. It offers several customizable options, but more advanced custom features may prove difficult to implement, since there is no official and complete documentation. Stepmania represented a good starting point to develop our project, but is greatly lacking in usability aspects, so it would have been impossible for us to use it as it is. Therefore, starting from the Stepmania source code and from a theme available online (*Moonlight* theme), we created a set of customized UIs (graphics, fonts, text strings, etc.) and automated scripts, representing the Carpet Diem theme of the game. Our main goal was to provide an

---

[3] https://www.lua.org/.

accessible and usable theme, both for therapists and for children with ID. To this end, the original Stepmania environment was modified by:

- Removing all the interface elements that were a potential source of confusion and error for the therapist who controls the system
- Removing interface elements that were unnecessary and could disturb the subject participating in the training
- Removing game-modalities that are not consistent with the current training program.

Moreover, we designed ex novo the game programs as described in Sect. 4.3

Carpet Diem: A desktop Rich Client Application built using the JavaFX 8 graphic user interface framework. We developed this application with two main goals: (i) Supervising Stepmania execution; (ii) Gathering and managing user information and collecting data from play sessions.

These goals are achieved through three key components:

a. The database access layer
b. The graphic user interface (GUI)
c. The Stepmania 5 Controller

The data access layer consists of a set of Java classes specialized in the management of a local MySQL database. Through this component, Carpet Diem manages the connection to the database and the business logic application to read and write data. Through the Controller component, the application performs two separate tasks as autonomous processor threads:

- A Starter thread that triggers the execution of Stepmania configured with the user data selected via the GUI, including the associated theme.
- A Controller thread that checks the presence of player data in order to update the database. Moreover, it can also terminate the execution of Stepmania. This thread runs in the background, but leaves a trace of its activity in the GUI, so the user can easily monitor the application. At a predefined time interval, the Controller checks whether the data file size has changed (in which case the results are read from the file and the database is updated).

Figure 3 shows a screenshot of the Carpet Diem User Interfaces during the starting phases.

Fig. 3. Carpet Diem application, screenshot

4.3 Design of Cognitive-Motor Training Programs

Stanish and Frey [20] summarized eight suggestions for motivating and engaging people with cognitive disabilities in performing physical activities:

(a) Include activities of different intensities
(b) Include strategies to motivate users and positively reinforce task completion
(c) Include fun activities and social interaction
(d) Involve participants in activity selection and decision-making
(e) Select age-appropriate activities
(f) Prefer inclusive environments considering participants' preferences
(g) Tune each activity to individual skills
(h) Consider setting goals and monitoring progress over time.

We attempted to apply all these suggestions as described in the following.

Music, especially for children and adolescents, can motivate the subject to participate in and enjoy training interventions. We used Stepmania, which encourages physical activity via music, offering a base for motivation and engagement (**b, c**).

The system enables one to define the user profile and assign the training path according to personal needs (age, intensity) and preferences (**a, e, f, g**), in order to provide simple interaction for ensuring participants' satisfaction.

The system provides automatic monitoring over time, recording users' performance data (**h**).

The Cognitive-Motor Training program consists of choreographies, i.e., steps synchronized with music tracks and guided by video instruction. Synchronism helps the player to reduce the cognitive load required to coordinate the visual component with the motor component and makes the game more fun. This element works very well in typical subjects and is the basis of the success of exergame programs, but can be a challenge for people with cognitive disabilities. For these reasons, the system implements different levels of difficulty to make the game increasingly challenging while supporting user success. Moreover, synchronism does not influence the score weight during the early training levels, but it affects the score at the advanced levels (**g**).

Song tracks were selected in collaboration with therapists in order to be suitable for the subject's age, and are quite varied in order to meet individual preferences (**e, f**). In addition, each selected track has a strong rhythm base (such as Latin American songs) in order to be easily perceived and it was elaborated in order to reduce disturbance, cut duration (all tracks are about 2 min long) and individuate the BPM (beats per minute), to associate it with the choreography. One constraint was having the BPM constant in each song to simplify the choreography's execution, helping familiarize the users with the rhythm (**a, e**). Lastly, participants were actively involved in the selection of preferred songs (**d**).

4.4   Cognitive Implications in Game Play

Actions tracked by the dance-pad are: (1) steps in the basic four directions (DX/SX/UP/DOWN); (2) holds (steps pressed for a long time) and (3) jumps (simultaneous pressing of two directional arrows). Stepmania depicts these elements on the screen through arrows of different styles (see Fig. 1b) in order to ask the user to perform them. Each element flows on the screen, forcing the player to pay attention, and the cognitive load required can be considerable.

People with intellectual disability often have difficulty sustaining attention, so our system implements choreographies involving only steps in four directions without holds or jumps. The flow of arrows on the screen defines each choreography, which was defined with the help of the project therapists. When each arrow flowing from the bottom of the screen arrives on a target arrow on the top of the screen, the player must step on the corresponding arrow of the dance-pad. Players receive feedback for each step performed (perfect, good, miss) and a final summary at the end of the song.

Levels of difficulty may increase if the user performs the choreography correctly. Each level results from the combination of two variables: how many steps per second players must perform on the target location (step execution time), and type of steps (variability between one step and the next). Specifically, for each track, four levels of difficulty (Beginner, Easy, Medium and Advanced) were identified to meet two main requirements: provide a progression flow by adapting times and difficulties to individual needs, and diversify the offer to satisfy different individuals' skills (**e, g**).

1. *Beginner:* the tracks were split into four sub-sections of about 30 s. Each one consists in repeating only one step many times (30 s step DX, 30 s step SX, 30 s step UP, 30 s step DOWN). The step execution time is sustained since the step is always the same one but repeated for a long time.

2. *Easy:* the tracks were split into five subsections of about 24 s. Each one consists in repeating a combination of two steps many times. Step execution time is sustained since step instructions are simple and repeated for a long time.
3. *Medium:* the tracks were split into subsections of different duration. Each one consists in a simple combination of steps. Step execution time is low, and the difficulty is mainly expressed by step variability (BPM/4).
4. *Advanced:* the tracks have been split into subsections of different durations. Each one consists in a more complex combination of steps with a sustained step execution time (BPM/2).

Cognitive demand on performing such types of choreographies mainly rely on executive functions, including planning and implementing strategies for performance, monitoring performance, using feedback to adjust future responses, vigilance, and inhibiting task-irrelevant information.

5 Pilot Test

In order to collect feedback and observe the interaction with real users, we tested the platform with six children (two male and four female) aged 7–10 years and expressing mild or moderate severity of intellectual disability due to different conditions such as Down Syndrome, George Syndrome, or other rare genetic diseases.

The test was carried out at the Institute of Neuropsychiatry IRCCS-Stella Maris Foundation in Pisa. The Institute of Neuropsychiatry takes care of children and adolescents expressing the main and most frequent pathologies of the nervous system and of the mind. It was our point of reference both for the collection of the training system requirements and for the preliminary verification of the prototype realized.

The test was organized to involve one child at a time in two phases to achieve two main goals: (i) collect preliminary feedback on the system's acceptability; (ii) evaluate sustainability over time.

A dedicated space was set up inside the room where children usually attend traditional therapy sessions. The children were not informed about the test but were simply invited by a therapist to perform the game. During the first phase of the test, the system was presented to each child, observing their responses to the proposed tasks. Some children accepted playing with the therapist without hesitation and waiting for instructions. They seemed involved in the game but did not really understand the existing connection between what was shown on the screen and the dance-pad. However, they tried to perform the task following the therapist's verbal instructions, properly prompted. Some other children needed more time to be cooperative. After some training, only a few children executed the proposed steps correctly, but all six users began to look at the screen to receive instructions, showing better accuracy in identifying the step to perform.

We realized, during this first phase, that: (i) The number of steps per second needed to be harmonized with the steps' variability; (ii) Certain step combinations (including the step *down*) were difficult to perform (compromising balance) due to the difficulty in mentally perceiving the dance-pad and its arrows' location.

These observations were valuable for improving the design of tasks and choreographies for the second phase, when we wished to observe how subjects reacted to a sustained demand for work, i.e., an intensive intervention session scheduled three times a week for 2 weeks. The dance-pad seemed to be highly motivating for all the users. Even when the tutor asked for a high frequency of usage, it was not perceived as an imposition nor as a repetitive and boring task. Despite the very good acceptance, intensive frequency intervention (three times a week) was difficult to propose at the clinic: often sessions were canceled or rescheduled due to unforeseen family and health problems. To resolve this issue, we plan to reproduce the training environment at home with the addition of an Internet connection to supervise the remote intervention. In this case, in order to calibrate the sequences' complexity and collect qualitative data, we also expect to use a video camera.

The 2-week study confirmed the importance of motivation and involvement in task execution during the play sessions. In similar studies involving older people needing cognitive-motor training to prevent risk of falling [3, 11, 16], personal awareness of the importance of training had a relevant role. In our target group, this key factor is lacking so finding alternatives to maximize user engagement is crucial. As suggested in literature, "compelling the persons to accept a physical activity condition without promoting (ensuring) their self-determination and independence could cause those persons considerable stress and anxiety" [6, 15]. In that sense, adapting stimuli to the subject's abilities and preferences could be the best approach to reducing stress, improving user cooperation and making the training program successful.

Moreover, environmental aspects enriching the game area could contribute to a positive overall experience. As an example: (i) the monitor where instructions are provided should be larger in order to improve user engagement; (ii) music has to be clear and clean (without distortions); (iii) additional stimuli such as different background colors associated with each song could enhance the emotional status of the subject without interfering with the main stimulus.

6   Conclusion and Future Work

This paper describes an accessible technology-enhanced environment for cognitive-motor training of subjects with intellectual disabilities. Compared to the state of the art, our contribution (i) proposes a tool suitable for an early intervention, addressing a target population of children and teenagers with mild or moderate disability; (ii) offers a low-impact (economic and technological) system reproducible in non-research contexts.

The platform is based on Stepmania, a free and freely available interactive video game, allowing a high degree of customization and integration into more complex systems such as the cognitive-motor training system described herein. The overall aim of the system is to maximize the involvement of the target population, offering physical exercise under cognitive load, and exploiting the potential of music and videogames in terms of engagement, motivation and pleasantness.

Preliminary results achieved with six children involved in the pilot test are encouraging and provide more insight into key factors for designing cognitive-motor training programs in order to motivate children with intellectual disability and ensure a pleasant experience.

In the future, we plan to carry out a 3-month user test with an improved version, involving ten subjects aged 7–14 years expressing mild to moderate cognitive disability. A pre/post cognitive-motor assessment through standardized scales to evaluate the effects of this cognitive-motor training intervention in terms of

(1) *Positive/negative influence in cognitive skills*: attention, auditory memory, spatial memory
(2) *Positive/negative influence in motor skills:* balance, coordination, speed, fluidity
(3) *Fitness measures* quantifiable with the calories burned stepping with the dance-pad compared to baseline condition would enable the analysis of the system's effectiveness.

Acknowledgments. We thank the participants in the pilot test and Fondazione Pisa, which funded the project.

References

1. Bartlo, P., Klein, P.J.: Physical activity benefits and needs in adults with intellectual disabilities: systematic review of the literature. Am. J. Intellect. Dev. Disabil. **116**(3), 220–232 (2011)
2. Brach, J.S., Van Swearingen, J.M., Perera, S., Wert, D.M., Studenski, S.: Motor learning versus standard walking exercise in older adults with subclinical gait dysfunction: a randomized clinical trial. J. Am. Geriatr. Soc. **61**, 1879–1886 (2013). https://doi.org/10.1111/jgs.12506. PMID: 24219189
3. Douglass-Bonner, A.: Exergame efficacy in clinical and non-clinical populations: a systematic review and meta-analysis. In: Medicine 2.0 Conference. JMIR Publications Inc., Toronto (2013)
4. Fedewa, A.L., Ahn, S.: The effects of physical activity and physical fitness on children's achievement and cognitive outcomes: a meta-analysis. Res. Q. Exerc. Sport **82**(3), 521–535 (2011)
5. Fernhall, B., Pitetti, K.H., Rimmer, J.H., McCubbin, J.A., Rintala, P., Miller, A.L., et al.: Cardiorespiratoy capacity of individuals with mental retardation including down syndrome. Med. Sci. Sports Exerc. **28**, 366–371 (1996)
6. Lancioni, G.E., Singh, N.N., O'Reilly, M.F., Sigafoos, J., Alberti, G., Perilli, V., Zimbaro, C., Boccasini, A., Mazzola, C., Russo, R.: Promoting physical activity in people with intellectual and multiple disabilities through a basic technology-aided program. J. Intellect. Disabil. (2016). https://doi.org/10.1177/1744629516684986
7. Lin, J.D., Lin, P.Y., Lin, L.P., Chang, Y.Y., Wu, S.R., Wu, J.L.: Physical activity and its determinants among adolescents with intellectual disabilities. Res. Dev. Disabil. **31**(1), 263–269 (2010)
8. Lotan, M., Isakov, E., Kessel, S., Merrick, J.: Physical fitness and functional ability of children with intellectual disability: effects of a short-term daily treadmill intervention. Sci. World J. **4**, 449–457 (2004)
9. Lotan, M., Henderson, C.M., Merrick, J.: Physical activity for adolescents with intellectual disability. Minerva Pediatr. **58**(3), 219–226 (2006)

10. Merom, D., Ding, D., Stamatakis, E.: Dancing participation and cardiovascular disease mortality: a pooled analysis of 11 population-based British cohorts. Am. J. Prev. Med. **50**(6), 756–760 (2016)
11. Pichierri, G., Wolf, P., Murer, K., de Bruin, E.D.: Cognitive and cognitive-motor interventions affecting physical functioning: a systematic review. BMC Geriatr. **11**(1), 29 (2011)
12. Rimmer, J.H., Yamaki, K.: Obesity and intellectual disability. Dev. Disabil. Res. Rev. **12**(1), 22–27 (2006)
13. Rizzo, A.A., Buckwalter, J.C., Van der Zaag, C.: Virtual environment application in clinical neuropsychology. In: Stanney, K. (ed.) The handbook of virtual environments, pp. 1027–1064. Erlbaum Publishing/Rogers-Wallgre, New York (2002)
14. Rizzo, A.A., Kim, G.J.: A SWOT analysis of the field of VR rehabilitation and therapy. Presence Teleoperators Virtual Environ. **14**, 119–146 (2005)
15. Russell, V.A., Zigmond, M.J., Dimatelis, J.J., Daniels, W.M., Mabandla, M.V.: The interaction between stress and exercise, and its impact on brain function. Metab. Brain Dis. **29**(2), 255–260 (2014)
16. Schoene, D., Valenzuela, T., Lord, S.R., de Bruin, E.D.: The effect of interactive cognitive-motor training in reducing fall risk in older people: a systematic review. BMC Geriatr. **14**(1), 107 (2014)
17. Schoene, D., Valenzuela, T., Toson, B., Delbaere, K., Severino, C., Garcia, J., Lord, S.R.: Interactive cognitive-motor step training improves cognitive risk factors of falling in older adults–a randomized controlled trial. PLoS ONE **10**(12), e0145161 (2015)
18. Sibley, B.A., Etnier, J.L.: The relationship between physical activity and cognition in children: a meta-analysis. Pediatr. Exerc. Sci. **15**(3), 243–256 (2003)
19. Staiano, A.E., Calvert, S.L.: Exergames for physical education courses: physical, social, and cognitive benefits. Child. Dev. Perspect. **5**, 93–98 (2011)
20. Stanish, H.I., Frey, G.C.: Promotion of physical activity in individuals with intellectual disability. salud pública de méxico **50**, s178–s184 (2008)
21. Temple, V.A.: Barriers, enjoyment, and preference for physical activity among adults with intellectual disability. Int. J. Rehabil. Res. **30**, 281–287 (2007)
22. Theill, N., Schumacher, V., Adelsberger, R., Martin, M., Jancke, L.: Effects of simultaneously performed cognitive and physical training in older adults. BMC Neurosci. **14**, 103 (2013). https://doi.org/10.1186/1471-2202-14-103. PMID: 24053148
23. Tomporowski, P.D., Davis, C.L., Miller, P.H., Naglieri, J.A.: Exercise and children's intelligence cognition and academic achievement. Educ. Psychol. Rev. **20**, 111–131 (2008)
24. Vaughan, L., Giovanello, K.: Executive function in daily life: age-related influences of executive processes on instrumental activities of daily living. Psychol. Aging **25**(2), 343 (2010)
25. Woodmansee, C., Hahne, A., Imms, C., Shields, N.: Comparing participation in physical recreation activities between children with disability and children with typical development: a secondary analysis of matched data. Res. Dev. Disabil. **49**, 268–276 (2016)

A Robot-Based Cognitive Assessment Model Based on Visual Working Memory and Attention Level

Ali Sharifara[✉], Ashwin Ramesh Babu, Akilesh Rajavenkatanarayanan,
Christopher Collander, and Fillia Makedon

Heracleia Human Centered Computing Laboratory,
Department of Computer Science and Engineering, University of Texas at Arlington,
Arlington, TX 76019, USA
{ali.sharifara,makedon}@uta.edu,
{ashwin.rameshbabu,akilesh.rajavenkatanarayanan,
christopher.collander}@mavs.uta.edu

Abstract. Vocational assessment is the process of identifying and assessing an individual's level of functioning in relation to vocational preparation. In this research, we have designed a framework to evaluate and train the visual working memory and attention level of users by using a humanoid robot and a brain headband sensor. The humanoid robot generates a sequence of colors and the user performs the task by arranging the colored blocks in the same order. In addition, a task-switching paradigm is used to switch between the tasks and colors to give a new instruction to the user by the robot. The humanoid robot displays guidance error detection information, observes the performance of users during the assessment and gives instructive feedback to them. This research describes the profile of cognitive and behavioral characteristics associated with visual working memory skills, selective attention and ways of supporting the learning needs of workers affected by this problem. Finally, the research concludes the relationships between visual working memory and attentional level during different level of the assessment.

Keywords: Human robot interaction · Visual working memory assessment
Computer vision · Sequence learning · Socially assistive robots

1 Introduction

Visual Working Memory (VWM) is considered as a limited capacity system for storing, manipulating, and utilizing, visual information, which is fundamental for many cognitive tasks or further processing [12]. It is important for reasoning and guidance of decision making and behavior. In addition, working memory helps users to hold information long enough to put the information to use. Working memory capacity is an evaluation of individual differences in the efficiency with complex cognitive functions [18]. In addition, weak working memory may affect the learning

© Springer International Publishing AG, part of Springer Nature 2018
M. Antona and C. Stephanidis (Eds.): UAHCI 2018, LNCS 10907, pp. 583–597, 2018.
https://doi.org/10.1007/978-3-319-92049-8_43

process and overall performance, especially in the work place, and may cause events resulting in injury or even death.

The human brain processes information by paying attention and reacting accordingly to all types of sensory inputs, including visual data [8]. The concept of attention is considered as a brain mechanism, which is developed to ensure that the most significant information is chosen for further processing. This selective attention is a significant process in the vision system [6]. However, with the lack of attention, the limitation of information processing capacity in the human brain stops the brain from receiving information for further processing.

Visual working memory is considered as part of the cognitive system in which memory and attention interact with each other in order to solve complicated cognition problems [18]. The challenge can be presented by sort of visual tasks of remembering the order of items. Therefore, this task provides an ideal context for studying working memory capacity to control the contents of attention.

The human brain constantly produces several electrical signals from different activities such as thinking, learning, sleeping, etc. [20]. These signals can be detected from outside of brain through several sensors [20]. Over the last few years, there has been a growth of affordable devices for electroencephalographic (EEG) recording systems and these devices allow scientists to access the raw data for research purposes [23]. MUSE is one of the devices which can detect a range of brainwave in an active manner [23]. Brainwaves are usually divided into five bands including Delta, Theta, Alpha, Beta, and Gamma waves [21]. According to Adjouadi et al., Beta waves occur when alert, actively thinking, or problem solving [1]. Using these waves can help obtain the level of attention during performing specific tasks. These sensors have been used as a complement for the assessment along with a humanoid robot.

The existence of low-cost humanoid robots allows the researchers in the robotics community to explore further research in human-robot interaction (HRI). In addition, robots are able to simulate and imitate many human functions continuously without getting tired [17]. They can observe, communicate, move, sense their environment, respond to changes, etc. In this research, we have used a humanoid robot in order to instruct, observe, and evaluate the user for the specific tasks. The reasons why a humanoid robot is used are included, but not limited to following; First, in many cases robots do not have the background of users which can affect the result of assessment and they can provide feedback unlimitedly. Second, robots are able to perform tiring and dangerous tasks. Third, robots in industry are able to work at a constant speed without breaks or delay.

The main contribution of the present research is to verify the effects of cognitive training and proving feedback during a working memory assessment in work stations by using humanoid robots. We have collected data from several sensors of the human brain as well as several parameters during the assessment including the number of errors, delay, speed, and level of attention. In addition, a survey is given to each subject which participated in the assessment to ask about their experience with the assessment and the results are provided in the results and discussion sections.

The present section provides an introduction about the visual working memory and monitoring attention assessment as well as introduction to human brain signals and the

NAO robot which have been used for this study. The following sections of the paper are dedicated to the thorough analysis and representation of the proposed application. In Sect. 2, we address the influences of related work, which had similar assessment. Section 3 introduces the hardware and sensors which have been used. Section 4 provides the game overview and includes visual working memory and monitoring attention assessments. Section 5 describes the methods which have been used to conduct this study including computer vision methods, and task switching paradigm. Section 6 discusses the experimental results. Section 7 is a discussion of the study. Finally, in Sect. 8, we provide a summary of the work that was conducted and we mention the challenges and plans for future work.

2   Related Work

Techniques developed in recent years provide a reasonable degree of choice in the nature and level of detail of the working memory assessment which are now also open to a wider range of users. One new development is that working memory problems can now been assessed indirectly, using knowledge of the workers' behavior while performing tasks.

The NAO humanoid robot is being used as an intelligent assistant for several studies and is capable of color recognition, voice recognition, and face recognition [10, 14] These Nao robots are extensively used in recent researches in the field of rehabilitation and training.

Simonov and Delconte proposed an approach where the NAO robot was used for rehabilitation training and assessment with minimal human supervision. The paper aims at providing a humanoid robot based assessment for rehabilitation such as pulmonary rehabilitation in Chronic Obstructive Pulmonary Disease (COPD) patients. The NAO robot is implemented with an automated judgment functionality to assess how the rehabilitation exercise matches the pre-programed sequence. The authors were able to achieve complete monitoring of the patients with minimal human supervision [19].

Shamsuddin et al. proposes a robot-based assessment and training for autistic children who had impaired intelligence. Authors have proved that using a humanoid robot for interaction augments their communication skills. After training the children with the NAO robot, assessments show that 4 among 5 children exhibited a decrease of autistic behavior with credits going to the human like appearance of the robot [16].

Similar research is being done to improve and assess the short term working memory over the past decades. With the improvement of technology, researchers aim to utilize them in order to increase the speed and efficiency of the assessments.

A popular research conducted by Lorenzo et al. proposed an approach for work memory assessment and response inhibition through "First person shooter" game. The game requires the players to rapidly react to fast moving objects and auditory stimuli. The working memory is assessed with two set of people, one having experience with FPS games and the other group did not. Results proved that the impulsivity and updating of the task relevant information was much higher with experienced people [4].

Similarly, Daneman and Carpenter have taken a different approach of assessing working memory capacity through reading and comprehending. With the developed system, the authors were able to prove that poor readers are less efficient that they can maintain less information in their working memory. The assessment was made with tests that involved facts retrieval, words recall and pronominal references [5].

Westerberg et al. examined the effects of working memory assessment in adults affected by stroke. Authors claim that statistically significant training effects were observed on the non-trained tests for the working memory and attention. They also claim that more than one year after stroke, systematic working memory training can significantly improve attention [22].

Belpaeme et al. proposed a multi-modal approach for child-robot interaction using NAO robot to build social bonds. Authors claim that, robot that is built to communicate with humans have greater impacts in creating bonds with the humans. The authors explain about techniques to increase the effectiveness in interaction [2].

Our proposed framework combines working memory assessment approaches with Socially Assistive Robotics (SAR) in order to evaluate cognitive function and visual working memory among users (workers) in industries to reduce or prevent death or injuries due to weakness in working memory or cognitive function.

3   Hardware and Sensors

In the following sections, the hardware and sensors which have been used for this study are described including the humanoid robot, the vision system and the brain sensing headband.

3.1   Humanoid Robot

Nao is a humanoid robot, which is developed by Aldebaran, and is used for research and education purposes [9]. NAO equipped with several sensors that it uses to sense its environment. For example, the Nao robot has sonar sensors to verify the distance of objects in its vicinity and tactile sensors on its head and body which are triggered when they get touched by a user. These sensors provided capability of communication between user and robot [9]. The Nao humanoid robot is shown in Fig. 1.

Fig. 1. Aldebaran's Nao robot is an autonomous, programmable humanoid robot.

3.2 NAO's Vision System

The vision system uses the built-in cameras in the robot. The Nao robot is equipped with two different cameras. One of them is located in the forehead (top) and the other one is located at the mouth level (bottom). The top camera scans the horizontal direction, while the bottom camera focuses on the floor. Both cameras provide 640×480 up to 960×1280 resolution at 30 frames per second [9]. For this research, the bottom camera is used in order to perform computer vision processing including object and color detection.

3.3 Brain Sensing Headband

Electroencephalogram (EEG) is one of the rich sources of information for accessing to brain electrical activities [11]. An extensive amount of research has been done using professional EEG hardware in a wide variety of contexts and applications. However, with the development of cheap, easy to use EEG hardware, using EEG as a human-computer interface for many types of applications has become plausible. There are several sensors associated with the headband for collecting EEG waves including reference, forehead, and Smart-sense Conductive Rubber ear sensors. In this research, we have used MUSE in order to measure attention level based on brain signals. The signals give the degree of attention and concentration of users while performing the assessment. The Nao robot receives these values and the feedback and training will be given to user based on the values which received from the MUSE.

4   Game Overview

A rehabilitation training requires the ability to adapt to a changed living and working environment. In order to train and evaluate workers' cognitive function in industries a robot-based assessment is designed. This assessment is implemented to evaluate the visual working memory and cognitive function of users. The game starts with an easy task and the level of difficulty of the game will be increased gradually according to users' performance. The humanoid robot observers and collects data in order to provide feedback. Feedback can be visual, verbal, and immediate. In the following section the details of assessment are provided.

4.1   Visual Working Memory Assessment

A humanoid robot is used as an instructor for a vocational assessment task. The main reason which a humanoid robot is used, is to provide visual and verbal feedback while user performing the assessment. The assessment starts with showing a random sequence of different colors for three (initial value) seconds. By passing each level to another, the level of difficulty will be increased. In addition, the assessment contains task-switching to replace a color with a different color and user needs to remember this substitution. The assessment has three levels of difficulty including easy, medium, and hard. The levels and number of each blocks which are associated to each level are provided in Table 1.

Table 1. Levels of difficulty.

Levels	Number of blocks	Difficulty level
1	2–4	Easy
2	5–6	Medium
3	7–8	Hard

The data collected during the assessment will be used in order to give feedback and decrease the level of difficulty of the game, in case a user needs more attention and concentration. As can be seen from Fig. 2, user is performing the task and Nao robot is observing to give constructive feedback during the assessment.

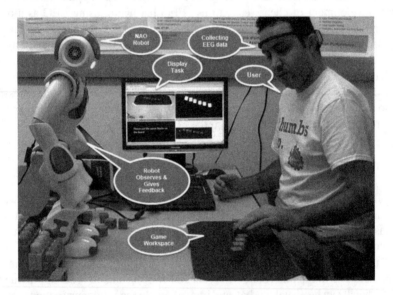

Fig. 2. Visual working memory assessment. In each level, the robot displays a sequence of colors on a monitor for 3 s and it disappears. User needs to imitate the task in front of humanoid robot and robot observes and gives feedback based on user's performance. (Color figure online)

The level of difficulty of the assessment being increased gradually based on the user's performance. If user performs well, in each level, it increases the level of difficulty by adding more blocks for the assessment. If user does not perform well, the robot encourages user by showing the blocks again and reading the order of colors to pursue the user to complete the task. The robot records the number of errors, delay, EEG data, and task completion time of the assessment for further analysis. In the following section, the methods which have been used to implement the assessment are provided.

5   Methods

5.1   Proposed Architecture

The proposed architecture contains several parts including computer vision, robot feedback, and analysis. Figure 3 illustrates the proposed system architecture.

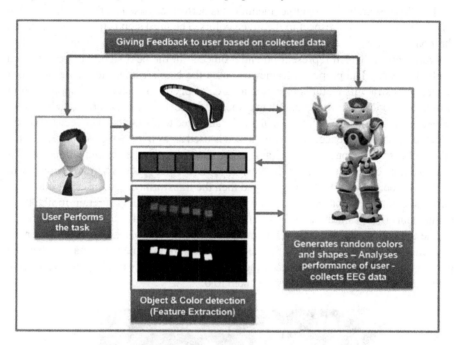

Fig. 3. Proposed architecture. Robot generates sequence of tasks and user performs the task. Robot instructs and observers the task. (Color figure online)

5.2   Task Switching

Task switching is considered as regular shifts between cognitive tasks [13]. For this purpose, several models have used to examine the brain mechanisms underlying individual differences specific to the selection of representations that use cognitive control in task switching. In this research, we have used several techniques for task switching including switching the colors during the assessment, and switching color with plain text. For instance, it may ask user to use red instead of blue for the given model. In this case, user needs to memorize and switch the colors while doing the exercise.

5.3   Computer Vision Methods

In this section, the computer vision methods which have been used in this assessment are described. The computer vision methods for the proposed framework consist of edge detection, image segmentation, object detection, and color detection. The procedure starts with edge detection. Edge detection is one of the important components in several vision systems such as object recognition and image segmentation algorithms [7]. For the edge detection purpose, Canny edge detector is used to locate the edges of the board and the objects on the board. The second method in the process is image segmentation. The main aim of image segmentation is to divide a digital image into meaningful regions [15]. In this research, the image segmentation is performed based on the pixels in region which are similar with respect to the given colors. The third step is to detect objects on the board. The goal was achieving a scalable object detection by predicting a set of bounding boxes, which represent potential objects. In the next step, a color detection method is used. The proposed framework uses the Nao's camera to capture the user model and extract its features based on an area of pixels to detect and respond to user actions. A coordinate transformation may then be deployed to detect corresponding color values from camera data, which can in turn be analyzed to distinguish between the colors of detected objects. Hence, HSV color space is used as well as histogram threshold. the HSV color space is one of the suitable color spaces for image segmentation [3]. The captured image by the camera of the robot is in RGB color space. Therefore, image will be transformed into HSV color space and then the transformed image is split into three different components based on intensity and color to obtain the histogram for the three components (hue, saturation and value). The threshold value is individually applied to all the three components. Lastly, the morphological operations are performed for the extraction of the desired region. Figure 4 illustrates an intermediary image, where all pixels classified as object (using the range in channel H already established) were set to value 255, and non-object pixels were fixed to 0.

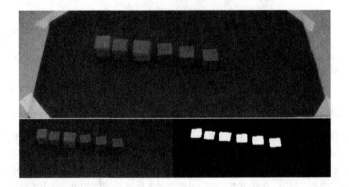

Fig. 4. User input model-in each level, robot captures the board and analyses the number and color of blocks. (Color figure online)

As can be seen from Fig. 4, there are several objects on the board, and with the aforementioned methods their types, colors and the number of objects will be obtained.

Figure 5 illustrates the method of obtaining user model as well as generating robot model. Once they have given, robot compares two models in real-time to give feedback to user. In the last level, there is color-switching paradigm. In this case, the instruction is different with normal condition. In this case, robot asks user to change certain color with another color.

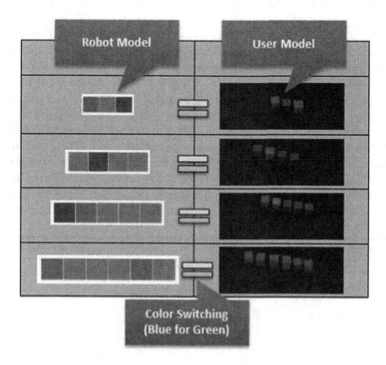

Fig. 5. Robot and user models. Two models are compared in real-time based on the number of blocks as well as their colors. (Color figure online)

5.4 Feedback Mechanism

In many cases, it is better to simplify a process than to train people to cope with the intricacy. Feedback should be considered to be a way of simplifying the interaction between the user and the robot. In this assessment, there are three different types of feedback which robot will provide based on the user performance. The feedbacks are Visual, verbal, and instant based on the design and user models. The design mode is the model created by robot and shows to user of how the order of blocks should be and the user model is the model of the system, as built up by the user during user interaction with the system. The visual feedback shows the task to user visually, meanwhile verbal feedback reads the task for user verbally after completing each level. The instant feedback alerts users immediately if they are making error or if they need to pay more attention. This feedback mainly receives the data from brain waves to alert user to avoid many mistakes due to lack of concentration.

5.5 Procedures

The procedure to evaluate and collect data from subjects received approval from The University of Texas at Arlington with reference No. IRB 2017-0563. In order to test and evaluate the accuracy of our proposed framework, we recruited 20 participants (13 males and 7 females) to perform the task in front of a humanoid robot with two different conditions for training and assessment purposes. The first condition was with error detection disabled. Users started the task without getting any feedback and the number of errors and their speed recorded for training purposes of the user. The second condition was with error detection enabled. The user needed to imitate the model which generated by robot in any step and the robot automatically detected completion status and number of errors to notify user in real-time. All twenty participants were subject to do the same task with the same condition. For each condition, the participants were asked to play the visual working memory assessment in front of a NAO robot and to put the blocks on the board based on robot models. In the following, the Pseudocode of how the assessment performs and showing how robot instructs, observes, and provides feedback.

Algorithm 1. Pseudocode for how the robot instructs, observes, and provides feedback

```
1:  procedure VISUAL WORKING MEMORY ASSESSMENT
2:    Number_of_Errors ← 0
3:    Min_Attention ← 0.1
4:    Max_Number_Blocks ← 8
5:    Init_NumBlocks ← 3
6:    Init_Level ← 1
7:  Start:
8:    Attention_Level ← Gets_From_Sensors (btwn 0 and 1)
9:    if Attention_Level < Min_Attention then
10:       goto Start
11: Assessment Process:
12:   Robot_Model ← Generates by Robot
13: Display Task:
14:   output ← Robot_Model
15:   User_Model ← obtained from user
16:   if Robot_Model <> User_Model then
17:       NumberofErrors ← NumberofErrors + 1
18:       output ← feedback
19:       goto Display Task.
20:   Init_NumBlocks ← Init_NumBlocks + 1.
21:   Init_Level ← Init_Level + 1.
22:   if (Init_NumBlocks <> Max_Number_Blocks) then
23:     goto Assessment Process
24:   End
```

---

6 Experimental Results

We used a 2×2 factorial within-subjects experimental design. The independent variables were the user's gender, environment, and user's attention level. The dependent variables were the time taken to complete the task, number of errors, ease of use, ease of understanding, ease of instruction, satisfaction, and usefulness. The task completion time, number of errors made during assessment were recorded for each level. After completion of each assessment, each participant was asked to fill out a questionnaire asking them for feedback about their experience with each condition using the questions shown in Table 2. The questionnaire consisted of 4-point Likert-Type Scale Response, with 1 indicating the most positive response and 4 indicating the most negative response.

Table 2. Survey results.

Question	Strongly agree	Agree	Uncertain	Disagree
Ease of assessment	34%	60%	0%	6%
Ease of visual feedback	45%	40%	15%	0%
Ease of verbal feedback	30%	50%	20%	0%
Ease of user interface	20%	50%	15%	15%
Ease of wearing sensors	55%	30%	15%	0%
Environment condition	50%	50%	0%	0%
Level of involvement	45%	50%	5%	0%
Ease of task-switching	35%	55%	5%	5%
Sufficient given time	25%	45%	25%	5%
Satisfy with the assessment	50%	50%	0%	0%

There are several metrics that have been measured including number of errors, attention level, and task completion time.

As can be inferred from Table 3, the mean value of attention level is higher among females when they perform a cognitive task, meanwhile the error rate among females is slightly higher than males in the same assessment. However, the difference is not significant based on attention level which is less than 0.03.

Table 3. Error rate and attention level based on gender.

Metric/gender	Male	Female
Number of errors (mean)	1.77	2
Attention level (mean)	0.65	0.68

Figures 6, 7, and 8 show the performance of three selected users. The first two figures show that if a user has a lower attention level, or it start to drop, the performance of the user will decline. This will result in a higher probability of an error occurring, especially in tasks of a higher difficulty. The third figure shows that when a user maintains a relatively high level of attention, then no errors are likely to occur.

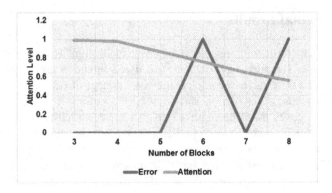

Fig. 6. The correlation between attention level and error.

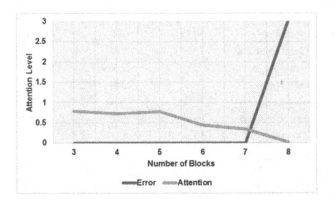

Fig. 7. The correlation between attention level and error.

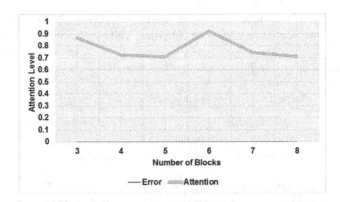

Fig. 8. The correlation between attention level and error.

Figure 9 illustrates the average attention level of each user compared to the total number of errors committed. This once again shows that users, regardless of gender, will make more errors when their attention level starts to decrease.

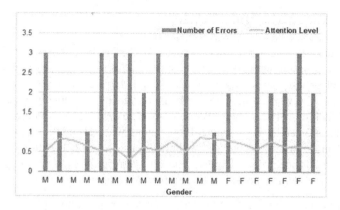

Fig. 9. The correlation between gender, attention level and error for all participants.

7 Discussion

The primary objective of this research was to assess visual working memory based on several parameters including task completion time, attention level and cognitive function, while testing visuospatial memory among workers in industries by using humanoid robots as an instructor and EEG sensors for collecting attention level. Therefore, the following predictions are made for our hypotheses:

- MH1: Participants evaluate the robot instructions as more suitable for visual feedback than verbal feedback.
- MH2: Participants evaluate the high attention level as the most suitable parameter for visual working memory assessment.
- MH3: Participants report better preference when they get encouraging and positive feedback from a robot.
- MH4: Task-switching paradigm is a challenging parameter for participants.
- MH5: Participants report that they perform better when they get more than three seconds to memorize the order of 4 to 8 blocks.

In our assessment, the results from survey suggest participants were more encouraged by getting visual feedback than verbal feedback. The results supported our first hypothesis (MH1). In addition, participants performed better when they pay more attention on a vocational assessment task, which supported our second hypothesis (MH2). The results from survey also support our third hypothesis (MH3) which proves that positive feedback encourages users during the assessment. We also can infer that color-switching increase the challenges to the assessment which supports the forth hypothesis (MH4). Finally, from the survey and results, it can be derived that as the users get more time, they perform better for visual working assessment tasks.

8   Conclusion and Future Work

Robot-Assisted tasks are increasingly being used to train and improve social skills and cognitive functions among workers in industries. In this research, we have proposed an interactive robot-based vocational assessment method in order to assess and train visual working memory of workers in industries by increasing the difficulty of the tasks at each level and switching between them. We have used computer vision methods for object and color detection and using humanoid robot along with several sensors for collecting EEG data to make interactive connection between user and robot. Future work can add more challenges to the tasks which users need to perform. Followings are some of the future work which will be considered by authors for future extension.

- Applying machine learning, particularly reinforcement learning in order to produce the process more intelligent and interactive based on the previous data which is collected from subjects.
- Applying emotion detection to capture emotions (sadness, happiness, anger, and the neutral state) during the assessment based on human face to provide better feedback.

Acknowledgments. This work is supported in part by the National Science Foundation under Grant NSF-CNS 1338118. Any opinions, findings, and conclusions or recommendations expressed in this publication are those of the author(s) and do not necessarily reflect the views of the National Science Foundation.

References

1. Adjouadi, M., Cabrerizo, M., Yaylali, I., Jayakar, P.: Interpreting EEG functional brain activity. IEEE Potentials **23**(1), 8–13 (2004)
2. Belpaeme, T., Baxter, P.E., Read, R., Wood, R., Cuayáhuitl, H., Kiefer, B., Racioppa, S., Kruijff-Korbayová, I., Athanasopoulos, G., Enescu, V., Looije, R.: Multimodal child-robot interaction: building social bonds. J. Hum. Robot Interact. **1**(2), 33–53 (2012)
3. Chang, C.H., Wang, S.C., Wang, C.C.: Vision-based cooperative simultaneous localization and tracking. In: IEEE International Conference on Robotics and Automation (ICRA), Shanghai, China, pp. 5191–5197 (2011)
4. Colzato, L.S., van den Wildenberg, W.P., Zmigrod, S., Hommel, B.: Action video gaming and cognitive control: playing first person shooter games is associated with improvement in working memory but not action inhibition. Psychol. Res. **77**(2), 234–239 (2013)
5. Daneman, M., Carpenter, P.A.: Individual differences in working memory and reading. J. Verbal Learn. Verbal Behav. **19**(4), 450–466 (1980)
6. Dobnikar, A., Lotrič, U., Šter, B. (eds.): Adaptive and Natural Computing Algorithms: 10th International Conference, ICANNGA 2011, Proceedings. Springer, Heidelberg (2011). https://doi.org/10.1007/978-3-642-20282-7
7. Dollár, P., Zitnick, C.L.: Structured forests for fast edge detection. In: Proceedings of the IEEE International Conference on Computer Vision, Sydney, Australia, pp. 1841–1848 (2013)
8. Hamadicharef, B., Zhang, H., Guan, C., Wang, C., Phua, K.S., Tee, K.P., Ang, K.K.: Learning EEG-based spectral-spatial patterns for attention level measurement. In: IEEE International Symposium Circuits and Systems, ISCAS 2009, pp. 1465–1468. IEEE, Vancouver, May 2009

9. Hu, Y., Sirlantzis, K., Howells, G., Ragot, N., Rodríguez, P.: An online background subtraction algorithm deployed on a NAO humanoid robot based monitoring system. Robot. Auton. Syst. **85**, 37–47 (2016)
10. Ismail, L., Shamsuddin, S., Yussof, H., Hashim, H., Bahari, S., Jaafar, A., Zahari, I.: Face detection technique of Humanoid Robot NAO for application in robotic assistive therapy. In: IEEE International Conference on Control System, Computing and Engineering (ICCSCE), pp. 517–521. IEEE, Penang (2011)
11. Lay-Ekuakille, A., Vergallo, P., Griffo, G., Conversano, F., Casciaro, S., Urooj, S., Bhateja, V., Trabacca, A.: Entropy index in quantitative EEG measurement for diagnosis accuracy. IEEE Trans. Instrum. Meas. **63**(6), 1440–1450 (2014)
12. Mance, I., Vogel, E.K.: Visual working memory. Wiley Interdisc. Rev. Cogn. Sci. **4**(2), 179–190 (2013)
13. Monsell, S.: Task switching. Trends Cogn. Sci. **7**(3), 134–140 (2003)
14. Nguyen, T.L., Boukezzoula, R., Coquin, D., Benoit, E., Perrin, S.: Interaction between humans, NAO robot and multiple cameras for colored objects recognition using information fusion. In: 8th International Conference on Human System Interactions (HSI), pp. 322–328. IEEE, Warsaw, June 2015
15. Roy, P., Goswami, S., Chakraborty, S., Azar, A.T., Dey, N.: Image segmentation using rough set theory: a review. Int. J. Rough Sets Data Anal. (IJRSDA) **1**(2), 62–74 (2014)
16. Shamsuddin, S., Yussof, H., Ismail, L.I., Mohamed, S., Hanapiah, F.A., Zahari, N.I.: Humanoid robot NAO interacting with autistic children of moderately impaired intelligence to augment communication skills. Procedia Eng. **41**, 1533–1538 (2012)
17. Shamsuddin, S., Yussof, H., Miskam, M.A., Hamid, A.C., Malik, N.A., Hashim, H.: Humanoid robot NAO as HRI mediator to teach emotions using game-centered approach for children with autism. In: HRI 2013 Workshop on Applications for Emotional Robots (2013)
18. Shipstead, Z., Harrison, T.L., Engle, R.W.: Working memory capacity and the scope and control of attention. Atten. Percept. Psychophys. **77**(6), 1863–1880 (2015)
19. Simonov, M., Delconte, G.: Humanoid assessing rehabilitative exercises. Methods Inf. Med. **54**(2), 114–121 (2015)
20. Sousa, D.A.: How the Brain Learns. Corwin Press, Thousand Oaks (2016)
21. Veniero, D., Vossen, A., Gross, J., Thut, G.: Lasting EEG/MEG aftereffects of rhythmic transcranial brain stimulation: level of control over oscillatory network activity. Front. Cell. Neurosci. **9**, 477 (2015)
22. Westerberg, H., Jacobaeus, H., Hirvikoski, T., Clevberger, P., Östensson, M.L., Bartfai, A., Klingberg, T.: Computerized working memory training after stroke–a pilot study. Brain Inj. **21**(1), 21–29 (2007)
23. Wiechert, G., Triff, M., Liu, Z., Yin, Z., Zhao, S., Zhong, Z., Lingras, P.: Evolutionary semi-supervised rough categorization of brain signals from a wearable headband. In: 2016 IEEE Congress on Evolutionary Computation (CEC), pp. 3131–3138. IEEE, Vancouver (2016)

Effects of E-Games on the Development of Saudi Children with Attention Deficit Hyperactivity Disorder Cognitively, Behaviourally and Socially: An Experimental Study

Doaa Sinnari[1]([⊠]), Paul Krause[1], and Maysoon Abulkhair[2]

[1] Faculty of Engineering and Physical Sciences, University of Surrey,
Guildford, UK
{d.sinnari,p.krause}@surrey.ac.uk
[2] Information Technology Department, King Abdulaziz University (KAU),
Jeddah, Kingdom of Saudi Arabia
mabualkhair@kau.edu.sa

Abstract. Attention Deficit Hyperactivity Disorder (ADHD) is a set of behavioural characteristics disorder, such as inattentiveness, hyperactivity and/or impulsiveness. It can affect people with different intelligent abilities, and it may affect their academic performance, social skills and generally, their lives. Usually, symptoms are not clearly recognized until the child enters school, most cases are identified between the ages 6 to 12. In the kingdom of Saudi Arabia (KSA), ADHD is a widely spread disorder among young children. Usually, they suffer from distraction and lack of focus, and hyperactivity, which reduce their academic achievements. As technology have been used in classrooms to facilitate the information delivery for students, and to make learning fun; some of these technologies have actually been applied in many schools in KSA with normal students, but unfortunately no studies were reported by the time of writing this paper. Specifically, there are no studies done for using any type of technology to help Saudi students with ADHD reaching up their peers academically. Because of that, our focus in this study is to investigate the effect of using technology, particularly e-games, to improve Saudi children with ADHD cognitively, behaviourally and socially. As well as evaluating the interaction between those children with the game interface. Thus, the investigation done through exploring the interaction of web-based games that runs on Tablets. The respondents are 17 ADHD children aged from 6–12 in classroom settings. The study involves focussing on interface of the games stimulate different executive functions in the brain, which is responsible for the most important cognitive capacities, such as: Sustained Attention, Working Memory, and Speed of Processing. Ethnographic method of research was used, which involved observing students' behaviour in classroom, to gather information and feedback about their interaction with the application. National Institutes of Health (NIH) tests were used in pre- and post- intervention to measure improvements in attention, processing speed and working memory. Students' test scores of main school subjects were taken pre- and post-intervention to measure enhancement in academic performance. Results show that using the application significantly improve

© Springer International Publishing AG, part of Springer Nature 2018
M. Antona and C. Stephanidis (Eds.): UAHCI 2018, LNCS 10907, pp. 598–612, 2018.
https://doi.org/10.1007/978-3-319-92049-8_44

cognitive capacities for participants, which affected their academic grades in Math, English and Science, as well as its positive influence on their behaviour. In addition, the application's interface was found easy to use and subjectively pleasing. As a conclusion, the application considered effective and usable.

Keywords: ADHD · Cognition · HCI · Interactive · Games

1 Introduction

The first thing that parents think about when their child reach the age of understanding is searching for an educational institute that develops his/her knowledge and cognition so he/she can enjoy a bright and a successful future. They start their search by looking for a school that have a good reputation, with qualified teachers who have excellent educational experience in delivering information and skills development. Highly qualified teachers can identify the different levels of their students and classify them based on their understanding of the curriculum, through observation and assessment. In fact some of the students have learning issues that might affect their overall academic progresses and achievements.

Some of the issues that students could suffer from are caused by a behavioural condition called Attention Deficit Hyperactivity Disorder (ADHD). In simple words, the child with ADHD is hyperactive and sometimes impulsive; additionally he/she has attention problems, disorganized, and faces difficulties in finishing tasks. These symptoms could be reflected at school as difficulty in managing impulsive manners, not paying attention to teachers in classroom, poor skills in mathematics, and may struggle in reading [23]. ADHD was discovered a long time ago, but now it becomes easier to recognize on individual cases because of the awareness of some teachers and parents about it. We can say that it is widely spread among students especially from pre-school until 12th grade; this is supported by the findings of the American Psychiatric Association (APA) that acknowledges seven percent of school students are diagnosed with ADHD [13].

In school environment, the teacher has a significant role in recognizing the students with ADHD symptoms. On the other hand, teachers must be equipped with the knowledge for dealing with ADHD students using the best ways and strategies; to ensure providing those students with equal learning chances. It is recommended for teachers to improve their teaching/instructional methods as well as using different kinds of interventions for children with ADHD. Also, using certain methods for attracting their ADHD students' attention such as sounds, bright colours, animations, or images. Stimulate teamwork, theatrical presentations, choice making, peer tutoring, and create competition among students through contests and other creative methods [15].

In the last ten years, and with the advance utilization of technology in our daily life, schools and educational institutions introduced the latest technology in their educational systems as effective tools to assist in the academic development of their students. Laboratories are equipped with computers and devices, classrooms have been updated to include technical tools and devices to assist delivering information in an interesting way. Students uses different applications to understand mathematical problems, to produce creative short movies, to organize agenda and much more [16].

Some teachers and researchers admitted handheld devices and mobile phones to the classroom as new type of technological tools, which have proved their effectiveness in the development of skills of the average student. This came right after the emergence of several free and paid applications and games, some are educational and some are just for fun. The use of mobile devices and tablets in education allows students to access the information at any time and any place. Now, the teacher is no more the central source inside the classroom, instead he/she became the supervisor and the assistant in this open-source technical context [7].

It is good to utilize these technologies for ADHD students to improve some of their deficiencies, and to be a replacement of traditional strategies and interventions [6, 11, 17]. Few researches have been done in investigating the use of technologies and applications such as computer based games to improve ADHD students' academic performance. Additionally, more research should be done to explore whether the computer games could develop their skills, and solve some of the behavioural and cognitive problems for ADHD diagnosed children.

1.1   Statement of Purpose

In the kingdom of Saudi Arabia (KSA), ADHD is a widely spread disorder among young children, between the ages 6–12 years. Usually, they suffer from distraction, lack of focus, and hyperactivity, which put them back academically. They do not fully understand the lessons, due to lack of attention, but not because a mental illness. ADHD students are a little bit slower in delivering tasks on time than normal students; thus they can be frustrated to their teachers and parents.

Many suggested educational interventions and traditional approaches were applied in classrooms by educators, as we will demonstrate in literature. Even medical treatments are not desirable any more by parents. No denial of the positive effectiveness and improvement of some of these methods on the overall academic level of ADHD child, no recovery will be made rather than a smart way to let the child be more involved in class and to be more organized.

Now, technologies are considered an integral part of anyone life, especially children; they always use them whether they watch their favourite shows on TV, or play one of the entertaining or educational games on handheld devices. Many studies had brought the use of technology in classrooms [4, 5, 22]; to facilitate the delivery of information for students, to prompt collaboration among students with each other, and to make learning fun. Several types of technologies used to enhance and facilitate the educational process, such as the use of electronic boards, data display devices, speakers and microphones, teaching and learning applications using smart devices etc.

Some of these technologies were actually been applied in many schools in KSA with normal students, but unfortunately no studies were reported by the time of writing this paper. Specifically, there are no studies done for using any type of technology to help ADHD students, in KSA, to reach up their peers academically. Existing ADHD applications and games must be investigated, to verify their effectiveness toward improving disordered children.

The contributions of this work are as follows: (1) we investigated the effectiveness of an e-game, using tablets, on ADHD students; regarding improvement in their abilities and skills, (2) as well as evaluated the usability, acceptability and adaptability of the game interface by observing children's behaviour while interacting with the game.

2 Related Work

Media, such as TV, movies, cartoons, video recordings, internet and games, has its major influence on the learning and behaviour of children [1]. So, an inactive environment may be unbearable for children who are hyperactive. In fact, children find it hard to sit still for a short period of time in classroom, and they involve in activities that demand listening and thinking [16]. Because of that, it is essential to incorporate technology in the learning process to grasp children attention, thus it will be reflected on their achievements. In our study we focus on the effect of using tools and games; to improve some of the weaknesses associated with ADHD disorder. Follows a review from literature on some of the tools, applications, and games that could help in the improvement of children with ADHD.

2.1 Tablets

Touch screen devices, or so called tablets, are powerful portable technologies that have been used recently in many fields, especially in learning. In the last few years, tablets were, and still, considered as productive learning tools used inside and outside school settings to assist education. They provide innovative use and direct access to a fortune of many resources. Many educational applications (apps) were developed with the help of teachers and educators for the transformation of learning [7].

One of the main benefits of tablets is that they support learning anywhere, anytime; that changes the traditional concept where the classroom is the essential learning place controlled by the teacher instructions during a typical school day [7]. These devices offer users an access to a wider and more variable source of learning resources and knowledge than what is offered in ordinary classrooms.

Many studies have proven the benefit of using tablets, such as the "iPad", in enhancing the learning procedure inside and outside school, in fact, these studies suggest to consider this technology not just as an "educational tool" rather than a "cognitive tool" [7]. They also provided the evidence that using iPads in classroom, by students, to improve engagement and enthusiasm, enhance collaboration and one-to-one tutoring, and improve learning outcome. For instance, a study by Wrońska [25], has verified that using an iPad-based tool helped ADHD students with reading comprehension. In this study, the iPad was selected to be used as the "tool" of experiment, owing to its "significant and very positive impact on learning" [8].

2.2 Applications and Games for ADHD

Most adults and even children find it very easy to download any application, from the App Store, on their tablets or mobile devices, by a single touch on the screen. Applications, such as games, health tracking, news, social media, educational and other different categories, are considered now as essential needs of daily life. Over 3 million apps, for iOS (iPhone operating system) and android systems, are available to download in leading App Stores such as Apple and Google play, as published in the Statistics Portal in July 2015 [21]. Many applications were adopted in schools and institutions that provide educational tools and skills development, most of these apps are classified as 'Education' in the iTunes App Store [20]. Lots of developing companies are tending to design usable and effective educational applications, with taking into account certain design features that support diverse learners' needs, even for students who have different learning experience either with disabilities or disorders [18].

Recently, technological tools via educational applications are integrated into school programs, by researchers and curriculum developers, to help students of all capabilities overcome learning obstacles, especially students with certain disorders and needs. Many applications have been found useful in facilitating the student's school day and organizing his daily life [18]. Students with ADHD constantly need to be reminded, notified, instructed multiple of times; so, using alarm applications, for instance, would be helpful [9, 14]. Other applications and games were found to enhance the students' academic level and develop some of their skills. After reviewing literature, Table 1 list some of the most popular applications and games used by children diagnosed with ADHD [3, 12, 17, 19, 24];

Table 1. Tablet applications for ADHD children from reviewed literature

Name of App	Type	Description
Homeroutines Alarmed-reminder timers inClass My Homework	Time Management	Create checklists Set alarm Reminders Notifications
Audio-notes recorder Event Countdown Audio note recorder-notepad Dragon Dictation Speak It To Me Talkulator Voice Dream Reader	Audio Application	Record notes Voice recognition Talking calculator Reading lists
Evernote Notability Knowtes MindNode	Note Taking Apps	Take notes and photos, generate to-do lists Record vocal reminders Support handwriting Word processing Document translator A drawing tool
iearnedthat-lite ireward	Behavioral Apps	Reinforce positive behaviors using visual rewards Develop desirable behaviors by working towards tangible goals

(*continued*)

Table 1. (*continued*)

Name of App	Type	Description
TooLoud Too Noisy Kibits Collaboration Show Me	Classroom Apps	Monitor classroom noise level Graphical presentations of the background noise level in a room in an exciting and engaging way Createcollaboration rooms share media Turn your iPad into interactive whiteboard
Mathtopia+ iWriteWords LetterForms	Math and Handwriting Apps	Math game Handwriting exercises
Play Attention SmartBrain Technologies ADHD Kids Trainer KAPEAN Lumosity ACTIVE TARLAN	Cognitive, Executive Functions Applications (games)	Neurofeedback technology that allow you to control the computer by mind/attention alone using tools such as helmets – Improving Student Attention – Enhancing Academic Skills – enhance social skills

Serious games such as Play Attention, KAPEAN, Lumosity, TARLAN, and ACTIVATE have been found effective by researchers [3, 12, 17, 19, 24]. They provide mini games, with attractive animations and sounds, which train different parts of the brain. By experiment, researchers found significant improvements in one or more executive function(s) such as attention, behavioural skills, as well as social skills. In addition, these improvements had a great impact on the academic levels of these children [3, 12, 17, 19, 24].

So, after revising some of the applications and games with their assumed purposes, we selected ACTIVATE to be the instrument to study the interaction effect for ADHD designed applications to improve the cognitive, behavioural and social abilities and skills of ADHD children specifically in Saudi Arabia. We selected ACTIVATE since it is suitable for targeted young children with ADHD. In addition, it targets the eight core cognitive capacities, essentially: Sustained Attention, Working Memory, and Speed of Information Processing. Thus, our focus in this study is to investigate the effect of using technology, particularly e-games such as ACTIVATE, to improve Saudi children with ADHD cognitively, behaviourally and socially. A more detail about the selected instrument will be presented in the next section.

3   Methodology

Our goal is to investigate the user interface for e-games that could be used by young children with ADHD at school to increase their attention, processing speed, working memory and control their hyperactivity. The web based instrument was selected to be run on iPad devices by ADHD diagnosed children aged from 6–12 in a classroom settings. Details about measures used, participants, instruments/software specifications, and the experiment method will be discussed in following sections.

3.1 Measures

Data was gathered from five sources: Conner's rating scale, teachers and parents interviews, observations and notes taking during the experiment, short talks with the participants after each session and after finishing the experiment, and finally, gathered data by the system itself such as: error rate, duration, scores, etc.

Conner's rating scale was used in this study, by the researcher, to measure the child's behaviour and habits as a preliminary screening for ADHD. Not only does this help to diagnose children who otherwise may have been overlooked, but it also offers a point of comparison for those who do suffer from ADHD [10].

Teachers' and parents' interviews were done at various stages. In the beginning, teachers' interviews helped in selecting the proper participants for our experiment, by pointing those who have some attention or hyperactivity problems within class, (we must mention that severe learning difficulties cases are excluded from this study owing to concentrating on ADHD symptoms only). After that other interviews with same teachers gradually took place to sense any improvements in their behaviour and academic performance during regular classes. Regarding parents' interviews, nearly all of them were done through phone, but we were fortunate to meet some of the mothers at schools. General information was collected, about the student's behaviour, their social skills, whether diagnose with ADHD or not, any medications etc. Later on, couple of interviews were done to see if the student was positively affected by the application, and whether the parents sensed any enhancements in their daughter's life. Feedback from interviews was very supportive and beneficial for this study, it added value to the outcomes.

During testing sessions, the researcher tried not to interact with students unless there were any technical problems or any difficult query from any student, also it was necessary to maintain control in class due to their movements and loud voices. Ethnographical method was used as our quantitative measure, observations and note-taking took place for each participant as a separate case. The researcher documented their conversations during playing with games, their most important reactions and attitudes, problems they faced, the way they helped each other, their hand movements and gestures, and their opinions and judgments about the games. The study analysis included qualitative measures as well. The National Institutes of Health (NIH) have recommended to measure the amount of enhancement in cognitive skills for each student using the NIH toolbox [24]. It was used to gather data about the students' improvements during the experiment. Pre-tests were taken before using the application, and post-tests after finishing the required sessions. Finally, the application generates four individual reports for each participant during the whole experiments. Each presents numerical and statistical data about the level reached, errors done, correct and wrong clicks, time for reaction and the progress of each executive function. These reports were very helpful in analysing and evaluating the interaction. In addition it highlights the points of strengths and weaknesses for each participant, as well as listing some of the effective teaching tips, for each case, to be passed to their teachers.

3.2 Participants

The intervention took place in classroom settings by a group of female students aged between 6 and 12 years old. It is important to indicate that the nature of KSA environment separates males from female, due to culture and tradition custom, in some organizations, including educational. Because of that, as a female researcher, the possible and easy choice was to work with female students.

For our case studies, two international schools approved to participate in the experiment. The researcher intentionally selected international schools due to the interface language for ACTIVATE, which is English. A survey was distributed among the parents that contained Conner's scale to assess ADHD. The goal was to initially discover if there were signs for ADHD to those whom are not yet diagnosed, and also to detect if there were actually diagnosed ADHD cases. After detecting students with ADHD symptoms, a consent forms were sent to their parents explaining the application, its assumed benefit, sessions timing and how long the experiment will take. Eventually 17 families signed and agreed for their daughters to participate. So 17 students enrolled, out of 25 who are identified to have signs of ADHD but choose not to participate in the experiment, due to family restrains. For Ethical reasons and anonymity, codes were used instead of their real names. The first school was Al-Hammra international school – English sector, six students participated, one student from the 1st grade (Std 1H), three from 2nd grade (Std 2LB, Std 3K, Std 4LW), one from 3rd grade (Std 5T), and one from the 4th (Std 6M). The second school was Al-Bayan model school – English sector, eleven students participated, one student from the 4th grade (Std 17LH), four from the 5th grade (Std 7JN, Std 8LN, Std 9LS, Std 10JR), and six from the 6th grade (Std 11RG, Std 12I, Std 13RL, Std 14T, Std 15D, Std 16RF). Background information on participants is listed in Table 2.

The ADHD Type for each case was diagnosed depending on the most noticeable symptoms and signs which were observed frequently by teachers and parents, and by using DSM-IV-TR criteria for ADHD [2]. The participants were seated together in a classroom, each with an iPad, with an encouragement to think aloud.

Table 2. Background information on participants

Student	Age year	ADHD type	Any medication
Std 1H	6	Inattentive	No
Std 2LB	7	Inattentive	No
Std 3K	7	Inattentive	Yes
Std 4LW	7	Combined	No
Std 5T	8	Inattentive	No
Std 6M	9	Hyperactivity	No
Std 7JN	10	Combined	No

(continued)

Table 2. (*continued*)

Student	Age year	ADHD type	Any medication
Std 8LN	11	Hyperactivity	No
Std 9LS	10	Hyperactivity	No
Std 10JR	10	Combined	No
Std 11RG	12	Inattentive	No
Std 12I	11	Inattentive	No
Std 13RL	12	Inattentive	No
Std 14T	11	Hyperactivity	No
Std 15D	11	Hyperactivity	No
Std 16RF	12	Combined	No
Std 17LH	9	Combined	No

3.3   Instrument Interface Specification

ACTIVATE is a web-based application that provide certain brain-training exercises for children with ADHD to enhance and develop their learning skills in classroom settings. The research presented in [24] identified the executive functions, which is divided into eight core cognitive capacity: Sustained Attention, Working Memory, Speed of Information Processing, Response Inhibition, Cognitive Flexibility, Category Formation, Pattern Formation, and Multiple Simultaneous Attention. These capacities can be strengthen, in children with ADHD, by stimulating them through the system. The application has three portals: teacher, student, and test portals [24].

The educator can manage his students with their accounts through the Teacher Portal. Monitoring their scores in games and progress, their error rate and response speed. In addition, the teacher can compare tests results of each student to measure improvements. Finally, the system generates reports for student which gives details about their strength and weakness, and how much they improved since they begin using the application.

The Student Portal contains six games that target eight cognitive skills necessary for executive functions. The games train the student's ability to move between different tasks, remember sequences, classify items, and reinforce thinking strategies. The games' theme is about being in an island that been discovered by Captain Blue feather and his crew, the student must help them complete levels and collect scores. The Captain introduces each game and gives audio instructions, to help students to understand their tasks. These tasks range from feeding the crew, categorizing items, helping animals and more. Figure 1 represent sample of games offered to students. Each game have hundreds of challenging levels, students are allowed to play each game within five minutes only, four or six games per session according to session timing.

Fig. 1. Sample games in ACTIVATE application

In the Test Portal, students undertake three tests pre- and post- the intervention, which are recommended from the National Institutes of Health (NIH), to measure the amount of enhancement in cognitive skills for each student. These tests are done by each participant at the beginning and the end of the training program. The NIH toolbox contains Flanker Task Test, Working Memory Test, and Go/No-Go Test. These kind of assessments can help teachers to measure the amount of cognitive growth in real-time data, and analysis the amount of success, that effected the academic future of students.

3.4   Method

In day one, first session, students logged in the test portal and done all three tests to measure their cognitive levels before the intervention. In the next session, they start playing with the games. The target was to complete one thousand minutes of playing, each class must stick to a training schedule of exercise sessions, twenty or thirty minutes per session, from three to five times a week. The schedule was flexible and could be simply modified to meet the demands of any school. The sessions start easy and short to sustain students' enthusiasm, then gradually begin to increase the difficulty level. However, the level of difficulty is set up or down every ten to fifteen seconds to meet the student's abilities based on their error rate, reaction time, and accuracy. Each student pick up an iPad, login their accounts, and start playing one of the six games. The students could play four to six games depending on time provided. The application then automatically terminate the sessions when time is up. There is an animated timer for students to track time. Instant feedback in both wrong and right answers. Colours, sounds, animated objects, all these features were motivating and stimulating the students while playing.

After the intervention, approximately four months later, the students logged in the test portal again to redo the three tests to measure the improvements gained. As mentioned before, pre- and post- intervention subjects' scores were collected from teachers to measure enhancement in the academic performance.

4   Results and Discussion

Our main objective was to evaluate the effectiveness of game-based technology developed to help ADHD students to overcome their attention, processing problems, and to trigger their cognitive capacities. Follows a discussion of the quantitative results, generated by the system and NIH tests, as well as the qualitative findings from the researcher observations.

4.1   Measuring Improvements

Throughout testing, the system generates quantitative data that help in detecting the average of development in cognitive capacities for each student. Table 3 demonstrates each student's improvement in the eight core cognitive capacities throughout the whole testing period.

Table 3. Improvement averages in cognitive capacities of participants

Core cognitive capacities							
Participants	Sustained attention	Response inhibition	Speed of processing	Cognitive flexibility	Working memory	Formation and use	Pattern recognition
Std 1H	7%	30%	33%	0	0	0	31%
Std 2LB	12%	26%	54%	30%	10%	0	0
Std 3K	18%	0	7%	19%	37%	0	33%
Std 4LW	12%	14%	54%	19%	60%	0	0
Std 5T	25%	80%	16%	0	7%	0	0
Std 6M	25%	40%	31%	60%	10%	0	0
Std 7JN	32%	7%	28%	83%	0	0	39%
Std 8LN	35%	64%	80%	42%	0	0	66%
Std 9LS	22%	39%	85%	42%	0	0	66%
Std 10JR	60%	0	70%	42%	7%	50%	66%
Std11RG	70%	47%	39%	29%	7%	0	0
Std 12I	34%	4%	24%	42%	0	0	0
Std 13RL	15%	0	55%	42%	0	64%	20%
Std 14T	9%	29%	68%	22%	0	98%	80%
Std 15D	25%	23%	71%	15%	0	0	88%
Std 16RF	15%	29%	55%	42%	0	0	51%
Std 17LH	25%	0	55%	42%	7%	23%	0

Cognitive capacities marked by zero "0" could not be calculated, as the student did not reach the required level in the games. In fact, all participants got zero "0" in cognitive capacity called "Multiple Simultaneous Attention", which is eliminated from table, due to unreached required levels; In normal children, we could see how difficult for them to do multiple things in the same time, so in contrast, it is harder for ADHD children to concentrate on one thing rather than multiple things.

Furthermore, it is obvious, from the results presented in Table 3, that students have improved in the main cognitive capacities such as: sustain attention, processing speed and cognitive flexibility. However, the average of improvement varies between students due to severity of impairments, in addition, it is said to be an improvement even if it was a slightly increase in measurements [24].

By looking at the percentages presented in Table 3, for instance: Std 3K is slow in terms of processing tasks (speed of processing 7%), with lack in focus (sustain attention 18%). Furthermore, when a subject is changed she seems to be stuck in the previous subject (low cognitive flexibility 19%), but on the other hand, she has a very good memory (working memory 37%) and she is good in guessing and figuring things out (pattern recognition 33%).

The least beneficiary from the intervention was (Std 1H), even though she gets the minimum improvement percentages, but her progress was noticeable by her teachers and parents. Other teachers were impressed by her good marks and unusual focusing in the class. Her attention and concentration has improved 7% than before, her speed of processing also improved 33%; she thinks and replies faster now. Also, she enhanced in math by 33% (in pattern recognition).

Another student, (Std 9LS), improved her attention by 22%, she got the highest improvement in processing speed (85%), her teacher acknowledged that she understands better and faster. Her mother noticed that she is more organized in studying than before, and generally in her life, not surprising, her cognitive flexibility has improved 42%.

(Std 10JR) was the perfect model of this experiment, she has transformed from a very hyperactive inattentive student to a better student in all standards. Teacher complained earlier about her uncontrollable behaviour in class, she moves a lot, her low academic level, unorganized, impulsive with her friends, and she does not focus at all. The results showed that after four months of using the brain training games, she is 60% more focus and calm, has enhanced in language and math (formation and use 50%, pattern recognition 66%). she understands and do what she is asked to do immediately (processing speed 70%).

Overall, the improvements in cognitive capacities for all students were remarkable. By calculating the averages, we found that sustain attention has improved by 23%, response inhabitation by 28%, speed of processing by 49%, and cognitive flexibility by 38%. The capacities will continue to improve as long as students continue to play. Actually, a lot of parents have asked on behalf of their daughters to continue using the brain training system due to the notable changes they have touched in their children behaviours and skills.

4.2   NIH Tests Results

In addition to previous data, other data was generated from tests; students took NIH tests in the first and in the last session to measure their improvement. Accuracy and reaction time were the main parameters in those tests.

In the first test, flanker task, students done very well in the congruent trails. 99% of students select the correct arrow direction with 100% accuracy, with an acceptable reaction time (RT). In the pre-test more than half of the students select the correct direction with an average accuracy 72% and average RT (1645 ms). While in the post test, after intervention, nearly 98% of the students select the correct direction with 100% accuracy, and faster reaction time RT with an average of (1163 ms). The accuracy and RT have been clearly enhanced after intervention. We can say that the average of overall enhancement in the flanker test is by 20%.

In the Go/No Go test, we considered No Go results due to its difficulty to hold back when no action must be done. Before intervention, the average of correct "no goes" was 52%, while after intervention, the average of correct "no goes" was 74%. In the case of Std 1H, we noticed that the score of her pre-test is better than her score in the post test by 5%, which considered normal in ADHD students due to their lack of focusing during the test; despite that, she showed significant progress in response inhabitation and processing speed in Table 3, and that is what Go/No Go test measures. The average of overall improvement in this test is 24%.

In the third test, working memory test, the pre-test have shown weakness in the working memory function before intervention, since the average of accuracy was 15%. While the post test scores have shown significant improvements with an average of 27% of accuracy.

After discussing and analysing the quantitative data generated by the system, in Sects. 4.1 and 4.2, and depending on the level of remarkable improvements measured, we can say that the system is effective. This is clearly shown from the positive influence on the behaviour of students as teachers and parents declared, and on their academic level.

5 Conclusion

In this study we investigated the interaction of e-games system to measure its effectiveness and whether it could help ADHD children to overcome their impairments, and to improve their cognitive capacities that could affect skills and behaviour. The system consists of six different brain training games, each trigger one or two cognitive capacities. The iPad was used as the tool of the study. Seventeen students were selected, from two international schools in Jeddah city, which have clear signs and symptoms of ADHD. Testing took place in school settings, in-class sessions. Students played three sessions a week, for 20 min for each session. NIH tests were done pre and post intervention, to measure improvements.

The results have shown significant improvements in behaviour and skills quantitatively and qualitatively. Their academic levels have been enhanced and evolved. As evaluation results show, students found the games easy to use and pleasant. Students went through levels in a reasonable reaction time.

So we strongly encourage ADHD children to play with such games, developed specially to enhance their abilities and skills, owing to the probable benefit that may positively change their lives.

Acknowledgments. First of all, I would like to thank my two supervisors for their support and guidance. They were there in each step, and helped me whenever I needed them. Secondly, my deepest thanks to Professor Bruce Wexler for allowing me to test ACTIVATE application without any fees, supporting me by sharing his published papers, made a helpful connection to the IT team of C8 Science Company and for being a great consultant too. Also, I would like to thank the ministry of education of Saudi Arabia in Jeddah for giving me the green light to apply a field experiment in different governmental schools. In addition, I Thank Dr. Fatimah Abu Zarifa, Dr. Rafa bin Laden, Faridah Farsi, Elham Ezzy and all school staff members for allowing the experiment to take place in their schools, giving me all the authorities I needed to make this experience succeed. Special thanks to Amal Al-Attas, Maiadah Emarah, Noora Pastukhova to arranging sessions timing and place, they facilitate contacting the parents of the participants as well. Finally, thanks to my parents, husband, friends, and family for all the support I got from them.

References

1. Blumberg, F.C., Brooks, P.J. (eds.): Cognitive Development in Digital Contexts. Academic Press, London (2017)
2. Brown, T.E.: Executive functions and attention deficit hyperactivity disorder: implications of two conflicting views. Int. J. Disabil. Dev. Educ. **53**(1), 35–46 (2006)
3. Cooper-Kahn, J., Dietzel, L.: Apps to support executive functioning, pp. 1–7 (2015). Accessed from esc4 website. http://www.esc4.net/Assets/executive-function-apps.pdf
4. Edyburn, D.L.: Rethinking assistive technology. Spec. Educ. Technol. Pract. **5**(4), 16–23 (2004)
5. Fails, J.A.: Mobile collaboration for young children: reading and creating stories. Doctoral dissertation, University of Maryland, College Park (2009)
6. Foster, M.E., Anthony, J.L., Clements, D.H., Sarama, J., Williams, J.M.: Improving mathematics learning of kindergarten students through computer-assisted instruction. J. Res. Math. Educ. **47**(3), 206–232 (2016)
7. Goodwin, K.: Report: Use of Tablet Technology (iPads) in the Classroom State of New South Wales, Department of Education and Communities, NSW Curriculum and Learning Innovation Centre (2012). www.clic.det.nsw.edu.au
8. Heinrich, P.: The iPad as a tool for education: A study of the introduction of iPads at Longfield Academy, Kent. NAACE: The ICT Association, Nottingham (2012)
9. Irvine, M.J.: Outcome evaluation of a time management smartphone application: a pilot study (2013)
10. Kessler, R.C., Adler, L., Barkley, R., Biederman, J., Conners, C.K., Demler, O., Spencer, T.: The prevalence and correlates of adult ADHD in the United States: results from the National Comorbidity Survey Replication. Am. J. Psychiatry **163**, 716–723 (2006)
11. Kourakli, M., Altanis, I., Retalis, S., Boloudakis, M., Zbainos, D., Antonopoulou, K.: Towards the improvement of the cognitive, motoric and academic skills of students with special educational needs using Kinect learning games. Int. J. Child Comput. Interact. (2016)
12. Kumaragama, K., Dasanayake, P.: iOS Applications (apps) for Attention Deficit Hyperactivity Disorder (ADHD/ADD): a preliminary investigation from Australia. J. Mob. Technol. Med. **4**(2), 33–39 (2015)
13. Langberg, J.M., Epstein, J.N., Urbanowicz, C.M., Simon, J.O., Graham, A.J.: Efficacy of an organization skills intervention to improve the academic functioning of students with attention-deficit/hyperactivity disorder. Sch. Psychol. Q. **23**(3), 407 (2008)

14. Langereis, G., Hu, J., Gongsook, P., Rauterberg, M.: Perceptual and computational time models in game design for time orientation in learning disabilities. In: Göbel, S., Müller, W., Urban, B., Wiemeyer, J. (eds.) Edutainment/GameDays-2012. LNCS, vol. 7516, pp. 183–188. Springer, Heidelberg (2012). https://doi.org/10.1007/978-3-642-33466-5_21

15. Loe, I.M., Feldman, H.M.: Academic and educational outcomes of children with ADHD. J. Pediatr. Psychol. 32(6), 643–654 (2007)

16. Lundholm-Brown, J., Dildy, M.E.: Attention-deficit/hyperactivity disorder: an educational cultural model. J. Sch. Nurs. 17(6), 307–315 (2001)

17. Martínez, F., Barraza, C., González, N., González, J.: KAPEAN: understanding affective states of children with ADHD. J. Educ. Technol. Soc. 19(2), 18–28 (2016)

18. O'Connell, T., Freed, G., Rothberg, M.: Using Apple technology to support learning for students with sensory and learning disabilities. WGBH Educational Foundation (2010)

19. Olounabadi, A.A.: TARLAN: a simulation game to improve social problem-solving skill of ADHD children. Doctoral dissertation, University of Canterbury (2014)

20. Shuler, C.: iLearnII: An Analysis of the Education Category of the iTunes App Store. The Joan Ganz Cooney Center at Sesame Workshop, New York (2012)

21. Statista   (2015).   http://www.statista.com/statistics/276623/number-of-apps-available-in-leading-app-stores/61

22. Tavakkoli, A., Loffredo, D., Ward Sr., M.: Lessons from game studies to enhance gamification in education. In: Proceedings of the 18th World Multi-conference on Systemics, Cybernetics, and Informatics, Orlando, FL (2014)

23. Vicini, E.: Methods for Students with ADHD Improving the Success of All Students, Saint Mary's College of Maryland (2011)

24. Wexler, B.E.: Integrated brain and body exercises for ADHD and related problems with attention and executive function. Int. J. Gaming Comput. Mediated Simul. (IJGCMS) 5(3), 10–26 (2013)

25. Wrońska, N., Garcia-Zapirain, B., Mendez-Zorrilla, A.: An iPad-based tool for improving the skills of children with attention deficit disorder. Int. J. Environ. Res. Public Health 12, 6261–6280 (2015). https://doi.org/10.3390/ijerph120606261

Audiovisual Design of Learning Systems for Children with ASD

Rafael Toscano and Valdecir Becker[✉]

Informatics Center, Federal University of Paraiba, João Pessoa, Brazil
audiovisualdesign@lavid.ufpb.br

Abstract. The increasing use of information and communication technologies for children with Autism Spectrum Disorder (ASD) establishes a complex media, interaction and learning scenario not currently supported by models of communication, computation, and pedagogy. Moving forward on this theme, this work proposes a model of interactions for problem description, planning, and production of systems for teaching skills and abilities to children with ASD. The proposed model arises from theoretical integration between Audiovisual Design framework with Taxonomy Instructional Objectives. In addition to theoretical input, a systematic review of the state of the art reveals a shared nature of media, among individuals with ASD, family members, clinical and educational professionals. Four stages of interaction were identified. In this way, this research contributes to teaching strategies that integrate levels of interaction from cognitive, affective and psychomotor domains, that impact the generation of contents and adaptive systems for the needs of children with ASD.

Keywords: Autism · Learning · Taxonomy · Goals · Audiovisual Design

1 Introduction

The relationship among individuals and technological artifacts has become increasingly closer, expanding meanings and possibilities of interaction. By incorporating everyday life, actions and goals, media devices become integrated with people's cultural, social and cognitive processes, in different scenarios and variable uses.

Considering applications of information and communication technologies (ICTs) we can highlight the use in educational processes, formal or otherwise, clinical and assisted technologies. ICTs have been used with a focus on information, culture and teaching assistance, both for individuals with typical development and for people with some level of cognitive, motor or even learning disorders, such as dyslexia, Attention Deficit Hyperactivity Disorder (ADHD) and Autism Spectrum Disorder (ASD), which is the focus of this research [1].

ASD is defined as an invasive developmental disorder that arises in childhood and has as main characteristics delay in acquisition of language, social interaction and restrictive and repetitive interests [1]. ASD is also recognized by neurobiological features that accompany the individual from fetal formation to adult life, [1, 2]. The deficits are extensive and not limited to social life. Instruments and mediation technologies daily challenge individuals with ASD. To face this issue, innumerable

M. Antona and C. Stephanidis (Eds.): UAHCI 2018, LNCS 10907, pp. 613–627, 2018.
https://doi.org/10.1007/978-3-319-92049-8_45

approaches involving stimulus, teaching and development are used in multisensory relationships between individual, tools and the environment (context).

Strictly speaking about individuals with ASD, the use of digital systems has been recognized as an effective approach to improve quality of life, cognitive and behavioral development. For example, in the survey conducted by The National Professional Development Center on Autism Spectrum Disorder (NPDC) it is possible to identify digital technologies among the 27 evidence-based strategies proven by this Center [3].

The convenience of inclusion of digital artifacts in teaching process can also be perceived in the Appy Autism project promoted by Orange Foundation, in which software are classified according to system, device, scientific proof (when available) and fields of action. Among the areas mapped by the platform are verbal communication, alternative or augmentative communication, apprehension (skills to learn and how to learn), reading, emotions and social behaviors, as well as support materials for relatives and caregivers. As a complementary strategy to solutions mapping, Orange Foundation also promotes courses to stimulate families and professionals to use ICTs.

In parallel with initiatives outside academic context, such as Appy Autism, scientific literature reports effectiveness and predisposition in education systems mediated by digital systems instead of direct interpersonal expositions [4–21]. Interventions assisted by digital technologies and teaching processes that aim to supplement deficits inherent to children with ASD can be classified [7] as: (a) Mixed reality games, using audio and video to integrate augmented or virtual reality to expand perception of facts, events and behaviors; (b) Robots, as agents to stimulate social interaction; (c) Applications dedicated to specific gaps, such as digital boards of alternative communication. In general, these technologies have incorporated partially clinical requirements and playful interests of individuals with ASD [12].

The state of the art about audiovisual systems and Autism shows outcomes in reduction and acquisition (intensive and functional) of skills and competences. Evaluating the studies [4–21], one can notice a lack of theoretical contribution to delimit media, interaction and learning variables present in this scenario. This absence can also be related to the fact that isolated theories of communication, computation and pedagogy used in the studies do not contemplate the complexity of planning and producing systems to attend to the individuals with ASD.

In order to address this gap, the present study aims to initiate a theoretical intersection between Audiovisual Design model and Taxonomy of Instructional Objectives. A graphic framework is presented to describe and systematize aspects that allow us to design, plan and produce systems that meet both the interests of individuals and learning demands.

This paper is organized as follows: Sect. 2 presents models for teaching processes development in digital environments for individuals with ASD; Sect. 3 presents theoretical discussions that support the model proposed in this work; Sect. 4 describes the integration between Audiovisual Design and Taxonomy of Instructional Objectives; discussions about proposed model are presented in Sect. 5; Finally, in Sect. 6 the final considerations, limitations and future perspectives are presented.

2   Related Work

Many studies discuss directly or indirectly media technology use for education. One of the most significant is Instructional Design (ID) [22]. It is a conceptual approach that integrates educational planning into an online education processes using ICTs, from student's point of view. For these authors, the process of constructing a learning object goes through four stages: (I) An analysis about needs and constraints; (II) Design and development, the stage of planning and elaboration of artifacts; (III) Implementation, the stage at which teachers are trained to use the system and students to use the provided artifacts; (IV) Evaluation, the stage which involves reviewing and maintaining studied objects. The above referred study [22] and others that define ID, contribute to the comprehension of the big picture of how educational objects can be developed. Despite the relevance of ID, the theory does not provide means to understand aspects related to how interactions with media systems impact the learning of individuals with or without ASD.

Another method, Diversity for Design (D4D), addresses neurodiversity, the atypical cognitive and neural profile of individuals with ASD [23]. This framework provides technological solutions focused on individual's capacities instead of their limitations. D4D proposes an integration of participatory design practices with clinical and pedagogical intervention strategies of the Treatment and Education of Autistic and related communication handicapped Children (TEACH). In general, the authors suggest that insertion of ICTs should be based on the conception of autism as a mode of being (culture) and on particular aspects of individuals, such as, abilities, skills or comorbidities associated with the disorder.

D4D contributes to media interaction scenarios proposing a process of artifacts development with participation of individuals with ASD, focusing on their interests and potentialities. However, the framework does not support teaching and learning processes, nor how recurrent use of media impacts the students. The central part of D4D's contribution is designing artifacts from skills. As an example of aptitudes that should be considered, the authors highlight the creative state of individuals for specific areas, which are different from person to person: Focus on elements of interest; Strong systematization and organization of elements; High storage capacity; Spatial and visual skills [23].

Other study pertinent to the scope of this work is the process for designing interfaces for autistic users (ProAut), [24]. Similar to D4D, ProAut proposes insertion of individuals with ASD into the process of constructing media educational objects. The authors combined principles of participatory design and user-centered design and synthesized the following processes: initial prototype design; prototype evaluation and refinement; recommendations or guidelines; final prototype. Therefore, ProAut's contribution consists of a dynamic categorization of guidelines for media development teams.

Initially the authors mapped, based on scientific literature, guidelines for production of graphical interfaces applied to individuals with ASD. Secondly, they suggested the use of data bases of participatory design to increase the user experience value. In order to structure such recommendation system, the authors developed an online data base named Guidelines ProAut. Researchers, professionals and other people interested in the subject can use the system to share and to validate recommendations for creation of digital interfaces for individuals with ASD [25]. The most important guidelines are: Avoid the use of elements that may distract or interfere with attention; Be succinct; Allow up to five attempts before revealing the correct answer in evaluation contexts; Use visual equivalences for texts; Use markings that facilitate reading flow, such as lists.

Reviewing the methods and models described in this section, one can notice that the studies have sought to list practices to help professionals and researchers in computing, design and education fields to develop digital artifacts. The described studies also suggest the inclusion of requirement surveys from individuals with ASD point of view. These studies provide contributions to the use of media in interaction and learning scenarios. However, all approaches focus on general perspectives or on specific parts of artifacts development, such as scenario analysis and requirement survey. This indicates a room for further studies that enlarge the discussion in media studies and how to evaluate the process of interaction and learning.

3   Media, Interaction and Learning

Audiovisual Design (AD) methodology integrates principles from Media Studies to Human Computer Interaction (HCI) [26]. AD describes a set of variables and levels of relationships that an individual develops throughout his experience with mediatic processes. The authors consider four roles people can assume throughout their process of media fruition: Audience, Synthesizer, Modifier and Producer. Each role has elements that permit individuals to extrapolate common behaviors, then assuming the enhanced role 'Player'.

Audience: The basic role individuals can assume in AD model. Individuals are inertial to content or have low action possibilities, such as channel tuning or searching for on line videos. Motivations and media consumption remain relatively private.

Synthesizer: In this role individuals have developed an identity relationship with content. Individuals' behavior is based on interaction in on line media. They share content and experience in social spheres, thematic or professional interaction networks, mainly on social media.

Modifier: This role consists of part of Synthesizers which, expanding their relation of identity, motivation and diffusion, handles skills and abilities to elaborate new meanings for artifacts with a high rate of personalization. Practical examples are: to improve a downloaded movie translating and adding subtitles, and remix music to create new songs.

Producer: The Producer is responsible for content creation. This role can be assumed by individuals in formal media institutions, home or private generation of content, or part of the modifiers that have developed the identity personalization in content that results in completely new products.

Player: Refers to the individual who fully uses the interaction tools available within each level, being an 'enhancement' within each role. They seek content that will bring challenges and make them, even in isolation, think and do something. This role is identified with "early adopters" or "early users", i.e. people who take the risks of using a new technology and, thus, contribute to its development. As examples, we mention a Producer creating new distribution channels (Player-Producer); a Modifier creating a new product based on different media, such as a cartoon from images other people have taken (Player-Modifier); a Synthesizer acting as a fan and searching posts in many blogs, sites or social media to share them with their own social media contacts (Player-Synthesizer); an individual who looks for easter eggs or other hidden content in off-line media, such as DVD or Blu-ray discs, and engages in its content (Player-Audience).

Each of the roles corresponds to the graph shown in Fig. 1. Such representation is important to understand the integration and complementarity between the elements.

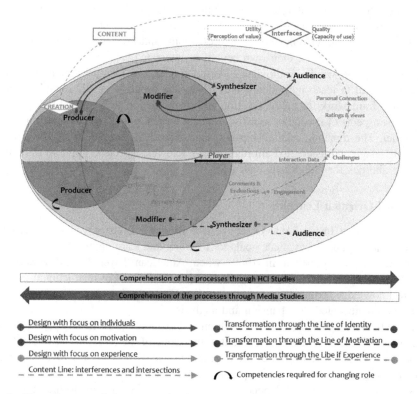

Fig. 1. Flow diagram of the process in the Audiovisual Design (AD) (Source: Audiovisual Design Research Group).

The relationships inherent in these roles occur through four Lines of Design: (a) Content, with relationships that vary (and add up) according to the role played by the individual: subjective relations at Audience level; engagement in Synthesizer level;

appropriation in Modifier level; creation for Producer; and challenges for Player; (b) Identity, which bases the personal relationship with content; (c) Motivation, which leads to engagement; and (d) Experience, which links fruition to advanced use of interactive features, which should provide practical experience with content and interfaces.

The Lines of Design allow us to understand that individuals, throughout their relationship of fruition, develop cumulative skills and abilities. Cumulative abilities are mostly associated with role alternation, either by inertia stimuli triggered by attention, analysis and interpretation, or action, through affordances that establish value and utility to interact in other levels, [26, 27].

According to the Audiovisual Design model, individuals need to have a "set of skills" appropriate to technological affordances to achieve role changes. These competencies are divided into assimilating: physical affordances, i.e. perceptions of the physical environment, such as devices and peripherals of interaction, and symbolic or narrative environments; the meanings of interaction (cognitive affordances); and the notion of utility (functional affordances). Thus, the change between levels of interaction is determined by understanding, in each role, what actions are available, which a Producer expects individuals should take or avoid, and how they can transform the content and/or artifacts for their own benefit or interests [27].

Analyzing the whole Audiovisual Design model, we identify potential relevant elements useful to teach individuals with ASD. The proposal of AD includes a comprehensive framework for media creation and manipulation. It is natural that thematic or specific aspects of special or assistive education scenarios do not naturally integrate the model. The dynamic relationship between individual and system, as well as the Lines of Design and its context affordances, are relevant aspects to apply in training or teaching abilities for individuals with ASD.

3.1 Goal-Oriented Learning

The Taxonomy of Instructional Objectives, or Bloom's Taxonomy, is a pedagogical tool to identify, plan and evaluate goals for teaching and learning process [28]. Studies about this taxonomy began in 1948, when American Psychological Association (APA) initiated a research to evaluate and propose standards of instructional goals to acquire knowledge, competences and attitudes. From the initial publication, several researchers contributed to expansion and analysis.

In 2001 APA updated and revised Bloom's Taxonomy [29]. In this paper, we use the new classification and when pertinent to the scope of the research, we return to the history as well as to the impact of the updates. The revised taxonomy maintains three domains, cognitive, affective and psychomotor. Each domain has objectives in a hierarchy of complexity and dependency, always from the simplest to the most complex goal.

The cognitive domain consists of the process of knowledge acquisition and its stages. This domain has been developed since beginning of the above mentioned studies, has undergone revision and has been applied by several researchers in contexts such as use digital media in children, adults an organizational education. Its goals are: Remember; Understand; Apply; Analyze; Evaluate; and Create. Complementary, the affective domain is related to individuals' emotions, behaviors and values. Its goals are: Receive; Respond; Value; organize; and Characterize.

The Psychomotor domain incorporates discussions about reflexes, perception, physical abilities, improved movements and non-verbal communication [30–32] In this domain, goals vary depending on the context. For example, for [31] the elements are: Imitation, Manipulation, Precision, Articulation, and Naturalization. On the other hand, the study [30] considers: Perception, Set, Guided Response, Mechanism, Complex Response, Adaptation and Origination. The research [32] considers: Reflex Movement, Basic Fundamental Movement, Perceptual Abilities, Physical Abilities, Skilled Movement and Non-Discursive Communication.

The objective of Bloom's Taxonomy is to build lists of elements to plan teaching and learning process. One resource used is to associate verbs with each mentioned goals. In addition to connections between objectives and verbs present in three domains, the taxonomy specifically proposes four dimensions of knowledge to cognitive domain, as shown in Table 1.

Table 1. Cognitive process in the revised taxonomy.

Knowledge dimension	Cognitive process dimension					
	Remember	Understand	Apply	Analyze	Evaluate	Create
Factual	Goal 1					
Conceptual		Goal 2	Goal 2			
Procedural					Goal 3	
Metacognitive	Knowledge		Competence		Skill	

Source: [33]

The dimensions of knowledge are: (a) Effective or Factual, related to basic content individuals should have to solve problems; (b) Conceptual, that is, the interrelation of basic elements in an elaborated context in which individuals would be able to discover or posses knowledge of classification and categorization; (c) Procedural, linked to methods, criterion or technique to accomplish something; (d) Metacognitive, linked to recognition of cognition, that is, the individuals' self-knowledge about their ability to connect, process and, for example, develop strategies for problem solving activities.

Finally, we can understand the conceptual proposal of Taxonomy of Instructional Objectives as a theoretical framework that allows us to assign variables in teaching process and apply general goals to contextualized verbs and learning needs. Other considerations and examples of applications will be explained in the section of analysis and theoretical intersection proposition.

3.2   Shared Interaction

A systematic review of scientific literature about audiovisual systems and ASD patients, [4–21] indicates recurrent uses of multiple-baseline design method to evaluate four scenarios, or general interaction contexts: C1 - Baseline; C2 - Intervention session; C3 - Maintenance; C4 - Generalization.

The Baseline (C1) is disclosed as a stage of observation of potentialities, needs and interests of individuals with ASD. The Intervention Session (C2) applies for the instant individuals are introduced to the solution (content and technology) and are invited to interact with media (body and mind). After the first intervention contact, users undergo application activities and revision of the initial modeling, step known as Maintenance (C3).

The frequency of Maintenance sessions varies according to patient's abilities, to complexity of given tasks and, as suggested by some studies, to media supports used to interact [4, 11, 15]. When they reach satisfactory pre-established indices, children begin the Generalization stage (C4). At this point, the set of skills induced by media usage is already reproduced by the child. New activities of application and context variation are introduced. Throughout the whole intervention, researchers alternate among different interaction technologies, considering skills and abilities are changing.

Based on the evaluated literature, the complexity of interaction processes, in systems for learning purposes for individuals with ASD, can be noticed in aspects such as (a) time, the interventions last for weeks or months to achieve results; (b) resources, such as space, equipment and professionals; or (c) technical requirements, through solutions or services that require customization and updating. Another aspect identified is that individuals with ASD like to share their interactions and media uses with other subjects, such as clinicians or education professionals and responsible, in many cases represented by their mothers [1].

How these people exchange information influence requirements and priorities of technologies and interaction design. During intervention sessions, it was found that a greater use of contents that serve clinical and educational interests, instead of helping the general ludic wellbeing of the patient [12]. However, the opposite is observed in day to day use of contents. Limited and repetitive uses of media are common. For example, it is recurrent among children with ASD to reproduce several times music videos and cartoons, based on visual and sound stimulus.

No modularity or content adaptability aspects were identified to meet these two motivations in the ICTs solutions reviewed in articles [4–21]. Thus, it is possible to perceive opportunities of theoretical contribution for creation of interactive audio and video systems that meet both utility relations and clinical value perception, as well as the ludic interests and potentialities of individuals.

4   AD Applied to Bloom's Taxonomy

From the intersection between elements of Audiovisual Design and Taxonomy of Instructional Objectives, we propose a graph that integrates these concepts. Two starting points are relevant to integrate these models: cumulative relations of inertia and production of content and meanings (Fig. 2). Another relevant aspect is the similarity between Bloom's Taxonomy domains and Affordance concepts used in AD.

An initial grouping of elements, due to simple identification of inertia and action, represents the foundation of the model proposed in this paper. Metrics of media composition, interaction and learning are different in those two theoretical discussions. However, this primary association aligns the different nature of each element. While for

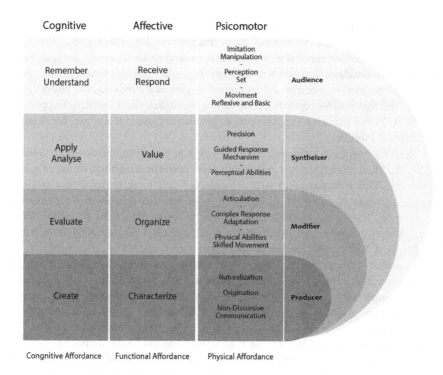

Fig. 2. Intersection between AD and Bloom's taxonomy

media context (AD), reception role represents an initial stage, its equivalent in Taxonomy of Instructional Objectives are the goals Remember and Understand, Receptivity and Response, Imitation, Perception and Reflex Movement. Considering domains and Affordances, both perspectives incorporate requirements that had to be achieved for progression of roles and learning. Both AD and Bloom's Taxonomy maintain a convergence among the importance of cognitive, affective or motivational, and psychomotor elements in interaction process.

According to Fig. 2, the first level represents the Audience. At this stage individual receives the flow of information about the subject to be learned using basic skills. On the cognitive domain it is individuals' responsibility to "react" to stimulus of media based on their cultural and cognitive repertoire to understand and remember the meanings and contexts of information. For example, an activity that teaches geometric shapes and has a blue triangle needs individuals to be able to recognize language (verbal, sound, visual) and retake the meaning of "blue", if it was already learned. Similarly, in affective domain individuals are characterized with Receptiveness and Responsiveness. In psychomotor domain, even with the three classifications, the essence of "reaction" and reception at private level is maintained. The Psychomotor goals inherent to audience are: Imitation and physical manipulation of models or stimuli made by the media; Perception and group; Basic movements and extreme reflexes.

At the second level, individuals already interact with content on a personal or primary level, but decide to expand their relations to larger contexts. While for Audiovisual Design this expansion is necessarily linked to social levels, for learning it is up to the Synthesizer to interact with content from other points of view, associations potentially stimulated by content and mediators or simply by individuals' motivations. Therefore, the Synthesizer consists of the following objectives: Cognitive (Apply and Analyze); Affective (Receive); Psychomotor (Precision, Guided Response, Mechanism and Perceptual Abilities).

At Modifier's stage individuals have a very high personalized relation with content. For AD, Modifiers correspond to individuals who perform a cumulative list of added competences. This understanding is also perceived in Bloom's Taxonomy goals. It represents a greater engagement, transposing processes and aspects of the content to other contexts. Therefore, Modifier consists of the following goals: Cognitive (Synthesize); Affective (Organize); Psychomotor (Articulation, Complex Response, Adaptation, Physical Ability and Skilled Movement).

The fourth level describes the Producer. At this stage individual reaches the apex of action becoming responsible for content generation and appropriations of new meanings. For example, let's say a given system teaches the step-by-step procedure of paper folding in order to teach geometry. Going through all processes, individual will acquire abilities to manage skills, competencies and processes to achieve other purposes, such as setting up a simple origami. In this case the Producer would be the individual who has the ability to abstract skills, needs for creation or application of new contents and meanings. In this way, the producer is constituted of the following goals: Cognitive (Create); Affective (Characterize); Psychomotor (Naturalization, Origin, Non-discursive Communication).

By comparing Producer's profile between AD and Bloom's Taxonomy it is possible to identify a difference in cause and effects relationships. For AD, Producer can be either someone who starts a move from Audience and expands his level of interaction, or an individual who, for his/her own motivations, generates a primary new content. On the other hand, for Bloom's Taxonomy, individuals always start from initial levels then to progress to synthesize, manipulate, and create. As the focus of learning systems in this paper is teaching, monitoring and developing skills and competences, these two perspectives can be appended as follows: while the individual uses the system to learn progressively, he creates his own repertoire and shapes options and recommendations for the process.

Besides these four levels presented, the Audiovisual Design has the Player as an enhanced role for all others. Using the same principle of inertia and action as applied to other roles, it is not possible to establish a parallel with the Taxonomy of Instructional Objectives. Thus, the identification of Players who compound teaching scenarios should be analyzed in specific contexts, such as training skills for young teens with ASD.

5 Audiovisual Teaching Systems for Children with ASD

As communication and media processes, teaching methods also have surpassed the paradigm that only one agent is the sender or holder of information and all others are receivers. While in AD the production of content can be done by companies or autonomous individuals, for pedagogical context the manipulation of knowledge also has a flexible environment, in which the learner is considered and stimulated to produce and interfere in knowledge.

Evaluating the use of technologies by individuals with ASD, one characteristic is common: the interaction is based on collaboration between children with ASD and those responsible or professionals who act as mediators of the whole process. The notion of mediator of interactions or learnings is common in psychology, HCI and education.

One important line of thought about mediation and technologies is based on studies developed by Vygotsky [34]. This author understands every individual has a zone of real competences and one of potentials. The difference between the two regions is called proximal zone. This interval represents opportunities for mediation between the individual who is learning and the environments (contexts) or other persons with higher knowledge. Teaching children with ASD demands a mediator, or an individual who contributes to the interaction, adds elements, and in some cases, leads the experience. This individual carries notion of encourage, influence and, sometimes, subversion of values. To him, one can also attribute the Player role, defined in Audiovisual Design. Thus, in the context of the use of information and communication technologies, family members and clinical or educational professionals, can be the Players within this interaction model. This 'Player-mediator', who takes part in interaction, impacts the lines of motivation, identity and experience. In other words, he plays a central role in the whole teaching and learning processes.

Affordances can be taught by Producers and learned by individuals, based on sharing experiences with other users, or by their own practical experience. It is necessary to take into account the contributions of mediation and interaction scenarios throughout the affordances learning process in intervention education systems. For example, during the four stages of interaction (Baseline, Intervention, Maintenance and Generalization) stimulus and objectives are influenced by variations in the mediators profiles, sometimes family, sometimes professionals. These mediators can act as reinforcers, when the student has autonomy, or as an action modeler, when the student has very low autonomy.

The generation of audiovisual systems, the focus of this paper, focuses on particularities of skills training that children with ASD are exposed to. In this way, it is necessary to understand that pedagogical project of intended content should contemplate cognitive, affective and psychomotor goals through acts (verbs) that are tangible both to the mediator and to the system, to identify, store and process information. Thus, teaching efficacy is related to how content is exploited and modified by children's action, depending on their competencies or difficulties. As motivations of interaction vary according to interaction scenarios, modularity and adaptability of content by the system become relevant.

Content modularity and adaptability are linked to scenario, including interaction objective (ability to be learned), and to participants (individual with ASD and mediator). For example, while the child is in an intervention session with the mediator (professional), taking initial contacts with the subject to be learned, it is natural that clinical rigor about fulfillment of skills and competences prevail in content. On the other hand, while individual is in maintenance sessions, manipulating the system alone or mediated by family members, it is the natural ludic, aesthetic, and affective motivations that predominate to engage him to continue the process.

Thus, the design of audiovisual systems for training individuals' abilities should:

A. Map individuals' difficulties and competences through the subject to be learned;
B. Segment the content (ability) and relate it to levels of interaction and learning in cognitive, affective and psychomotor domains using verbs or easily identifiable actions;
C. Establish equivalences of reception and interaction to content and device to meet the fulfillment of verbs and objectives which produce the intended ability;
D. Design variation of content to meet different use and mediation scenarios.

The synthesis of these steps contemplates interaction design that the individual with ASD will find when using the system. It is important to emphasize the process of moving from Audience (inertia) to Producer (action) is extremely dynamic and cyclic. Individuals, after acquiring new competences and skills, start new patterns of interpretation, synthesis and creation of meanings.

In addition, the interaction is not necessarily linked to only one device, content or technology. To achieve the goals of each domain, different interaction experiences can be used. For example, individual can initiate learning about "how to start dialogues" at the Audience level watching a television in therapist's office, move to games or simulators on home computer, and finally use audio or video in practical exercises in social context. In these cases, what delimits the amount of processes, devices and formats of content exposure are factors like individual's competences and difficulties; complexity of given tasks and feasibility or technical and financial availability.

The potential of integrating aspects of media, interaction and learning with the objective of describing, planning and executing audiovisual content systems for teaching and training skills and competences for individuals with ASD is remarkable. Since current models do not comprise mediated scenarios of interventions, we believe the strategy proposed in this paper, to juxtapose AD through levels of interaction to the parameterization of Bloom's Taxonomy domains and objectives, represents a strong contribution to address the gaps identified in the literature.

6   Conclusions

The use of Information and Communication Technologies for intervention and teaching processes for children with Autism Spectrum Disorder establishes a new condition of media, interaction and learning currently not supported by models of communication, computation and pedagogy. Aiming to fill this gap, this paper proposes a theoretical integration between Audiovisual Design model and Taxonomy of Instructional

Objectives. The Audiovisual Teaching Systems for children with ASD is a theoretical framework to erect media use in teaching process of individuals with ASD.

A systematic review about correlated publications identified the use and evaluation through four stages: Baseline, Intervention, Maintenance and Generalization. In addition, it has been found that this process is shared with clinical or educational mediators and family members. By integrating those two theoretical bases, using an equivalence about interaction and learning stages and relating them to the domains of cognition, affectivity and executive or motor functions, this paper proposed a scheme that connects each level of interaction to learning goals. The proposal also integrates content adaptability through four Lines of Design with the mediation nature.

This outcome contributes to current discussions, as it opens a dialogue between media and interaction aspects that can structure and enhance teaching methods to teach competences and skills for individuals with ASD. The model allows construction of pedagogical projects using media artifacts, based on observable objectives (actions) of cognitive, affective and psychomotor domains. Affordances and media interaction paths, which vary from the audience (personal layer and relatively inert) to the sphere of production (creation of social and functional meanings), complete the description. Finally, the proposed framework can facilitate dialogues between professionals in the technology fields and therapists, aiming the creation and use of audio and video based systems.

The scenarios described in this research highlight the demand for more studies about variables present at specific moments in interaction and learning processes. As future suggestions, we perceive potential for expansion of the study including dialogues with fields such as multimodal literacy studies, activity theory, hybrid learning, among other discussions that expand the understanding of complex interaction processes. Finally, this study can guide researches that evaluate and improve existing systems using validation with users.

References

1. Rotta, N.T., Ohlweiler, L., dos Santos Riesgo, R.: Transtornos da Aprendizagem: Abordagem neurobiológica e multidisciplinar. Artmed, Porto Alegre, Brasil (2016)
2. Mintz, M.: Evolution in the understanding of Autism Spectrum Disorder: historical perspective. Indian J. Pediatr. 84, 44–52 (2017). https://doi.org/10.1007/s12098-016-2080-8
3. Wong, C., Odom, S.L., Hume, K.A., Cox, A.W., Fettig, A., Kucharczyk, S., Brock, M.E., Plavnick, J.B., Fleury, V.P., Schultz, T.R.: Evidence-based practices for children, youth, and young adults with Autism Spectrum Disorder: a comprehensive review. J. Autism Dev. Disord. 45, 1951–1966 (2015). https://doi.org/10.1007/s10803-014-2351-z
4. Zhen, B., Blackwell, A.F., Coulouris, G.: Using augmented reality to elicit pretend play for children with autism. IEEE Trans. Vis. Comput. Graph. 21, 598–610 (2015). https://doi.org/10.1109/tvcg.2014.2385092
5. Macpherson, K., Charlop, M.H., Miltenberger, C.A.: Using portable video modeling technology to increase the compliment behaviors of children with autism during athletic group play. J. Autism Dev. Disord. 45, 3836–3845 (2015). https://doi.org/10.1007/s10803-014-2072-3

6. Özen, A.: Effectiveness of siblings-delivered iPad game activities in teaching social interaction skills to children with Autism Spectrum Disorders. Kuram ve Uygulamada Egit. Bilim. **15**, 1287–1303 (2015). https://doi.org/10.12738/estp.2015.5.2830

7. Bartolome, N.A., Zapirain, B.G.: Cognitive rehabilitation system for children with Autism Spectrum Disorder using serious games: a pilot study. Biomed. Mater. Eng. **26**, S811–S824 (2015). https://doi.org/10.3233/BME-151373

8. Jouen, A.-L., Narzisi, A., Xavier, J., Tilmont, E., Bodeau, N., Bono, V., Ketem-Premel, N., Anzalone, S., Maharatna, K., Chetouani, M., Muratori, F., Cohen, D.: GOLIAH (Gaming Open Library for Intervention in Autism at Home): a 6-month single blind matched controlled exploratory study. Child Adolesc. Psychiatry Ment. Health **11**, 17 (2017). https://doi.org/10.1186/s13034-017-0154-7

9. Eder, M.S., Diaz, J.M.L., Madela, J.R.S., Mag-usara, M.U., Sabellano, D.D.M.: Fill me app: an interactive mobile game application for children with autism. Int. J. Interact. Mob. Technol. **10**, 59 (2016). https://doi.org/10.3991/ijim.v10i3.5553

10. Lee, S.Y., Lo, Y., Lo, Y.: Teaching functional play skills to a young child with Autism Spectrum Disorder through video self-modeling. J. Autism Dev. Disord. (2017). https://doi.org/10.1007/s10803-017-3147-8

11. Malmberg, D.B., Charlop, M.H., Gershfeld, S.J.: A two experiment treatment comparison study: teaching social skills to children with Autism Spectrum Disorder. J. Dev. Phys. Disabil. **27**, 375–392 (2015). https://doi.org/10.1007/s10882-015-9420-x

12. Malinverni, L., Mora-Guiard, J., Padillo, V., Valero, L., Hervás, A., Pares, N.: An inclusive design approach for developing video games for children with Autism Spectrum Disorder. Comput. Hum. Behav. **71**, 535–549 (2017). https://doi.org/10.1016/j.chb.2016.01.018

13. Spriggs, A.D., Gast, D.L., Knight, V.F.: Video modeling and observational learning to teach gaming access to students with ASD. J. Autism Dev. Disord. **46**, 2845–2858 (2016). https://doi.org/10.1007/s10803-016-2824-3

14. Fridenson-Hayo, S., Berggren, S., Lassalle, A., Tal, S., Pigat, D., Meir-Goren, N., O'Reilly, H., Ben-Zur, S., Bölte, S., Baron-Cohen, S., Golan, O.: "Emotiplay": a serious game for learning about emotions in children with autism: results of a cross-cultural evaluation. Eur. Child Adolesc. Psychiatry 1–14 (2017). https://doi.org/10.1007/s00787-017-0968-0

15. Miltenberger, C.A., Charlop, M.H.: The comparative effectiveness of portable video modeling vs. traditional video modeling interventions with children with Autism Spectrum Disorders. J. Dev. Phys. Disabil. **27**, 341–358 (2015). https://doi.org/10.1007/s10882-014-9416-y

16. Jung, S., Sainato, D.M.: Teaching games to young children with autism spectrum disorder using special interests and video modelling. J. Intellect. Dev. Disabil. **40**, 198–212 (2015). https://doi.org/10.3109/13668250.2015.1027674

17. Ryan, C., Furley, P., Mulhall, K.: Judgments of nonverbal behaviour by children with high-functioning Autism Spectrum Disorder: can they detect signs of winning and losing from brief video clips? J. Autism Dev. Disord. **46**, 2916–2923 (2016). https://doi.org/10.1007/s10803-016-2839-9

18. Durango, I., Carrascosa, A., Gallud, J.A., Penichet, V.M.R.: Interactive fruit panel (IFP): a tangible serious game for children with special needs to learn an alternative communication system. Univers. Access Inf. Soc. **17**, 51–65 (2017). https://doi.org/10.1007/s10209-016-0517-5

19. Rice, L.M., Wall, C.A., Fogel, A., Shic, F.: Computer-assisted face processing instruction improves emotion recognition, mentalizing, and social skills in students with ASD. J. Autism Dev. Disord. **45**, 2176–2186 (2015). https://doi.org/10.1007/s10803-015-2380-2

20. Craig, A.B., Brown, E.R., Upright, J., DeRosier, M.E.: Enhancing children's social emotional functioning through virtual game-based delivery of social skills training. J. Child Fam. Stud. **25**, 959–968 (2016). https://doi.org/10.1007/s10826-015-0274-8
21. Edwards, J., Jeffre, S., Jeffre, S., Rinehart, N.J., Barnett, L.M.: Does playing a sports active video game improve object control skills of children with autism spectrum disorder? J. Sport Heal. Sci. **1** (2016). https://doi.org/10.1016/j.jshs.2016.09.004
22. Fiilatro, A., Piconez, S.C.B.: Design instrucional contextualizado (2004)
23. Benton, L., Vasalou, A., Khaled, R., Johnson, H., Gooch, D.: Diversity for design: a framework for involving neurodiverse children in the technology design process. In: Proceedings of the 32nd Annual ACM Conference on Human Factors in Computing Systems - CHI 2014, pp. 3747–3756. ACM Press, Toronto (2014)
24. Hiléia, Á., Melo, S., Barreto, R.: ProAut: Um Processo para Apoio de Projetos de Interface de Produtos de Software para Crianças Autistas. Cad. Informática **9**, 27–41 (2016)
25. da Silva Melo, Á.H., Fernandes, C.A.A.B., da Silva Jardim, M.S., da Silva Barreto, R.: Modelo 3C de Colaboração aplicado ao uso de um repositório para o desenvolvimento de interfaces para autistas. In: 14º SBSC - Simpósio Brasileiro de Sistemas Colaborativos Modelo, pp. 1471–1485. XXXVII Congresso da Sociedade Brasileira de Computação (2017)
26. Becker, V., Gambaro, D., Ramos, T.S.: Audiovisual design and the convergence between HCI and audience studies. In: Kurosu, M. (ed.) HCI 2017. LNCS, vol. 10271, pp. 3–22. Springer, Cham (2017). https://doi.org/10.1007/978-3-319-58071-5_1
27. Becker, V., Gambaro, D., Ramos, T.S., Toscano, R.M.: The development of media affordances in the audiovisual design. In: de Abreu, J.F., Guerrero, M.J.A., Almeida, P., Silva, T. (eds.) Proceedings of the 6th Iberoamerican Conference on Applications and Usability of Interactive TV - jAUTI 2017, pp. 91–103. UA Editora, Aveiro (2017)
28. Bloom, S.B.: Taxonomy of Educational Objectives. David Mckay, New York (1956)
29. Krathwohl, D.R.: A revision of Bloom's taxonomy: an overview. Theory Pract. **41**, 212–218 (2002). https://doi.org/10.1207/s15430421tip4104_2
30. Harrow, A.: A Taxonomy of Psychomotor Domain – A Guide for Developing Behavioural Objectives. David Mckay, New York (1972)
31. Dave, R.H.: Developing and Writing Behavioural Objectives. Educational Innovators Press, Tucson (1970)
32. Simpson, E.J.: The Classification of Educational Objectives in the Psychomotor Domain. Gryphon House, Washington, DC (1972)
33. Ferraz, A.P.D.C.M., Belhot, R.V.: Taxonomia de Bloom: revisão teórica e apresentação das adequações do instrumento para definição de objetivos instrucionais. Gestão & Produção **17**, 421–431 (2010). https://doi.org/10.1590/s0104-530x2010000200015
34. Vygotsky, L.S.: Mind in Society: The Development of Higher Psychological Processes. Harvard University Press, Harvard (1978)

Assisting, Not Training, Autistic Children to Recognize and Share Each Other's Emotions via Automatic Face-Tracking in a Collaborative Play Environment

Pinata Winoto, Tiffany Y. Tang[✉], Xiaoyang Qiu, and Aonan Guan

Media Lab, Department of Computer Science, Wenzhou Kean University,
Wenzhou, China
{pwinoto,yatang,qiux}@kean.edu

Abstract. One of the core characteristics of Autism Spectrum Disorder (ASD) is the presence of early and persistent impairments in social-communicative skills; and among the diagnostic characterization, difficulty in recognizing faces and interpreting facial emotions have been reported at all stages of development in ASD. Till now, an overwhelming number of previous works focus on training children with ASD on emotion recognition mostly via face perception and learning. Few published works have attempted on designing *assistive* tools to help the population recognize the emotions expressed by each other and make the emotion labels aware among each other, which motivates our present study. Drawn from results from our previous works, in this paper, we offer a collaborative play environment to inform autistic children each other's emotions with an aim to engage them happily and with much less stress. The emotion recognition is accomplished through a mounted motion capture camera which can capture users' facial landmark data and generate emotion labels accordingly.

Keywords: Collaborative game · Face-tracking · Emotion recognition
Autism spectrum disorder · Children

1 Introduction and Background

One of the core characteristics of Autism Spectrum Disorder (ASD) is the presence of early and persistent impairments in social-communicative skills (APA 2013); and among the diagnostic characterization, difficulty in recognizing faces and interpreting facial emotions have been reported at all stages of development in ASD (among many (Harms et al. 2010; Baron-Cohen et al. 1993; Gross 2004; Hobson 1986). However, these earlier works on face perception and emotion recognition functions have produced inconsistent results (Picard 2009; Peterson et al. 2015; Gross 2004; Dawson et al. 2010; Nuske et al. 2013), thus, research in this area remains inconclusive to date (Webb et al. 2016; Weigelt et al. 2013; Peterson et al. 2015). Nuske et al. urges more empirical studies to be conducted at various contexts of an *"emotion communication system"* (2013).

© Springer International Publishing AG, part of Springer Nature 2018
M. Antona and C. Stephanidis (Eds.): UAHCI 2018, LNCS 10907, pp. 628–636, 2018.
https://doi.org/10.1007/978-3-319-92049-8_46

Meanwhile, despite these inconsistent and inconclusive results, in response to the population's diminished functions in recognizing emotion, a number of computer-assisted applications have been developed to train face perception, emotion mimicking and demonstration skills (among numerous, (Harrold et al. 2014; Golan et al. 2010, Kouo and Egel 2016; Rice et al. 2015; Lacava et al. 2007; Lierheimer and Stichter 2012; McHugh et al. 2011; Hopkins et al. 2011)).

However, in our present study, instead of training autistic children emotion recognition skills, we offer a collaborative play environment to inform autistic children each other's emotions with an aim to engage them happily and with much less stress. As Baron-Cohen put it in 1993 that a training environment *"cannot expect learning to proceed smoothly or even to occur at all if the information is in a form that causes distress or is even painful"* (p. 3527, (Baron-Cohen et al. 1993)). The emotion recognition is accomplished through a mounted motion capture camera, the Intel RealSense™ which can capture users' facial landmark data and generate emotion labels accordingly.

The organization of this paper is as follows. In Sect. 2, we provide discussions on previous works in order to position our research in the research context. In Sect. 3, the first version of the game will be presented along with a short discussion on our pilot study. Finally, we will discuss our current plan and conclude our paper in Sect. 4.

2 Related Work

2.1 Emotion Recognition Training Games for Children with ASD

According to a recent white paper, there are more than two million children with ASD in China (Colorful deer 2015). Chinese children with ASD, like their western counterpart, have difficulty experiencing emotion, and communicating with others, which have posed a serious problem for their families and the society (Cong 2010). To the best of our knowledge, there is no dedicated computerized emotion-recognition training program in China. Yet, it has been recognized that early intervention on face perception and emotion recognition skills for children with ASD is very crucial (Rehg 2011, 2013; Webb et al. 2016).

Computer-aided Learning (CAL) for autism has been heralded to offer a very consistent and predictable environment to the users (Colby 1973; Golan et al. 2007; Yamamoto and Miya 1999; Moore and Calvert 2000; Bölte et al. 2006). Hence, there does not lack of such computer assisted training and remediation environment where English remains the main communication language (Harrold et al. 2014; Golan et al. 2010; Kouo and Egel 2016; Rice et al. 2015; Lacava et al. 2007; Lierheimer and Stichter 2012; McHugh et al. 2011; Hopkins et al. 2011; Bölte et al. 2006; Golan et al. 2015). The faces used in almost all of these training applications are posed by typically developing (TD) individuals. For example, Natalie et al. developed an iPad game, *CopyMe*, as a serious offline single-player game for children to learn emotions through observation and mimicry (Harrold et al. 2014). In particular, a player is asked to mimic the photo expression in *CopyMe* (posed by TD individuals) in order to advance to the next level. In the small-scale pilot study, some individuals with ASD struggled to make expressions which is consistent to one of the core impairments the population exhibit. Hence, the validity of the training approach in *CopyMe* remains unknown; the authors did propose to include more player inputs to complement the insufficiency of the facial expression.

These previous studies find that computer-based intervention is more suitable than the paper-based intervention for the young children (Harrold et al. 2014), and more complex social skills including complex emotion recognition can improve with CAL approach (Golan et al. 2010; Golan and Baron-Cohen 2006; Lacava et al. 2007; Young and Posselt 2012).

2.2   Faces Posed by Children with ASD for Emotion Recognition Training Games: Current Progress

Almost all of the prior works make trainings on either animated faces or posed faces by TD individuals (Tang 2016) mainly due to the population's persistent and noted impairments in posing recognizable facial expression (Brewer et al. 2015; Grossman et al. 2013; Weimer et al. 2001) and recognizing emotions (among many, (Baron-Cohen et al. 1993; Gross 2004; Harms et al. 2010). Some clinical, neurological and behavioral works emerged to address the issue on the emotion recognition skills on faces posed by individuals with ASD (among many, recent ones (Brewer al 2015; Capps et al. 1993; Faso et al. 2015; Stagg et al. 2014)). Some computerized approach relying on capturing facial expression posed by individual with ASD has emerged (Tang and Winoto 2017; Tang et al. 2017); our understanding on it is very limited (Tang 2016) and more works are expected which motivates our current study.

Our game is similar to that described in (Harrold et al. 2014), but ours will distribute the emotion labels through on-screen visualization to another player (see Fig. 3 on the current design). Therefore, our game could provide greater flexibility and generate less stress for children engaging in the play environment and foster more natural collaboration accordingly.

2.3   Computational Sensing Based on Facial Landmark Data for Automatic Emotion Recognition

While emotion recognition research is mature and emergingly popular thanks to the recent rekindled interest in deep learning field, however, learning emotion labels based on autistic facial data is rare (Tang et al. 2017).

According to (Rehg 2011, 2013), it is very labor-intensive to acquiring social and communication behavioral data. Computational sensing could play a key role in transforming the measurement, analysis, and understanding of such human behavior (Rehg 2011, 2013, Tang et al. 2017). In our previous study, we rely on the Microsoft Kinect motion sensor (v2) to capture autistic children's skeleton data (Winoto et al. 2016); however, due to the interferences between multiple sensors, it is too computational costly to adopt such a system at home. Rehg pointed out that widespread availability and increasingly low cost of sensor technology makes it possible to capture a multimodal portrait of behavior through video, audio, and wearable sensing (Rehg 2011). (Tang et al. 2017) mounted a portable motion camera, the Intel RealSense™ to learn and generate autistic children's emotion labels during their cartoon-watching sessions. The generated emotion tags were then compared with the manually labeled ones by the special education teacher or their parents who were at present for validation purpose.

While their studies offer an early glimpse of such automatic emotion recognition via face-tracking on autistic facial landmarks (Tang et al. 2017), it is different from present study in that in our proposed game, no human intervention is needed. Instead, the game is expected to make adjustment based on autistic children's behaviors

3   Our Game

3.1   Early Design of the Game

Our Game and Playing Rules Our proposed game is a multiplayer feeding game, where two players need to feed some fishes in a simulated aquarium (see Fig. 1). Each player will play on a PC connected to another one through LAN. In addition, player's information will be shown to others on the game screen (or teachers or other children in the environment) using various light colors and intensity without overstimulating autistic children (see Fig. 2). Our game is intended to help children with autism to express their own emotion or to detect other's emotion, and can also allow people with typical development (TD) be informed of it.

Fig. 1. The user interface of the game (version one)

Fig. 2. Two players are seen playing the game together

Behavioral Data Collection for Game Tuning and Computational Sensing. Our system will also record the players' in-game action (playing) and other behavioral data (such as speech and prosody characteristics) which can be used to automatically adjust some game parameters (such as playing speed so as to maximize game playability). These behavioral data, meanwhile, can further be computed for teachers and clinical doctors to understand children's behavioral patterns (Winoto et al. 2016; Rehg 2011, 2013; Picard 2009; Tang et al. 2017).

Pilot Testing and User Feedbacks. The first version of the game has been tested by two adults; feedbacks were given on the user interface design aspects (Fig. 2). Figure 3 lists the new game design with a story.

A pilot study is scheduled later in the summer.

Player 1 is responsible for selecting the corresponding fish feed for feeding with appropriate voice hints. It aims to improve the emotion recognition ability and observation ability of the children with ASD.

USER 1　　　USER 2

Player 2 is expected to make a corresponding facial expression after Player 1 feeding a fish correctly.

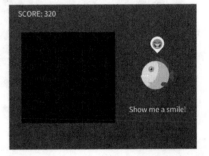

Fig. 3. The updated design

3.2 Emotion Recognition via Face-Tracking

Players' facial expression is captured via an Intel RealSense™ motion capture camera; computation and generation of emotion labels is then accomplished through the API provided by RealSense™. Four movements in the face and head areas are supported in the *FaceExpression* Module provided in the API: *eye brow movement, mouth movement, head movement,* and eye movement. For example, the "Smile Score" computed based on mouth movement data returns a value between 0 (no smile at all) to 100 respectively. The collected data include the timestamp associated with continuous micro-mouth movements (Fig. 4) when the player's face remains in the detected area.

31	0	12.58.08.902	17
32	0	12.58.08.920	14
33	0	12.58.08.962	27
34	0	12.58.08.977	34
35	0	12.58.08.991	29
124	0	12.58.10.846	24
125	0	12.58.10.862	19
126	0	12.58.10.882	29
127	0	12.58.10.902	24
128	0	12.58.10.921	25
129	0	12.58.10.939	33
130	0	12.58.10.961	38
131	0	12.58.10.982	32
132	0	12.58.11.001	31
133	0	12.58.11.026	23
134	0	12.58.11.046	34
135	0	12.58.11.062	31
136	0	12.58.11.080	23
137	0	12.58.11.106	23
138	0	12.58.11.122	24

Fig. 4. The mouth movement data collected associated with smile score

This computation is different from our previous work where we designed light-weight emotion-recognition algorithm to compute and generate emotion index based on Face Action Units (AUs) (Tang et al. 2017). It is unclear which approach yields to more accurate results even though assessment of such emotion labels remains to be a challenging issue (Tang 2016; Tang and Winoto 2017).

4 Discussion and Further Work

Much heterogeneity is apparent in emotion recognition and processing in ASD, more empirically studies need to be conducted. Previous attempts on computer assisted emotion recognition and face perception training applications had built upon the *theory of mind (ToM)* which has been empirically investigated to significantly improve the abilities in children with ASD (Weigner and Depue 2011). However, the ecological validity of such results, across population, is unknown. In this paper, stead of pursing research down this path, we offer a collaborative play environment to inform autistic children each other's emotions with an aim to engage them happily and with much less stress. The emotion recognition is accomplished through a mounted motion capture camera which can capture autistic children's facial landmark data and generate emotion labels accordingly.

Although the research described in this paper offers an early glimpse of one of the few earliest attempts down this path, it is our hope that the experiment and knowledge emerged from such an early attempt would help to inform remediation strategies of this kind to target emotion-related difficulties in order to help individuals with ASD to lead emotionally rich lives during their social interaction within the population and with TD individuals.

Acknowledgments. The authors acknowledge the financial support to this research by Wenzhou-Kean University's Student Partnering with Faculty (SpF) Research Program (WKU201718017). Thanks also go to Carl Guanxing Chen and Alex Xi Yang for implementing the system, and their assistance during pilot testing.

References

American Psychiatric Association: Diagnostic and Statistical Manual of mental disorders: DSM-5. Washington, DC (2013)

Baron-Cohen, S., Spitz, A., Cross, P.: Can children with autism recognize surprise? Cogn. Emot. **7**, 507–516 (1993)

Bölte, S., Hubl, D., Feineis-Matthews, S., Prvulovic, D., Dierks, T., Poustka, F.: Facial affect recognition training in autism: can we animate the fusiform gyrus? Behav. Neurosci. **120**(1), 211 (2006)

Brewer, R., Biotti, F., Catmur, C., Press, C., Happé, F., Cook, R., Bird, G.: Can neurotypical individuals read autistic facial expressions? Atypical production of emotional facial expressions in autism spectrum disorders. Autism Res. **9**(2), 262–271 (2015)

Capps, L., Kasari, C., Yirmiya, N., Sigman, M.: Parental perception of emotional expressiveness in children with autism. J. Consult. Clin. Psychol. **61**(3), 475–484 (1993)

Colby, K.M.: The rationale for computer-based treatment of language difficulties in nonspeaking autistic children. J. Autism Child. Schizophr. **3**(3), 254–260 (1973)

Colorful deer Children's behavior modification center. China's autism education and rehabilitation industry development status report. Beijing Normal University Publishing House (2015)

Dawson, G., Webb, S.J., McPartland, J.: Understanding the nature of face processing impairment in autism: insights from behavioral and electrophysiological studies. Dev. Neuropsychol. **27** (3), 403–424 (2010)

Cong, Y.: The world of children with autism: no emotional behavior rigid memory. China Youth Daily (2010)

Faso, D.J., Sasson, N.J., Pinkham, A.E: Evaluating posed and evoked facial expressions of emotion from adults with autism spectrum disorder. J. Autism Dev. Disord. 1–15 (2015)

Golan, O., LaCava, P.G., Baron-Cohen, S.: Assistive technology as an aid in reducing social impairments in autism growing up with autism: working with school-age children and Adolescents. pp. 124–142 (2007)

Golan, O., Baron-Cohen, S.: Systemizing empathy: teaching adults with Asperger syndrome or high-functioning autism to recognize complex emotions using interactive multimedia. Dev. Psychopathol. 18(02), 591–617 (2006)

Golan, O., Ashwin, E., Granader, Y., McClintock, S., Day, K., Leggett, V., Baron-Cohen, S.: Enhancing emotion recognition in children with autism spectrum conditions: an intervention using animated vehicles with real emotional faces. J. Autism Dev. Disord. 40(3), 269–279 (2010)

Golan, O., Sinai-Gavrilov, Y., Baron-Cohen, S.: The Cambridge mindreading face-voice battery for children (CAM-C): complex emotion recognition in children with and without autism spectrum conditions. Mol. Autism 6, 22 (2015)

Gross, T.: The perception of four basic emotions in human and nonhuman faces by children with autism and other developmental disabilities. J. Abnormal Child Psychol. 32(5), 469–480 (2004)

Grossman, R.B., Edelson, L.R., Tager-Flusberg, H.: Emotional facial and vocal expressions during story retelling by children and adolescents with high-functioning autism. J. Speech Lang Hear. Res. 56(3), 1035–1044 (2013)

Harrold N., Tan, C.T., Rosser, D., Leong, T.W.: CopyMe: a portable real-time feedback expression recognition game for children. In Proceedings of the CHI 2014 Extended Abstracts on Human Factors in Computing Systems (CHI EA 2014), pp. 1195–1200 (2014)

Harms, M.B., Martin, A., Wallace, G.L.: Facial emotion recognition in autism spectrum disorders: a review of behavioral and neuroimaging studies. Neuropsychol. Rev. 20(3), 290–322 (2010)

Hobson, R.P.: The autistic child's appraisal of expressions of emotion. J. Child Psychol. Psychiatry 27, 321–342 (1986)

Hopkins, I., Gower, M., Perex, T., Smith, D., Amthor, F., Casey Wimsatt, F., Biasini, F.: Avatar assistant: improving social skills in students with an ASD through a computer-based intervention. J. Autism Dev. Disord. 41(11), 1542–1555 (2011)

Kouo, J.L., Egel, A.L.: The effectiveness of interventions in teaching emotion recognition to children with autism spectrum disorder. Rev. J. Autism Dev. Disord. 3(3), 254–265 (2016)

Lacava, P.G., Golan, O., Baron-Cohen, S., Myles, B.S.: Using assistive technology to teach emotion recognition to students with Asperger syndrome: a pilot study. Remedial Spec. Educ. 28(3), 174–181 (2007)

Lierheimer, K., Stichter, J.: Teaching facial expressions of emotion. Beyond Behav. 21(1), 20–27 (2012)

McHugh, L., Bobarnac, A., Reed, P.: Brief report: teaching situation-based emotions to children with autistic spectrum disorder. J. Autism Dev. Disord. 41, 1423–1428 (2011)

Moore, M., Calvert, S.: Brief report: vocabulary acquisition for children with autism: Teacher or computer instruction. J. Autism Dev. Disord. 30(4), 359–362 (2000)

Nuske, H.J., Vivanti, G., Dissanayake, C.: Are emotion impairments unique to, universal, or specific in autism spectrum disorder? A Comprehensive Review Cogn. Emot. 27(6), 1042–1061 (2013)

Peterson, C.C., Slaughter, V., Brownell, C.: Children with autism spectrum disorder are skilled at reading emotion body language. J. Exp. Child Psychol. 139, 35–50 (2015)

Picard, R.W.: Future affective technology for autism and emotion communication. Philos. Trans. R. Soc. B Biol. Sci. 364, 3575–3584 (2009)

Rehg, J.: Behavior imaging: using computer vision to study autism. In Proceedings of IAPR Conference on Machine Vision and Application (MVA 2011), pp. 14–21 (2011)

Rehg, J.: Behavior imaging and the study of autism. In: Proceedings of the 15th ACM on International conference on multimodal interaction (ICMI 2013), pp. 1–2 (2013)

Rice, L.M., Wall, C.A., Fogel, A., Shic, F.: Computer-assisted face processing instruction improves emotion recognition, mentalizing, and social skills in students with ASD. J. Autism Dev. Disord. **45**(7), 2176–2186 (2015)

Stagg, S., Slavny, R., Hand, C., Cardoso, A., Smith, P.: Does facial expressivity count? How typically developing children respond initially to children with autism. Autism **18**(6), 704–711 (2014)

Tang, T.Y.: Helping neuro-typical individuals to "Read" the emotion of children with autism spectrum disorder: an internet-of-things approach. In: Proceedings of the 15th ACM Interaction Design and Children Conference (ACM IDC 2016), pp. 666–671. ACM Press, Manchester (2016)

Tang, T.Y., Winoto, P., Chen, C.: Emotion recognition via face tracking with RealSense 3D camera for children with autism. In: Proceedings of the 16th ACM Interaction Design and Children Conference (ACM IDC 2017), pp. 533–539. ACM Press (2017)

Tang, T.Y., Winoto, P.: An Internet of Things Approach to "Read" the Emotion of Children with Autism Spectrum Disorder. John Wiley & Sons, Hoboken (2017). in Press

Webb, S.J., Neuhaus, E., Faja, S.: Face perception and learning in autism spectrum disorders. Q. J. Exp. Psychol. **70**(5), 970–986 (2016)

Weigelt, S., Koldewyn, K., Kanwisher, N.: Face recognition deficits in autism spectrum disorders are both domain specific and process specific. PLoS ONE **8**(9), e74541 (2013). https://doi.org/10.1371/journal.pone.007454

Weigner, P.M., Depue, R.A.: Remediation of deficits in recognition of facial emotions in children with autism spectrum disorders. Child Family Behav. Ther. **30**(1), 20–31 (2011)

Weimer, A., Schatz, A., Lincoln, A., Ballantyne, A., Trauner, D.: "Motor" impairment in asperger syndrome: evidence for a deficit in proprioception. J. Dev. Behav. Pediatr. **22**(2), 92–101 (2001)

Winoto, P., Chen, C.G. Tang, Y.T.: The development of a Kinect-based online socio-meter for users with social and communication skill impairments: a computational sensing approach. In: Proceedings of IEEE International Conference on Knowledge Engineering and Applications (ICKEA'2016), pp. 139–143. IEEE (2016)

Yamamoto, J., Miya, T.: Acquisition and transfer of sentence construction in autistic students: analysis by computer-based teaching. Res. Dev. Disabil. **20**(5), 355–377 (1999)

Young, R.L., Posselt, M.: Using the transporters DVD as a learning tool for children with autism spectrum disorders (ASD). J. Autism Dev. Disord. **42**(6), 984–991 (2012)

Research on the Interactive Design
of Wearable Devices for Autistic Children

Minggang Yang[(✉)] and Xuemei Li[(✉)]

School of Art, Design and Media, East China University of Science
and Technology, M. Box 286, No. 130, Meilong Road, Xuhui District,
Shanghai 200237, China
yangminggang@163.com, 1165541916@qq.com

Abstract. According to the "Development report on China's autism education and rehabilitation industry", the autistic children aged 0–14 years old may exceed more than 2 million in China. With the development of science and technology, autistic children have drawn more attention. The treatment of autistic children is becoming more and more diverse. Since wearable products are portable, real-time and interconnected, they have advanced rapidly in recent years. It has been applied to the treatment of autistic children in the field of medicine. But the impact of the existing wearable medical products on the body and mind of the patients is not comprehensive. There are no effective interaction design specification systems. Therefore, further improving and studying the interactive mode of wearable devices for autistic children have important theoretical value and practical significance.

This paper first studied physiological and psychological characteristics of autistic children and obstacles they encounter in their lives through the methods of literature and documentation, interview and observation. Next, the classification and characteristics of wearable devices are generalized, and the characteristics and elements of the interactive design of wearable devices are summarized. In addition, this paper also carries out detailed case analysis of the current wearable products, and summarizes the shortage of the present products. Finally, system network diagram in respect with wearable device medical services for autistic children is proposed, combining the interactive information flow of the wearable device service system with autistic children centered, and sums up the wearable device interaction design specification in terms of autistic children in the end, and proposes feasible ideas and suggestions for interactive design.

Keywords: Wearable devices · Autistic children · Interaction design

1 Introduction

Autism, also known as lonely illness, proposed by American clinical scientist Kanner, it is a lifelong developmental disorder with unknown cause, which has seriously hindered children's learning, language communication, emotional expression and social development. The number of autism increases rapidly and the total amount is astonishing in the world. The incidence of autism, from one in ten thousand, one in

M. Antona and C. Stephanidis (Eds.): UAHCI 2018, LNCS 10907, pp. 637–649, 2018.
https://doi.org/10.1007/978-3-319-92049-8_47

thousand, one in hundred, to 1/68 in 2014 (released by American disease control and prevention center), and then to 1/45 in 2016 (released by American national center for health statistics survey). According to "Development report on China's autism education and rehabilitation industry II (2017)", the incidence of autism in China is also 1%. This means that there may be more than 10 million of the autistic population and 2 million of the autistic children among the population of 1.38 billion in China, and growing at nearly a speed of 200 thousand per year. The increase in the number of reported cases is shocking, but there are no successful cured cases so far. Although there is no cure yet, a correct intervention measure can make these children reduce their symptoms in some way, there is hope for them to live their own independent life with long-term intervention therapy.

Wearable devices are portable devices that can be directly worn on people, or integrated into clothing and ornaments. Combining the wearable sensor with the mobile communication, integrate chip technology, communication technology, and intelligent interactive technology, through Bluetooth, Wi-Fi, Zig Bee (wireless communication technology), NFC (Near Field Communication, near distance wireless communication technology) and other ways to connect, to make portable electronic devices with the functions of collecting, processing, and transmitting data [1]. At present, the researches on wearable devices in China are mainly focused on the technical level, most of them develop this technology in a business perspective, there are few studies on wearable device design in respect of the medical point of view, such as the field of autism treatment. The medical field has applied wearable products to the treatment process of autistic children due to the advantages of portable, real-time and interconnected, but since this is an interdisciplinary field, multidisciplinary cooperation requirements (medicine, psychology, product design, etc.) and professional knowledge restrict the further development of this field. In addition, the influences of current wearable medical products on patients' body and mind are not comprehensive, and there are no effective interactive design standard systems in terms of design. Therefore, this paper has summarized effective methods for the interactive design of wearable products for autistic children on the basis of previous studies, to propose some direction for future improvement of product interaction in this field.

2 Concept of Children with ASD

2.1 The Concept of Autism

Autism is a series of disorders of inter behavior, usually happens before the age of three. Due to poor understanding of communication and relationship with others, which leads to cognitive impairment and emotional disorder in children. The most distinctive differences between the people with autism and normal people are in three aspects of social interaction, language communication and imagination [2]. In *Fifth revision of the manual for the diagnosis and statistics of mental diseases* published by The America Psychological Association in 2013, calls Autism, Asperger syndrome, childhood disintegrative disorder and pervasive developmental disorder to be classified together as

Autism Spectrum Disorders, that is what we often said ASD. The subject in this study is that children with autism.

2.2 Life Disorder in Autistic Children

Social Communication Disorder. In social communication, autistic children usually lack communication with others, do not have proper communication skills, and lack of security attachment relationship with parents, etc. [3]. As infant, the patients have the behavior of avoiding eye contact, do not expect to be held up and close to people, and have no interest and reaction to sound [3]. As in early childhood, the children still avoid eye contact, have no response when being called, cannot contact in a proper way and establish partnerships with children of the same age [3]. With the growing age and improvement of the condition, the children may become friendly and emotional to their parents and fellow, but still lack interest and behavior for actively contacting with others [3]. Although some children are willing to communicate with others, they are unclear about the social distance, lack of normal reaction to the emotions of others, and cannot adjust their behaviors according to social situations.

Language Communication Disorder. The backward language development shows in the following aspects: (1) Nonverbal communication disorder: children often cry or scream to express physical and psychological discomfort, cannot express oneself by nodding head, shaking head and waving hands normally and so on. (2) Verbal communication disorder: there are obvious obstacles in the communication of children's speech, including: ① language comprehension is damaged in varying degrees; ② verbal communication development is slow or undeveloped, some of the children had expressive language before the age of 2–3, but gradually decreased and even disappeared completely; ③ language form and content abnormality: children often have mimicry, stereotyped repetition, often use wrong grammatical structure and personal pronouns, and the intonation, the speed, the rhythm, the stress, and so on are also abnormal; ④ the ability to use speech is impaired, rare to communicate with words, and cannot raise and maintain the topic, or talk only by repeated phrases, entangled in the same topic [4].

Narrow Interest. The children lack interest in toys and games that general children are fond of, but particularly interested in things that are usually not toys, such as round, rotatable things like wheel, bottle cap, and so on [3]. Some children also have attachment to non-life objects such as plastic bottles and sticks. The behaviors of the children are often very rigid, often with stereotyped and strange behaviors, such as: repeated bouncing, staring hands in front of the eyes, or walk with the tip of the feet etc.

3   Concept of Wearable Devices

3.1   Classification and Characteristics of Wearable Devices

Wearable devices are an emerging market with great potential, it has ushered more vigorous development momentum since 2013. With more wearable devices are put into the market, wearable devices are gradually accepted by the public and integrated into various industries. Health and medical field is recognized as one of the most potential areas and the largest market size for the development of wearable devices. At present, the common wearable devices in the market can be divided into four categories of head-wearing type, wristband-wearing type, portable-wearing type and body-wearing type according to the way of wearing. Implantable type of wearable devices is still in the R&D stage. Different styles of wearing have different features, as shown in Table 1.

Table 1. Classification and characteristic analyze for existing wearable devices

Classification according to wearing methods	Characteristic	Representative products
Head-wearing type	Information can be displayed in the user's natural field of vision; The use of bone conduction or headphones to send private sound signals; Closely related to the user's vision and head movement	Google glasses, Melon head ring
Wristband-wearing type	Display screen is small or do not have display screen; Measurable pulse, blood pressure, and other parameters; closely related to the body movement of the user; The use of low power communication technology (such as Bluetooth) in conjunction with mobile App; Auxiliary tool (such as receiving phone calls) as traditional mobile intelligent device	Apple Watch, Samsung Galaxy Gear
Portable-wearing type	Display screen is small or do not have display screen; Can be used as external device for mobile equipment; The use of low power communication technology (such as Bluetooth) in conjunction with mobile App	Oxyful Intelligent Wallet, Copycat Bluetooth anti lost device
Body-wearing type	Display screen is small or do not have display screen; Wear directly on the body; Combined with daily wearing	Hexoskin: Intelligent sports T-shirt Nike+ Sports shoes, etc.
Implantable type	Directly implanted in the user's body, and no intuitive feeling, and it is still at the exploratory stage.	Online pill that can communicate directly with doctor

3.2   Analysis of the Interactive Elements of Wearable Devices

Compared with other products, the biggest advantage of wearable devices is portability, but because of this advantage characteristic of wearing directly on the body, there are many challenging requirements for its design and development, such as safety, comfort, durability, interactive convenience, information transmission effectiveness, data acquisition accuracy, energy consumption persistence, even social acceptance of device wearing and use behavior and so on need to be considered. All of these are required for the human-computer interaction design of wearable devices.

In respect of human-computer interaction, sensing technology is widely used in wearable devices, and people gradually accept the interactive mode based on sensing. The use of sensor based interaction is not only the advantage of wearable device's easy access to body information, but also a good solution to the problems of wearable device's small visual interface and difficult to touch. Speech, gesture, eye movement recognition and other interactive ways become the main form of interaction of wearable devices, and form multimodal interaction mode of combined use of variety of interactive ways. For example, users wearing Google glasses can control photograph by blinking or voice control, start glass display time by raising the head, and bone conduction can transmit private sound signals and so on. The interaction with the mobile phone and the network is not the direct operation of the user, but is also the important interactive content between the wearer and the wearable device. Under the circumstances that most devices have handset applications, the interacting between people and wearable devices is more like interacting with input and output devices in many ways, many of the functional operations behind it are completed in mobile phone applications or in the cloud.

However, for the special group of children with autism, the design of the interactive mode of wearable devices is facing a huge test. Consideration of the physiological and psychological characteristics of autistic children determines the feasibility of interactive approach. As an intermediate tool to assist the normal life of autistic children, the role of wearable devices is crucial.

4   Research Status

4.1   Literature Review

The design and promotion of wearable devices have been a hot topic in recent years. The electronic product design has appeared the big trend of wearable and intelligent along with the development of hardware technology. However, these devices are just touching the surface of the achieved function of the wearable device, and there are not enough people to notice the marginalized population of the society, at the same time, the designers often lack a deep understanding of the special population, especially the study of the psychological and behavioral characteristics of the special group of autistic children. Therefore, there are many difficulties that need to be overcome in the application of wearable devices to the treatment of autistic children.

There are considerable achievements in the interaction design of wearable devices and treatment on autistic children in foreign countries, which have very important reference and promoting significance for the follow-up research work. For example, Harrison et al. [5] studied the timeliness of the visual response to wearable devices at different parts of the body in respect of information transmission. Aziz et al. [6] adopted Kansei engineering this powerful emotion extraction mechanism to evaluate children's mood, the final result is to find the use of humanoid robot therapy to help autistic children find the best treatment to use humanoid robots. Mintz et al. [7] explored the mediation elements to help autistic children obtain social cognition and life skills by using intelligent mobile tools. Dunne and Smyth [8] studied the awareness levels of sensory stimulation from wearable devices by the user in terms of perception and cognition. Dunne and Smyth believe that being "forgotten" and providing cognitive help are important aspects of wearable. Profita et al. [9] studied the social acceptance of the interaction of other people wearing devices in public places, and the position where the appropriate control interface is placed on the body, that has reference value for the design of the wearable devices based on the body interaction.

In China, the development of wearable devices focuses on the fashion commercial products of sports products, however, in recent years, the research on intervention therapy for autistic children has also gradually gained social attention. Studies by Chen et al. [10] show that the education intervention through human computer interaction is a feasible new way to realize the recovery of autistic children. The experimental results show that human computer interactive learning can arouse children's interest and increase participation, and multimodal signals attract attention more than single mode, the adjustment of learning activity according to the individual learning state can effectively improve the social interaction ability of autistic children. Jiang et al. [11] designed and achieved ProCom wearable system that helps autistic patients build social distance awareness, this system can provide assistance to patients at any time, in any environment, without the aid of environmental devices and participation of others.

It can be seen that the theory of intervention treatment on autistic children with wearable devices has gradually gained attention, most important of all, as the difficulties of the new technology continue to break, wearable devices are turning to multiple development perspectives, the application and practice will be more extensive among the special population. However, the theory and research of wearable devices interactive design related to children's autism are not abundant, and there are still large development spaces.

4.2 Typical Case Analysis

At present, the existing wearable medical devices for autistic children at home and abroad are still relatively small, and the development ability is relatively weak, most of the available devices provide services for monitoring the physical condition of autistic children for parents or doctors, the most core requirements for the group of autistic children are often not met. Awake Labs company has developed a Reveal wristband for autistic children (see Fig. 1). It has built-in heart rate sensor, skin conduction sensor, and temperature sensor, can sort and record the data collected by these sensors together with App equipped by smart phone, form anxiety changes chart with time changes, and record high anxiety time, to help identify which behavior pattern leads to the breakdown of children's behavior.

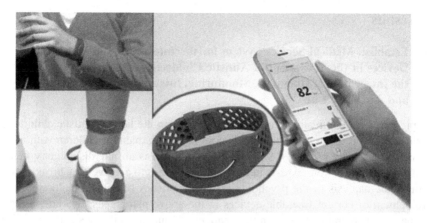

Fig. 1. Reveal smart wristband for autistic children

Fig. 2. Google glasses assist in expression recognition

Researchers at Stanford University have made new breakthroughs on the Google glasses relative to the Reveal smart wristband. Researchers have used high-tech, such as machine learning and artificial intelligence, to help children with autism better understand facial expressions (see Fig. 2), and distinguish others' emotions, including happiness, sadness, anger, etc. They no longer have to speculate about the emotions of the others, simple text information is prompted in the corner of the screen to explain the mood represented by others' expression for the wearers. The modified Google glasses direct the effective information to the wearers from the angle of the autistic children, instead of providing monitoring function only, it can directly participate in the daily life of the patient and provides effective social assistance.

5   Results

5.1   Establish Medical Service System for the Intervention of Wearable Devices in the Treatment of Autistic Children, to Realize the Integration of Diagnosis, Monitoring, Intervention and Treatment and Auxiliary Life

The prospects for the treatment of wearable devices in the field of autistic children are considerable, and the use of wearable devices in the treatment of children with autism will be more widely used in the future. But since this is an interdisciplinary field, it needs mutual efforts from experts in different disciplines to achieve new breakthrough. Through the analysis of the psychological characteristics of autistic children and the development of current wearable devices in the above paragraphs, this article argues that the use of wearable devices in the treatment of autistic children should establish a fixed mature medical service system, to realize the integration of diagnosis, monitoring, intervention treatment and auxiliary life for children with autism (as shown in Fig. 3). Wearable medical devices can be used to monitor and diagnose autistic children and to serve as social auxiliary tool in the lives of children, such as helping patients communicate with children of the same age. Parents or caregivers can understand the situation in real time through the mobile phone App, and the mobile App automatically uploads information to the cloud record. When the patient has an abnormal situation, the wearable device can transmit information directly to the doctor; the doctor can also understand the daily condition of the patient through checking at the information recorded in the cloud, in order to be assure treatment situation of the patient and formulates more accurate treatment plan.

In the long run, the treatment of autistic children is a long-term medical process and takes a lot of manpower and time; therefore, the integration into a perfect treatment service system brings out its advantages. Assemble various functional modules together with the help of wearable devices, and exerting the role of each module at different times and in different cases of children, which greatly saves manpower and time.

5.2   The Interactive Information Flow Network of Wearable Devices Service System from the Angle of Autistic Children

Through the previous case analysis of existing medical products, it can be seen that the intervention treatments of most wearable devices for autism are still in the monitoring part. In other words, the current problems focused by wearable devices are monitoring and understanding the physical information related to the patient. Information receivers are doctor, caregiver or parents, the service object of wearable devices is not the patient himself and there is no direct input. This is the current short board for wearable devices used to treat children autism. Of course, this is also limited by the development of the current medical and technological fields, but with the unceasingly intensive study of autism in children and continuous strengthening of hardware technology, this paper argues that the design of wearable devices with the patient as the main object can be achieved.

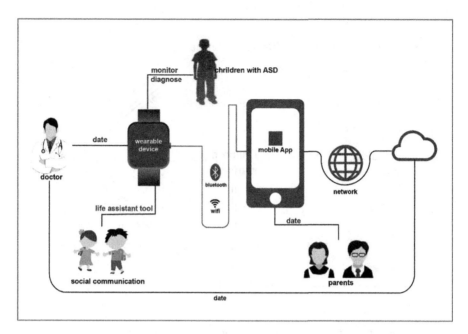

Fig. 3. Network diagram of autism medical service system for wearable device

This paper suggests that intervention therapy for children with autism through wearable devices in the future needs to be considered and designed from the patients' perspective (as shown in Fig. 4). From the previous analysis of the psychological cognition of children with autism, it can be understood that the patient has barriers on external cognition and cannot obtain and understand the external information correctly, and strong input of information can stimulate to trigger the child lose control of emotions. Therefore, in this case, wearable devices need to play a role of n information interpreter between the outside environment and the patient. Wearable devices take the initiative to obtain information from the outside world and transform it into the form that the patient is easy to accept, and thereby guide the patient to correctly recognize the received external information and can direct the patient to have corresponding responses.

In addition, in the whole closed loop information flow guidance network diagram, parents or caregivers can manipulate wearable devices through the mobile terminal, and acquire corresponding information feedback to understand the physical and mental condition of the children. The doctors in hospital can also get corresponding data feedback through wearable devices to achieve timely diagnosis and treatment. In sum, the information flow interaction of the whole service system is centered on autistic children, and the emphasis is on realizing autistic children to get correct external cognition through wearable devices to assist them to complete their daily social life.

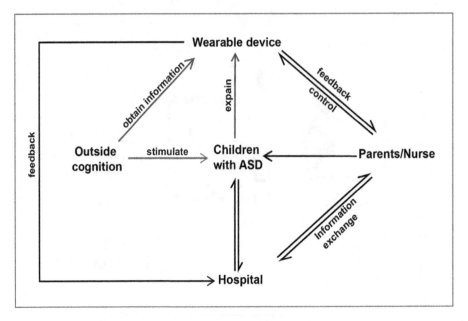

Fig. 4. Interactive information flow guide diagram of wearable devices service system

5.3   Wearable Devices Interaction Design Specification for Autistic Children

Wearable devices, while improving portability and wearable, also bring great challenges to interactive design, which include the problems of interface narrowing, even without interface, the sensitivity of the body interaction and so on. However, the difficulty is significantly increased for the special group of autistic children. Therefore, these factors should be fully considered in the interaction design to find the unique design specification.

Taking Account of the Acceptance of Operation Mode. The most common application of the interactive mode of wearable devices is sensing technology, which is also the advantage of wearable devices, it can understand the user's body information timely and effectively by using sensing technology, at the same time, it casts off the limitation of interface interaction, to make wearable devices to be more compact and convenient integrated in user's daily wearing. The interaction of wearable devices perform functional operations by gestures, voice and eye movements, therefore the social acceptability of these actions should take full consideration. And for the special group of autistic children, their psychological and physiological characteristics should also be considered fully, whether they can accept such operation method and the degree of acceptance. For example, when the patient communicate with children of the same age by using wearable devices, the way patient get help from wearable devices should be taken into account thoroughly, to reduce the difference between autistic child and other partners to the greatest extent. Moreover, children with autism present very quiet, so it is unrealistic to allow the patient to achieve manipulating wearable devices by voice directly, other interactive ways can be converted to induce the patient to increase the frequency of using the language.In addition, the wearable devices advocated by this article are to provide auxiliary functions for children in their daily activities, therefore, in order to support the effective implementation of the task in different situations, this paper believes that wearable devices should have "micro action, multiplex mode, and more intelligent" on the treatment of children autism as the design direction of operation mode. "Micro action" avoids some large operating gestures, which is easy accepted by the patient, and reduces psychological difference with other children. "Multiplex mode" refers to richer information input mode, that is, the combination of multiple interactions. "More intelligent" means wearable devices can achieve obtain information from the environment more intelligently, to satisfy the requirements of the patient actively through data analysis.

Increasing the Sense of Authenticity with Scene Fusion. One of the purposes of the treatment of autistic children is to make the children better handle the outside information and the correct understanding of the living environment. Noiprawat and Sahachaiseri [12] studied environmental factors for strengthening the development of autistic children, and conclude that building good environment can enhance and promote the healthy development of autistic children, and the aim is to encourage autistic children to learn and produce self-motivation to do things in the environment. From this study, it can be seen that the correct environmental induction plays vital function in the treatment of autistic children. The wearable devices based on sensing interaction not only include identifying the child's manipulative input and collecting data from the human body through the sensor, but also include collection of environmental data, and feedback to the sensual system of the child after analyzed and processed. This implies the information inputs of the wearable devices are wide-ranging, one part comes from the active input of the child, and the other comes from the active collection of environmental information by the wearable devices. A large part of them includes actions and behaviors in children's daily life and some elements in living environment, which are not necessarily the intention of children's operation devices. For instance, the action of child's looking around the scenery will be regarded as user behavior input by head wearing type wearable devices. Thus it can be seen, the interactive design of wearable devices should ensure to have sufficient contact with the real use of the situation (environment, action, and goal) of the child, to more accurate and convenient use of environmental information for wearable devices, and intelligently integrate digital information into the environment, assist autistic children's daily life in more realistic means of expression. With the unceasingly application of augmented reality and virtual reality technology, the means of combining the real living environment with the elements of the virtual environment have been relatively mature, which can be used as way of realization for providing more realistic information explanation for autistic children.

Simplifying Interaction and Reducing Interference. Through the previous analysis of the psychological characteristics of children with autism, it can be understood that, most children do not have the ability to deal with this information when faced with the stimulation of a large number of external information, they will show neglect attitude or overly concentrated on one of these information, more seriously, will be emotionally out of control. Therefore, the information output of the wearable devices must be relatively single, reducing the interference of unnecessary visual information. The wearable devices that rely on the interaction of the display interface must ensure the simplicity and rationality of the information in the interface. For example, the case of using Google glasses to assist the life of autistic children, the interface of Google glasses will remain in people's visual field when they are worn, therefore, it is necessary to ensure that the information provided is streamlined and can be accepted by children. Furthermore, it is inevitable that the operations mentioned earlier are more intelligent. The man-machine active interaction is relatively weak due to the consideration of the psychological characteristics of children with autism, so, on the one hand, the operation of human active interaction should be simplified to make wearable devices provide services more intelligent and reduce the trouble of choice for children. On the other hand, guiding the children to increase active behavior through their favorite elements, this is the process of guiding children to develop normal behavior and the significance of intervention in the treatment of autism through wearable devices.

6   Conclusion and Discussion

This article explores the interactive design of wearable products from the perspective of autistic patients. This is a fundamental method to find the way to help treat autism, compared to previous product design, the wearable devices only act as the transmitter and receiver of the third party information, directly start from the perspective of autistic children, and have more direct practical significance. In this paper, network diagram of autism medical service system for wearable devices is proposed, interactive information flow of wearable device service system centered on autistic children is sorted out, and finally, concluded the design specification of wearable device interaction for children with autism. In summary, this article searches the optimal interaction mode between the patients and wearable devices from the perspective of patients throughout, expects to provide theoretical basis and new ideas for the interactive design of wearable medical products for children with autism, and plays a positive role for the happy life of autistic children and the stability and prosperity of society.

References

1. Lu, Y., Xie, H.: Wearable devices in medical applications. Chin. J. Med. Instrum. **41**(03), 213–215 (2017)
2. Bigham, S., Boucher, J., Mayes, A., et al.: Assessing recollection and familiarity in autistic spectrum disorders: methods and findings. Autism Dev. Disord. **40**(07), 878–889 (2010)
3. Geschwind, D.H.: Advances in autism. Annu. Rev. Med. **60**, 367–380 (2009)
4. Chen, S., Bai, X., Zhang, R.: The symptom, diagnosis and treatment for autism spectrum disorder. Adv. Psychol. Sci. **19**(01), 60–72 (2011)

5. Harrison, C., Lim, B., Shick, A., Hudson, S.: Where to locate wearable displays? Reaction time performance of visual alerts from tip to toe. In: Proceedings CHI, pp. 941–944 (2009)
6. Aziz, A.A., Moganan, F.F.M., Ismail, A., et al.: Autistic children's Kansei responses towards humanoid-robot as teaching mediator. Procedia Comput. Sci. **76**, 488–493 (2015)
7. Mintz, J., Branch, C., March, C., et al.: Key factors mediating the use of a mobile technology tool designed to develop social and life skills in children with autistic spectrum disorders. Comput. Educ. **58**(01), 53–62 (2012)
8. Dunne, L., Smyth, B.: Psychophysical elements of wearability. In: Proceedings of CHI 2007, pp. 299–302 (2007)
9. Profita, H., Clawson, J., Gilliland, S., et al.: Don't mind me touching my wrist: a case study of interacting with on- body technology in public. In: Proceedings of ISWC 2013, pp. 89–96 (2013)
10. Chen, L., Wang, G., Zhang, K.: Design and realization of human-computer interaction learning activity to improve the social interaction ability of children with autism. e-Education Research 2005, pp. 106–117 (2017)
11. Jiang, X., Chen, Y., Liu, J.: Cognitive wearable system for autistic patients. J. Zhejiang Univ. Eng. Sci. **4**, 637–647 (2017)
12. Noiprawat, N., Sahachaiseri, N.: The model of environments enhancing autistic children's development. Procedia Soc. Behav. Sci. **5**, 1257–1261 (2010)

Understanding Fine Motor Patterns in Children with Autism Using a Haptic-Gripper Virtual Reality System

Huan Zhao[1]([✉]), Amy Swanson[2], Amy Weitlauf[2], Zachary Warren[2], and Nilanjan Sarkar[3]

[1] Electrical Engineering and Computer Science Department, Vanderbilt University, Nashville, TN 37212, USA
huan.zhao@vanderbilt.edu
[2] Treatment and Research Institute for Autism Spectrum Disorders (TRIAD), Vanderbilt University, Nashville, TN 37212, USA
[3] Mechanical Engineering Department, Vanderbilt University, Nashville, TN 37212, USA

Abstract. Many children with Autism Spectrum Disorders (ASD) experience deficits in fine motor skills as compared to their typically developing (TD) peers. It is possible that the differences in fine motor patterns of children with ASD may provide useful insight into clinical diagnosis and intervention of ASD. This paper presents a preliminary study that used machine learning approaches to recognize the motor patterns exhibited by children with ASD based on their fine motor data obtained during carefully designed manipulation tasks in a virtual haptic environment. Six children with ASD and six TD children (aged 8–12) participated in a study that presented a series of fine motor tasks using a novel Haptic-Gripper virtual reality system. The results revealed that the identification accuracy of several machine learning approaches such as k-Nearest Neighbor (k-NN) and Artificial Neural Network (ANN) are encouraging and can reach up to 80%, indicating the potential of such an approach in ASD identification and intervention.

Keywords: Autism · Fine motor pattern · Haptic virtual reality system
Machine learning

1 Introduction

When referring to Autism spectrum disorder (ASD), people always focus on the core deficits of ASD in social communication and interaction [1]. However, the high prevalence of motor impairments and delays among ASD population cannot be overlooked [2]. Previous studies have noted several motor abnormalities of children with ASD, including atypical gait, postural control and upper limb movements [3, 4]. In particular, atypical fine motor control, such as the abnormalities in eye hand coordination, grasping and reaching, and less accurate manual dexterity, is found among children with ASD [5, 6].

© Springer International Publishing AG, part of Springer Nature 2018
M. Antona and C. Stephanidis (Eds.): UAHCI 2018, LNCS 10907, pp. 650–659, 2018.
https://doi.org/10.1007/978-3-319-92049-8_48

Early diagnosis and early enrollment in ASD intervention can offer many benefits, including increase treatment outcomes, earlier educational planning, and appropriate resources for health improvement [7]. However, ASD diagnosis is a difficult and complex task due to the wide range of symptoms involved. Currently, ASD diagnosis relies on the clinical evaluation of autism-specific behaviors via standardized interviews, observations and questionnaires, which is often time- and resource-consuming [8]. As a growing number of studies evidence the existence of atypical motor patterns in children with ASD, understanding and exploring the motor signatures in children with ASD provide a new methodology to facilitate early ASD diagnosis [9].

Computer-aided systems (e.g., robots and tablets) have been increasingly applied in ASD intervention taking advantage of providing an engaging intervention environment as well as recording objective and quantitative performance data [10–12]. The equipment with specific sensors to detect and measure motor information is easily accessible in recent days. Instead of using paper materials for motor function assessment, such as Beery VMI [13] and Mullen Scales [14], motor tasks in the form of computer tasks/games are more likely to be accepted among children with ASD, and are able to provide computational measures enabling the exploration of motor patterns using pattern recognition approaches.

The preliminary study presented in this paper aimed at investigating whether fine motor information is useful to identify children with ASD, and to look for the most discriminant fine motor features that distinguish the children with ASD from TD children. In this study, we employed a novel Haptic-Gripper virtual reality system, which provided fine motor tasks that required grip, hold, reach and touch manipulations from the participants, and recorded the manipulation data, such as grip force and movement location. We recruited six children with ASD and six TD children for this study, each of whom independently performed eight fine motor tasks with minimal disturbance. The recorded data from these tasks were then analyzed using several well-known machine learning approaches to obtain the fine motor patterns that could discriminate children with ASD from their TD peers. We expected that properly trained classification models based on fine motor patterns could be a practical predictor for the future ASD diagnosis.

The paper is organized as follows. Section 2 provides the details of the Haptic-Gripper virtual reality system. Section 3 describes the methods of data acquisition and data analysis. Section 4 presents the study results. Finally, in Sect. 5, we summarize the contributions of the current work along with its limitations and future potential.

2 The Haptic-Gripper Virtual Reality System

The Haptic-Gripper virtual reality System is an interactive system that we developed from a prototype used in a previous project [15] to provide virtual hand manipulation tasks for fine motor skill training of children with ASD. The system is able to conveniently set up at any place with computers, and allows the users to perform tasks under more comfortable and natural conditions that might provide more spontaneous and reliable data. From the feedback of the previous project, the children with ASD showed great interest in such a haptic system and were found to be engaged in the virtual tasks. We thus used this Haptic-Gripper virtual reality system in this study to provide virtual fine motor tasks by adapting the gripper size and redesigning the virtual tasks for the target participants. The Haptic-Gripper virtual reality system allows users to manipulate (e.g., move, grip and feel) objects in the virtual tasks by using a customized tool, named Haptic Gripper (see Fig. 1), and simultaneously records quantitative data regarding the users' manipulative behaviors (e.g., grip force and hand location).

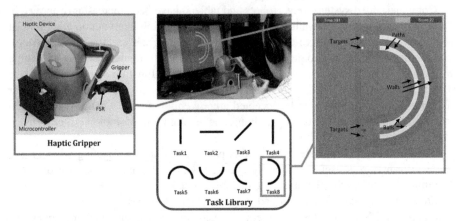

Fig. 1. A child was performing the Task 8 using the Haptic Gripper in the Haptic-Gripper virtual reality system.

In this study, we used this system to acquire fine motor data of participants from eight virtual fine motor tasks (see Fig. 1). In each task, the participant controlled two balls in a group (moving in parallel along the paths), and tried to make them go through the paths without hitting the walls, and to reach the two sets of targets at the both ends of the paths. At the beginning of the task, the grouped balls appeared at one end of the paths. Participants were asked to first touch the targets near the other end of the paths, and then go back through the paths to touch the targets near the start point. These tasks provided haptic feedback to improve the sense of immersion. For instance, if the balls collide with the walls, the participant would feel the resistance and friction from the walls.

All eight tasks required movement manipulation that controlled the location of the grouped balls, and grip manipulation that adjusted the inner distance of the grouped balls to fit the location of the paths. The Haptic Gripper was the tool for the participants to manipulate the grouped balls in the tasks. It was implemented by augmenting a Geomagic Touch Haptic Device [16] with a 3D-printed gripper consisting of force sensing resistors (FSRs) from Interlink Electronics [17]. Thus it was able to detect the gripper location and map the location data to those of the controlled balls, as well as to detect the grip force and use the force data to adjust the inner distance of the grouped balls with the following pre-defined logic:

$$Balls\_Distance = \begin{cases} small\_Distance & f \in [0N, 2.96N) \\ medium\_Distance & f \in [2.96N, 5.5N) \\ large\_Distance & f \in [5.5N, \infty) \end{cases} \quad (1)$$

All tasks required participants to grip with force within medium range i.e., [2.96N, 5.5N) in order to pass the parallel paths with fixed medium distance. This force range was determined based on the grip force of Grade 4 children used in handwriting [18].

Figure 1 illustrates the use of the Haptic-Gripper virtual reality system and the task types we used in this study. A child grabbed the gripper and put her thumb and index finger on the press plates. She moved the gripper and applied appropriate grip force to move the grouped balls through the white paths to touch the targets and get rewards. Eight tasks with paths of different shapes were prepared in the task library and were loaded automatically after one task was completed.

3   Method

The purpose of this study was to investigate whether virtual tasks that involved fine motor activities could contribute to the classification of children with ASD from their TD peers using machine learning approaches. The study was approved by the Institutional Review Board of Vanderbilt University.

3.1   Participants

We recruited six participants with ASD and six TD participants through a research registry of the autism center of Vanderbilt University. The participants with ASD had confirmed diagnoses by a clinician based on the Diagnostic and Statistical Manual of Mental Disorders (DSM-IV-TR) criteria [19]. The Stanford-Binet Intelligence Scales, Fifth edition (SB-5) [20] was employed to measure the intellectual functioning (IQ) of the participants, while the Social Responsiveness Scale, Second Edition (SRS-2) [21] was completed by participants' parents to index the ASD symptoms of their children. The participants' characteristics are shown in Table 1. From the table, we can see that participants in ASD group and TD group were similar regarding IQ and age.

Table 1. Participants' characteristics.

Metrics	ASD group	TD group	$t(10)$	p
	Mean (SD)	Mean (SD)		
Age	9.66 (1.36)	10.73 (1.91)	-1.12	.288
IQ	106 (7.1)	97.50 (11.91)	1.50	.164
SRS-2 T score	71.17 (11.18)	44.5 (6.53)	5.05	<.001

3.2 Procedure

The experimenters first introduced the Haptic-Gripper virtual reality system to the participants and explained how to perform the tasks using the Haptic Gripper. Because none of participants had used the haptic device before, they were allowed to participate in practice tasks with instructions from the experimenters to get familiarized with the system. Next, the participants started the tasks on their own from Task1 to Task8 in that order, and were allowed to take a rest between tasks.

3.3 Feature Extraction

The Haptic-Gripper virtual reality system collected four types of performance metrics at 50 Hz. These metrics included:

- Task Duration: the time one participant took for completing one task.
- Hit Number: the times of the grouped balls hitting the walls.
- Grip Force: a set of force data one participant applied in one task.
- Location: a set of location data of the grouped balls in one task.

From the Location data, we derived the Speed metric that were a set of movement speed data of the grouped balls in one task. We also generated the "Root-Mean-Square Error (RMSE)" metric to indicate the motion stability, which measured the distance between the location of the ball and the center of the path. In addition, by dividing each task into two sub-processes: (1) go forward through the paths (GO process), and (2) go backward through the paths (BACK process), we derived sub-metrics for each sub-process. For instance, "D_GO" represented the duration of completing the "go forward" sub-process, while "D_BACK" for the "go backward" sub-process.

In this study, we only considered time domain features that were frequently employed in the activity recognition literature [22]. For each type of metric, we extracted several features. We also combined some features when appropriate. Table 2 includes the final chosen performance metrics and corresponding features extracted from these metrics. For Task Duration, Hit Number and RMSE, except for the original data, we extracted the "difference" feature, which was defined as the difference between the BACK process data and GO process data. As for the Grip Force and Speed, we extracted more features, such as the mean, median, standard deviation, etc.

3.4 Feature Selection and Classification

The number of the overall extracted features was 59. We first ranked all features by F-values using one-way analysis of variance (ANOVA) test [23], and generated a feature list that arranged all features in descending order of F-values. Since some features were redundant to improve the accuracy of the classification model, we reduced the highly-related features (correlation > 0.9) to a single feature with a higher F-value, and finally obtained 35 features. To select the most discriminative features, we conducted the model training and evaluation on a subset of the feature list, where the subset size increased from 1 to 35. The feature subset was constructed by iteratively inserting a feature from the top of the feature list to the feature subset.

Table 2. Performance metrics and features.

Types	Metrics	Features
Task duration (D)	D, D_GO, D_BACK	Original metric, difference
Hit number (H)	H, H_GO, H_BACK	
RMSE (E)	E, E_GO, E_BACK	
Grip force (F)	F, F_GO, F_BACK	Difference, mean, median, standard deviation, coefficient of variation (COV), interquartile range, skewness, kurtosis, mean/median absolute deviation (mad), maximum
Speed (V)	V, V_GO , V_BACK	

We trained six classifiers (Table 3) on our dataset (96 samples), and used the leave-one-subject-out cross validation for model evaluation. The classification accuracy was evaluated using F_1 score, which considered the precision (P) and the recall (R) of the classification results. The F_1 score for each model was computed as:

$$F_1 = 2 \times \frac{P \times R}{P + R},$$
$$P = \frac{TP}{TP + FP}, R = \frac{TP}{TP + FN}, \tag{2}$$

where TP was the number of ASD samples that were correctly classified as the member of ASD group, FP was the number of TD samples that were incorrectly classified as the member of ASD group, and FN was the number of ASD samples that were incorrectly classified as the member of TD group.

Table 3. Classification methods.

Classifiers	Parameters
Decision Trees	CART algorithm
Random Forest	50 random trees
Naïve Bayes	Gaussian
k-Nearest Neighbor (k-NN)	k = 7, Euclidean distance
Artificial Neural Network (ANN)	1 hidden layer (4 neurons)
Support Vector Machine (SVM)	Radial basis function kernel

4   Results

Figure 2 shows the classification results of six classifiers with respect to the number of features. Table 4 lists the maximum scores for each classifier. The results indicated that all classifiers can achieve maximum accuracies within 67–80% by considering appropriate features. The k-NN and ANN classifiers had the best performance with the maximum accuracy of 80%, when the k-NN classifier used the top one feature (Mean of Grip Force during the BACK process) and the ANN classifier used the top six features. The Naïve Bayes and the Random Forest classifiers had the second best performance with the maximum accuracy of 75%, when they separately used the top 5 and 11 features. The SVM and Decision Trees classifiers had lower accuracies of 71% and 67% respectively.

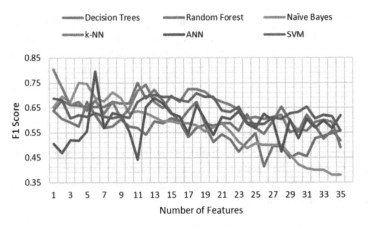

Fig. 2. Classification results for six classifiers with respect to the number of features.

According to the results of the ANOVA test, the top 10 features (all with $p < .05$) are related to the Grip Force (six features) and Speed data (four features). It suggested that Grip Force and Speed data provided much information for improving the classification of participants with ASD. The boxplots of the top 10 features (see Fig. 3) indicated that the ASD group applied significantly smaller Grip Force than the TD group (BACK_Fmean, Fmedian, GO_Fmedian). During the BACK process, the TD group increased much more Grip Force than the ASD group (DIFF_Fmean, DIFF_Fmedian), and reduced the variability of Grip Force much more than the ASD group (DIFF_Fmeanmad). In addition, during the GO process, the ASD group had greater Speed than the TD group (GO_Vmean), and had a lower kurtosis of Speed (GO_Vkurtosis). During the BACK process, the TD group reduced the COV of Speed much more than the ASD group (DIFF_Vcov). During the whole process, the ASD group had greater variability of Speed than the TD group (Vmeanmad).

Table 4. Classification results evaluated by F_1 score.

Classifiers	# Features	Max F_1
Decision Trees	5	0.67
Random Forest	11	0.75
Naïve Bayes	5	0.75
k-Nearest Neighbor (k-NN)	1	0.80
Artificial Neural Network (ANN)	6	0.80
Support Vector Machine (SVM)	18	0.71

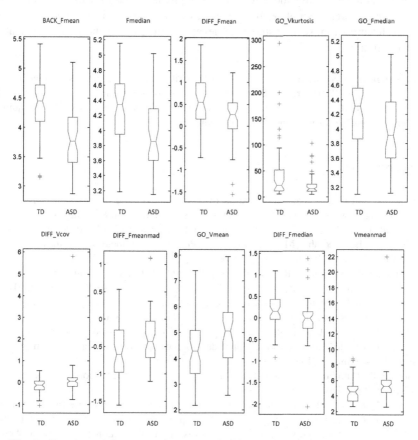

Fig. 3. Boxplots of the top ten features ranked by F-values using the ANOVA test.

5 Conclusion

In this paper, we present a preliminary study evaluating the effectiveness of using fine motor information for ASD identification, and achieved up to 80% accuracy using machine learning approaches. The results revealed the differential fine motor patterns were related to the grip force and movement speed of children with ASD, supporting the notion that motor differences can be a predictor for ASD diagnosis. It is worth noting that the Grip Force data that have not been sufficiently analyzed in existing studies were shown to contain most useful information to improve classification accuracy. The study also offered insights on the potential of computer-aided systems for ASD diagnosis and intervention, which offer benefits in recording objective measures and providing an engaging, low-cost and non-intrusive environment.

While the results of our study is encouraging, it is limited due to small sample size and feature types. The follow-up work will include recruiting a larger population with younger participants, developing more virtual fine motor tasks with different levels of difficulties, and integrating more features to improve the classification performance. This area of research has not yet been explored in depth and it is possible to combine tasks and features from several studies to develop a more comprehensive classification test in the future.

Acknowledgment. We would like to thank all the children and their parents for their participation in this study. We are grateful for the support provided by the National Institutes of Health under Grant 1R01MH091102-01A1 and Grant 1R21MH111548-01 for this work. The authors are solely responsible for the contents and opinions expressed in this manuscript.

References

1. Baio, J.: Prevalence of autism spectrum disorders: autism and developmental disabilities monitoring network, 14 Sites, United States, 2008. Morbidity and Mortality Weekly Report. Surveillance Summaries. vol. 61, no. 3. Centers for Disease Control and Prevention (2012)
2. Ming, X., Brimacombe, M., Wagner, G.C.: Prevalence of motor impairment in autism spectrum disorders. Brain Dev. **29**(9), 565–570 (2007)
3. Doumas, M., McKenna, R., Murphy, B.: Postural control deficits in autism spectrum disorder: the role of sensory integration. J. Autism Dev. Disord. **46**(3), 853–861 (2016)
4. Mari, M., et al.: The reach–to–grasp movement in children with autism spectrum disorder. Philos. Trans. R. Soc. Lond. B Biol. Sci. **358**(1430), 393–403 (2003)
5. David, F.J., et al.: Coordination of precision grip in 2–6 years-old children with autism spectrum disorders compared to children developing typically and children with developmental disabilities (2012)
6. Gowen, E., Hamilton, A.: Motor abilities in autism: a review using a computational context. J. Autism Dev. Disord. **43**(2), 323–344 (2013)
7. Koegel, L.K., et al.: The importance of early identification and intervention for children with or at risk for autism spectrum disorders. Int. J. Speech-Lang. Pathol. **16**(1), 50–56 (2014)
8. Filipek, P.A., et al.: The screening and diagnosis of autistic spectrum disorders. J. Autism Dev. Disord. **29**(6), 439–484 (1999)
9. Trevarthen, C., Delafield-Butt, J.T.: Autism as a developmental disorder in intentional movement and affective engagement. Front. Integr. Neurosci. **7**, 49 (2013)
10. Zhao, H., Swanson, A., Weitlauf, A., Warren, Z., Sarkar, N.: A novel collaborative virtual reality game for children with ASD to foster social interaction. In: Antona, M., Stephanidis, C. (eds.) UAHCI 2016. LNCS, vol. 9739, pp. 276–288. Springer, Cham (2016). https://doi.org/10.1007/978-3-319-40238-3_27
11. Zheng, Z., et al.: Design of an autonomous social orienting training system (ASOTS) for young children with autism. IEEE Trans. Neural Syst. Rehabil. Eng. **25**(6), 668–678 (2017)

12. Zhao, H., Swanson, A., Weitlauf, A., Warren, Z., Sarkar, N.: Design of a tablet game to assess the hand movement in children with autism. In: Antona, M., Stephanidis, C. (eds.) UAHCI 2017. LNCS, vol. 10277, pp. 555–564. Springer, Cham (2017). https://doi.org/10.1007/978-3-319-58706-6_45

13. Beery, K.E., Natasha Beery, N.A.B.: The Beery-Buktenica Developmental Test of Visual-Motor Integration: Beery VMI with Supplemental Developmental Tests of Visual Perception and Motor Coordination: Administration, Scoring and Teaching Manual, 6th edn. NSC Pearson, Minneapolis (2010)

14. Mullen, E.M.: Mullen Scales of Early Learning. AGS, Circle Pines (1995)

15. Zhao, H., Zheng, Z., Swanson, A., Weitlauf, A., Warren, Z., Sarkar, N.: Design of a haptic virtual system for improving fine motor skills in children with autism. In: Nunes, I. (ed.) International Conference on Applied Human Factors and Ergonomics. Springer, Cham (2017). https://doi.org/10.1007/978-3-319-60366-7_20

16. The Geomagic Touch Haptic Device. http://www.geomagic.com/en/products/phantom-omni/overview

17. Interlink Electronics. http://www.interlinkelectronics.com/FSR402.php

18. Schwellnus, H., et al.: Writing forces associated with four pencil grasp patterns in grade 4 children. Am. J. Occup. Ther. 67(2), 218–227 (2013)

19. Diagnostic and Statistical Manual of Mental Disorders: Quick Reference to the Diagnostic Criteria from DSM-IV-TR, 4th edn. American Psychiatric Association, Washington D.C. (2000)

20. Roid, G.H.: Stanford-Binet Intelligence Scales. Riverside Publishing, Itasca (2003)

21. Constantino, J.N., Gruber, C.P.: Social Responsiveness Scale (SRS). Western Psychological Services, Los Angeles (2007)

22. Lara, O.D., Labrador, M.A.: A survey on human activity recognition using wearable sensors. IEEE Commun. Surv. Tutor. 15(3), 1192–1209 (2013)

23. Howell, D.C.: Statistical Methods for Psychology. Cengage Learning, Boston (2012)

Evaluating the Accessibility of Scratch
for Children with Cognitive Impairments

Misbahu S. Zubair[1,2(✉)], David Brown[1], Thomas Hughes-Roberts[1],
and Matthew Bates[2]

[1] School of Science and Technology, Nottingham Trent University,
Nottingham, UK
{misbahu.zubair,david.brown,
thomas.hughesroberts}@ntu.ac.uk
[2] Software Engineering Department, Bayero University, Kano, Nigeria
mszubair.se@buk.edu.ng, matthew.bates@ntu.ac.uk

Abstract. Research on the use of interactive media as learning tools for children with cognitive impairments has focused mainly on employing predesigned
content, rather than constructing new content. Visual programming tools could
potentially provide cognitively impaired children with a platform that can enable
them to create their own interactive media. However, very little is known about
the accessibility of the tools. This study uses a novel approach to evaluate the
accessibility of Scratch (a visual programming tool) for children with cognitive
impairments by employing a Grounded Theory research method. The study was
conducted with 9 participants: 2 special education teachers and 7 cognitively
impaired children over a period of ten weeks. The children's usage of Scratch
was documented through screen capturing. In addition, semi structured interviews were conducted with the two teachers. Grounded Theory based analysis
was performed using QSR NVivo, which led to the identification of: accessibility issues; causal conditions; contexts; strategies employed to tackle issues;
and consequences. Thus, the findings of this research contribute to existing
knowledge on the accessibility of visual programming tools and elucidate the
experience of cognitively impaired children while using the tools.

Keywords: Accessibility · Visual programming · Cognitive impairments
Scratch · Grounded Theory

1 Introduction

Over the past two decades, there has been much interest in the use of interactive media
as learning tools. Due to their interactive, entertaining and engaging nature, they have
been successfully employed as learning aids for children with cognitive impairments.
They have been applied in teaching curriculum subjects such as mathematics [1], as
well and independent living skills [2] with positive results. More recently though,
research on the use of interactive media for learning has been moving towards creating
rather than consuming pre-designed content [3]. One of the main forces driving this
movement is the availability of easy to use creative software, among which are Visual
Programming (VP) tools.

© Springer International Publishing AG, part of Springer Nature 2018
M. Antona and C. Stephanidis (Eds.): UAHCI 2018, LNCS 10907, pp. 660–676, 2018.
https://doi.org/10.1007/978-3-319-92049-8_49

A VP language "allows the user to specify a program in a two (or more) dimensional fashion" [4]. VP tools integrate a VP language and an environment that supports the visualization of program execution. Recently, several visual programming tools have been developed to improve children's access to programming skills at an early age; they include Scratch [5] and Alice [6].

Scratch allows users to create interactive and media rich projects such as animated stories, games, and music videos. It is free and open source, and can be used either online, or through its offline desktop application [5]. Scratch projects are made up of media (2D backdrops and sprites, and sounds) and scripts. Media can be built, imported or created within Scratch, and scripts are made up of blocks of instructions. The main aim of Scratch is "to introduce programming to those with no previous programming experience" [7]. Hence its features such as the use of visual blocks, single-window user interface layout with multiple panes, minimal command set, and its no error approach to error handling. It focuses less on direct instructions and encourages learning through exploration. Therefore, Scratch provides a sandbox environment with few rules and no restrictions as to what one can create (Fig. 1).

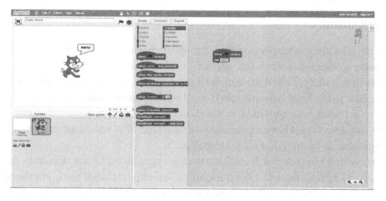

Fig. 1. A screenshot of a Scratch project created on the Scratch website.

VP tools like Scratch can potentially play an important role in learning and teaching for those with cognitive impairments. They can provide a platform for fostering creativity, improving communication skills, building new interests, learning computational and problem-solving skills, and ultimately lead to inclusion. However, conducted literature review showed little is being done to utilize them as learning aids for children with cognitive impairments. Furthermore, very little is known about their accessibility to individuals that face the difficulties associated with cognitive impairments.

This paper presents a study conducted with the aim of evaluating the accessibility of Scratch for children with cognitive impairments. With the objectives of identifying the difficulties they face, and the effects of those difficulties. The section that follows discusses the research methodology used, the participants, and the process of data collection and analysis. Findings of the study are presented in detail in the third section, followed by a section that reflects on the findings and their implications. Conclusion and future work are presented in the fifth and final section.

2 Methodology

The aim of this study is to evaluate the accessibility of Scratch for children with cognitive impairments. Due to the nature of the participants and the research goal, a Grounded Theory [8] approach was followed. Grounded Theory "consists of a systematic yet flexible guidelines for collecting and analysing qualitative data to construct a theory from the data themselves" [9]. It is best suited for situations where the goal is to understand, from the perspective of people, how they understand and deal with challenging situations. It does not require a prior hypothesis to focus research on [10], hence it can be applied in situations where very little is known about the issue to be researched.

Although this method has its origins in social sciences, it has been adopted by researchers outside the field, including HCI researchers [11–13].

2.1 Participants

Six special education schools catering for individuals with different needs and age groups were contacted within the greater Nottinghamshire area, and one agreed to participate in the study. Given the nature of the population with regards to diversity and unique needs, the school was consulted in choosing participants for the study. A criterion for inclusion was provided to the school; participants should be less than 18 years old, are able to and have experience using a web browser on a computer and have been diagnosed as being cognitively impaired.

A class which consisted of 8 students was recommended by the school as the group that's stands to benefit the most from a study of this kind. Out of the eight members of the class, seven participated in the study and one was disqualified because of his inability to use a web browser. Participants were aged between thirteen and fourteen years old and comprised of four females and three males. Table 1 below shows the participants' profiles provided by the class teacher.

Table 1. Participants' diagnosed cognitive impairment and fine motor skills.

Participant	Cognitive impairment	Fine motor skills
P1	Autism spectrum disorder, moderate learning disability	Poor
P2	Autism spectrum disorder, moderate learning disability	Good
P3	Moderate learning disability	Poor
P4	Severe learning disability	Good
P5	Autism spectrum disorder, moderate learning disability	Good
P6	Autism spectrum disorder, moderate learning disability	Good
P7	Autism spectrum disorder, severe learning disability	Good

Two of the participating children have been diagnosed with learning disability only. Learning disability affects an individual's ability to understand information, communicate, and learn new things (both academic and non-academic). It can also affect one's attention, memory, coordination, social skills, and emotional maturity [14]. Its nature, i.e. moderate or severe, determines how adverse the difficulties are on the individual.

The remaining five participating children have been diagnosed with both learning disability and autism spectrum disorder. Autism spectrum disorders (ASD) refer to a range of conditions that result in difficulties interacting appropriately with others, possessing language and communication disorders and peculiarities, struggling with changes in the environment, and peculiar repetitive behaviour [15]. However, being a spectrum disorder, individuals with ASD tend to have unique needs and requirements.

Two class teachers (T1 and T2), one male and one female, also participated in the study. Between them, they had an average of more than eleven years of experience in teaching children with special needs.

2.2   Data Collection and Analysis

Even though the most common sources of data used in grounded theory are collected through interviews and observations, almost any form of written, observed and recorded data can be used [16]. This study employed a combination of video screen capture and semi-structured interviews.

Screen capture is performed using software that "records the actions, sounds and movements that take place on electronic monitors" [17]. A free and open source screen capturing software (Camstudio [18]) was used for screen capturing in this study. It was used to collect empirical data on the interactions between the participants and Scratch.

Participants were introduced to Scratch and its features in an introductory session that lasted for one hour. In each of the ten weeks that followed, at least two of the seven participating children used Scratch to create stories during a 45-min storytelling session. Storytelling was chosen by the class teachers because of its potential in improving the participants' communication skills. Graphical guides for accomplishing common tasks (based on previous stories participants have created) were designed and provided to participants. The guides consisted of scripts for participants to duplicate, and instructions written in communication symbols. The researcher acted as a participant observer, and at least one teaching assistant was available to support participants per session. All sessions were held in the participants' classroom, using their classroom laptops, and were screen captured using Camstudio. To tackle this methods limitation of capturing only onscreen data [19], audio data of participants interacting with their environment was included in the recordings.

As recommended in Grounded Theory, data collection and analysis were conducted simultaneously. The process usually starts with transcribing data, then coding. Coding is the process of assigning words or phrases that capture or summarize the concepts present within a portion of language based or visual data [20]. The grounded theory coding method defined by Corbin and Strauss [16] was used in this study. It has three stages: open, axial and selective coding. Concepts are identified from data and allocated codes during open coding. Related concepts are then combined to form categories. Axial coding is conducted next, this phase involves further developing categories of data and finding relationships that exist between categories and sub categories [21], using the "coding paradigm" of conditions, context, strategies and consequences [16]. The final coding phase is selective coding, it involves the unification of all categories around a central category; the central phenomenon of the study. A descriptive narrative, which has the central category at its centre is then developed [22]. Constant comparison should be done until additional data adds no new knowledge about the concepts and categories generated i.e. saturation has been reached.

Data analysis in this study was done using QSR Nvivo 11 [23] data analysis software. All video screen capture data was watched three times, first to transcribe interesting observations, then to code them as concepts, and lastly to identify and verify relationships between concepts. Concepts were combined into sub categories and categories. As the study concerned accessibility, all accessibility issues identified in the data were scrutinized to determine their causal conditions, the context in which they occurred, the strategies adopted by participants in the situation, and their consequences. However, saturation was reached before a theory was fully formed.

Based on the emerging theory from the screen capture data analysed, semi-structured interviews were conducted with the two class teachers. In Grounded Theory, where focus is on data collection for the sake of creating a theory, semi-structured interviews are valuable tools for researchers to target concepts that they consider relevant for their theory. Collected data was analysed in the same way the screen capture data was, and used to verify and complete the theory.

During this process more than 70 concepts were identified. After comparing and verifying data with data, a theory was developed with 5 main categories, 20 sub-categories and 69 concepts.

3 Findings

Following an iterative and rigorous process of coding, comparing codes, and verification with the data itself, concepts were categorized into phenomena, causal conditions, context, strategies and consequences. Phenomena represents the study's main interest, which is accessibility issues in this case. Accessibility issues observed in this study were classified into two types, user interface (UI) related and cognition related issues. The study's findings lead to the creation of a theoretical model of how these accessibility issues affect the use of scratch by children with cognitive impairments.

In the sub-sections that follow, each category is discussed in detail. Examples of observations from the screen capture videos as well as quotations established from the interview transcripts are used to support interesting discussions. Although both types of accessibility issues belong to one category, they have been presented separately for clarity. A table showing a category's subcategories (if any), concepts, and an example of a concept's occurrence follows each category discussion. Observations and quotations include one or more of the following individuals: a participant (P1–7), the researcher conducting the session, a teaching assistant (TA) and a class teacher (T1–2). Finally, the theoretical model is presented.

3.1 UI Related Issues

These accessibility issues are directly related to how the Scratch user interface is designed, and how it is interacted with. They are discussed below, and summarised in Table 2.

Table 2. UI related issues, with observation examples for selected concepts.

UI related issues		
Sub-category	Concept(s)	Example
Recognising buttons	- Difficulty differentiating shrink and grow - Difficulty deleting sprite - Difficulty deleting script - Difficulty importing sprite - Difficulty importing backdrop	Difficulty importing sprite example: at the start of his fourth session, P2 couldn't find the button for adding new characters on the interface
Differentiating blocks	- Drags wrong block	Drags wrong block: while following the provided guide in the first session, P3 dragged and used a 'switch costume' block instead of a 'say' block
Differentiating links	- Difficulty finding backdrop category - Difficulty finding block category - Difficulty finding sprite category	Difficulty finding backdrop category: in his first session, P7 could not find the link to 'Underwater' backdrop category
Switching area	- Difficulty changing area - Difficulty differentiating tabs	Difficulty changing area: in her third session, P4 could not switch from 'Scripts' to 'Sounds' area
Dragging	- Difficulty dragging sprites - Difficulty dragging blocks - Difficulty rearranging blocks in script	Difficulty rearranging blocks in script: in her first session, P4 struggled to drag a block above another block
Selecting	- Difficulty selecting tool - Difficulty switching active sprite - Difficulty switching active costume	Difficulty switching active costume: in her second session, P1 struggled to activate a sprite thumbnail by dragging unintentionally instead of clicking

Recognising Buttons. Findings from this study revealed that at one point or another all participants struggled to recognise buttons on the user interface. Buttons for importing media such as sprites and backdrops caused difficulties at the beginning of sessions but seemed to be easier to identify with time. However, participants continuously struggled with differentiating buttons for shrink, grow and delete tools. In one scenario observed, to shrink the size of a knight sprite, P2 repeatedly chose and used the grow tool, which did not produce the intended results.

Differentiating Links. Links in Scratch can be used to access collections of similar items. For example, when importing backdrops or sprites, links ease the process of locating items by grouping images into themes or categories. This study observed that participants rarely utilised this feature while working alone. Participants had to be advised to use the feature to locate specific items. For example, in one instance, P7 was trying to add a dragon sprite to his story, a TA advised P7 to look in 'Fantasy'. P7 then clicked on two wrong links, before the TA pointed him to the right link.

Another use for links in Scratch is to access block categories. When instructing participants, it was observed that they were only able to identify block category links when they were associated with a colour (block categories are colour coded). Simply using the text associated with the category's link was not enough. For example, in one session, P2 asked for help on integrating a sound into his story, he was instructed to click to the 'Sound' block category, he then hovered over 'Looks' for a few moments until the link was associated with a colour. However, it was observed that although all categories are coded with unique colours, some of the colours are similar. As a result, some categories were difficult to identify even when associated with colours.

Differentiating Blocks. Scratch uses a unique colour to identify each category of blocks, which means all the blocks within a category have the same colour. Although a few blocks are labelled with both text and a symbol, most blocks' unique identifier is their text label. Observations showed participants in this study struggled to differentiate blocks of the same category. This was recorded in both cases where participants were following instructions, and when participants were creating their own scripts.

Switching Area. Most Scratch projects require users to move continuously between the scripts, sounds and costumes area using tabs. However, some participants kept finding themselves stuck in one area and unable to switch to another. For example, when P7 customised a sprite in the costumes area and wanted to get back to the scripts area, he attempted that by trying to minimise the browser, when that didn't work he clicked the browsers 'Back' button, that brought up a 'Save' message box and the attention of a TA who showed P7 how to switch areas using tabs.

Other observations showed the struggle of participants who understood the purpose of the tabs but could not tell one from the other. Those participants used trial and error to find the area they were looking for.

Dragging. Participants, especially those with fine motor skills difficulties struggled with dragging items within the Scratch interface. They had difficulties positioning their sprites when setting up their stories, as well as dragging blocks to create scripts. However, when it came to rearranging blocks in a script, observations showed all participants faced difficulties in dragging a block to a new position.

Selecting. To use tools such as grow, shrink, delete and tools within Scratch's paint editor, one must first click on the required tool to select it. Participants with poor fine motor skills also found this task difficult. Especially when the tool is small and/or closely positioned to another tool. Another group of items of that were difficult to select were sprite thumbnails for switching active sprite or choosing an active sprite for a costume. In these situations, participants were observed to be dragging slightly, when their intention was to click.

3.2   Cognition Related Issues

These accessibility issues are related to the cognitive processes required to efficiently use Scratch. They are discussed below, and summarised in Table 3.

Table 3. Cognition related issues, with observation examples for selected concepts.

Cognition related issues		
Sub-category	Concept(s)	Example
Defining instruction	- Project executed without script - Expecting a sprite to make use of another sprite's script	Program executed without script: in his second session, P7 repeatedly executed his project after adding a 'ghost' sprite and wondering why it was not moving
Structuring and sequencing	- Difficulty reinitializing sprite position - Difficulty sequencing actions and events - Difficulty translating idea to Scratch project	Difficulty sequencing actions and events: in her first session, P5 struggled to sequence a conversation between three characters in her story
Staying on track	- Abandons original story - Repeats customizing character - Repeats adding character - Repeats moving character - Repeats resizing character	Repeats resizing character: in her first session, P4 spent time growing then shrinking her sprites repeatedly

Defining Instruction. In Scratch, each component of a project that has a behaviour needs to have that role explicitly defined using scripts. On many occasions observed, participants expected their sprites to perform some form of action with no script defined. Participants that faced this difficulty were observed to execute their projects without adding any script again and again, or expect a script assigned to one sprite to also work on another just by activating the second sprite.

Structuring and Sequencing. All participants, at one point or another struggled with structuring and sequencing the events in their stories. When participants were creating stories in the moment, without any initial plans, they seemed to lack the direction and guidance they needed to develop ideas into their projects, and easily went back to recreating old storylines from previous sessions.

   When participants had a predetermined story to create, they faced other kinds of difficulties. Such as struggling to correctly sequence the actions of sprites, and on fewer occasions, struggling to reinitialise the positions of sprites after execution.

Staying on Track. This study observed that participants were easily distracted from the goal of creating a story. This happened usually because of a discovery within the software in form of media, a feature of the software, or a new skill. The discovery then led to loosing focus on the overall story to focus on one aspect or abandoning the story altogether. For example, when P5 was introduced to Scratch's paint editor, she spent the next 13 min modifying her sprites.

   However, not all recorded instances of participants getting distracted were due to distractions from within Scratch, distractions from the participants' surroundings have also been recorded. For example, during one session P6 was in the middle of creating a story when he overhead a conversation about choosing a Scratch username for P7, P6 then abandoned his story to add sprites related to the username mentioned.

3.3   Causal Conditions

These conditions lead to the occurrences of accessibility issues. They are discussed below, and summarised in Table 4.

Table 4. Causal conditions of accessibility issues with observation examples for selected concepts.

Causal conditions		
Sub-category	Concept(s)	Example
Text labels as identifiers	- Difficulty with reading or spelling - Difficulty reading labels	Difficulty reading labels: when directed to look in 'People' to find a 'diver' sprite, P2 could not recognize the right link
Similar colours in proximity	- Difficulty processing visual data - Difficulty differentiating similar colours	Difficulty differentiating similar colours: while following the guide in her second session, P1 was confused by two categories that are represented by different shades of the same colour
Lack of templates	- Need for concrete structure - Poorly developed story	Poorly developed story: P4's second session's story consisted of a backdrop, three characters and no script
Lack of constraints	- Need for focus and clarity - Repetitive behaviour	Repetitive behaviour: in his fourth session, P7 kept adding characters to his story for the first half of his session
Mouse input	- Difficulty interacting with mouse	Difficulty interacting with mouse: in her first session, P3 used two hands to drag objects on screen

Text Labels as Identifiers. Throughout this study, participants struggled with aspects of Scratch that required reading and writing skills. Links and blocks that are identified using text labels were a constant source of struggle for participants. Their writing and spelling difficulties were also evident when they attempted to input or change block inputs, e.g. when inputting the text to be displayed by a 'Say' block.

Similar Colours in Proximity. Although using colours helped participants recognise and differentiate objects, using similar colours to differentiate objects within proximity defeated the purpose. This was mostly observed when participants were trying to locate a block category coded with a colour that's unique, yet similar to that of other categories. A possible reason for this confusion may be found in the interview excerpt below:

> *".... even without visual impairment, visual processing is quite a difficult thing for them."* (T1)

Lack of Templates. Although Scratch provides a guide for creating example projects, it does not provide a structure or template for creating a project. This led to participants having difficulty in developing their story ideas or structuring them in the right way within Scratch. T1 mentions how participants can be helped in that aspect using concrete objects:

> *"... that's where students struggle, having that imagination. By having props, that's sort of your concrete, real bit"* (T1)

Templates or interactive guides could have been applied as a concrete frame in the scenario, for participants to build projects around.

Lack of Constraints. One of the most appealing features of Scratch is that it has no restrictions on what users can create. But for the participants in this study, this might be a disadvantage due to the difficulty they have staying focused. T1 explains why having focus is important, and how it's implemented in the classroom, below:

> *"We do that already with our curriculum planning don't we, because if we give ourselves a title that we want, and then that sort of immediately gives you a bit of focus, a bit of clarity... for example, if you are doing a story, and you said 'Right, we are doing something about the sea', then obviously that gets rid of a load, and that's what you are trying to do. Otherwise there is far too much choice out there. But in saying that, what we try and do here is get it to be student led, so what are you interested in, talk to the students about it"* (T1)

Lack of constraints did not just affect participants that found it difficult to stay focused on tasks, but also those participants that were repetitive in performing tasks, choosing characters, story themes, etc. T2 discusses how the lack of constraint affected P7 and how restrictions may help, below:

> *"he can't move on, like his favourite colour is red and he has to paint everything red... if he was working with the same 10 set of characters, what would happen if he uses the program and those 10 characters weren't there, he'd have to use something else."* (T2)

With Scratch's sandbox nature, users with characteristics similar to participants of this study are likely to get side-tracked from their original goals.

Mouse Input. Participants, especially those with poor fine motor skills struggled with mouse operations such as dragging, double clicking and even clicking. Clicking was especially difficult on objects that can be clicked as well as dragged. T1 explains why one participant struggles with mouse operations in the excerpt below:

> *"...she would find it extremely difficult just to pick something up off the table, because she doesn't have that depth in perception. If you are using a mouse, for it to register your finger, you can't be sort of up and down."* (T1)

Scratch being a drag and drop environment, relies highly on mouse input, hence caused a lot of difficulties to this group of participants.

3.4 Context

It was observed that different usability issues occurred in different contexts of usage, they are discussed below, and summarised in Table 5.

Table 5. Context for the occurrences of accessibility issues with observation examples of selected concepts.

Context		
Sub-category	Concept(s)	Example
Adding and modifying media	- Dragging sprite - Adding sprite - Adding sound - Customising sprite - Resizing sprite - Adding backdrop - Deleting sound - Deleting Sprite	Adding backdrop: in his first session, P2 was trying to locate a backdrop fit for a medieval story
Planning and implementing story	- Changing story plot - Changing story character(s) - Changing story setting - Assigning roles and instructions - Integrating interests - Deciding on storyline/characters/setting	Integrating interests: in his second session, P7 was dedicated to creating a story set in his favourite place (deep blue sea)
Scripting	- Locating category - Locating block - Adding block - Rearranging script - Deleting block - Inputting values into block	Locating block: in his first session, P7 tried to locate a block for changing the colour of his sprite

Adding and Modifying Media. Identified UI related issues mostly occurred during two aspects of using Scratch, the first is when participants were working with media e.g. sprites and backdrops. At this stage participants were interested in locating, adding or positioning, and may choose to customize imported media to fit their needs. The mentioned operations required identifying links, buttons, tools, selecting, and may also require dragging.

Scripting. The second aspect of Scratch that triggered UI related difficulties is scripting. In creating scripts for their stories, participants had to select the right script, locate the right block category, identify the right block and drag it to the scripting area.

Planning and Implementing Story. Cognition related accessibility issues affected participants trying to breakdown their story ideas into components that can be represented within Scratch. This involved building up a setting, characters and storylines.

For instance, structuring and sequencing difficulties were mostly observed when participants added sprites and were trying to decide how best to organize and add scripts to them. Difficulties with staying focused on the other hand were mostly recorded when participants were integrating their interests in the story such as specific characters or themes, or when they decided to implement changes to their stories.

3.5 Strategies

Observations showed that participants used one of four strategies when they faced difficulties. The strategies are discussed below, and summarised in Table 6.

Table 6. Strategies employed when accessibility difficulties are faced with examples of selected concepts.

Strategy	
Concept(s)	Example
- Idle - Retry - Ask for help - Move to another task	Move to another task: in her first session, P4 could not find the 'paint bucket' tool to edit her sprite in Scratch's paint editor, she decided to resize all her sprites

Idle. This strategy was more common among participants with communication difficulties. When facing an issue, or when they were not sure how to proceed after completing a task, these participants normally became idle. For example, during a session where P1 was creating a story about a dragon and pony, she became idle after adding the pony sprite and its corresponding script, until she was noticed by the researcher.

Ask for Help. Other participants reacted to difficulties by asking for help from either the TA or the researcher. Participants asked for help in performing tasks ranging from navigating the user interface to implementing a storyline. For instance, when P2 was trying to locate a diver to include in his story, he asked the researcher who advised him to look under the 'People' category.

Retry. Retrying was another strategy used by participants to tackle difficulties, mainly UI related ones. Observations showed how participants attempted clicking or dragging multiple times until they achieved their objective, tried out multiple tools until the right one was chosen, had a look at different links to find the right group of media etc.

Move to Another Task. The last strategy that was observed is moving to another task. In some cases, it was employed as a second strategy, after being idle for a while or retrying with no success. Participants then moved to a different task which may be related or unrelated to their current project.

3.6   Consequences

Consequences show the actions taken by the researcher or TA to address accessibility issues, or a strategy. They are discussed below, and summarised in Table 7.

Table 7. Consequences of facing accessibility issues or employing strategy, with observation examples for selected concepts.

Consequences		
Sub-category	Concept(s)	Example
Participant is kept on track	- Participant is asked to share plans - Discussing participant's story	Discussing participant's story: when P3 was found idle in her first session, the researcher asked what her characters were up to, and she attempted to add scripts to illustrate
Participant is instructed	- Participant follows instructions - Participant performs task after receiving explanation	Participant follows instructions: in his second session, P2 followed the researcher's instruction to create an animation of a shark opening and closing its jaws
Task is performed for participant	- Script is created for participant - Sprite is resized for participant - Tool is selected for participant - Tab is changed for participant - Sprite is deleted for participant	Script is created for participant: a disappearing script was created for P3 in her first session

Participant is Kept on Track. When a TA or the researcher noticed a participant that is idle, taking too much time on a single task, or performing tasks not related to their story, they tried to get the participant back on track and provide help where necessary. This was done by drawing the participant's attention to other aspects of the story using questions or discussion. For example, when P5 was caught up in editing her character, she was simply asked questions about the characters role in the story, and P5 got interested again in creating the story not just the character. This was noticed to be an efficient way of reminding participants of other aspects of the project that they needed to work on.

Participant is Instructed. The researcher or TA provided guidance to participants that asked a question or were seen to be idle. The process usually started by the researcher or TA confirming what the participant wanted to achieve, and then providing an explanation that can help achieve that goal, if that failed then step by step guidance was provided on how to achieve the goal.

Task is Performed for Participant. Lastly, in cases where the participant tried multiple times alone, or under instruction to achieve a goal unsuccessfully, the researcher or TA performed the task while the participant watched. This was the approach that was taken during a session where after P4 unsuccessfully attempted to rearrange blocks in a script.

3.7   Theoretical Model

Based on the findings presented in Sects. 3.1–3.6, the theoretical model shown below was generated to explain the experiences of participants in this study while using Scratch to create stories (Fig. 2).

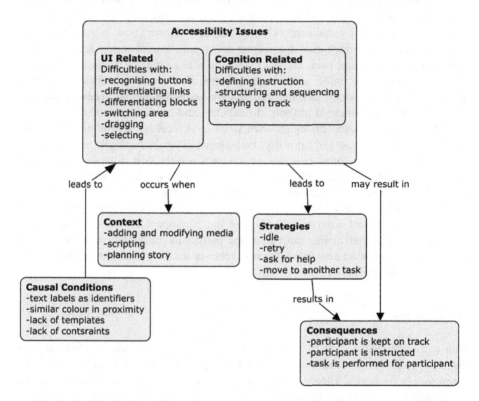

Fig. 2. A theoretical model showing how accessibility issues affect the use of Scratch.

4   Discussions

This study used a Grounded Theory approach to evaluate the accessibility of Scratch, and how that affects its usage by children with cognitive impairments. Findings uncovered two types of accessibility issues faced by participants, those that were caused by the design of the UI and how it was interacted with, and those that had to do with the cognitive processes of using Scratch.

It was discovered that participants had trouble locating and identifying buttons, links and blocks. Although Scratch uses colours to differentiate objects, not all objects are uniquely identified by colours. In cases where colours are unique it was found that similar colours within proximity easily confused participants. Although few buttons and blocks are identified with text and symbols, text labels are the main unique identifiers used by Scratch. They were difficult for participants to recognise due to reading difficulties and led to most of the difficulties identifying objects on the UI. Difficulties of this kind usually occurred when participants were working with media (adding, modifying) or blocks.

Even though the difficulties associated with the UI outnumber those related to cognition, the latter was more difficult to tackle and had greater impact on participants' goal of creating stories. Scratch is well known for the freedom it provides its users to create projects, while that can be considered good for creativity, it's not necessarily helpful to this study's participants. Due to this lack of restriction, some participants frequently strayed off track after discovering new media objects or new features. Other participants on the other hand chose to focus on a task or keep repeating an action. With no template to build around, participants also found it difficult to define instructions and behaviour, structure projects and sequence actions. These difficulties resulted in non-goal oriented projects, distractions, and creative difficulties.

Participants employed strategies when faced by difficulties depending on the participant's characteristics, and difficulty. Participants either became idle, retried, asked for help or moved to another task. Staying on track was the only difficulty that did not lead to any strategy by the participant and was only identified by either the researcher or a TA, who then tried to get the participant back on track.

Consequences occurred as a result of a participant facing a difficulty or employing a strategy. They ranged from simply keeping the participant on track, providing an explanation for a participant, instructing the participant in simple steps on how to perform a task, to, if all else failed, the researcher or teaching assistant performing the task for the participant.

5   Conclusion

The aim of this study was to evaluate the accessibility of Scratch for children with cognitive impairments. The study used a novel approach to accessibility evaluation by employing a Grounded Theory research method. The resulting findings make original contributions to knowledge on the accessibility of visual programming tools, and shed light on the experiences of users with cognitive impairments. Not only are the accessibility issues reported, their causes, practices of users when faced with difficulties and measures taken to help users are also reported upon. This provides guidance on best practices while using such tools in similar contexts, but more importantly it provides accessible design suggestions for visual programming environments suitable for those with cognitive impairments.

It should be acknowledged that this study has its limitations and they are as follows. First, extensive programming was not taught to participants before or during the study and participants had no previous programming experiences, rather participants were guided to create simple programming scripts that they required to create stories of the complexity that they normally created before using Scratch. Therefore, programming difficulties were not considered, but difficulties related to following programming guides were included. Secondly, even though teaching assistants provided guidance and help to participants during sessions, they were not themselves trained on how to use Scratch, which meant they were also required to learn and experiment with the software as part of the sessions. However, despite this limitation, there were few instances where a teaching assistant was unsure on how to guide participants, and in those cases the researcher was asked for support. Lastly, it should be noted that the participants in this study represent only a small group of individuals with cognitive impairments, which means that all needs and requirements of children with cognitive impairments while using Scratch may not have been addressed in this study.

Future work should focus on investigating how specific cognitive impairments, for example Autism Spectrum Disorders, affect the accessibility of Scratch as a storytelling tool. By focusing on one type of impairment, specific characteristics, needs and requirements that need to be considered to make Scratch accessible can be better understood.

References

1. Brown, D.J., Ley, J., Evett, L., Standen, P.: Can participating in games based learning improve mathematic skills in students with intellectual disabilities? In: 2011 IEEE 1st International Conference on Serious Games and Applications for Health (SeGAH), pp. 1–9 (2011)
2. Brown, D., Standen, P., Saridaki, M., Shopland, N., Roinioti, E., Evett, L., Grantham, S., Smith, P.: Engaging students with intellectual disabilities through games based learning and related technologies. In: Stephanidis, C., Antona, M. (eds.) UAHCI 2013. LNCS, vol. 8011, pp. 573–582. Springer, Heidelberg (2013). https://doi.org/10.1007/978-3-642-39194-1_66
3. Papert, S.: Situating constructionism. Constructionism 36, 1–11 (1991)
4. Myers, B.: Taxonomies of visual programming and program visualization. Vis. Lang. Comput. 1(1), 97–123 (1990)
5. Scratch - Imagine, Program, Share. https://scratch.mit.edu/. Accessed 12 Jan 2018
6. Alice – Tell Stories. Build Games. Learn to Program. https://www.alice.org/. Accessed 12 Jan 2018
7. Maloney, J., Resnick, M., Rusk, N., Silverman, B., Eastmond, E.: The scratch programming language and environment. ACM Trans. Comput. Educ. 10(4), 1–15 (2010)
8. Glaser, B., Strauss, A.L.: Discovery of Grounded Theory Strategies for Qualitative Research. Taylor and Francis, Abingdon (1967)
9. Charmaz, K.: Constructing Grounded Theory. Sage, Thousand Oaks (2014)
10. Strauss, A., Corbin, J.: Grounded theory methodology. In: Handbook of Qualitative Research, pp. 273–285. Sage Publications, Inc., Thousand Oaks (1994)
11. Devkar, S., Lobo, S., Doke, P.: A grounded theory approach for designing communication and collaboration system for visually impaired chess players. In: Antona, M., Stephanidis, C. (eds.) UAHCI 2015. LNCS, vol. 9175, pp. 415–425. Springer, Cham (2015). https://doi.org/10.1007/978-3-319-20678-3_40
12. Elliott, G., Jones, E., Barker, P.: A grounded theory approach to modelling learnability of hypermedia authoring tools. Interact. Comput. 14(5), 547–574 (2002)
13. Gasson, S., Waters, J.: Using a grounded theory approach to study online collaboration behaviors. Eur. J. Inf. Syst. 22(1), 95–118 (2013)
14. Learning disability - Live Well - NHS Choices. https://www.nhs.uk/Livewell/Childrenwithalearningdisability/Pages/Whatislearningdisability.aspx. Accessed 12 Jan 2018
15. Simpson, R.L., de Boer-Ott, S.R., Smith-Myles, B.: Inclusion of learners with autism spectrum disorders in general education settings. Top. Lang. Disord. 23(2), 116–133 (2003)

16. Corbin, J.M., Strauss, A.L.: Basics of Qualitative Research : Techniques and Procedures for Developing Grounded Theory. Sage, Thousand Oaks (2015)
17. Goodwin, S.: Using screen capture software for web site usability and redesign buy-in. Libr. Hi Tech **23**(4), 610–621 (2005)
18. CamStudio - Free Screen Recording Software. http://camstudio.org/. Accessed 12 Jan 2018
19. Thorsteinsson, G., Page, T.: Piloting new ways of collecting empirical data. In: ICT in education: reflections and perspectives (2007)
20. Saldaña, J.: The Coding Manual for Qualitative Researchers. Sage, Thousand Oaks (2016)
21. Corbin, J.M., Strauss, A.: Grounded theory research: procedures, canons, and evaluative criteria. Qual. Sociol. **13**(1), 3–21 (1990)
22. Adams, A., Lunt, P., Cairns, P.: A qualitative approach to HCI research. In: Research Methods for Human-Computer Interaction. Cambridge University Press, Cambridge (2008)
23. NVivo qualitative data analysis software | QSR International. https://www.qsrinternational. com/nvivo/home. Accessed 12 Jan 2018

Author Index

Aasheim, Marius Wiker II-397
Abulkhair, Maysoon I-598
Aceves, Luis I-493
Aguirrezabal, Andoni II-48
Ahmad, B. I. I-133
Al-khazraji, Sedeeq I-205
Almeida, Leonelo Dell Anhol I-3
Alqasemi, Redwan II-48, II-58
Alsaggaf, Maha I-311
Altendorf, Eugen I-216
Amano, Nao II-3
Amat, Ashwaq Zaini I-463
Andrade, Rossana M. C. I-365
Andreadis, Alessandro II-187
Araki, Iori II-308
Arceo, Patrick I-146
Atzori, Barbara II-15

Babar, Ayesha II-246
Bailin, Emma S. II-28
Bajireanu, Roman II-102
Bamasag, Omaimah I-311
Baranauskas, Maria Cecília Calani I-38
Barandiarán, Xabier II-519
Bargagna, Stefania I-571
Barreto, Armando I-228, I-299, II-149
Barroso, João II-262, II-320, II-330, II-530
Bates, Matthew I-660
Bauer, Corinna M. II-28
Becker, Valdecir I-613
Bennett, Christopher R. II-28
Bernal, Jonathan I-299
Bernardo, Ruben II-262
Beuscher, Linda I-192
Bex, Peter J. II-28
Beyene, Wondwossen M. II-397
Bica, Paulo II-102
Bienhaus, Diethelm I-433
Bodenhagen, Leon II-366
Bolivar, Santiago II-39
Bonacin, Rodrigo II-226
Bondioli, Mariasole I-475
Borges, Jorge II-530
Bosse, Ingo K. II-409

Bozgeyikli, Evren II-48, II-58
Bozgeyikli, Lal "Lila" II-48, II-58
Brown, David I-660
Bühler, Christian I-503
Buzzi, Maria Claudia I-475, I-571
Buzzi, Marina I-475, I-571

Caber, Nermin II-201
Cabral, Ruben II-347
Cabrita, Cristiano II-214
Çağıltay, Kürşat I-542
Camenar, Leticia Maria de Oliveira I-3
Cardoso, Pedro J. S. II-102, II-214, II-421
Carine, Kanani II-246
Carneiro Araújo, Maria da Conceição I-273
Chang, Hsien-Tsung II-574, II-583
Chang, Tian-Sheuan II-386
Chen, Jean-Lon II-386
Chen, Jiatyan II-437
Chen, Weiqin I-63
Chen, Yi-Cheng II-574
Chicanelli, Rachel T. I-18
Chu, Shaowei I-327
Cipolla Ficarra, Francisco V. II-450, II-463
Cipolla Ficarra, Miguel II-450
Clarkson, P. John II-201
Collander, Christopher I-583
Correia, Diogo II-330
Cruz, Dario II-214

da Conceição Júnior, Vicente Antônio I-178
Damasio Oliveira, Juliana I-337, I-401
David, Darren Goldwin I-146
de Borba Campos, Marcia I-337, I-401, II-553
de Faria Borges, Luciana C. Lima I-18, I-178
de Freitas Guilhermino Trindade, Daniela II-171
de Godoi, Tatiany Xavier II-171
de Macedo, Claudia Mara Scudelari I-355
de Podestá Gaspar, Renata II-226
de Santana, Vagner Figueredo I-38
de Souza, Patricia C. I-18

Deja, Jordan Aiko   I-146
del Rio Guerra, Marta   I-493
DeLong, Sean   I-160
Dirks, Susanne   I-503
do Nascimento, Diego de Faria   I-3
Domingues, Fernanda   I-355
dos Santos Nunes, Eunice P.   I-178
Dubey, Rajiv   II-48, II-58

Eckhardt, Jennifer   I-50
Eika, Evelyn   I-107, I-287
Englebienne, Gwenn   II-366
Evers, Vanessa   II-366

Fan, Jing   I-192
Ferati, Mexhid   II-246
Ferrari, Ambra   II-87
Ferreira, Gabriel   II-262
Ficarra, Maria V.   II-450, II-463
Flemisch, Frank O.   I-216
Friend, Michelle   II-486
Fu, Bo   I-91
Fujita, Kosuke   II-285

Gan, Patrick Lawrence   I-146
Garcea, Giacomo   II-87
Garzotto, Franca   I-517
Gelsomini, Mirko   I-517
Giudice, G. Bernard   I-243
Giudice, Nicholas A.   I-243
Gjøsæter, Terje   I-63
Godsill, S. J.   I-133
Goethe, Ole   II-475
Gonçalves, Vinícius P.   II-226
Gottlieb, Timothy K.   II-28
Graf von Spee, Rudolf   I-216
Greenberg, Jesse   I-385
Guan, Aonan   I-628
Guerino, Guilherme Corredato   II-171
Guerreiro, Pedro   II-421
Güleç, Mustafa   I-542

Hall, Margeret   II-486
Hamidi, Ali   II-246
Hara, Sachiko   II-274
Hariharan, Dhananjai   I-205
Hirotomi, Tetsuya   I-530, II-274
Ho, Wei-Ling   II-583
Hsu, Chia-Yu   II-574

Huenerfauth, Matt   I-205
Hughes-Roberts, Thomas   I-660

Jono, Yusuke   II-3
Justino, Elsa   II-530

Kaletka, Christoph   I-50
Kanetsuku, Haruka   II-274
Kara, Ersin   I-542
Katkoori, Srinivas   II-58
Keates, Simeon   I-75
Khakurel, Jayden   I-91
Kinoshita, Fumiya   II-3, II-285
Kitamura, Kazuki   II-122
Knutas, Antti   I-91
Kratky, Andreas   II-496
Krause, Markus   II-486
Krause, Paul   I-598
Kressin, Lori   II-511
Kreutzer, Michael   I-433
Krüger, Norbert   II-366
Kuo, Chen-li   II-160

Lam, Roberto   II-102
Langdon, Patrick M.   I-133, II-201
Lauro Grotto, Rosapia   II-15
Leporini, Barbara   I-571
Li, Xuemei   I-637
Lien, Pei-Jung   II-583
Lin, Shu-Yu   II-574
Lin, Yu-Wen   II-583
Linke, Hanna   II-409
Liu, Sicong   I-551
Liu, Xinxiong   I-450
Lourenço, Alvaro   II-132
Lu, Guoying   I-121
Lucena Jr., Vicente F.   II-132
Luna, Álvaro   II-519

MacKenzie, I. Scott   I-160, I-420
Makedon, Fillia   I-583
Maldonado, Jose   II-149
Mantovani, Fabrizia   II-87
Marczak, Sabrina   I-401
Martin Gutierrez, Jorge   I-493
Martins, Márcio   II-530
Matarazzo, Vito   I-517
Matsuura, Shu   II-541
McKenna, H. Patricia   II-295

Medola, Fausto Orsi   I-107, I-287
Melkas, Helinä   I-91
Mendes Damasceno, Rafael   I-337
Mendes, Luís   II-262, II-330
Mendoza, Eulogia   II-450
Merabet, Lotfi B.   II-28
Merlin, José Reinaldo   II-171
Mesquita, Lana   I-365
Messeri, Andrea   II-15
Messina, Nicolo'   I-517
Meyer, Ronald   I-216
Mion, Lorraine C.   I-192
Miyanaga, Kazuya   II-285
Miyao, Masaru   II-3
Miyata, Akihiro   II-308
Monteiro, Jânio   II-214, II-421
Moore, Emily B.   I-385
Morisaki, Saki   II-122
Mörtberg, Christina   II-246
Murai, Shota   II-340

Nagamune, Kouki   II-78
Neves, Álvaro   II-262
Newhouse, Paul   I-192
Norberto de Souza, Osmar   II-553

Occhiuto, Daniele   I-517
Ohta, Kazuki   II-122
O-larnnithipong, Nonnarit   I-228
Oliveira, Luís M. R.   II-214
Omokawa, Reika   II-541
Ortega, Francisco R.   I-228, I-299, II-39,
    II-149

Palani, Hari Prasath   I-243
Pallavicini, Federica   II-87
Paredes, Hugo   II-320
Paulino, Dennis   II-320
Pei, Yu-Cheng   II-386
Pelagatti, Susanna   I-475
Pelka, Bastian   I-50, II-409
Peng, Mei   I-327
Penicheiro, Paulo   II-262
Penzenstadler, Birgit   I-91
Pepe, Alessandro   II-87
Pereira, António   II-262, II-330
Pereira, João A. R.   II-102
Pereira, Rúben   II-330
Perrone, Erico   I-571

Piatti, Alice Elena   I-571
Picelli Sanches, Emilia Christie   I-355
Pichiliani, Mauro C.   I-256
Pinto, Nelson   II-214
Porras, Jari   I-91
Postal, Juliana   II-132

Qiu, Xiaoyang   I-628
Quiroga, Alejandra   II-463

Rabadão, Carlos   II-330
Radianti, Jaziar   I-63
Raij, Andrew   II-48, II-58
Rajavenkatanarayanan, Akilesh   I-583
Ramesh Babu, Ashwin   I-583
Ratchatanantakit, Neeranut   I-228
Reis, Arsénio   II-320, II-530
Ribeiro, Carlos Eduardo   II-171
Rishe, Naphtali D.   I-299, II-39
Ritzel Paixão-Côrtes, Walter   II-553
Rocha Façanha, Agebson   I-273
Rocha, Tânia   II-530
Rodrigues, João M. F.   II-102, II-214, II-421
Roque, Ryan Christopher   I-146

Sahashi, Katsuya   II-340
Sánchez, Jaime   I-273, I-365
Sandnes, Frode Eika   I-107, I-287
Santos, Marcelino B.   II-347
Sardo, João D. P.   II-102
Sarkar, Arpan   I-560
Sarkar, Nilanjan   I-192, I-463, I-560, I-650
Semião, Jorge   II-214, II-347
Senette, Caterina   I-475, I-571
Sgarbi, Ederson Marcos   II-171
Shams, Fatimah   I-311
Sharifara, Ali   I-583
Sinnari, Doaa   I-598
Smith, Taliesin L.   I-385
Somoza Sanchéz, Vella V.   II-366
Stangherlin Machado Paixão-Côrtes,
    Vanessa   I-337, II-553
Sugiura, Akihiro   II-122
Sundarrao, Stephen   II-48
Suvei, Stefan-Daniel   II-366
Swanson, Amy   I-463, I-560, I-650

Takada, Hiroki   II-3, II-122, II-285
Takada, Masumi   II-3, II-285

Takahashi, Yasutake   II-340
Takata, Keisuke   II-78
Tanaka, Kunihiko   II-122
Tang, Tiffany Y.   I-628
Tangnimitchok, Sudarat   I-228
Tanimura, Toru   II-3
Tarre, Katherine   II-149
Tayeb, Muna   I-311
Teixeira Borges, Olimar   I-337, I-401
Teixeira, Isabel C.   II-347
Teixeira, J. Paulo   II-347
Teófilo, Mauro   II-132
Torres, Nicholas   I-299
Toscano, Rafael   I-613
Touyama, Hideaki   II-285
Trujillo, Amaury   I-571
Tsai, Tsai-Hsuan   II-574, II-583
Tseng, Kevin C.   II-386

Unceta, Alfonso   II-519

Vagnoli, Laura   II-15
Varghese Jacob, Sibu   I-420
Vassigh, Shahin   II-149
Veiga, Ricardo J. M.   II-102
Viana, Windson   I-273
von Zabiensky, Florian   I-433
Vroon, Jered   II-366

Wade, Joshua   I-560
Wang, Chih-yuan   II-160
Wang, Hui   I-551
Wang, Shishun   I-121
Wang, Tongshun   II-308
Wang, Wanru   I-450
Warren, Zachary   I-463, I-560, I-650
Weitlauf, Amy   I-463, I-560, I-650
Whiting, Brent   II-591
Winoto, Pinata   I-628
Wong, Alice M. K.   II-386
Wu, Chung-Yu   II-386
Wu, Yinyun   I-121

Xi, Yan   I-551

Yan, Wei-Cheng   II-574, II-583
Yang, Minggang   I-637
Yu, Ming-Chun   II-583

Zambon, Riccardo   II-187
Zanacchi, Andrea   II-87
Zancan, Breno Augusto Guerra   II-171
Zhang, Ting   I-121
Zhao, Huan   I-650
Zock-Obregon, Maia   II-39
Zubair, Misbahu S.   I-660

Printed in the United States
By Bookmasters